ELEVENTH EDITION

Textiles

Sara J. Kadolph

Iowa State University

PEARSON

Boston   Columbus   Indianapolis   New York   San Francisco   Upper Saddle River
Amsterdam   Cape Town   Dubai   London   Madrid   Milan   Munich   Paris   Montreal   Toronto
Delhi   Mexico City   Sao Paulo   Sydney   Hong Kong   Seoul   Singapore   Taipei   Tokyo

Editor in Chief: Vernon Anthony
Editorial Assistant: Doug Greive
Director of Marketing: David Gesell
Senior Marketing Manager: Alicia Wozniak
Marketing Assistant: Les Roberts
Associate Managing Editor: Alexandrina Benedicto Wolf
In-house Production Liaison: Alicia Ritchey
Operations Specialist: Deidra Skahill
Art Director: Diane Ernsberger
Cover Designer: Diane Lorenzo

Image Permission Coordinator: Silvana Attanasio
Cover Art: Photo Researchers, Inc.
Lead Media Project Manager: Karen Bretz
Full-Service Project Management: Thistle Hill Publishing
    Services, LLC
Copy Editor: Thistle Hill Publishing Services, LLC
Composition: S4Carlisle Publishing Services
Printer/Binder: Courier Kendallville, Inc.
Cover Printer: Lehigh-Phoenix Color
Text Font: 45 Helvetica Light

Credits and acknowledgments borrowed from other sources and reproduced, with permission, in this textbook appear on appropriate page within text.

Library of Congress Cataloging-in-Publication Data

Kadolph, Sara J.
    Textiles / Sara J. Kadolph.—Eleventh ed.
        p. cm.
    Includes bibliographical references and index.
    ISBN–13: 978–0–13–500759–4 (casebound)
    ISBN–10: 0–13–500759–3 (casebound)
    1. Textile industry.   2. Textile fibers.   3. Textile fabrics.   I. Title.
    TS1446.K33 2009
    677—dc22

                                                                2009050124

10 9 8 7 6 5 4 3 2 1

Prentice Hall
an imprint of

www.pearsonhighered.com

ISBN-13: 978-0-13-500759-4
ISBN-10: 0-13-500759-3

brief contents

contents

SECTION III: Yarns

SECTION V: Finishing

SECTION VI: Other Issues Related to Textiles

Appendixes

preface

Philosophy of This Book

Textiles provides students with a basic knowledge of textiles so that they understand how textiles are produced and how appropriate performance characteristics are incorporated into materials and products. With this knowledge, they have the foundation they need to make informed decisions regarding textile materials and products and to communicate effectively with team members in the workplace, suppliers, contractors, and buyers. A solid understanding of textile components (fibers, yarns, fabrics, and finishes), the interrelationships among these components, and their impact on product performance is necessary to fulfill day-to-day responsibilities in many careers in the textile, apparel, and interior segments of the global textile complex.

Serviceability of textiles and textile products is the fundamental principle emphasized throughout the book. I discuss the contributions of each component as it is incorporated in or combined with other components in a textile product. I stress interrelationships among the components. Basic information regarding how each component is processed or handled helps in understanding product performance and cost. Production of textiles is a complex process dealing with a wide variety of materials and techniques. To understand textiles, students need a basic understanding of the choices and technology involved.

This book will help students:

- use textile terminology correctly;
- know laws and labeling requirements regulating textile distribution;
- understand the impact of production processes and selection of components on product performance, cost, and consumer satisfaction;
- recognize the forces that drive product and process developments;
- identify fiber type, yarn type, and fabrication method;
- predict fabric or product performance based on a knowledge of fibers, yarns, fabrication methods, and finishes in conjunction with informative labeling;
- select textile components or products based on specified end uses and target market expectations for performance and serviceability;
- select appropriate care for textile products;
- understand some of the issues related to sustainability and environmental quality related to textiles, their production, use, care, and disposal;
- develop an interest in and appreciation of textiles.

Understanding textiles cannot be achieved only by studying this book; it also requires working with fabrics. Numerous learning activities included in the chapters make use of fabric swatches. The numbers in the activities refer to the swatches in the Basic Swatch Kit available with this book.

Organization of This Book

Each section of the book focuses on a basic component or aspect of fabrics and textile products or on general issues important to the use of, production of, or satisfaction with textile products. Sustainability and environmental issues are included in almost every chapter. Each section is complete and can be used in any order desired. The four main sections follow the normal sequence used in the production of textiles: fiber, yarn, fabrication, and finishing.

The first section of the book introduces the study of textiles and the global textile complex and approaches product development from a textile perspective. Section Two focuses on fibers and their production, serviceability, effect on product performance, and use. Several new fibers and new generic classifications have been added to this section. Smart textiles and nanotechnology have been added. Section Three focuses on yarn production, yarn types, the relationship of yarn type to product performance and serviceability, sewing and embroidery threads, and rope. More types of novelty or fancy yarns have been added. Section Four examines fabrication methods. These chapters are organized by basic fabrication method, standard or classic fabric names and types, and the relationships between fabrication and product performance. Areas that were confusing have been clarified. Section Five deals with finishes, grouped by type or effect. Dyeing and printing are also included, as well as problems that consumers and producers experience with dyed or printed fabrics. Section Six deals with other issues related to textiles. One chapter focuses on care of textile products, new cleaning products and processes, and associated sustainability and environmental concerns. Another chapter investigates legal, sustainability, and environmental concerns. The final chapter discusses career opportunities requiring knowledge of textiles and has been extensively revised to reflect the ever-changing career opportunities in the textile and apparel industries.

This book assumes that the student requires basic information regarding textiles in order to perform professional responsibilities and communicate with other professionals in an intelligent and informed manner. Hence, the book is designed to be of use as a textbook and to become a valued component of a professional's reference library. Key terms are defined in both the text and the glossary. The glossary includes more than basic or classic fabric names as well as a pronunciation guide. Fiber modifications, finishes, and terminology related to performance have been incorporated. The extensive index will help individuals locate information needed for class or on the job. Appendix A lists fiber names in several languages that may be encountered in the global textile complex. Appendix B lists fibers that are no longer produced in the United States. Appendix C lists selected trade names for fibers, yarns, fabrics, finishes, and cleaning procedures. Appendix D is a map of the world that students can use to understand the global nature of the textile complex. Appendix E provides definitions from the Federal Trade Commission for care label terms. A shorter list of such terms is now in Chapter 20. Appendix F provides stain removal guidelines.

Features of This Book

Instructors and students have always liked this book's summary and reference tables and charts, the presentation of information in a clear and consistent fashion, the emphasis on serviceability, and the numerous illustrations, graphics, and photographs. I tried to strengthen these things in this revision. The flowcharts from previous editions have been maintained, with some revisions. I revised, reorganized, or updated tables where necessary or where students or colleagues suggested improvements.

Although the basic content and flavor of *Textiles* remain intact, the changes help students recognize and focus on the most important material. Objectives and key terms for each chapter were updated so that students will be able to identify and understand the major concepts. After reading and studying each chapter, students should be able to define each term in the key terms list and describe how terms relate to each other and to the chapter content. Additional review questions provide students with an opportunity to test their level of understanding, focus on key concepts or applications, and integrate the information. I updated the list of readings for students who would like to investigate topics beyond the scope of the book. Many of these readings are technical in nature. There are a few articles on textiles in the popular press, but these often include little substantive information. Hence, the most valuable articles and books tend to be those written from a technical perspective.

Major Changes and Additions

The emphasis in this revision has been on updating and adding material where new processes or concerns have developed in the professional workplace, in the global textile complex, or among consumers. I added explanations, expanded discussions, and clarified concepts in areas where students had indicated the need or where colleagues expressed or suggested improvements. Terminology incorporates an industry perspective so that professionals can understand and communicate with other professionals. The pronunciation guide included with some words in the glossary will help professionals pronounce and use terms correctly. I kept the expanded index to facilitate the book's use as a resource by professionals who need to locate information quickly regarding a specific term,

process, or product. Color photographs and diagrams make the text more interesting and concepts easier to understand.

The book continues to focus on the three major end uses of textiles: apparel, interiors, and technical products. However, many changes have been made in the text. Technological advances and new industry and societal concerns that have arisen or have increased in importance since the last edition are included. Several topics have been reorganized to more closely represent industry practices or to enhance learning. New fibers have been added to the fiber section.

The discussion of dyeing and printing has separated the resist dyeing methods from printing methods. The discussion of finishing is organized so as to make it understandable to students. In some cases, this approach combines mechanical and chemical finishes—an anathema to the textile purist, but an approach that works well with students. Nanotechnology and changes in chemicals and processes reflect the ever-increasing interest in sustainability.

The chapter on career opportunities has been extensively revised. This discussion is intended to help students understand careers and how they will apply their knowledge of textiles and textile products in their professional work. It should help students gain a better understanding of careers and how professionals interact with each other. Although this chapter may not be assigned in a beginning textile course, students might read the chapter on their own to explore career possibilities and use the information when considering career options other than those that are most obvious to the consumer.

Learning Activities and a case study are included with every chapter. The Learning Activities were developed to make use of the Basic Swatch Kit available to be purchased at a discount with this book. Other Learning Activities have been developed to allow students to discuss topics in small groups or use the textiles they are wearing as learning tools. I tried to keep these activities independent of additional resources. Key concepts for each chapter have been emphasized. Review questions have been included at the end of each main section of the book to encourage students to connect textile components to product characteristics and performance.

Supplements

Instructor Resources

- **Instructor's Manual** that includes an updated outline of the material for each chapter, a revised list of suggested activities, and sample test questions in a variety of formats.
- **PowerPoint Presentation** for use in lectures or as a supplement to class activities.
- **Online Instructor's Resource Center** to access supplementary materials online. Instructors need to request an instructor access code. Go to **www.pearsonhighered.com/irc,** where you can register for an instructor access code. Within 48 hours after registering, you will receive a confirming e-mail, including an instructor access code. Once you have received your code, go to the site and log on for full instructions on downloading the materials you wish to use.

Student Resources

- **Swatch Kit** that is packaged in a 3-ring binder and includes 126 fabric swatches, master list of the fabric swatches (with fabric name, description, and fiber content), heavyweight mounting sheets, linen tester/stitch counter, and Textile Companion CD with more than 1300 fabric images.
- **MyTextilesLab** is an exciting new online digital resource that will contain cutting edge videos, animations, comprehensive digital fabric glossary, audio pronunciation guide, career interviews, learning activities, and assessment materials.

Acknowledgments

I used the comments and contributions of many students and colleagues in preparing this revision. I find students' comments help the most in evaluating the approach, wording, and style of presentation, and therefore I appreciate hearing from any student or faculty member about the book. Thanks to retired faculty Nancy Owens and Barbara Harger, who were generous in sharing their perspectives and suggestions for improvements. Both positive and negative comments are incredibly helpful and invaluable in revising the book. I would especially like to thank Sara Marcketti and Carmen Keist of Iowa State University for their suggestions and perspectives. Thanks to reviewers for their comments and suggestions: Heather Akou, Indiana University; Deborah Carlson, Cleveland Institute of Art; Melinda Cowen, Florida State University; Yehia Elmogahzy, Auburn University; Kay Grise, Florida State University; Robert Gruber, Drexel University; George Hodge, North Carolina State University; Janice Lessman-Moss, Kent State University; Sara Marcketti, Iowa State University; Ajoy Sarkar, Colorado State University; and Patricia Walton, Georgia Southern University. Great thanks to my sister, Lora Camacho, who kept me fed and the house clean while I worked on this edition. And finally, thanks to Clementine, Silkie, Imp, and Sampson, who reminded me that 5 p.m. is feeding time—every day!

Revising this book is always an exciting challenge. I enjoy the opportunity to explore the textiles literature in more depth than university responsibilities usually allow. I enjoy sharing the exciting area of textiles with so many others. I hope that this book hooks you on textiles as the third edition of this book did for me when I was a college sophomore just beginning to learn about textiles.

Sara J. Kadolph

About the Author

Sara J. Kadolph is a full professor of Textiles and Clothing at Iowa State University in Ames, Iowa, where she has taught for 30 years. She teaches several courses related to textiles: chemistry, dyeing, quality assurance, and conservation. Dr. Kadolph is the recipient of numerous teaching, advising, and professional awards including teaching excellence awards from the International Textiles and Apparel Association, Iowa State University, and the Iowa Association of Family and Consumer Sciences. She holds the Donna R. Danielson Professorship in Textiles and Clothing. She is a Fellow of the International Textiles and Apparel Association and a Wakonse Fellow.

Dr. Kadolph has consulted with companies in the textile complex to solve quality problems, educate product development/design teams, select materials, assess textile performance, write specifications, and develop quality assurance programs. Her teaching and research scholarship has been published in the *Clothing and Textiles Research Journal,* the *Journal of the Society of International Natural Dyeing,* the *Journal of the Korean Society for Clothing Industry, The Journal of Consumer Education,* the *Journal of Family and Consumer Sciences,* the *International Journal of Clothing and Science Technology,* and others. Her *Textiles* book with Pearson Education is used in colleges and universities throughout the world. She is currently working on two other books related to textiles for Pearson Education.

Textiles

1 Introduction

2 Product Development from a Textile Perspective

Introduction to TEXTILES

SECTION I

INTRODUCTION

CHAPTER OBJECTIVES

- To recognize the diversity in textiles and textile products.
- To understand the value of developing a professional knowledge of textiles.
- To recognize how textile apparel, interior, and technical products enhance quality of life.
- To understand the global nature of the textile complex.

1

Imagine apparel that responds to cold weather by releasing heat and keeping your skin dry while you are cross-country skiing, that protects you from sunburn while hiking in a national park, that protects police from knife slashes, and that reduces diaper rash and body odor! Imagine technical textiles that filter hazardous waste, bacteria, and parasites from drinking water; that keep pets and livestock safer and healthier; that keep roadbeds smooth longer; that help wounds heal; and that enable astronauts to work outside their spacecraft! Imagine fibers so tiny they are sized by nanometers (1×10^{-9} m) or so large that they can cut through plant stems, or fibers that are based on research about spider webs! You will learn about all these amazing textiles, innovative research in the industry, and more in this book.

This book is divided into several sections. Section 1 is divided into two chapters. Chapter 1 introduces the study of textiles by defining terms, providing examples of textile products, surveying the diversity of textiles, and describing the importance of the textile complex to the global economy. Chapter 2 describes basic characteristics of textiles, the manner in which textiles and textile products are developed and used, and how consumers assess their satisfaction with them.

The majority of the book is devoted to basic information about textile materials, with an emphasis on fibers, yarns, fabric construction, finishes, and coloration. These interdependent elements found in most textiles contribute to the beauty or aesthetics, durability, care, cost, appearance retention, safety, function, and comfort of textile products.

Much of the terminology used in this book may be new to students, and many facts must be memorized. It takes time and effort to understand and recognize the fine differences among fibers, yarn and fabric structures, and finishes and coloration methods. You will have to examine many fabrics closely in order to develop this ability. Often, a single term is used to describe a wide range of fabrics. For example, velvet can be produced by knitting, weaving, tufting, and flocking. Woven velvet is used for skirts and dresses. Heavier weight woven velvets and warp-knit velvets are used for upholstery. Flocked and tufted velvet are less expensive and used for less expensive upholstered furniture.

To apply a knowledge of textiles, an understanding of the basics is essential. The emphasis is on fundamental concepts and commercially significant fibers, yarn and fabric types, finishes, coloration techniques, and production methods. Principles of textile production are included to help the student develop a better understanding of, and appreciation for, the textile industry. Because of the quantity of information included in this book, it will be a useful resource for individuals seeking careers in the global textile complex.

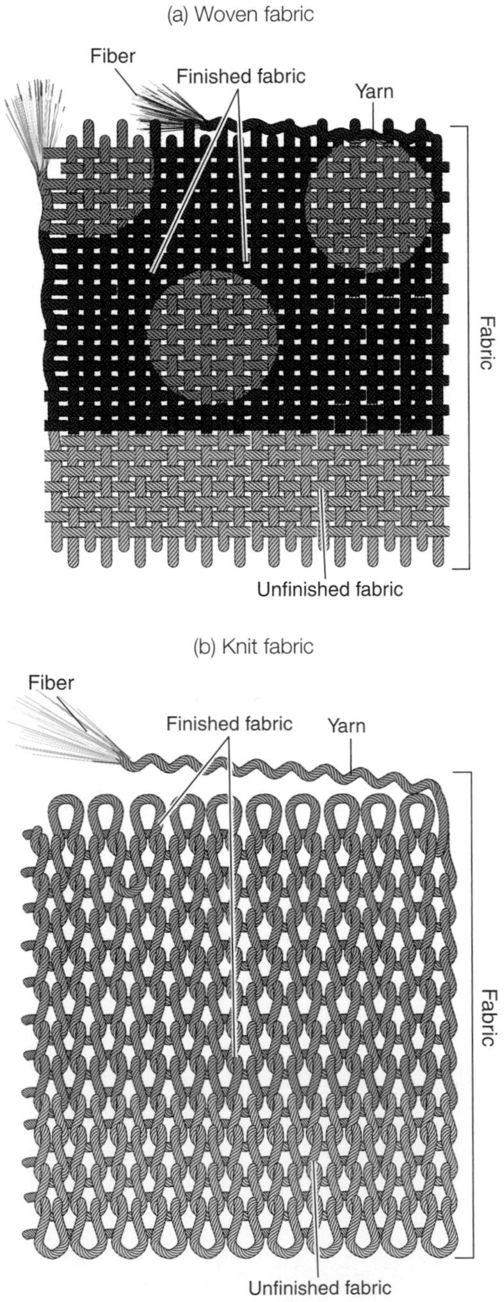

Textiles and Textile Products

But what are textiles? To know what textiles are and to understand textiles, several basic terms must be defined:

Textile A term originally applied only to woven fabrics, now generally applied to any flexible material that is composed of thin films of polymers or of fibers, yarns, or fabrics or products made of films, fibers, yarns, or fabrics.

Polymer A very large molecule made by connecting many small molecules together. Almost all fibers are polymers made of organic materials, but some polymers are formed into thin films and used as textiles. For example, vinyl upholstery is a film, often applied to a more traditional textile knit or woven material for added durability.

Fiber Any substance, natural or manufactured, with a high length-to-width ratio possessing suitable characteristics for being processed into fabric; the smallest component, hairlike in nature, that can be separated from a fabric. Fibers can be absorbent (like cotton and rayon), stretchy (like spandex), warm and bulky (like wool), or very strong and abrasion resistant (like nylon and polyester). (See Figure 1.1.)

(a) Woven fabric

Fiber
Finished fabric
Yarn
Fabric
Unfinished fabric

(b) Knit fabric

Fiber
Finished fabric
Yarn
Fabric
Unfinished fabric

Figure 1.1 The components of a fabric: fiber, yarn, structure, and finish.

Yarn An assemblage of fibers that is twisted or laid together so as to form a continuous strand that can be made into a textile fabric. Yarns can be used to make a fabric that is smooth and slick like satin or soft and fuzzy like brushed denim. (See Figure 1.1.)

Fabric A flexible planar substance constructed from solutions, fibers, yarns, or fabrics, in any combination. (See Figure 1.1.) Fabrics range from lightweight and sheer chiffon scarves to heavy and sturdy denim to rigid and firm carpeting to technical products. (See Figures 1.2 and 1.3.)

Gray goods (grey or greige goods) Any fabric that has not been finished. Consumers rarely see gray goods, except for home sewers and quilters who may work with muslin.

Coloration Any dyeing or printing process used to add color with dyes or pigments to a textile. Coloration adds interest and fashion appeal to apparel and interiors. (See Figure 1.1.)

Finish Any process that modifies appearance or enhances performance of gray goods (unfinished fabric). Some finishes make the fabric more comfortable such as brushing velveteen to produce the soft surface. With other finishes, the consumer cannot determine the presence of a finish. For example, a pair of cotton slacks may have a stain-resistant finish that makes stains easier to remove, but the consumer will not be able to see the finish and will only know of its presence if such information is included on labels or tags. (See Figure 1.1.)

Soft goods Products constructed of textiles and other flexible materials including apparel, interior textiles, and technical textiles.

Smart textiles (also known as **smart fabrics**, **interactive textiles** or **intelligent textiles**) sense and react to the environment or stimuli of an electrical, chemical, thermal, mechanical, magnetic, or other nature. While smart textiles are an area undergoing rapid change, many new smart textiles are of interest to government agencies, the military, and consumers. Smart textiles deliver medication in slow controlled doses, monitor pulse and body temperature, promote safety with sensors that identify seat occupancy in vehicles, and keep wearers comfortable by promoting heat loss in warm weather and minimizing heat loss in cooler weather. In the future, some smart textiles may clean themselves. Research in its early stages has found chemicals that can be applied to the surface of fabrics to break down soil and kill microorganisms that cause odor. Smart textiles also offer the potential for reducing design and product piracy and counterfeit products.

Technical or **industrial textiles** include a broad range of materials that are widely used in special applications of a technical nature and that are generally not considered apparel or interiors. Table 1.1 lists examples of technical textiles. Technical textiles contribute to quality of life. For example, the automotive industry uses textiles for tire cords for a durable tire that produces a comfortable ride; seat upholstery and carpeting for comfort, style, and easy care; head liners and window runners for noise reduction and a finished interior; seat belts and shoulder harnesses for safety; reinforcement fibers in molded plastic parts to reduce weight and cost; and fan belts, gaskets, and seals to improve function and efficiency.

Some textiles are encountered every day while others are never directly used or seen by most people. Everyday textile products include **apparel** (clothing and fashion accessories like bags and shoes made from flexible materials), **interior textiles** (including upholstered furniture, carpets and rugs, wall coverings, draperies and curtains, table linens, and towels and bed linens; also known as **interior furnishings** or **home fashions**), and technical and industrial textiles found in the home like toothbrushes and bandages and wraps to immobilize or support wrists and ankles in first aid kits, and in the car (seat belts, trunk liners, and gaskets and belts in the engine). Technical textiles include fabrics that reduce environmental damage (woven and nonwoven landscape erosion control fabrics) and protect other buildings and pedestrians during demolition of buildings (woven and nonwoven demolition screen fabrics). Medical textiles include warp knit replacement veins, graphite fibers to lubricate replacement joints, impermeable gloves and bandages that protect against infection, and filter membranes in artificial kidney machines.

Most textiles are made of fibers that are processed into yarns and woven or knit into fabrics. Coloration and finishing add value, enhance appearance, or improve performance.

Table 1.1 Examples of Technical and Industrial Textiles Grouped by End Use Category

Personal Hygiene	Transportation	Environment	Medical
Tooth and hair-brushes	Tire cords	Erosion barriers	Support wraps
Medicated pads	Road bed underlays	Weed-control fabrics	Casts
Makeup brushes	Bicycle helmets	Pond liners	Surgical masks
Nail buffers	Interiors for planes, buses, cars, and trucks	Snow and silt fences	Sutures
Incontinence pads	Seat belts and air bags	Drainage screens	Arteries
Feminine hygiene products	Brake linings	Shore protectors	Examination gowns
Cotton balls	Gaskets and seals	Oil-spill-control barriers	Bandages
Dental floss	Convertible tops	Air and water filters	Dialysis filters
			Gloves
Food	**Animal Care**	**Agriculture**	**Protective Gear**
Bags and sacks	Leashes	Bags and sacks	Ballistic vests
Bakery filters	Blankets	Ropes	Heat/fire-resistant suits
Coffee filters	Saddles	Hoses and belts	Impact-resistant helmets
Packaging materials	Stall liners	Bale coverings	Chemical-resistant gloves
Tea bags	Restraints	Tractor interiors	Abrasion-resistant gloves
	Pet bed liners	Plant covers and tree wraps	Hazmat suits
Sports and Recreation	**Manufactured Goods**	**Miscellaneous Products**	**Building Materials**
Helmet liners	Hoses	Artificial flowers/plants	Insulation
Protective pads	Belts	Banners and flags	Covers for wiring
Balls	Loading dock covers	Book bindings	Drop cloths
String for rackets	Tarpaulins	Candle wicks	Pool liners and covers
Tents	Paint rollers	Casket linings	Wall coverings
Backpacks	Wipes	Communication lines	Venetian blinds
Life jackets	Carpet backing	Felt-tip pens	Window screens
Rafts and boat hulls	Mailing envelopes	Lampshades	Gaskets and seals
Sails	Duct tape backing	Mops and dusting cloths	Duct tape
Fishing line and nets	Conveyor belts	Sandbags	Awnings
Artificial playing surfaces	Silk-screen mesh	Personal computer boards	Moisture barriers

▶ **Learning Activity 1**

Select Fabric #1 from your swatch kit. Dismantle it so that you have a fiber and a yarn. Describe the differences and similarities between these components. Compare what you have written with the definitions for fiber, yarn, and fabric. Identify an end use that would be appropriate for this fabric and explain your reasoning.

(See Figures 1.2 and 1.3.) Many of these astonishing textiles were not possible before the development of manufactured fibers. It is challenging to envision what our lives would be like without them.

The field of textiles is ever-changing. Textiles are modified in response to changes in fashion, consumer demand, production costs and processes, government standards for safety and environmental quality, research developments, innovations in the industry, and international trade. These influential factors and historical developments related to the textile industry are identified. Some changes occur quickly, but others might take several years of basic and applied research to engineer new fibers, new end uses, or meet challenging criteria for unusual performance conditions or applications. As consumers and industry expectations become more sophisticated, demands for textile product performance expand.

Astronauts traveled to the moon in 28-layer space suits with nylon water-cooled underwear. Life is prolonged by replacing worn-out or damaged body parts with textiles such as polyester arteries and velour heart valves. Ballistic- and slash-resistant vests protect police and soldiers, and shoulder and seat belts make travel safer. Three-dimensional, inflatable structures protect us from desert heat and arctic cold.

Technical textiles surround us. We brush our teeth, hair, and clothes with bristles made of synthetic or natural fibers. Buildings are warmer with fiberglass insulation and polyethylene film wind and moisture barriers. Roads last longer with synthetic nonwoven underlays that minimize shifting of the road base and development of potholes. Soil is conserved with fiber erosion-control barriers of woven or nonwoven fabrics. Wiring is insulated with fiberglass-woven braids.

Athletic performance is enhanced with carbon reinforcement fibers in golf clubs and tennis rackets and with body-condensing swimwear. Injuries are minimized with padded protective helmets, shoulder and knee pads, gloves specific to the sport, and footwear that protects the foot and ankle while enhancing performance. The next time you are in a store that specializes in sporting goods, outdoor recreation, or athletic performance, examine the wide range of footwear and gloves available—each designed for a specific activity. Body parts are protected with support wraps of woven or knit fabrics.

Farmers and ranchers protect crops and livestock with textile barrier fabrics. Fine mesh nets protect fruit from insects while textile braids are used for leads for show horses and cattle. Fruits and vegetables are packaged in net bags. Outdoor activities take place under tents and awnings to protect us from sun and rain. Manufactured goods are transported on conveyor belts made of composite textiles. At the gas station, gas is pumped through a fibrous filter and a fabric-supported hose. Our lives would be very different if all technical textiles were to disappear.

The apparel industry uses a wide range of textiles in products for consumers. Apparel ranges from soft and absorbent apparel for newborn infants, to easy-care and colorful apparel

Figure 1.2 A photodegradable erosion control blanket (pictured) is an example of a technical textile.
SOURCE: Courtesy of North American Green.

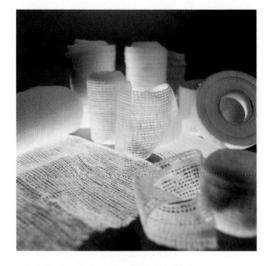

Figure 1.3 Medical fabrics, woven tapes, and webbing for use in orthopedic/prosthetic and other medical applications.
SOURCE: Courtesy of Bally Ribbon Mills.

▶ **Learning Activity 2**

Make a list of the textile products you have used today. Group your list by apparel, interior textiles, or technical textiles. (It might be helpful to consult Table 1.1 when identifying the technical textiles.) Compare your list with those of others in your class. What are some of the common and not so common items on the lists? Discuss how textiles have contributed to your quality of life. What parts of your day would not have been possible without these textile products? Has anyone worn or used any smart textiles today? If yes, ask them to describe or display the textile product and explain what it does.

for toddlers, to comfortable and stylish apparel for office workers, to rugged and durable apparel for farmers and factory workers, to high fashion and elegant apparel for weddings and celebrations. Human performance in sports is further enhanced by selecting textiles that help remove perspiration from the surface and maximize heat loss in warm weather or that minimize heat loss in cold or windy weather. Fabrics used in apparel include the fabric consumers see when shopping for and using apparel as well as nonwoven support materials and woven or knit elastic narrow fabrics that help maintain the shape and appearance of the garment.

The interior textiles industry also uses a wide range of textiles in home and contract interiors. Examples include wall and window coverings; office panels; upholstery; mattresses, mattress pads, and pillows; carpeting and rugs; and table, bed, and bath linens. Nonwoven support materials and fiberfills are used in the interiors industry to enhance the comfort and appearance of upholstered furniture.

Textiles are soft goods and include apparel, interior, and technical items. They add variety and interest to our activities and make our lives more comfortable and safer.

The Global Textile Complex

The textile complex developed from an arts and crafts industry perpetuated by guilds in the early centuries, through the Industrial Revolution in the 18th and 19th centuries when the emphasis was on mechanization and mass production, to the 21st century, with its emphasis on science, technology, quality, and cost efficiency. In the last century, manufactured fibers and modified textured yarns were developed. New fabrications were created, knits became a major fabric for apparel and interiors, and many finishes and sophisticated textile production and marketing systems were developed.

Sustainability concerns have resulted in a renewed interest in the impact of the production, use, cleaning, and disposal of textiles. Nylon carpets and polyester beverage bottles that used to go to landfills are being recycled into textile products. Consider the environmental impact of buying a cotton shirt that is labeled "machine wash/machine dry" versus a silk shirt that is labeled "dry clean only." Which is better for the environment? Why is it better for the environment? Our increasing awareness of the limits of world resources are driving research with focuses on renewable resources, lower energy and water use in the production and finishing of textiles, modifying cleaning processes for consumers and commercial establishments, and recycling. New chemicals and processes are being investigated for finishing and cleaning textiles. General government policies and trade practices are being reevaluated to make global textile production more sustainable.

The **textile complex** is the global mix of related industries that provide soft goods for the world's population. Figure 1.4 includes several dimensions of the textile complex that relate most closely to textile materials: the natural and manufactured fiber producers, yarn spinners and throwsters who create plied or textured yarns, fabric mills that weave and knit fabric, tufters who make some carpet and upholstery fabrics, fiberweb or nonwoven fabric producers, finishers and dyers who add to the appearance and determine the color of fabrics in the market, equipment producers, and many others. While many dimensions of the textile complex are not evident to the average individual, huge segments of the world population are involved in the development, engineering, design, production, evaluation, marketing, and transportation of textiles and textile products.

The United States and Europe were once major players in the development and production of synthetic fibers. While research and fiber production continue in the United States and Europe, Korea and Japan are current leaders in research. China, India, and parts of eastern Europe are undergoing rapid growth in research and production.

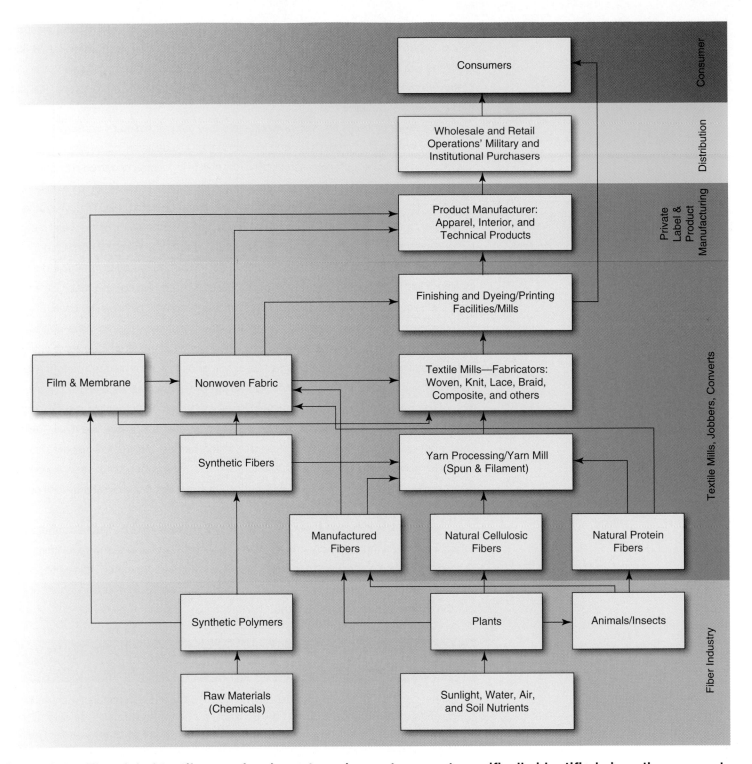

Figure 1.4 The global textile complex. Imports and exports are not specifically identified since they can enter or exit the complex at every stage.

At one time, many textile products were domestic products, meaning that they were produced and sold within a single country. While a domestic industry remains in many parts of the world, many portions of the textile complex are involved globally with the export and import of textile components, product components, or finished products. **Globalization** refers to companies purchasing from and/or selling to multiple sites in the world and applies to many industries, including the textile complex. Globalization requires use of advanced technology to satisfy a wide variety of consumers and coordinate purchasing, manufacturing, and distribution to multiple locations worldwide. While the textile complex has had an international perspective for centuries including early silk and spice/natural dye trade routes, globalization as it is now practiced is a twentieth century development. Many of the textile products sold in the United States are produced in other countries in a process known as offshore production, just one of many aspects of globalization.

Many textile products are well traveled before they are purchased by consumers. A cotton T-shirt may include fiber grown by cotton farmers in the United States, converted into yarns and knit into fabric in China, cut and assembled into the shirt in Indonesia, and dyed and embroidered in India. Maintaining records of the information required for product labels can be a challenge.

While thousands of jobs have moved offshore where production costs are lower, other jobs have been created to ensure that products manufactured in other parts of the world meet customer expectations for design, size, production, and quality standards; that the products are appropriately labeled; and that they do not present a hazard to the consumer. The process of making a textile product is long and involved. Descriptions of the desired materials and their characteristics and performance are written so that appropriate materials are used.

However, with access to the global market, many more options are now available for every type of textile product. The wide variety of products in the market has created some challenges in the selection of apparel and interior textiles. Many items look alike but their performance and care differ significantly. Without specific knowledge of textiles, it is impossible to know what factors are important for specific end uses. Knitted fabrics look like woven fabrics, vinyl and polyurethane films look like leather, and acrylic and polyester fabrics look like wool. Traditional cotton fabrics may be polyester or polyester/cotton blends. Consumers expect that items offered for sale are appropriate for the end use. It is the responsibility of those who work in the global textile complex to work to ensure the consumer trust is not damaged by poorly performing textile products.

To make textile selection easier for consumers, the textile industry has set standards and established quality-control programs for many textile products. Laws and regulations inform consumers of fiber content and care requirements and protect them from unsafe textiles, improperly labeled merchandise, and other unfair trade practices. Other laws and regulations protect the environment and regulate trade.

The global textile complex is one of the world's largest industries and has a significant impact on the world economy.

► Learning Activity 3

Make a list of the countries identified on the labels of the textile products you have with you today. Group them by type, country, and part of the world, such as shirt, Haiti/Central America. Consult the world map in Appendix D to determine the location of many of the countries. Compile your results with those of your classmates. Do you see specific trends regarding product types, countries, or parts of the world? What factors might influence these trends? What are the factors that sway your textile product purchases that might also influence these trends?

► Learning Activity 4

Examine the labels of several textile products and identify the kinds of information provided. Compile the information found by the class. Discuss why that information is required and how consumers might use that information.

Energy and water use, energy and water conservation, environmental quality, sustainability, noise abatement, health, and safety issues are challenges that affect all industries. Efforts to meet standards set by governments affect consumers by increasing the amount of information at point of purchase, raising prices for merchandise, limiting the choices available, and improving product and environmental quality.

Textile fabrics can be beautiful, durable, comfortable, and easy-care. Understanding the components used in textile products and their production will provide a better basis for textile selection, a better understanding of product limitations, and a more satisfied consumer.

▶ Learning Activity 5

Search the yellow pages of a local phone directory or the ads in a newspaper or magazine and identify the types of businesses that include apparel, interior textiles, and technical textiles and products within their merchandise mix or services provided. Discuss the range of business and product types and their impact on the local and global economies.

key terms

Apparel 7
Coloration 7
Fabric 7
Fiber 6
Finish 7
Globalization 11
Gray, grey, or greige goods 7

Home fashions 7
Industrial textiles 7
Intelligent textiles 7
Interactive textiles 7
Interior furnishings 7
Interior textiles 7
Polymer 6

Smart textiles 7
Soft goods 7
Technical textiles 7
Textile 6
Textile complex 10
Yarn 7

review questions

1. Define the key terms, explain the differences among them, and describe how these terms relate to textiles.

2. How do textiles contribute to quality of life?

3. Consult Figure 1.4 and explain the parts of the textile complex that would have been involved in producing and marketing a 100 percent cotton towel.

4. Identify five things you do that are made possible, safer, or easier because of today's textiles.

5. Find an example of each of the following textiles that you come into contact with on a regular basis: film, fiber, yarn, and fabric. Identify the items that are a new textile application for you. Why are these items considered textiles?

6. Identify your current career goal and describe where it would fit within the global textile complex in Figure 1.4.

7. What are the differences between apparel or interior textiles and technical textiles?

8. What are smart textiles? Do you own or use any items that are considered to be smart textiles?

9. Explain how each of the following would use knowledge of or information about textiles (It might be beneficial to scan the discussion of careers in Chapter 22):
   a. Designer of children's casual or play clothes
   b. Product development specialist for a specialty retailer for menswear
   c. Stylist for a catalog company that sells sportswear
   d. Technical designer for a discount store's bedding line
   e. Buyer for junior apparel for a department store
   f. Interior designer for an architectural firm that specializes in office buildings and corporate headquarters

PRODUCT DEVELOPMENT from a TEXTILE PERSPECTIVE

CHAPTER OBJECTIVES

- To describe the role of textiles in product development.
- To apply the serviceability components to textiles and textile products.
- To introduce environmental concerns and sustainability concepts related to the global textile complex.
- To link product serviceability and textile performance with target market needs and expectations.
- To identify information sources used in product development.

2

Product development refers to the design and engineering of a product so that it has the desired serviceability characteristics, appeals to the target market, can be made within an acceptable time frame for a reasonable cost, and can be sold at a profit. Product development encompasses a range of activities and differs widely by companies and segments of the global textile complex. It may involve selecting interior textiles for a room, developing or creating completely new fibers or finishes, determining new end uses for current or new textiles, selecting materials to incorporate into apparel or interior or technical products, developing new styles or design features, modifying current styles, or altering competitors' styles. The product development process involves many areas of specialized knowledge, ranging from understanding product characteristics that appeal to a specific target market or address specific needs of a target market to knowing how to produce the item so that it meets consumers' needs. Important factors for successful product development include understanding customers and consumers, product innovation, product management, and textile materials. Because of the large role that the textile complex plays in the global economy and the shorter product life span compared with that of many other consumer and technical products, textile product development has become an expensive, but essential element.

In assessing target market or consumer expectations, a firm needs to understand its consumers, their shopping preference, lifestyle, values, and factors that influence purchase decisions. Some firms have specialized market-research divisions that help identify consumer expectations. In other firms, product-development specialists, designers, and merchandisers are responsible for identifying consumer expectations, designing the product line, selecting materials, sourcing, and developing purchasing and production specifications. Many firms also work with forecasting companies to ensure success in product development. Color and fashion trend forecasting may be done 18 to 24 months in advance. Forecasting companies and organizations research trends and sell their services to designers, manufacturers, retailers, and others. To forecast color, industry experts meet periodically to discuss and identify colors for each season and product type. Color cards are produced for residential and contract interiors; packaging; automotive applications; women's, men's, and children's wear; and other markets where color is an important factor in selling the product. Fashion trend forecast information includes silhouette, fabric swatches to demonstrate fabric type and texture, color cards, and periodic newsletters with current fashion information tailored to specific product categories or markets.

To survive and thrive in the global economy, firms in the textile complex must develop management strategies that enable them to recognize and capitalize on opportunities within the market. Product development includes a range of activities. Basic research may lead to new fibers. Applied research may focus on minimizing environmentally harmful by-products from dyeing and finishing. Blue jeans may be redesigned to provide a more fashion-forward look. New fabric designs and colorways may be created for contract window treatments. Understanding textile characteristics and serviceability is essential for product development so that materials or fabrics used in a product meet consumers' expectations and needs. Some innovations such as microfibers (fibers with very small diameters, introduced in Chapter 6) transformed some existing product types (blouses with softer drape and hand), created new product lines that increased company markets (production of both regular and micro-fibers), and broadened existing product lines (tights and hosiery combining regular and micro-fibers). Other innovations such as soil-resistant finishes resulted in product improvements that improved performance (resist soiling), solved problems (better cleaning of oily soils), or added perceived value to some products (soil-resistant dress slacks would look new longer). Innovations solve new problems or meet new market needs, such as ultraviolet-resistant fabrics that reduce sun exposure. Innovations that reduce costs or respond to consumer demand include garment dyeing in colors that are selling well.

Significant changes are occurring in textile product development and the global textile complex. While Europe and the United States once dominated textile and textile product production and design, that dominance is faltering. Worldwide developments include the increasing importance of Japanese designers, technology-rich fabrics from South Korea and Taiwan, and a developing international fashion industry in India. China has developed a five-year plan to restructure its industry and develop technology-rich synthetics and desirable Chinese apparel brands with outsourcing to other countries like Bangladesh.

Denim is a long-term classic fabric with a strong fashion component and will be one example used to illustrate the variables that may be considered in selecting or developing a fabric. Denim is a basic fabric used for such diverse products as jeans, skirts, shorts, jackets, hats, bags, upholstery, wall coverings, and bed sheets. Denim can differ in fiber content from all cotton to blends of cotton and polyester to all wool. Denim can be made from new, unused cotton fiber, or polyester fiber recycled from beverage bottles. The yarns in denim can be made in many sizes by several processes. Denim can be made in many weights, from very heavy to relatively light. It can be finished to look crisp and new or faded and stressed. Denim can be dyed or printed in a variety of colors or patterns, including the traditional indigo blue. All these variations related to fabrics mean that many decisions are made during product development to determine the look and performance of the fabric and the product. Understanding the effects of decisions related to fiber and yarn type, fabric type and weight, and fabric finishes on product serviceability is one responsibility of the product-development team.

Product-development decisions occur throughout the textile complex to determine what is available in the market. When designers, merchandisers, producers, or engineers select one fabric or fiber or yarn type over another, they determine the product's performance, appearance, appeal, and cost. Factors such as fabric weight, stiffness, hand, texture, yarn structure and process, fiber content, fiber modifications, coloration method, and finishes should be considered in decision making. Of course, analysis is an important step in product development to diminish risk and improve the product through laboratory analysis, wear tests in which consumers use the product in real or realistic settings, test marketing, or focus group discussions with sample products.

Sometimes, design firms negotiate with fabric producers so that some part of the fabric—for example, the color—is exclusive or confined to that firm. *Confinement* means that only one firm can use that color, pattern, or fabric. Some large retailers or manufacturers control such a significant market share that fabric producers willingly modify their processes to meet the buyer's preferences. Some fabric firms in the interiors market produce custom-designed fabrics or custom colors. However, many firms are small and must work with fabrics available on the open market.

▶ Learning Activity 1

Visit three or more different stores that sell denim jeans. Walk around the store and examine at least four different denim jean styles in each store. Describe the target market for each store. Identify similarities and differences among the jeans by store type. Compile the information gathered by the class and identify some basic factors related to product innovation for denim jeans.

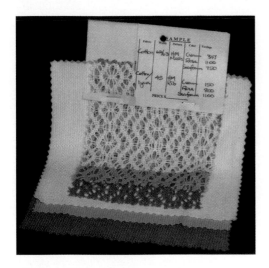

Figure 2.1 Fabric presentation swatches showing an assortment of fabric structures and colors.

Product development drives many factors related to textile products and sustainability.

Fabrics are presented in a variety of formats so that designers can observe a fabric's appearance and drape, examine fabric texture and hand, and consider how an assortment of related fabrics work together (Figure 2.1). *Assortment* refers to a group of fabrics that share a commonality of design, structure, or color. For example, an assortment could consist of fabrics of the same structure available in a range of colors or one color available in several fabrications. Information may be limited to a fabric's style number, width, fiber content, and weight, or additional information related to yarn size, yarn spinning method, weave structure, and finishes may be provided. Adherence to fire safety codes also may be provided for some interior and apparel fabrics. Fabric information helps product developers determine its appropriateness for the product and target market and determine production requirements.

Designers and product-development specialists examine many fabrics when developing a product line. Designers may be attracted to a specific fabric because of its hand, color, texture, drape, or other factor. But they also consider their target market and their company's product line and mission. In order for their company to make a profit and stay in business, the products must satisfy consumers' expectations for serviceability and performance.

Serviceability and the Consumer

Serviceability describes the measure of a textile product's ability to meet consumers' needs. The emphasis of serviceability is on understanding the target market and relating target market needs to product serviceability. The serviceability concepts that are used to organize the information are aesthetics, durability, comfort, safety, appearance retention, care, environmental concerns, sustainability, and cost.

Aesthetics addresses the attractiveness or appearance of a textile product. Does the item look pleasing and appropriate for its end use? Does it make the right statement for the target market? Aesthetics includes texture, luster, pattern or motif, color, opacity, drape, stiffness, and surface characteristics.

Durability describes the manner in which the product withstands use, that is, the length of time the product is considered suitable for the use for which it was purchased. Will the consumer be satisfied with how well it wears, how strong it is, and how long it remains attractive? Is the product strong, tear and abrasion resistant, snag-proof, and pill resistant?

Comfort addresses the way textiles affect heat, air, and moisture transfer, and the way the body interacts with a textile product. **Safety** considers a textile's ability to protect the body from harm. Is this item comfortable for its end use in terms of absorbency, temperature regulation, hand, and so on? Will its comfort change with use or age? How does it feel? Is it safe to use or wear?

Appearance retention considers how the product maintains its original appearance during use and care. Will the item retain its new look with use and cleaning? Will it resist wrinkling, shrinkage, abrasion, soiling, stretching, pilling, sagging, or other changes with use? Will it age quickly or slowly?

Care describes the treatment required to maintain a textile product's original appearance and cleanliness. Does the item include a recommended care procedure? Is the care procedure appropriate to maintain the product's new or nearly new look? Are these recommendations appropriate considering its end use, cost, and product type? Is the care reasonable for the product and target market?

Environmental concerns focus on the effect that the production, use, or disposal of a textile has on the environment. **Sustainability** describes practices and policies that reduce environmental pollution and do not exploit people or natural resources in meeting the lifestyle needs of the present without compromising the future. Sustainability deals with the life cycle impact of products. **Life cycle impact** examines the way the production, use, care, and disposal of a product affects the environment and the people involved with the product. How has the production of this item affected the environment and the people involved in its production? How will its recommended care affect the environment? Can this product, its components, or its packaging materials be recycled? Do the product or its packaging contain any recycled materials? Have the product or its components been evaluated for environmental concerns and sustainability? Can the individuals or company producing this product earn a living or make a profit? Are the fibers rapidly renewable without concentrating their impact within one segment of the agricultural or manufacturing segment?

Textile production has been linear: producing a textile product and delivering it to the consumer as quickly and inexpensively as possible. Sustainability is adding another dimension to this process. New factors are entering the product development process—what are the short- and long-term effects of producing, using, and disposing of this product? If the thread, fabric, and trim are all made of a single fiber, will that make it easier to recycle this product? Can this product be used to create new products?

Cost is the amount paid to acquire, use, maintain, and dispose of a product. Additional factors that should be considered include how much it will cost to care for this product during its lifetime and the product's inherent attributes. Cost is very important to many consumers, but cost will not be discussed in much depth in this book because many outside factors, such as how a product is promoted and sold, greatly influence purchase price. Fabric cost is only one component of the cost of a finished product. For example, estimates for costs for a woven fabric include 21 percent for fibers, 20 percent for yarn production, 29 percent for weaving, 14 percent for finishing, and 16 percent for dyeing or printing.

These serviceability concepts provide a framework for combining textile knowledge with consumers' expectations to develop an understanding of textiles. When consumers discuss textile products, they often touch on these concepts, although their terms may not precisely match some of the more technical terms used in this book. One consumer may describe the needs for a particular product as inexpensive, easy care, nice looking, comfortable in hot weather, and long-lasting. While this list may not address all eight aspects of serviceability, the comments do address cost (inexpensive), care (easy care), aesthetics and appearance retention (nice looking), comfort (comfortable in hot weather), and durability (long-lasting). Another consumer might focus more on a product with lower environmental impact and express concerns about the safety components of the product. Is the fiber recycled or can it be recycled? Is there excessive packaging with the product that adds cost without adding value to the product? Will it meet safety standards for children's sleepwear? Consumers evaluate their purchases and determine their satisfaction with products based on these concepts, which will be used throughout the book to relate textile characteristics and performance to consumer expectations.

> Serviceability includes aesthetics, durability, comfort, appearance retention, care, and cost. Environmental concerns and sustainability are additional factors of importance in product development.

▶ Learning Activity 2

Select a textile product you are wearing. Describe your general expectations when you purchased this item and group them by serviceability concepts. Prioritize the serviceability concepts from most to least important. Describe your degree of satisfaction with this product. In what serviceability areas has performance been satisfactory and in what areas could it be improved?

Performance

Performance describes the manner in which a textile, textile component, or textile product responds to use or how it responds when exposed to some mechanical or environmental factor that might adversely affect it. Mechanical factors include abrasion, impact, or pulling forces. Environmental factors include such diverse things as extremely warm or cold temperatures, intense light, and frequent and prolonged wetting. Because performance measures are used in making product-development decisions, methods have been developed to make such assessments. These methods are referred to as *standard test methods* so that everyone assessing performance will follow the same procedure and use identical equipment in the process. For example, we can assess how much fading or loss of strength occurs when a textile is exposed to a known amount of artificial light for a certain time. We can measure how much force will cause a textile to tear. We can assess whether a fabric will bleed when washed and how much a fabric will shrink when machine-washed and machine-dried using a regular cycle with hot water.

Each material in a textile product influences the overall performance of the product. That is, textile product performance cannot be determined solely on a single component such as fiber content or fabric structure. Although these two product characteristics are important and can have a significant impact, product performance can be enhanced or negated by other factors such as yarn type and finish, and product fit, construction, or design.

Retail sleeping bags will be used as an example to illustrate differences in products, target markets, and expectations (Figure 2.2). Sleeping bag A is sold at a specialty store that carries products for outdoor enthusiasts. This bag is mummy-shaped, with an outer cover of water-repellent ripstop nylon taffeta, a filling of high-volume goose down, and an inner lining of polyester modified to enhance warmth and comfort. Bag A is very lightweight and can be compressed and packed in a relatively small space. It is expensive and requires special care because of the down filling. This bag is designed to be used outdoors without the added protection of a tent or other structure.

Sleeping bag B is a more traditional sleeping bag sold in a discount store. The outer layer is a cotton/polyester blend print cloth with a printed pattern that would appeal to a young child, the fiberfill is polyester, and the inner layer is cotton/polyester flannel. Bag B will not be as warm or as expensive as bag A. It is designed to be used indoors by a child. It is easy to care for and can be machine-washed and machine-dried.

Sleeping bag C is sold through a mail-order catalog and also has a traditional shape. It incorporates a specially modified polyester fiberfill for warmth without weight; it has a solid dark-green polyester/cotton poplin outer cover and a plaid yarn-dyed cotton flannel for the inner layer. Bag C is more expensive than bag B and is also easy to care for. Bag C would appeal to an adult who is interested in a warm, comfortable sleeping bag to be used in a tent or other structure and who does not have a lot of time to shop.

The three sleeping bags differ in their materials, in their serviceability and performance, and in the way they are marketed to their specific target market.

T-shirts provide another example of variations in products, target markets, and expectations (Figure 2.3). A wide variety of T-shirts exists on the market to meet the needs and expectations of consumers. T-shirt A is a basic, no-frills 50 percent cotton/50 percent polyester T-shirt of a solid navy blue sold in a discount store. It is a simple tube knit jersey fabric with no side seams. It will be worn for physical labor such as construction work or yard and garden work, so the target market expects the shirt will be labeled machine wash and machine dry. Other expectations include a shirt that is durable and comfortable. T-shirt B, sold at specialty shops for teenage consumers, is a more fashion forward 95 percent cotton/5 percent spandex blend T-shirt with lace neckline trim, shorter

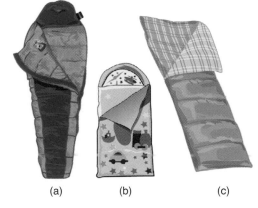

Figure 2.2 Sleeping bags:
(a) mummy-shaped,
(b) traditional-shaped (for child),
and (c) traditional-shaped (for adult).

(a)   (b)   (c)

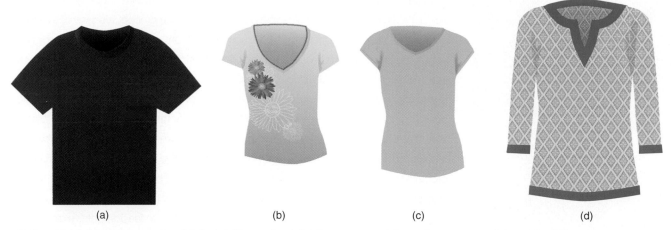

Figure 2.3 T-shirts: (a) work shirt, (b) V-neck shirt for teens, (c) active-wear shirt, (d) office-wear shirt.

sleeves, and more body-hugging fit for casual outings and class. The fabric in this T-shirt is a patterned jersey knit in a fashion-forward yellow-green that is screen printed with a floral pattern. T-shirt C is made with specially engineered comfort polyester. This T-shirt is designed for rock climbing to wick moisture from the body, dry quickly, and protect against ultraviolet exposure. This polyester T-shirt is made of a mesh knit to enhance comfort. This T-shirt would be sold by an athletic or outdoor activity specialty store. T-shirt D is an all-silk baby pique knit with three-quarter-length sleeves and a split neckline for office and white-collar work. The fabric design incorporates several shades of blue, making it easy to match with slacks, skirts, and jackets. This T-shirt would be available from a mail-order catalog or Web site. Each fiber or blend listed here contributes a unique set of performance characteristics to the shirt. Additional aspects related to product performance that can be tried out during product development include yarn type and structure, fabric knit structure, type of support materials and decorative trims, and dyes and finishes.

Fabric performance may be assessed by the fabric producer, the firm buying the fabric, or an outside firm that specializes in assessing fabric performance. Unfortunately, some firms do not assess fabric performance, increasing the risk that products will not meet performance expectations or will fail in consumers' hands. For example, products that incorporate two or more fabrics of different colors may exhibit problems with color bleeding during laundering if the designer is not aware of this performance problem. If one fabric bleeds in laundering, then all products that combine both fabrics into a single product incorporate this inherent flaw. These products are likely to produce consumer dissatisfaction with the product, complaints, and returns. By failing to assess how the two fabrics interact, the designer has created an unsatisfactory product and an expensive failure for the company.

In some product and performance categories, such as the flammability of interior textiles in public-use areas and the flammability of children's sleepwear, performance testing is required by law. Products that do not meet minimum safety standards are banned from the market.

▶ Learning Activity 3

Use Fabrics #2, 8, and 25 from your swatch kit. Identify the similarities and differences in their structure, weight, and appearance. Identify an apparel product that might be made using each fabric. Describe an appropriate target market and its serviceability expectations for each product. How might these fabrics be modified to make them more appropriate for the end use and target market? How would these modifications be a factor in product development? Which of these modifications would be considered innovative? What new products might make use of this innovation?

Figure 2.4 Samples from performance testing: snagging (top) and resistance to sunlight (bottom) with faded portion on left side.

Understanding textiles will contribute to developing serviceable products that perform well for consumers.

Fabric performance often is assessed following standard industry procedures so that performance values for fabrics can be compared. In these procedures, one or more small pieces of fabric are tested for performance on a specific criterion, such as snagging or fading (Figure 2.4). Assessing fabric performance helps in selecting fabrics appropriate for the target market and the firm. Some firms have developed specifications or written descriptions describing minimum performance measures for fabrics used in their products. Their performance specifications are based on understanding their target market's expectations. These specifications help the firm ensure that the fabrics they buy and the products they turn out meet their target market's expectations for performance. Although performance testing eliminates many material-selection problems, it is not an absolute guarantee that all products will be perfect, since some problems may be related to accidents or spills that involve a tiny portion of a fabric.

Product quality has become an important dimension in the competitive global marketplace. But the term is difficult to define because it means different things to consumers and producers. *Quality* generally refers to the sum total of product characteristics such as appearance, end use, performance, material interactions within the product, consistency among identical products, and freedom from defects in construction or materials. Throughout this book, measures and dimensions of fabric quality will be addressed. Keep in mind that fabric quality is only one component of product quality. Fabric quality addresses the fabric used to produce the product. Other factors beyond the scope of this book, such as design and construction, also influence product quality.

It must be stressed that neither this book nor any course or combination of courses in textiles will provide the "best" single answer for any specific end use. This book will not answer the question, "What is the best combination of fiber and yarn type, fabrication method, and finish for (fill in the name of a product)?" The answer to the question is based on understanding a specific target market and end use, current fashion, lifestyle, budget, access to the market, and so on. However, this book will provide a wealth of information for developing and selecting products to meet a wide variety of target market needs.

Information Sources

Information related to textiles and the selection of textile and other materials to be used in textile products can be found in textbooks, technical journals, industry or trade publications, and on the World Wide Web. Technical publications include such journals as *America's Textiles International*, *AATCC Review*, and *Textile Research Journal*. Trade publications such as *DNR* (www.wwd.com) and *Home Furnishings News* (http://www.hfnmag.com) are available online. The World Wide Web includes many sites that provide technical information and fabric assortments. Many producers and retailers provide information about their products on their Web sites. Of course, it remains the responsibility of the reader to determine the validity and accuracy of the information and to apply it in a professional and appropriate manner.

▶ Learning Activity 4

Examine current newspapers and magazines for articles related to textiles and textile products. Describe the topic and its relationship to textiles. Who is the target market for the publication? How would the article inform the public about textiles and textile products or persuade the public to purchase a textile product?

key terms

review questions

1. Define product development and describe how it determines what is on the market.

2. Identify consumer expectations for each serviceability concept for the following products and target markets:
   a. Carpet in a fast-food restaurant in an upscale shopping mall
   b. Shirt/blouse for a retail management trainee
   c. Housecoat/robe for a resident in a physical rehabilitation center
   d. Upholstery for chairs in a medical clinic's waiting room
   e. Adhesive bandage for a college student's heel blister

3. Explain the relationships among serviceability, product performance, and product development.

4. Compare the type of textile information available in a technical journal, in a trade publication, and on the Internet.

5. Using the serviceability concepts, debate the advantages and disadvantages from a consumer's perspective of an organic cotton T-shirt versus a polyester T-shirt made from recycled beverage bottles.

6. List six questions that would help you determine the life cycle impact of a pair of cotton slacks.

7. Identify five questions a friend or relative might ask before purchasing the following items:
   a. an apparel item, such as a shirt
   b. an interior textile item such as a placemat

8. Compare the two lists in Question 7 and describe how and why they are different. Now, consider how the questions might differ if the consumer represented a different target market or socioeconomic group. What are the factors that might explain these differences?

9. Identify three sources of information about textiles and textile products other than the Internet. For each source, explain why you selected it, the kinds of information it includes, the bias of the information, and how consumers and professionals might access these sources.

10. Identify five characteristics that you use in determining the quality of a textile product. As you learn more about textiles, add characteristics or details to your list.

section review questions

1. Identify which of these items would be considered a textile. Explain your classification.
   a. Grocery store reusable bag
   b. Dog leash
   c. Vinyl umbrella
   d. Polo shirt
   e. Store awning
   f. Tennis ball
   g. Biking shorts

2. Describe the serviceability factors important for each of the textiles identified in Question 1.

3. Explain how product development might be used to improve the performance or cost for each of the items in Question 1.

4. Explain how product development and the global textile complex work together.

5. Explain why sustainability and environmental impact are becoming increasingly important in decision making regarding product development.

Case Study

Product Development*

A menswear company developed a coat that retailed for $325, a new and higher price point for the company. Because of strong sales for that specific coat, they developed a line of coats for the following season that would retail for $300 to $500. When the economic downturn occurred in 2008, many retailers who had placed orders for the more expensive line cancelled their orders. The owners of the menswear company worked quickly to save their business and focused on products that would retail for less than $200. They reduced fabric costs by negotiating lower prices and finding new suppliers, decreased embellishment on some products, trimmed shipping costs by no longer airmailing goods to/from China, and diminished the number of yarns per inch for part of their shirt line. Other changes related to marketing and management also occurred within the company.

DISCUSSION QUESTIONS

1. What elements of product development are incorporated in this case study?

2. How would the changes in the materials used in the menswear line alter product serviceability and consumer satisfaction?

3. Which is more important to consumers: cost, serviceability, or quality? How do consumers measure product quality? How do they estimate serviceability of textile products?

4. How will the changes the company made in their product line affect the companies that supplied the materials and the individuals working for those companies?

*Binkley, C. (2009, February 12). Inside a fashion label's scramble to survive. *The Wall Street Journal*, D8.

suggested readings

Anon. (2007, February 26). Avoiding global collapse. *Chemical and Engineering News, 85*, (9), 51.

Borland, V. S. (2004). Color works. *Textile World, 154*(1), 48–50.

Chapman, K. (2003). Where design begins. *AATCC Textile Review, 3*(4), 40–42.

Colchester, C. (2007). *Textiles Today: A Global Survey of Trends and Traditions*. New York: Thames & Hudson.

Fletcher, K. (2008). *Sustainable Fashion and Textiles: Design Journeys*. London: Earthscan.

Glock, R. E., & Kunz, G. I. (2005). *Apparel Manufacturing: Sewn Product Analysis*, 4th ed. Upper Saddle River, NJ: Prentice-Hall.

Kadolph, S. J. (2007). *Quality assurance for textiles and apparel*, 2nd ed. New York: Fairchild Publications.

McDonough, W., & Braungart, M. (2002). *Cradle to Cradle*. New York: North Point Press.

Powell, N. B., & Cassill, N. L. (2006). New textile product development: Processes, practices, and products. *Journal of the Textile Institute, 97*(2), 155–166.

Strickland, M. (2008). A detailed manufacturer's guide to successful retail product development and on-time deliveries—From a retailer's perspective. *AATCC Review, 8*(1), 30–33.

Winchester, S. C. (1994). Total quality management in textiles. *Journal of the Textile Institute,* 85, pp. 445–459.

Yaeger, J. I., & Teter-Justice, L. K. (2000). *Textiles for Residential and Commercial Interiors*, 2nd ed. New York: Fairchild Publications.

3 Textile Fibers and Their Properties

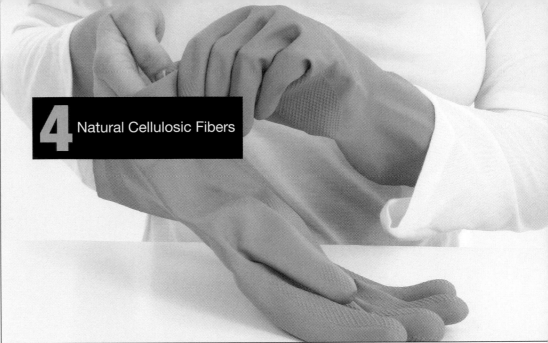

4 Natural Cellulosic Fibers

5 Natural Protein Fibers

6 The Fiber-Manufacturing Process

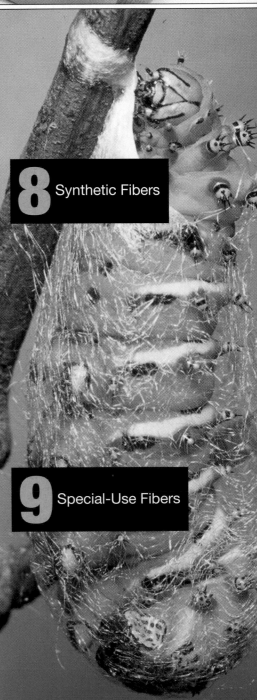

8 Synthetic Fibers

9 Special-Use Fibers

7 Manufactured Regenerated Fibers

FIBERS

 3

 5

 5

 6

 7

 8

 9

SECTION

TEXTILE FIBERS and THEIR PROPERTIES

CHAPTER OBJECTIVES

- To understand terms describing textile fibers and their properties.
- To use terminology correctly.
- To understand the relationships between fiber structure and fiber properties.
- To relate fiber performance to end-use requirements and expectations.
- To identify commonly used fibers through simple identification procedures.

3

Understanding fibers and their performance is essential because fibers are the basic unit of most fabrics. Fibers influence product aesthetics, durability, comfort, appearance retention, care, environmental impact, sustainability, and cost. Successful textile fibers must be readily and continuously available and cost-effective. They must have sufficient strength, pliability, length, and cohesiveness to be processed into yarns, fabrics, and products that satisfy customer needs.

Textile fibers have been used to make fabric for several thousand years. Until 1885, when the first manufactured fiber was produced commercially, fibers were produced by plants and animals. The fibers most commonly used were wool, flax, cotton, and silk. These four natural fibers continue to be used and valued today, although their economic importance relative to all fibers has decreased. **Natural fibers** are those that are in fiber form as they grow or develop and come from animal, plant, or mineral sources. **Manufactured** (or **man-made**) **fibers** are made into fiber form from chemical compounds produced in manufacturing facilities and include such fibers as acrylic used in sweaters and awnings and aramid used in bullet-proof vests and brake liners. See Table 3.1 for a list of natural and manufactured fibers. Several new fibers on the market are made from plant materials, but these new fibers are not considered natural

> **Natural fibers** are in fiber form as they grow or develop and come from animal, plant, or mineral sources. **Manufactured** (or **man-made**) **fibers** are made into fiber form from chemical compounds produced in manufacturing facilities.

Table 3.1 Fiber Classification Chart*

NATURAL FIBERS			MANUFACTURED FIBERS			
Cellulosic	**Protein**	**Mineral**	**Cellulosic**	**Protein**	**Synthetic Fibers**	**Mineral**
Seed: Cotton	Wool	Asbestos	Acetate	Azlon	Acrylic	Glass
Coir	Silk		Bamboo		Aramid	Metal/Metallic
Kapok	Cashmere/Pashmina		Lyocell		Elastoester	Carbon
Milkweed	Llama		Rayon		Elasterell-p	Ceramic
	Alpaca		Seaweed		Fluoropolymer	Stainless steel
Bast: Flax	Vicuña				Lastol	
Hemp	Guanaco				Modacrylic	
Ramie	Angora				Nylon	
Jute	Camel				Olefin	
Kenaf	Mohair				PBI	
Hibiscus	Yak				PBO	
	Fur				PLA	
Leaf: Abaca	Qiviut				Polyester	
Piña	Spider silk				Polyimide	
Sisal					Rubber	
Henequen					Spandex	
Other: Rush					Sulfar	
Sea grass					Vinal	
Maize/corn husks					Vinyon	
Rush						
Palm fiber						
Wicker						

*See individual fiber chapters for more complete lists. Only select fibers are included here.

> ▶ **Learning Activity 1**

Look at the labels in your clothes and other textile products you have with you today. Locate where the fibers listed on the labels fit in Table 3.1. Discuss fiber categories represented by product categories such as casual tops, dressy tops, lingerie and underwear, active or athletic wear, casual bottoms, dressy bottoms, outerwear, accessories, book bags/backpacks and purses, and other items. Do you think this distribution is typical for your age group and occupation? How might it differ for other age groups and occupations?

fibers because the starting material does not resemble a fiber. One of the azlon fibers, Soysilk, is made from by-products of tofu production, while PLA, a fiber made from plant sugars, is currently made using fermented corn starch. Bamboo fiber is made from cellulose processed from bamboo stalks.

Many textile processes—spinning, weaving, knitting, dyeing, and finishing of fabrics—were developed for the natural fibers. Weaving and knitting for making fabrics, spinning for producing yarns, and dyeing and finishing to make fabrics more attractive with better consumer performance have been modified for use with manufactured fibers. New processes have been developed specifically for manufactured fibers and sometimes modified for use with natural fibers. For example, *spinning* is also the term used to describe extruding manufactured fibers. Most of the techniques for producing nonwovens have been developed for manufactured fibers.

For example, silk has always been a highly prized fiber because of its smoothness, luster, and softness. Early efforts in manufacturing fibers focused on duplicating silk. Rayon (called *artificial silk* until 1924) was the first fiber to be manufactured. Acetate and nylon also were introduced originally in silklike fabrics.

Many manufactured fibers were developed in the 20th century. Advances have been made in the manufactured-fiber industry, such as modifications of the original or parent fibers, to provide fibers with better properties for specific end uses. The manufactured fibers most commonly used in contemporary apparel and fabrics for interiors include polyester, nylon, olefin, acrylic, rayon, lyocell, and acetate. Fibers for special and technical applications include spandex, aramid, PBI, and sulfar. From time to time, new modifications or new fibers are introduced.

Fiber Properties

Fibers contribute to fabric performance. For example, strong fibers contribute to the durability of fabrics; absorbent fibers are used for apparel that comes into contact with the skin and for towels and diapers; fire-resistant fibers are used for children's sleepwear and firefighters' gear. While consumers may describe textile properties with such terms as *durable, easy care, comfortable*, and *strong*, a professional in the field needs to have a broader and more exact vocabulary. This section will introduce many new terms or provide more precise definitions of terms consumers often use.

Predicting and understanding fabric performance begins with the fiber. Knowledge of fiber properties will help determine a fiber's contribution to fabric and product performance. Fiber properties are determined by their physical structure, chemical composition, and molecular arrangement. Although this chapter focuses on fiber properties, several fabric properties will be included because they need to be understood early in the study of textiles.

Some attributes of fibers are desirable and some are not, often depending on the end use and product. The following list of characteristics of a low-absorbency fiber includes consumer advantages and disadvantages:

- Static cling can occur.
- Dries rapidly.
- Has a cool and slick hand.
- Feels clammy next to the skin.
- Waterborne soils do not stain.
- Liquids wick along the fiber's surface, but absorbency is low.
- Does not shrink when machine-washed and machine-dried.
- Does not require ironing after washing.
- Difficult to dye, but dyes are colorfast to washing.

While fiber plays a major role in the characteristics of a product, other components are also contributors. Fibers are used to produce yarns and nonwoven or fiberweb fabrics. The type of yarn and its structure influence hand and performance. For example, yarns made from short fibers may be comfortable, but they tend to pill. The process used to produce the fabric influences the product's appearance and texture, performance during use and care, and cost. Coloration adds color by dyeing or printing. Finishes alter the fabric's hand, appearance, and performance. These four components (yarn, fabric structure, coloration, and finish) will be discussed in detail in the chapters in Sections 3, 4, and 5.

Because cotton is a common consumer fiber, it is often used as a standard in the industry. It might be helpful to compare cotton's performance to that of other fibers when examining or studying Tables 3.4 through 3.8.

Fiber properties are determined using specialized equipment and following specified procedures called *standard test methods*. Assessment of specific fiber properties is important in selecting an appropriate fiber for the end use.

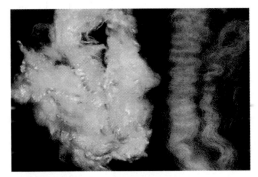

Figure 3.1   Staple fibers: manufactured (left) and natural (right).

Physical Structure

The physical structure, or morphology, can be identified by observing the fiber using a microscope. In this book, photomicrographs, in which fibers are magnified 250 to 1,000 times, show details of a fiber's physical structure. In addition, fiber dimensions influence fabric characteristics and performance and the process that will be used in producing a finished fabric.

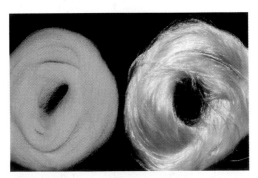

Figure 3.2   Manufactured filaments: textured bulk yarn (left) and smooth filament yarn (right).

Length   Fibers are sold by the fiber producer as staple, filament, or filament tow. **Staple fibers** are short fibers measured in inches or centimeters (Figure 3.1). They range in length from less than 2 to 46 cm (0.5 inch to 18 inches). Except for silk, all the natural fibers are available only in staple form. Staple fibers are used to product spun yarn fabrics. Cotton percale used in sheets, shirts, and blouses is an example of a spun yarn fabric.

Filaments are long, continuous fiber strands of indefinite length, measured in miles or kilometers. They may be either monofilament (one filament) or multifilament (a number of filaments). Filaments may be smooth or bulked (crimped in some way), as shown in Figure 3.2. Smooth filaments are used to produce silklike fabrics; bulked filaments are used in more cottonlike or wool-like fabrics. Silk crepe de chine, acetate taffeta, polyester satin, and polyester gabardine are examples of filament yarn fabrics. **Filament tow**, produced as a loose rope of several thousand fibers, is crimped or textured, and cut to staple length.

When examining a fabric with staple fibers, the fabric will have a soft or matte luster and feel fuzzy, and fiber ends protrude above the surface when the fabric is viewed closely. If the fabric is folded and the folded area is viewed over a contrasting surface, the fiber ends can be seen, making the edge of the fabric look slightly fuzzy or hazy. When a yarn is unraveled from these fabrics, short fiber ends can be seen protruding from the yarn. When the yarn is untwisted, short fibers can be pulled from the yarn and the fibers may vary slightly in their length. No fiber is as long as the yarn or the piece of fabric from which the yarn was raveled.

Smooth filament yarns will produce a fabric that is shiny, lustrous, smooth, and slick. No fiber ends can be seen on the surface. When a yarn is removed, it usually takes fewer turns to unravel it. The only fiber ends that exist are where the fabric has been cut and the fibers are as long as that piece of fabric. If the fabric is folded and viewed over a contrasting surface, the edge of the fabric will look sharper or crisper than that of a spun yarn fabric. If the filament yarn has been textured or bulked, it will resemble spun yarns in some aspects and filament yarns in other aspects. The fiber ends only occur where the fabric is cut and the yarns are as long as that piece of fabric. But the hand is not as smooth and slick and the surface will not look as flat and even as a smooth filament yarn fabric. Consumers will not see filament tow. Filament tow is used to produce spun yarns—either of a single fiber type or blends such as cotton and polyester chambray for shirts or wool and acrylic herringbone for skirts and trousers.

Diameter Fiber diameter greatly influences a fabric's performance and hand (how it feels). Large fibers are crisp, rough, and stiff. Large fibers also resist crushing—a property that is important in products such as carpets. Fine fibers are soft and pliable. Fabrics made with fine fibers drape more easily and are more comfortable next to the skin. Large fibers are used to produce durable products such as book bags and luggage. Fine fibers are used to produce softer and more comfortable products such as apparel and bed linens.

Natural fibers like cotton, ramie, wool, and silk are subject to growth irregularities and are not uniform. In natural fibers, fineness is one factor in determining quality—fine fibers are of better quality. Fineness is measured in micrometers (a micrometer is 1/1000 millimeter or 1/25,400 inch). The diameter range for some natural fibers is 16 to 20 micrometers for cotton, 12 to 16 for flax, 10 to 50 for wool, and 11 to 12 for silk.

For manufactured fibers like rayon, nylon, and polyester, diameter is controlled at several points during production. Manufactured fibers can be made uniform in diameter or can be thick and thin at regular intervals throughout their length. The fineness of manufactured fibers is described as denier or tex. **Denier** is the weight in grams of 9,000 meters of fiber or yarn. When used to describe a fiber, denier refers to the fineness or coarseness of the fiber—small

▶ Learning Activity 2

Use Fabrics #3, 5, and 6 from your swatch kit. Identify the fiber lengths in each fabric as filament or staple. Suggest one or two textile products that might be made using each fabric. Describe the serviceability for each product that would be related to fiber length. Explain your reasoning. From the clothes you are wearing and the other textile products you have with you today, identify the items that are made from staple fibers and those made from filament fibers. How does the serviceability of those items relate to fiber length?

numbers describe fine fibers; large numbers describe coarse fibers. **Tex** is the weight in grams of 1,000 meters of fiber or yarn. Staple fiber is sold by denier and fiber length; filament fiber is sold by the denier of the yarn or tow.

Both systems are weight per length systems. However, specific gravity has an effect on fiber size. Fibers that are dense, like rayon with a specific gravity of 1.48, will generally have a larger tex or denier number than lighter weight, less dense fibers such as olefin with a specific gravity of 0.90 or nylon with a specific gravity of 1.14. If samples of all three fibers had the same diameter measurement and all were 9,000 meters long, the denier would be largest for rayon and smallest for olefin because of the differences in specific gravity of these three examples.

Denier per filament (dpf) is a way of identifying fiber size; it is often used when describing or specifying yarns. Dpf is calculated by dividing the yarn size by the number of filaments: 40 denier yarn/20 filaments = 2 denier per filament. Fine cotton, cashmere, or wool is 1 to 3 denier; average cotton, wool, or alpaca is 5 to 8 denier; carpet wool is 15 denier. Most apparel fibers range from 1 to 7 denier, although much smaller fibers are also available. Carpet fibers may range from 15 to 24 denier. Technical fibers exhibit the broadest range, from less than 1.0 to several thousand, depending on the end use. For example, fibers used for weed trimmers and towropes are much larger than those used for absorbent layers in diapers or for fabrics to polish lens for glasses and microscopes.

Denier is related to end use. Apparel fibers do not make serviceable carpets, and carpet fibers do not make serviceable garments. Soft and pliable apparel fibers would make a carpet with poor crush resistance. Technical fibers are produced in various deniers, depending on the end use. Selecting the appropriate size fiber for the end use is important. Fibers that are too large for apparel are stiff and uncomfortable, while fibers that are too small for interior and technical products will wear out too quickly and may not provide sufficient strength and durability for the end use.

Cross-Sectional Shape The cross-sectional shape of a fiber affects luster, bulk, body, texture, and hand. Figure 3.3 shows common cross-sectional shapes. These shapes include round, dog-bone, triangular, lobal, multisided, or hollow. Round fibers are common in natural fibers and easy to produce for manufactured fibers. Round fibers have a small surface area and may magnify soil. Triangular or trilobal fibers are better at hiding soil. Almost all carpet fiber is trilobal or some other shape modification so that soil is not as readily seen. Round carpet fibers, except for natural fibers like wool, are not used because they make the carpet look dirtier than trilobal fibers.

▶ Learning Activity 3

Use Fabrics #7, 8, 11, 20, 119, and 120 from your swatch kit. Organize the fibers (not the yarns) from smallest diameter to largest diameter. (A magnifying glass, pick glass, or microscope might help with this assessment.) Suggest textile products that might be made using each fabric. Describe the serviceability for each product that would be related to fiber size. Explain your reasoning. Count the number of filament fibers in a yarn of one of the filament yarn fabrics used in this activity. How would the serviceability change if fewer and larger fibers were used? Or if more and smaller fibers were used? Consider the textile products you have with you today. Make a list of those items starting with those with the smallest diameter to those with the largest diameter. How does the serviceability of those items relate to fiber diameter?

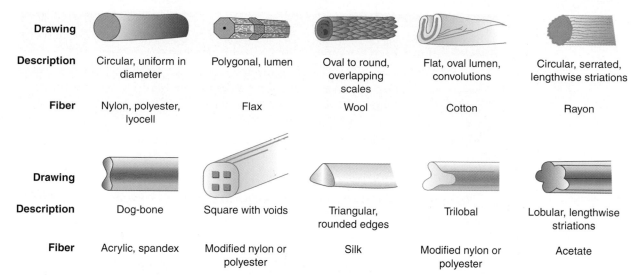

	Drawing				
Description	Circular, uniform in diameter	Polygonal, lumen	Oval to round, overlapping scales	Flat, oval lumen, convolutions	Circular, serrated, lengthwise striations
Fiber	Nylon, polyester, lyocell	Flax	Wool	Cotton	Rayon

	Drawing				
Description	Dog-bone	Square with voids	Triangular, rounded edges	Trilobal	Lobular, lengthwise striations
Fiber	Acrylic, spandex	Modified nylon or polyester	Silk	Modified nylon or polyester	Acetate

Figure 3.3 Cross-sectional shapes and fiber contours.

The natural fibers derive their shape from (1) the way the cellulose is built up during plant growth (cotton), (2) the shape of the hair follicle and the formation of protein substances in animals (wool), or (3) the shape of the orifice through which the insect extrudes the fiber (silk).

The shape of manufactured fibers is controlled by the shape of the spinneret opening and the spinning method. The size, shape, luster, length, and other properties of manufactured fibers can be modified by changes in the production process. More details about these modifications will be discussed in chapters focusing on manufacturing fibers.

Surface Contour Surface contour describes the outer surface of the fiber along its length. Surface contour may be smooth, serrated, striated, or rough, and it affects luster, hand, texture, and apparent soiling of the fabric. Figure 3.3 also shows surface contours of selected fibers. Surface contour can make fabrics comfortable or prickly to touch and easier or more difficult to clean. Many people prefer to wear cotton next to the skin because its slightly irregular contour is more pleasing to the skin. Coarser wool fibers feel prickly next to the skin because of their size and small scales along the outer edge of the fiber.

Crimp Crimp may be found in textile materials as fiber crimp or fabric crimp. **Fiber crimp** refers to the waves, bends, twists, coils, or curls along the length of the fiber. Fiber crimp increases cohesiveness, resiliency, resistance to abrasion, stretch, bulk, and warmth. Crimp increases absorbency and skin-contact comfort but reduces luster. Fibers with lots of crimp like wool are warmer than fibers with little crimp like cotton. Crimp helps trap air within the fabric and next to the skin, making the fabric warmer. Inherent crimp occurs in wool. Inherent crimp also exists in an undeveloped state in bicomponent manufactured fibers in which it is developed in the fabric or the garment (such as a sweater) with heat or moisture during finishing.

Do not confuse fiber crimp with **fabric crimp** (the bends caused by distortion of yarns due to weaving and knitting). When a yarn is unraveled from a fabric, fabric crimp can easily be seen in the yarn and in fibers removed from the yarn.

Fiber Parts Except for silk, the natural fibers have three distinct parts: an outer covering called a *cuticle* or *skin*; an inner area; and a central core that may be hollow.

> ### ▶ Learning Activity 4

Use Fabric #11 from your swatch kit. Unravel two yarns from the fabric. Place one yarn aside. Untwist the other yarn and examine the fibers for fiber crimp. (A magnifying glass, pick glass, or microscope might help with this examination.) Compare the fiber crimp of the fibers from the untwisted yarn with the fabric crimp of the yarn that you had set aside earlier. Describe the frequency and depth of both types of crimp.

The manufactured fibers are less complex in structure. They usually consist of a skin and a core.

Chemical Composition and Molecular Arrangement

All matter is made of chemicals. Chemicals make up the air we breathe, the compounds we use to wash our dishes, the books we read, tires we ride on, and the textiles we wear and use. The nature of the chemical and its structure determine its physical properties. This is true for all substances, including fibers. Because of the number of fibers in the market, a classification system has been developed. (See Table 3.1.) As you can see by this table, fibers are classified into groups by two criteria: source (natural or manufactured) and chemical composition. Fibers in a **generic group** have similar chemical compositions. The properties of fibers in one generic group differ from those in another group. For example, fibers based on plants (cellulose) tend to be absorbent, heavy, heat resistant, prone to wrinkling, damaged by acids and mildew, and highly flammable. Fibers based on synthetic organic compounds called *esters* (polyester) tend be nonabsorbent, lightweight, resistant to wrinkling, resistant to most chemicals, and melt when exposed to flames or high heat.

Fibers are composed of billions of atoms bonded together in millions of long molecular chains. The molecular chains are created by **polymerization**, when small molecules—monomers—are joined together to form a long chain, or **polymer**. The length of the polymer varies just as the length of fibers varies. The number of molecules connected in a chain is defined as the **degree of polymerization**. Long chains indicate a high degree of polymerization and a high degree of fiber strength. This knowledge was used to develop some of the very strong fibers on the market like the modified olefin fibers. Short molecular chains produce fibers with lower strength, such as rayon. Molecular chains are too small to be seen, even with the assistance of an optical microscope.

Molecular chain length also may be described by molecular weight, a factor in properties such as fiber strength and extensibility. Fibers with longer chains or higher molecular weights are stronger and more difficult to pull apart than fibers with shorter chains or lower molecular weights.

Molecular chains have different configurations within fibers. When the chains are arranged in a random or disorganized way within the fiber, they are **amorphous**. When the molecular chains are organized parallel to each other, they are **crystalline**. Molecular chains that are parallel to each other and to the fiber's lengthwise axis are oriented. Most molecular chains that are oriented have a high degree of **orientation** (highly oriented). Fibers that are highly oriented are also highly crystalline. However, highly crystalline fibers are not necessarily highly oriented (Figure 3.4). Fibers vary in their proportion of oriented, crystalline, and amorphous regions.

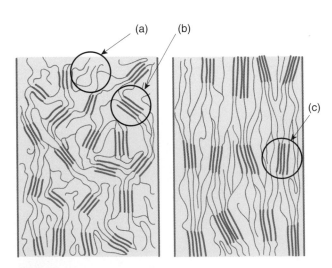

Figure 3.4 Polymers: (a) amorphous area; (b) crystalline, but not oriented, area; (c) oriented and crystalline area.

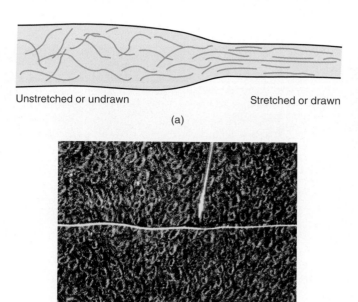

Unstretched or undrawn   Stretched or drawn

(a)

(b)

Figure 3.5 (a) Stretching or drawing a fiber affects its molecular arrangement and diameter; (b) nylon fiber, before drawing (left of the pin), after drawing (right of the pin).

The polymers in manufactured fibers are in a random, unoriented state immediately after production. **Stretching**, or **drawing**, causes the chains to slide and become more parallel to each other and to the longitudinal axis of the fiber. It also reduces fiber diameter and compacts the molecules (Figure 3.5). Fiber properties affected by crystallinity and orientation include strength, elongation, moisture absorption, abrasion resistance, and dyeability.

Amorphous fibers such as wool, cotton, and rayon are relatively weak and easily elongated. These fibers also have poor elasticity and good moisture absorbency, dyeability, and flexibility.

Highly oriented and crystalline fibers are strong and stiff. They do not stretch much or easily, but they recover from stretch quickly. They tend to be nonabsorbent and difficult to dye. Highly oriented and crystalline fibers include polyester, nylon, and aramid.

Molecular chains are held close to one another by intermolecular forces called **hydrogen bonds** and **van der Waals forces**. The closer the chains are to each other, the stronger the bonds are. Hydrogen bonding is the attraction of positive hydrogen atoms of one chain to the negative oxygen or nitrogen atoms of an adjacent chain. The van der Waals forces are weak bonds between atoms that are physically close together. Hydrogen bonding and van der Waals forces occur in the crystalline areas and help make crystalline polymers stronger than amorphous polymers.

Fibers differ in their physical structure, chemical composition, and molecular arrangement. These differences are used to distinguish among fibers by generic names. These differences mean each fiber or blend of fibers in a product influence the serviceability of that product.

Serviceability

Textile serviceability includes the concepts of aesthetics, durability, comfort, safety, appearance retention, care, environmental concerns, sustainability, and cost that were introduced in Chapter 2. Properties that relate to each concept are presented in Table 3.2.

Learning the definitions of the properties will contribute to a more in-depth understanding of textile fiber performance. The tables in this chapter compare various performance aspects among fibers. Relating past experience with fabrics made of a specific fiber will contribute to a better understanding of fiber performance and serviceability.

Table 3.2 Fiber Properties

Fiber Property	Is Due To	Contributes to Fabric Property
Abrasion resistance is the ability of a fiber to resist damage from rubbing or surface contact.	Tough outer layer, scales, or skin Fiber toughness Flexible molecular chains	Durability Abrasion resistance Resistance to splitting or pilling
Absorbency or **moisture regain** is the percentage of moisture a bone-dry fiber will absorb from the air when at standard temperature and relative humidity.	Chemical composition Amorphous areas	Comfort, warmth, water repellency, absorbency, static buildup Dyeability, soiling Shrinkage Wrinkle resistance
Aging resistance is resistance to deleterious changes over time.	Chemical structure	Fabric and product storage
Allergenic potential is the ability to cause physical reactions such as skin redness.	Chemical composition, additives	Comfort
Chemical reactivity describes the affect of acids, alkalis, oxidizing agents, solvents, or other chemicals.	Polar groups of molecules Chemical composition	Cleaning requirements Ability to take certain finishes
Cohesiveness is the ability of fibers to cling together during spinning.	Crimp or twist, surface contour	Resistance to raveling Resistance to yarn slippage
Compressibility is resistance to crushing.	Molecular structure, fiber diameter, and stiffness	Crush and wrinkle resistance
Cover is the ability to conceal or protect.	Crimp, curl, or twist Cross-sectional shape	Fabric opacity Cost—less fiber needed
Creep is delayed or gradual recovery from elongation or strain.	Lack of side chains, cross links, strong bonds; poor orientation	Streak dyeing and shiners in fabric
Density and **specific gravity** are measures of the weight of a fiber. **Density** is the weight in grams per cubic centimeter. **Specific gravity** is the ratio of fiber mass to an equal volume of water at 4°C.	Molecular weight and structure	Warmth without weight Loftiness Fabric buoyancy
Dimensional stability is the ability to retain a given size and shape through use and care. Includes **shrinkage resistance,** which is the ability of a fabric to retain its original dimensions during cleaning.	Physical and chemical structure, coatings	Shrinkage, growth, care, appearance
Drape is the manner in which a fabric falls or hangs over a three-dimensional form.	Fiber size and stiffness	Appearance Comfort
Dyeability is the fiber's receptivity to coloration by dyes; dye affinity.	Amorphous areas and dye sites, chemical structure	Aesthetics and colorfastness
Elasticity is the ability of a strained material to recover its original dimensions immediately after removal of stress.	Chemical and molecular structure: side chains, cross links, strong bonds	Fit and appearance; resiliency
Elastic recovery is the degree to which fibers will recover from strain.	Chemical and molecular structure: side chains, cross links, strong bonds	Processability of fabrics Resiliency and creep
Electrical conductivity is the ability to transfer electrical charges.	Chemical structure: polar groups	Poor conductivity, static, fabric cling
Elongation is the ability to be stretched, extended, or lengthened. Varies with conditions (wet/dry) and temperatures.	Fiber crimp Molecular structure: molecular crimp and orientation	Increased tear strength Reduced brittleness Provides "give"
Flammability describes how a fabric reacts to ignition sources.	Chemical composition	Fabric's ability to ignite and burn
Flexibility is the ability to bend repeatedly without breaking.	Flexible molecular chain	Stiffness, drape, comfort

Table 3.2 Fiber Properties (continued)

Fiber Property	Is Due To	Contributes to Fabric Property
Hand is the way a fiber feels, a tactile sensation: silky, harsh, soft, crisp, dry.	Cross-sectional shape, surface properties, crimp, diameter, length	Fabric hand
Heat conductivity is the ability to transfer heat through a fabric.	Crimp, chemical composition Cross-sectional shape	Comfort: cooling effect
Heat retention is the ability to retain heat or insulate.	Crimp, chemical composition Cross-sectional shape	Comfort: warming or insulating effect
Heat sensitivity is the ability to shrink, soften, or melt when exposed to heat.	Chemical and molecular structure Fewer intermolecular forces and cross links	Determines safe cleaning and pressing temperatures
Hydrophobic describes fibers with low affinity or attraction for water.	Chemical composition	Soiling, comfort, care Static build-up
Hydrophilic or **hygroscopic** describes fibers with a strong affinity or attraction for water.	Chemical composition Amorphous areas	Soiling, comfort, care
Light resistance is the ability to withstand degradation from sunlight.	Chemical composition Additives	Fabric durability
Loft, or **compression resiliency,** is the ability to spring back to original thickness after being compressed.	Fiber crimp Stiffness	Springiness, good cover Resistance to flattening
Luster is the light reflected from a surface. More subdued than shine; light rays are broken up.	Smoothness of fiber, yarn, and/or fabric Fiber length, shape, or additive	Luster
Mildew resistance is resistance to the growth of mold, mildew, or fungus.	Low moisture absorption and chemical composition	Storage
Moth resistance is resistance to insect damage.	Chemical composition	Storage
Oleophilic describes fibers with a strong affinity or attraction for oil.	Chemical composition	Soiling; care; appearance
Pilling is the formation of balls of fiber on the fabric surface.	Fiber strength High molecular weight	Pilling Unsightly appearance
Resiliency is the ability to return to original shape after bending, twisting, compressing, or a combination of deformations.	Molecular structure: side chains, cross links, strong bonds	Wrinkle recovery, crease retention, appearance, care
Specific gravity—see **Density**		
Stiffness, or rigidity, is resistance to bending or creasing.	Chemical and molecular structure	Fabric body, low drape characteristics Difficult to make spun yarns
Strength is the ability to resist stress and is expressed as **tensile strength** (pounds per square inch) or as **tenacity** (grams per denier). Breaking tenacity is the number of grams of force to break a fiber.	Molecular structure: orientation, crystallinity, degree of polymerization	Durability, tear strength, sagging, pilling Sheerest fabrics possible with strong, fine fibers
Sunlight resistance is the ability to withstand degradation from sunlight.	Chemical composition Additives	Fabric durability
Texture is the nature of the fiber or fabric surface.	Physical structure	Luster, appearance, comfort
Translucence is the ability of a fiber, yarn, or fabric to allow light to pass through the structure.	Physical and chemical structure	Appearance, cover
Wicking is the ability of a fiber to transfer moisture along its surface.	Chemical and physical composition of outer surface	Makes fabrics comfortable Moisture transport

Aesthetic Properties

A textile product should be appropriate in appearance for its end use. Aesthetic properties relate to the way senses such as touch and sight contribute to the perception of the textile. In evaluating the aesthetics of a textile product, the consumer usually determines whether the appearance is appropriate for the end use.

Cover is the ability of a fiber to conceal or protect. Fibers that are opaque, like cotton, can be used to produce relatively lightweight fabrics like batiste with good opacity. **Translucence** is the ability of a textile to allow light to pass through it. Fibers that are transparent or translucent like nylon or polyester must be altered by additives during production or by changing their cross section to provide good cover.

Luster results from the way light is reflected by a surface (Figure 3.6). Shiny or bright fabrics reflect a great amount of light. Lustrous fabrics reflect a fair amount of light and are used in formal apparel and interiors. Matte, or dull, fabrics reflect little light and are used most frequently for less formal looks in apparel and interiors. Silk fabrics are usually lustrous. Cotton and wool fabrics are usually matte. The luster of manufactured fibers can be varied during manufacturing. Fibers with high luster are referred to as bright fibers. (*Bright* is used here to describe luster, not color intensity.) Low-luster fibers are dull fibers. Medium-luster fibers are semibright or semidull. Yarn and fabric structure, and finish may change fabric luster.

Drape, a fabric characteristic, is the way a fabric falls over a three-dimensional form like a body or table. Fine fibers produce a softer drape than coarse fibers. Fibers influence fabric drape to a degree, but yarns and fabric structure are usually more important in determining drape. Chiffon is soft and free-flowing, chintz falls in graceful folds, and satin is stiff and heavy.

Texture describes the nature of the textile's surface. It is identified by both visual and tactile senses. Textiles may have a smooth or rough texture. Natural fibers tend to give a fabric more texture than manufactured fibers because of the variations inherent in the structure of natural fibers. Yarns, finishes, and fabric structure also greatly affect texture. Consider the differences in texture among cotton jersey for T-shirts, nylon and spandex tricot for women's swimwear, cotton terrycloth for bath towels, nylon taffeta for umbrellas, and acrylic rib knit for sweaters.

Hand is the way a textile feels to the skin. Hand is often described using adjectives such as warm or cool, bulky or thin, and slick or soft. Hand may be evaluated by feeling a fabric between the fingers and thumb. Both human assessment and instrument measures are used to determine suitability for an end use. Hand is important for designers and consumers. Imagine walking into an area with bolts of fabric on counters or garments on racks and not touching anything!

Durability Properties

A durable textile product should last a period of time adequate for its end use. Durability properties can be tested in the laboratory, but laboratory results do not always accurately predict performance when used by consumers.

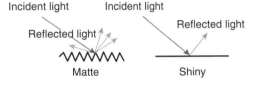

Incident light   Incident light

Reflected light   Reflected light

Matte   Shiny

Figure 3.6 Smooth surfaces reflect light in a straight line and are lustrous; rough surfaces reflect light at various angles and are dull.

Table 3.3 Fiber Ratings Related to Performance

Rating	Abrasion Resistance	Thermal Retention	Resiliency	Light Resistance
Excellent	Aramid	Wool	Nylon	Glass
	Fluoropolymer	Acrylic	Wool	Acrylic
	Nylon	Modacrylic		Modacrylic
	Olefin	Polyester		Polyester
	Polyester			
Good	Saran	Olefin	Olefin	Sulfar
	Spandex	Nylon	Acrylic	Lyocell
	Flax	Aramid	Modacrylic	Flax
	Acrylic		Polyester	Cotton
	PBI			Rayon
	Sulfar			PBI
	Cotton			
	Silk			
Moderate	Wool	Silk	Silk	Triacetate
	Rayon	Spandex		Acetate
				Olefin
Poor	Vinyon	Flax	Lyocell	Nylon
	Acetate	Cotton	Flax	Wool
	Glass	Lyocell	Cotton	Silk
		Rayon	Rayon	
		Acetate	Acetate	

Abrasion resistance is the ability of a textile to withstand the rubbing it gets during use (Table 3.3). Abrasion is measured by rubbing a textile against a surface and measuring the change in strength or appearance. Abrasion can occur when the textile is fairly flat, such as walking on a rug. Edge abrasion can occur when the textile is folded, as when a pant hem rubs on a sidewalk. Flex abrasion can occur when the textile is moving and bending, as in shoelaces that wear out where they are laced through the shoe. **Flexibility**, the ability to bend repeatedly without breaking, is an important property related to abrasion resistance. Some fibers like silk and wool have superior flexibility, while others like glass break very quickly after very few bends and are not used for apparel or other consumer products because the broken bits of fiber are irritating to the skin.

Pilling is the formation of balls of fiber on the fabric surface. Pilling most often occurs when fibers of differing abrasion resistance, such as cotton and polyester, are combined in one fabric. With abrasion, short pieces of the less resistant cotton breaks off and becomes entangled with the more abrasion-resistant polyester, forming little balls of fiber on the surface. These little pills are not only unattractive, but can be uncomfortable, too.

Strength is the ability to resist stress. **Tenacity**, or tensile strength, is the ability of a textile to withstand a pulling force (Table 3.4). Tenacity is measured by securing both ends of the fiber in clamps and measuring the force needed to break or rupture the fiber. (*Breaking tenacity*

Table 3.4 Fiber Properties Related to Performance

Rating	Fiber Tenacity (Grams/Denier)*	Absorbency**	Density or Specific Gravity (Grams/CC)***	Elongation****	Elastic Recovery*****
High	Glass (9.6/6.7) Aramid (4.0–5.3/3.0–4.1) Lyocell (4.8–5.0/4.2–4.6) Silk (4.5/2.8–4.0)	PBI (15) Wool (13–18) Flax (12) Rayon, viscose (11.5–12.5) Lyocell (11.5) Silk (11) Rayon, HWM (11)	Glass (2.48–2.69) Fluoropolymer (2.1)	Rubber (500) Spandex (400–700) Olefin (70–100)	Spandex (99 at 50%) Rubber (98 at 50%) Wool (99)
Medium	Nylon (3.5–7.2/3.0–6.5) Flax (3.5–5.0/6.5) Olefin (3.5–4.5) Cotton (3.5–4.0/4.5–5.0) Sulfar (3.0–3.5) PBI (2.6–3.0/2.1–2.5) Rayon, HWM (2.5–5.0/3.0) Polyester (2.4–7.0) Acrylic (2.0–3.0/1.8–2.7) Fluoropolymer (2.0)	Cotton (7–11) Aramid (6.5) Acetate (6.3–6.5) Melamine (5.8) Nylon (2.8–5.0) Modacrylic (2.5) Spandex (1.3)	Lyocell (1.56) Cotton (1.52) Flax (1.52) Rayon, viscose (1.48) Rayon, HWM (1.48) PBI (1.43) Melamine (1.40) Aramid (1.38–1.44) Sulfar (1.37) Modacrylic (1.35) Polyester (1.34–1.38) Vinyon (1.33–1.43) Acetate (1.32) Wool (1.32)	Acrylic (35–45/41–50) Sulfar (35–45) Nylon 6 (30–90/42–100) Modacrylic (30–60) PBI (25–30/26–32) Acetate (25–45/35–50) Wool (25/35) Aramid (22–32/20–30) Silk (20/30)	Modacrylic (99 at 2%) Nylon 6 (98–100) Olefin (96 at 5%) Rayon, HWM (96 at 2%) Rayon, regular (95 at 2%) Acrylic (92) Silk (90) Lyocell (88) Nylon 6,6 (82–89)
Low	Modacrylic (1.7–2.6/1.5–2.4) Melamine (1.8) Wool (1.5/1.0) Acetate (1.2–1.4/1.0–1.3) Rayon, viscose (1.0–2.5/0.5–1.4) Vinyon (0.7–1.0) Spandex (0.7–1.0) Rubber (0.34)	Acrylic (1.0–1.5) Rubber (0.8) Sulfar (0.6) Polyester (0.4) Vinyon (0.1) Olefin (0.01–0.1) Fluoropolymer (0.0) Glass (0.0)	Silk (1.26) Spandex (1.2) Acrylic (1.17) Nylon (1.13–1.14) Rubber (1.1) Olefin (0.90–0.91)	Nylon 6,6 (16–75/18–78) Lyocell (14–16/16–18) Vinyon (12–125) Polyester (12–55) Melamine (12) Rayon, HWM (9–18/20) Rayon, regular (8–14/16–20) Fluoropolymer (8.5) Glass (3.1/2.2) Cotton (3–7/9.5) Flax (2.0/2.2)	Polyester (81) Cotton (75) Flax (65) Acetate (48–95 at 4%)

*Numbers in parentheses are in grams per denier for staple fibers with unmodified cross sections. The first number is for dry fibers; the second number is for wet fibers. If there is only one number, there is no difference in performance between wet and dry fibers.

**Expressed as moisture regain (percentage of the moisture-free weight at 70°F (21°C) at 65% relative humidity).

***Ratio of weight of a given volume of fiber to an equal volume of water.

****A 10% minimum elongation is desirable for ease in textile processing. For fibers that are available in several lengths and modifications, the values are for staple fibers with unmodified cross sections.

*****Percent recovery at 3% stretch, unless otherwise noted. The first number is performance at standard conditions of 65% relative humidity, 70°F or 21°C; the second number is when wet. If only one number is given, the performance is the same at standard conditions and when wet. Percent recovery for some specialty fibers is not given because values are low or this aspect of performance is not critical for the more common end uses.

for a fiber is the force, in grams per denier or tex, required to break the fiber.) The tenacity of a fiber when it is wet may differ from the tenacity of that same fiber when it is dry. Although fabric strength depends, to a large degree, on fiber strength, yarn and fabric structure are additional factors affecting fabric strength. Strength may also be described by the force needed to rip a fabric (tearing strength) or to rupture a fabric (bursting strength). Textile products that will be used wet, like washcloths, are made of cotton and other fibers that are stronger when wet.

Cohesiveness, that ability of fibers to cling together during spinning, can be a factor in durability. Fibers with good cohesiveness tend to resist raveling or slipping during use. Cotton and wool have good cohesiveness while silk and polyester have poor cohesiveness.

Elongation refers to the degree to which a fiber may be stretched without breaking. It is measured as percent elongation at break (see Table 3.4) by measuring the change in length and comparing that to the original length. Elongation should be considered in relation to elasticity. Highly oriented and highly crystalline fibers do not elongate much when a force is applied. However, when that force is released, they recover quickly to their original length or very close to their original length. Aramid, used in ballistic vests, is a fiber that has very low elongation.

Comfort and Safety Properties

A textile product should be comfortable when it is worn or used. This is primarily a matter of personal preference and individual perception of comfort under different environmental conditions and degrees of physical activity. The complexities of comfort depend on characteristics such as absorbency, heat retention, density, and elongation.

Absorbency is the ability of a fiber to take up moisture from the body or from the environment. It is measured as moisture regain where the moisture in the material is expressed as a percentage of the weight of the moisture-free material (see Table 3.4). **Hydrophilic** fibers absorb moisture readily. **Hydrophobic** fibers have little or no absorbency. Hydrophobic fibers tend to be **oleophilic**, meaning that they have a strong affinity or attraction for oil. Oleophilic fibers tend to bond quickly and tightly with oil, making cleaning more of a problem. **Hygroscopic** fibers absorb moisture without feeling wet. Absorbency is related to static buildup; problems with static are more likely to develop in hydrophobic fibers because they do not conduct electrons readily. Absorbency is a measure of the increase in mass when a fiber is exposed to humid air. Cotton, a hydrophilic fiber, is often used for casual work apparel and children's wear because it absorbs moisture readily. Nylon and polyester, hydrophobic fibers, are often used for the outer layer in raincoats. Wool, a hygroscopic fiber, is often used in winter apparel because it will absorb the moisture of perspiration during physical activity or moisture from melting snow without feeling wet next to the skin. Fibers that have good absorbency also tend to have good **dyeability**, meaning that they are receptive to coloration by dyes. Fibers that absorb water quickly dye well and have good dye affinity.

Fibers with good absorbency also tend to be good electrical conductors. **Electrical conductivity** is the ability to transfer electrical charges. Absorbent fibers do not build up static charge readily and do not attract lint or create problems with static cling.

Wicking is the ability of a fiber to transfer moisture along its surface. Fibers that wick well are not very absorbent. Moisture is transported along the surface rather than being absorbed into the fiber. Fibers with good wicking characteristics can produce comfortable products because the moisture is pulled away from the skin by wicking to the outer surface of the fabric where evaporation can occur. Smart textile modifications of polyester and olefin make use of this characteristic and are used in comfortable apparel for athletic competitions.

Heat or **thermal retention** is the ability of a textile to hold heat (see Table 3.3). Because people want to be comfortable regardless of the weather, a low level of thermal retention is favored in hot weather and a high level in cold weather. This property is affected by fiber, yarn, and fabric structure and layering of fabrics. Bulky fibers like wool or acrylic are often used for sweaters and winter hats and scarves because they retain heat well. Heat conductivity is the opposite of heat retention. **Heat conductivity** is the ability to transfer heat through a fabric. Cotton is popular in summer apparel because it has good heat conductivity and helps the body release heat quickly.

Heat sensitivity describes a fiber's reaction to heat (Table 3.5). Since some fibers soften and melt and others are heat resistant, these properties identify safe pressing temperatures. Electrical line personnel seldom wear synthetics like nylon or polyester since these heat-sensitive fibers shrink and melt with heat, a potential problem when working near high-voltage power lines.

Table 3.5 Heat Sensitivity*

Fibers That Do Not Melt	Pressing* Recommendations in °F (°C)
Natural Fibers	
Cotton	425 (218)
Flax	450 (232)
Silk	300 (149)
Wool	300 (149)
Manufactured Fibers	
Aramid	Do not press**
Fluoropolymer	Do not press**
Lyocell	400 (205)
Melamine	Do not press**
Modacrylic	200–250 (93–121)
PBI	Do not press**
Rayon	375 (191)
Fibers that Melt	**Pressing Recommendations in °F (°C)**
Manufactured Fibers	
Acetate	350 (177)
Acrylic	300 (149)
Glass	Do not press**
Nylon 6	300 (149)
Nylon 6,6	350 (177)
Olefin	150 (66)
Polyester PET	325 (163)
Polyester PCDT	350 (177)
Spandex	300 (149)

*Lowest setting on irons is 185–225°F. Settings on irons and presses correspond to recommended temperatures for pressing and may be designated by common apparel fiber names.

*These technical fibers are rarely used in products that might require pressing.

Flammability describes how a fabric reacts to ignition sources and how it burns. Fabrics that are highly flammable are banned from interstate commerce in the United States and many other countries because of the safety risk they pose. See Chapter 21 for more information.

Density or **specific gravity** is a measure of fiber weight per unit volume (see Table 3.4). Lower-density fibers can be made into thick fabrics that are more comfortable than high-density fibers that result in heavy fabrics. Fibers with the same diameter may not have the same denier or tex value since fiber density affects weight. Take a 100 percent cotton and a 100 percent polyester fabric identical in fabric structure, yarn structure and size, and number of yarns per inch. Since cotton has a higher density than polyester, the all-cotton fabric will be heavier. Also refer back to the discussion earlier in this chapter regarding fiber size and fiber density.

Allergenic potential is the ability to cause physical reactions such as skin redness resulting from exposure to the fiber. While many individuals claim an allergy to wool, most are not allergic, but are very sensitive to the prickle caused by coarser wool fibers. Chemicals used in finishing and dyeing can cause allergic reactions in some individuals.

Appearance-Retention Properties

A textile product should retain its appearance during use, care, and storage.

Resiliency is the ability of a textile to return to its original shape after bending, twisting, or crushing (see Table 3.3). Resilient fibers usually produce resilient fabrics. An easy test for resiliency is to crunch a fabric in your hand and watch how it responds when you open your hand. Fabrics that do not wrinkle easily and spring back after compression are resilient and wrinkle resistant. A fabric that wrinkles easily stays crumpled in your hand. When it is flattened out, wrinkles and creases are apparent. Because of the poor wrinkle resistance of cotton, finishes have been developed to improve their resilience. (See Chapter 18.) In the standard test for resiliency, a fabric is twisted and compressed for a set length of time. The number and sharpness of the wrinkles are evaluated to assess resiliency.

Compressibility is resistance to crushing. Fibers, like cotton, that are easily compressible tend to wrinkle easily but can produce heavy and compact fabrics, like denim. Fibers, like wool, that do not compress easily, do not wrinkle easily and produce bulky fabrics. **Loft** or **compression resiliency** is the ability to spring back to the original thickness after being compressed. Loft is important for pile fabrics, most knits, and carpets and rugs.

Dimensional stability is the ability of a fabric to retain its original size and shape through use and care, which is desirable. It includes the properties of shrinkage resistance and elastic recovery. Fabrics are carefully measured, cleaned, and measured again. Dimensional change is calculated based on the difference between the original measurements and the after-cleaning measurements. Fabrics and products that are dimensionally stable maintain their size and shape throughout their life.

Shrinkage resistance is the ability of a fabric to retain its original dimensions throughout care. It is related to the fabric's reaction to moisture or heat. Items that shrink may no longer be attractive or suitable for their original end use. Most textile products exhibit their greatest shrinkage during the first cleaning cycle, but some products continue to shrink each time they are cleaned. Residual shrinkage refers to additional shrinkage that may occur after the first care cycle.

Elasticity or **elastic recovery** is the ability of a textile to return to its original dimension or shape after elongation (see Table 3.4). It is measured as the percentage of return to original length. Elastic recovery varies with the amount of elongation and with the length of time the fabric is stretched. Fibers with poor elastic recovery, like cotton and rayon, tend to produce fabrics that stretch out of shape. Fibers with good elastic recovery, like nylon and polyester, tend to produce fabrics that maintain their shape. **Creep** is a delayed or gradual recovery from elongation. Creep may be seen in the difference in fit between denim shorts at the end of one day of wearing and the fit at the beginning of the next day of wearing. The shorts may have gotten looser during the day as they were worn and stretched. Because of the low and slow elastic recovery of cotton (creep), the shorts will probably be a little tighter fitting the next day.

Some fibers age more slowly than others. **Aging resistance** is resistance to deleterious changes over time. Spandex and other elastic fibers have poor aging characteristics. Over time, these fibers become stiff, rigid, and brittle. When stretched, the spandex fiber breaks and the fabric remains stretched out. Other fibers, such as cotton, can be stored for years without suffering significant damage.

Mildew resistance and moth resistance can be especially important when textiles are stored. **Mildew resistance** is the resistance to the growth of mold, mildew, or fungus. If cotton and other plant fibers are stored in humid and warm conditions, mildew, mold, or fungus growth can occur. While the odor can be unpleasant, these microorganisms can also permanently damage textiles. **Moth resistance** is resistance to insect damage, including moths, beetles, crickets, roaches, and spiders. Problems with insects are most often encountered during storage of textile products.

Resistance to Chemicals

Different fibers react differently to chemicals. Some are quite resistant to most chemicals; others are resistant to one group of chemicals but easily harmed by others. Resistance to chemicals and chemical reactivity determines the appropriateness of care procedures and end uses for fibers as well as selection of appropriate dyes and finishes for fabrics and products. Table 3.6 summarizes fiber reactions to acids and alkalis. Acids are compounds that yield hydrogen ions to alkalis in chemical reactions. Alkalis (bases) are compounds that remove hydrogen ions from acids and combine with the acid in a chemical reaction. The average consumer can come in contact with acids in the kitchen (fruit and vegetable juice, vinegar, and salad dressings), the bathroom (some medications, skin and hair treatments, and first aid supplies), outdoors (grass stains), and garage (battery acid). Alkalis are also encountered by consumers in the bathroom and laundry (soaps and detergents), kitchen (baking soda or sodium bicarbonate), and cleaning supplies (household ammonia and borax). While the reaction of fibers to other chemicals like organic solvents (fingernail polish remover) and inorganic salts (deicing salt) is important, these reactions are more important in terms of end use and cleaning—issues that are addressed during product development.

Resistance to Light

Light or **sunlight resistance** is the ability to withstand degradation from natural or artificial light. Exposure to light may damage fibers. The energy in light, especially in the ultraviolet region of the spectrum, causes irreversible damage to the chemical structure of the fiber. This damage may appear as a yellowing or color change, a slight weakening of the fabric, or, eventually, the complete disintegration of the fabric (see Table 3.3). Fibers with good light resistance are used where exposure to light, especially sunlight, is high. For example, acrylic is often used in awnings because of its high light resistance. Tenacity is measured before and after exposure to light. A loss in strength indicates ultraviolet damage to the fiber.

Table 3.6 Effect of Acids* and Alkalis**

Fiber	Acid	Alkali
Natural Fibers		
Cotton	Harmed	Resistant
Flax	Harmed	Resistant
Silk	Harmed by strong mineral acids, resistant to organic acids	Harmed
Wool	Resistant	Harmed
Manufactured Fibers		
Acetate	Unaffected by weak acids	Little effect
Acrylic	Resistant to most acids	Resistant to weak alkalis
Aramid	Resistant to most acids	Resistant
Glass	Resistant	Resistant
Lyocell	Harmed	Resistant
Modacrylic	Resistant to most acids	Resistant
Nylon	Harmed, especially nylon 6	Resistant
Olefin	Resistant	Highly resistant
PBI	Resistant	Resistant to most alkalis
Polyester	Resistant	Degraded by strong alkalis
Rayon	Harmed	Resistant to weak alkalis
Spandex	Resistant	Resistant
Sulfar	Resistant	Resistant

*Examples of acids: organic (acetic, formic); mineral (sulfuric, hydrochloric).

**Examples of alkalis: weak (ammonium hydroxide); strong (sodium hydroxide).

Environmental Concerns and Sustainability

Environmental concerns refer to the way the production, use, care, and disposal of a fiber or textile product affects the environment. Many consumers assume that natural fibers have less of an environmental impact than do manufactured or synthetic fibers. The environmental concerns related to each fiber are far more complex. The factors differ with each fiber or process and may differ depending on the region of the world where a fiber is produced. Natural fibers' impact on soil conservation, use of agricultural chemicals, disposal of animal waste, water demands, cleaning requirements, and processing create environmental problems. Since very few textile products are disposed of in a manner that allows for biodegradation, natural fibers do not even have that advantage in modern society.

Sustainability describes practices and policies that reduce environmental pollution and do not exploit people or natural resources in meeting the lifestyle needs of the present without compromising the future. While the environmental concerns and sustainability for each of the major consumer fibers will be discussed in Chapters 4–9, it is important to remember some basic concepts and issues. Cotton and polyester account for more than three-fourths of the global textile fiber market. With this degree of concentration in only two fibers, the agricultural and manufacturing segments dependent on them concentrate the potential for

Chemical reactivity of fibers determines several factors: care, end use, coloration process, and finishing.

environmental and economic problems. These large segments are less responsive to change in global markets and provide fewer consumer choices. Distributing this market among a more diverse group of fibers would have a greater impact on local economies and offer greater consumer choice. The **cradle to cradle** concept is an environmentally intelligent design framework that examines the overall impact of the production, use, care, disposal, and recycle potential of products, including textile products, from economic, industrial, and social perspectives.

Care Properties

Treatments that are required to maintain the new look of a textile product during use, cleaning, or storage are referred to as **care**. Improper care can result in items that are unattractive, not as durable as expected, uncomfortable, or unusable. Fiber reactions to water, cleaning chemicals, heat in pressing and drying, and special storage requirements will be discussed in each fiber chapter.

Cost

Cost is affected by how a fiber is produced, the number and type of modifications present, and how the fiber is marketed. Cost will be addressed in general terms for each fiber. Actual costs for fibers are related to supply of and demand for the fiber as well as costs of raw materials used to grow or produce each fiber. Fiber costs are only a small percentage of the cost that a consumer pays for a textile product.

Fiber Property Charts

The fibers within each generic family have individual differences. These differences are not reflected in the tables in this chapter, except in a few specific instances. The numerical values are averages, or medians, and are intended as a general characterization of each generic group.

Fiber Identification

The procedure for identifying fibers in a fabric depends on the nature of the sample, the experience of the analyst, and the facilities available. Because laws require the fiber content of most apparel and interior textiles to be indicated on the label, the consumer may only need to look for identification labels. If a professional wishes to confirm or verify the label information, simple solubility and burn tests may be used. These procedures differ in their effectiveness in identifying fibers. Microscopic appearance is most useful for natural fibers. Solubility tests and sophisticated spectroscopic analyses are most effective for manufactured fibers.

Visual Inspection

Visual inspection of a textile for appearance and hand is always the first step in fiber identification. It is no longer possible to make an identification of the fiber content by appearance and hand alone, because manufactured fibers can resemble natural fibers or other manufactured fibers. However, observation of certain characteristics is helpful. These characteristics are apparent to the unaided eye and are visual clues used to narrow the number of possibilities.

1. **Length of fiber.**   Untwist the yarn to determine fiber length. Any fiber can be made in staple length, but not all fibers can be filament. For example, cotton and wool are always staple and never filament.

2. **Luster or lack of luster.**   Manufactured fiber luster may range from harsh and shiny to dull and matte.

3. **Body, texture, hand.**   These factors indicate whether the fiber is soft to hard, rough to smooth, warm to cool, or stiff to flexible and relate to fiber size, surface contour, stiffness, and cross-sectional shape.

Burn Test

The burn test can be used to identify a fiber's general chemical composition, such as cellulose, protein, mineral, or synthetic (Tables 3.1 and 3.7). Blends cannot be identified by the burn test. If visual inspection is used along with the burn test, fiber identification can be carried further. For example, if the sample is cellulose and also filament, it is probably rayon; but if it is staple, a positive identification for a specific cellulosic fiber cannot be made.

Work in a safe, well-ventilated area or under a hood. Remove paper and other flammable materials from the area. Check apparel and hair to ensure that they will not put the analyst at risk. Follow these general directions for the burn test:

1. Ravel out and test several yarns from each direction of the fabric to determine if they are the same fiber type. Differences in luster, twist, and color suggest that there might be more than one generic fiber in the fabric.

2. Hold the yarn horizontally, as shown in Figure 3.7. It is helpful to roll long pieces of yarn into a flat ball or clump, as shown in the figure. Use tweezers to protect your fingers. Move the yarns slowly into the edge of the flame and observe what happens. Repeat this step several times to check your results.

Microscopy

Knowing the physical structure of fibers will be of use when using a microscope in fiber identification. Identification of natural fibers is best done by microscopy. For the best accuracy,

Figure 3.7   Fiber identification by the burn test.

Table 3.7 Identification by Burning

Fibers	When Approaching Flame	When in Flame	After Removal from Flame	Ash	Odor
Cellulose (Cotton, Flax, Lyocell, Rayon)	Does not fuse or shrink from flame	Burns with light gray smoke	Continues to burn, afterglow	Gray, feathery, smooth edge	Burning paper
Protein (Silk, Wool)	Curls away from flame	Burns slowly	May self-extinguish	Crushable black ash	Burning hair
Acetate	Melts and pulls away from flame	Melts and burns	Continues to burn and melt	Brittle, black, hard bead	Acrid, harsh, sharp odor
Acrylic	Melts and pulls away from flame	Melts and burns	Continues to burn and melt	Brittle, black, hard bead	Chemical odor
Glass	No reaction	Does not burn	No reaction	Fiber remains	None
Modacrylic	Melts and pulls away from flame	Melts and burns	Self-extinguishes, white smoke	Brittle, black, hard bead	Chemical odor
Nylon	Melts and pulls away from flame	Melts and burns	May self-extinguish	Hard gray or tan bead	Celerylike
Olefin	Melts and pulls away from flame	Melts and burns	May self-extinguish	Hard tan bead	Chemical odor
PLA	Melts and pulls away from flame	Melts and burns with slight white smoke	May self-extinguish	Hard tan or gray bead	Slightly acrid odor
Polyester	Melts and pulls away from flame	Melts and burns	May self-extinguish	Hard black bead	Sweet odor
Spandex	Melts but does not pull away from flame	Melts and burns	Continues to melt and burn	Soft black ash	Chemical odor

examination of both the lengthwise appearance (longitudinal) and crosswise appearance (cross section) of an unknown fiber is best. Photomicrographs of fibers (longitudinal and cross-sectional views) are included in Chapters 4–9. Consult those chapters for identifying characteristics of the natural fibers. Manufactured fibers are more difficult to identify because many of them look alike, and their appearance may be changed by variations in the manufacturing process. Positive identification of the manufactured fibers by microscopy is not possible.

The following are directions for using the microscope:

1. Clean the microscope lens and the glass slide and cover glass.
2. Place a drop of distilled water or glycerin on the slide.
3. Untwist a yarn and place several fibers from the yarn on the slide. Cover with the cover glass and tap to remove air bubbles. (Make sure you are examining several individual fibers, not a yarn.)
4. Place the slide on the stage of the microscope. Focus with low power first. If the fibers have not been well separated, it will be difficult to focus on a single fiber. Center the fiber or fibers in the viewing field. Then move to a lens with greater magnification. As magnification increases, the size of the viewing field decreases. Thus, if fibers are not in the center of the field when a higher magnification is selected, they may disappear from the viewing field.
5. If a fabric contains two or more fiber types, examine both warp and filling yarns.

Use Fabrics #9, 30, and 39 from your swatch kit. Follow the instructions for preparing a slide and using the microscope. Describe what you see through the microscope for Fabric #9. Repeat the process for Fabrics #30 and #39. What are the differences you see about each fiber? Watch for discussions in Chapters 4, 5, 6, and 8 that describe the microscopic appearance of these fibers.

Solubility Tests

Solubility tests are used to identify the manufactured fibers by generic class and to confirm identification of natural fibers. Two simple tests, the alkali test for wool and the acetone test for acetate, are described in Chapters 5 and 7, respectively.

Table 3.8 lists solvents from weakest to strongest. Place the specimen in the liquid in the order listed. Although many solvents will dissolve some fibers, following this order will help in identifying the specific fiber. Stir the specimen for 5 minutes and note the effect. Fiber, yarns, or small pieces of fabric may be used. Remember that the liquids are hazardous—handle them with care! Use chemical laboratory exhaust hoods, gloves, aprons, and goggles.

Fiber identification is required on product labels and helps professionals and consumers select appropriate products for end uses. If labels are not present or if fiber content must be verified, visual inspection, burn and solubility tests, and microscopy can be used.

Table 3.8 Solubility Tests

Solvent (In Order of Increasing Strength)	Fiber Dissolved
Acetic acid, 100%, 20°C	Acetate
Acetone, 100%, 20°C	Acetate, modacrylic, vinyon
Hydrochloric acid, 20% concentration, 1.096 density, 20°C	Nylon 6; nylon 6,6; vinal
Sodium hypochlorite solution, 5%, 20°C	Silk and wool (silk dissolves in 70% sulfuric acid at 38°C), azlon
Xylene (meta), 100%, 139°C	Olefin and saran (saran in 1.4 dioxane at 101°C; olefin is not soluble), vinyon
Dimethyl formamide, 100%, 90°C	Spandex, modacrylic, acrylic, acetate, vinyon
Sulfuric acid, 70% concentration, 38°C	Cotton, flax, rayon, nylon, acetate, silk
Cresol (meta), 100%, 139°C	Polyester, nylon, acetate

key terms

review questions

1. Define each of the key terms listed in Table 3.2.

2. Differentiate between the following pairs of related terms:
   a. Elongation and elasticity
   b. Absorbency and wicking
   c. Loft and resiliency
   d. Heat conductivity and heat sensitivity
   e. Hand and texture
   f. Cover and translucence
   g. Care and chemical sensitivity
   h. Strength and abrasion resistance
   i. Drape and stiffness
   j. Electrical conductivity and cohesiveness

3. How would performance change when a fiber's shape is changed from round to trilobal?

4. What differences in performance might you expect from fibers used to produce a T-shirt, a carpet in a movie theater, and an outdoor flag?

5. Describe polymerization and the possible arrangements of molecules within fibers. List four aspects of performance that might be expected for each combination you describe.

6. What would be an efficient procedure to identify the fiber content of an unknown fabric?

7. Look through your clothes and make three lists: items that only include natural fibers (cotton, hemp, ramie, wool, or silk); items that include only manufactured and synthetic fibers (rayon, lyocell, bamboo, acrylic, polyester, nylon, and spandex); and items that combine both natural and manufactured fibers. Describe the number and type of items in each list and how restricted your wardrobe might be without the manufactured fibers. (Remember when creating your lists that elastic bands usually incorporate a manufactured fiber.) If you find a fiber that you cannot identify, check Table 3.1 to determine the classification of the fiber in question.

8. Consider textile products that you have discarded recently. Did these products fail because of some performance problem? If yes, identify the performance problem using one or more of the key terms discussed in this chapter. If you remember the fiber content of the failed product, consult the tables in this chapter to determine a fiber type that might have resulted in better performance in this area. Explain why another fiber might provide better performance.

9. Select two of the fiber property summary lists. Explain what the numbers represent and how that information describes fiber performance. For each summary, explain if a higher value might be more or less desirable for a textile product.

10. Select one of the serviceability concepts and identify how cotton compares to polyester in terms of performance in this category.

11. Explain the fiber characteristic(s) that has the greatest influence on these fiber properties. Some properties influence other properties, too. Search out the properties that influence other properties and identify how one property affects another. Explain how the characteristic could be manipulated to enhance performance. For example, density is related to molecular weight and structure. Density could be altered by increasing or decreasing molecular weight or expanding molecular structure.
    a. Absorbency
    b. Cohesiveness
    c. Elasticity
    d. Flexibility
    e. Hand
    f. Loft
    g. Luster
    h. Pilling
    i. Strength
    j. Texture
    k. Wicking

12. Explain why most natural fibers are available as staple only, but most manufactured and synthetic fibers are available in either staple or filament form.

13. For apparel on a hot summer day, which would you prefer—a fiber that absorbs perspiration quickly or one that wicks perspiration? Explain your response.

14. For apparel on a cold, windy day, which would you prefer—a fiber with good heat retention or a fiber with good heat transference? Explain your response.

Case Study
Diapers and Incontinence Products*

Baby diapers are lightweight, inexpensive, thin, strong, and attractive; prevent leaks; fit in the leg area; minimize skin chafing and diaper rash; feel soft; and control odor. The market for incontinence products extends to adults. Adult incontinence results from age, obesity, injury, surgery, or disease and affects hundreds of millions of people worldwide. Incontinence products for adults have different performance requirements. While absorbency, fit and movement with the body, including good elongation and elasticity, soft hand, odor control, strength, and thinness are key, other demands include

the ability to pull or wick moisture from the skin, discreet and quiet products (no rustle as with baby diapers), nonbinding or chafing, nonallergenic, durable, and abrasion resistant. Innovation is a growing factor for the adult market. Smart textiles with reactive nano-coatings would protect against the acid of urine and bacteria that cause skin rashes, and diagnostic components would inform about the wearer's health. Smart technology is currently used in diapers, creating an uncomfortable cooling when the child wets, thus encouraging use of the toilet.

DISCUSSION QUESTIONS

1. Find the textile properties used in this discussion that are defined in Table 3.2.

2. Explain these terms in your own words.

3. Describe how these properties contribute to product performance for incontinence products.

4. Search through the terms in Table 3.2 and identify additional terms that might apply to diapers and incontinence products.

5. What are some of the environmental and sustainability issues that use of and production of incontinence products create?

*Thiry, M. C. (2008). Baby grows up. *AATCC Review, 8*(2), 22–28.

suggested readings

ASTM International. (2008). *Annual Book of ASTM Standards*, Vol. 7. West Conshockon, PA: ASTM International.

Fletcher, K. (2008). *Sustainable Fashion and Textiles: Design Journey*. London: Earthscan.

Hethorn, J., & Ulasewicz, C. (2008). *Sustainable Fashion: Why Now?* New York: Fairchild Books.

McDonough, W., & Braungart, M. (2002). *Cradle to Cradle: Remaking the Way We Make Things*. New York: North Point Press.

Thiry, M. C. (2008). Baby grows up. *AATCC Review, 8*(2), 22–28.

Thiry, M. C. (2004). Built to last. *AATCC Review, 4*(12), 8–11.

Thiry, M. C. (2005). From ready to win to ready to wear. *AATCC Review, 5*(9), 18–22.

Thiry, M. C. (2007). Lightning on a small scale. *AATCC Review, 7*(11), 18–23.

Tortora, P. G., & Merkel, R. S. (1996). *Fairchild's Dictionary of Textiles*, 7th ed. New York: Fairchild Publications.

NATURAL CELLULOSIC FIBERS

CHAPTER OBJECTIVES

- To identify cellulosic fibers.
- To understand characteristics common to all cellulosic fibers.
- To understand characteristics and performance unique to the commonly used cellulosic fibers.
- To know the basic steps in processing these fibers.
- To integrate the properties of natural cellulosic fibers with market needs.

4

All plants contain fibrous bundles that give strength to the stem and root, pliability to the leaves, and cushioning or protection to developing seeds. In some plants, these fibrous bundles can be removed from the plant in an easy and economical process and used in textile products. These natural cellulosic fibers are classified according to the plant component from which they are removed (Table 4.1): seed, stem (bast), leaf, or miscellaneous component (root, bark, husk, or moss). While hundred of plant fibers have been used since humans first discovered how to work with fibers, this chapter will focus on the ones that are significant in the global textile complex or that offer potential for future growth as plant fibers. Figure 4.1 shows where the fibers in this chapter are produced.

Table 4.1 Natural Cellulosic Fibers

Seed Fibers	Bast Fibers	Leaf Fibers	Miscellaneous Fibers
Cotton	Flax	Piña	Rush
Kapok	Ramie	Abaca	Sea grass
Coir	Hemp	Sisal	Maize
Jute	Milkweed	Henequen	Palm fiber
	Kenaf		
	Hibiscus		
	Nettle		
	Bamboo		

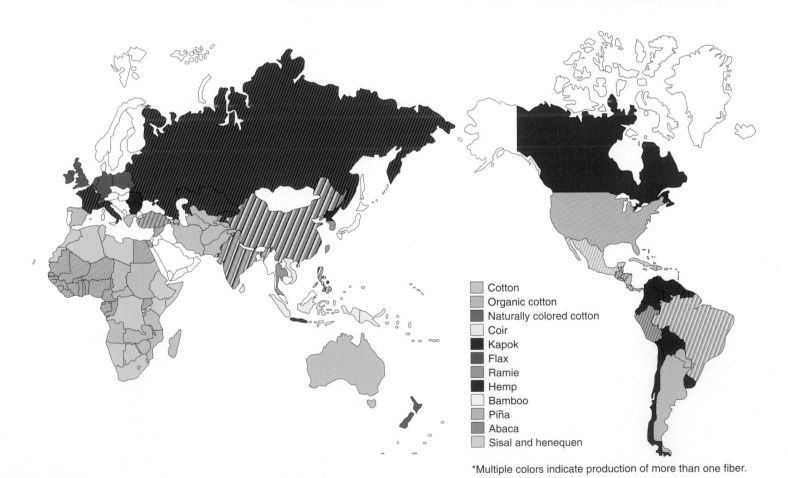

Cotton
Organic cotton
Naturally colored cotton
Coir
Kapok
Flax
Ramie
Hemp
Bamboo
Piña
Abaca
Sisal and henequen

*Multiple colors indicate production of more than one fiber.

Figure 4.1 Countries where natural cellulosic fibers are produced.

Cotton, a **seed fiber**, grows within a pod or boll from developing seeds. Flax, a **bast fiber**, is obtained from the stem and root of the plant. Sisal, a **leaf fiber**, is removed from the veins or ribs of a leaf. Fiber from other plant components such as Spanish moss and cedar bark were used by Native Americans, but are not currently used in commercial products.

These fibers are all cellulosic, but they differ in the percentage of cellulose present and in their physical structure. While the arrangement of the molecular chains in these fibers is similar, it varies in orientation and length. Thus, performance characteristics related to these aspects differ. Fabrics made from these fibers differ in appearance and hand but have a similar reaction to chemicals and require similar care. Properties common to all cellulosic fibers are summarized in Table 4.2.

All cellulose fibers contain carbon (C), hydrogen (H), and oxygen (O). The basic monomer of cellulose is *glucose*. The figure to the right shows two glucose units (the second one is inverted) that repeat thousands of times to form cellulose. This two-glucose repeating unit is called *cellobiose*. The chemical reactivity of cellulose is related to the hydroxyl groups (–OH) of the glucose unit. The hydroxyl group reacts readily with moisture, dyes, and many finishes. Chemicals such as chlorine bleach damage cellulose by attacking the oxygen atom between the two ring units or within the ring, rupturing the chain or ring.

This chapter discusses major natural cellulosic fibers and those of more limited use that may be present in imported goods or that may be encountered during travel or in certain careers. While several of these fibers may not be common in apparel, they are important in the interiors industry and may be used as reinforcement fibers in composites. Many other natural cellulosic fibers will not be discussed because of their minimal commercial use.

Some fibers that are derived from plants (bamboo, corn starch, and soy fibers) are not included in this chapter because they are made from noncellulosic parts of the plant or are not found in fiber form in the plant. They must undergo several chemical and manufacturing steps to become fibers and are included in Chapter 7.

Table 4.2 Properties Common to All Cellulosic Fibers

Properties	Importance to Consumer
Good absorbency	Comfortable for warm weather wear and activewear and interiors
	Good for towels, diapers, and activewear
Good conductor of heat	Sheer fabrics cool for warm-weather wear
Ability to withstand high temperature	Fabrics can be sterilized; no special precautions necessary in pressing
Low resiliency	Fabrics wrinkle badly unless finished for wrinkle recovery
Low loft; good compressibility	Dense, high-count fabrics possible
	Wind-resistant fabrics possible
Good conductor of electricity	No static buildup
Heavy fibers (density of 1.5)	Fabrics are heavier than comparable fabrics of other fibers
Harmed by mineral acids, minimal damage by organic acids	Remove acid stains immediately
Attacked by mildew	Store clean items under dry conditions
Resistant to moths, but eaten by crickets and silverfish	Store clean items under dry conditions
Flammable	Ignite quickly, burn freely with an afterglow and gray, feathery ash; loosely constructed garments should not be worn near an open flame; interior textiles should meet required codes
Moderate resistance to sunlight	Draperies should be lined

Seed Fibers

Seed fibers develop in the seedpod of the plant. In order to use the fiber, it must be separated from the seed. (The seed is used to produce oil and animal feed.) By far the most important seed fiber is **cotton**. This section discusses cotton and some minor seed fibers.

Cotton

Cotton is an important cash crop in more than 80 countries. Its combination of properties—pleasing appearance, comfort, easy care, moderate cost, and durability—makes cotton ideal for warm-weather apparel, activewear, work clothes, upholstery, draperies, area rugs, towels, and bedding. Even though other fibers have encroached on former cotton markets, the cotton look is maintained. Cotton is also a major component of many blend fabrics.

Cotton cloth was used by the people of ancient China, Egypt, India (where the cotton spinning and weaving industry began), Mexico, and Peru. In the Americas, naturally colored cotton was used extensively.

Cotton was grown in the southern U.S. colonies as soon as they were established. Throughout the 1600s and 1700s, cotton fibers were separated from cotton seeds by hand in a very time-consuming and tedious job. A worker could separate only one pound of cotton fiber from the seeds in a day.

When Eli Whitney mechanized the saw-tooth cotton gin in 1793, things changed. The gin could process 50 pounds of cotton in a day and more cotton could be prepared for spinning. Within the next 20 years, a series of spinning and weaving inventions in England mechanized fabric production. The southern states were able to meet Britain's greatly increased demand for raw cotton. By 1859, U.S. production was 4.5 million bales of cotton—two-thirds of the world's production. Cotton was the leading U.S. export. During the time of rapidly expanding cotton production in the south, most U.S. fabrics were spun and woven in New England.

The picture again changed dramatically during the U.S. Civil War. U.S. cotton production decreased to 200,000 bales in 1864, and Britain looked to other countries to fill the deficit. After the war, western states began producing cotton and the southern states built spinning and weaving mills. Between World War I and World War II, most of the New England mills moved south. Factors influencing this move included proximity to cotton producers, less expensive power and nonunion labor, and relocation incentives from state and local governments. By 1950, 80 percent of the mills were in the south. However, during the 1980s and 1990s, most of these mills closed because of increased costs and competition from imports.

Production of Cotton Cotton grows in any place where the growing season is long and the climate is temperate to hot with adequate rainfall or irrigation. Cellulose will not form if the temperature is below 70°F. In the United States, cotton is grown south of a line from southern Virginia to central California.

The major producers of cotton in the world are China (32.0 percent), India (21.8 percent), the United States (12.2 percent), Pakistan (7.8 percent), and Brazil (5.7 percent). In 2007 the worldwide production of cotton was over 113 million bales (480 pounds per bale). Mechanization and weed control reduce the number of hours required to produce a bale of cotton, thereby increasing productivity.

Factors affecting the U.S. production of cotton include the value of the dollar as compared with other currencies, imports of cotton goods, changes in government incentives for growing cotton, weather conditions, and comparable changes in other countries.

Cotton grows on bushes 3 to 6 feet high. After the blossom drops off, the *boll* or seedpod begins to grow. Inside the boll are seven to eight seeds with several hundred thousand cotton fibers. Each cotton seed may have as many as 20,000 fibers growing from its surface. When the boll is ripe and about the size of a walnut, the fluffy white fibers expand as they grow and eventually split open the boll (Figure 4.2).

Cotton is most often picked by machine (Figure 4.3). This cotton contains many immature fibers—an inescapable result of mechanically stripping the cotton plant. After picking, the cotton is pressed into a brick weighing approximately 22,000 pounds and taken to a **gin** to separate the fibers and the seeds. In a saw gin, the whirling saws pick up the fiber and carry it to a knifelike comb, which blocks the seeds and permits the fiber to be carried through (Figure 4.4). The fibers, called **lint**, are pressed into bales weighing 480 pounds each and sold to spinning mills or exported.

After ginning, the seeds are covered with very short fibers—$\frac{1}{8}$ inch in length—called **linters**. The linters are removed from the seeds and are used to a limited extent as raw material in producing rayon and acetate. Linters are used to stuff small decorator pillows and are used in automotive upholstery, mops, candlewicks, blankets, mattresses, twine, rugs, and medical supplies. Linters are also converted into cellophane, photographic film, fingernail polish, and methylcellulose used in makeup and chewing gum. The seeds are crushed to obtain cottonseed oil and meal used in food and livestock feed, pharmaceuticals, and soap stock. The hulls are used in animal feed, fertilizer, garden mulch, and oil drilling mud to plug leaks in oil wells.

Recent advances in plant breeding have produced cottons that are insect-, herbicide-, and stress-tolerant. Cotton breeders have focused their efforts on improving fiber strength and length. These changes have contributed to higher processing speeds, finer and more uniform yarns, and more durable fabrics. Efforts in plant breeding continue to focus on producing cotton varieties with better resistance to insects, disease, herbicides, fungi, and drought and with enhanced properties for ease of processing, higher reactivity for dyes, and improved product performance. Some bioengineered cotton plants have been developed that incorporate a tiny percentage of polyester in the fiber. In addition, some plant breeders are working to improve the performance characteristics and color options of naturally colored cotton.

Physical Structure of Cotton

Although some naturally colored cotton is produced, most raw cotton is creamy white in color. The cotton fiber is a single cell, which grows from the seed as a hollow tube over one thousand times as long as it is thick.

Length Staple length is very important because it affects how the fiber is handled during the spinning process, and it relates to fiber fineness and fiber tensile strength. Longer cotton fibers are finer and make stronger yarns. Length is determined by removing a sample from a bale of cotton, sorting the fibers by length, and calculating the average staple length and the variation of length or uniformity ratio.

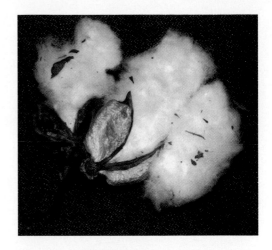

Figure 4.2 Opened cotton boll.
SOURCE: Courtesy of National Cotton Council of America.

Figure 4.3 Harvester in a cotton field.
SOURCE: Courtesy of John Deere.

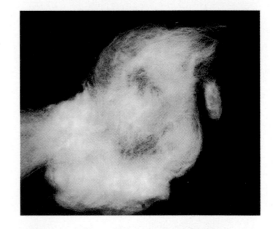

Figure 4.4 Cotton fiber (left) removed from the seed (right).

Cotton fibers range in length from $\frac{1}{2}$ to 2 inches, depending on the genetic variety. Three groups of cotton are commercially important:

1. Upland cottons (*Gossypium hirsutum*, the predominant type of cotton produced in the United States) are $\frac{7}{8}$ to $1\frac{1}{4}$ inches in length and were developed from cottons native to Mexico and Central America. Approximately 97 percent of the U.S. crop is an Upland variety.

2. Long-staple cottons, which are $1\frac{5}{16}$ to $1\frac{1}{2}$ inches in length, were developed from Egyptian and South American cottons. Varieties include American Pima, Egyptian, American Egyptian, and Sea Island cottons. Cotton from the *Gossypium barbadense* variety is grown in the southwestern United States and is about 3 percent of the crop.

3. Short-staple cottons, *Gossypium arboreum* and *Gossypium herbaceum*, are less than $\frac{3}{4}$ inch in length and are produced primarily in India and eastern Asia.

Long-staple fibers are considered to be of higher quality and are used to produce softer, smoother, stronger, and more lustrous fabrics. Because their perceived value is higher, they are sometimes identified on the label or tag as **Pima**, **Supima**, **Egyptian**, or **Sea Island**. Or they may be referred to as *long-staple* or *extra-long-staple* (*ELS*) cotton.

Distinctive Parts The cotton fiber is made up of a cuticle, primary wall, secondary wall, and lumen (Figure 4.5). The fiber grows to almost full length as a hollow tube before the secondary wall begins to form.

The **cuticle** is a waxlike film covering the primary, or outer, wall. The secondary wall is made up of layers of cellulose (Figure 4.6).

The layers deposited at night differ in density from those deposited during the day; this causes growth rings, which can be seen in the cross section. The cellulose layers are composed of fibrils—bundles of cellulose chains—arranged in a spiral that sometimes reverses direction. These reverse spirals (Figure 4.7) contribute to the development of convolutions that affect the fiber's elastic recovery and elongation. They are also 15 to 30 percent weaker than the rest of the secondary cell wall.

Cellulose is deposited daily for 20 to 30 days, until, in the mature fiber, the fiber tube is almost solid. The **lumen** is the central canal, through which nourishment travels during fiber development. When the fiber matures, dried nutrients in the lumen may result in dark areas that are visible under a microscope.

Convolutions **Convolutions** are ribbonlike twists that characterize cotton (Figure 4.8). When the fibers mature and force the boll open, they dry out and the central canal collapses. Reverse spirals in the secondary wall cause the fibers to twist. The twist forms a natural texture that enables the fibers to cling to one another. Thus, despite its short length, yarn spinning is easy with cotton. However, the convolutions may trap soil, requiring vigorous cleaning to remove it. Long-staple cotton has about 300 convolutions per inch; short-staple cotton has less than 200.

Fineness Cotton fibers vary from 16 to 20 micrometers (microns) in diameter. The cross-sectional shape varies with the maturity of the fiber. Immature fibers tend to be U-shaped, with a thin cell wall. Mature fibers are more nearly circular, with a thick cell wall and a very small central canal or lumen. Every cotton boll contains some immature fibers that can create problems in spinning and dyeing. Figure 4.8 illustrates the variation in size and shape of the fibers.

Color Cotton is available in a range of colors. Naturally creamy white is highly desirable because it can be dyed or printed to meet fashion and consumer needs. These fibers may yellow with age. If it rains just before harvest, cotton becomes grayer.

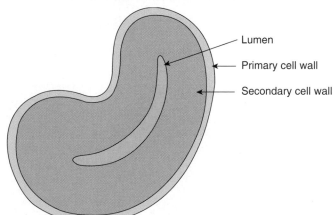

Lumen
Primary cell wall
Secondary cell wall

Figure 4.5 **Cross section of mature cotton fiber.**

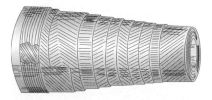

Figure 4.6 **Layers of cellulose (schematic).**

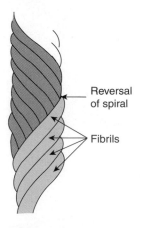

Reversal of spiral

Fibrils

Figure 4.7 **Reverse spirals in cotton fiber.**

Naturally colored cotton fibers have been cultivated for thousands of years. As commercial production replaced hand processes, these fibers declined in importance. By the early 20th century, they had become difficult to find. However, with the current interest in minimizing environmental impact and sustainability concerns, interest in naturally colored cottons has resurfaced. Naturally colored cottons produce less fiber per acre, but sell for about twice the price of white cotton. Naturally brown, rust, red, beige, and green colored cottons are commercially available. These colors deepen with age and care, which is contrary to the aging process of most dyed or printed fabrics (Figure 4.9). Colored cottons are shorter, weaker, less absorbent, and have less uniform properties than do white cotton, but improvements are expected as plant breeders concentrate on enhancing these properties. These cottons also have higher metal content than white cottons, probably because of the natural pigments in the fiber. Naturally colored cottons are produced in Russia, India, South and Central America, Africa, and the United States. Plant breeders continue to work to add blue, lavender, and yellow to the current list of naturally colored cottons. Naturally colored cotton has lower environmental impact, especially in yarn and fabric finishing processes.

Picking and ginning affect the appearance of cotton fibers. Carefully picked cotton is cleaner. Well-ginned cotton is more uniform in appearance and color. Poorly ginned cotton contains brown flecks of trash, such as bits of leaf, stem, or dirt, that decrease fiber quality. Fabrics made from such fibers include utility cloth and may be fashionable when a "natural" look is popular.

Classification of Cotton
Grading and classing of cotton is done by hand and by machine HVI (high-volume instrument) systems. Fiber characteristics, including staple length and color of the cotton from the bale, are compared with standards prepared by the U.S. Department of Agriculture.

Cotton classification describes the quality of cotton in terms of staple length, grade, and character. Fiber-length classifications for cotton include very-short-staple cotton (less than 0.25 inch), short-staple cotton (0.25 to 0.94 inch), medium-staple cotton (0.94 to 1.13 inches), ordinary long-staple cotton (1.13 to 1.38 inches), and extra-long-staple cotton (1.38 inches). *Staple length* is based on the length of a representative bundle of fibers from a bale of cotton. There are 19 staple lengths, ranging from less than $^{13}/_{16}$ inch to $1^{1}/_{8}$ inches and beyond. A sample classified as $^{15}/_{32}$ inch is likely to have fibers ranging in length from $^{1}/_{8}$ inch to $^{13}/_{16}$ inches, as shown in Figure 4.10.

There are 39 grades of cotton. *Grade* refers to the color of the fiber and the absence of dirt, leaf matter, seed particles, motes or dead fibers, and tangles of fiber called *neps*. Mote fibers do not absorb dyes, lower fiber quality, and cause defects in fabrics. The best-quality grade is lustrous, silky, white, and clean. The predominant grade of cotton produced in the United States is strict low-middling cotton. *Strict* in this case means "better than."

This grading system is used primarily for the creamy white fibers that dominate the market. Color is described as white, light-spotted, spotted, tinged, or yellow. Color is also described in terms of lightness to darkness: plus, light gray, and gray. This factor is a combination of grayness and the amount of leaf bits present in white cotton grades.

Character includes such fiber aspects as maturity, smoothness and uniformity of fibers within the bale, fiber fineness, strength, and convolutions. Micronaire values, which reflect both fineness and maturity, are assessed by forcing air through a standard weight plug of cotton fibers compressed to a fixed volume. Lower micronaire results indicate less mature and coarser fibers, while higher values indicate more mature and finer fibers. Character identifies the amount of processing necessary to produce a good white fabric for commercial use. Because of yearly variations in growing conditions and in geographic locations, yarn and fabric producers carefully select and blend cottons so that the cotton fabrics and products are as uniform from year to year as possible.

Figure 4.8 Photomicrographs of cotton: cross-sectional view (left), longitudinal view (right).
SOURCE: Courtesy of the British Textile Technology Group.

Figure 4.9 Naturally colored cotton fibers and fabrics. New swatch (top) becomes darker with laundering (bottom).

Figure 4.10 Cotton classed as 1$\frac{5}{32}$ inch contains fibers that range in length from $\frac{1}{8}$ inch to 1$\frac{5}{8}$ inches.

SOURCE: Courtesy of U.S. Department of Agriculture.

Cotton is a commodity crop. It is sold by grade and staple length. Strict low-middling cotton is used in mass-produced cotton goods and in cotton/synthetic blends. Better grades of cotton and longer-staple cotton are used in better-quality shirtings and sheets. Extra-long-staple (ELS) American Egyptian cotton usually is identified by the terms *Pima* and *Supima* on labels for sweaters, blouses, shirts, underwear, sheets, and towels.

Chemical Composition and Molecular Arrangement of Cotton

Cotton, when picked, is about 94 percent cellulose; in finished fabrics it is 99 percent cellulose. Like all cellulose fibers, cotton contains reactive hydroxyl groups. Cotton may have as many as 10,000 glucose monomers per molecule connected in long linear chains and arranged in a spiral form within the fiber. Chain length (average number of glucose monomers per molecule) contributes to fiber strength.

Cotton can be altered by using chemical treatments or finishes. *Mercerization* (treating yarns or fabrics with sodium hydroxide [NaOH]) causes a permanent physical change. The fiber swells and creates a rounder cross section. Mercerization increases absorbency and improves the dyeability of cotton yarns and fabrics. Liquid ammonia is used as an alternative to several preparation finishes, especially mercerization. Fabrics treated with ammonia have good luster and dyeability. When these fabrics are treated to be wrinkle-resistant, they are not as stiff and harsh as mercerized wrinkle-resistant fabrics.

Properties of Cotton

Cotton is a comfortable fiber. Appropriate for year-round use, it is the fiber most preferred for many interiors and for warm-weather apparel, especially where the climate is hot and humid. Reviewing the fiber property tables in Chapter 3 will help when comparing cotton's performance to that of other fibers.

Aesthetics Cotton fabrics certainly have consumer acceptance. Their matte appearance and low luster are the standards that have been retained with many blends used in apparel and interiors.

Long-staple cotton fibers contribute luster to fabrics. Mercerized and ammonia-treated cotton fabrics have a soft, pleasant luster resulting from the finishes; cotton sateen's luster is due to a combination of fabric structure and finishing.

Drape, luster, texture, and hand are affected by choice of yarn size and type, fabric structure, and finish. Cotton fabrics range from soft, sheer batiste to crisp, sheer voile to fine chintz to sturdy denim and corduroy.

Durability Cotton is a medium-strength fiber, with a dry breaking tenacity of 3.5 to 4.0g/d (grams per denier). It is 30 percent stronger when wet. Long-staple cotton produces stronger yarns because there are more contact points among the fibers when they are twisted together. Because of its higher wet strength, cotton can be handled roughly during laundering and in use.

Abrasion resistance is good; heavy fabrics are more abrasion-resistant than thinner fabrics. Fiber elongation is low (3 percent), with low elasticity.

Comfort Cotton makes very comfortable fabrics for skin contact because of its high absorbency, soft hand, and good heat and electrical conductivity. Static buildup is not a problem. It has no surface characteristics that irritate the skin. Cotton has a moisture regain of 7 to 11 percent. When cotton becomes wet, the fibers swell and become more pliant. This property makes it possible to give a smooth, flat finish to cotton fabrics in pressing or finishing and makes high-count woven fabrics water-repellent. However, as cotton fabrics absorb more moisture in cool, damp conditions, they feel wet or clammy and eventually may become uncomfortable.

Still, cotton is good for use in hot and humid weather. The fibers absorb moisture and feel good against the skin in high humidity. The fiber ends in the spun yarn hold the fabric slightly off the skin for greater comfort. Moisture passes freely through the fabric, thus aiding evaporation and cooling.

Appearance Retention Overall appearance retention for cotton is moderate. It has very low resiliency. The hydrogen bonds holding the molecular chains together are weak, and when fabrics are bent or crushed, particularly in the presence of moisture, the chains move freely to new positions. When pressure is removed, these weak internal forces cannot pull the chains back to their original positions, so the fabrics stay wrinkled. Creases can be pressed in and wrinkles can be pressed out, but wrinkling during use and care remain a problem. However, cotton fibers can be given a durable-press finish or blended with polyester and given a durable-press finish so they do not wrinkle as easily. Unfortunately, these finishes decrease fiber strength and abrasion resistance.

Cotton's poor resiliency means that it is seldom used in pile rugs or carpets. However, on-going research is attempting to improve cotton's performance in this significant market.

All-cotton fabrics shrink unless they have been given a durable-press finish or a shrinkage-resistant finish. Untreated cottons shrink less when washed in cool water and drip-dried; they shrink more when washed in hot water and tumble dried in a hot dryer. When they are used again, they may stretch out slightly—think of cotton denim jeans or fitted cotton sheets.

Shrinkage should be low for all-cotton fabrics that have been given a wrinkle-resistant or durable-press finish or that have been treated for shrinkage. However, more effort may be needed with handwoven or short-staple cotton fabrics, unless the label includes specific information about shrinkage.

Elastic recovery is moderate. Cotton recovers 75 percent from a 2 to 5 percent stretch. This means that cotton stays stretched out in areas of stress, such as in the elbow or knee areas of garments.

Care Cotton can be washed with strong detergents and requires no special care during washing and drying. White cottons can be washed in hot water. Many dyed cottons retain their color better if washed in warm, not hot, water. If items are not heavily soiled, cool water cleans them adequately. Cotton releases most soils readily, but soil-resistant finishes are desirable for some interior and apparel uses. Use of chlorine bleach is appropriate for spot removal, but should not be used on a regular basis because excessive bleaching weakens cellulosic fibers.

Less wrinkling occurs in the dryer if items are removed immediately after drying. Cotton fabrics respond best to steam pressing or ironing while damp. Fabric blends of cotton and a heat-sensitive fiber need to be ironed at a lower temperature to avoid melting the heat-sensitive fiber. Cotton is not thermoplastic; it can be ironed safely at high temperatures. However, cotton burns readily.

Table 4.3 Summary of the Performance of Cotton in Apparel and Interior Textiles

Aesthetics	Attractive	Appearance Retention	Moderate
Luster	Matte, pleasant	Resiliency	Poor
Drape	Soft to stiff	Dimensional stability	Moderate
Texture	Pleasant	Elastic recovery	Moderate
Hand	Smooth to rough		
Durability	Good	Recommended Care	Machine-wash and machine-dry (apparel)
Abrasion resistance	Good		
Tenacity	Good		Steam- or dry-clean with caution (interior textiles)
Elongation	Poor		
Comfort	Excellent		
Absorbency	Excellent		
Thermal retention	Poor		

Cotton draperies should be dry-cleaned. Cotton upholstery may be steam-cleaned, with caution. If shrinkage occurs, the fabric may split or rupture where it is attached to the frame.

Cottons should be stored clean and dry. In damp or humid conditions, mildew can form. Mildew digests cellulose and may cause holes if enough time elapses. If textiles smell of mildew, they can be laundered or bleached to remove the odor. But if the mildew areas are visible dark or black spots, they indicate permanent and excessive fiber damage.

Cotton is harmed by acids. Fruit and fruit juice stains should be treated promptly with cold water for easy removal. Cotton is not greatly harmed by alkalis. Cotton is resistant to organic solvents, so it can be safely dry-cleaned.

Cotton oxidizes in sunlight, which causes white and pastel cottons to yellow and all cotton to degrade. Some dyes are especially sensitive to sunlight, and when used in window-treatment fabrics the dyed areas disintegrate.

Table 4.3 summarizes cotton's performance in apparel and interior textiles.

Environmental Concerns and Sustainability of Cotton Since cotton is a natural fiber, many environmentally sensitive consumers believe it is a good choice. However, although cotton is a renewable resource, it cannot be produced without some environmental impact. Mainstream farming methods that produce conventional cotton make extensive use of agricultural chemicals to fertilize the soil, fight insects and disease, control plant growth, and strip the leaves for harvest. Excess rain can create problems with runoff contaminated with these chemicals, many of which are toxic to other plants, insects, animals, and people. While cotton growers in developed countries have modified agricultural practices to reduce use of

▶ **Learning Activity 2**

Select an item of apparel you or a class partner is wearing that is all cotton. Identify one or more performance aspects of the product related to each of the serviceability concepts (aesthetics, durability, comfort, appearance retention, care). Has the performance of the product been satisfactory? Explain performance satisfaction and performance problems in terms of fiber characteristics.

agrichemicals and soil erosion and genetically modified cotton is grown, which significantly can reduce the amount of pesticides used, that is not the case for all parts of the world.

Cotton that is harvested by machine is often treated with defoliant chemicals to remove the leaves. Machine-picked cotton usually also includes impurities such as seeds, dirt, and plant residue, which requires more effort in cleaning. Hand-picked cotton does not include these components, but children are sometimes used as slave labor to pick cotton.

Cotton is a water-intensive crop requiring at least 20 inches of rain per year. Sometimes this cotton is marketed as rain-fed cotton. But in many areas of the world where rainfall is low or irregular, irrigation is used. Excessive irrigation can upset the water table or the water level in the soil. In some geographic regions, irrigation is so extremely inefficient, up to 50 percent of the water is wasted. Irrigation has created problems in some parts of the world for people and environments dependent on rivers and lakes. So much water can be diverted for cotton production that rivers disappear and lakes dry up, destroying ecosystems and forcing communities to move away from their traditional homes to the irrigated areas.

Tilling the soil contributes to soil erosion by water and wind. Efforts to improve the production of cotton are focusing on use of locally adapted varieties that require fewer agricultural chemicals and less irrigation, wide crop rotation to avoid depleting the soil of necessary nutrients, and mechanical and manual weed control as opposed to chemical herbicides.

Genetically modified (GM) cotton is well established because of its resistance to certain insect pests and tolerance of herbicides. There is some concern about large-scale production of GM cotton in terms of its unknown long-term environmental and health effects. Concern about GM crops and their impact on nonpest insects is an issue. Environmentalists also are concerned about the potential of insects developing resistance to GM crops. However, GM cotton does reduce the use of pesticides and is tolerant of herbicides. Benefits of GM cotton include less use of pesticides, yields equal to or higher than conventional cotton, no loss in fiber quality, less soil erosion because of less tilling of the soil, and higher incomes for producers.

Cotton is produced in many parts of the world and is a major cash crop in more than 80 countries. This means that farmers raise cotton to produce income for their families. When cotton prices and production are good, their incomes increase. However, when cotton prices or production falls, incomes suffer a similar decrease. Droughts, decreasing prices for cotton, disease, or insect problems can create significant hardships for cotton farmers—regardless of the size of their farm. In some parts of the world, a significant portion of the labor involved in hand harvesting cotton is performed by forced child labor. Many segments of the global textile complex deplore this practice and refuse to source cotton from areas that violate minimum age laws.

Cotton seeds are processed into food used to prevent malnutrition in part of Central American and Africa.

In an effort to provide consumers and producers with more information at the point of purchase, several terms are used to describe cotton grown under more environmentally friendly conditions. **Organic cotton** is produced following state fiber-certification standards on land where organic farming practices have been used for at least three years. No synthetic commercial pesticides or fertilizers are used in organic farming. Integrated pest management programs help decrease use of pesticides. The BASIC (biological agricultural systems in cotton) program uses approximately 70 percent fewer pesticides and is an alternative to organic cotton. **Transition cotton** is produced on land where organic farming is practiced, but the three-year minimum has not been met. **Green cotton** describes cotton fabric that has been washed with mild natural-based soap but has not been bleached or treated with other chemicals, except possibly natural dyes. The term **conventional cotton** describes all other cottons.

Figure 4.11 Organic cotton and linen washcloth. Fibers are grown without the aid of commercial fertilizers, herbicides, or insecticides. No bleaches or dyes were used in producing the fabric.

Some retailers and manufacturers have made a commitment to use only organic cotton in their products (Figure 4.11). Organic and transition cottons are more expensive than conventional cotton. The additional costs are related to the lower fiber yield per acre, requirements for processing in facilities that are free of hazardous chemicals, and the smaller quantities of fibers that are processed and sold.

Cotton also uses large quantities of water, energy, and chemical compounds to clean the fiber and to finish and dye the fabrics. Soil or trash is removed from the raw cotton fiber before it is processed into yarn. Opening cotton bales can generate significant amount of dust that if not removed from the air can result in lung disorders for people who work in that part of the building.

In order to add color in dyeing and printing, cotton is bleached in a chemical and water solution and rinsed. Dyes, pigments, and finishing chemicals add to the consumer appeal of cotton products. All these steps make extensive use of water, other chemicals, and heat. Although the industry has improved recycling, reduced waste, and cleaned up wastewater, the net environmental effect of processing cotton continues to be a concern.

Identification of Cotton Microscopic identification of cotton is relatively easy. Convolutions are easily seen along the fiber. Burn tests will verify cellulose, but a more precise identification is not possible with this procedure. Fiber length helps in determining content, but long fibers can be broken or cut shorter. Cotton is soluble in strong mineral acids, like sulfuric acid.

Uses of Cotton Cotton is the single most important apparel fiber in the United States. All-cotton fabrics are used when comfort is of primary importance and appearance retention is less

▶ Learning Activity 3

Work in groups of four. Two students discuss the advantages of increasing use of cotton for apparel, interiors, and technical products. Two students discuss the concerns related to the sustainability of cotton. Switch roles and repeat the discussion. Identify four major points each side identified.

▶ Learning Activity 4

Use a small portion of the fiber from the small self-sealing bag labeled Cotton or three to four yarns from Fabric #48 from your swatch kit. Following the procedures described in Chapter 3, examine the fibers using the microscope to see the convolutions and variations among the cotton fibers. Identify the maturity of the fiber—mature fibers are very rounded, while immature fibers are flatter.

▶ Learning Activity 5

Use a small portion of the fiber from the small self-sealing bag labeled Cotton or three to four yarns from Fabric #48 from your swatch kit. Following the procedures and safety precautions described in Chapter 3, conduct a burn test. Describe the ease of ignition, the color and odor of the smoke, and the color and texture of the cooled ash. Compare your results with those included in Table 3.7 or with the chart on the sheet with the fiber bags in your swatch kit.

important, or when a more casual fabric is acceptable. Cotton blended with polyester in wrinkle-resistant fabrics is widely marketed. These blends retain cotton's pleasant appearance, have the same or increased durability, are less comfortable in conditions of extreme heat and humidity or high physical activity, and have better appearance retention as compared with 100 percent cotton fabrics. However, removal of oily soil is a greater problem with blends.

Cotton is a very important interiors fabric because of its versatility, natural comfort, and ease of finishing and dyeing. Towels are mostly cotton—softness, absorbency, wide range of colors, and washability are important in this end use. Durability can be increased in the base fabric, as well as in the selvages and hems, by blending polyester with the cotton. However, the loops of terry towels are 100 percent cotton so that maximum absorbency is retained.

Sheets and pillowcases of all-cotton or cotton/polyester blends are available in percale, flannelette, dobby and jacquard weaves, jersey, and muslin. A range of blend levels and counts are available. Cotton blankets and bedspreads can be found in a variety of weights and fabric types.

Draperies, curtains, upholstery fabrics, slipcovers, rugs, and wall coverings are made of cotton. Cotton upholstery fabrics are attractive and durable, comfortable, easy to spot-clean, and retain their appearance well. Resiliency is not a problem with the heavyweight fabrics that are stretched over the furniture frame. Cotton is susceptible to abrasion, waterborne stains, and shrinkage if cleaning is too vigorous or incorrect. Small accent rugs made from cotton can be machine-washed.

Medical, surgical, and sanitary supplies are frequently made of cotton. Since cotton can be autoclaved (heated to a high temperature to sanitize it), it is widely used in hospitals. Absorbency, washability, and low static buildup are also important properties in these uses.

Technical uses include abrasives, book bindings, luggage and handbags, shoes and slippers, tobacco cloth, and woven wiping cloths. Recycled denim scraps are used to create paper currency.

Cotton Incorporated is an organization that promotes the use of cotton by consumers. It also promotes the use of all-cotton and NATURAL BLEND™ fabrics with at least 60 percent cotton (Figure 4.12). The National Cotton Council is an organization of producers, processors, and manufacturers.

NATURAL BLEND®

Figure 4.12 Seal of Cotton trademark (top) for 100 percent cotton fabrics and apparel and NATURAL BLEND trademark (bottom) used for fabrics and apparel made of at least 60 percent cotton.

SOURCE: Courtesy of Cotton Incorporated.

Other Seed Fibers

Coir

Coir is obtained from the fibrous mass between the outer shell and the husk of the coconut (*Cocos nucifera*). It is sometimes sold as coco fiber. The long, curly fibers are removed by soaking the husk in saline water. Coir, which is very stiff, is naturally cinnamon-brown. It can be bleached and dyed. It has good resistance to abrasion, water, and weather. Available from Sri Lanka, coir is used for indoor and outdoor mats, rugs, floor tiles, and brushes. Its stiff, wiry texture and coarse size produce fabrics whose weave, pattern, or design is clearly visible. These floor textiles are extremely durable and blend with interiors of many styles.

> ▶ **Learning Activity 6**

Select three technical end uses for cotton and explain its performance characteristics that make it appropriate for those end uses.

Kapok

Kapok is obtained from the seed of the Java kapok (silk cotton) tree (*Eriodendron anfractuosum*) or the Indian kapok tree (*Bombax malabarica*). The fiber is lightweight, soft, hollow, and very buoyant, but it quickly breaks down. The fiber is difficult to spin into yarns, so it is used primarily as fiberfill in some imported items from Java, South America, and India. Researchers in India are studying ways of blending kapok with cotton for apparel uses.

Milkweed

Milkweed (*Asclepias incarnate* and *A. syrica*) produces a soft, lustrous, hollow-floss seed hair fiber resembling kapok. Milkweed has been used for fiberfill in comforters, personal flotation devices, and upholstery. It is very difficult to spin into yarns because it is so weak, smooth, and straight. Milkweed is also known as silkweed fiber and asclepias cotton.

Bast Fibers

Bast fibers come from the stem of the plant, near the outer edge (Figure 4.13). Hand labor may be used to process bast fibers, and production has flourished in countries where labor is cheap. Since the fiber extends into the root, harvesting is done by pulling up the plant with mechanical pullers or cutting it close to the ground to keep the fiber as long as possible. Cut fibers are approximately 10 percent shorter than pulled fibers. After harvesting, the seeds are removed by pulling the plant through a machine in a process called **rippling**.

Bast fibers lie in bundles in the stem of the plant, just under the outer covering or bark. They are sealed together by a substance composed of pectins, waxes, and gums. To loosen the fibers so that they can be removed from the stalk, the pectin must be decomposed by a bacterial rotting process called **retting**. The process differs for individual fibers, but the major steps are the same. Fiber quality can be greatly affected by the retting process. Retting can be done in the fields (dew retting) or in stagnant ponds, pools, or tanks (water retting), where the temperature and bacterial count can be carefully controlled with special enzymes or with chemicals such as sodium hydroxide. Chemical retting is much faster than any other method. However, extra care must be taken or the fiber can be irreversibly damaged. Retting can create problems with water quality if the retting water is released directly into streams or lakes. Dew retting is done in many areas because of its minimal environmental impact.

After the stems have been rinsed and dried, the woody portion is removed by **scutching**, a process that breaks or crushes the outer covering when the stalks are passed between fluted metal rollers. Most of the fibers are separated from one another, and the short and irregular fibers are removed by **hackling**, or combing. This final step removes any remaining woody portion and arranges the fibers in a parallel fashion. Figure 4.14 shows the plant or fiber at each step in processing.

Bast fibers characteristically have thick-and-thin variations in their appearance when processed into yarns and fabrics. This occurs because fiber bundles are never completely separated into individual or primary fibers.

Because the processing of bast fibers is time-consuming and requires specialized machinery, researchers have developed ways of speeding up the process and minimizing the need for

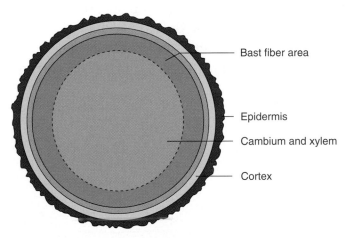

Figure 4.13 Bast fibers are located toward the epidermis of the plant stem.

Bast fiber area

Epidermis

Cambium and xylem

Cortex

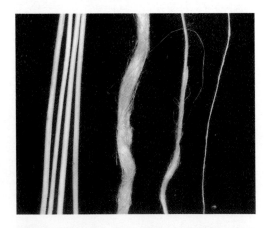

Figure 4.14 Flax fiber at different stages of processing: plant stems before retting, fiber after hackling, fiber during yarn processing, bleached linen yarn (left to right).

special equipment. **Cottonizing** reduces a bast fiber to a length similar to that of cotton. These cottonized fibers can be processed on equipment designed for cotton but may lack some of their more traditional characteristics related to hand, luster, and durability. Flax, ramie, and hemp are bast fibers that are frequently cottonized.

Flax

Flax is one of the oldest documented textile fibers. Fragments of linen fabric have been found in prehistoric lake dwellings in Switzerland; linen mummy wraps more than 3,000 years old have been found in Egyptian tombs. The linen industry flourished in Europe until the 18th century. With the invention of power spinning, cotton replaced flax as the most important and widely used fiber.

Today, flax is a prestige fiber as a result of its limited production and relatively high cost. The term **linen** refers to fabric made from flax, but, that term may be misused when it refers to fabrics of other fibers made of thick-and-thin yarns with a heavy body and crisp hand. *Irish linen* always refers to fabrics made from flax. (Because of its historic wide use in sheets, tablecloths, and towels, the word *linen* is used to refer to table, bed, and bath textiles.)

The unique and desirable characteristics of flax are its body, strength, durability, low pilling and linting tendencies, pleasant hand, and thick-and-thin texture. The main limitations of flax are low resiliency and lack of elasticity.

Most flax is produced in Western Europe, in Belgium, France, Italy, Ireland, the United Kingdom, Germany, the Netherlands, and Switzerland. Flax is also produced in Russia, Belarus, and New Zealand.

Structure of Flax
Individual fiber cells, called *ultimates*, are spindle-shaped with pointed ends and a center lumen. The primary fiber of flax averages 5.0 to 21.5 inches in length and 12 to 16 micrometers in diameter. Flax fibers (*Linum usitatissium*) can be identified microscopically by crosswise markings called **nodes** or *joints* that contribute to its flexibility (Figure 4.15). The nodes may appear to be slightly swollen and resemble the joints in a stalk of corn or bamboo. The fibers have a small central canal similar to the lumen in cotton. The cross section (Figure 4.15) is many-sided or polygonal with rounded edges. Immature fibers are more oval in cross-section with a larger lumen.

Flax fibers are slightly grayish when dew retted and more yellow when water retted. Because flax has a more highly oriented molecular structure than cotton, it is stronger than cotton.

Flax is similar to cotton in its chemical composition (71 percent cellulose). Compared to cotton, flax has a longer polymer (a higher degree of polymerization) and greater orientation and crystallinity.

Short flax fibers are called **tow**; the long, combed, better-quality fibers are called **line**. Line fibers are ready for wet spinning into yarn. The tow fibers must be carded before dry spinning into yarns for heavier fabrics for interior textiles.

Properties of Flax
Review the fiber property tables in Chapter 3 to compare the performance of flax with that of other fibers.

Aesthetics Flax has a high natural luster that is softened by its irregular fiber bundles. Its luster can be increased by flattening yarns with pressure during finishing.

Because flax has a higher degree of orientation and crystallinity and a larger fiber diameter than cotton, linen fabrics are stiffer in drape and harsher in hand. Finishes that wash and air blow the fabric produce softer and more drapeable fabrics.

Figure 4.15 Photomicrographs of flax: cross-sectional view (left), longitudinal view (right).
SOURCE: Courtesy of the British Textile Technology Group.

Durability Flax is strong for a natural fiber. It has a breaking tenacity of 3.5 to 5.0g/d when dry that increases to 6.5g/d when wet. Flax has a very low elongation of approximately 7 percent. Elasticity is poor, with a 65 percent recovery at only 2 percent elongation. Flax is also a stiff fiber. With poor elongation, elasticity, and stiffness, repeatedly folding a linen item in the same place will cause the fabric to break. The nodes contribute greatly to flexibility, but they are also the weakest part of the fiber. Flax has good flat abrasion resistance for a natural fiber because of its high orientation and crystallinity.

Comfort Flax has a high moisture regain of 12 percent, and it is a good conductor of electricity with no static buildup. Flax is also a good conductor of heat, so it makes an excellent fabric for warm-weather wear. Flax has the same high specific gravity (1.52) as cotton.

Care Flax is resistant to alkalis, organic solvents, and high temperatures. Linen fabrics can be dry-cleaned or machine-washed and bleached with chlorine bleaches. For upholstery and wall coverings, careful steam cleaning is recommended to avoid shrinkage. Linen fabrics have low resiliency and often require pressing. They are more sunlight-resistant than cotton.

Crease-resistant finishes are used on linen, but the resins may decrease fiber strength and abrasion resistance. The wrinkling characteristics of linen make it easy to recognize. Linen fabrics must be stored dry; otherwise mildew will become a problem.

Table 4.4 summarizes flax's performance when used in apparel or interior textiles.

Environmental Concerns and Sustainability of Flax Flax has less of an environmental impact than does cotton. The production of flax requires fewer agricultural chemicals like fertilizer and pesticides, and irrigation is seldom required. But the practice of pulling the plants

Table 4.4 Summary of the Performance of Flax in Apparel and Interior Textiles.

Aesthetics	Excellent
Luster	High
Texture	Thick-and-thin
Hand	Stiff
Durability	Good
Abrasion resistance	Good
Tenacity	Good
Elongation	Poor
Comfort	High
Absorbency	High
Thermal retention	Good
Appearance Retention	Poor
Resiliency	Poor
Dimensional stability	Moderate
Elastic recovery	Poor
Recommended Care	Dry-clean or machine-wash (apparel)
	Steam- or dry-clean (interior textiles.)

during harvest in order to get longer fibers contributes to soil erosion. Removing the fiber from the stem requires significant amounts of water, but recycling is often used. Depending on the type of retting used, disposal of chemicals and contaminated water are other areas of concern. Changes in retting practices have occurred because of environmental issues. Dew and enzyme retting are more sustainable practices than water retting. Hand labor used in some areas where flax is produced needs to be monitored to avoid exploitation of workers.

Identification Tests Flax burns readily in a manner very similar to that of cotton. Fiber length is an easy way to differentiate between these two cellulosic fibers. Cotton is seldom more than 2.5 inches in length; flax is almost always longer than that. However, cottonized flax will be more difficult to identify. Flax is also soluble in strong acids.

Uses of Linen The Masters of Linen, an organization that promotes the use of linen, has developed a trademark to identify linen (Figure 4.16). Linen is used in bed, table, and bath items, in other interior items for home and commercial use, in apparel, and in technical products. Linen fabrics are ideal for wallpaper and wall coverings up to 120 inches wide because their irregular texture adds interest, hides nail holes or wall damage, and muffles noise. Linen fabrics are used in upholstery and window treatments because of their durability, interesting and soil-hiding textures, and versatility in fabrication and design.

Linen apparel includes items for warm-weather use, high fashion, casual, and professional wear. Technical products include luggage, bags, purses, and sewing thread.

In 1998, The Center for American Flax Fiber (CAFF) was established in South Carolina. Its goal is to establish a U.S. flax industry that emphasizes short-staple or cottonized flax.

Figure 4.16 Linen symbol of quality.
SOURCE: Courtesy of Masters of Linen/USA.

▶ Learning Activity 7

Use a small portion of the fiber from the small self-sealing bag labeled Flax or a yarn from Fabric #1 from your swatch kit. Following the procedures described in Chapter 3, examine the fibers using the microscope to see the nodes and variations among the flax fibers. Describe the differences in surface contour and structure between flax and cotton.

▶ Learning Activity 8

Use a small portion of the fiber from the bag labeled Flax or three to four yarns from Fabric #1 from your swatch kit. Following the procedures and safety precautions described in Chapter 3, conduct a burn test. Describe the ease of ignition, the color of the smoke, the color and texture of the ash, and the smell of the smoke. Compare your results with those included in Table 3.7 or with the chart on the sheet with the fiber bags in your swatch kit. Describe the similarities and differences between your results with cotton and linen.

▶ Learning Activity 9

Select an end use for flax other than apparel. Explain its performance characteristics that make it appropriate for that end use.

Other Bast Fibers

Ramie

Ramie is also known as rhea, grasscloth, China grass, and Army/Navy cloth. It has been used for several thousand years in China. The ramie plant (*Boehmeria nivea*) is a tall perennial shrub from the nettle family that requires a hot, humid climate. Ramie is fast-growing and can be harvested as frequently as every 60 days. Thus, several crops can be harvested each year. Because it is a perennial, it is cut, not pulled. It has been grown in the Everglades and Gulf Coast regions of the United States, but it is not currently produced in those areas.

Ramie fibers must be separated from the plant stalk by **decortication,** in which the bark and woody portion of the plant stem are separated from the fiber (83 percent cellulose). Because this process required a lot of hand labor, ramie did not become commercially important until less expensive mechanized ways of decorticating ramie were developed. Because ramie is a relatively inexpensive fiber that can be cottonized and blends well with many other fibers, ramie or ramie blend items are common in the United States. Ramie is produced in China, Brazil, the Philippines, South Korea, Taiwan, Thailand, and India. Ramie must be degummed by boiling in a weak alkaline solution to remove the wax and pectin along the cell walls and separate the fiber bundles.

Properties of Ramie Ramie is a white, long, fine fiber with a silklike luster. It is similar to flax in absorbency, density, and microscopic appearance (Figure 4.17). Because of its high molecular crystallinity and orientation, ramie is stiff and brittle. Like flax, it will break if folded repeatedly in the same place. Consequently, it lacks resiliency and is low in elasticity and elongation potential. Ramie can be treated to be wrinkle-resistant.

Ramie is one of the strongest natural fibers known; its strength increases when it is wet. It is resistant to insects, rotting, mildew, and shrinkage. Its absorbency is good, but it does not dye as well as cotton. Ramie can be mercerized to enhance dye absorbency. Ramie does not retain color well unless it is dry-cleaned.

Uses Ramie is used in many imported apparel items, including sweaters, shirts, blouses, and suits. Ramie is important in interiors for window treatments, pillows, and table linens. It is often blended with other natural fibers in levels greater than 50 percent ramie for many apparel and interior uses. It is used in ropes, twines, nets, banknotes, cigarette paper, and geotextiles for ground-cover fabrics for erosion control.

Table 4.5 summarizes ramie's performance in apparel and interior textiles.

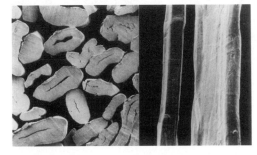

Figure 4.17 Photomicrographs of ramie: cross-sectional view (left), longitudinal view (right).
SOURCE: Courtesy of the British Textile Technology Group.

Hemp

The history of hemp is as old as that of flax. **Hemp** resembles flax in macroscopic and microscopic appearance; some varieties of hemp are very difficult to distinguish from flax. Although hemp is coarser and stiffer than flax, processing and cottonizing can minimize these differences. Hemp fibers can be very long—3 to 15 feet. It is processed in a manner similar to flax with similar environmental issues. Alternatives to regular retting are enzyme retting and steam explosion. In steam explosion, steam is used to break apart the fiber and the woody stem. While the process shortens the staple length and reduces its strength, hemp processed in this manner is easier to process on cotton spinning equipment.

Depending on the processing used to remove the fiber from the plant stem, it may be naturally creamy white, brown, gray, almost black, or green. It is 78 percent cellulose and can be

Table 4.5 Summary of the Performance of Ramie in Apparel and Interior Textiles.

Aesthetics	Good
Luster	Matte
Texture	Thick-and-thin
Hand	Stiff
Durability	Moderate
Abrasion resistance	Moderate
Tenacity	Good
Elongation	Moderate
Comfort	Good
Absorbency	High
Thermal retention	Moderate
Appearance Retention	Poor
Resiliency	Poor
Dimensional stability	Poor
Elastic recovery	Poor
Recommended Care	Dry-clean or machine-wash

machine-washed and dried. The plant produces three types of fibers. The bast fibers from the outer region of the stalk are the longest and finest. These are the fibers most often used in 100 percent hemp and blend fabrics with linen, cotton, or silk for apparel and interiors. The inner two fibers are shorter and most often used in nonwovens and other technical applications. The innermost woody core fibers are used for mulch and pet and animal bedding. Hemp is resistant to ultraviolet light and mold. It has only 5 percent elongation, the lowest of the natural fibers.

The high strength of hemp makes it particularly suitable for twine, cordage, and thread. Hemp is resistant to rotting when exposed to water. Although hemp had been an important technical fiber for centuries, its importance began to decline in the late 1940s because of competition from synthetic fibers and regulations controlling the production of drugs—hemp (*Cannabis sativa*) is a close relative of marijuana. New varieties of hemp grown for fiber have less than 1 percent of the compound tetrahydrocannabinol (THC, the hallucinatory agent in marijuana) and are of no value as a source of the drug. Hemp activists and promoters are working to lift the ban on producing hemp for fiber in several countries.

Because of its comfort and good absorbency (8 percent), hemp is used for some apparel and interiors. Hemp is environmentally friendly and does not require the use of pesticides during its production. It grows so quickly that it smothers weeds. Its root system minimizes soil erosion. Approximately 20 to 30 percent of the hemp plant is fiber. Hemp produces 250 percent more fiber than cotton and 600 percent more fiber than flax on the same land. Most hemp fiber is imported from China and the Philippines, but it is also grown in cooler climates in Italy, France, Chile, Russia, Poland, India, and Canada. Commercial production of hemp is not allowed in several countries, including the United States. Hemp is found in hats, shirts, shoes, backpacks, T-shirts, and jeans. Hemp also is used as a paper fiber and as litter and bedding for animals. In some areas, it is being grown on land to extract such pollutants as zinc and mercury from the soil. Oil from hemp seeds is used to make cooking oil, cosmetics, and plastic.

Jute

Jute was used as a fiber in Biblical times and probably was the fiber used in sackcloth. **Jute,** which is 61 percent cellulose, is one of the cheapest natural textile fibers. It is grown throughout Asia, chiefly in India and Bangladesh. The primary fibers in the fiber bundle are short and brittle, making jute one of the weakest of the cellulosic fibers.

Jute is creamy white to brown in color. While soft, lustrous, and pliable when first removed from the stalk, it quickly turns brown, weak, and brittle. Jute has poor elasticity and elongation.

Jute is used to produce sugar and coffee bagging, carpet backing, rope, cordage, and twine, but it is facing strong competition from olefin for these end uses. Because jute is losing its market, it is being investigated as a reinforcing fiber in resins to create preformed low-cost housing and in geotextiles.

Burlap or hessian is used for window treatments, area rugs, and wall coverings. Jute has low sunlight resistance and poor colorfastness, although some direct, vat, and acid dyes produce fast colors. It is brittle and subject to splitting and snagging. It also deteriorates quickly when exposed to water. Jute is occasionally used in casual apparel like walking shorts.

Kenaf

Kenaf is a soft bast fiber from the kenaf plant. The fiber is long, light yellow to gray, and harder and more lustrous than jute. Like jute, it is used for twine, cordage, and other technical purposes. Kenaf is produced in Central Asia, India, Africa, and some Central American countries. Kenaf is being investigated by researchers as a source of paper fiber and in blends with cotton.

Hibiscus

Hibiscus is from the same general botanical family as cotton—the Malvaceae family. The plant (*Hibiscus ficulneus*) grows as a tall shrub in tropical and subtropical regions. While it is commercially grown and used for clarifying sugarcane juice, the waste material has been studied for its fiber potential. As with other bast fibers, retting is required to extract the fiber from the plant stem. Hibiscus fiber can be bleached and has good fastness when dyed with direct dyes. The fiber is stronger than jute and has a potential for use in bags, rugs, and some apparel items when used in blends.

Nettle

Nettle fiber known as aloo or allo is removed from the plant stem of the Himalayan giant nettle plant (*Giradinia diversifolia*). The fiber is stripped from the stem, boiled for several hours, air dried, and handspun into yarns. The hollow fiber looks and feels similar to raw flax. The nettle plant is a perennial that grows without the use of fertilizers or pesticides. The fiber is used for technical products like bags and ropes as well as for apparel and interior textiles. Because the fiber is hollow, it has good insulating characteristics.

Another nettle fiber from the stinging nettle (*Urtica cannabina L.*) plant stems was widely used in Europe until the 15th century when cotton began to replace it because of easier processing. Stinging nettle is being investigated in Europe as a potentially sustainable fiber. The plant can be grown in areas where the soil or climate is not conducive for the production of cotton. Nettle must be pond retted for a few weeks and mechanically separated from the plant stem. Degumming in an acidic water bath is required. Nettle is 48 percent cellulose. It is similar in shape to ramie, coarser than jute, and stronger than ramie. Current plant breeding programs are attempting to improve fiber characteristics.

Bamboo

There are two types of **bamboo** fiber on the market. The type that is removed from the bamboo culms (above-ground stems of the plant) will be discussed here. The other bamboo fiber is regenerated from bamboo pulp and will be discussed in Chapter 7. The natural bamboo fiber (as opposed to the regenerated bamboo rayon fiber) maintains its natural resistant to microbes. The fiber is also absorbent, but has a somewhat coarse hand. This type of bamboo is not usually found in the apparel or interiors market. Bamboo is a type of grass that grows quickly without the use of pesticides or fertilizer. Most bamboo is harvested on a regular basis from managed farms where the land is not tilled and irrigation is not needed. Natural bamboo does not threaten wild bamboo forests or natural habitats. Most bamboo is processed in China.

Leaf Fibers

Leaf fibers are those obtained from the leaf of a plant. Most leaf fibers are long and fairly stiff. In processing, the leaf is cut from the plant and fiber is split or pulled from the leaf. Most leaf fibers have limited dye affinity and may be used in their natural color. Several leaf fibers are being used in composites in the European automotive industry.

Piña

Piña is obtained from the leaves of the pineapple plant. The fiber is soft, lustrous, and white or ivory. Since piña is highly susceptible to acids and enzymes, rinse out acid stains immediately and avoid detergents or enzyme presoaks. Hand washing is recommended for piña. The fiber produces lightweight, sheer, stiff fabrics. These fabrics are often embroidered and used for formal and wedding wear in the Philippines. Piña is also used to make mats, bags, table linens, and other apparel (Figure 4.18). Current research is aimed at producing a commercially competitive piña fiber that can be blended with other fibers.

Abaca

Abaca is obtained from a member of the banana tree family (*Musa textilis*). Abaca fibers are coarse and very long; some may reach a length of 15 feet. Abaca is off-white to brown in color. The fiber is strong, durable, and flexible. It is used for ropes, cordage, floor mats, table linens, some wicker furniture, and apparel. It is produced in Central America and the Philippines. Abaca is sometimes referred to as Manila hemp, even though it is not a true hemp.

Sisal and Henequen

Sisal and **henequen** are closely related plants. They are grown in Africa, Central America, and the West Indies. Both fibers are smooth, straight, and yellow. They are used for better grades of rope, twine, and brush bristles. However, since both fibers are degraded by salt water, they are not used in maritime ropes.

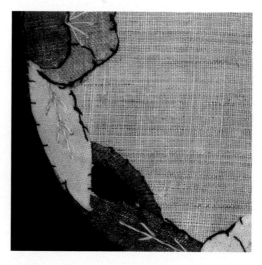

Figure 4.18   Piña place mat.

Sisal is used for upholstery, carpet, and custom rugs that can be hand painted for a custom look. Sisal provides a complementary texture and background for many interior styles. Sisal may be used by itself or in blends with wool and acrylic for a softer hand. The dry extraction cleaning method (see Chapter 20) is recommended. Sisal is used in wall coverings, especially in heavy-duty commercial applications, because of its durability and ease of application to a variety of surfaces. Unfortunately, sisal has a tendency to shed and fade out and it absorbs waterborne stains.

Other Cellulosic Materials

Other cellulosic materials are important in interiors. **Rush** (stems of a marsh plant), **sea grass** from China and Vietnam, and **maize** or **cornhusks** are used in accent rugs because of their resistance to dry heat and soil. Rush and **palm fiber** seats are often used on wooden frame chairs for a natural look. Yarns made from paper (wood pulp) add interest and texture to wall coverings for interiors. Wooden slats and grasses are found in window treatments. Grasses are especially appealing for wall coverings; the variable weights, thicknesses, and textures add a natural look to interiors. They can be applied to any type of wall surface, treated to be flame retardant, and colored to match the decor.

Wicker furniture is commonly made from tightly twisted paper yarns, rattan, and other such natural materials as sea grass, abaca (banana leaf), and raffia. Wall panels and wall coverings are being produced from shredded straw, bark, and old telephone books because of the interesting texture and shading produced by these materials.

Bacteria produce cellulose with an extremely uniform structure, high water-holding capacity, and multidimensional strength. At present, bacterial cellulose is used in medicine as a covering for severe burns and other skin injuries.

▶ Learning Activity 10

Select one of the minor bast or leaf fibers. Identify an end use for this fiber and explain its performance characteristics that make it appropriate for that end use.

▶ Learning Activity 11

Use Fabrics #1, 3, 41, and 53 from your swatch kit. Check the key for the swatch kit and determine the fiber content of each swatch. Identify an end use for each fabric and describe the serviceability of that product based on fiber content. Examine Figure 4.1 and locate one or more countries where each of these fibers might have been produced.

▶ Learning Activity 12

Identify a cellulosic fiber that could be promoted as a more sustainable replacement for cotton for many end uses. Explain why it is more sustainable. What are the roadblocks preventing this fiber from taking over more of cotton's market share? What are the properties in which this fiber is better than cotton? What are the properties in which this fiber is not as good as cotton? How would you market this fiber to convince consumers that this is a sustainable alternate to cotton?

key terms

review questions

1. Explain the properties that are common to all cellulosic fibers.

2. To what fiber aspects are differences among cellulosic fibers attributed?

3. Compare the performance characteristics of the following fiber pairs:
   a. Ramie and cotton
   b. Flax and hemp
   c. Cotton and hemp

4. Identify a cellulosic fiber that would be an appropriate choice for each of the following end uses and explain why you selected that fiber:
   a. Sheets for a double bed in master bedroom
   b. Tablecloth for an expensive ethnic restaurant
   c. Area rug for a designer's showroom
   d. Woman's sweater for summer wear
   e. Socks for an active 4-year-old child
   f. Corduroy slacks for a student

5. Explain the differences among naturally colored cotton, organic cotton, green cotton, transition cotton, and conventional cotton.

6. Consider the distribution of fibers present in your wardrobe. Explain which natural cellulosic fibers are present. For each cellulosic fiber, locate one or more countries where the fiber is produced. Describe your degree of satisfaction or dissatisfaction with each fiber's performance. What are the general areas where the products excel in performance, and what are the general areas where problems in performance exist? (Keep these issues in mind when reading Chapter 10 and the discussion on fiber blends and Chapter 18 and the discussion of several special-purpose finishes.)

7. Explain why most cotton that is produced is white or off-white in color. What are the advantages and disadvantages of white versus naturally colored cotton?

8. Identify six issues related to cotton and sustainability concepts.

9. Compare the processing needed to separate fibers from the plant component for each of these groups: seed fibers, bast fibers, and leaf fibers.

10. Which of these fibers has the lowest impact on the environment: seed fibers, bast fibers, or leaf fibers? Why?

Case Study

Colored Cotton*

Natural colored cotton has been raised in Central and South America, the Caribbean, Africa, and India for thousands of years. Because longer staple white cottons are easier to spin and dye and more adaptable to industrial spinning technology and market demands, colored cottons were less desirable until recently. Colored cotton plants are often grown as perennials and are more pest resistant. Many indigenous people grow colored cottons using low-impact farming practices to provide a source of family income. Plants are being developed to maintain the fiber color while improving the fiber's performance and spinnability. Complaints from commercial white cotton growers about the colored cotton cross-fertilizing with white cotton resulted in shutting down most of the colored cotton production in the United States. Other issues related to colored cotton fibers mixing in with white cotton fibers during yarn processing. For these reasons, little colored cotton is grown and processed in the United States. Most colored cotton is imported from such South American countries as Peru.

DISCUSSION QUESTIONS

1. What properties of white cotton would be desirable in colored cotton?

2. Why would producers object to colored cotton mixing in with white cotton yarns? What kinds of problems might that create in producing and finishing fabric?

3. What grades of white cotton apply to colored cotton? How would the grades and classification system be modified for the colored cottons?

4. Examine the fibers in small self-sealing bags labeled Cotton and Fox Fibre® Cotton or three to four yarns from Fabrics #57 and 108 from your swatch kit. What similarities and differences do you see and feel between these two examples of cotton?

5. How would a market for colored cotton impact small farmers in Peru? What are some sustainability and environmental issues that should be considered for these farmers?

*Rhoades, C. H. (2008). Colored cotton. *Spin-Off, 32*(2), 52–58.

suggested readings

Anonymous (1997, March). Cotton: Still the core fiber for consumer textiles. *Textile Month*, pp. 32–34.

Borland, V. S. (2002). From flower to fabric. *Textile World, 152*(10), 52–55.

Burnett, P. (1995, February). Cotton naturally. *Textile Horizons*, pp. 36–38.

Fletcher, K. (2008). *Sustainable Fashion and Textiles: Design Journey*. London: Earthscan.

Gordon, S., & Hsien, Y-L. (Ed.) (2007). *Cotton: Science and Technology*. Cambridge, England: Woodhead.

Hann, M. A. (2005). Innovation in linen manufacture. *Textile Progress, 37*(3), 1-42.

Hethorn, J., & Ulasewicz, C. (2008). *Sustainable Fashion: Why Now?* New York: Fairchild Books.

Huang, G. (2005). Nettle (*Urtica cannabina L.)* fibre, properties, and spinning practice. *Journal of the Textile Institute, 96*(1), 11–15.

Kang, S. Y., & Epps, H. H. (2008). Effect of scouring on the color of naturally-colored cotton and the mechanism of color change, *AATCC Review, 8*(7), 38–43.

Kerr, N. (1999, January/February). Evaluating textile properties of Alberta hemp. *Canadian Textile Journal*, pp. 36–38.

Kimmel, L. B., & Day, M. P. (2001). New life for an old fiber: Attributes and advantages of naturally colored cotton. *AATCC Review, 1*(10), 32–36.

McEvoy, G. (1994–1995, December/January). Linen: One of the world's oldest fibers is ideal for the '90s. *Canadian Textile Journal*, pp. 20–21.

Pandey, S. (2007). Ramie fibre: Part 1. Chemical composition and chemical properties. *Textile Progress, 39*(1).

Ramaswamy, G. (1995–1996, Winter). Kenaf for textiles: Revival of an old fiber. *Shuttle, Spindle, & Dyepot, 27*(1), 28–29.

Rhoades, C. H. (2008). Colored cotton. *Spin-Off, 32*(2), 52–58.

Rivoli, P. (2005). *The Travels of a T-Shirt in a Global Economy*. Hoboken, NJ: John Wiley & Sons.

Schuster, A. M. H., & Walker, H. B. (1995, July/August). Colorful cotton! *Archaeology, 48*(4), 40–45.

Thiry, M. (2007). Detecting the fiber. *AATCC Review, 7*(12), 18–21.

Thiry, M. (2007). Fibers in contention. *AATCC Review, 7*(12), 22–23.

Watkins, P. (2008). Cotton's future, *Textiles, 35*(1), 8–10.

Yafa, S. (2005). *Big Cotton*. New York: Viking.

NATURAL PROTEIN FIBERS

CHAPTER OBJECTIVES
- To know the characteristics common to protein fibers.
- To recognize the differences in characteristics and performance among the common protein fibers.
- To understand the processing of natural protein fibers.
- To integrate the properties of natural protein fibers with market needs.
- To identify natural protein fibers.

5

Natural protein fibers are of animal origin: wool and specialty wools are the hair and fur of animals, and silk is the secretion of the silk caterpillar. Figure 5.1 shows the countries that produce the majority of the natural protein fibers. The natural protein fibers are luxury fibers today. Silk, vicuña, cashmere, and camel hair have always been in this category. Wool is a widely used protein fiber, but production rates have decreased and cost has increased. Some individuals also use the protein fibers from their pet cats and dogs in hand-spun woven or knit textile products.

Protein fibers are composed of various amino acids that have been formed in nature into polypeptide chains with high molecular weights, containing carbon (C), hydrogen (H), oxygen (O), and nitrogen (N). Protein fibers are amphoteric, meaning that they have both acidic and basic reactive groups. The protein of wool is keratin, whereas that of silk is fibroin. The types and percentages of amino acids differ between wool and silk. There are more types of amino acids in wool and fewer types of amino acids in silk. The amino acids in wool tend to have larger molecular side groups compared to those found in silk. This difference means that the wool molecule is bulkier and less compact compared to the silk molecule. Because the side groups in wool are more likely to form temporary bonds with other side groups, wool has better resiliency. Wool contains sulfur while silk does not. Amino acids that contain sulfur are especially attractive to insects, thus explaining why wool is more prone to insect damage. Silk and wool differ in some properties because of their different physical and molecular structures.

To the left is a simple chemical formula for an amino acid, where R refers to a simple organic functional group.

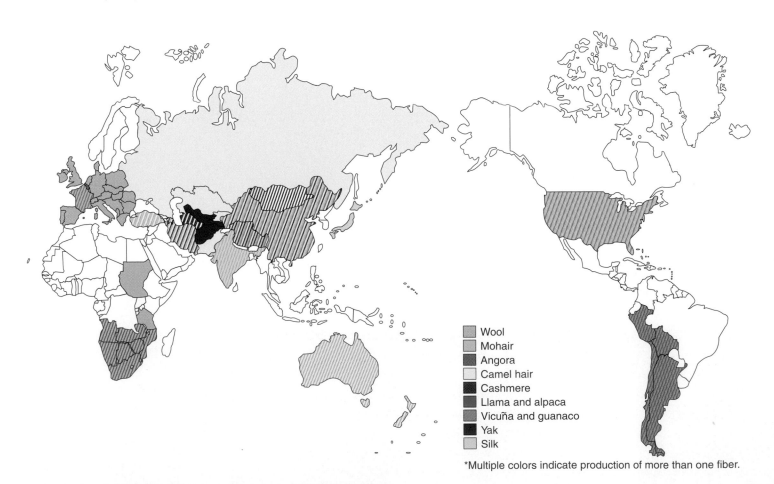

Figure 5.1 Countries that produce natural protein fibers.

Table 5.1 Properties Common to all Protein Fibers

Properties	Importance to Consumer
Resiliency	Resist wrinkling. Wrinkles disappear between uses. Fabrics maintain their shape.
Hygroscopic	Comfortable, protects from humidity in cool, damp climate. Moisture prevents brittleness in carpets.
Weaker when wet	Handle carefully when wet. Wool loses about 40 percent of its strength and silk loses about 15 percent when wet.
Specific gravity	Fabrics feel lighter than cellulosics of the same thickness.
Harmed by alkali	Use neutral or only slightly alkaline soap or detergent. Perspiration weakens the fiber.
Harmed by oxidizing agents	Chlorine bleach damages fiber so should not be used. Sunlight causes white fabrics to yellow.
Harmed by dry heat	Wool becomes harsh and brittle and scorches easily with dry heat. Use steam. White silk and wool will yellow.
Flame resistance	Do not burn readily and self-extinguish; have odor of burning hair; form a black, crushable ash.

▶ Learning Activity 1

Examine Table 5.1. Explain these properties in terms of a jacket to wear in an office building. How do these terms relate to the concept of serviceability?

Protein fibers have some common properties because of their similar chemical composition (Table 5.1). These fibers absorb moisture without feeling wet; they are **hygroscopic**. This phenomenon explains why items made from protein fibers are comfortable to use. Hygroscopic fibers minimize sudden temperature changes at the skin. In the winter, when people go from dry indoor air into damp, cold outdoor air, wool absorbs moisture and generates heat, insulating the wearer from the cold.

Wool

Because of wool garments and interior textiles' high initial cost and the cost of their care, many consumers consider them to be investments. These factors have encouraged the substitution of acrylic, polyester, or wool/synthetic blends in many products. However, wool's combined properties are not equaled by any manufactured fiber: ability to be shaped by heat and moisture, good moisture absorption without feeling wet, excellent heat retention, water repellency, feltability, and flame-retardancy.

Wool was one of the earliest fibers to be spun into yarns and woven into fabric. Wool was one of the most widely used textile fibers before the Industrial Revolution. Sheep were probably among the first animals to be domesticated. The fleece of primitive sheep consisted of a long, hairy outercoat (kemp) and a light, downy undercoat. The fleece of present-day domesticated sheep is primarily the soft undercoat. The Spanish developed the Merino sheep, whose fleece contains no kemp fiber. Some kemp is still found in the fleece of all other sheep breeds.

Sheep raising on the Atlantic seaboard began in the Jamestown, Virginia, colony in 1609 and in the Massachusetts settlements in 1630. From these centers, the sheep-raising industry spread rapidly. In 1643 in the Massachusetts Bay colony, the New England textile industry got its start when English wool combers and carders began to produce and finish wool fabric. Following the U.S. Civil War, sheep production expanded with the opening of free grazing lands

Figure 5.2 Merino sheep.

west of the Mississippi. By 1884, the peak year, 50 million sheep were found in the United States; the number of sheep has declined steadily since then.

Production of Wool

In 2007, wool was produced by Australia (22.5 percent), New Zealand (18.8 percent), China (18.8 percent), and Eastern Europe (10.0 percent). The United States ranked tenth, with only 0.8 percent of world production. Worldwide production was 4,678 million pounds of raw wool fiber.

Merino sheep produce the most valuable wool (Figure 5.2). Australia produces about 43 percent of the Merino wool. Good-quality fleeces weigh 15 to 20 pounds each. Merino wool is 3 to 5 inches long and very fine. It is used to produce high-quality, long-wearing products with a soft hand and luster and good drape.

Fine wool is produced in the United States by four breeds of sheep: Delaine-Merino, Rambouillet, Debouillet, and Targhee. The majority of this fine wool is produced in Texas and California. It is 2½ inches long. These fine wools are often used for products that compete with higher-priced Merino wools.

The greatest share of U.S. wool production is of medium-grade wools removed from animals raised for meat. These wools have a larger diameter than the fine wools and a greater variation in length, from 1½ to 6 inches. They are used for products such as carpeting, where the coarser fiber contributes high resiliency and good abrasion resistance. The fifteen breeds of sheep commonly found in the United States vary tremendously in appearance and type of wool produced. Sheep are raised throughout the United States but most are raised in the west.

Sheep are generally sheared once a year, in the spring. The fleece is removed in just minutes with power shears that look like large barber's shears. A good shearer can handle 100 to 225 sheep per day. The fleece is removed in one piece with long, smooth strokes, beginning at the legs and belly. After shearing, the fleece is folded together and bagged to be shipped to market.

As alternatives to shearing, both a chemical feed additive and an injection have been developed. When digested, the feed additive makes the wool brittle. Several weeks later, the fleece can be pulled off the sheep. The injection causes the sheep to shed the fleece a week or so later. Both alternatives decrease shearing costs.

Newly removed wool is **raw wool** or **grease wool,** which contains between 30 and 70 percent by weight of such impurities as sand, dirt, grease, and dried sweat (*suint*). Removing these impurities produces **clean** or **scoured wool**. The grease is purified to *lanolin* and used in creams, cosmetics, soaps, and ointments.

Grading and sorting are two marketing operations that group wools of like character together. **Grading** is evaluating the whole fleece for fineness and length. In **sorting**, a single fleece is separated into sections of fibers of different quality. The best-quality wool comes from the sides, shoulders, and back; the poorest wool comes from the lower legs. Wool quality helps determine use. For example, fine wool works well in a lightweight worsted fabric, while coarse wool works well in carpets. Fineness, color, crimp, strength, length, and elasticity are characteristics that vary with the breed of the sheep. However, genetic engineering of sheep may alter the physical characteristics and performance properties of wool.

Types and Kinds of Wool

Many types of wool are used in yarns and fabrics. Although breeds of sheep produce wools with different characteristics, labels on wool products rarely state that information; the fiber is simply identified as wool. The term *wool* legally includes fiber from such animals as sheep, Angora and Cashmere goats, camel, alpaca, llama, and vicuña.

Sheared wool is removed from live sheep. Pulled wool is taken from the pelts of meat-type sheep. Recycled wool is recovered from worn apparel and cutters' scraps. **Lamb's wool** comes from animals less than 7 months old. This wool is finer and softer. It has only one cut end; the other end is the natural tip (Figure 5.3). Lamb's wool is usually identified on a label.

Wool is often blended with less expensive fibers to reduce the cost of the fabric or to extend its use. The Federal Trade Commission defines label terms for wool garments as follows:

Virgin wool—wool that has never been processed. Use of the single term *wool* implies a virgin wool and is a helpful marketing tool.

Wool—new wool or wool fibers reclaimed from knit scraps, broken thread, and noils. (Noils are short fibers that are removed in making worsted yarns.)

Recycled wool—scraps of new woven or felted fabrics that are **garnetted** (shredded) back to the fibrous state and reused. Shoddy wool comes from old apparel and rags that are cleaned, sorted, and shredded. Recycled wool may be blended with new wool before being respun and made into fabrics.

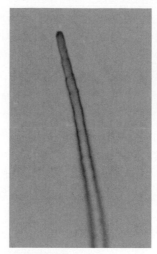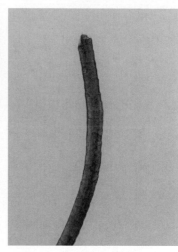

Figure 5.3 Lamb's wool fiber: natural tip (left), cut tip (right).

Recycled wool is important in the textile complex. However, these fibers may be damaged by the mechanical action of garnetting and/or wear. The fibers are not as resilient, strong, or durable as new wool, yet the fabrics made from them perform well. The terms *recycled wool* and *virgin wool* on a label do not refer to the quality of the fiber but to the past use of the fiber.

Quality of wool is based on fiber fineness, length, scale structure, color, cleanliness, and freedom from damage caused by environment or processing. The coarse fiber content of wool may be determined because the coarser fibers contribute to the prickle that may occur when wearing wool garments. The best-quality wools are white, clean, long, free of defects and coarse fibers, and contain small-diameter fibers with a regular scale structure. The Federal Trade Commission also defines superfine wools so labels claiming a superfine wool content must meet strict guidelines for fiber size.

Physical Structure of Wool

Length
The length of Merino wool fibers ranges from $1\frac{1}{2}$ to 5 inches, depending on the animal and the length of time between shearings. Long, fine wool fibers, used for worsted yarns and fabrics, have an average length of $2\frac{1}{2}$ inches. *Worsted* refers to a compact yarn and implies longer fibers and greater uniformity of fiber length after it undergoes a combing process. The shorter fibers, which average $1\frac{1}{2}$ inches in length, are used in woolen fabrics. *Woolen* describes a softer and more loosely twisted yarn and implies shorter, less uniform in length, and less parallel fibers. Some sheep breeds produce coarse, long wools (5 to 15 inches in length) used in specialty and hand-crafted fabrics.

The diameter of wool fiber varies from 10 to 50 micrometers. Merino lamb's wool may average 15 micrometers in diameter. The wool fiber has a complex structure, with a cuticle, cortex, and medulla (Figure 5.4).

Medulla
When present, the **medulla** is a microscopic honeycomb-like core containing air spaces that increase the insulating power of the fiber. It may appear as a dark area when seen through a microscope, but is usually absent in fine wools.

Cortex The **cortex** is the main part of the fiber. It is made up of long, flattened, tapered cells with a nucleus near the center. In natural-colored wools, the cortical cells contain *melanin*, a colored pigment.

The cortical cells on the two sides of the wool fiber react differently to moisture and temperature. These cells are responsible for wool's unique three-dimensional **crimp**, in which the fiber bends back and forth and twists around its axis (Figures 5.5 and 5.6). Crimp may be as high as 30 per inch for fine Merino wool to as low as 1 to 5 per inch for low-quality wool.

This irregular lengthwise waviness gives wool fabrics three important properties: cohesiveness, elasticity, and loft. Crimp helps individual fibers cling together in a yarn, which increases the strength of the yarn. Elasticity is increased because crimp helps the fiber act like a spring. As force is exerted on the fiber, the crimp flattens so that the fiber becomes straighter. Once the force is released, the undamaged wool fiber gradually returns to its crimped position. Crimp also contributes to the loft or bulk that wool yarns and fabrics exhibit throughout use.

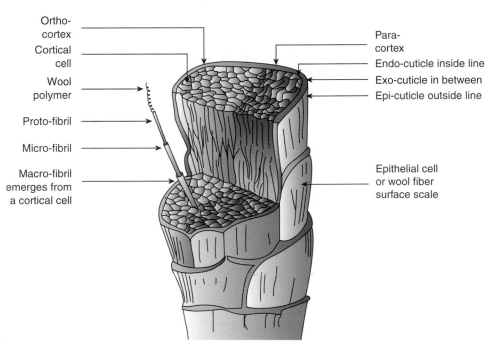

Figure 5.4   Physical structure of wool fibers.
SOURCE: Courtesy of E. P. G. Gohl. From *Textile Science* (1983) by E. P. G. Gohl and L. D. Vilensky. Published by Longman Cheshire, now Addison Wesley Longman Australia Pty. Limited.

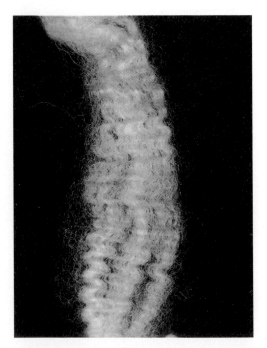

Figure 5.5   Natural crimp in wool.

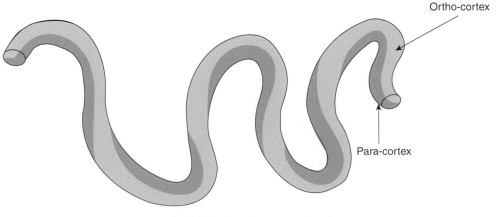

Figure 5.6   Three-dimensional crimp of wool fiber.
SOURCE: Courtesy of E. P. G. Gohl. From *Textile Science* (1983) by E. P. G. Gohl and L. D. Vilensky. Published by Longman Cheshire, now Addison Wesley Longman Australia Pty. Limited.

Wool is a **natural bicomponent fiber**; it has two different cell types or two components with slightly different properties in the cortex. This bicomponent nature is best illustrated by describing how wool reacts to moisture. One side of the fiber swells more than the other side, decreasing the fiber's natural crimp. When the fiber dries, the crimp returns.

Wool can be compared to a giant molecular coil spring. It has excellent resiliency when the fiber is dry and poor resiliency when it is wet. If dry wool fabric is crushed, it tends to spring back to its original shape when the crushing force is released. Wool can be stretched up to 30 percent longer than its original length. Recovery from stretching is good, but it takes place more slowly when the fabric is dry. Since steam, humidity, and water hasten recovery, wool items lose wrinkles more rapidly when exposed to a steamy or humid environment.

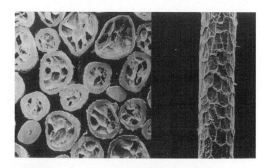

Figure 5.7 Photomicrograph of wool: cross-sectional view (left) and longitudinal view (right).
SOURCE: Courtesy of the British Textile Technology Group.

Cuticle The cuticle consists of an epicuticle and a dense, nonfibrous layer of **scales**. The epicuticle is a thin, nonprotein membrane that covers the scales. This layer gives water repellency to the fiber but is easily damaged by mechanical action. In fine wools, the scales completely encircle the shaft and each scale overlaps the bottom of the preceding scale, like parts of a telescope. In medium and coarse wools, the scale arrangement resembles shingles on a roof or scales on a fish (Figure 5.7). The free edges of the scales project outward and point toward the tip of the fiber. The scales contribute to wool's abrasion resistance and felting property, and they can irritate sensitive skin.

Felting, a unique and important property of wool, is based on the structure of the fiber. Under mechanical action—combining agitation, friction, and pressure with heat and moisture— adjacent wool fibers move rootward and the scale edges interlock. This prevents the fiber from returning to its original position and results in shrinkage, or felting, of the fabric. **Feltability** refers to the ability of fibers to mat together.

The movement of the fibers is speeded up and felting occurs more rapidly under severe conditions. Wool items can shrink to half their original size. Lamb's wool felts more readily than other wools. In soft, knit fabrics the fibers are more likely to move, so these fabrics are more susceptible to felting than are the firmly woven fabrics. While felting is an advantage in making felt fabric directly from fibers without spinning or weaving, it makes the laundering of wool more difficult. Treatments to prevent felting shrinkage are available (see Chapter 18).

Chemical Composition and Molecular Arrangement of Wool Wool fiber is a cross-linked protein called **keratin**. It is the same protein that is found in horns, hooves, and in human hair and fingernails. Keratin consists of carbon, hydrogen, oxygen, nitrogen, and sulfur. These

> ### Learning Activity 2

Supplies needed:

- Wool fiber, wool yarn, or wool fabric. Make sure it has not been finished to be machine washable. Some wool yarn is marketed as feltable.
- Paper or fabric towels
- Squirt bottles with water and shampoo or detergent added

Take a small handful of wool fiber, a 6-inch piece of wool yarn, or a piece of wool fabric. Wet the wool with water with shampoo or detergent added to speed wetting. Work the wool with your hands rolling it back and forth or around. After several minutes, examine the result. Is it felted? Can you separate the individual fibers? Explain what happened.

combine to form over 17 different amino acids. Five amino acids are shown in Figure 5.8. The flexible molecular chains of wool are held together by natural cross links—cystine (or sulfur) linkages and salt bridges—that connect adjacent molecules.

Figure 5.8 resembles a ladder, with the cross links analogous to the crossbars of the ladder. This simple structure can be useful in understanding some of wool's properties. Imagine a ladder that is pulled askew. When wool is pulled, its cross links help it recover its original shape. However, if the cross links are damaged, the structure is destroyed and recovery cannot occur.

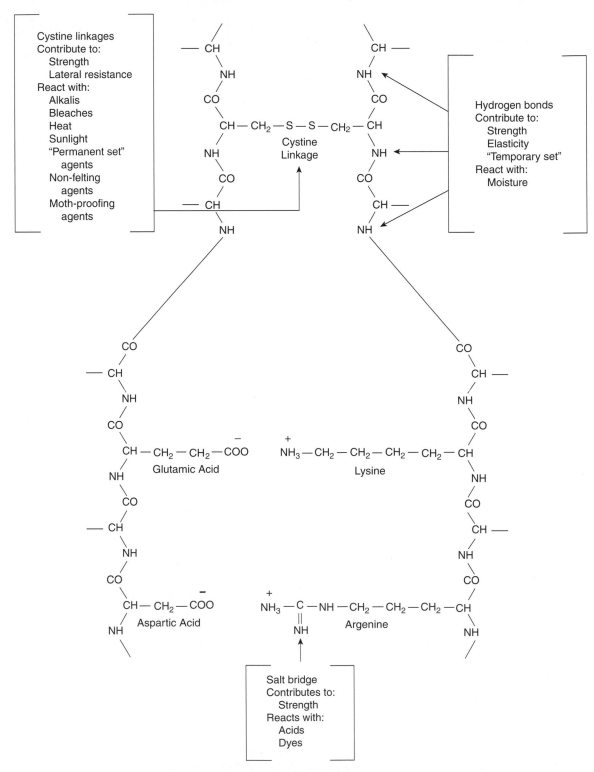

Figure 5.8 Structural formula of the wool molecule.

A more realistic model of wool's molecular structure would show this ladder like structure alternating with a helical structure. About 40 percent of the chains are in a spiral formation, with hydrogen bonding occurring between the closer parts. The ladderlike formation occurs at the cystine cross links or where other bulky amino acids meet and the chains cannot pack closely together. The spiral formation works like a spring and contributes to wool's resiliency, elongation, and elastic recovery. Figure 5.9 shows the helical structure of wool.

The cystine linkage is the most important part of the molecule. Any chemical, such as alkali, that damages this linkage can destroy the entire structure. In finishing wool, the linkage can be broken and then reformed. Pressing and steaming can produce minor modifications of the cystine linkage. Careless washing and exposure to light can destroy the links and damage the fiber.

Shaping of Wool Fabrics

Shaping of Wool Fabrics Wool fabrics can be shaped by heat and moisture—a definite plus in producing wool products. Puckers can be pressed out; excess fabric can be eased and pressed flat or rounded as desired. Pleats can be pressed with heat, steam, and pressure, but they are not permanent to washing.

Hydrogen bonds are broken and reformed easily with steam pressing. The newly formed bonds retain their pressed-in shape until exposed to high humidity, when the wool returns to its original shape.

Properties of Wool

Reviewing the fiber property tables in Chapter 3 will help in understanding wool's performance.

Aesthetics

Aesthetics Because of its physical structure, wool contributes loft and body to fabrics. Wool sweaters, suits, carpets, and upholstery are the standard "looks" by which manufactured fiber fabrics are measured.

Wool has a matte appearance. Shorter wool fibers are sometimes blended with longer wool fibers, specialty wools such as mohair, or other fibers to modify the fabric's luster or texture.

Drape, luster, texture, and hand can be varied by choice of yarn structure, fabric structure, and finish. Sheer wool voile, medium-weight printed wool challis, medium-weight flannels and tweeds, heavyweight coating, upholstery fabrics, and wool rugs and carpets demonstrate the range of possibilities.

Durability

Durability Wool fabrics are durable. Their moderate abrasion resistance stems from the fiber's scale structure and excellent flexibility. Wool fibers can be bent back on themselves 20,000 times without breaking, as compared with 3,000 times for cotton and 75 times for rayon. Atmospheric moisture helps wool retain its flexibility. Wool carpets, for example, become brittle if the air is too dry. The crimp and scale structure of wool fibers make them so cohesive that they cling together to make strong yarns.

Wool fibers have a low tenacity, 1.5 g/d dry and 1.0 g/d wet. The durability of wool fibers relates to their excellent elongation (25 percent) and elastic recovery (99 percent). When stress is put on the fabric, the crimped fibers elongate as the molecular chains uncoil. When stress is removed, the cross links pull the fibers back almost to their original positions. The combination of excellent flexibility, elongation, and elastic recovery produces wool fabrics that can be used and enjoyed for many years.

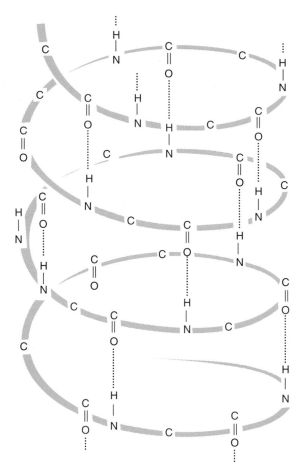

Figure 5.9 **Helical arrangement of the wool molecule.**
SOURCE: Courtesy of Australian Wool Services.

Comfort Wool is more hygroscopic than any other fiber, with a moisture regain of 13 to 18 percent under standard conditions. In a light rain or snow, wool resists wetting and the water runs off or beads on the fabric surface. This should be no surprise since wool evolved to protect sheep from severe weather. Wool dries slowly enough that the wearer is more comfortable than in any other fiber.

Wool is a poor conductor of heat, so warmth from the body is not dissipated readily. Outdoor sports enthusiasts have long recognized the superior comfort provided by wool. Wool's excellent resiliency contributes to its warmth. Since wool fibers recover well from crushing, fabrics remain porous and capable of trapping air. This "still" air is an excellent insulator because it keeps body heat close to the body.

Some people are allergic to the chemical components of wool; they itch, break out in a rash, or sneeze when they touch wool. For others, the harsh edges of coarse, low-quality wools are irritating and uncomfortable.

Wool has a medium specific gravity (1.32). People often associate heavy fabrics with wool since it is used in fall and winter wear, when the additional warmth of heavy fabrics is desirable. Lightweight wools are very comfortable in the changeable temperatures of spring and early fall.

One way to compare fiber densities is to think of blankets. A winter blanket of wool is heavy and warm. An equally thick blanket of cotton would be even heavier (cotton has a higher density), but not as warm. A winter blanket of acrylic would be lighter in weight (acrylic has a lower density than either wool or cotton). Personal preferences will help determine which fiber to choose.

Appearance Retention Wool is a very resilient fiber. It resists wrinkling and recovers well from wrinkles. (It wrinkles more readily when wet.) Wool maintains its shape fairly well during normal use. Wool apparel may be lined to help maintain garment shape.

When wool fabrics are dry-cleaned, they retain their size and shape well. When wool items are hand-washed, they need to be handled carefully to avoid shrinkage. Follow the care instructions for washable woolens.

Wool has an excellent elastic recovery—99 percent at 2 percent elongation. Even at 20 percent elongation, recovery is 63 percent. Recovery is excellent from the stresses of normal usage. Wool carpet maintains an attractive appearance for years.

Care Wool does not soil readily, and the removal of soil from wool is relatively simple. Grease and oils do not spot wool fabrics as readily as with fabrics made of other fibers. Wool items do not need to be washed or dry-cleaned after every use. Layer wool garments with washable ones next to the skin to decrease odor pickup.

Gentle use of a firm, soft brush not only removes dust but also returns matted fibers to their original position. Damp fabrics should be dried before brushing. Garments require a rest period between wearings to recover from deformations. Hang the item in a humid environment or spray it with a fine mist of water to speed recovery.

Wool is very susceptible to damage when it is wet. Its wet tenacity is one-third lower than its relatively low dry strength. When wet, its breaking elongation increases to 35 percent and resiliency and elastic recovery decrease. The redeeming properties of dry wool that make it durable in spite of its low tenacity do not apply when it is wet, so handle wet wool very gently.

Dry cleaning is the recommended care method for most wool items. Dry cleaning minimizes potential problems that may occur during hand or machine washing. Incorrect care procedures can ruin an item.

Some items can be hand-washed if correct procedures are followed. Use warm water that is comfortable to the hand. Avoid agitation; squeeze gently. Support the item, especially if it is knit, so it does not stretch. Air-dry it flat. Do not machine or tumble dry or felting will occur. Woven or knit items that are labeled "machine-washable" are usually blends or have been finished so they can be laundered safely (see Chapter 18). Special instructions for these items often include use of warm or lukewarm water, a gentle cycle for a short period of time, and drying flat.

Chlorine bleach, an oxidizing agent, damages wool. One can verify this by putting a small piece of wool in fresh chlorine bleach and watching the wool dissolve. Wool is also very sensitive to alkalis, such as strong detergents. The wool reacts to the alkali by turning yellow; it then becomes slick and jelly like and finally dissolves. If the fabric is a blend, the wool in the blend disintegrates, leaving only the other fibers.

Wool is attacked by moth larvae and other insects. Regular use of mothballs or crystals is discouraged due to the toxic nature of these pesticides. However, they should be used when evidence of insects is apparent, such as when moths or traces of larvae are seen. Moth larvae also eat, but do not digest, any fiber that is blended with wool. Unless mothproofed, wool fabrics should be stored so that they will not be accessible to moths. Wool fabrics should be cleaned before storage.

Wool burns very slowly and is self-extinguishing. It is normally regarded as flame-resistant. This is one of the reasons why wool is so popular with interior designers. However, when wool is used in public buildings, a flame-retardant finish may be needed to meet building code requirements.

Table 5.2 summarizes wool's performance in apparel and interior textiles.

▶ Learning Activity 3

Use Fabrics #11, 39, 61, 66, and 69 from your swatch kit. Identify an end use for each fabric and describe the serviceability for each product. How would the serviceability change if the fabric were made from cotton or another natural cellulosic fiber? Use Figure 5.1 and locate a country of production for each of the wool fabrics. Remember, coarser wools may not be imported from Australia or New Zealand.

Table 5.2 Summary of the Performance of Wool in Apparel and Interior Textiles

Aesthetics	Variable
Luster	Matte
Durability	High
Abrasion resistance	Moderate
Tenacity	Poor
Elongation	High
Comfort	High
Absorbency	High
Thermal retention	High
Appearance Retention	High
Resiliency	High
Dimensional stability	Poor
Elastic recovery	Excellent
Recommended Care	Dry-clean (apparel)

Environmental Concerns and Sustainability of Wool

Since wool is a natural fiber, many consumers believe it is environmentally friendly. Although wool can be viewed as a renewable resource, it is not produced without any impact on the environment. Sustainable management of natural and physical resources is a challenge for sheep growers. Sheep graze pastures so closely that soil erosion can occur if care is not taken to avoid overgrazing. Disposal of animal waste is another concern. Sheep manure is frequently spread over the ground to return nutrients to the soil. However, excessive applications can create problems during spring thaw or after heavy rains with runoff contaminated with the manure. In addition, sheep producers have traditionally opposed programs that contribute to the survival of wolves and other natural predators. Other sustainability issues relate to the treatment of sheep, shearing practices, and health and back problems associated with shearing hundreds of sheep daily.

Sheep are susceptible to some diseases that can be transmitted to humans. Most of these diseases are of concern only to sheep producers; consumers of wool products are not at risk. However, customs officials and importers check imported wools from some countries for diseases that can be transmitted via contaminated fibers. Fibers contaminated in this way will not be imported. Consumers should not be concerned with imported items purchased in the United States, but they should exercise caution when purchasing wool products in some other countries.

Sheep are also susceptible to parasitic infections. Treatment to prevent the infection makes use of pesticides, either through injection or as a surface application as either a pour-on liquid treatment or the animal is dipped in a bath. If the liquid pesticide is disposed of improperly, contamination of lakes, streams, and other water systems can occur. The pesticides used are highly toxic to aquatic life.

Organic wool is from sheep that are fed organically grown feed, graze on land not treated with pesticides, and not dipped in synthetic pesticides. Only a small percentage of the wool produced is organic, but interest in organic wool is growing.

Merino sheep have wrinkled skin, especially around the tail area. These wrinkles tend to collect moisture and urine and are attractive areas for flies to lay eggs. To prevent this problem, ranchers sometimes remove the excess skin from this area. This treatment is more common with organic wool since the treatment is used to control flies because insecticides are prohibited with organic wool. Animal right activists object to this practice and to the shearing of fiber from any animal.

Because of concerns about how sheep and other animals are treated, some companies use barcodes to enable consumers to trace the path wool takes from the grower through the production process. Criteria regarding animal health and welfare, long-term environmental respect, and fiber quality standards must be met for products that bear these codes. Promotional organizations accredit growers who meet specific standards related to fiber quality and animal welfare; environmental, social, and economic values; and trace the wool from grower through manufacturer. Some of these wools are organic, while others are free-range (meaning that the sheep graze in open pastures).

Other environmental issues relate to the intensive use of water, energy, and chemicals to clean the greasy wool fiber, produce the fabrics, and finish and dye them. Wool is the only fiber that requires hot water or solvent cleaning before being processed into a yarn. The cleaning process produces wool grease sludge with a high pollution index. While the wool grease is usually reclaimed for use as lanolin, pesticides applied to the wool may remain in the grease. When an organic solvent is used in cleaning raw wool, it is reclaimed and recycled.

Many wool products require dry cleaning. Some dry-cleaning solvents have been identified as possible carcinogens and restrictions regarding workplace exposure exist. See Chapter 20 for more information on dry cleaning.

Uses of Wool

Only a small amount of wool is used in the United States. In 2007 domestic consumption of wool comprised only a fraction of a percent of all fiber used in the United States. The most important use of wool is for adult apparel.

Wool suits perform well and look great. They fit well because they can be shaped through tailoring. The durable fabrics drape well. They are comfortable under a variety of conditions and retain their appearance during wear and care. Suits are usually dry-cleaned to retain their appearance and shape. Suit materials are also made of synthetic fiber/wool blends.

The Wool Bureau has adopted two symbols to assist in the promotion of wool. The Woolmark® is used on all 100 percent wool merchandise that meets their quality specifications; the Woolblend® mark is for blends with at least 60 percent wool. Both symbols are shown in Figure 5.10.

Even though the amount of wool used in interiors is low, wool constitutes the standard by which carpet appearance is judged. A major use of wool is in carpets and custom rugs, often special-order or one-of-a-kind rugs. Wool rugs can be machine-woven (Axminster or Wilton types), hand-woven, or hand-hooked. Most rugs are imported, although some are made in the United States. Wool carpets and rugs are more expensive than those made from other fibers because the rich color, texture, and appearance of wool are appreciated and valued. Wool carpets and rugs account for less than one-fifth of the floor-coverings market.

Both wool and wool-blend fabrics are used in upholstery because of their aesthetic characteristics, good appearance retention, durable nature, and natural flame resistance. For residential use, no additional flame-retardant treatment may be necessary; but for many commercial and contract uses, wool or wool-blend upholstery fabric may require a flame-retardant finish.

Handcrafted wall hangings and woven tapestries are often made of wool because textile artists like the way the fiber handles. Designers, artists, and consumers appreciate the way the finished item looks and wears.

Many school laboratories have fire-safety blankets made of wool. Stadium blankets and throws are often made of wool for warmth and an attractive appearance.

Wool is used in felts as foundation pads under heavy machinery to help decrease noise and vibration as well as for other uses. Tiny balls of wool that absorb up to 40 times their weight in oil are used to clean up oil spills. Wool mulch mats are used for landscape and horticultural weed control.

WOOLMARK   WOOLMARK
                  BLEND

Figure 5.10   Woolmark®
and Woolmark blend®
symbols of quality.
SOURCE: Courtesy of Australian Wool Innovation Limited.

Table 5.3 Groupings of Specialty Wools

Goat Family	Camel Family	Others
Angora goat—mohair	Camel hair	Angora rabbit—angora
Cashmere goat—cashmere and pashmina	Llama	Fur fibers
	Alpaca	Musk ox—qiviut
	Vicuña	Yak
	Guanaco	

Specialty Wools

Most specialty wools are obtained from the goat, rabbit, and camel families (Table 5.3). Specialty wools are available in smaller quantities than sheep's wool and are usually more expensive. Like all natural fibers, specialty wools vary in quality. Most specialty wool products require dry cleaning.

Specialty wool fibers are of two kinds: the coarse, long outer hair and the soft, fine undercoat. Coarse fibers are used for interlinings, upholstery, and some coatings; the fine fibers are used in luxury coatings, sweaters, shawls, suits, dresses, and interior textiles.

Mohair

Mohair is the hair fiber of the Angora goat. Major producers are South Africa, the United States, Turkey, and Lesotho. Texas is a major producer, but most U.S. mohair is exported. The goats (Figure 5.11) are usually sheared twice a year, in the early fall and early spring. Each adult goat yields about 5 pounds of fiber. The fiber length is 4 to 6 inches if sheared twice or 8 to 12 inches if sheared once a year. Approximately 12 percent of the crop is kid (baby goat) mohair, and the remaining 88 percent is adult mohair.

Mohair fibers are slightly coarse (average diameter of 25 microns for kid mohair and 40 microns for adult mohair) and have a circular cross section. Scales on the surface are scarcely visible, and the cortical cells may appear as lengthwise striations. There are some air spaces between the cells that give mohair its lightness and fluffiness. Few fibers have a medulla.

Mohair is a very resilient fiber because it has fewer scales than wool and no crimp. Mohair fibers are smoother and more lustrous than wool fibers (Figure 5.12). Mohair is very strong and has a good affinity for dyes. The washed fleece is a lustrous white. Mohair is less expensive than many other specialty wools. Mohair's chemical properties are very similar to those of wool. Mohair makes a better novelty loop yarn than wool or the other specialty hair fibers.

Mohair's good resiliency is used to advantage in hand-knitting yarns, pile fabrics, and suitings. Because it resists crushing and pilling, it is used in flat and pile upholstery fabrics and hand-produced floor coverings. Its natural flame resistance, insulation, and sound absorbency make it ideal for specialty drapery applications. Blankets of mohair blends retain heat well. Mohair is used to produce natural-looking wigs and hairpieces. Mohair is often blended with wool to add sheen and texture to apparel and interior textiles.

Figure 5.13 shows the quality symbol used on all mohair products that meet performance standards established by the Mohair Council of America.

Figure 5.11 Angora goats produce mohair fibers.
SOURCE: Peter Anderson © Dorling Kindersley, courtesy of Odds Farm Park, High Wycombe, Bucks.

Figure 5.12 Photomicrograph of mohair: cross-sectional view (left) and longitudinal view (right).
SOURCE: Courtesy of the British Textile Technology Group.

Figure 5.13 Mohair symbol of quality.
SOURCE: Courtesy of the Mohair Council of America.

Qiviut

Qiviut (ké-ve-ute), a rare and luxurious fiber, is the underwool of the domesticated musk ox (Figure 5.14). A large musk ox provides about 6 pounds of wool each year. The fiber can be used just as it comes from the animal, for it is protected from debris by the long guard hairs and has low lanolin content. Qiviut resembles cashmere in hand and texture but is much warmer. The fleece is not shorn but is shed naturally and is removed from the guard hairs as soon as it becomes visible. Producers in Alaska and Canada raise musk ox and harvest the fiber. Qiviut is expensive and used to produce handcrafted items by fiber artists, Inuit, and other Native American people.

Angora

Angora is the hair of the Angora rabbit produced in Europe, Chile, China, and the United States (Figure 5.15). It is harvested up to four times a year by plucking or shearing. Fiber yield and quality vary with the rabbit and its health and breed, and ranges from 8 to 30 oz. Of the four breeds of Angora rabbits, the two most common types are English and French. English Angoras produce a fine silky fiber; French Angoras produce a coarser fiber.

The white or naturally colored fiber is very fine (13 microns), fluffy, soft, slippery, and fairly long. Angora does not take dye well and usually has a lighter color than other fibers with which it is blended. It is often blended with wool to facilitate spinning because the slick fiber has poor cohesiveness. Angora is used in apparel such as sweaters and suitings and in knitting yarn.

If a label states "rabbit hair," this means the fiber is from a common rabbit, not an Angora rabbit. Rabbit hair is often used to make felt for hats, but it is too short to make into yarns for woven or knit fabrics.

Camel Hair

Camel hair is obtained from the two-humped Bactrian camel. Major producers of camel hair include China, Mongolia, Iran, Afghanistan, Russia, New Zealand, Tibet, and Australia. Camel hair is an excellent insulator. The hair is collected as it is shed or sheared from the animals. A camel produces about 5 pounds of hair a year.

Because camel hair gives warmth without weight, the finer fibers are valued for apparel. They are often used in blends with sheep's wool, which is dyed the tan color of camel hair. Camel hair is used in coats or jackets, scarves, and sweaters. Blankets of camel hair and wool are also available.

Cashmere

Cashmere is produced by the small cashmere goat (*Capra hircus laniger*) raised in China, Mongolia, Tibet, Afghanistan, and Iran. Cashmere production is a main source of income for the herders in these countries. The fibers vary in color from white to gray to brownish gray. The goat has an outercoat of long, coarse hair and an innercoat of down. The hair usually is combed by hand from the animal during the molting season. In dehairing, the coarse hair is separated from the fine fibers (13–18 microns). The downy fine fibers make up only a small part of the fleece, usually about one-half pound per goat. The fiber is solid, with no medulla and with fine scales. Cashmere is graded by color, tensile strength, and freedom from contamination with other fibers or plant residue. Cashmere is used for sweaters, coats, suits, jackets, loungewear, and blankets. Fabrics are warm, buttery in hand, and have beautiful draping

Figure 5.14 The musk ox of Alaska produces qiviut fiber.
SOURCE: Geoff Brightling © Dorling Kindersley.

Figure 5.15 The Angora rabbit produces a soft, luxurious fiber.
SOURCE: Steve Shott © Dorling Kindersley.

characteristics. Cashmere is more sensitive to chemicals than wool. *Pashmina* is a fine cashmere fiber originally produced in parts of northern India, Kashmir, and Pakistan. Cashmere is sometimes mistaken for *shahtoosh*, an illegal fiber harvested from slaughtered Tibetan chiru antelopes. The chiru is on the endangered species list. Sometimes, cashmere is blended with less expensive sheep's wool. When labels indicate a blend, no legal problem exists. However, this is a fraudulent practice when the label does not indicate that the product is a blend.

Cashgora is a new fiber resulting from the breeding of feral cashmere goats with Angora goats in New Zealand and Australia. Although the International Wool Textile Organization has adopted *cashgora* as a generic fiber term, it is not recognized around the world. The fiber is coarser than cashmere and not as lustrous. It is used primarily in less expensive coatings and suits.

Cashmere fiber, because of its high price and high demand by consumers, has been subject to fraud of several kinds. Items labeled 100 percent cashmere or pure Mongolian cashmere may be blended with other fibers such as wool or yak, may be a coarser and lower quality cashmere, or may be a fine wool with no cashmere present. Because of these problems, the Mongolian Fibermark Society has been established to uphold the purity and quality of Mongolian cashmere and ensure that items bearing the label meet strict quality and authenticity standards. In addition, the Federal Trade Commission defines cashmere so labels claiming cashmere content must also meet strict guidelines for fiber size and species.

Llama and Alpaca

Llama and **alpaca** are domesticated animals of the South American branch of the camel family (Figure 5.16). The fiber from their coats is 8 to 12 inches in length and is noted for its softness, fineness, and luster. The natural colors range from white to light fawn, light brown, dark brown, gray, and black. The fibers are used for apparel, handcrafts, and rugs. Because alpaca is soft, it is often used for apparel. However, it is more difficult to dye than most other specialty wools. For this reason, it is often used in its natural colors. Scales are less pronounced, so felting is not as big a problem as with other wools. Its soft hand, beautiful luster, and good draping characteristics are appreciated by fashion designers. Llama is coarser and most often used for coats, suitings, ponchos, and shawls. As with wool, fibers from the younger llama and alpaca are finer and softer.

Vicuña and Guanaco

Vicuña and **guanaco** are rare wild animals of the South American camel family. In the past, the animals were killed to obtain the fiber. Now, they are sheared in a manner similar to that of sheep. Vicuña and guanaco are now protected. Vicuña is one of the softest, finest (13 micron), rarest, and most expensive of all textile fibers. The fiber is short, very lustrous, and light cinnamon in color. Research is under way to produce genetic crosses of alpaca and vicuña. Currently, vicuña are classified as a threatened species. The Peruvian government labels products

Figure 5.16   The Llama from South America is prized for its fiber.
SOURCE: Courtesy of Kim Eve.

> ## ► Learning Activity 5

Use Fabric #38 from your swatch kit. Identify an end use for the fabric and describe its serviceability. Locate a country where this protein fiber could have been produced.

containing vicuna to guarantee that the animals were captured, sheared alive, released, and will not be sheared again for two years. A large portion of the profit from the sale of vicuña is returned to the villagers. However, poaching continues to be a problem.

Yak

Yak fiber is produced by a large ox found in Tibet and Central Asia. The fiber, which is collected by combing out during the spring molt, is smooth and lustrous. Yak is often used in apparel and rope and tent covers in its native area. Yak fiber is used in the international market because it is mixed with the much more expensive cashmere to extend its use and lower the cost. It is coarser than cashmere and dark brown or black in color.

Silk

Silk is a natural protein fiber. It is similar to wool in that it is composed of amino acids arranged in a polypeptide chain, but it has no cross links. Silk is produced by the larvae of a moth.

According to Chinese legend, silk culture began in 2640 B.C., when Empress Hsi Ling Shi became interested in silkworms and learned how to reel the silk and weave it into fabric. Through her efforts, China developed a silk industry and a 3,000-year monopoly. Silk culture later spread to Korea and Japan, westward to India and Persia, and then to Spain, France, and Italy. Silk fabrics imported from China were coveted in other countries; in India, Chinese fabrics were often unraveled and rewoven into looser fabrics or combined with other fibers to produce more yardage from the same amount of silk filament. Several attempts at sericulture were made in the United States, but none were successful. A few villages in Mexico have been producing silk since the Spanish introduced it in the sixteenth century. Today, the major producers of silk are China, India, and Japan.

Figure 5.17   Silkworm eggs or graine.
SOURCE: Courtesy of Careyn Armitage.

Silk is universally accepted as a luxury fiber. The International Silk Association of the United States emphasized this by its slogan "Only silk is silk." Silk has a combination of properties not possessed by any other fiber: It has a dry tactile hand, unique natural luster, good moisture absorption, lively suppleness and draping qualities, and high strength.

The beauty and hand of silk and its high cost are probably responsible for the development of the manufactured fiber industry. Silk is a solid fiber with a simple physical structure. It is this physical nature of silk that some manufactured fibers attempt to duplicate. Most successful are those manufactured fibers with a triangular cross section and fine size.

Production of Silk

Sericulture is the production of cultivated silk, which begins when the silk moth lays eggs on a specially prepared paper (Figure 5.17). (The cultivated silkworm is usually *Bombyx mori*.) When the eggs hatch, the caterpillars, or larvae, are fed fresh, young mulberry leaves (Figure 5.18).

Figure 5.18   Silkworms feeding on mulberry leaves.
SOURCE: Courtesy of Careyn Armitage.

Figure 5.19   Silk cocoons.
SOURCE: Courtesy of Careyn Armitage.

Figure 5.20   Reeling of silk.

After about 35 days and four moltings, the silkworms are approximately 10,000 times heavier than when hatched and are ready to begin spinning a cocoon, or chrysalis case. A straw frame is placed on the tray and the silkworm starts to spin the cocoon by moving its head in a figure eight. The silkworm produces silk in two glands and forces the liquid silk through *spinnerets*, openings in its head. The two strands of silk are coated with a water-soluble protective gum, **sericin**. When the silk comes in contact with the air, it solidifies. In 2 or 3 days, the silkworm will spin approximately 1 mile of filament and will completely encase itself in a cocoon (Figure 5.19). The silkworm then metamorphoses into a moth. Usually the silkworm is killed (stifled) with heat before it reaches the moth stage.

If the silkworm is allowed to reach the moth stage, it is used for breeding additional silkworms. The moth secretes a fluid that dissolves the silk at one end of the cocoon so that it can crawl out. These cocoons cannot be used for filament silk yarns and the staple silk produced from them is less valuable.

To obtain filament silk, the cocoons that have been stifled are sorted for fiber size, fiber quality, and defects, then brushed to find the outside ends of the filaments. Several filaments are gathered together and wound onto a reel. This process, referred to as **reeling**, is performed in a manufacturing plant called a *filature*. Each cocoon yields approximately 1,000 yards of usable silk filament. This is **raw silk**, or **silk-in-the-gum**, fiber. Several filaments are combined to form a yarn. The operators in the filature must carefully join the filaments so that the diameter of the reeled silk remains uniform in size. Uniformly reeled filament silk is the most valuable (Figure 5.20).

As the fibers are combined and wrapped onto the reel, twist can be added to hold the filaments together. Adding twist is referred to as *throwing,* and the resulting yarn is called a *thrown yarn*. The specific type of yarn and amount of twist relate to the fabric to be produced. The simplest type of thrown yarn is a *single*, in which three to eight filaments are twisted together to form a yarn. Used for filling yarns in many silk fabrics, singles may have two or three twists per inch.

Staple silk is produced from cocoons in which the filament broke or in which the moth was allowed to mature and come out. It is also produced from the inner portions of the cocoon. This silk is known as **silk noils**, or *silk waste*. It is degummed (the sericin is removed) and spun like any other staple fiber, or it is blended with another staple fiber and spun into a yarn. Spun silk is less expensive, less durable, more likely to pill, and of lower quality than filament silk.

Wild silk production is not controlled. Although many species of wild silkworms produce wild silk, the two most common are *Antheraea mylitta* and *Antheraea pernyi*. The silkworms feed on oak and cherry leaves in the wild and produce fibers that are much less uniform in texture and color. The fiber is most often brown, but yellow, orange, and green also occur. Researchers are investigating the feasibility of producing fabrics from these naturally colored silks.

Since the cocoons are harvested after the moth has matured, the silk cannot be reeled and must be used as spun silk. **Tussah** silk is the most common type of wild silk. It is coarser, darker, and cannot be bleached. Hence, white and light colors are not available in tussah silk. *Tasar* is a type of wild silk from India. Some fabrics are sold simply as wild silk. The term "raw silk" is sometimes used incorrectly to describe these fabrics.

Duppioni silk is another type of silk that results when two silkworms spin their cocoons together. The yarn is irregular in diameter with a thick-and-thin appearance. It is used in such linenlike silk fabrics as shantung.

Silk fabric descriptions may include the term *momme*, the standard way to describe silk fabrics. **Momme**, pronounced like "mummy" and abbreviated mm, describes the weight of the silk. One momme (momie or mommie) weighs 3.75 grams. Most silk fabrics are produced in several weights. Higher numbers describe heavier fabrics. Other terms such as *habutai* or *crepe* describe the yarn and fabric structure. Silk fabrics are often graded for their degree of evenness, fiber or yarn size, and freedom from defects. Grade A refers to the highest grade, only about 10 percent of the silk produced.

Japan is known for its high-quality silks. India produces handwoven wild silks with a pronounced texture. Thailand's handwoven iridescent silks are created by using two yarn colors in weaving the fabric. With over 30 countries producing silk, there is a wide range of silk types and qualities on the market. *Pure silk* and *pure dye silk* describe 100 percent silk fabrics that do not contain any metallic weighting compounds. See Chapter 21 for more information on labeling silk fabrics.

Physical Structure of Silk

Silk is the only natural filament fiber. It is a solid fiber, smooth but irregular in diameter along its shaft. The filaments are triangular in cross section, with rounded corners (Figure 5.21). Silk fibers are very fine—1.25 denier/filament (dpf). Wild silks are slightly coarser, with slight striations along the length of the fiber.

Chemical Composition and Molecular Structure of Silk

The protein in silk is **fibroin**, with 15 amino acids in polypeptide chains. Silk has reactive amino (NH_2) and carboxyl (COOH) groups. Silk has no cross linkages and no bulky side chains. The molecular chains are not coiled, as in wool, but are pleated and packed closely together. Silk's high orientation contributes to its strength. Its elasticity is due to some amorphous areas between the crystalline areas.

Properties of Silk

Consult the fiber property tables in Chapter 3 when comparing the performance of silk to that of other fibers. Table 5.4 compares silk and wool.

Aesthetics Silk can be dyed and printed in brilliant colors. Since it is adaptable to a variety of fabrication methods, it is available in many fabric types for interior and apparel uses. Because of cultivated silk's smooth but slightly irregular surface and triangular cross section, its luster is soft, with an occasional sparkle. It is this luster that has been the model for many manufactured fibers. Fabrics made of cultivated silk have a smooth appearance and a luxurious hand. Silk has a smooth, soft hand, but it is not as slippery as many synthetic fibers.

Wild silks have a duller luster because of their coarser size, less regular surface, and the presence of sericin. Fabrics made of wild silk have a more pronounced texture.

In filament form, silk has poor covering power. Before the development of strong synthetic fibers, silk was the only strong filament, and silk fabrics were often treated with metallic salts such as tin, a process called **weighting**, to produce better drape, covering power, and dye absorption. Unfortunately, these historic weighted silks aged quickly because excessive amounts of metallic salt were used. Figure 5.22 shows a 19th-century silk bodice that has shattered (disintegrated) as a result of the weighting chemicals added during production. Although this

Figure 5.21 Photomicrographs of silk fiber: cross-sectional view (left) and longitudinal view (right).
SOURCE: Courtesy of the British Textile Technology Group.

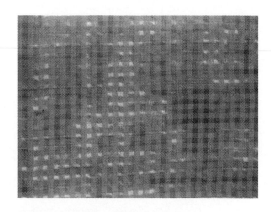

Figure 5.22 Close-up of shattered bodice (c. 1885) of weighted silk gingham. Note that only the weighted yarns (yellow) have disintegrated.

Table 5.4 Comparison of Wool and Silk

Property	Wool	Silk
Abrasion resistance	Moderate	Moderate
Breaking tenacity (dry; wet)	Low (1.5 g/d; 1.0 g/d)	High (4.5 g/d; 2.8–4.0
Breaking elongation (dry; wet)	Medium (25%; 35%)	Medium (20%; 30%)
Absorbency	High (13–18%)	High (11%)
Thermal retention	Excellent	Moderate
Specific gravity	Medium (1.32)	Medium (1.25)
Resiliency	Excellent	Moderate
Elastic recovery at 3% stretch	High (99%)	Medium (90%)
Resistance to strong acids	More resistant	More sensitive
Resistance to alkalis	Harmed	Harmed
Resistance to light	Poor	Poor
Fiber length	1.5–5 inches	Natural filament; available in staple form
Fiber fineness (micrometers)	10–50	11–12

problem is sometimes referred to as dry rot, it is more commonly known as "shattered silk" by museum specialists. At present, no treatment exists to reduce the damage and save garments with this inherent problem. Silk has **scroop**, a natural rustle, which can be increased by treatment with an organic acid such as acetic or tartaric acid.

Durability Silk has moderate abrasion resistance. Because of its end uses and cost, silk seldom receives harsh abrasion. Silk is one of the strongest natural fibers, with a tenacity of 4.5g/d dry. It may lose up to 20 percent of its strength when wet. It has a breaking elongation of 20 percent. It is not as elastic as wool because there are no cross linkages to retract the molecular chains. When silk is elongated by 2 percent, its elasticity is only 90 percent. Thus, when silk is stretched even a small amount, it does not return to its original length but remains slightly stretched.

Comfort Silk has good absorbency, with a moisture regain of 11 percent. Silk may develop static cling because of the smoothness of the fibers and yarns and the fabric weight. Silk fabrics are comfortable in summer. Like wool, silk is a poor conductor of heat so that it is comfortably warm in the winter. The weight of a fabric is important in heat conductivity—sheer fabrics are cool, whereas heavy fabrics are warm. Silk is smooth and soft and not irritating to the skin. The density of silk is 1.25g/cc, producing strong and lightweight silk products. Weighted silk is not as durable as regular silk and wrinkles more readily.

Appearance Retention Silk has moderate resistance to wrinkling. Because silk's recovery from elongation is low, it does not resist wrinkling as well as some other fibers.

Silk fibers do not shrink. Because the molecular chains are not easily distorted, silk swells only a small amount when wet. Fabrics made from true crepe yarns shrink if laundered, but this is due to the yarn structure, not the fiber content.

Care Dry cleaning solvents do not damage silk. Dry cleaning may be recommended for silk items because of yarn types, dyes with poor fastness to water or laundering, or product or fabric-construction methods. Washable silk items can be laundered in a mild detergent solution with gentle agitation. Since silk may lose up to 20 percent of its strength when wet, care should be taken with wet silks to avoid any unnecessary stress. Silk items should be pressed after laundering. Pure dye silks should be ironed damp with a press cloth. Wild silks should be dry-cleaned and ironed dry to avoid losing sericin and fabric body. Silk interior textiles are generally cleaned by the dry extraction method.

Silk may water-spot easily. Before hand- or machine-washing, test in an obscure place on the item to make sure the dye or finish does not water-spot. Silk can be damaged and yellowed by strong soaps or detergents (highly alkaline compounds) and high temperatures. Chlorine bleaches should be avoided. Cleaning agents containing hydrogen peroxide and sodium perborate are safe to use if the directions are followed carefully.

Silk is resistant to dilute mineral acids and organic acids. A crepelike surface effect may be created by the shrinking action caused by some acids. Silk is weakened and yellowed by exposure to sunlight and perspiration. For this reason, interior textiles of silk should be protected from direct exposure to sunlight. Silks may be attacked by insects, especially carpet beetles. Items should be stored clean because soil may attract insects that do not normally feed on silk.

Weighted silks deteriorate even under ideal storage conditions and are especially likely to break at the folds. Historic items often exhibit a condition known as shattered silk, in which the weighted silk is disintegrating (see Figure 5.22). The process cannot be reversed.

Table 5.5 summarizes silk's performance in apparel and interior textiles.

Environmental Concerns and Sustainability of Silk

Silk is a natural fiber and a renewable resource. Sericulture uses leaves of the mulberry tree. These trees grow in regions where the soil may be too poor to grow other crops or in small and irregular spaces. The trees help retain soil and contribute to the income of small farms. Mulberry trees are severely pruned when the leaves are harvested and the trees do not achieve a natural shape. Since mulberry trees are deciduous, leaves are available for only part of the year and silk production is limited to one generation each year.

Table 5.5 Summary of the Performance of Silk in Apparel and Interior Textiles

Aesthetics	Variable
Luster	Beautiful and soft
Durability	High
Abrasion resistance	Moderate
Tenacity	High for natural fibers
Elongation	Moderate
Comfort	High
Absorbency	High
Thermal retention	Good
Appearance Retention	Moderate
Resiliency	Moderate
Dimensional stability	High
Elastic recovery	Moderate
Recommended Care	Dry-clean (apparel) or dry extraction clean (interior textiles)

> ## ► Learning Activity 7

Use Fabrics #5, 19, 36, and 68 from your swatch kit. Identify an end use for each fabric and describe the serviceability for each product. How would the serviceability change if the fabric were made from cotton or another natural cellulosic fiber? Use Figure 5.1 and locate a country where these silk fibers might have been produced.

Silkworms are susceptible to disease and changes in temperature. Research is underway to increase silk production by developing disease-resistant varieties, producing artificial diets, and controlling internal environments to induce year-round production. Researchers are also examining the production of naturally colored silks that do not require the use of chemical dyes.

Silkworms are raised for the silk they produce. Most are killed before they have matured in order to harvest filament silk. Because of this, some animal rights activists avoid purchasing or using silk items. Some small quantities of organic, vegetarian, peace, or cruelty-free silk are available from cocoons where the mature silk moth is allowed to leave the cocoon. Wild silk cocoons are harvested after the moth has left the cocoon and are found in open forests with no use of hazardous chemicals. Wild silk is lower in quality than conventional silk because of its staple length.

Silk production is labor-intensive and is concentrated in regions where labor costs are low. When silk prices fall, these regions suffer accordingly. Child labor may be used in producing silk. However, in many areas, silk production allows families to work together and each member's work contributes to a better economic situation for the family. In the villages of Mexico, silk production provides economic freedom for women and boosts family income. Efforts to mechanize the production of silkworms could have a pronounced impact on regions that have traditionally relied on hand labor to produce silk.

Silk production makes extensive use of water and other chemicals to clean the fiber and remove sericin. Silk sericin is removed from the silk in a hot water bath (degumming). The waste water is usually discharged into the ground water system without any treatment. Some factories that degum silk have developed water treatment procedures so that the water returned to the environment is clean. Although the use of chemical finishes is relatively low for silk, the use of dyes is high. Dyeing silk requires use of heat, water, dyes, and other chemicals. Environmental regulations are minimal in some parts of the world where silk is processed, and disposal of chemicals is done with little regard for the environment. Although not all silk products require dry cleaning, many do. Dry-cleaning solvents may harm the environment, and their use and disposal are restricted. For more information on dry cleaning, see Chapter 20.

Uses of Silk

Silk has a drape, luster, and texture that may be imitated by synthetic fibers, but cannot be duplicated exactly. Because of its unique properties and high cost, silk is used primarily in apparel and interior products. Other factors that contribute to the continued popularity of silk are its appearance, comfort, and strength. Silk is extremely versatile, and it can be used to create a

> ## ► Learning Activity 8

Is silk a sustainable fiber? Identify the positive and negative aspects of silk in terms of sustainability. Explain your answer.

variety of fabrics, from sheer, gossamer chiffons to heavy, beautiful brocades and velvets. Because of silk's absorbency, it is appropriate for warm-weather wear and active sportswear. Because of its low heat conductivity, it is also appropriate for cold-weather wear. Silk underwear, socks, and leggings are popular due to silk's soft hand, good absorbency, and wicking characteristics. Silk is available in a range of apparel from one-of-a-kind designer garments to low-priced discount store shirts.

Silk and silk blends are equally important in interior textiles. Silk is frequently used in upholstery, wall-covering fabrics, and wall hangings. Some designers are so enamored with silk that they drape entire rooms in it. Silk blends are often used in window-treatment and upholstery fabrics because of their soft luster and drape. The texture and drape of wild and duppioni silks make them ideal for covering ceilings and walls. Occasionally, beautiful and expensive handmade rugs are made of silk. Liners for sleeping bags, blankets, and bedsheets of silk feel warm, soft, and luxurious next to the skin.

Silk is also used in the medical field for sutures, prosthetic arteries, and fibroin-based scaffolds and grafts. The scaffold provides support for regenerating ligaments, tendons, and other bodily connective tissue. It has been successful in restoring full functionality following some injuries.

Spider Silk

For several years, researchers have been intrigued with the dragline silk produced by some spiders of the *Nephila* and *Araneus* families because of their exceptional strength, elasticity, and light weight. This silk can be magnetized, conducts electricity, and is stable to high temperatures. The protein of **spider silk** is *spidroin*, but each spider spins several kinds of silk. Capture silk is highly elastic and hydroscopic, while dragline silk is very strong for its fine size. It is difficult to produce quantities of the spider silk for research purposes because spiders are territorial and kill each other before spinning much silk. Spider farms are simply not possible. Researchers are studying the plausibility of using a transgenic silkworm in which some of the silkworm genes have been replaced with spider genes to produce the dragline spider silk. Other researchers have worked with genetically modified goats. The dragline silk would be used in technical products that require exceptional strength and elasticity. Possible applications include civil engineering and road construction applications, protective clothing, and for bone and tendon repair in the medical field.

Identification of Natural Protein Fibers

Natural protein fibers can be identified with a microscope fairly easily. Wool fibers have scales that are visible along the edge and, if the fiber is white or pastel, may be seen throughout the length of the fiber. It is difficult to distinguish among the wool fibers because of their similar

▶ Learning Activity 10

Use Fabric #11 from your swatch kit. Following the procedures described in Chapter 3, examine the fibers using the microscope to see the scales of the wool fiber. Repeat the process with Fabric #38. Describe the differences and similarities of the microscopic appearance of both fibers.

▶ Learning Activity 11

Use Fabric #5 from your swatch kit. Following the procedures described in Chapter 3, examine the fibers using the microscope to see the slightly irregular appearance of silk. Compare the appearance of silk with that of wool and cashmere.

▶ Learning Activity 12

Use a small portion of the fiber from the small self-sealing bags labeled Silk, Wool, and Mohair or three to four yarns from Fabrics #4, 11, and 38 (cashmere) from your swatch kit. Following the procedures and safety precautions described in Chapter 3, conduct a burn test of these samples. Describe the ease of ignition, the color and odor of the smoke, and the color and texture of the cooled ash. Compare your results with those included in Table 3.7 or with the chart on the back of the sheet with the fiber bags in your swatch kit. Use Figure 5.1 and locate a country where the mohair fiber might have been produced.

▶ Learning Activity 13

Use a small portion of the fiber from the small self-sealing bags labeled Silk, Wool, and Mohair or three to four yarns from Fabrics #4, 11, and 38 (cashmere) from your swatch kit. Following the procedures and safety precautions described in Chapter 3, place each sample in a container of chlorine bleach. Describe what happens. Record how long it takes for the fiber samples to dissolve.

appearance. For example, it is easy to distinguish wool from cotton, but it is difficult to distinguish sheep's wool from camel hair. Correct identification of the various specialty wools is difficult but necessary because of fraudulent blends that are labeled "100 percent cashmere" or other luxury fiber. Silk can be identified with a microscope, but with greater difficulty. Since silk is a natural fiber, its surface is not as regular as that of most manufactured fibers. The trilobal cross section may not be apparent, but the fiber has slight bumps or other irregularities.

Natural protein fibers are soluble in sodium hypochlorite. In the burn test, these fibers smell like burning hair. However, the odor is so strong that a very small percentage of protein fiber produces a noticeable hair odor. Hence, the burn test is not reliable for blends, nor will it distinguish among the protein fibers.

key terms

review questions

1. Describe the similarities in the properties common to all protein fibers.

2. For the products listed below, describe the properties of wool and silk that some manufactured fibers attempt to duplicate:
   a. Carpeting
   b. Blanket
   c. Blouse
   d. Interview suit (wool)
   e. Interview suit (silk)

3. Compare the performance characteristics of the following fiber pairs:
   a. Wool and angora
   b. Cashmere and silk
   c. Mohair and llama

4. Identify a natural protein fiber that would be appropriate for each of the end uses listed below and describe the properties that contribute to that end use:
   a. Area rug in front of a fireplace
   b. Upholstery for corporate boardroom
   c. Suit for business travel

   d. Tie with small print pattern
   e. Casual sweater

5. To what fiber aspects are the differences in properties among the natural protein fibers attributed?

6. Consider the distribution of fibers present in your wardrobe. Explain which natural protein fibers are present and how you are satisfied or dissatisfied with their performance. Use Figure 5.1 and locate a country of production for each of the natural protein fibers represented in your wardrobe.

7. Explain why wool is not more commonly used in apparel. What are the reasons you do not own more wool items?

8. Would one of the other animal fibers be able to compete with wool in the market? Why or why not?

9. Select two animal fibers other than wool. Explain the differences and similarities between these fibers and wool in terms of processing and performance.

10. Although silk production was attemped in many parts of the world in the 16th through the 19th centuries, it usually failed. Propose five reasons why silk production might not succeed in an area.

Case Study
Merino Wool*

Merino wool is treasured for its dense, fine, crimped fibers and is the standard by which all other wool fibers are judged. Wool is graded by fineness, length, luster, and weight. Hand spinners often buy fleece in the grease from local sheep producers and have to degrease it before spinning. Spinners also sort the wool into piles based on location within the fleece and remove waste, dirt, and vegetable matter before spinning. After sorting and cleaning, wool can be blended with mohair, silk, and other fibers before spinning.

DISCUSSION QUESTIONS

1. Why is degreasing necessary before spinning fiber into yarn? What kinds of problems might be encountered if the wool is not clean before attempting to spin a yarn?

2. Why do spinners sort the fleece before beginning working with it? How does this hand sorting practice relate to the practice used in commercial facilities?

3. Describe the serviceability of a Merino wool yarn. How would the serviceability differ if 50 percent of the fibers were mohair or silk or cotton?

4. What are the environmental concerns that should be considered for wool?

5. Why is locally available wool fleece considered sustainable? How would an individual interested in local wool locate a source for it?

*Vester, P. J. (2005/2006). Merino: A golden fleece. *Shuttle, Spindle, and Dyepot, 37*(1), 43–47.

suggested readings

Collins, K. (2008). South America's wild ones, vicuña and guanaco. *Spin-Off, 32*(4), 78–84.

De Roy, T. (2002, January/February). Return of the golden fleece. *International Wildlife*, pp. 12–19.

Fletcher, K. (2008). *Sustainable Fashion and Textiles: Design Journey*. London: Earthscan.

Franck, R. R. (ed.) (2001). *Silk, Mohair, Cashmere, and Other Luxury Fibres*. Cambridge, England: Woodhead Publishing.

Gilman, V. (2003, June 16). The silk road. *Chemical and Engineering News*, p. 27.

Greer, S., Banks-Lee, P., & Jones, M. (2007). Physical and mechanical properties of chiengora fibers. *AATCC Review, 7*(5), 42–46.

Hearle, J. W. S. (2007). Protein fibres: 21st century vision, *Textiles, 34*(2), 14–18.

Hethorn, J., & Ulasewicz, C. (2008). *Sustainable Fashion: Why Now?* New York: Fairchild Books.

Parker, J. (1991). *All About Silk: A Fabric Dictionary and Swatchbook*. Seattle, WA: Rain City Publishing.

Rheinberg, L. (1991). The romance of silk. *Textile Progress, 21*(4), 1–43.

Rhoades, C. H. (2007). Bactrian camel. *Spin-Off, 31*(3), 50–57.

Ryder, M. L. (1997). Silk: The epitome of luxury. *Textiles Magazine*, 1, pp. 17–21.

Smirfitt, J. (1996). Lamb's wool. *Textiles Magazine*, 2, pp. 18–19.

Thiry, M. (2007). Detecting the fiber. *AATCC Review, 7*(12), 18–21.

Thiry, M. (2007). Fibers in contention. *AATCC Review, 7*(12), 22–23.

Vester, P. J. (2005/2006). Merino: A golden fleece. *Shuttle, Spindle, and Dyepot, 37*(1), 43–47.

Wallack, R. L. (2008). Cashmere: From the land of mystery. *AATCC Review, 8*(5), 28–31.

the
FIBER-MANUFACTURING
PROCESS

CHAPTER OBJECTIVES

- To describe the process of manufacturing fibers.
- To identify the differences and similarities among natural and manufactured fibers.
- To understand how fibers are modified and the resulting changes in product performance.
- To explain why fibers are engineered for specific end uses.

6

The natural fibers do not possess a perfect combination of characteristics, performance, availability, or cost. Because of this, the manufacture of new fibers has been described for centuries. In 1664, Robert Hooke suggested that if the proper liquid were squeezed through a small aperture and allowed to congeal, a fiber like silk might be produced. In 1889, the first manufactured fiber (from a solution of cellulose by Count Hilaire de Chardonnet) was shown at the Paris Exhibition. In 1910, rayon fibers were first commercially produced in the United States. Acetate was first commercially produced in 1924. These first manufactured fibers made it possible for consumers to have silklike fabrics at low cost. In 1939, the first synthetic fiber, nylon, was made. Since that time, many more generic fibers with numerous modifications have appeared on the market.

A **manufactured fiber** is any fiber derived by a process of manufacture from a substance that at any point in the process is not a fiber. There are many different manufactured fibers available today. The differences among the fibers are due to the chemistry of the polymer. Because it is very difficult for consumers to differentiate among these fibers based on their appearance or hand, generic names are used to identify each specific type. Generic names are not the same as trade names. **Generic name** refers to the family of manufactured or synthetic fibers that have a similar chemical composition, are based on fiber chemistry, and are approved by the Federal Trade Commission (Table 6.1). **Trade names** are companies' names for fibers and may be used in promotion and marketing. Certification requirements for use of a trade name or trademark allow the owner to set minimum performance standards for a product that carries

> **Manufactured** fibers are derived by a process of manufacture from a substance that at any point in the process is not a fiber. **Generic name** refers to the family of manufactured or synthetic fibers that have a similar chemical composition, based on fiber chemistry. **Trade names** are companies' names for fibers.

▶ Learning Activity 1

Develop a list of the criteria that would make a perfect fiber for a specific end use or product. Compare your list to the fiber property charts in Chapter 3. Which fiber(s) come(s) closest to being your perfect fiber? What are the performance areas where this fiber is less than perfect? Explain the performance areas where synthetic and manufactured fibers excel and where natural fibers excel. Are these areas the same or different?

Table 6.1 Generic Names for Manufactured Fibers

Cellulosic	Noncellulosic and Synthetic		Mineral
Acetate	Acrylic	Nylon	Glass
Triacetate*	Anidex*	Nytril*	Metallic
Rayon	Aramid	Olefin	
Lyocell	Azlon*	PBI	
Bamboo*	Elasterell-p	PLA	
	Elastoester	Polyester	
	Fluoropolymer	Rubber	
	Lastol	Saran	
	Lastrile*	Spandex	
	Melamine	Sulfar	
	Modacrylic	Vinal*	
	Novoloid*	Vinyon*	

*Not produced in the United States.

> ## ▶ Learning Activity 2

Examine the list of fibers in Table 6.1. Make a list of the fibers whose names you recognize and a list of fibers whose names you do not recognize. Review the names on your second list. Place these fibers in one of three categories: elastic fiber, special use fiber, and rarely used fiber. Skim through Chapters 7, 8, and 9 to determine if your placement was correct.

> ## ▶ Learning Activity 3

Use Fabrics #20, 25, 42, 45, and 82 and the key from your swatch kit. Identify which of the terms identifying these fabrics are generic fiber names and which are trade names or trademarks. Check Table 3.1 to determine which of these fibers are natural, manufactured, and synthetic. Appendix C might also be of use in determining generic and trade names.

the trade name or trademark. Trade names for generic fibers, like Tencel lyocell, are used less often, while trade names for special fiber modifications, like Supplex nylon, are used widely to promote products.

There are two types of manufactured fibers: regenerated and synthetic. Manufactured regenerated fibers will be discussed in Chapter 7 and manufactured synthetic fibers will be discussed in Chapters 8 and 9.

The impact of manufactured fibers on the consumer and the technical markets has far exceeded original predictions. The first manufactured fibers were aimed at people who could not afford the expensive natural fibers like silk. Yet manufactured fibers have caused tremendous changes in the way people live and the things they do. End uses that in the past were simply not possible are now commonplace because of the use of manufactured fibers. Many fashions are directly related to manufactured fibers. The combination of fit and performance found in spandex and nylon biking shorts, swimwear, and leotards is not possible with any combination of natural fibers. The common use of carpeting in homes, businesses, and other facilities is related to the low cost and good performance characteristics of nylon, olefin, and other manufactured fibers. Carpets of wool are too expensive and do not possess the characteristics appropriate for the many ways carpets are used today. Manufactured fibers in roadbed underlays, communication cables, and replacement human body parts are examples of new end uses for fibers. Manufactured fibers have revolutionized daily life!

Manufactured fibers possess the unique ability to be engineered for specific end uses. For that reason, many of these fibers are highly versatile and found in an amazing array of products. With an expanded understanding of polymer chemistry and fiber production, many problems in the original fiber have been overcome through changes in the polymer, production, or finishing steps.

With current lifestyles, it is not possible to return to only natural fibers. Table 6.2 summarizes the use of manufactured fibers in the United States in 2007. In the United States, manufactured fibers comprise 83 percent of the fiber market: 50 percent for apparel, 89 percent for interior textiles (98 percent for floor coverings), and 91 percent for technical products. Amazingly, the manufactured-fiber industry uses only approximately 1 percent of the nation's oil and natural gas supplies. The industry is highly efficient. One 300-acre polyester facility can produce as much fiber as 600,000 acres of cotton.

Table 6.2 Use of Manufactured Fibers

Use Category	Percentage	Use Category	Percentage
Sheer hosiery	96	Carpet	98
Socks/anklets	22	Other interior textiles	74
Sweaters	65	Tires	99
Craft yarn	80	Hose, technical	88
Underwear	40	Belting, technical	82
Lingerie	78	Medical, surgical uses	89
Robes and loungewear	78	Nonwovens	100
Pile fabrics	100	Fiberfill	100
Linings	95	Felts	85
Apparel lace	100	Filtration	96
Narrow fabrics	82	Rope, etc.	92
Top-weight apparel	41	Sewing thread	53
Bottom-weight apparel	37	Reinforcement, paper and tape	67
Other apparel	85	Reinforcement, plastic and electrical	24
Bedspreads and quilts	52	Coated fabrics	86
Blankets	38	Transportation fabrics	96
Sheets	39	Narrow fabrics, technical	88
Towels	7	Bags, bagging	97
Window treatments	67	Miscellaneous	87
Upholstery	66		

Fiber Spinning

It took years to develop the first fiber-spinning solutions and invent mechanical devices to convert the solutions into filaments. The first solutions were made from dissolved cellulose. In the 1920s and 1930s scientists learned how to build long-chain molecules from simple starting materials.

The raw material is a natural product such as cellulose or protein, or it is a synthetic polymer. These raw materials are dissolved in liquid chemicals and made into thick solutions called **spinning solution** or **dope**. For some synthetic polymers such as nylon and polyester, the polymer is formed, cooled, and broken into small pieces or chips. The chips are heated until they form a liquid **melt**, and the melt is used to form the fiber.

All manufactured-**fiber-spinning** processes are based on these three general steps:

1. Preparing a viscous dope (a thick solution) or a melt
2. Forcing or extruding the dope or melt through an opening in a spinneret to form a fiber
3. Solidifying the fiber by coagulation, evaporation, or cooling

Extrusion is forcing or pumping the spinning solution through the tiny holes of a spinneret, a very important step in the spinning process. A **spinneret** is a small thimblelike nozzle made of platinum or stainless steel (Figure 6.1). Spinnerets are costly, and new developments are closely guarded secrets. The making of the tiny holes, usually with laser beams, is the critical part of the process. Round holes are common, but many other shapes are also used (see Figure 3.3).

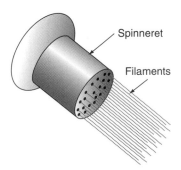

Spinneret

Filaments

Figure 6.1 Spinneret showing extrusion of filament fibers.

Each hole in the spinneret forms one fiber. **Filament fibers** are spun from spinnerets with 350 holes or less. When these fibers are grouped together and slightly twisted, they make a **filament yarn. Filament tow** is an untwisted rope of thousands of filament fibers. This rope is made by combining the fibers from many spinnerets, each of which may have thousands of holes. The tow is crimped and converted into staple by cutting or breaking to the desired length. (See Chapter 10 for methods of breaking filament tow into staple fibers.)

Spinning Methods

Spinning is done by three basic methods, which are compared briefly in Figure 6.2. Details of each method are described in later chapters.

Wet Spinning: Acrylic, Lyocell, Rayon, Spandex

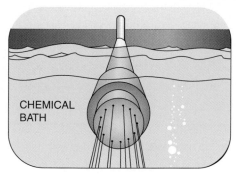

1. Raw material is dissolved by chemicals.
2. Fiber is spun into chemical bath.
3. Fiber solidifies when coagulated by bath.

Oldest process
Most complex
Weak fibers until dry
Washing, bleaching, etc., required before use
Solvent may be recovered and reused

Dry Spinning

Acetate, Acrylic, Modacrylic, Spandex (Major Method)

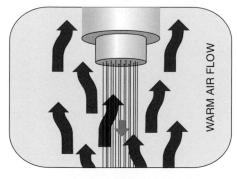

1. Resin solids are dissolved by solvent.
2. Fiber is spun into warm air.
3. Fiber solidifies by evaporation of the solvent.

Direct process
Solvent required
Solvent recovery required
No washing, etc., required

Melt Spinning: Nylon, Olefin, Polyester, Saran

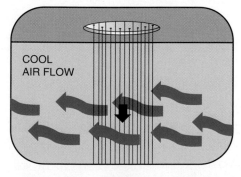

1. Resin solids are melted in autoclave.
2. Fiber is spun into the air.
3. Fiber solidifies on cooling.

Least expensive
Direct process
High spinning speeds
No solvent, washing, etc., required
Fibers shaped like spinneret hole

Figure 6.2 Methods of spinning manufactured fibers.

SOURCE: Courtesy of American Fiber Manufacturers Association, Inc.

The process of developing a new fiber is long and expensive and requires a huge investment before any profit can be realized. First, a research program develops the new fiber. Then a pilot plant is built to translate laboratory procedures to commercial production. Fibers produced by the pilot plant are tested to determine end uses and evaluate suitability. When the fiber is ready, a commercial plant is built.

A patent on the process gives the producer 17 years of exclusive rights to the use of the process—time to recover the initial cost and to make a profit. The price per pound during this time is high, but it drops later. The patent owner can license other producers to use the process. Continuing research and development programs address problems that arise and produce modifications for special end uses.

Fiber Modifications

One advantage of the manufactured fibers is that each step of the production process can be precisely controlled to modify the fiber. Modifications result from a producer's continuing research program to address any limitations, explore each fiber's potential, and develop properties that will expand the fiber's versatility. Specific modifications can be selected to improve fiber performance in many areas including hand, comfort, soil resistance, and sunlight resistance to reduce problems or improve performance for specific products. For example, nylon fibers for carpeting are modified so that they are soil-resistant, cross-dyeable, flame-retardant, antistatic, and larger and more crush-resistant with a nonround cross-section that hides soil.

The **parent fiber** is the fiber in its simplest, unmodified form. It is often sold as a commodity fiber by generic name only, without benefit of a trade name. Other terms for parent fiber include *regular*, *basic*, *standard*, *conventional*, or *first-generation fiber*.

Modifications of the parent fiber may be sold under a brand or trade name. Modifications may also be referred to as *types, variants*, or *x-generation fibers*, where the *x* could be any number such as second, fifth, or tenth generation.

There are five general ways that a **fiber modification** can be made.

1. The size and shape of the spinneret can be changed to produce fibers of different sizes and shapes.
2. The fiber's molecular structure and crystallinity can be changed to enhance fiber durability.
3. Other compounds (additives) can be added to the polymer or dope to enhance fiber performance.
4. The spinning process can be modified to alter fiber characteristics.
5. In a more complex modification, two polymers can be combined as separate entities within a single fiber or yarn.

Spinneret Modifications

Because fiber size often dictates end use, it is not surprising that changing the fiber size is a common modification. The simplest way to change fiber size is by changing the size of the opening in the spinneret. Other ways of changing fiber size include a controlled stretching or drawing after fiber extrusion or a controlled rate at which the solution is extruded through the spinneret. Finer fibers, those with a denier of less than 7, are most often used for apparel. Deniers ranging from 5 to 25 are used in interior textiles. Technical applications have the widest range of denier, ranging from less than 1 for polishing lenses for glass and optical applications to

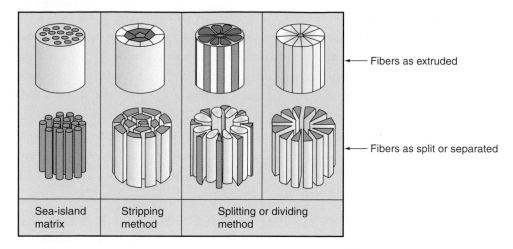

Fibers as extruded

Fibers as split or separated

| Sea-island matrix | Stripping method | Splitting or dividing method |

Figure 6.3 Typical methods of splitting or separating microfibers.
SOURCE: Courtesy of American Association of Textile Chemists and Colorists.

several thousand for ropes and fishing line. Because technology is able to produce fibers with extremely tiny sizes, the term **macrofiber** is used to describe fibers with a denier greater than 1.0. **Microfibers** are fibers with deniers of less than 1.0; most range from 0.5 to 0.8 denier per filament (dpf). **Ultrafine fibers** are less than 0.3 dpf. Larger-sized fibers are used where greater strength, abrasion resistance, and resiliency are required. For example, carpet fibers with deniers in the range of 15 to 24 are more resilient. Higher-denier fibers resist crushing better than lower-denier fibers.

Microfibers and ultrafine fibers are produced by modifying the spinning technique or by splitting or separating the filaments. Figure 6.3 shows several fiber types. Polyester ultrafine fibers with modified cross sections with slight fiber irregularities are sometimes referred to as **shin-gosen**, a Japanese term that means new synthetic fiber. Technical innovations in fiber production and processing result in products with exceptional consumer performance characteristics. In apparel and interiors, these fibers mimic the appearance and hand of silk.

A yarn of microdenier fibers or microfibers may have as many as four times more fibers than a regular fiber yarn of the same size. Microdenier generic fibers include polyester, nylon, acrylic, and rayon in apparel and interiors in staple and filament form. Fabrics made from these fibers are softer and are more drapeable, silklike, comfortable, and water-repellent.

Microfibers may be present by themselves in fabrics or in blends with no more than 60 percent natural or other manufactured fibers in order to retain the microfiber's characteristics. End uses include coats, blouses, suits, sleepwear, active sportswear, hosiery, upholstery, window treatments, bedding, and wall coverings. These very fine fibers required modifications in yarn-spinning frames, looms and sewing machines, and dyeing and finishing techniques.

Mixed-denier filament bundling combines fibers of several denier sizes in one yarn (Figure 6.4). Microfibers (0.5 dpf) contribute the buttery hand to the fabric, while the macrofibers or regular denier fibers (2.0 dpf) contribute drape, bounce, and durability. When the fabric is laundered, the macrofibers shrink slightly, forcing the microfibers to the fabric's surface and enhancing the hand.

Even smaller than microfibers, **nanofibers** are fibers with cross sections measuring less than 1,000 nm. (One nanometer is 1×10^{-9} meters.) A human hair is 80,000 nm. Nanofibers are on a much smaller scale than regular or macrofibers used in most apparel and interior textiles. (See Figure 6.5.) *Nanotubes* are hollow nanofibers. Nanofibers are made by several techniques including those discussed with micro- and ultrafine fibers. Another

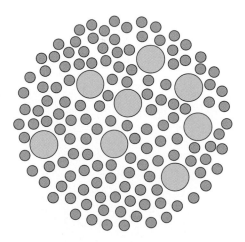

Figure 6.4 Cross section of yarn combining microfibers and macrofibers.

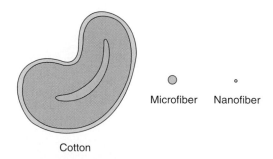

Microfiber   Nanofiber

Cotton

Figure 6.5 Comparison of fiber size (not to scale): cotton fiber (apparel), microfiber, and nanofibers.

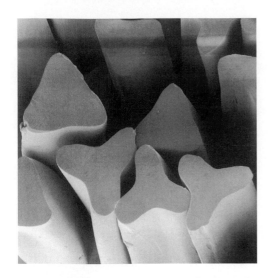

Figure 6.6   Stereoscan of trilobal nylon.

SOURCE: Courtesy of E. I. du Pont de Nemours & Company.

technique, **electrospinning**, forces the fiber through a tiny spinneret opening into an electric field. Nanofibers and nanotubes have high surface-to-volume ratios, small pore size, flexible surface functions, biocompatibility, and enhanced mechanical and electrical properties. Nanofibers and nanotubes are currently being used in protective apparel, safety harnesses, and filtration for technical and medical applications. Smart textiles make use of nanofibers, nanotubes, and nanotechnology to produce materials that react to the environment. Micro-, ultrafine, and nanofibers are also used in technical applications where extremely fine fibers are needed. (For additional nanotechnology applications in the textile complex, see Chapters 9, 15, and 18.)

Fiber Shape Changing the cross-sectional shape is the easiest way to alter a fiber's mechanical and aesthetic properties. This is usually done by changing the shape of the spinneret hole. Many shapes are possible: flat, trilobal, quadrilobal, pentalobal, triskelion, cruciform, cloverleaf, and alphabet shapes such as Y and T (see Figure 3.3).

The *flat shape* was an early variation. Ribbonlike "crystal" acetate and "sparkling" nylon are extruded through a long, narrow spinneret hole. Flat fibers reflect light much as a mirror does and produce fabrics with a glint or sparkle.

The **trilobal shape** is widely used in both nylon and polyester fibers (Figure 6.6). It is spun through a spinneret with three triangularly arranged slits. The trilobal shape produces a fabric with a beautiful silklike hand, subtle opacity, soil-hiding capacity, built-in bulk without weight, heightened wicking action, silklike sheen and color, crush resistance in heavy deniers, and good textured crimp.

Other fiber shapes that produce similar characteristics are *triskelion* (a three-sided configuration similar to a boat propeller), *pentalobal*, *octolobal*, and *Y-shaped*. Multilobal fibers improve hydrophilic, wicking, and moisture management properties, making them more comfortable for athletic apparel and sportswear.

Thick-and-thin fiber types vary in their diameter along their length as a result of uneven drawing or stretching after spinning. The resulting fabrics have a texture like duppioni silk or linen. The thick nubby areas dye a deeper color to create interesting tone-on-tone color effects. Many surface textures are possible by changing the size and length of the slubs.

Hollow or multicellular fibers imitate the air cells of some animal hair, which provides insulation in cold weather, and the hollow feathers of ducks, which produce buoyancy in water. Air cells and hollow filaments in manufactured fibers are made by adding gas-forming compounds to the spinning solution, by injecting air as the fiber is forming, or by modifying the shape of the spinneret holes. For example, when the spinneret hole is in a C shape or as two half circles, the dope flows slightly on extrusion so that the perimeter closes up and the center remains hollow.

Molecular Structure and Crystallinity Modifications

Manufacturers can change the molecular structure and degree of orientation and crystallinity of fibers, engineering them for specific end uses. Slight changes can improve performance for an end use. Some modifications occur in the physical arrangement of the polymer within the fiber. Nanoparticles can be used to control crystallinity and orientation when uniformly distributed through the spinning solution. Nanoclay particles increase crystallinity and orientation for melt spun fibers. Other modifications occur in the selection of the compounds used to produce the polymer in order to change the polymer chain length.

Controlled stretching of fibers immediately after extrusion produces **high-tenacity fibers**. Fiber strength is increased (1) by drawing or stretching the fiber to align or orient the molecules and strengthen the intermolecular forces, and/or (2) by chemical modification of the fiber polymer to increase the degree of polymerization. These procedures will be discussed in more detail in Chapters 7 and 8.

Low-pilling fibers are engineered to reduce their flex life by slightly reducing the molecular weight of the polymer chains (decreasing the number of mers in a chain). When flex-abrasion resistance is reduced, the fiber pills break off almost as soon as they are formed and the fabric retains its smooth appearance. These low-pilling fibers are not as strong as other types, but they are durable enough for apparel uses, especially knits. (Review the discussion of molecular weight in Chapter 3.)

Binder staple is a semi-dull, crimped polyester with a very low melting point. Binder staple develops a thermoplastic bond with other fibers under heat and pressure and is used in fiberwebs and related uses. For example, in nonwoven interlinings in apparel, the binder staple is mixed with regular staple fibers. When the mixture is heated, the binder staple melts and, upon cooling, bonds the regular fibers together.

Low-elongation modifications are used to increase fabric strength and abrasion resistance when weaker fibers are blended with stronger fibers, as in cotton/polyester blends. Low elongation results from changing the balance of tenacity and extension. High-tenacity fibers have lower elongation properties. These fibers elongate less so that weaker cotton fibers are not stretched beyond the breaking point during use in work apparel and other items that receive hard wear.

Shape memory fibers, a type of smart textile, are being developed to have the capacity to change shape in a predefined way. Chemical groups are incorporated in the fiber's polymer during polymerization. These groups are sensitive to heat, light, or other stimuli and are designed to conform to a specific shape when activated by the stimuli. These polymers are often referred to as active polymers, meaning that they react to stimuli in the environment.

Additives to the Polymer or Spinning Solution

Fiber additives include introducing a new or modified monomer to the polymer chain so that it is a part of the polymer or adding a compound to the polymer solution or dope so that it is included in the fiber but not as part of the polymer chain. When too much of the additive is used, it adversely affects physical fiber characteristics such as strength and hand.

Delustering A basic fiber reflects light from its smooth, round surface. It is referred to as a **bright fiber**. (Note that here *bright* refers to high luster, not intense color.) To **deluster** a fiber, titanium dioxide—a white pigment—is added to the spinning solution before the fiber is extruded. In some cases, the titanium dioxide can be mixed at an earlier stage when the resin polymer is being formed. The degree of luster is controlled by varying the amount of delusterant, producing dull or semi-dull fibers. Figure 6.7 shows yarns of different lusters.

Delustered fibers can be identified microscopically by the presence of dark spots within the fiber (see Figure 6.7). The particles of pigment absorb light or prevent reflection of light. Energy from absorbed light breaks fiber bonds causing degradation or tendering. For this reason, bright fibers reflect light and suffer less light damage and are better for use in window-treatment fabrics. The strength of a delustered fiber is slightly less than that of a bright fiber. Rayon, for example, is 3 to 5 percent weaker when it is delustered.

(a)

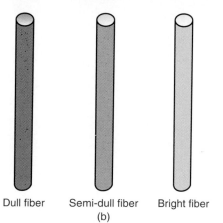

Dull fiber   Semi-dull fiber   Bright fiber
(b)

Figure 6.7 (a) Polyester yarns (left to right: dull, semi-dull, bright); (b) fibers as they would look under a microscope.

Solution Dyeing or Mass Pigmentation

Solution dyeing, or **mass pigmentation**, is the addition of colored pigments or dyes to the spinning solution. Thus, the fiber is colored when it emerges from the spinneret. These fibers are referred to as *solution-dyed*, *mass-pigmented*, *dope-dyed*, *spun-dyed*, or *producer-colored*. If the color is added before the fiber hardens, it is called *gel dyeing*. Solution dyeing provides color permanence that is not obtainable in any other way. The lightfastness and washfastness are usually excellent. Because the color is uniformly distributed throughout the fiber, color changes resulting from use are minimal.

Because of the difficulty in obtaining a truly black dye with good colorfastness properties, black pigments are often the first ones to be used. Other colors are produced as suitable colorfast pigments are developed.

Solution-dyed fibers cost more per pound than uncolored fibers. This difference may be offset later by the cost of yarn or piece (fabric) dyeing. The solution-dyed fibers are used in upholstery, window treatments, and apparel. One disadvantage of the solution-dyed fibers is that the manufacturer must carry a large inventory to be able to fill orders quickly. The manufacturer is also less able to adjust to fashion changes in color because it is not possible to strip color from these fibers and redye them.

Whiteners and Brighteners

Whiteners and **brighteners** are added to the spinning solution to make fibers look whiter and resist yellowing. The additive is an optical bleach or fluorescent dye that reflects more blue light from the fabric and masks yellowing. These whiteners are permanent in washing and dry cleaning. They also eliminate the need for bleaching.

Cross Dyeable

Cross-dyeable, or *dye-affinity*, **fibers** are made by incorporating dye-accepting chemicals into the molecular structure. Some of the parent fibers are nondyeable; others do not accept certain classes of dyes well. The cross-dyeable types were developed to correct this limitation. The dye-affinity fibers are far easier to dye than their parent fibers. Several dye-accepting chemicals can be used so that a combination of types of cross-dyeable fibers is used in a product such as carpet. The carpet can be produced and a pattern developed based on the dyes selected.

Do not confuse cross-dyeable fibers with solution-dyed fibers. Cross-dyeable fibers are not colored when they emerge from the spinneret, while solution-dyed fibers emerge as colored fibers.

Antistatic Fibers

Static builds up as a result of electron flow. Fibers conduct electricity according to how readily electrons move in them. If a fiber has an excess of electrons, it is negatively charged and it is attracted to something that is positively charged—anything that has a deficiency of electrons. This attraction is illustrated by the way some apparel clings to the body. Water is a good conductor of electrons and dissipates static. Because many synthetic fibers have low water absorbency, static charges build up rapidly but dissipate slowly during dry weather or when fabrics have been rubbed or tumbled together. If the fibers can be made wettable, the static charges will dissipate quickly and annoying static buildup will be minimal.

The **antistatic fibers** give durable protection because the fiber is made wettable by incorporating an antistatic compound—a chemical conductor—as an integral part of the fiber. The compound is added to the fiber-polymer raw material so that it is evenly distributed throughout the fiber. It changes the fiber's hydrophobic nature to a more hydrophilic one and raises the moisture regain so that static is dissipated more quickly. The moisture content of the air should be sufficient to provide moisture for absorption—even cotton builds up static if the air is too dry. Static control is also achieved by incorporating a conducting core into a fiber (Figure 6.8).

The soil-resistant benefits of the antistatic fibers are outstanding. The antistatic fibers retard soiling by minimizing the attraction and retention of dirt particles, and the opacity and luster in the yarn have soil-hiding properties. Soil redeposition in laundry is dramatically reduced. Oily stains, even motor oils, are released more easily.

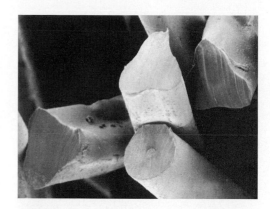

Figure 6.8 Antistatic polyester.
SOURCE: Courtesy of E. I. du Pont de Nemours & Company.

Sunlight-Resistant Fibers Ultraviolet light causes fiber degradation as well as color fading. When ultraviolet light is absorbed, the damage results from a reaction between the radiant energy and the fiber or dye. Stabilizers such as nitrogenous compounds may be added to the dope to increase **sunlight resistance (SLR)**. These stabilizers must be carefully selected for the fiber–dye combination. The SLR fibers are especially important for window treatments and other interior textiles in glass office buildings and car interiors. Delustered fibers are more sensitive to sunlight than bright fibers, so the SLR fibers are usually bright.

Flame-Resistant Fibers Fibers with this modification provide better protection for consumers than flame-retardant finishes applied to fabric surfaces (see Chapter 18). Some **flame-resistant fibers** are inherently flame-retardant because of their chemical composition. These include aramid, novoloid, modacrylic, glass, PBI, saran, sulfar, and vinyon. Other flame-retardant fibers are produced by changing the polymer structure or by adding flame-retardant compounds to the spinning solution. These fiber modifications make the fibers inherently flame-retardant.

Antibacterial Fibers **Antibacterial** or **antimicrobial fibers** protect textiles from bacteria, mildew, and other micbrobial growth, odor, and fiber damage. Chemical compounds that kill bacteria and other microbes or discourage their growth or function are incorporated in the spinning solution prior to extrusion or incorporated in fibers during spinning. Several organic and inorganic compounds are used. However, there is some concern that bacteria may develop resistance to some of these compounds. Many compounds remain effective for the life of the product, but a few diminish in effectiveness over time.

The antibacterial properties of modified acrylic, acetate, polyester, nylon, and olefin are permanent and will not wash out. Some fibers with these modifications inhibit odor-causing bacteria in hosiery, underwear, and air filters. Other modified fibers are used to minimize microbes' long-term persistence on textiles and create more hygienic surfaces. Some products made with these modified fibers may require frequent washing to remove microbial debris and allow the additive to work on living microbes. Antibacterial topical or surface finishes are also frequently used (see Chapter 18).

Modifications in Fiber Spinning

When producers started to make staple fiber, mechanical crimping was done to broken filaments and later to filament tow to make the fibers more cohesive and thus easier to spin into yarns. Other techniques give permanent crimp to rayon and acetate and provide bulk or stretch to both filament and staple fibers.

Crimping of fibers is important in many end uses: for cover and loft in bulky knits, blankets, carpets, battings for quilted items, and pillows, and for stretch and recovery from stretch in hosiery and sportswear.

For wet-spun fibers, coagulating the fiber in a slightly modified bath can produce crimp. A skin forms immediately around the fiber and bursts, and a thinner skin forms over the rupture. Crimp develops when the fiber is immersed in water. Melt-spun fibers with a helical or spiral crimp are produced by cooling one side of the fiber faster than the other side as the fiber is extruded. This uneven cooling causes the fiber to curl. The same effect can be achieved by heating one side of the fiber during the stretching or drawing process. This helical crimp has more springiness than the conventional mechanical sawtooth crimp. These fibers are used where high levels of compressional resistance and recovery are needed.

For thermoplastic fibers, the spinneret holes are drilled at an angle and turbulence is introduced where the polymer is extruded so that one side of the fiber has uneven internal tensions. This uneven tension produces a fiber with a helical or zigzag crimp.

Complex Modifications

Bicomponent Fibers A **bicomponent fiber** is a fiber consisting of two polymers that are chemically different, physically different, or both. When the two components represent two different generic classes, the fiber is **bicomponent-bigeneric**. Bicomponent fibers may be of several types. Bilateral fibers are spun with the two polymers side by side. In core-sheath fibers, one polymer is surrounded or encircled by another polymer. In matrix-fribil fibers, short fibrils of one polymer are embedded in another polymer (Figure 6.9). In composite fibers, the

A thick liquid is forced through tiny nozzles to form fibers. Manufactured fibers can be modified to make them better for specific end uses. Common modifications affect drape and durability (fiber size), appearance (shape, luster, color, whiteness, and dyeability), and performance (strength, pilling, elongation, antistatic, sunlight resistance, flame resistance, and antibacterial).

> ## ▶ Learning Activity 4
>
> Use Fabrics #7, 9, 27, 32, 37, and 119 and the key from your swatch kit. Identify the fiber content and an end use for each fabric. Identify one or more fiber modifications that would be appropriate for the manufactured or synthetic fibers in the fabric. It might be helpful to make a list of the characteristics of a first-generation fiber and compare that list to the characteristics you can see and feel in each of these fabrics.

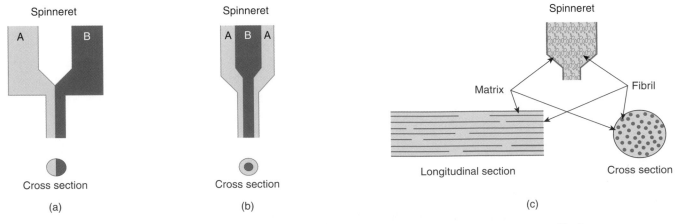

Figure 6.9 Bicomponent fiber structure: (a) bilateral, (b) core-sheath, (c) matrix-fibril.

fibrils, tubes, or particles are nano-sized. They are sometimes referred to as nanostructured composite fibers.

The original discovery that the two sides of a fiber react differently when wet was made by studying wool in 1886. In 1953, it was discovered that this behavior was the result of wool's bicomponent nature produced by different growth rates and chemical composition. This differential behavior was the key to producing bilateral bicomponent fibers with latent or inherent crimp.

For example, bilateral acrylic fibers can be spun straight and knit into a sweater. When exposed to heat, one side of the fiber shrinks, creating a helical crimp. The fiber's reaction to water occurs during laundering. As the fiber gets wet, one side swells and the crimp straightens out. As the crimp relaxes, the sweater increases in size. The crimp returns as the sweater dries, and it will regain its original size if properly handled. Sweaters of this type should not be drip-dried or placed on a towel to dry because the weight of the water and the resistance of the towel prevent the sweater from regaining its original size. To dry the sweater correctly, either machine-dry it at a low temperature or place it on a smooth, flat surface and bunch it up to help the crimp recover.

An example of a bicomponent-bigeneric antistatic fiber is a fiber with a polyester core surrounded by a sheath of a polyester copolymer impregnated with carbon nanoparticles. This fiber is used where static can create a potential explosion hazard or where static creates a nuisance. It is used in interior, apparel, and technical applications. Another bicomponent fiber has a core of polyester with an exterior of ethylene vinyl alcohol that promotes cooling. In another example combining polyester and nylon, fadeless brightly colored fibers are produced. The iridescent color observed depends on the viewing angle because of the different optical properties of the two polymers. Applications include formal apparel, embroidery thread, and other fashion end uses.

Composite fibers may incorporate such fillers as clay, metal oxides, and carbon black. Some of these additives were discussed earlier in this chapter. When the fillers are nanosized, the fibers have better performance and potential new applications. Adding clay nanoparticles will produce a strong, composite fiber with high electrical, heat, chemical, and flame resistance and the ability to block ultraviolet light. Nanoparticles of metal oxides in composite fibers produce fibers with antimicrobial, antistatic, and ultraviolet light blocking functions.

Nanostructures in fibers can result in products with lower weight, better insulation, and high cracking resistance. The nanosized voids in the fiber can be filled with medicine, fragrance, or biological agents to protect the wearer. Nanostructures are developed by incorporating organic solvents with low boiling points and supercritical liquids in the polymer melt. When the temperature is raised or the pressure lowered, the tiny drops of liquid expand.

See Chapter 10 for a discussion of blended-filament yarns that are another example of a complex fiber modification.

Performance Fibers Fiber modifications that provide comfort and improve human performance are important in active sportswear. With recent advances in fiber and fabric technology, more efficient materials produce lighter-weight, more comfortable products. Several materials may be combined into one product to manage moisture or wick perspiration away from the skin, to provide warmth or insulation, to decrease friction and increase speed, and to protect from wind, rain, or snow.

The moisture-management material may be a synthetic fiber with good wicking characteristics, like polyester or olefin. An alternative is a fiber with hydrophilic molecules permanently grafted onto the surface that allow for cooling by evaporation during vigorous exercise. Another alternate is embedding nanoparticles in the fiber to produce evaporation cooling. Fiber research and development continues to focus on improving insulation. While fiber insulators build on the principle of trapped air for warmth, advances in fiber size, configuration, and placement have resulted in a variety of products that are soft, breathable, and fashionable. Microfibers provide incredibly warm, soft, and lightweight insulation. These fibers are used in outerwear, pillows, quilts, blankets, sleeping bags, and window treatments to minimize heat transfer. Fabrics made of microfibers with a special finish are waterproof and breathable.

More information on specific fiber performance and trade names is provided in the appropriate sections of Chapters 7, 8, and 9. Finishes that enhance these performance fibers are discussed in Chapter 18. Additional aspects of performance fabrics are discussed in Chapters 12 through 15, with fabrication methods.

Environmental Concerns and Sustainability of Manufactured Fibers

Consumers may criticize manufactured fibers because they are perceived to be harmful to the environment. Although it is true that many synthetic fibers are processed from petroleum sources, they use only a small fraction of the by-products of the production of gasoline and fuel oils. Fibers like nylon, polyester, and olefin are produced from natural gases or from butadiene, a by-product of refining crude oil. Fibers from naturally occurring polymers, like rayon from wood pulp, contribute to excess acid in the air and surface water. Some practices of harvesting trees to be processed into wood pulp—such as clear-cutting timber, cutting old-growth forests, and overharvesting national forests—are criticized by environmentalists.

Concerns with manufactured fibers regarding crude oil and hazardous chemical spills, recycling, health, and safety are real and cannot be ignored or minimized. Government regulations, concern for safety, the economic necessity of reducing costs, and public image concerns have resulted in significant efforts on the part of fiber producers to minimize the negative environmental aspects of fiber production. Modified fiber-production processes use fewer hazardous chemicals and recycle the chemicals. Record-keeping practices document the production and disposal of waste materials. Materials that were disposed of at one time are now recycled within the company or sold to other companies for their use. The generation of hazardous waste and waste-disposal problems has been reduced significantly. Besides minimizing the impact on the environment, these practices reduce costs and benefit the consumer with lower retail prices. Some fiber modifications enhance fiber finishing and further minimize use of hazardous chemicals.

Consumers are also concerned with the disposal of manufactured fibers that do not degrade naturally. Natural fibers will eventually degrade if exposed to nature. However, with current landfill waste-disposal, fibers do not degrade. This is as true for cotton as it is for polyester. Although the concern for synthetics in landfills is valid, consumers should be equally concerned about natural fibers.

Recycling of synthetic fibers is very important to the fiber industry. Polyester fibers produced from preconsumer and postconsumer waste include a range of products from underwear to carpeting. Items with trade names, such as Polartec Recycled, DyerSport E.C.O., and Fortrel EcoSpun, are popular with environmentally conscious consumers. Some products labeled "100 percent recyclable" will be taken back by the manufacturer and recycled when the consumer disposes of them.

Manufactured fibers made from plant materials, like rayon, acetate, lyocell, bamboo, and PLA, are renewable. However, their production raises sustainability concerns. Some synthetic fibers offer a potential for recycling, but additives and other materials present in textile products make recycling more difficult. Watch for sustainability and environmental discussions in Chapters 7, 8, and 9.

Manufactured-Fiber Consumption

In 1928, manufactured fibers accounted for 5 percent of fiber consumption in the United States; now, manufactured fibers comprise over 64 percent of world textile consumption and 83 percent of U.S. textile consumption. See Figure 6.10 to compare consumption of manufactured fibers, cotton, and wool. As new manufactured and synthetic fibers appear on the market, choices expand and performance options grow. Consumers continue to value natural fibers, but in many end uses manufactured fibers are clearly superior and provide textile solutions not possible in the 1920s. Many new technical products and technical applications appear with the development of each new fiber.

Manufactured Versus Natural Fibers

Manufactured fibers provide performance options not possible with natural fibers. These performance options will be discussed in Chapters 7 through 9. It is important to recognize that manufactured fibers are incredibly versatile and modified to meet a wide range of performance expectations. Manufactured fibers also can be produced quickly in the quantity and quality needed to meet demand in the market. A comparison of natural and manufactured fibers is shown in Table 6.3.

> Manufactured fibers comprise over 64 percent of world textile consumption and 83 percent of U.S. textile consumption.

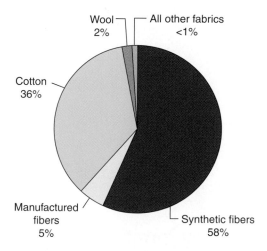

Figure 6.10 Worldwide fiber production.

SOURCE: Data from Fiber Economics Bureau of the American Fiber Manufacturing Association.

Table 6.3 Comparison of Natural and Manufactured Fibers

Category	Natural	Manufactured
Production	Seasonal; stored until used	Continuous
Quality	Varies due to weather, nutrients, type, insects, or disease	Uniform
Uniformity	Lacking	Can be manipulated depending on end use
Physical structure	Related to plant or animal source	Depends on fiber-spinning processes and after-treatments
Chemical composition	Varies with plant or animal source	Depends on starting materials and molecular structure
Properties	Inherent; but can be changed by yarn, fabrication, or finishes	Inherent; but can be changed by varying spinning dope and conditions, yarn, fabrication, or finishes
Length	Mostly staple; silk is the only filament	Any length
Versatility	Not as versatile	Versatile; changes can be made quickly
Absorbency	Highly absorbent	Absorbency related to fiber chemistry or modification
Heat sensitivity	Not heat sensitive	Many are heat-sensitive, but some are heat-resistant
Heat settability	Requires fabric finish	Many can be heat-set
Research, development	By trade organizations	By individual companies as well as by trade and promotion organizations
Size	Depends on type and variety	Any size can be produced

SOURCE: Courtesy of the Fiber Economics Bureau, a division of the American Fiber Manufacturers Association.

▶ Learning Activity 7

Use Table 6.3 and make a list of the positive and negative aspects of natural and manufactured fibers. Is one group better than the other? Explain why you answered as you did.

key terms

Antibacterial fibers   121
Antimicrobial fibers   121
Antistatic fibers   120
Bicomponent-bigeneric fiber   122
Bicomponent fiber   122
Binder staple   119
Bright fibers   119
Cross-dyeable fibers   120
Deluster   119
Electrospinning   126
Extrusion   114
Fiber additives   119
Fiber modification   116
Fiber spinning   114
Filament fiber   115

Filament tow   115
Filament yarn   115
Flame-resistant fibers   121
Generic name   112
High-tenacity fibers   119
Hollow or multicellular fibers   118
Low-elongation modifications   119
Low-pilling fibers   119
Macrofiber   117
Manufactured fiber   112
Mass pigmentation   120
Melt   114
Microfiber   117

Mixed-denier filament bundling   117
Nanofiber   117
Parent fiber   116
Shape memory fibers   119
Shin-gosen   117
Solution dyeing   120
Spinneret   114
Spinning solution or dope   114
Sunlight resistance   121
Thick-and-thin fibers   118
Trade names   112
Trilobal shape   118
Ultrafine fiber   117
Whiteners or brighteners   120

review questions

1. Explain, in general terms, how a manufactured fiber is produced.

2. How can properties and characteristics of manufactured fibers be manipulated? Why is this not possible or more difficult with natural fibers?

3. What are the three most common spinning methods used to produce manufactured fibers? Explain briefly how they differ and give an example of an apparel or interiors fiber produced by each of these methods.

4. What characteristics of manufactured fibers can be modified? Identify an end use that would benefit from each modification. How are these modifications achieved?

5. Do fiber modifications reduce fiber performance in any area? If so, what are the modifications that produce problems? What are the problems produced?

6. What modifications would be appropriate for each end use listed below? Explain how these modifications would enhance performance.
   a. Carpeting for restaurant floor
   b. Window treatment for office building
   c. Woman's slip
   d. Ski coat
   e. Fiberfill for quilt batting
   f. Tow rope

7. Explain the differences among macro-, micro-, ultrafine, and nanofibers.

8. Explain the difference between a generic fiber and a trade name. Give an example of each. How are these terms used to market textile products?

9. Explain the differences and similarities between these pairs of terms:
   a. Solution dyeing and cross-dyeable
   b. Bright fiber and brightened fiber
   c. Sunlight resistant and flame resistant
   d. Generic fiber and bigeneric fiber

10. Why are manufactured fibers produced as filaments and sometimes cut into staple?

Case Study
Brand Logos and Counterfeiting*

Counterfeiting is copying exact or nearly exact designs and materials to sell at lower prices. Counterfeiting of textiles and textile products has occurred for decades, costing retailers, designers, and manufacturers millions of dollars of lost revenue. A company that provides custom-designed covert marking systems has developed a method for embedding a brand logo or other information within a fiber. (See Figure 6.11.) The mark is claimed to be permanent. Company detectors and software can read the marks by scanning an area of the textile product, such as a seam.

The process uses bicomponent and Sea Island matrix technology used to produce microfibers. The logo is incorporated throughout the length of the fiber and appears on the cross section. These synthetic fibers of 10–30 microns can be incorporated in sewing or embroidery thread or periodically woven into the fabric. The fibers may be blended with other fibers.

DISCUSSION QUESTIONS

1. Describe how this development would reduce counterfeiting and why it is important to the global textile complex.

2. How does the fiber size described here relate to apparel and interior textiles? (You might have to explore information in other fiber chapters.)

3. Explain how this development would fit within the main categories of this chapter: fiber spinneret modification, molecular structure and crystallinity modification, additive to the polymer or spinning solution, modification of fiber spinning, or complex modification.

*Rodie, J. B. (2007, November/December). Marked for authenticity. *Textile World News* (www.textileworld.com).

Figure 6.11 A company logo embedded in the fibers to reduce counterfeiting.

SOURCE: ARmark™ Authentication Technologies LLC.

suggested readings

Anonymous. (1998, August). Fiber makers top 130. *Textile World*, pp. 69–98.

Colchester, C. (2007). *Textiles Today: A Global Survey of Trends and Traditions*. New York: Thames & Hudson.

Fletcher, K. (2008). *Sustainable Fashion and Textiles: Design Journey*. London: Earthscan.

Hethorn, J., & Ulasewicz, C. (2008). *Sustainable Fashion: Why Now?* New York: Fairchild Books.

Holme, I. (2008, May/June). Nanosurfaces gain ground. *Textile Horizons*, p. 13.

Holme, I. (2005, January). Nanotechnologies for textiles, clothing, and footwear. *Textile Magazine*, 7–11.

Karst, D., & Yang, Y. (2006), Potential advantages and risks of nanotechnology for textiles. *AATCC Review, 6*(3), 44–48.

Lenox-Kerr, P. (1998, November). How to make filaments with intrinsic crimp. *Technical Textiles International*, pp. 22–24.

McCurry, J. W. (1996, August). Stretch, durability, and style among fiber trends. *Textile World*, pp. 39–46.

Patanaik, A., Anandjiwala, R. D., Rengasamy, R. S., Ghosh, A., & Pal, H. (2007). Nanotechnology in fibrous materials: A new perspective. *Textile Progress, 39*(2), 67–120.

Qian, L. (2004). Nanotechnology in textiles: Recent development and future prospects, *AATCC Review, 4*(5), 14–16.

Rawnitzkey, M. (1994, September). How synthetics became real. *Industrial Fabric Products Review*, pp. 49–50, 52, 54.

Reichard, R. S. (2008). Textiles 2008: Blueprint for survival. *Textile World, 158*(1), 22–32.

Rodie, J. B. (2007, November/December). Marked for authenticity. *Textile World News* (www.textileworld.com).

Roshan, P., & Roshan, S. P. (2005). Electrospinning: A breakthrough technology. *The Textile Journal, 122*(1), 14–16.

Rupp, J. (2008, November/December). Man-made fibers: New attitude. *Textile World News* (www.textileworld.com).

Thiry, M. C. (2007). Small scale: Huge potential. *AATCC Review, 7*(6), 22–27.

Wei, Q., Mather, R., Ye, F., Huang, F., & Xu, W. (2005, December). The functionalization of the surface of polymer nanofibres. *Technical Textiles International,* pp. 21–23.

Williams, J. F., & Cho, U. (2005). Antimicrobial functions for synthetic fibers: Recent developments. *AATCC Review, 5*(4), 17–21.

MANUFACTURED REGENERATED FIBERS

CHAPTER OBJECTIVES

- To understand the processes used to produce manufactured regenerated fibers.
- To know the properties of rayon, lyocell, acetate, and other regenerated fibers.
- To relate fiber properties to end uses for rayon, lyocell, acetate, and other regenerated fibers.

7

Manufactured regenerated fibers or regenerated fibers are produced from naturally occurring polymers of cellulose or protein, but processing is needed to convert them into fiber form.

Manufactured regenerated fibers or regenerated fibers are produced from naturally occurring polymers. These polymers do not occur naturally as fibers; processing is needed to convert them into fiber form. The starting materials for these fibers are cellulose and protein. The majority of this chapter will focus on the cellulosic fibers—rayon, lyocell, and acetate—which are used in apparel, interiors, and technical products. Regenerated fibers made from protein are discussed at the end of the chapter.

Cellulosic Regenerated Fibers

Rayon

Rayon was the first regenerated cellulosic fiber and many processes were developed. A few of these continue today. It was developed before scientists knew how molecular chains were developed in nature or how they could be produced in the laboratory. Frederick Schoenbein discovered in 1846 that *cellulose* pretreated with nitric acid would dissolve in a mixture of ether and alcohol, but the resulting fiber was highly explosive. In 1889 in France, Count Hilaire de Chardonnet made rayon by changing the nitrocellulosic fiber back to cellulose. This dangerous and difficult process was discontinued in 1949.

In 1890, Louis Despeissis discovered that cellulose would dissolve in a cuprammonium solution, and in 1919 J. P. Bemberg made a commercially successful cuprammonium rayon. In 1891, in England, Cross, Bevan, and Beadle developed the viscose method.

Commercial production of viscose rayon in the United States began in 1910. The fiber was sold as artificial silk until the name *rayon* was adopted in 1924. Viscose filament fiber, the fiber's original form, was a brightly lustrous fiber. Rayon was only produced as a filament until the early 1930s, when a textile worker discovered that broken waste rayon filament could be used as staple fiber. In 1932, machinery was designed to crimp filament tow and cut it into staple fiber. Rayon was originally used in crepe and linenlike apparel fabrics. The high-twist crepe yarns reduced the rayon's bright luster. Other early rayon fabrics included transparent velvet, sharkskin, tweed, challis, and chiffon.

Commercial production of viscose and cuprammonium rayon continues. Regular rayon produced in the United States is a *viscose rayon*. Some imported rayon is labeled viscose, and rayon made using the *cuprammonium process* may be labeled as *cupra rayon* under the trade name Bemberg®.

The physical properties of rayon remained unchanged until 1940, when high-tenacity (HT) rayon was developed. Zinc added to the spinning bath slowed polymer regeneration while the fiber was drawn, thus increasing orientation and crystallinity. Continued research led to high-wet-modulus rayon. Production in the United States started in 1955.

High-wet-modulus or HWM rayon has different characteristics from regular or viscose rayon. While HWM rayon is a viscose rayon, in common usage, *viscose rayon* refers to the weaker fiber. HWM rayon is also called high-performance (HP) rayon, or polynosic rayon, and some products may be labeled *polynosic* or *modal* rather than rayon. A few labels describe modal rayon as beech wood fiber. Beech is a fast-growing softwood tree often harvested from managed timbers or woodlands.

Production of rayon is not expected to increase significantly because of the high cost of replacement machinery and the cost of wet spinning. Rayon is no longer the inexpensive fiber it once was—now it is comparable in price to cotton.

Table 7.1 Spinning Process for Viscose and HWM Rayon

Regular or Viscose		High-Wet-Modulus
1. Blotterlike sheets of purified cellulose		1. Blotterlike sheets of purified cellulose
2. Steeped in caustic soda (a strong alkali)		2. Steeped in weaker caustic soda
3. Liquid squeezed out by rollers		3. Liquid squeezed out by rollers
4. Shredder crumbles sheets		4. Shredder crumbles sheets
5. Aged 50 hours		5. No aging
6. Treated with carbon disulfide to form cellulose xanthate, 32% CS_2		6. Treated with carbon disulfide to form cellulose xanthate, 39–50% CS_2
7. Mixed with caustic soda to form viscose solution		7. Mixed with 2.8% sodium hydroxide to form viscose solution
8. Solution aged 4–5 days		8. No aging
9. Solution filtered		9. Solution filtered
10. Pumped to spinneret and extruded into acid bath		10. Pumped to spinneret and extruded into acid bath
10% H_2SO_4	Spinning bath	1% H_2SO_4
16–24% Na_2SO_4		4–6% Na_2SO_4
1–2% $ZnSO_4$		
120 meters/minute	Spinning speed	20–30 meters/minute
45–50°C	Spinning bath temperature	25–35°C
25%	Filaments stretched	150–600%

Production of Rayon Wet spinning is the most common method of producing rayon. Purified cellulose is chemically converted to a viscous solution, forced through spinnerets into a bath, and returned to solid 100 percent cellulose filaments (see Figure 6.2). Table 7.1 compares the processes for making **viscose rayon** (regular rayon) and high-wet-modulus rayon. Process differences produce fibers with different properties. The high-wet-modulus process maximizes chain length and fibril structure.

Physical Structure of Rayon Regular viscose is characterized by lengthwise lines called striations. The cross section is a serrated or indented circular shape (Figure 7.1) that develops from loss of solvent during coagulation and subsequent collapse of the cross section. This serrated shape is an advantage in dyeing because it increases the fiber's surface area. HWM and cupra rayons have rounder cross sections.

Filament rayon yarns range from 80 to 980 filaments per yarn and vary in size from 40 to 5000 denier. Staple fibers and tow range from 1.5 to 15 denier. Micro rayon fibers are also available. Staple fibers are crimped mechanically or chemically. Rayon fibers are naturally very bright, which limits use to more formal apparel and interior textile items. Use of delustering pigments (see Chapter 6) solves this problem. Solution-dyed fibers are also available.

Chemical Composition and Molecular Arrangement of Rayon

Rayon—a manufactured fiber composed of regenerated cellulose, as well as manufactured fibers composed of regenerated cellulose in which substituents have replaced not more than 15 percent of the hydrogens of the hydroxyl groups.

—*Federal Trade Commission*

Rayon is a manufactured fiber composed of regenerated cellulose.

Table 7.2 Comparison of Cotton, Rayon, and Lyocell

Properties	Cotton	Regular Rayon	HWM Rayon	Lyocell
Fibrils	Yes	No	Yes	Yes
Molecular chain length	10,000	300–450	450–750	—
Swelling in water, %	6	26	18	—
Average stiffness	57–60	6–50	28–75	30
Tenacity, grams/denier				
Dry	4.0	1.0–2.5	2.5–5.0	4.3–4.7
Wet	5.0	0.5–1.4	3.0	3.8–4.2
Breaking elongation, %	3–7	8–14	9–18	14–16

Rayon is 100 percent cellulose and has the same chemical composition and molecular structure as the natural cellulose found in cotton or flax, except that the rayon polymer chains are shorter and less crystalline. Because it is manufactured, rayon does not have the cellular structure that is found in the natural fibers. Cellulose from the wood pulp breaks down during the aging steps in rayon production, shortening the polymer chains. When the solution is spun into the acid bath, regeneration and coagulation take place rapidly. Stretching aligns the molecules to give strength to the filaments. In high-wet-modulus rayon, aging is eliminated, resulting in slightly longer molecular chains. Because the acid bath is less concentrated, there is slower regeneration and coagulation to achieve more stretch and greater molecular orientation. Since HWM rayon retains its microfibrilar structure, its performance is more similar to that of cotton than to that of regular rayon. Table 7.2 compares cotton with the rayons.

Properties of Rayon Rayon fibers are highly absorbent, soft, comfortable, easy to dye, and versatile. Fabrics made of rayon have a unique soft drape that designers love for apparel and interior textiles. Rayon has many technical applications, too. Table 7.3 summarizes rayon's performance in apparel and interior textiles. Review the tables in Chapter 3 to compare the performance of rayon to that of the other fibers.

Aesthetics Since its luster, length, and diameter can be controlled, rayon can be made into fabrics that resemble cotton, linen, wool, and silk. Rayon can be engineered with physical characteristics similar to those of other fibers in a blend. If it is used instead of cotton or blended with cotton, rayon can simulate the look and length of mercerized long-staple cotton. Rayon has an attractive, soft, fluid drape. Sizing may be added to increase the body and hand. Cupra rayon has a more silklike hand and luster and may be found in smaller deniers.

Durability Regular rayon is a weak fiber that loses about 50 percent of its strength when wet. The breaking tenacity is 1.0 to 2.5 g/d. Rayon has a breaking elongation of 8 to 14 percent dry and 20 percent wet; rayon will stretch slightly before breaking and is more sensitive to damage when wet. It has the lowest elastic recovery of any fiber, meaning that products tend to stretch out in areas of stress and do not recover well when the stress is removed. All of these factors are due to the amorphous regions in the fiber. Water readily enters the amorphous areas, causing the molecular chains to separate as the fiber swells, breaking the hydrogen bonds and distorting the chains. When water is removed, new hydrogen bonds form, but in a distorted state. Cupra rayon is not as strong as HWM rayon, but it is stronger than viscose rayon.

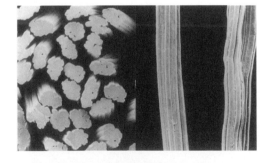

Figure 7.1 Photomicrographs of viscose rayon: cross-sectional view (left), longitudinal view (right).
SOURCE: Courtesy of the British Textile Technology Group.

Table 7.3 Summary of the Performance of Rayon in Apparel and Interior Textiles

	Regular Rayon	HWM Rayon
Aesthetics	Variable	Variable
Durability	Poor	Moderate
Abrasion resistance	Poor	Moderate
Tenacity	Poor	Moderate
Elongation	Moderate	Poor
Comfort	Excellent	Excellent
Absorbency	High	Excellent
Thermal retention	Poor	Poor
Appearance Retention	Poor	Moderate
Resiliency	Poor	Poor
Dimensional stability	Poor	Moderate
Elastic recovery	Poor	Moderate
Recommended Care	Dry-clean	Machine-wash
		Dry-clean

HWM rayon has a more crystalline and oriented structure so that the dry fiber is relatively strong. It has a breaking tenacity of 2.5 to 5.0 g/d, a breaking elongation of 9 to 18 percent dry and 20 percent wet, and an elastic recovery greater than that of cotton.

Comfort Rayon makes very comfortable, smooth, soft fabrics that are not irritating to the skin. Rayon is absorbent, with a moisture regain of 11.5 to 12.5 percent that eliminates static except under extreme conditions. Thermal retention is low, meaning that rayon is good for warm-weather wear, but not as good for cold-weather wear.

Appearance Retention The resiliency of rayon is low. This can be improved in HWM rayon fabrics by adding a wrinkle-resistant finish, but with a loss of strength and abrasion resistance. The dimensional stability of regular rayon is low. Fabrics may shrink or stretch and have low elastic recovery. The performance of HWM rayon is better. It exhibits moderate dimensional stability that can be improved by shrinkage-control finishes. The fiber is less likely to stretch out of shape and has moderate elastic recovery.

Care Regular rayon fabrics have limited washability because of their low strength when wet. Unless rayon fabrics are resin-treated, they have a tendency to shrink progressively. Most regular rayon fabrics should be dry-cleaned. Another reason to dry-clean rayon is the use of sizing during finishing to increase fabric body and hand that water-spot or streak after wetting with water.

The HWM rayon fabrics have greater washability. Their stability and strength are equal to that of cotton. They can be mercerized and finished to minimize shrinkage. They also wrinkle less than regular rayon in washing and drying.

The care of interior textiles of rayon or rayon blends poses some real problems. Although many items can be cleaned with water-based compounds, the lack of labels on many interior

Rayon was first introduced to consumers as an artificial silk fiber. Compare the similarities and difference in serviceability between silk and rayon. What were the factors that made artificial silk successful in the market in the early twentieth century?

textiles makes this a gamble. Items may shrink, water-spot, or lose color when cleaned. Manufacturers and suppliers of interior textiles rarely distinguish among regular or HWM rayons, making it difficult for professionals to recommend appropriate care for these products. Thus, as a general recommendation, rayon interior textiles should be cleaned when necessary, but with the understanding that the results may not be completely satisfactory.

The chemical properties of rayon are similar to those of the other cellulosic fibers. They are harmed by acids, resistant to dilute alkalis, and not affected by organic solvents. They can be safely dry-cleaned. Rayon may be damaged by silverfish and mildew. Rayon is not greatly harmed by sunlight. Since it is not thermoplastic, it can withstand high-temperature pressing. Rayon burns readily like cotton.

Environmental Concerns and Sustainability of Rayon Although rayon is produced from a naturally occurring polymer, significant processing is needed to produce a usable fiber. Most rayon is produced from wood pulp from fast-growing softwood trees. Some of the wood is harvested from tree farms located on marginal agricultural land. However, other wood used to produce rayon is cut from mature forests. Environmental issues related to cutting trees include clear-cutting—all trees in an area are cut, with no trees remaining to hold soil and provide a habitat for birds, animals, insects, and other plants; cutting old-growth forests that may provide habitat for endangered species; and harvesting trees in national forests at minimal cost to lumber companies.

Processing wood pulp uses large quantities of acid and other chemicals that may contribute to water and air pollution. While the process may be described as carbon neutral (the plants' growing cycle absorbs an equal amount of carbon dioxide as is lost at harvest), air emissions of sulfur, nitrous oxides, carbon disulfide, and hydrogen sulfide produce high pollution indices if discharged without treatment. Water emissions include organic matter, nitrates, phosphates, iron, zinc, oil, and grease. The water is low in dissolved oxygen, creating problems for aquatic life.

Regulations for air and water quality have changed how some rayon is produced. Cuprammonium rayon is no longer made in the United States because producers could not meet water- and air-quality requirements. The chemicals used to process rayon into fiber and to clean it after extrusion are sometimes recovered and recycled, but these additional steps are costly to perform and monitor. Producers have reduced pollutant emissions like hydrogen sulfide and carbon disulfide, decreased wastewater effluent, and use closed chemical systems so that up to 99 percent of the waste liquor can be recovered.

Sustainable alternatives include lyocell or rayon made from managed forests, rayon processed without chlorine-containing bleach, zinc sulfate, and catalytic chemicals containing cobalt or manganese.

Rayon, a regenerated cellulose fiber, is biodegradable. However, current landfill practices prevent natural degradation of buried materials. Rayon is not generally recycled. Since rayon fibers are used in many sanitary products, including disposable diapers, disposal of these products is an issue. Producing consumer goods from rayon makes extensive use of water, dyes, and finishing chemicals. Depending on how items have been finished, they may require dry cleaning. Solvents used in dry cleaning present additional hazards to the environment. See Chapter 20 for more information on dry cleaning.

Uses of Rayon Rayon is mostly used in woven fabrics, especially in apparel and interior textiles such as draperies and upholstery. Rayon also is used in nonwoven fabrics where absorbency is important. These items include technical wipes and medical supplies, including bandages, diapers, and sanitary napkins and tampons. Hollow cuprammonium rayon is used in dialysis machines to filter waste products from blood.

Types and Kinds of Rayon The only way to determine a specific type of rayon is by the trade name, such as Modal or Bemberg. Unfortunately, trade names for rayon are seldom used as a marketing tool with consumers. Besides HWM rayons, other types include solution-dyed, modified cross section, intermediate- or high-tenacity, optically brightened, high absorbency, hollow, and microfibers. In addition, there are several flame-retardant rayons, including Visil rayon, which contains silica. It is used for interior textiles for which stringent flammability standards exist and for protective apparel.

Lyocell

The development of **lyocell** was prompted in part by concern about rayon's negative environmental impact. When first introduced in the early 1990s, lyocell was marketed as a type of rayon, but now it is a separate generic fiber. Lyocell is produced in both Europe and the United States.

Production of Lyocell Wet spinning is used to produce lyocell (Figure 7.2; and see Figure 6.2). The cellulose polymer is dissolved in a liquid, amine oxide, and spun into a weak bath of amine oxide rather than a weak acid bath as for rayon. Amine oxide, a solvent with low toxicity and low skin irritation, dissolves the cellulose in wood pulp without changing the nature of the cellulose. After spinning, the fiber is washed and dried. The solvent is recovered, purified, and recycled. This process results in a fiber that is more like cotton than any other manufactured fiber. Table 7.2 compares the properties of cotton, rayon, and lyocell.

Physical Structure of Lyocell Lyocell does not collapse on itself as rayon does and has a more rounded cross section and smoother longitudinal appearance (Figure 7.3). Lyocell is available in a variety of deniers and lengths. Filament yarns are available in various numbers of filaments per yarn, depending on end use. Staple fibers and tow range from less than 1.0 to 15 denier per filament and are mechanically crimped for use in blends and other staple fiber products.

Chemical Composition and Molecular Arrangement of Lyocell

Lyocell—a manufactured fiber composed of solvent-spun cellulose.

—*Federal Trade Commission*

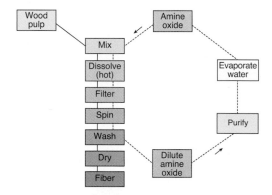

Figure 7.2 **Wet spinning process for lyocell.**
SOURCE: Courtesy of Lenzing Fibers.

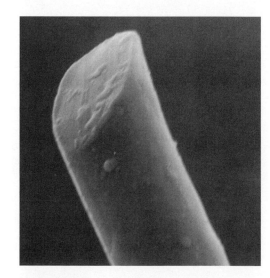

Figure 7.3 **Photomicrograph of lyocell.**
SOURCE: Courtesy of Lenzing Fibers.

Lyocell is 100 percent cellulose, with the same chemical composition and molecular structure as that found in natural cellulose, but without the cell structure of the natural plant fibers. The polymer chain length is longer than that of rayon, but not as long as that of cotton. Drawing the fibers after spinning increases the orientation and crystallinity and makes lyocell more durable.

Properties of Lyocell The properties of lyocell fibers are more like those of cotton than any of the other regenerated cellulose fibers. Lyocell fabrics possess a soft, flowing drape that attracts designers. Lyocell is used in apparel, interior, and technical products. Table 7.4 summarizes lyocell's performance in apparel and interior textiles. Compare the performance of lyocell with that of the other fibers as presented in the tables in Chapter 3.

Aesthetics As with all manufactured fibers, the luster, length, and diameter of lyocell can be varied depending on the end use. Lyocell can be used by itself or blended with any natural or manufactured fiber. It can be processed in a variety of fabrications and finishes to produce a range of surface effects. With its ability to fibrillate under certain conditions, lyocell offers unusual combinations of strength, opacity, and absorbency.

Durability Lyocell performs more like cotton than rayon. The strongest of the cellulosic fibers, its breaking tenacity is 4.8 to 5.0 g/d dry and 4.2 to 4.6 g/d wet, only a 12 percent loss in strength. Its dry breaking elongation is 14 to 16 percent, and its wet elongation is 16 to 18 percent. Because of its unique combination of soft hand and good durability characteristics, it produces comfortable, long-lasting apparel and interiors. Its high strength, especially when wet, offers some unusual possibilities for wet processing and finishing. Applications that require high wet strength are ideal for lyocell. When abraded, its tendency to fibrillate (split lengthwise into tiny fibrils) produces a fuzzy, hairy texture that is distracting on smooth fabrics.

Comfort Lyocell is another soft, smooth fiber that makes comfortable apparel and interiors. With a regain of 11.5 percent, problems with static are not likely. Its soft hand and high absorbency make lyocell ideal for apparel that comes in contact with the skin and in interior textiles. As with all other cellulosic fibers, thermal retention is poor.

Table 7.4 Summary of the Performance of Lyocell in Apparel and Interior Textiles

Aesthetics	Variable
Durability	Good
Abrasion resistance	Good
Tenacity	Good
Elongation	Poor
Comfort	Excellent
Absorbency	Excellent
Thermal retention	Poor
Appearance Retention	Moderate
Resiliency	Moderate
Dimensional stability	Good
Recommended Care	Dry-clean or machine-wash, gentle

Appearance Retention Lyocell's resiliency is moderate; it will wrinkle, but not as severely as rayon. The dimensional stability of lyocell is good. It shrinks, but it does not exhibit the progressive shrinkage of some regular rayons. Its tendency to fibrillate with abrasion may create problems with fuzziness, pilling, or other surface changes over time. Elastic recovery is superior to rayon and acetate.

Care Products made of lyocell can be either machine-washed on a gentle cycle or dry-cleaned. Abrasion from machine-washing of dark or intensely colored lyocell fabrics may produce an unacceptable alteration of hand and irregular color. Gentle agitation minimizes this problem. Dry cleaning is successful and does not alter the color or hand that may occur with machine washing.

Lyocell is sensitive to acids and resistant to dilute alkalis and most organic solvents. Because of its cellulosic nature, lyocell is sensitive to damage by mildew and some insects.

Environmental Concerns and Sustainability of Lyocell

Lyocell is produced from wood pulp and spun into a solvent bath in a closed-loop manufacturing process that recovers and reprocesses 99.5 percent of the amine oxide solvent, a nontoxic, noncorrosive chemical. The chemicals used for the production of lyocell are significantly less hazardous to the environment than those used for the production of viscose rayon. Because the solvent is recycled efficiently and the wood is harvested from fast-growing eucalyptus trees farmed for this end use, lyocell is more environmentally friendly than rayon and acetate.

The cellulose of lyocell is biodegradable. If the fiber is disposed of in landfills, however, it will not degrade. Lyocell is not recycled. As with the other cellulosic fibers, producing consumer goods from lyocell makes extensive use of water, dyes, and finishing chemicals. Depending on how items have been finished, they may require dry cleaning. Solvents used in dry cleaning present additional hazards to the environment. See Chapter 20 for more information on dry cleaning.

Uses of Lyocell

Lyocell, more expensive per pound compared to viscose rayon, is found in a variety of products: professional business wear, leotards, hosiery, casual wear, upholstery, and window-treatment fabrics. It is used in blends with wool, cotton, and other manufactured fibers. In manufacturing of glass and other items, lyocell is used in conveyer belts because of its strength and softness. In a fibrillated form, lyocell is used for filters, printers' blankets, specialty papers, and medical dressings.

Types and Kinds of Lyocell

Because lyocell is a relatively new fiber, there are fewer modifications available for lyocell as compared with the number of modifications for other manufactured fibers. As the fiber gains market share, more modifications are expected. Current modifications related to fiber size and length enable it to be blended with other fibers. A cross-linked lyocell, Tencel 100A, exhibits significantly fewer problems with fibrillation.

> ## ▶ Learning Activity 3
>
> Compare the production processes for rayon and lyocell in terms of sustainability and environmental concerns. Is one of these two fibers more sustainable? If yes, explain your choice.

Compare and contrast the production and serviceability of viscose rayon and lyocell. Identify an end use for these two fibers and explain why each fiber is appropriate for that end use.

Acetate

Acetate originated in Europe. Using a technique that produced a spinning solution for a silk-like fiber, the Dreyfus brothers experimented with acetate in Switzerland. They went to England during World War I and perfected the acetate dope as a varnish for airplane wings. After the war, they perfected the process of making acetate fibers. In 1924, acetate became the second manufactured fiber to be produced in the United States.

More problems had to be solved with the acetate process than with the rayon processes. Acetate is a different chemical compound. Primary acetate (**triacetate**) contains no hydroxyl groups; modified or secondary acetate (acetate fiber) has only a few hydroxyl groups. Because of the unique chemistry of the fibers, they could not be dyed with any existing dyes. Disperse dyes were developed especially for acetate and triacetate.

Acetate was the first **thermoplastic**, or **heat-sensitive fiber**. Consumers were confronted with fabrics that melted under a hot iron—something they had never experienced before. This was at a time when consumers were accustomed to ironing all apparel. The problem was further compounded when manufacturers introduced acetate as a kind of rayon.

Still another problem with acetate was **fume or pollution fading**—a condition in which certain disperse dyes changed color (blue to pink, green to brown, gray to pink) when exposed to atmospheric fumes, now referred to as atmospheric pollutants. Solution-dyeing corrected this problem and is used for many manufactured fibers. In 1955, an inhibitor greatly improved dye performance under all conditions that cause fading. However, fume or pollution fading continues to be a problem.

Production of Acetate The basic steps in the acetate manufacturing process are listed in Table 7.5. Triacetate was produced until the end of 1986, when the last triacetate plant was closed because the Environmental Protection Agency (EPA) banned use of the solvent methylene chloride. Some triacetate is imported into the United States, so it is important to know that triacetate is a thermoplastic fiber. It can be heat-set for resiliency and dimensional stability and is machine-washable.

Table 7.5 Acetate Manufacturing Process

1. Purified cellulose from wood pulp or cotton linters
2. Mixed with glacial acetic acid, acetic anhydride, and a catalyst
3. Aged 20 hours—partial hydrolysis occurs
4. Precipitated as acid-resin flakes
5. Flakes dissolved in acetone
6. Solution is filtered
7. Spinning solution extruded in column of warm air; solvent recovered
8. Filaments are stretched and wound onto beams, cones, or bobbins ready for use

Physical Structure of Acetate Acetate is available as staple or filament. Much more filament is produced because it gives a silklike look. Staple fibers are crimped and usually blended with other fibers. The cross section of acetate is lobular or flower petal–shaped. The shape results as solvent evaporates when the fiber solidifies in spinning. Notice in Figure 7.4 that the lobes may appear as a false lumen. The cross-sectional shape can be varied. Flat filaments give glitter to fabrics.

Chemical Composition and Molecular Arrangement of Acetate

Acetate—a manufactured fiber in which the fiber-forming substance is cellulose acetate. Where not less than 92 percent of the hydroxyl groups are acetylated, the term triacetate may be used as a generic description of the fiber.

—Federal Trade Commission

Acetate, an ester of cellulose, has a different chemical structure from rayon or cotton. In acetate, two hydroxyl groups are replaced by bulky acetyl groups (see Figure 7.5) that prevent highly crystalline areas. There is less attraction between the molecular chains due to a lack of hydrogen bonding. Water molecules do not penetrate as readily, contributing to acetate's lower absorbency and dye affinity. Acetate is thermoplastic.

Properties of Acetate Acetate has a combination of properties that make it a valuable textile fiber. It is low in cost and has good draping qualities. Table 7.6 summarizes acetate's performance in apparel and interior textiles. Reviewing the tables in Chapter 3 will help in comparing the performance of acetate with that of the other fibers.

Aesthetics Acetate has been promoted as a beauty fiber. It is widely used in satins, brocades, and taffetas, in which fabric luster, body, drape, and beauty are more important than durability or ease of care. Acetate maintains a good white color, an advantage over silk.

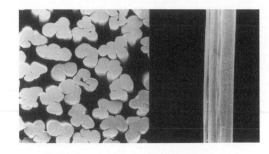

Figure 7.4 Photomicrographs of acetate fiber: cross-sectional view (left), longitudinal view (right).
SOURCE: Courtesy of the British Textile Technology Group.

Glucose → Acetate

Figure 7.5 Chemical structure of acetate.

Acetate is a manufactured fiber in which the fiber-forming substance is cellulose acetate.

Table 7.6 Summary of the Performance of Acetate in Apparel and Interior Textiles

Aesthetics	Excellent
Luster	High
Drape	High
Texture	Smooth
Hand	Smooth
Durability	Poor
Abrasion resistance	Poor
Tenacity	Poor
Elongation	Moderate
Comfort	Moderate
Absorbency	Moderate
Thermal retention	Moderate
Appearance Retention	Poor
Resiliency	Poor
Dimensional stability	Moderate
Elastic recovery	Poor
Recommended Care	Dry-clean

Durability Acetate is a weak fiber, with a breaking tenacity of 1.2 to 1.4 g/d. It loses some strength when wet. Other weak fibers have some compensating factor, such as wool's good elastic recovery or rayon's high absorbancy, but acetate does not. Acetate has a breaking elongation of 25 percent. Since acetate has poor resistance to abrasion, a small percentage of nylon is sometimes combined with acetate to produce a stronger fabric.

Comfort Bcause acetate is smooth and slick, it is often used for linings for coats and jackets, making them easier to put on over long-sleeved shirts and blouses and adding a finished look to the garment. Acetate has a moisture regain of 6.3 to 6.5 percent and is subject to static buildup. The fiber is extremely soft, with no allergenic potential. Thermal retention is poor.

Appearance Retention Acetate fabrics are not very resilient and wrinkle during use. Wrinkles from washing are extremely difficult to remove—even with a hot iron. Acetate has moderate dimensional stability. The fibers are weaker when wet and can be shrunk by excess heat. Elastic recovery is low, 58 percent, so areas of stress do not recover well.

Care Acetate should be dry-cleaned unless other care procedures are identified on the care label. Acetate is resistant to weak acids and to alkalis. It can be bleached with hypochlorite or peroxide bleaches, but these are seldom used in the home. Acetate is soluble in acetone. Acetate cannot be heat-set at a temperature high enough to give permanent shape to fabrics or a durable embossed effect.

Acetate is thermoplastic and heat-sensitive; it becomes sticky at low ironing temperatures (177 to 191°C, 350 to 375°F) and melts at 230°C (446°F). Triacetate has a higher melting point than acetate.

Acetate has better sunlight resistance than silk or nylon but less than the cellulose fibers. It is resistant to moths, mildew, and bacteria.

Comparison with Rayon

Rayon and acetate are the two oldest manufactured fibers and have been produced in large quantities, filling an important need for less-expensive fibers in the textile complex. They lack the easy care, resilience, and strength of the synthetics and have had difficulty competing in uses for which these characteristics are important. Rayon and acetate have some similarities because they are made from the same raw material, cellulose. The manufacturing processes differ, so the fibers differ in their individual characteristics and uses. Table 7.7 compares rayon, lyocell, and acetate.

Environmental Concerns and Sustainability of Acetate

Acetate is produced from cellulose and requires a significant amount of processing to produce a usable fiber. The same concerns identified in the discussion of rayon apply to the wood pulp used to produce acetate. Because acetate is dry-spun, it is easier for producers to reclaim and reuse the solvent. With current environmental regulations and economic pressures, solvent recovery and reuse is standard practice in the production of acetate. Acetate fiber is less likely to degrade naturally as compared with rayon and is not recycled. Acetate is usually dyed with disperse dyes that require special chemical carriers during dyeing. Acetate items usually require dry cleaning. The solvents

Table 7.7 Comparison of Rayon, Lyocell, and Acetate

Rayon (Viscose)	Lyocell	Acetate
Wet-spun	Solvent-spun	Dry-spun
Regenerated cellulose	Regenerated cellulose	Chemical derivative of cellulose
Serrated cross section	Rounded cross section	Lobular cross section
More staple produced	Staple and filament produced	More filament produced
Scorches	Scorches	Melts
High absorbency (12.5%)	High absorbency (11.5%)	Fair absorbency (6.4%)
No static	No static	Static
Ignites quickly, burns readily	Ignites quickly, burns readily	May initially shrink from flame, burns quickly, may drip
Not soluble in acetone	Not soluble in acetone	Soluble in acetone
Technical uses—absorbent products, dialysis	Technical products, filters	Few technical uses, fiberfill
Color may crock or bleed	Color may crock or bleed	Color may fume- or pollution-fade
Mildews	Mildews	Resists mildew
Moderate cost	Higher cost	Low cost
Poor resiliency	Moderate resiliency	Poor resiliency
Low strength (1.0–2.5 g/d dry; 0.5–1.4 g/d wet)	Higher strength (4.8–5.0 g/d dry; 4.2–4.6 g/d wet)	Low strength (1.2–1.4 g/d dry; 1.0–1.3 g/d wet)
Moderate abrasion resistance	Good abrasion resistance	Poor abrasion resistance
Chlorine bleaches can be used	Chlorine bleaches can be used	Chlorine bleaches can be used
Moderate light resistance	Moderate light resistance	Moderate light resistance
1.48–1.54 g/cc	1.56 g/cc	1.32 g/cc
Harmed by strong acids	Harmed by strong acids	Harmed by strong acids
Resistant to alkalis and most solvents	Resistant to alkalis and most solvents	Resistant to most alkalis; soluble in many solvents
95% elastic at 2% elongation	Unknown	48–65% elasticity at 4% elongation
7–14% breaking elongation dry; 20% wet	14–16% breaking elongation dry; 16–18% wet	24–45% breaking elongation dry; 35–50% wet

▶ Learning Activity 5

Make a list of the performance characteristics of acetate that are different from those of rayon, the natural cellulosic fibers, and the natural protein fibers. Describe how a consumer from the 1920s would be challenged by her or his first purchase of an item of acetate. Would the consumer know it was acetate and that acetate was not a natural fiber? (Check in Chapter 21 regarding laws related to fiber content labeling.)

used in dry cleaning present additional hazards to the environment. See Chapter 20 for more information on dry cleaning.

Uses of Acetate While it is a minor fiber, acetate is used in apparel, interior, and technical products. One important use of acetate is in lining fabrics. The aesthetics of acetate—its luster, hand, and body—its relatively low cost, and its ease in handling contribute to its wide use here. However, since acetate is not a durable fiber, the fabric must be carefully selected for the end use or the consumer will be dissatisfied with the product.

Acetate is very important in drapery fabrics. Sunlight-resistant modifications contribute to the fiber's popularity here, as do its luster and soft drape. Antique-satin fabrics made of blends of acetate and rayon are very common. Fabrics of 50 percent acetate and 50 percent cotton are used for draperies that match bedspreads or lightly used upholstery. Acetate and acetate-blend fabrics come in an amazing assortment of colors—nearly any decor can be matched. Another use of acetate is in fabrics for formalwear, such as dresses and blouses in moiré taffeta, satin, and brocade.

Other important uses of acetate fabrics include bedspreads and quilts, fabrics sold for home sewing, ribbons, and cigarette filters. Absorbent antibacterial acetate is used in personal hygiene products, fiberfill, and filters. One of the largest technical uses for acetate is as a cigarette filter. Since acetate is not biodegradable, discarded cigarette butts thrown on the ground create environmental problems.

Types and Kinds of Acetate Types of acetate are solution-dyed, flame-retardant, sunlight-resistant, fiberfill, textured filament, modified cross section, antibacterial, and thick-and-thin slublike filament.

Other Regenerated Cellulosic Fibers

Bamboo fiber from the woody bamboo grass (*Bambuseae* spp.) is produced in China. Bamboo is promoted as a sustainable fiber. It grows naturally in many parts of the world as a dense thicket that crowds out weeds. It has few problems with insect pests. Because of these two characteristics, it is grown with no agrichemicals like herbicides and insecticides needed. It can be harvested once a year and is a good income source for people in many isolated rural areas. Because the thicket expands by underground shoots, the soil is not disturbed by heavy machinery when harvesting the stalks or starting new plants. Bamboo is produced at farmed plantations so protected natural habitats are not disturbed. Bamboo production encourages preservation of cultural heritage, cultural traditions related to growing bamboo, and many handcrafts.

There are two types of bamboo fiber: one that is removed from the bamboo stems and one that is regenerated from bamboo pulp that should be labeled bamboo rayon. The regenerated bamboo rayon is the most common on the market and the focus of this discussion. (For a discussion of natural bamboo fiber, see Chapter 4.) Regnerated bamboo is harvested from bamboo, a type of grass plant that grows quickly without the use of fertilizer or pesticides. The plant requires four to five years to reach the harvest stage. The fiber production process is similar to that used for lyocell using pulp from managed farms. Most of them practice sustainable production and preserve wild bamboo forests and natural habitats. Regenerated bamboo has a soft hand and silky texture. Bamboo is durable with good breathability and comfort characteristics. Its microporous cross section allows for good wicking of perspiration and good absorption of dyes. Claims that the fiber is naturally antimicrobial have not been substantiated by independent researchers. Considering the processing that may occur with the regnerated form, it is unlikely that bamboo rayon is antimicrobial. Bamboo is used for sweaters, toweling, blankets, T-shirts, socks, lightweight blouses and shirts, wallpaper, and curtains. Bamboo is used by fiber artists to produce one-of-a-kind apparel and interior items.

Bamboo fiber that is regenerated from bamboo pulp should be labeled bamboo rayon.

Seaweed fiber is a marine plant fiber produced using a process similar to that for lyocell. Seaweed (from *Ascophyllum nodosom*) is added to the lyocell spinning solution in relatively low percentages. The manufacturers claim that minerals and vitamins from seaweed are absorbed through the skin. The fiber is soft, breathable, and comfortable next to the skin. There are two forms sold under the tradename SeaCell®: active and pure. SeaCell® active contains silver, which is an effective antimicrobial agent for bras, underwear, sportswear, workwear, carpets, bedding, towels, craft yarn, nonwovens, and hygiene products. SeaCell® pure does not include the antimicrobial agent and is used in apparel and interior textiles.

Additional source materials being investigated as potential regenerated fibers include rice and wheat straw, native prairie grasses, and corn husks.

Other Regenerated Fibers

Alginate fibers are polysaccharides processed from brown seaweed. They are short fibers used primarily for wound dressings because they protect while allowing healing to occur. Another fiber with medical applications is chitosan, produced from the exoskeleton of crustaceans and insects. Both fibers are antimicrobial, biocompatible with human tissue, biodegradable, and biorenewable.

Several fibers from regenerated protein are available in the market. These fibers are **azlon**, which is "a manufactured fiber in which the fiber-forming substance is composed of any regenerated naturally occurring proteins." However, they are most often sold under trade names. Soya or soy fiber, often sold as SoySilk®, is made from soybean waste from the tofu manufacturing process. SoySilk is durable with a soft hand, wonderful drape, good colorfastness, excellent absorbency, and good comfort and thermal retention. It is used in imported apparel and by fiber artists. Soya fiber is sometimes referred to as vegetable cashmere because of its soft hand. Because of its desirable characteristics and low cost in comparison to silk and cashmere, it can be used in blends to resemble the more expensive fibers or in place of them. Silk Latte® and Milkofil® are made from casein, the protein in milk. These fibers have a soft hand and take dye well, but ares not quite as durable as soy fiber. Both soy and milk fibers are renewable and biodegradable (see Figure 7.6).

Figure 7.6   Silk Latte® fibers and cone of SoySilk® yarn.

While producers of both fibers claim they are good for the environment, that is not necessarily the case. Both fibers are renewable, but the production of the raw materials require extensive use of land and water in processing. Milk is produced by cattle that have a significant carbon footprint; they eat large quantities of feed to produce milk and generate significant amounts of methane gas and manure. Soybeans require extensive use of agrichemicals: herbicides to control weeds, fertilizer to promote heavy yields, pesticides to kill insects that damage soy plants, and fungicides to reduce disease. In addition, soy is genetically modified for resistance to adverse growing conditions, to improve yield, and to reduce sensitivity to herbicides. Some individuals object to the use of genetically modified organisms (GMOs).

> ► **Learning Activity 6**
>
> Compare the advantages and disadvantages in terms of sustainability for azlon fibers produced from such protein sources as soybeans and milk.

Identification of Regenerated Fibers

The regenerated cellulosic fibers appear similar microscopically. Rayon and acetate have striations and irregular cross sections. Lyocell is more rounded and smoother. Rayon and lyocell burn like cotton or flax. Acetate burns freely, melts, and decomposes to a black char.

Solubility is an easy way to identify acetate. The **acetone test** is specific for acetate, since none of the other fibers dissolves in acetone. See the fiber identification discussion in Chapter 3 for information about the acetone test.

▶ Learning Activity 7

Use Fabrics #21 and 45 from your swatch kit. Following the procedures described in Chapter 3, examine the fibers using the microscope to see the striations along the length of the fibers.

▶ Learning Activity 8

Use a small portion of the fiber from the small self-sealing bags labeled rayon, acetate, and lyocell or three to four yarns from Fabrics #21, 25, and 45 from your swatch kit. Following the procedures and safety precautions described in Chapter 3, conduct a burn test of these samples. Describe the ease of ignition, the color and odor of the smoke, and the color and texture of the cooled ash. Compare your results with those included in Table 3.7 or with the chart on the sheet with the fiber bags in your swatch kit.

▶ Learning Activity 9

Use a small portion of the fiber from the small self-sealing bags labeled rayon, acetate, and lyocell or three to four yarns from Fabrics #21, 25, and 45 from your swatch kit. Following the procedures and safety precautions described in Chapter 3, conduct a solubility test using acetone for these samples. Record your results. Did all three samples dissolve in the acetone?

key terms

Acetate   140
Acetone test   146
Azlon   145
Bamboo   144
Fume or pollution fading   140
Heat-sensitive fiber   140

High-wet-modulus rayon   132
Lyocell   137
Manufactured regenerated fiber   132
Rayon   132
Seaweed fiber   145

Striations   133
Thermoplastic fiber   140
Triacetate   140
Viscose rayon   133
Wet spinning   133

review questions

1. How do the properties of the manufactured cellulosic fibers rayon, lyocell, and acetate differ from those of the natural cellulosic fibers?

2. Explain the difference in properties among viscose rayon, HWM rayon, and lyocell.

3. What is modal and how does it compare to HWM rayon?

4. Explain the problems that consumers can face when caring for rayon and acetate.

5. Natural cellulosic fibers can be machine washed and dried and ironed with a hot iron. How does the care differ with rayon, lyocell, and acetate?

6. Lyocell is more sensitive to abrasion compared to many other fibers. Explain what happens with lyocell and how that characteristic is used to advantage for some end uses for lyocell.

7. How can the manufactured regenerated fibers be changed to enhance their performance for specific end uses?

8. For each end use listed here, identify a fiber discussed in this chapter that would be appropriate. Indicate why you selected that fiber as well as any fiber modifications that might enhance the fiber's performance for that end use.
   a. Inexpensive kitchen wipes
   b. Draperies for formal dining room
   c. Lining for suit jacket
   d. Summer-weight suit

9. Explain why bamboo should be labeled "rayon from bamboo" or "bamboo rayon."

10. Describe why bamboo, azlon such as soy or soya, and lyocell are considered sustainable fibers. What are the sustainability and environmental concerns with rayon and acetate?

Case Study
Eco-Fashion*

Eco-fashion is touted as including organic cotton, soy, bamboo, hemp, and other natural materials that are produced without the use of pesticide and fertilizer. The bamboo fiber is grown on family farms in China, processed into yarn there, and imported to South Carolina where it is knit into sweaters, baby blankets, T-shirts, socks, and other items. People often assume bamboo apparel will be similar to burlap and are pleasantly surprised when they first experience it. Soy is another eco-friendly fiber that was first produced in the mid-twentieth century, but is now gaining popularity because of its sustainability. Soy fiber is available in sweaters and other casual and active wear. However, the biggest hurdle that the eco-fashions face is their higher retail prices.

DISCUSSION QUESTIONS

1. Is the bamboo fiber described above a manufactured regenerated fiber or is it a natural fiber? (See the discussion of bamboo in this chapter and in Chapter 4.)

2. Describe the aspects of organic cotton, bamboo, soy, and hemp that make them eco-friendly. Is there anything about these fibers in terms of their enviromental impact that eco-conscious consumers should be aware of?

3. Do you own any textile products made of these fibers? What convinced you to buy or not buy them?

4. If you have eco-friendly textile products, what are the things you like about them? Dislike about them?

*Gaston, E. (2007, January 21). Bamboo for the body: Andrews Plant makes eco-fashion clothing. *The Sun News* (Myrtle Beach, SC).

suggested readings

Acetate properties. (1994, Autumn). *Textiles Magazine*, p. 24.

Fletcher, K. (2008). *Sustainable Fashion and Textiles: Design Journey*. London: Earthscan.

Ford, J. E. (1991). Viscose fibres. *Textiles*, 3, pp. 4–8.

Havich, M. M. (1999, June). New fabric stalks a market share. *America's Textiles International*, p. 66.

Hearle, J. W. S. (2007). Protein fibres: 21st century vision. *Textiles, 34*(2), 14–18.

Hethorn, J., & Ulasewicz, C. (2008). *Sustainable Fashion: Why Now?* New York: Fairchild Books.

Qin, Y. (2004). Novel anitmicrobial fibres. *Textiles, 31*(2), 14–17.

Reichard, R. S. (2008, Janurary/February). Textiles 2008: Blueprint for survival. *Textile World News* (www.textileworld.com).

Rodie, J. B. (2007, May/June). Spotlight on bamboo. *Textile World News* (www.textileworld.com).

Taylor, J. (1998, July/August). Tencel—a unique cellulosic fibre. *Journal of the Society of Dyers and Colourists*, 114, pp. 191–193.

Thiry, M. C. (2004). Back to nature—textile fibers come full circle. *AATCC Review*, 4(1), 7–11.

Tullo, A. H. (2008, September 29). Growing plastics, *Chemical and Engineering News*, 21–25.

Viscose rayon properties. (1994). *Textiles Magazine*, 2, p. 17.

Woodings, C. (2001, July/August). Regenerated cellulose—from commodity to specialty item. *Technical Textiles International*, pp. 3–6.

SYNTHETIC
FIBERS

CHAPTER OBJECTIVES

- To know the properties common to most synthetic fibers.
- To understand the processes used in producing synthetic fibers.
- To integrate performance characteristics of the common synthetic fibers with end-use requirements.
- To recognize the use of synthetics in apparel, interior, and technical products.

8

Synthetic fibers, the second type of manufactured fibers, have helped shape the world as we know it. The major difference between manufactured regenerated fibers and manufactured synthetic fibers is the raw material from which the fiber is formed. Regenerated fibers are produced from naturally occurring polymers. The polymers for synthetic fibers are synthesized or made from small simple molecules. Although sometimes referred to as *manufactured synthetic fibers*, *chemical fibers*, or *noncellulosic manufactured fibers*, synthetic fibers is the name most commonly used.

Synthetic Fibers: An Overview

The fiber-forming compounds used to produce synthetic fibers are made from basic raw materials, often petroleum-based chemicals or petrochemicals, using complex procedures that are beyond the scope of this book. The synthetic fiber industry is huge (Table 8.1) and growing larger. China, India, and several other countries in Asia have constructed new synthetic fiber production facilities over the past decade to meet growing internal and export demand for these fibers. In spite of this growth, it is estimated that less than 1 percent of the total petroleum-based compounds consumed in one year is used to make fibers.

Once the materials are available, they are polymerized or connected into an extremely long linear chemical called a *polymer*. For many fibers, the basic repeating unit of the polymer, the monomer, is fairly simple; for others, the repeating unit is more complex. Two basic polymerization processes are used: addition and condensation. In addition polymerization, a double bond between two adjacent carbon atoms in the repeating unit is broken and reforms as a single bond connecting two repeating units, until a long-chain polymer is formed. In condensation polymerization, as monomers combine, water or another small molecule is eliminated and is a by-product of this reaction (Figure 8.1).

Different chemical compounds are used to produce nylon, polyester, olefin, and acrylic. These four fibers are the most widely used of the synthetic fibers and are found in a wide variety of apparel, interior, and technical applications. The next chapter will focus on other synthetic fibers that have special properties and end uses. The synthetic fibers have many common properties and processes (Table 8.2).

Synthetic fibers are viewed negatively by some consumers for a variety of reasons: inappropriate end uses, poor fashion image, damage to the environment, and poor comfort characteristics. Marketing strategies have strengthened the industry and are changing the perception of these fibers. Synthetic fibers offer much in terms of high-tech versatility, easy care, durability, and high-fashion appeal. Research and development efforts continue to improve their performance, reduce their environmental impact, improve their sustainability, and expand their end uses.

(a) $3(A = B) \longrightarrow - A - B - A - B - A - B -$
Addition polymerization

(b) $3D - H + 3E - OH \longrightarrow - D - E - D - E - D - E - + 3H_2O$
Condensation polymerization

Figure 8.1 Polymerization: (a) addition and (b) condensation.

Table 8.1 Worldwide Demand for Fibers (in million pounds)

Fiber	2006	Percent
Cotton	56,674	34
Other natural fibers	3,025	2
Synthetic fibers	98,336	60
Manufactured cellulosic fibers	7,267	4
Total	165,302	100

Table 8.2 Properties Common to Synthetic Fibers

Properties	Importance to Consumers
Heat-sensitive	Fabrics shrink and melt when exposed to excess heat. Holes may appear. Pleats, creases, and three-dimensional shapes can be heat-set. Fabric can be stabilized by heat setting. Yarns can be textured for bulk. Furlike fabrics are possible.
Resistant to most chemicals	Used in technical applications in which chemical resistance is required.
Resistant to insects, fungi, and rot	Storage is no problem. Used in geotextiles, sandbags, fishing lines, tenting, etc.
Low moisture absorbency	Products dry quickly, resist waterborne stains. Poor comfort in humid weather. Difficult to dye. Static problems more likely. Does not shrink when wet.
Oleophilic	Oil and grease stains must be removed by dry-cleaning agents.
Electrostatic	Static cling and shocks may occur. Static sparks may pose risk of explosions or fires in unusual situations.
Abrasion resistance good to excellent (acrylics lowest)	Resistant to wear and holes. Used in many technical applications.
Strength good to excellent	Make good ropes, belts, and hosiery. Resist breaking under stress.
Resilience excellent	Easy-care apparel, packable for travel. Less wrinkling during wear. Resilient carpeting.
Sunlight resistance good to excellent (nylon modified to improve resistance)	Used in outdoor furniture, indoor/outdoor carpet, curtains/draperies, flags, banners, and awnings.
Flame resistance	Varies from poor to excellent. Check individual fibers.
Density or specific gravity	Most are lightweight. More product per unit mass.
Pilling	May occur in products made of staple fibers.

Common Properties of Synthetic Fibers

Heat Sensitivity Many synthetic fibers are heat-sensitive. **Heat sensitivity** refers to fibers that soften or melt with heat; those that scorch or decompose are *heat-resistant*. Awareness of heat sensitivity is important in manufacturing because of the heat in dyeing, scouring, singeing, and other finishing and production processes. Heat sensitivity is also important to consumers because of the heat encountered in washing, ironing, and dry cleaning.

Fibers differ in their level of heat sensitivity. These differences are shown in Table 3.5. If the iron remains in one spot too long, the heat builds up. When heat-sensitive fabrics get too hot, the yarns soften and pressure from the iron flattens them permanently (Figure 8.2). **Glazing** is the melting and flattening of yarns and fibers exposed to excess heat. While it is a disaster to the consumer if the iron is too hot, glazing is used in finishing to produce deliberate texture and surface effects.

Heat-sensitive fibers make altering apparel difficult because creases, seams, and hems are hard to press in or out. Fullness cannot be shrunk out for shaping, so patterns have to be adjusted. However, application of nanotechnology can be used to improve the heat resistance of synthetic fibers. Nanoclay dispersed in nylon and polyester improves their heat resistance.

Chemical Resistance Most synthetic fibers are resistant to most chemicals, including water, solvents, acids, and bases. Chemical resistance means that these fibers do not absorb water or other liquids, resist soiling by most soils, are more difficult to dye, and resist solvents. Low absorbency can create problems with comfort and static. Chemical resistance means a broader range of technical applications for synthetic fibers.

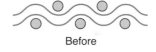
Before

After

Figure 8.2 Heat and pressure cause permanent flattening of the yarn. Glazing is a permanent change in fiber or yarn cross section.

Examine the list of properties in Table 8.2. Identify products where these properties would be used to enhance a product or where they might create a problem with a product. (In some instances, a property can be identified as both enhancing and problematic.)

Pilling Fiber tenacity affects **pilling**, the formation of tiny balls of entangled fiber ends on a fabric's surface. Pilling occurs on staple-fiber fabrics, where fiber ends entangle due to abrasion. The pills may break off before the item becomes unsightly, but most synthetic fibers are so strong that surface pills accumulate. Pills are of two kinds: lint and fabric. *Lint pills* are more unsightly because they contain not only fibers from the item but also fibers picked up during care, through contact with other fabrics in use and through static attraction. *Fabric pills* consist of fibers from the fabric and are less obvious. Pilling can be minimized by fiber modification or finishes.

To minimize pilling, compact weaves, high yarn twist or plied yarns, and longer-staple fibers are recommended. Resin finishes of cotton and fulling of wool also help prevent pilling.

Static Electricity Static electricity is generated by friction when a fabric is rubbed against itself or other objects. If the electrical charge is not removed, it builds up on the surface. When the fabric comes in contact with a good conductor, a shock, or electron transfer, occurs. This transfer may produce sparks that, in some environments, can cause explosions. Static tends to build up more rapidly in dry, cold regions.

Static attracts soil, dust, and lint that is unappealing. Brushing to remove the soil simply increases the problem. Static cling is another problem. Fabrics cling to equipment in production facilities; cutting and handling these fabrics are more difficult. Clothes cling to the wearer and are uncomfortable and unsightly. Antistatic finishes are applied to many fabrics at the factory, but they may not be permanent. Consumers can minimize static by using fabric softeners.

Additives to the spinning solution can reduce static build-up. Examples include additive that improve fiber absorbency or nanoparticles that improve electrical conductivity. Fibers that are modified to reduce static problems are more expensive than nonmodified fibers.

Oleophilic Fibers with low moisture absorption usually have a high affinity for oils and greases. They are **oleophilic**. Exposure to oily substances may cause these fibers to swell. Oily stains are very difficult to remove and may require prespotting with a concentrated liquid soap or a dry-cleaning solvent.

Common Manufacturing Processes

Melt Spinning Many synthetic fibers are melt-spun. The basic steps in **melt spinning** for filament and staple fibers made from filaments are shown in Figure 8.3. Melt spinning can be demonstrated by a simple laboratory experiment using flame, tweezers, and nylon or polyester fiber or fabric. Heat the fiber or fabric until some of it has melted, then quickly draw out the melt with tweezers as shown in Figure 8.4.

In commercial melt spinning, the melt is forced through heated spinneret holes. The fiber cools in contact with the air, solidifies, and is wound on a bobbin.

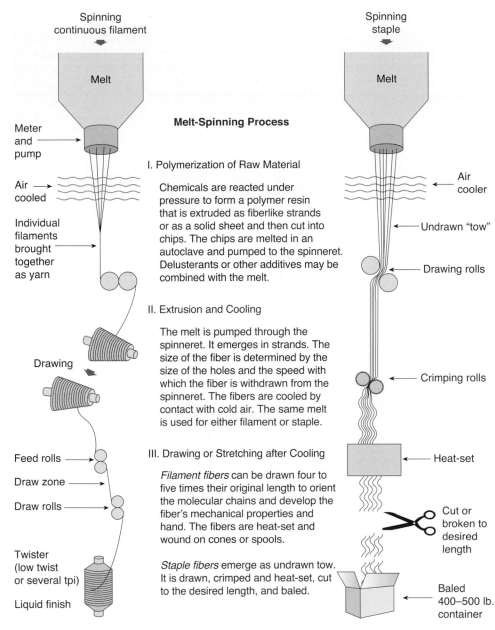

Melt-Spinning Process

I. Polymerization of Raw Material

Chemicals are reacted under pressure to form a polymer resin that is extruded as fiberlike strands or as a solid sheet and then cut into chips. The chips are melted in an autoclave and pumped to the spinneret. Delusterants or other additives may be combined with the melt.

II. Extrusion and Cooling

The melt is pumped through the spinneret. It emerges in strands. The size of the fiber is determined by the size of the holes and the speed with which the fiber is withdrawn from the spinneret. The fibers are cooled by contact with cold air. The same melt is used for either filament or staple.

III. Drawing or Stretching after Cooling

Filament fibers can be drawn four to five times their original length to orient the molecular chains and develop the fiber's mechanical properties and hand. The fibers are heat-set and wound on cones or spools.

Staple fibers emerge as undrawn tow. It is drawn, crimped and heat-set, cut to the desired length, and baled.

Figure 8.3 The melt-spinning processes: filament (left) and staple (right).

Drawing After extrusion of the fiber, its chainlike molecules are in an amorphous or disordered arrangement. The filament fiber is drawn to develop the desirable strength, pliability, toughness, and elasticity properties. Some fibers are cold-drawn; others must be hot-drawn. **Drawing** aligns the molecules in a more parallel arrangement and brings them closer together so they are more crystalline and oriented. The amount of draw (draw ratio) varies with intended use, determines the decrease in fiber size, and controls the increase in strength.

Heat Setting **Heat setting** is a process that uses heat to stabilize the shape and dimensions of yarns or fabrics made of heat-sensitive fibers. The yarn or fabric is heated to bring it to a temperature specific for the fiber being heat-set—the glass transition temperature (T_g). At this temperature the fiber molecules move freely to relieve stress within the fiber. Tension remains until the fiber has cooled, locking this shape into its molecular structure. After cooling, the fabric or yarn will be stable to any heat lower than that at which it was set. Higher temperatures may

Figure 8.4 Melt-spinning a synthetic fiber by hand.

Table 8.3 Heat Setting

Advantages	Disadvantages
Permanent embossed designs	"Set" creases and wrinkles are hard to remove in ironing or in garment alteration.
Permanent pleats and shape	Care must be taken in washing or ironing to prevent setting wrinkles.
Stable size, even for knits	
Crush-resistant pile	
Wrinkle-resistant apparel	

▶ **Learning Activity 2**

Compare the processes used to melt spin fibers with those used to wet or dry spin fibers. How do the processes compare in terms of sustainability and environmental impact?

▶ **Learning Activity 3**

Remove approximately one-third of the fiber in the small self-sealing bag labeled Polyester or three to four yarns from Fabric #9 from your swatch kit. Roll it into a small bundle and place the tip or edge of the bundle between the jaws of a tweezers. Following the safety precautions described in Chapter 3 for the burn test, slowly bring the fiber bundle towards the flame, but not close enough so it ignites. Melt the bundle in the heat. Once the bundle has melted, immediately remove it from the flame and use a second pair of tweezers to pull out a fiber from the melt.

Many synthetic fibers are melt-spun and modifications for size, shape, pilling, tenacity, and elongation are common.

cause shrinkage or other changes. Heat setting may be done at any stage of finishing, depending on the fiber's heat resistance and end use (Table 8.3).

Identification of Synthetic Fibers

Burn tests can be used to identify the presence of some synthetic fibers because of the melting and dripping that occurs. However, the burn test is not good for blends or for fibers that are flame-retardant or heat-resistant. The burn test also cannot be used to identify a specific generic fiber since the differences are minor or masked by fiber additives or finishes (see Table 3.7).

Microscopic appearance is not a reliable method to identify synthetic fibers because their appearance can be modified easily. Fibers in this group have no unique visible characteristics at either the microscopic or the macroscopic level. Photomicrographs included in this chapter clearly illustrate this.

Solubility tests are the only procedures that differentiate among the synthetic fibers. Table 3.8 lists solvents commonly used to identify synthetic fibers. Several solvents used to identify fibers are toxic and hazardous. Appropriate care should be taken when using any solvent.

Common Fiber Modifications

Fiber Shape and Size Since many synthetic fibers are melt-spun, changing the fiber's cross-sectional shape is relatively easy. Altering the shape of the spinneret hole changes fiber shape. Figure 3.3 illustrates several common modifications. Hollow fibers for fiberfill provide better thermal properties and lighter weight. For example, a 12-void fiber by Kuraray is 40 percent lighter than a fiber without the voids. Trilobal, pentalobal, and multilobal fibers are used for apparel and interiors, especially carpeting. Voided fibers hide soil on carpeting. Flat-ribbon fibers are used in formalwear and special-occasion apparel. Channel fibers are used in active sportswear to wick moisture away from the skin's surface. Fiber size can range from very large for technical applications to very small for apparel and interior textiles.

Microfibers are filament or staple fibers with a denier per filament (dpf) of less than 1.0; most are in the range of 0.5 to 0.7 dpf. These fibers are produced by conventional melt spinning, splitting bicomponent fibers, or dissolving one of the components of bicomponent fibers (see Figure 6.3). All three techniques provide commercially important microfibers for apparel, interior, and technical applications. End uses include fashion apparel, intimate apparel, performance athletic apparel, upholstery, wall coverings, bedding, window-treatment fabrics, medical uses, and wiping cloths for the precision and glass industries.

Nanofibers and nanotubes (hollow fibers) are much smaller than microfibers with diameters or cross sections less than 1,000 nanometers or 1×10^{-9} meters. Unfortunately, microfibers are sized based on the denier system (a weight per unit length system), while nanofibers are sized based on fiber diameter. Because of the incredibly tiny size, special spinning methods are used. Two methods are most common. In electrospinning, the polymer solution is extruded into a strong electrical field. In centrifugal spinning, the polymer solution is extruded in high centrifugal force. Nanofibers and nanotubes provide unusually high surface to volume ratios, flexibility in surface function, and enhanced mechanical and electrical properties.

> **Learning Activity 6**

From the list of common fiber modifications of synthetics, select two and explain how the modifications enhance product performance:

Low-Pilling Fibers **Low-pilling fibers** are engineered to minimize pill formation. By reducing the molecular weight slightly, the fiber's flex life is decreased. When flex abrasion resistance is reduced, fiber pills break off almost as soon as they are formed, thus maintaining the fabric's original appearance. The low-pilling fibers are not as strong as other fiber types, but are durable enough for most apparel and interior uses. They are especially applicable for soft knitting yarns. Some low-pilling fiber modifications are designed for blending with other fibers. For example, low-pilling polyester blends well with cotton, rayon, or lyocell.

High-Tenacity Fibers Even though synthetic fibers are known for their high strength, fiber tenacity can be increased for end uses in which high strength is needed, such as tow ropes, air bags, and parachute cords. Fiber strength can be increased in several ways. Drawing or stretching a fiber to align or orient the molecules strengthens the intermolecular forces. In addition, the molecular chain length can be varied by chemical modification or by changes in time, temperature, pressure, and catalysts used in the polymerization process. Long molecules are harder to pull apart than short molecules. Most **high-tenacity fibers** are produced by combining drawing with molecular-chain-length modifications. Composite fibers of nylon or polyester and nanoclay have improved breaking strength.

Low-Elongation Fibers Synthetic fibers often are blended with cellulosic fibers to add strength and abrasion resistance. However, the greater elongation potential of synthetic fibers can create more problems unless low-elongation varieties are used in the blend. Low-elongation varieties stretch less under force but are as strong as regular fibers. The primary end uses are apparel and interior items that receive hard use, such as work apparel and heavy-duty upholstery fabrics.

Synthetic Fibers

Nylon

Nylon was the first synthetic fiber and the first fiber developed in the United States. In 1928, the DuPont Company established a fundamental research program as a means of diversification. DuPont hired Dr. Wallace H. Carothers, an expert on high polymers, to direct a team of scientists. The team created many kinds of polymers, starting with single molecules and building them into long molecular chains. One team member discovered that a solution could be formed into a stable solid filament. This stimulated the group to concentrate on textile fibers. By 1939, DuPont was making polyamide fiber in a pilot plant. This fiber—nylon 6,6—was introduced to the public in women's hosiery, for which it was an instant success. The name *nylon* was chosen for the fiber, but the reason for that choice is not known. At that time there were no laws specifying generic names for fibers.

Nylon had a combination of properties unlike any other fiber in use in the 1940s. It was stronger and more resistant to abrasion; it had excellent elasticity and could be heat-set. Permanent pleats became a reality. For the first time, gossamer-sheer fabrics were durable and

Table 8.4 Comparison of Nylon 6,6 and Nylon 6

Nylon 6,6	Nylon 6
Made of hexamethylene diamine and adipic acid	Made of caprolactam

$$\left[\begin{array}{c} O \\ \| \\ C \end{array} (CH_2)_4 \begin{array}{c} O \\ \| \\ C \end{array} NH (CH_2)_6 NH \right]_n \qquad \left[NH (CH_2)_5 \begin{array}{c} O \\ \| \\ C \end{array} \right]_n$$

Characteristics	**Characteristics**
Heat setting 205°C (401°F)	Heat setting 150°C (302°F)
Pleats and creases can be heat-set at higher temperatures	Softening point 220°C (428°F)
Softening point 250°C (482°F)	Better dye affinity than nylon 6,6; takes deeper shades
Difficult to dye	Softer hand
	Greater elasticity, elastic recovery, and fatigue resistance
	Better weathering properties, including better sunlight resistance

PERFORMANCE				PERFORMANCE		
TENACITY DRY/WET	BREAKING ELONGATION, %	ELASTIC RECOVERY, %	FIBER TYPE	TENACITY DRY/WET	BREAKING ELONGATION, %	ELASTIC RECOVERY, %
5.9–9.8/5.1–8.0	15–28	89	High-tenacity filament	6.5–9.0/5.8–8.2	16–20	99–100
2.3–6.0/2.0–5.5	25–65	88	Regular-tenacity filament	4.0–7.2/3.7–6.2	17–45	98–100
2.9–7.2/2.5–6.1	16–75	82	Staple	3.5–7.2/—	30–90	100

machine-washable. Nylon's high strength, light weight, and resistance to chemicals made it suitable for technical products such as ropes, cords, sails, and parachutes.

As nylon entered more end-use markets, problems became apparent—static buildup, poor hand, poor comfort in skin-contact fabrics, and low resistance to sunlight. As each problem appeared, solutions were developed.

Production of Nylon Nylon or polyamides are made from various substances. The numbers after the word *nylon* indicate the number of carbon atoms in the starting materials. Nylon 6,6 is made from hexamethylene diamine with six carbon atoms and adipic acid, also with six carbon atoms.

While nylon 6,6 was being developed in the United States, scientists in Germany were working on nylon 6. It is made from a single six-carbon substance, caprolactam (Table 8.4).

Physical Structure of Nylon Nylon is available in multifilament, monofilament, staple in a variety of lengths, and tow in a wide range of deniers and shapes and as partially drawn or completely finished filaments. Fibers are produced in bright, semi-dull, and dull lusters, with varying degrees of polymerization and strengths.

Regular nylon has a round cross section and is uniform throughout the filament (Figure 8.5). Microscopically, the fibers look like fine glass rods. They are transparent unless they have been delustered or solution-dyed.

At first, the uniformity of nylon filaments was a distinct advantage over the natural fibers, especially silk. However, the perfect uniformity of nylon produced woven fabrics with a dead,

Figure 8.5 Photomicrographs of nylon fiber: cross-sectional view (left), longitudinal view (right).
SOURCE: Courtesy of the British Textile Technology Group.

Figure 8.6 Photomicrographs of trilobal nylon.
SOURCE: Courtesy of E. I. du Pont de Nemours & Company.

Figure 8.7 Nylon fiber with voids.
SOURCE: Courtesy of E. I. du Pont de Nemours & Company.

Nylon is a manufactured fiber in which the fiber-forming substance is any long-chain synthetic polyamide.

unattractive feel. Changing the fiber's shape reduces this condition. Nylon and other melt-spun fibers retain the shape of the spinneret hole. Thus, where performance is influenced by fiber shape, producers adjust the shape as needed. For example, in nylon carpets, trilobal fibers and square fibers with voids give good soil-hiding characteristics (Figures 8.6 and 8.7).

Chemical Composition and Molecular Arrangement of Nylon

Nylon—a manufactured fiber in which the fiber-forming substance is any long-chain, synthetic polyamide in which less than 85 percent of the amide linkages are attached directly to two aromatic rings.

$$\left[\begin{array}{c} C-NH \\ \| \\ O \end{array}\right]$$

—*Federal Trade Commission*

Nylons are **polyamides**; the recurring amide groups contain the elements carbon, oxygen, nitrogen, and hydrogen. Nylons differ in their chemical arrangement, accounting for slight differences in some properties.

The molecular chains of nylon are long, straight chains of variable length with no side chains or cross linkages. Cold-drawing aligns the chains so that they are oriented with the lengthwise direction and are highly crystalline. High-tenacity filaments have a longer chain length than regular nylon. Staple fibers are not cold-drawn after spinning, have lower degrees of crystallinity, and have lower tenacity than filament fibers.

Nylon is related chemically to the protein fibers silk and wool. Both have similar dye sites that are important in dyeing, but nylon has far fewer dye sites than wool.

Properties of Nylon Nylon's performance in apparel and interior fabrics is summarized in Table 8.5. Compare the performance of nylon to that of other fibers by reviewing the tables in Chapter 3.

Aesthetics Nylon has been very successful in hosiery and in knitted fabrics such as tricot and jersey because of its smoothness, light weight, and high strength. The luster of nylon can be

Table 8.5 Summary of the Performance of Nylon in Apparel and Interior Textiles

Aesthetics	Variable
Durability	Excellent
Abrasion resistance	Excellent
Tenacity	Excellent
Elongation	High
Comfort	Poor
Absorbency	Poor
Thermal retention	Moderate
Appearance Retention	High
Resiliency	High
Dimensional stability	High
Elastic recovery	Excellent
Recommended Care	Machine-wash (apparel)
	Dry extraction method (interior textiles)

selected for the end use—it can be lustrous, semilustrous, or dull. Trilobal nylons have a pleasant luster.

The drape of fabrics made from nylon can be varied, depending largely on fiber and yarn size and fabric structure selected. High-drape fabrics are found in draperies, in sheer overlays for lingerie, and in formalwear. Stiff fabrics are found in taffetas for formalwear, parkas, interiors, or technical uses. Very stiff fabrics include webbing for luggage handles and seat belts.

Smooth textures are common. Texture can be varied by using spun yarns or by changing the fabric structure. The hand frequently associated with nylon fabrics is smooth because of the filament yarn and compact structure. Textured-yarn fabrics are bulkier.

Nonround fibers are generally used in upholstery and carpets because round fibers magnify soil and look dirty quickly. Trilobal, pentalobal, and voided fibers are used because they hide soil—even though the product may be soiled, the soil is not apparent. In addition, voids and flat sides of the fibers scatter light, hiding the soil and closely duplicating the matte luster of wool and other natural fibers (see Figures 8.6 and 8.7).

Durability Nylon has outstanding durability. High-tenacity fibers are used for seatbelts, tire cords, ballistic fabric, and other technical uses. Regular-tenacity and staple fibers are used in apparel and interior textiles.

High-tenacity (HT) fibers are stronger but have lower elongation than regular-tenacity fibers. During production the high-tenacity fibers are drawn to a greater degree than are regular-tenacity fibers. Thus, the HT fibers are more crystalline and oriented. HT nylon fibers are used in technical products, such as towropes, where high strength and low elongation are essential.

In addition to excellent strength and high elongation, nylon has excellent abrasion resistance. A major end use for nylon is carpet (Table 8.6). The ideal carpet is durable, resilient, and resistant to pilling, shedding, fading, traffic, abrasion, soil, and stains. Nylon meets or exceeds many of these demands. Nylon is also popular in pile upholstery fabrics because of its good durability properties.

This combination of properties makes nylon the perfect fiber for women's hosiery. No other fiber has been able to compete with nylon for pantyhose. The high elongation and excellent elastic recovery of nylon account for its outstanding performance here. Hosiery is subjected to high degrees of elongation; nylon recovers better after high elongation than other fibers do. Nylon can also be heat-set, which helps it retain its shape during wear. Filament hosiery develops runs

Table 8.6 Comparison of Wool and Manufactured Carpet Fibers

Fiber Characteristic	Wool	Nylon
Diameter	Coarse	15–18 denier or blend of various deniers
Length	Staple	Staple or filament blend of various lengths
Crimp	Three-dimensional crimp	Sawtooth crimp, three-dimensional crimp, bicomponent, textured filament
Cross section	Round to oval	Round, trilobal, multilobal, voided square, 5-pointed star
Resiliency and resistance to crushing	Good	Medium to excellent
Resistance to abrasion	Good	Good to excellent
Resistance to waterborne stains	Poor	Good to excellent
Resistance to oily stains	Good	Poor, unless modified or treated
Fire retardancy	Good	Modified fiber or topical finish
Static resistance	Good	Poor to good, can be modified

because the fine yarns break and the knit loop is no longer secure. Sheer hosiery is less durable than opaque hosiery. Microfiber nylon hosiery is warmer and softer than regular hosiery.

Nylon is used for lining fabrics in some coats and jackets. Nylon linings are more durable; however, the cost is greater because of the greater difficulty in sewing and higher costs as compared with acetate fabrics. Nylon is not very durable as a curtain or drapery fabric because it is weakened by the sun. Sunlight- or ultraviolet-resistant modifications are available. These modified fibers are used in sheer curtains, draperies, car interiors, seatbelts, and other technical applications where sunlight exposure is high.

Comfort Nylon has low absorbency. Even though its moisture regain is the highest of the synthetic fibers (4.0 to 4.5 percent for nylon 6,6 and 2.8 to 5.0 percent for nylon 6), nylon is not as comfortable to wear as the natural fibers.

Compact yarns of filament nylon originally were used in men's woven sports shirts. The shirts became transparent when wet from perspiration and felt clammy, especially in warm, humid weather. Today, textured and spun yarns used in knit fabrics result in more comfortable shirts. Knit fabrics of nylon are more comfortable than woven nylon fabrics because heat and moisture escape more readily through the additional air spaces within the fabric. Polymer modifications are also available to improve the comfort of nylon apparel. A hydrophilic fiber with improved absorbency and wicking is used in thermal underwear, actionwear, footwear, and accessories.

The factors that make nylon uncomfortable in one set of conditions make it comfortable in other conditions. Nylon is widely used for wind- and water-resistant jackets, parkas, tents, and umbrellas. The smooth, straight fibers pack closely together in yarns that can be woven into a compact fabric with very little space for wind or water to penetrate.

Another disadvantage of low absorbency is the development of static electricity by friction at times of low humidity. This disadvantage can be overcome by using antistatic-type nylon fibers, antistatic finishes, or blends with high-absorbency, low-static fibers.

Static creates problems with comfort, soiling, and use. Antistatic fiber modifications and finishes are common carpet modifications. Sometimes, small amounts of metallic and carbon fibers are used to minimize static in carpets. Antistatic nylon is used in lining fabrics and slips.

With a specific gravity of 1.14, nylon is one of the lightest fibers on the market. When compared to polyester, nylon yields 21 percent more yardage per pound of fabric. This lighter weight corresponds to lighter products and lower costs for moving and finishing fabrics. Actionwear and sports gear take advantage of nylon's light weight and high durability.

Appearance Retention Nylon fabrics are highly resilient because they have been heat-set. The same process is used to make permanent pleats, creases, and embossed designs. Nylon carpet yarns are heat-set before they are incorporated into the carpet. Heat setting improves the excellent compressional resiliency of nylon fibers in the pile yarns. **Compressional resiliency** is the ability of the carpet fibers to spring back to their original height after being bent or otherwise deformed. Traffic paths do not develop quickly. In addition, depressions from heavy furniture are less likely to be permanent. Steaming these areas can minimize marks from heavy furniture. Most carpet fibers are made in a high denier, often 15 or greater because higher-denier fibers have improved compressional resiliency and appearance retention.

Shrinkage resistance is also high because of heat setting and because the low-absorbency fiber is not affected by water. Elastic recovery is excellent. Nylon recovers fully from 8 percent stretch; no other fiber does as well. At 16 percent elongation, it recovers 91 percent immediately. This property makes nylon an excellent fiber for hosiery, tights, ski pants, swimsuits, and other actionwear (see Table 8.4). Nylon does not wrinkle much in use, is stable, and has excellent elastic recovery, so it retains its appearance well during use.

Solution-dyed and sunlight-resistant carpet fibers are available for areas where fading, especially from exposure to sunlight, may be a problem. These carpets are specifically aimed at the low-priced contract/commercial markets and for automotive interiors. An ultraviolet-resistant nylon fiber is used in flags, life vests, and other technical applications.

Care Nylon introduced the concept of easy-care garments. Nylon fabrics retain their appearance and shape during use and care.

The wet strength of nylon is 80 to 90 percent of its dry strength. Wet elongation increases slightly. Little swelling occurs when nylon is wet. Compare the swelling of these fibers: nylon, 14 percent; cotton, 40 to 45 percent; and viscose rayon, 80 to 110 percent.

To minimize wrinkling, warm wash water, gentle agitation, and gentle spin cycles are recommended. Hot water may cause wrinkling in some fabrics. Wrinkles set by hot wash water can be permanent, but hot water may help remove greasy and oily stains.

Nylon is a *color scavenger*. White and light-colored nylon fabrics pick up color from other fabrics or dirt that is in the wash water. A red sock that loses color into the wash water of a load of whites will turn the white nylon fabrics pink that is difficult to remove. Prolonged use of chlorine bleach may cause yellowing of white nylon. Discolored nylon and grayed or yellowed nylon can be avoided by following correct laundry procedures.

Since nylon has low absorbency, it dries quickly. Hence, fabrics need to be dried for only a short time. Nylon reacts adversely to overdrying or dryers set on high heat. Figure 8.8 shows the melted and fused result of a nylon garment dried in an overheated gas dryer with socks of a different fiber content.

Nylon does have problems with static, particularly when the air is dry, so a fabric softener should be used in the washer or dryer. Nylon should be pressed or ironed at a low temperature setting, 270 to 300°F, to avoid glazing. Home-ironing temperatures are not high enough to press seams, creases, and pleats permanently in items or to press out wrinkles acquired in washing.

The chemical resistance of nylon is generally good. Nylon has excellent resistance to alkali and chlorine bleaches but is damaged by strong acids. Pollutants in the atmosphere can damage nylon or create problems with dyes used with nylon. Certain acids, when printed on the fabric, create a puckered effect. Nylon dissolves in formic acid and phenol.

Nylon is resistant to the attacks of insects and fungi. However, food soil on carpets may attract insects. Nylon has low resistance to sunlight. Bright fibers have better sunlight resistance than delustered fibers because the damaging energy is reflected and not absorbed. Sunlight-resistant modifications of nylon are available.

Carpet soiling can be a real problem. Soiling in carpets is related to fiber cross section, carpet color, and fiber opacity/translucence. Round cross sections magnify soil. Nonround cross sections, such as trilobal, pentalobal, and voided, hide soil (see Figures 8.6 and 8.7). Soil-resistant fiber modifications are used in carpeting to minimize soil adherence and permanent staining. In addition, many carpets now combine soil-resistant fiber modifications with soil-resistant finishes. See Chapter 18 for information on soil-resistant finishes for carpets.

Environmental Concerns and Sustainability of Nylon Nylon is resistant to molds, mildew, rot, and many chemicals. It is resistant to natural degradation and does not degrade quickly. Although most nylon is susceptible to damage from sunlight, the damage does not occur quickly enough to minimize disposal problems with nylon products. Nylon is processed from

Figure 8.8 The melted and fused remains of nylon garments dried in an overheated gas dryer.

petrochemicals, so there are concerns regarding the political, social, and pollution impact of the petrochemical industry: drilling in sensitive environments, pipelines and other transportation issues, oil spills, refinement and production of the chemicals from which nylon is made, and use of and disposal of hazardous chemicals. The production of nylon consumes more energy than does the production of polyester or cotton. Nitrous oxide, a greenhouse gas, is emitted from nylon production facilities.

The processing of nylon from raw fiber into finished product uses few, if any, chemicals to clean the fiber. This is because nylon and other synthetic fibers, unlike the natural fibers, are not contaminated with soil and other materials like leaf bits. Since nylon is a melt-spun fiber, no residue from chemical baths needs to be rinsed from the fiber and no solvents, like those used with wet- or dry-spun fibers, need to be reclaimed. In addition, less water, salt, and acid is used to dye the fiber. Removal of excess dye from nylon fabrics uses less water than for some common dyes used for natural and regenerated cellulose fibers. Chemical finishes are rarely needed to enhance consumer satisfaction with nylon products because the fiber can be engineered for specific end uses. Thus, once nylon fiber is produced, further processing of nylon has minimal impact on the environment.

Nylon is made from materials that are by-products of oil refineries. Nylon uses for its raw materials substances that were once considered waste products. Nylon recycling is a reasonable alternative to disposal. Two problems with recycling nylon relate to the presence of other materials added to the melt in producing the original material and the wide variety of nylon polymers on the market.

A commercial carpet recycling program economically converts nylon carpet fiber to caprolactam (a nylon 6 raw material). In other recycling programs for nylon carpet fiber, the fiber is shaved from the carpet's surface and mixed with plastic and concrete. The lightweight and durable composite materials of fiber and plastic or concrete are used to make recycled picnic tables and poured concrete foundations. Unfortunately, not all discarded nylon carpet is recycled. In addition, a significant percentage of the nylon use in carpet is applied to olefin or other backing materials so that recycling is complicated. Additives used to enhance performance of nylon carpet make recycling more challenging since dye, delusterant, and soil- and stain-resistant compounds will be present with most nylon carpet pile.

Uses of Nylon Nylon is one of the most widely used fibers in the United States. The single most important use of nylon is for carpets. Tufted carpets are an excellent end use for nylon because of its aesthetic appearance, durability, appearance retention, and ability to be cleaned in place. The combination of nylon fiber and the tufting process results in relatively low-cost and highly serviceable carpeting, contributing to the widespread use of carpeting in both residential and commercial buildings.

A second important use of nylon is for apparel. Lingerie fabrics are an end use for which nylon is an important fiber. The fabrics are attractive and durable, retain their appearance well, and are easy care. Panties, bras, nightgowns, pajamas, and lightweight robes are frequently made from nylon.

Women's sheer hosiery is an important end use of nylon. No other fiber has the combination of properties that make it ideal for that use. Very sheer hosiery is often 12 to 15 denier instead of a heavier-denier yarn or monofilament. Sheers give the look that is wanted, but they are less durable. Hosiery yarns may be monofilament or multifilament stretch nylon and plain or textured and regular or micro-denier in size.

Short socks or knee-high socks are sometimes made from nylon. Frequently they are nylon blends with cotton or acrylic. Nylon adds strength and stretch. Active sportswear and actionwear in which comfort stretch is important—leotards, tights, swimsuits, and ski wear—are other end uses for nylon. Nylon-taffeta windbreakers and parkas are common in cool and windy weather. Lining fabrics for jackets and coats can be made of nylon.

Some performance nylon fibers are modified to have a cottonlike hand with improved pilling resistance and are used in the inner layers of workwear, hunting apparel, and mountaineering apparel. Other nylons have been modified to be stain- and tear-resistant, quiet (making minimal rustling or other noise that might scare off game animals), quick-drying, and warm. These fabrics are used in outer layers of workwear and hunting and hiking apparel. Supplex is an INVISTA microfiber nylon that has been modified to be softer, more supple, and less bulky than regular nylon so that it provides greater freedom of movement in outerwear, beachwear, and actionwear. Supplex is wind-resistant, water-repellent, breathable, and durable.

Technical uses for nylon are varied. Nylon is used for the tire cord that goes rim to rim over the curve of some radial tires, but polyester, heat-resistant aramid, and steel are more common because nylon has a tendency to "flat-spot." Flat spotting occurs when a car has been parked for some time and a flattened place forms on the tire. The ride will be bumpy for the first mile or so until the tire recovers from flattening.

The average car uses 25 pounds of fiber, a good share of which may be nylon. Several nylon fabrics are used for car interiors: upholstery fabric (called *body cloth*), carpet for the interior, trunk lining, door and visor trims, head liners on interior roofs, and seatbelt webbing. Some are modified to be sunlight-resistant, heat-resistant, or high-tenacity. In addition, clutch pads, brake linings, yarns to reinforce radiator hoses and other hoses, and airbags are nylon.

Additional technical uses include parachute fabric, cords and harnesses, glider tow ropes, ropes and cordage, conveyor belts, fishing nets, mail bags, and webbings. The category of technical uses also includes consumer uses, sporting goods, and leisure fabrics. Consumer uses include umbrellas, clotheslines, toothbrush and hairbrush bristles, paintbrushes, and luggage. Leisure goods include soft luggage, backpacks, book bags, camera bags, golf bags, hunting gear, and horse blankets.

Nylon is important in sporting goods. It is used for tents, sleeping bags, spinnaker sails, fishing lines and nets, racket strings, backpacks, and duffle bags.

Nylon microfibers are used in apparel and interior textiles. These fibers are 26 to 36 percent softer than regular nylon fibers and range in size from 0.7 to 1.0 dpf, as compared with a denier of 2.0 dpf for regular nylon. The micro nylons are used in a variety of applications. These fibers are water-repellent, wind- and wear-resistant, vapor-permeable, and comfortable. They are used in 100 percent nylon formations and in blends with natural fibers like wool and cotton (Table 8.7).

Table 8.7 Nylon Microfibers

Producer	Trade Name	Size, dpf	End Use
Honeywell Nylon Inc.	Silky Touch	0.8	Lingerie, swimwear
INVISTA	Supplex	1.0	Woven actionwear
	MicroSupplex	0.7	Woven actionwear

Table 8.8 Types and Kinds of Nylon

Cross Section	Dyeability	Crimp or Textured	Other
Round	Acid dyeable	Mechanical crimp	Antistatic
Heart-shaped	Cationic dyeable	Crimp-set	Soil hiding
Y-shaped	Disperse dyeable	Producer textured	Bicomponent
8-shaped	Deep dye	Undrawn	Fasciated
Delta	Solution dye	Partially drawn	Thick-and-thin
Trilobal	Heather	Steam-crimped	Antimicrobial
Triskelion	Optically whitened	Bulked continuous filament	Sunlight-resistant
Trinode		Latent crimp	Flame-resistant
Pentagonal			Delustered
Hollow			High-tenacity
Voided			Cross linked
Microfibers			

Table 8.9 Some Trade Names and Producers

Nylon 6,6 Trade Names	Producer	Nylon 6 Trade Names	Producer
Anso (all options), Caprolan, Silky Touch, Ultra Touch, Zefsport, Zeftron (all options)	Honeywell Nylon Inc.	Antron (all options), Supplex, MicroSupplex, Solar Max, Stainmaster	INVISTA
Nylon 6	Beaulieu of America, Inc.	Ultron (all options), Wear-Dated	Solutia, Inc.

Types and Kinds of Nylon It has been said that as soon as a new need arose, a new type of nylon was produced to fill the need. This has led to a large number of types of nylon that are identified by trademarks.

The list in Table 8.8 illustrates many modifications of nylon. Table 8.9 lists trade names for several producers of nylon.

Polyester

The first polyester fiber, Terylene, was produced in England. It was first introduced in the United States in 1951 by DuPont. The outstanding wet and dry resiliency of polyester and its excellent dimensional stability after heat setting made it an instant favorite.

Sometimes referred to as the workhorse fiber, polyester is the most widely used synthetic fiber. Its filament form is extremely versatile, and its staple form can be blended with many other

Table 8.10 Properties of Polyester

Properties	Importance to Consumers
Resilient—wet and dry	Easy-care and packable apparel, interior textiles
Dimensional stability	Machine-washable
Sunlight-resistant	Good for curtains and draperies
Durable, abrasion-resistant	Technical uses, sewing thread, work clothes
Aesthetics superior to nylon	Blends well with other fibers, silklike

fibers, contributing desirable properties to the blend without destroying those of the other fiber. Its versatility in blending is one of the unique advantages of polyester.

The polyester polymer is endlessly engineerable, with many physical and chemical variations possible. These modified fibers improve the performance of the original polyester. The standard round shape can be easily modified to other shapes for different properties. High-tenacity staple polyester is used in durable-press fabrics to reinforce the cotton fibers that had been weakened by finishing. Other polyesters have a hand and absorbency more like the natural fibers. The properties of polyester are listed in Table 8.10.

Production of Polyester **Polyester** is produced by reacting dicarboxylic acid with dihydric alcohol. The fibers are melt-spun by a process very similar to the one used to make nylon. The polyester fibers are hot-drawn to orient the molecules and improve strength, elongation, and stress/strain properties. Since polyester is melt-spun, it retains the shape of the spinneret hole. Modifications in cross-sectional shape are inexpensive and easy to produce.

Physical Structure of Polyester Polyester fibers are produced in many types. Filaments are high- or regular-tenacity, bright or delustered, white or solution-dyed. The speckled appearance of some fibers may be due to delusterant. Delustered staple fibers are available in a range of deniers. They may be regular, low-pilling, or high-tenacity. Polyester is not as transparent as nylon fibers. It is white, so fibers normally do not need to be bleached. However, whiter types of polyester fibers have optical whiteners added to the fiber-spinning solution. Regular polyester fibers are smooth rodlike fibers with a circular cross section (Figure 8.9). A variety of cross-sectional shapes are produced: round, trilobal, octolobal, oval, hollow, voided, hexalobal, and pentalobal (star-shaped).

Chemical Composition and Molecular Arrangement of Polyester

Polyester fibers—manufactured fibers in which the fiber-forming substance is any long-chain synthetic polymer composed of at least 85 percent by weight of an ester

Figure 8.9 Photomicrographs of polyester: cross-sectional view (left), longitudinal view (right).
SOURCE: Courtesy of the British Textile Technology Group.

of a substituted aromatic carboxylic acid, including but not restricted to substituted terephthalate units, and para substituted hydroxybenzoate units,

$$P(-R-O-\underset{O}{\underset{\|}{C}}-C_6H_4-\underset{O}{\underset{\|}{C}}-O-), \qquad P(-R-O-C_6H_4-\underset{O}{\underset{\|}{C}}-O-).$$

Where the fiber is formed by the interaction of two or more chemically distinct polymers (of which none exceeds 85 percent by weight), and contains ester groups as the dominant functional unit (at least 85 percent by weight of the total polymer content of the fiber), and which, if stretched at least 100 percent, durably and rapidly reverts to its unstretched length when the tension is removed, the term *elasterell-p* may be used as a generic description of the fiber.

—*Federal Trade Commission*

Polyester fibers are made from terephthalate polymers: polyethylene terephthalate (PET), poly 1,4 cyclohexylene-dimethylene terephthalate (PCDT), polybutylene terephthalate (PBT), and polytrimethylene terephthalate (PTT). While the properties of each polymer differ, in most cases the differences are minor and do not result in noticeable changes in consumer performance. These polymers may be homopolymers or copolymers. Most copolymers are pill-resistant, lower-strength staple fibers used primarily in knits, blends, and carpets. Polyester fibers have straight molecular chains that are packed closely together and are well oriented, with very strong hydrogen bonds.

> Polyester is a manufactured fiber in which the fiber-forming substance is any long-chain synthetic polymer composed of an ester of a substituted aromatic carboxylic acid.

Properties of Polyester Polyester's performance in apparel and interior fabrics is summarized in Table 8.11. To understand polyester's performance in comparison with that of the other fibers, examine the tables in Chapter 3.

Aesthetic Polyester fibers blend well, maintaining a natural fiber look and texture, with the advantage of easy care for apparel and interior textiles. The fabrics look like the natural fiber in the blend; their appearance retention during use and care clearly illustrates the presence of polyester.

Table 8.11 Summary of the Performance of Polyester in Apparel and Interior Textiles

Aesthetics	Variable
Durability	Excellent
Abrasion resistance	Excellent
Tenacity	Excellent
Elongation	High
Comfort	Poor
Absorbency	Poor
Thermal retention	Moderate
Appearance Retention	High
Resiliency	Excellent
Dimensional stability	High
Elastic recovery	High
Recommended Care	Machine-wash (apparel)
	Dry extraction (interior textiles)

Thick-and-thin yarns of polyester and rayon give a linen look to apparel and interior fabrics. Wool-like fabrics are found in both summer-weight and winter-weight men's suit fabrics.

The trilobal polyester fibers resulted when researchers worked with a silk finishing company to develop a manufactured filament that would have the aesthetic properties of silk. This research found that the unique properties of silk—liveliness, suppleness, and drape of the fabric; dry "tactile" hand; and good covering power of the yarns—resulted from (1) the triangular shape of the silk fiber; (2) the fine denier per filament; (3) the loose, bulky yarn and fabric structure; and (4) the highly crimped fabric structure. These results were applied to polyester. Silklike polyesters are spun with a trilobal shape and made into fabrics processed by a silk-finishing treatment. They are unique because they can be treated with caustic soda that leaves a thinner, less uniform fiber, yarn, or fabric without basically changing the fiber.

Polyester microfibers are particularly suited to high-fashion apparel and interior items because of their versatility and durability. Designers find the microfibers' drape and hand exciting and challenging. Consumers are willing to pay the additional cost for products that incorporate microfibers. Microfibers yield softer and more drapeable fabrics than conventional fibers do. Figure 8.10 illustrates the differences among fiber sizes. Items of polyester microfibers, both 100 percent polyester and blends with other fibers, include coats, suits, blouses, dresses, active sportswear, wall coverings, upholstery, sleeping bags, tents, filters, and toweling. These very fine fibers exhibit unparalleled softness, fluidity, drape, and appearance. *Shin-gosen* polyesters are Japanese fibers that are the most silklike of the very fine polyesters because of slight irregularities along the fiber. Some modifications combine a microchannel with the trilobal cross section; others have tiny microcraters along the fiber's surface. The techniques used to produce the microfibers and *shin-gosen* fibers are similar, but not identical, and the resultant fibers have slightly different performance and appearance characteristics.

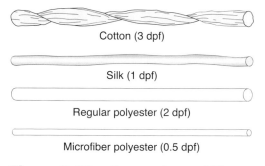

Figure 8.10 Comparison of fiber diameter: cotton, silk, regular polyester, and microfiber polyester.

Durability The abrasion resistance and strength of polyesters are excellent. Wet strength is comparable to dry strength. The high strength is produced by hot drawing to develop crystallinity and by increasing the molecular weight. Table 8.12 shows how the breaking tenacity of polyester varies with end use. The stronger fibers have been stretched more; their elongation is lower than that of the weaker fibers. This is particularly dramatic in the case of partially oriented filament fibers that are sold to manufacturers who stretch them more during the production of textured yarns. Their tenacity is 2.0 to 2.5 g/d, a lower strength than staple fibers, but with an elongation exceeding that of the other fibers, 120 to 150 percent. Sold in yarn form, these polyesters are known as POY, *partially oriented yarn*.

Because of its better sunlight resistance, polyester is often selected for end uses in which sunlight resistance is essential for durability, such as vehicle interiors, tarpaulins, and seatbelts.

Table 8.12 Performance Aspects of Modified Polyester Fibers

Fiber Modification	Tenacity, g/d	Breaking Elongation, %	End Use
High-tenacity filament	6.8–9.5	9–27	Tire cord, technical uses
Regular-tenacity filament	2.8–5.6	18–42	Apparel and interior textiles
High-tenacity staple	5.8–7.0	24–28	Durable-press items
Regular-tenacity staple	2.4–5.5	40–45	Apparel and interior textiles

Table 8.15 Summary of the Performance of Olefin in Apparel and Interior Textiles

Aesthetic	Variable
Luster	Medium
Durability	High
Abrasion resistance	Very good
Tenacity	High
Elongation	Variable
Comfort	Moderate
Absorbency	Poor
Thermal retention	Good
Appearance Retention	Excellent
Resiliency	Excellent
Dimensional stability	Excellent
Elastic recovery	Excellent
Recommended Care	Machine-wash, dry at low temperature (apparel)
	Dry extraction (interior textiles)

An acid-dyeable olefin is available, but dyed olefins comprise a tiny fraction of the market. Polypropylene is used in apparel, interiors, and technical products.

Properties of Olefin Olefin's performance in apparel and interior fabrics is summarized in Table 8.15. Review the fiber property tables in Chapter 3 to help understand the performance of olefin in comparison with that of the other fibers.

Aesthetics Olefin is usually produced with a medium luster and smooth texture, but the luster and texture can be modified depending on the end use. Many sizes of olefin fibers are available. Smaller fibers are available for interiors and apparel. Finer-denier fibers produce a softer, more natural drape.

Olefin has a waxy hand; crimped fibers with modified cross sections have a much more attractive hand and are most often used for apparel and interior textiles. Drape can be varied relative to end use by selection of fiber modification, fabric construction method, and finish.

Current olefins do not look artificial, as the early olefins did. Contemporary olefins are modified easily by changing cross section, fiber size, crimp, and luster. Olefin fibers are most often solution-dyed; many producers provide a wide variety of color choices for olefins designed for interiors or apparel. Some interior designers prefer olefin to most other fibers because of its attractive appearance and other positive performance aspects, coupled with its relatively low price as compared with similar products made from different fibers.

Durability Olefins may be produced with different strengths suited to the end use. The tenacity of polypropylenes ranges from 3.5 to 8.0 g/d; that of polyethylenes, from 1.5 to 7.0 g/d. Wet strength is equal to dry strength for both types. An ultra-high-strength olefin, Spectra by Honeywell, has a tenacity of up to 30 g/d and is used in technical products. Fibers produced for less demanding end uses have tenacities ranging from 4.5 to 6.0 g/d. Olefin fibers have very good abrasion resistance. Elongation varies with the type of olefin. For olefins normally used in apparel and interior textiles, the elongation is 10 to 45 percent, with excellent recovery. Upholstery and commercial carpets of olefin and olefin blends combine excellent performance with low cost.

Olefin products are durable and strong. With olefin's low density, it is possible to produce highly durable, lightweight products. Resistance to abrasion and chemicals is excellent. This combination of characteristics and low cost means that olefin is very competitive with other fibers with equal or superior durability. Olefin is ideal for end uses for which durability, low cost, and low density are critical, such as ropes and cables of great size or length.

Comfort Olefins are nonabsorbent, with a moisture regain of less than 0.1 percent. Because of this, most olefin fibers are mass-pigmented or solution-dyed. However, when modified nanoclay particles are incorporated in composite olefin fibers, it can be dyed. Olefins are nonpolar in nature and are not prone to static electricity. Because of its excellent wicking abilities, olefin is used in some active sportswear, socks, and underwear, and as a cover stock in disposable diapers. It does not absorb moisture and minimizes leakage. In cold-weather wear and active sportswear, olefin keeps the skin dry by wicking moisture away from the skin's surface.

Olefin has good heat retention. It is also the lightest of the textile fibers. Polypropylene has a specific gravity of 0.90 to 0.91; polyethylene, 0.92 to 0.96. This low specific gravity provides more fiber per pound for better cover. As producers learned to deal with its low softening and melting temperatures, difficulty in dyeing, and unpleasant hand, olefin is used in warm, light-weight sweaters and blankets. It takes 1.27 pounds of nylon or 1.71 pounds of cotton to cover the same volume as 1 pound of olefin.

An inner-layer barrier fabric of olefin is used in activewear. The barrier fabric combines wind resistance with air permeability and a good moisture vapor transport rate. **Moisture vapor transport rate (MVTR)** measures how quickly moisture vapor, such as evaporated perspiration, moves from the interior side of the fabric, next to the body, to the exterior. A high MVTR describes a fabric with good comfort characteristics, especially when the wearer is active.

Lastol, an elastic olefin, is a generic subclass fiber with superior stretch and recovery properties compared to other olefin fibers. Lastol has low levels of crystallinity, a different molecular structure, more resistance to solvents, and more tolerance of a wider range of temperatures. It is used in easy-care stretch apparel.

With modifications of cross section, crimp, and fiber size, olefin upholstery fabrics can be extremely comfortable. In upholstery, olefins with deniers of 1.7 to 2.0 produce comfortable textures. Olefin fibers with a similar small denier are used in apparel. Soft and lightweight olefin fibers with excellent wicking are prized by both amateur and professional athletes for the edge they contribute to performance.

Appearance Retention Olefin has excellent resiliency and recovers quickly from wrinkling. Shrinkage resistance is excellent as long as it is not heated. It also has excellent elastic recovery. Olefin retains its attractive appearance for years. Since the fiber can be heat-set, wrinkles are minimal. Crimp and other three-dimensional effects are permanent. The fiber does not react with most chemicals, so it does not soil or stain readily. Designers find olefin carpeting and upholstery fabrics ideal for a wide variety of end uses.

Care Olefins have easy-care characteristics that make them suited to a number of end uses. They dry quickly after washing. Dry cleaning is not recommended because olefins are swollen by common dry-cleaning solvents such as perchloroethylene (perc or PCE). Petroleum-based dry-cleaning solvents are acceptable for cleaning olefins, but if perc is used, the damage cannot be reversed.

Since olefin is not absorbent, waterborne stains are not a problem. The fiber does not pick up color from stains or items that bleed in the wash. The major problems with olefin relate to its oleophilic and heat-sensitive nature. Oily stains are extremely difficult to remove. Exposure to oil may cause the fiber to swell. Exposure to excess heat causes the fiber to shrink and melt. Interior items of olefin should never be treated with soil-removal agents that contain perc since this solvent will alter the appearance of any treated areas.

Olefins have excellent resistance to acids, alkalis, insects, and microorganisms. They are affected by sunlight, but stabilizers can be added to correct this disadvantage. Outdoor carpeting made of olefin fibers can be hosed off.

Olefins have a low melting point (325 to 335°F), which limits their use in apparel. Warm or cold water should be used for spot cleaning or washing. Olefin fabrics should be air-dried. Olefins should be dried and ironed at low temperatures.

Environmental Concerns and Sustainability of Olefin

Many environmental issues discussed with nylon also apply to olefin. See the earlier discussion in this chapter. Olefin is an easier fiber to recycle than most other fibers. It is extensively used in a basic unmodified form to protect bales of fiber and rolls of fabrics used in apparel and interior textiles. Many packaging materials and technical products used in other industries are also used in a basic form that can be melted and reused with minimal effort to purify and process them back into fiber form. Tyvek Protective Wear by DuPont Performance Materials is an example of a product made of 25 percent postconsumer recycled polyethylene.

Since olefin is seldom dyed, the environmental problems related to dyeing are minimal. Because olefin can be engineered for specific end uses, the problems related to recycling or disposing of finishing chemicals are of little concern.

Probably one of the most significant impacts of olefin on the environment is its use in products that protect the environment. Erosion-control fabrics used in landscaping and along highways protect newly seeded areas and prevent soil erosion. Weed-barrier fabrics and protective covers for vegetables and flowers minimize the use of herbicides and insecticides by farmers, gardeners, and homeowners. Hazardous-waste-transport containers are lined with Tyvek, an olefin product by DuPont Performance Materials.

Uses of Olefin

The American Polyolefin Association (APA) promotes the use of olefin and a positive image of the fiber. Olefin is found in an ever-widening array of end uses. In apparel, it is used for underwear, socks, sweaters, glove liners, and active sportswear. A fine-denier olefin is used in blends for pantyhose, saris, and swimwear. A microdenier olefin is used as a wind-, water-, and cold-barrier layer in active and outdoor wear. Thinsulate is a low-bulk, ultra-fine-microdenier fiberfill of olefin produced by 3M and used in footwear, ski jackets, and other outerwear for which a slim silhouette is desired.

In interior textiles, olefin is used by itself and in blends with other fibers in carpeting as face yarns; as nonwoven, needle-punched carpets and carpet tiles; and as upholstery, draperies, and slipcovers. Olefin has almost completely replaced jute in carpet backing because of its low cost, easy processing, excellent durability, and suitability for a wide variety of face yarns, end uses, and finishing procedures. It is used for nonwoven fabrics for furniture webbing because it is versatile, efficient, easy to handle, and economic. Antimicrobial and antifungal olefins are also used in woven mattress covers and contract floor coverings.

It is in technical applications that olefin really proves itself. Olefin's popularity is due to its versatility, serviceability, and low cost in a wide array of applications. Olefin makes an ideal geotextile—textiles that are used in contact with the soil. It is used to produce roadbed-support fabrics, like Petromat and Petrotak, that provide a water and particle barrier between road surfaces and the underlying soil foundation. Roadbed-support and stabilizer fabrics are used on roadways, rail lines, and parking lots to extend their life.

Table 8.16 Types and Kinds of Olefin Fibers

Heat-stabilized	Acid-dyeable
Light-stabilized	Solution-dyed
Modified cross section	Bicomponent
Pigmented	Fibrillated
Antimicrobial and antifungal	Soil-blocking
Flame-retardant	

Table 8.17 Comparison of Melt-Spun Fibers

	Nylon	Polyester	Olefin
Breaking tenacity, g/d	2.3–9.8 filament	2.8–9.5 filament	3.5–8.0 filament
	2.9–7.2 staple	2.4–7.0 staple	
Specific gravity	1.14	1.22 or 1.38	0.91
Moisture regain %	4.0–4.5	0.4–0.8	Less than 1
Melting point	482 or 414°F	540 or 482°F	325–335°F
Safe ironing temp	270–300°F	325–350°F	250°F to lowest setting
Effect of light	Poor resistance	Good resistance	Poor resistance

▶ Learning Activity 11

Olefin is not a common apparel fiber, but it is used for interiors and technical products. Use Fabric #96 and list three technical end uses that would be appropriate for this textile. Describe the properties of olefin that make it a good choice for these end uses.

Olefin is used in some car interiors for floor coverings, upholstery, headliners, sun visors, instrument panels, arm rests, package-shelf fabric, door and side panels, and carpeting in trunks and cargo areas. It is also a popular fiber in boats for interiors and finishing fabrics and as surface coverings on docks and decks. It is found in dye nets, cover stock for diapers, filter fabrics, laundry bags, sandbags, banners, substrates for coated fabrics, ropes, and twines. Tyvek is used in wall-panel fabrics, envelopes, and protective apparel. Table 8.16 lists modifications of olefin. Table 8.17 compares the characteristics of nylon, polyester, and olefin, the three melt-spun fibers discussed in this chapter.

Acrylic

Acrylonitrile, the substance from which **acrylic** fibers are made and from which the generic name is derived, was first made in Germany in 1893. The marketing of acrylic fibers frequently takes advantage of their wool-like characteristics. Terms like *virgin acrylic*, *mothproof*, and *moth-resistant* appeal to consumers but do not convey anything significant, since acrylics are inherently moth-resistant and are not currently recycled.

Production of Acrylic Some acrylic fibers are dry- or solvent-spun and others are wet-spun. In **dry spinning**, the polymers are dissolved in a suitable solvent, such as dimethyl formamide,

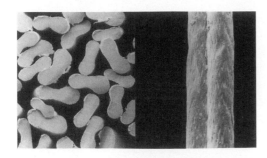

Figure 8.14 Photomicrographs of acrylic: cross-sectional view (left) and longitudinal view (right).
SOURCE: Courtesy of the British Textile Technology Group.

extruded into warm air, and solidified by evaporation of the solvent. After spinning, the fibers are stretched hot, 3 to 10 times their original length, crimped, and marketed as cut staple or tow. In **wet spinning**, the polymer is dissolved in solvent, extruded into a coagulating bath, dried, crimped, and collected as tow for use in the high-bulk process or cut into staple and baled.

Physical Structure of Acrylic The cross-sectional shape of acrylic fibers varies as a result of the spinning method used to produce them (Figure 8.14). Dry spinning produces a dog-bone shape. Wet spinning imparts a round or lima bean shape to some fibers. Differences in cross-sectional shape affect physical and aesthetic properties and thus can be a factor in determining appropriate end use. Round and lima bean shapes have a higher bending stiffness, which contributes to resiliency, and are appropriate for bulky sweaters and blankets. Dog-bone shape gives the softness and luster desirable for other uses.

All the production of acrylic fibers in the United States is staple fiber and tow. Staple fiber is available in deniers and lengths suitable for all spinning systems. Acrylic fibers also vary in shrinkage potential. Bicomponent fibers were first produced as acrylics. Some filament-yarn acrylic fabrics are imported, mostly in window treatments. MicroSupreme is a trade name for an acrylic microfiber made by Sterling Fibers Inc.

Chemical Composition and Molecular Arrangement of Acrylic

Acrylic fibers—manufactured fibers in which the fiber-forming substance is any long-chain synthetic polymer composed of at least 85 percent by weight acrylonitrile units.

$$\left[\begin{array}{c} -CH_2-CH- \\ | \\ CN \end{array} \right]$$

—Federal Trade Commission

Fibers of 100 percent polyacrylonitrile have a compact, highly oriented internal structure that makes them virtually undyeable. They are an example of a **homopolymer**, a fiber composed of a single substance. Schematically, a homopolymer could be diagrammed:

X X X X X X X X X X X X X X X   Homopolymer

Most acrylics are produced as **copolymers**, with up to 15 percent of the repeating units something other than acrylonitrile. This produces a more open structure and permits dye to be absorbed into the fiber. The other repeating units furnish dye sites that can be changed for specific dye classes so that cross dyeing is possible. The percentages of other repeating units and their arrangement in relation to each other will vary. Copolymer fibers are composed of two or more compounds and could be diagrammed:

XXXOXXXXXOXXXXXOXXX   Copolymer

In **graft polymer** acrylics, the other repeating unit does not become a part of the main molecular chain. It is a side chain attached to the backbone chain of the molecule. These molecular chains have a more open structure, less crystallinity, and better dye receptivity.

Some fibers have molecules with chemically reactive groups; others are chemically inert. A chemically inert molecule can be made reactive by grafting reactive groups onto the backbone. It could be diagrammed:

```
X X X X X X X X X X X X X X X X X X X X
    |             |             |
    C             C             C
```

Graft polymer

Copolymer acrylics are not as strong as the homopolymers or graft polymer acrylics. Since acrylics are used mostly in apparel and interiors, the reduced strength is not a major concern.

Acrylic is a manufactured fiber in which the fiber-forming substance is any long-chain synthetic polymer composed of acrylonitrile units.

Table 8.18 Summary of the Performance of Acrylic in Apparel and Interior Textiles

Aesthetics	Wool-like
Durability	Moderate
Abrasion resistance	Moderate
Tenacity	Moderate
Elongation	Moderate to high
Comfort	Moderate
Absorbency	Poor
Thermal retention	Moderate
Appearance Retention	Moderate
Resiliency	Moderate
Dimensional stability	Moderate
Elastic recovery	Moderate
Recommended Care	Machine-wash; follow care label (apparel)
	Dry-clean or dry-extraction method (interior textiles)

Properties of Acrylic Acrylic fibers are soft, warm, lightweight, and resilient. They make easy-care fabrics. Because of their low specific gravity and high bulk, the acrylics have been called the "warmth without weight" fibers. Acrylics have been successful in end uses, such as sweaters and blankets, that had been dominated by wool. They are superior to wool in their easy-care properties and are nonallergenic. Bulky acrylic yarns are popular in socks, fleece and fake-fur fabrics, and craft yarns. Table 8.18 summarizes the performance characteristics of acrylic. The fiber property tables in Chapter 3 compare the properties of acrylic to those of other fibers.

Aesthetics Acrylic fibers possess favorable aesthetic properties. They are attractive and have a soft, pleasant hand. Bulky spun yarns are usually textured to be wool-like. Indeed, acrylic fabrics imitate wool fabrics more successfully than any of the other manufactured fibers.

Apparel and interior items of all acrylic or acrylic blends are attractive. Their luster is matte as a result of delustering, the irregular cross-sectional fiber shape, and fiber crimp. Since these products are almost always staple fibers, their wool-like appearance is maintained. Bulky yarns and bicomponent fibers also contribute to the wool-like appearance and texture.

Durability Acrylics are not as durable as nylon, polyester, or olefin fibers, but in apparel and interior textiles, the strength of acrylics is satisfactory. Dry tenacity is moderate, ranging from 2.0 to 3.0 g/d. Abrasion resistance is also moderate. The breaking elongation is 35 percent. Elongation increases when the fiber is wet. The overall durability of acrylic fibers is moderate, similar to that of wool and cotton.

Interior textiles made from acrylics or acrylic blends are durable. They provide reasonable resistance to abrasion for upholstery fabrics. They are sufficiently strong to withstand laundering, dry cleaning, and dry-extraction cleaning, depending on the product. Pilling can be noticeable with staple fiber fabrics. However, low-pilling fiber modifications are available, and some fabric finishes reduce pilling.

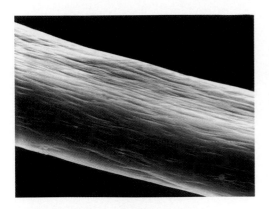

Figure 8.15 **Acrylic that is magnified 3000x shows a pitted and irregular surface.**

SOURCE: Courtesy of the British Textile Technology Group.

Table 8.19 Comparison of the Durability of Acrylic With That of Wool

Fiber Property	Acrylic	Wool
Abrasion resistance	Good	Fair
Breaking tenacity	2.0–3.0 g/d dry	1.5 g/d dry
	1.8–2.7 g/d wet	1.0 g/d wet
Breaking elongation	35%	25%
Elastic recovery	92%	99%

Carpets made with a blend of 88 percent nylon and 12 percent acrylic have high bulk and are more durable than nylon alone. The fibers are blended together in the carpet yarn, twisted, and heat-set. The high-shrinkage fiber modification shrinks and tightens the yarn tuft, producing good durability characteristics.

Because of its exceptional resistance to weathering, acrylic is widely used in awnings and tarpaulins. Table 8.19 shows that acrylic is comparable to wool in durability properties.

Comfort Compared to the other synthetic fibers, the surface of acrylic fibers is less regular and indented (Figure 8.15). In spite of the relatively low moisture regain of 1.0 to 2.5 percent, acrylics are moderately comfortable because of their irregular surfaces. Instead of absorbing moisture and becoming wet to the touch, acrylic fibers wick moisture to the fabric's exterior, where it evaporates more readily and cools the body.

Another factor that makes acrylics comfortable is that the fibers and yarns can be made with high bulk. Acrylic fibers can be produced with a latent shrinkage potential and retain their bulk indefinitely at room temperature. The resulting bulky fabrics retain body heat well, so they are warm in cold temperatures. Bulky knit sweaters are a common example of this.

The structure of the yarn and fabric can be modified to create a warmer or cooler product. In general, acrylics are more comfortable than nylon and polyester, but not as comfortable as cotton in hot, humid weather or as wool in cold or cool, humid weather.

The specific gravity of acrylic is similar to that of nylon. Thus, the fabrics are lightweight and durable. This means that bulky sweaters of acrylic are not as heavy as wool sweaters. Acrylic blankets are lighter than similar wool blankets.

Appearance Retention Acrylic fibers exhibit moderate resiliency and recovery from bending, so they resist wrinkling during use and care. They have moderate dimensional stability. When appropriate yarn and fabric structures are selected, the dimensional stability of acrylic fabrics is good. Acrylics shrink when exposed to high temperatures and steam; the fibers do not hold up well under hot, wet conditions.

Acrylic fibers cannot be heat-set like nylon and polyester because acrylic does not melt, but rather decomposes and discolors when heated. However, some acrylics can have pleats or creases set in that are not affected by normal use or care. With the careful application of heat and/or steam, the crease or pleats can be removed.

Acrylic also differs from nylon and polyester because of its poorer dimensional stability; fabrics may shrink or stretch during care. Acrylics will pill because the fibers fibrillate, or crack, with abrasion.

Acrylics and blends with acrylic maintain their appearance well. The bulk characteristics are permanent if the product receives the appropriate care. These fibers are less likely to mat than some fibers. With solution-dyeing of some upholstery, drapery, and awning fabrics, colors

Table 8.20 Comparison of Care for Acrylic and Wool

Fiber Property	Acrylic	Wool
Effect of alkalis	Resistant to weak alkalis	Harmed
Effect of acids	Resistant to most acids	Resistant to weak acids
Effect of solvents	Can be dry-cleaned	Dry cleaning recommended
Effect of sunlight	Excellent resistance	Low resistance
Stability	Generally retains shape	Subject to felting, shrinkage
Permanence of creases	Creases can be set and removed by heat	Creases set by heat and moisture—not permanent
Effect of heat	Thermoplastic—sticks at 450–490°F	Scorches easily, becomes brittle at high temperatures
Resistance to moths and fungi	Resistant	Harmed by moths; mildew forms on soiled, stored wool
Effect of water	None	May felt or mat, noticeable odor when wet

are permanent. Awning fabrics of solution-dyed acrylic are popular in finishing window exteriors, entries, and outdoor entertainment areas.

Care It is especially important to follow the instructions found on the care labels for acrylics. Table 8.20 compares the care for acrylic with that for wool. There are several basic acrylic fibers with slightly differing properties due to the polymer composition, manufacturing methods, and fiber modifications.

The acrylics have good resistance to most chemicals except strong alkalis and chlorine bleaches. This is not surprising; fibers containing nitrogen are usually susceptible to damage from alkali and chlorine. Except for the furlike fabrics, acrylic fabrics have good wash-and-wear characteristics. They do not wrinkle if handled properly and if directions on the care label are followed.

Some items made from high-bulk yarns of bicomponent fibers need to be machine-dried to regain their shape after washing. If they are blocked, dried flat, or drip-dried, they may be too large or misshapen. Rewashing and tumble drying should help restore the original shape.

Some acrylics can be dry-cleaned. However, with some fabrics the finish is removed, resulting in a harsh feel. Thus, care labels should be followed. Acrylics are resistant to moth damage and mildew and have excellent resistance to sunlight.

Following the recommended care procedures for acrylic or acrylic blend products is especially important for electric blankets made from acrylic. Electric blankets should never be dry-cleaned. Dry-cleaning solvents dissolve the protective coating on the wiring of the blanket, resulting in a high risk of electric shock or fire. Steam cleaning of draperies, upholstery, and carpeting is generally not recommended because acrylics may shrink.

▶ Learning Activity 12

Examine your wardrobe and home/apartment/dormitory. Make a list of the items that are all acrylic or a blend of acrylic and another fiber. (Be sure to consider things like upholstery and brushes in addition to apparel.) Select an item from your list and describe the characteristics of acrylic that have contributed to the serviceability of that textile product. How do these contributions enhance or detract from your satisfaction with the product? How could acrylic have been modified to reduce your areas of dissatisfaction?

Antimicrobial and antifungal acrylics are used in apparel, interior, and technical applications. Products include nursing uniforms, socks, shoe liners, sportswear, contract carpet and upholstery, surgical barrier fabrics, and technical filters.

Environmental Concerns and Sustainability of Acrylic

Acrylic is resistant to natural sources of degradation, including molds, mildew, rot, and many chemicals. Because acrylic is processed from petrochemicals, concerns include drilling in sensitive environments, oil spills, and disposal of hazardous chemicals. The chemicals from which acrylic is made require significant processing before they are polymerized to form acrylic. With wet- or dry-spun fibers, recycling of solvents is necessary to minimize the environmental impact. Wet-spun acrylics also require washing and drying to remove chemicals from the coagulating bath. Different types of acrylic are made from slightly different raw materials; potential hazards to the environment will differ depending on which raw materials and processes are used in production. Acrylic uses approximately 30 per cent more energy and substantially more water during production compared to polyester. Acrylic is not recycled. Because acrylics can be engineered for specific end uses, chemical finishing is not a concern. Acrylics may be dyed; processing of dye wastes is a concern.

Uses of Acrylic

Acrylic is a relatively minor fiber in terms of use. Although more acrylic is used in apparel, it is also important in interior and some technical products. Knitted apparel items of acrylic include fleece fabrics, sweaters, and socks. Occasionally, fleece fabrics of acrylic are used in jogging outfits and active sportswear. Acrylic pile fabrics and fun furs are used for coats, jackets, linings, or soft stuffed animals. Antistatic acrylics are used in apparel for computer clean rooms.

Craft yarns, another important end use of acrylic fibers, are often made of a heavier denier (5 to 6 denier). Many sweaters, baby garments, vests, and afghans are knitted or crocheted with these yarns. Acrylic yarns are also used for embroidery, weaving, and other crafts.

Upholstery fabrics have a wool-like appearance and may be flat-woven fabrics or velvets with good durability and stain resistance. Drapery fabrics of acrylic are resistant to sunlight and weathering. Acrylics are used in lightweight and winter-weight blankets. Carpets and rugs of acrylic or blends look more wool-like than several other synthetic fibers. Acrylic blankets, carpets, and rugs have easier care requirements and cost less than those of wool.

Acrylics are found in a number of technical uses for which their chemical and abrasion resistance and good weathering properties make them suitable: awnings and tarpaulins, luggage, boat and other vehicle covers, outdoor furniture, tents, filtration fabrics, carbon fiber precursors, office room dividers, and sandbags. When exposed to chemicals, fibers with good chemical resistance show little or no loss of physical structure or fiber properties. Sunbrella mass-pigmented acrylic awnings by Glen Raven Mills, Inc., withstand exposure to sun, wind, and rain for years without fading, cracking, hardening, peeling, or rotting. A cross-linked super-absorbent acrylic, Oasis, is used in nonwoven filters to remove water from fuels, solvents, and other organic liquids, in packaging for meats, and in gaskets and seals.

Types and Kinds of Acrylic

Sterling Fibers, Inc., is the only company that currently produces acrylic. Trade names include Creslan, BioFresh, MicroSupreme, and Weatherbloc. Fiber variants tailored for a specific end use are produced. See Table 8.21 for a list of fiber and yarn types available.

Table 8.21 Types and Kinds of Acrylic Fibers and Yarns

Homopolymer

Copolymer

Graft polymer

Bicomponent

Blends of various deniers

Blends of homopolymer and copolymer

Helical, nonreversible crimp

Reversible crimp

Surface modified

Variable cross section—round, acorn, dog-bone

Variable dyeability—cationic, disperse, acidic, basic

Solution-dyed

▶ Learning Activity 13

Use two of these fabrics from your swatch kit: #80, 86, 105, and 119. Use the swatch set key to verify that each fabric you selected incorporates acrylic. For your swatches, has acrylic been modified to resemble a natural fiber? If yes, which one and what modifications were done so that acrylic macroscopically resembles the natural fiber? Identify an end use for each sample and explain how acrylic would be a serviceable fiber for that end use. If two or more fibers are present in the fabric, how has acrylic been modified to make it more compatible with the other fiber(s)?

▶ Learning Activity 14

Identify the sustainability of these four fibers: nylon, polyester, olefin, and acrylic. How do these fibers compare to the sustainability of the manufactured or natural fibers? Are there any commonly used apparel or interior fibers that are fully sustainable? What are some of the concerns regarding sustainability of each group of fibers?

key terms

Acrylic   179

Compressional resiliency   162

Copolymer   180

Drawing   155

Dry spinning   179

Elasterell-p   170

Gel spinning   175

Glazing   153

Graft polymer   180

Heat sensitivity   153

Heat setting   155

High-tenacity fibers   158

Homopolymer   180

Lastol   177

Low-pilling fibers   158

Melt spinning   154

Moisture vapor transport rate   177

Nylon   158

Olefin   174

Oleophilic   154

Pilling   154

Polyamides   160

Polyester   166

Polyethylene   175

Polypropylene   175

Synthetic fibers   152

Wet spinning   180

1. Explain the differences in chemical composition between these groups of fibers:
   a. Polyamide (nylon) and polyester
   b. Polyethylene and polypropylene
   c. Acrylic and wool

2. Explain the differences in properties between the pairs of fibers listed in Question #1.

3. Describe the major performance characteristics of nylon, polyester, olefin, and acrylic.

4. Identify the spinning process used to produce nylon, polyester, olefin, and acrylic. How does the spinning process relate to the fiber's cross-sectional shape?

5. How do the characteristics of these fibers differ from those of the natural fibers and those produced from naturally occurring polymers?

6. Identify a synthetic fiber that would be an appropriate choice for each end use listed below and explain, using performance characteristics, why you selected that fiber:
   a. Carpet for department store boutique area
   b. Pantyhose
   c. Sweater vest for casual Friday
   d. Geotextile for use as roadbed underlay
   e. Lead rope for horses or ponies
   f. Upholstery fabric for theater seats

7. For each fiber selected for the end uses in Question #6, what problems might be encountered during the use or cleaning of that textile product? How do those problems relate to fiber characteristics?

8. For each fiber selected for the end uses in Question #6, explain fiber modifications that would be appropriate for that end use. How would those modifications enhance the serviceability of the textile product?

9. Many consumers assume that synthetic fibers are poor for the environment. Make a list of the factors about these fibers that would support consumers' assumptions. Make a second list of factors about these fibers that would refute consumers' assumptions.

10. Explain why polyester is frequently blended with cotton. What are the advantages and disadvantages of such blends?

11. What are the similarities and differences between silk and the microdenier modifications of nylon and polyester?

12. Polyester fleece has become a popular choice for colder climates. Explain the properties of polyester that make it a good choice for such a fabric.

Case Study

Green Apparel*

Uniforms for employees in the service industry are a multimillion-dollar-a-year business. Environmentally friendly uniforms are attracting interest from chains in the hospitality (restaurants, hotels, resorts, etc.) and service industries (cleaning, repair, delivery, etc.). Because of the daily use uniforms receive, they must be durable, easy care, and maintain an attractive and professional appearance throughout use. Environmentally friendly mix and match uniforms using recycled polyester fibers from plastic beverage bottles are one option. One large hotel and resort chain introduced new uniforms made from recycled polyester for their front desk and other customer service employees in 2009. The postconsumer beverage bottles are made into flakes, processed into filaments, spun into yarns, and woven into soft fabrics. The uniforms are machine washable and do not require professional laundering or dry cleaning. The hospitality chain has two collections—one for the hotels and one for the resorts. A customized look can be created based on location, climate, and décor. According to the company's president, the sustainable uniforms reflect the vision of being more mindful of the environment.

DISCUSSION QUESTIONS

1. How does the process for recycled polyester compare to that for new polyester?

2. How does recycled polyester, a petrochemical fiber, fit within the definition of sustainability?

3. How would you feel if you were an employee of this firm required to wear recycled polyester every day while working?

4. Go to the lobby of a nearby hotel or motel and observe the following: How easy is it to distinguish employees from guests? Is the staff required to wear uniforms? Is every staff member wearing identical uniforms? What does the attire of the staff say about the hotel? What are the general characteristics of the fabrics in the uniform—what does the fiber content look like?

*Vermillion, L. (2008, November). Dressed for sustainability. *Lodging Magazine*, 72.

suggested readings

Anonymous (1998). Corterra: a new polyester fibre. *Textiles Magazine*, 1, pp. 12–14.

Borland, V. S. (1998, January). Miracle fiber back in fashion. *American Sportswear and Knitting Times*, pp. K/A6, K/A8, K/A10.

Colchester, C. (2007). *Textiles Today: A Global Survey of Trends and Traditions*. New York: Thames & Hudson.

Fletcher, K. (2008). *Sustainable Fashion and Textiles: Design Journey*. London: Earthscan.

Ford, J. E. (1992). Acrylic fibres. *Textiles*, 2, pp. 10–14.

Ford, J. (1995). Polyolefin textiles. *Textiles Magazine*, 3, pp. 11–15.

Foster, L. E. (Ed.), (2006). *Nanotechnology: Science, Innovation, and Opportunity*. Upper Saddle River, NJ: Prentice Hall.

Havich, M. M. (1998, June). Performance power. *America's Textile International*, p. 90.

Hethorn, J., & Ulasewicz, C. (2008). *Sustainable Fashion: Why Now?* New York: Fairchild Books.

Jerg, G., & Baumann, J. (1990). Polyester microfibers: a new generation of fabrics. *Textile Chemist and Colorist*, 22(12), pp. 12–14.

Karst, D., & Yang, Y. (2006). Potential advantages and risks of nanotechnology for textiles, *AATCC Review,* 6(3), 44–48.

Qian, L., & Hinestroza, J. P. (2004), Application of nanotechnology for high performance textiles, *Journal of Textile and Apparel, Technology, and Management,* 4(1), 1–7.

Roshan, P., & Roshan, S. P. (2005, January/February). Electrospinning: A breakthrough technology. *The Textile Journal*, 14–16.

Tao, X. (Ed.), (2001). *Smart Fibres, Fabrics, and Clothing.* Cambridge, England: Woodhead Publishing.

The polycotton story. (1994, Winter). *Textiles Magazine*, pp. 8–11.

Vermillion, L. (2008, November). Dressed for sustainability. *Lodging Magazine*, 72.

Vonwiller, E. (2000, August). The secret life of industrial textiles. *America's Textiles International*, pp. 40–42.

Wei, Q., Mather, R., Ye, H., Huang, F., & Xu, W. (2005, December). The functionalization of the surface of polymer nanofibers. *Technical Textiles International*, 21–23.

SPECIAL-USE FIBERS

CHAPTER OBJECTIVES

- To differentiate among special-use fibers based on their elastomeric or protective characteristics.
- To recognize the importance of these fibers in apparel, interiors, and technical products.
- To integrate properties of special-use fibers with their uses.

9

This chapter focuses on fibers with unique characteristics. Some of these fibers are in common consumer products, but consumers may not be aware of them. Other fibers are used in technical applications and have contributed significantly to many scientific and engineering advances. The fibers are grouped by the purposes they serve: elastomeric or protective.

These fibers are produced in much smaller quantities as compared with the majority of the fibers discussed in previous chapters. They are used either in small quantities in products or in items with a relatively small market segment. For example, spandex may comprise as much as 20 percent of the fiber in a swimsuit or leotard. Graphite fiber may be used in the frame of a bicycle to add structural support. The potential for growth in this segment of the textile complex is excellent. The price per pound of these fibers can be very high compared with that of common apparel and interior fibers. Sustainability and the environmental impact of these fibers is relatively minimal because of their low production levels. Several of the protective fibers that will be discussed later in this chapter are frequently used to remove harmful chemicals from the environment, to monitor conditions as components of smart textiles, or to enable people to work in adverse or hazardous environments.

Elastomeric Fibers

An **elastomer** is a natural or synthetic polymer that, at room temperature, can be stretched repeatedly to at least twice its original length and that, after removal of the tensile load, will immediately and forcibly return to approximately its original length. Elastomeric fibers include spandex, rubber, elastoester, elasterell-p, lastol, and anidex. Anidex is no longer produced in the United States.

The type of stretch and elasticity required in a textile product depends on its end use. **Power stretch** is the ability of a fiber or fabric to exhibit high retractive forces that mold, support, or shape the body. This type of stretch is important in end uses for which holding power and elasticity are needed. Elastic fibers with a high retractive force are used to attain this kind of stretch. Some end uses are foundation garments, surgical-support garments, swimsuits, garters, belts, and suspenders.

Comfort stretch is the ability of a fiber or fabric to elongate slightly as the body moves and to recover a significant portion of that elongation when the stretching force is removed. This type of stretch is important in products for which only elasticity is desired. Comfort-stretch fabrics look like nonstretch fabrics. Their weight is lighter than that of power-stretch fabrics and they are used in apparel and interior textiles to enhance comfort and fit.

Rubber

Rubber—manufactured fiber in which the fiber-forming substance is comprised of natural or synthetic rubber, including:

1. A manufactured fiber in which the fiber-forming substance is a hydrocarbon such as natural rubber, polyisoprene, polybutadiene, copolymers of dienes and hydrocarbons, or amorphous (noncrystalline) polyolefins.
2. A manufactured fiber in which the fiber-forming substance is a copolymer of acrylonitrile and a diene (such as butadiene) composed of not more than 50 percent but at least 10 percent by weight of acrylonitrile units.

$$\left[-CH_2-CH- \atop \quad\quad | \atop \quad\quad CN \right]$$

Elastomers are natural or synthetic polymers that, at room temperature, can be stretched repeatedly to at least twice the original length and that, after removal of the tensile load, will immediately and forcibly return to approximately the original length. Elastomeric fibers include spandex, rubber, elastoester, elasterell-p, lastol, and anidex.

Power stretch is the ability of a fiber or fabric to exhibit high retractive forces that mold, support, or shape the body and is important in end uses for which holding power and elasticity are needed. **Comfort stretch** is the ability of a fiber or fabric to elongate slightly as the body moves and to recover a significant portion of that elongation when the stretching force is removed and is used in products for which only elasticity is desired.

The term **lastrile** may be used as a generic description for fibers falling in this category.

3. A manufactured fiber in which the fiber-forming substance is a polychloroprene or a copolymer of chloroprene in which at least 35 percent by weight of the fiber-forming substance is composed of chloroprene units.

$$\left[-CH_2-\underset{\underset{Cl}{|}}{C}=CH-CH_2- \right]$$

—Federal Trade Commission

Natural **rubber** is the oldest elastomer and the least expensive. It is obtained by coagulation of latex from the rubber tree *Hevea brasiliensis*. In 1905, sheets of rubber were cut into strips for yarns used in foundation garments. During and shortly after World War II, the first synthetic rubbers were developed. These synthetic rubbers are cross-linked diene polymers, copolymers containing dienes, or amorphous polyolefins. To develop their elastomeric properties, both synthetic and natural rubbers are vulcanized or cross-linked with sulfur. Both types have a large cross section. Round fibers are extruded, and rectangular fibers are cut from extruded film.

Rubber has an excellent elongation—500 to 600 percent—and excellent recovery. Its low tenacity—0.34 g/d—limits its use in lightweight garments. The finest rubber yarns must be three times as large as spandex yarns to be as strong. Because of rubber's low dye acceptance, hand, and appearance, it is covered by a yarn of another fiber or by other yarns in the fabric.

Rubber has been replaced in many uses by spandex, but it continues to be used in narrow elastic fabrics. Synthetic rubber is more common in these elastic fabrics than is natural rubber.

Even though antioxidants are added to the spinning solution, rubber lacks resistance to oxidizing agents and is damaged by aging, sunlight, oil, and perspiration. It is resistant to alkalis, but is damaged by heat, chlorine, and solvents. It should be washed with care and never dry-cleaned.

Neoprene, a type of synthetic rubber made from polychloroprene, is used as an elastomeric fiber or a supported elastic film. It is resistant to acids, alkalis, alcohols, oils, caustics, and solvents. It is found in protective gloves and apparel, wetsuits, framing for window glass, technical hoses and belts, anticorrosive seals and membranes, and coatings for wiring.

Spandex

The first manufactured elastic fiber, a spandex fiber called *Lycra*, was introduced in 1958. Spandex generated much interest because it was superior to rubber in strength and durability. Spandex is produced by Invista Inc. under the trade name of Lycra. Spandex is known as **elastane** in many other parts of the world; elastane is an acceptable alternative term for spandex in the United States according to the Federal Trade Commission.

Production Spandex fibers are made by reacting preformed polyester or polyether molecules with diisocyanate and polymerizing. Filaments are obtained by wet or solvent spinning. The spinning solution may contain delustering agents, dye receptors, whiteners, and lubricants.

Physical Structure Spandex is produced as monofilament or fused multifilament yarns in a variety of deniers. Monofilaments are round in cross section, whereas fused multifilaments are coalesced or partly fused together at intervals and are found in fibers with deniers of 40 and above (Figure 9.1). Spandex is delustered and is usually white or gray.

Figure 9.1 Photomicrographs of spandex: cross-sectional view (left), longitudinal view (right).
SOURCE: Courtesy of the British Textile Technology Group.

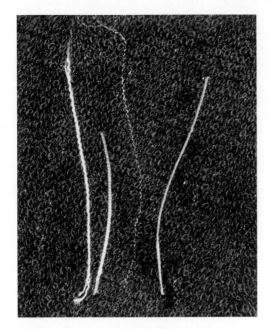

Figure 9.2 Comparison of several spandex fibers (left to right): spandex wrapped with cotton yarn (core spun), fused multifilament, three fine filaments used as a yarn, and dyed heavy-denier monofilament.

Spandex is a manufactured fiber in which the fiber-forming substance is a long-chain synthetic polymer consisting of a segmented polyurethane.

Deniers range from 20 to 4300. Twenty-denier spandex is used in lightweight support hosiery, in which a large amount of stretch is desirable. Much coarser yarns, 1,500 to 2,240 denier, stretch less and are used for support in hosiery tops, swimwear, and foundation garments (Figure 9.2).

Chemical Composition and Molecular Arrangement

Spandex—a manufactured fiber in which the fiber-forming substance is a long-chain synthetic polymer consisting of at least 85 percent of a segmented polyurethane.

—*Federal Trade Commission*

Spandex is a generic name, but it is not derived from the chemical name of the fiber, as are most of the manufactured fibers. The name was coined by shifting the syllables of the word *expand*.

Spandex consists of rigid and flexible segments in the polymer chain; the flexible segments provide the stretch, and the rigid segments hold the chain together. When force is applied, the folded, or coiled, flexible segments straighten out; when force is removed, they return to their original positions (Figure 9.3). Varying proportions of rigid and flexible segments control the amount of stretch.

Properties Table 9.1 compares the performance of spandex and rubber in apparel and interior fabrics. The tables in Chapter 3 include the performance characteristics of all the fibers.

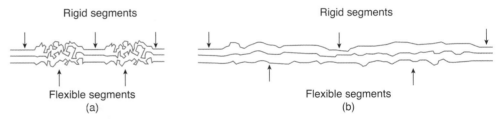

Figure 9.3 Spandex molecular chains: (a) relaxed, (b) extended.

Table 9.1 Summary of the Performance of Spandex and Rubber in Apparel and Interior Textiles

	Spandex	Rubber
Aesthetics	Moderate	Poor
Durability	Moderate	Poor
Abrasion resistance	Poor	Poor
Tenacity	Poor	Poor
Elongation	Excellent	Excellent
Comfort	Moderate	Poor
Appearance Retention	Good	Good
Resiliency	Good	Good
Dimensional stability	Good	Good
Elastic recovery	Excellent	Excellent
Recommended Care	Machine-wash or dry-clean	Wash with care

Table 9.2 Durability Factors of Spandex, Rubber, and Nylon

Fiber Property	Spandex	Rubber	Nylon
Breaking tenacity, g/d	0.6–0.9	0.34	3.0–9.5
Breaking elongation, %	400–700	500–600	23
Flex life	Excellent	Fair	Excellent
Recovery from stretch, %	99 (at 50% elongation)	97 (at 50% elongation)	100 (at 3% elongation)

Aesthetics Spandex is seldom used alone in fabrics. Other fibers produce the desired hand and appearance. Even in power-stretch fabrics for foundation garments and surgical hose, where beauty is not of major importance, nylon, cotton, or other fibers are used. The characteristics of spandex that contribute to beauty in fabrics are dyeability of the fiber and good strength, resulting in fashionable colors and prints in sheer garments.

Spandex needs no cover yarns since it takes dye. Eliminating the cover yarn reduces the cost and fabric weight, contributing to an attractive and comfortable lightweight fabric. However, in uses in which spandex will come in contact with the skin, it is normally covered.

Durability As shown in Table 9.2, spandex is more resistant to degradation than rubber. (Nylon is included in the table because it has more stretch than other manufactured filaments and illustrates differences between hard fibers and elastomeric fibers.)

Spandex is resistant to the body oils, perspiration, lotions, and cosmetics that degrade rubber. It also has good shelf life and does not deteriorate with age as quickly as does rubber. Its flex life is 10 times greater than that of rubber.

Comfort Spandex fibers have a moisture regain of 0.75 to 1.3 percent, making them uncomfortable for skin contact. Lighter-weight foundation garments of spandex have the same holding power as heavy garments of rubber. Spandex has a specific gravity of 1.2 to 1.25, which is greater than that of rubber. However, because of the greater tenacity of spandex, lower-denier yarns result in lightweight products.

Care Spandex is resistant to dilute acids, alkalis, bleaches, and dry-cleaning solvents. Spandex is thermoplastic, with a melting point of 446 to 518°F.

Spandex has superior aging resistance as compared with rubber, resists soiling, and has excellent elasticity and elongation properties. Spandex items retain an attractive appearance. However, over time, the coarser spandex fibers may rupture and work through the fabric. When ends of the thick fibers appear on the surface, those areas of the fabric have lost their elasticity and elongation properties. This problem, known as **grin-through**, cannot be remedied. It occurs most often in products that have aged or have been stressed to extremes (Figure 9.4).

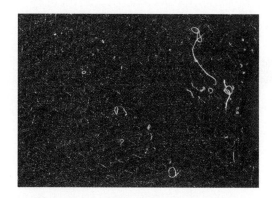

Figure 9.4 Grin-through in a swimsuit made of nylon and spandex.

Uses Spandex is used to support, shape, or mold the body or to keep textiles from stretching out of shape during use (Table 9.3). It is used primarily in knit foundation garments, actionwear, compression sportswear to reduce chafing and friction, intimate apparel, shapewear, hosiery, interiors, and narrow fabrics. It is used in chlorine-resistant and competitive swimwear, skiwear, leotards and other dancewear, leggings, biking shorts, and other body-fitting apparel. Higher percentages of spandex in these products provide greater body contouring or support properties. Spandex is also used in woven fabrics in a variety of end uses, but its use here is relatively small as compared with knits and is in

Table 9.3 Stretch Properties of Spandex

Major End Uses	Important Properties
Athletic apparel	Power stretch, washable
Foundation garments	Power stretch, washable, lightweight
Bathing suits	Power stretch, resistance to salt and chlorine, dyeable
Outerwear and sportswear	Comfort stretch
Support and surgical hose	Power stretch, lightweight
Elastic webbing	Power stretch
Slipcovers, bottom sheets	Comfort stretch, washable

response to fashion and comfort demands. It also has medical uses, such as surgical and support hose, bandages, and surgical wraps. It is used in fitted sheets and slipcovers. Blends of 2 to 40 percent spandex with other fibers are common.

Elastoester

An elastomer based on polyether-ester has been introduced by the Japanese textile firm Teijin, Ltd., under the trade name Rexe. **Elastoester** is a manufactured fiber in which the fiber-forming substance is composed of at least 50% by weight aliphatic polyether and at least 35% by weight polyester (Federal Trade Commission). The fiber has an elongation potential of 600 percent, a tenacity of 1.0 g/d, and elasticity of 80 percent at elongations over 200 percent. These properties are slightly less than the properties of spandex. However, elastoester is washable and has superior strength retention in wet heat and after treatment with alkalis. It is also superior in its resistance to chlorine bleach. It may be treated to increase dyeability and print clarity and to achieve a more silklike hand. It is used in fashion outerwear and fitted interior textiles.

Elasterell-p

Elasterell-p is an elastic bicomponent polyester with a helical coil. (See Chapter 8.) It has good inherent stretch with excellent recovery. The strong and durable fiber is easy care with a pleasing hand. Elasterell-p's stretch and recovery characteristics can be varied by adjusting spinning conditions so that the fiber can be more carefully engineered for specific end uses including active sportswear, leisure wear, and underwear. *Multelastester* is another term for this fiber.

Lastol

Lastol is an elastic cross-linked copolymer olefin with low but significant crystallinity, composed of at least 95 percent by weight of ethylene. (See Chapter 8.) It has superior stretch (500 percent) and recovery properties compared to other olefin fibers. Because it is more chemically stable than other olefins and more resistant to heat, it is used in activewear and other easy-care stretch apparel.

▶ Learning Activity 1

Identify an item you own that incorporates spandex. Explain how the serviceability of that item would change if rubber replaced the spandex. Would your satisfaction with the product change? If yes, how would it change?

Fibers with Chemical, Heat, or Fire Resistance

The protective fibers have specialized applications. In almost all cases, their costs are prohibitive for normal apparel and interior products. Some of these fibers cost over $60 per pound. Compare that with prices of about a $1 per pound or less than that for the fibers generally found in apparel and interior textiles, like cotton and polyester. Clearly, these fibers provide sufficient performance for their cost or they would not be used. With their unique resistance to chemicals, heat, and flame, protective fibers are very important as technical textiles. Many of these fibers are described as high-temperature fibers. This means that they can be used continuously at temperatures over 200°C without significant decomposition and retain the majority of their physical properties.

High-temperature fibers can be used continuously at temperatures over 200°C without significant decomposition and retain the majority of their physical properties.

Aramid

Aramid—a manufactured fiber in which the fiber-forming substance is a long-chain synthetic polyamide in which at least 85 percent of the amide linkages are attached directly to two aromatic rings.

$$(-C-NH-)$$
$$\|$$
$$O$$

—Federal Trade Commission

Nylon is a polyamide fiber; **aramid** is an aromatic polyamide fiber. DuPont chemist Stephanie Kwolek developed a nylon variant with exceptional heat and flame resistance. It was introduced in 1963 under the trade name Nomex nylon. DuPont introduced another variant of nylon in 1973 as Kevlar. Trade names for aramid fibers are *Nomex*, *Kevlar*, *Conex*, and *Fenilon*. Aramid has exceptional strength in addition to fire resistance. The Federal Trade Commission established the generic classification of aramid in 1974. An aromatic ring is a six-sided carbon compound with alternating double and single bonds represented in chemical notation as a circle in the six-sided ring. The location at which the amide linkages are attached determines the type of aramid and its properties. Nomex is a normal tenacity meta-aramid, or m-aramid, with a lower specific gravity and heat resistance and a higher regain compared to Kevlar, which is a high-tenacity para-aramid, or p-aramid (Table 9.4).

Aramid is a manufactured fiber in which the fiber-forming substance is a long-chain synthetic aromatic polyamide.

Table 9.4 Properties of Aramid

Property	m-Aramid	p-Aramid
Tenacity, dry	4.3–5.1 g/d—filament	21.5 g/d
	3.7–5.3 g/d—staple	
Specific gravity	1.38	1.44
Moisture regain, %	6.5	3.5–7.0
Effect of heat	Decomposes at 700°F	Decomposes at 900°F
	Very resistant to flame	Very resistant to flame
	Does not melt	Does not melt
Chemical structure	m-aramid	p-aramid

Figure 9.5 Photomicrographs of aramid: cross-sectional view (left), longitudinal view (right).
SOURCE: Courtesy of the British Textile Technology Group.

Figure 9.6 Technical products reinforced with aramid and carbon fibers: tent poles, belts, and brake pad.

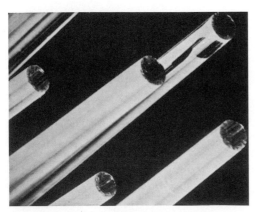

Figure 9.7 Photomicrograph of fiberglass.
SOURCE: Courtesy of Owens Corning.

Aramid can be wet- or dry-spun and is usually round or dog-bone shaped (Figure 9.5). Aramid has high tenacity and high resistance to stretch and to high temperatures. The fiber maintains its shape and form at high temperatures. Its resistance to most chemicals is good to excellent. It is only moderately resistant to sunlight. Aramids are oleophilic and prone to static buildup unless finished. Aramid fibers have excellent impact and abrasion resistance.

Kevlar aramid is lightweight and fatigue- and damage-resistant. It is five times stronger than steel on an equal-weight basis and 43 percent lower in density than fiberglass. Kevlar is used primarily in reinforcements of radial tires and other mechanical rubber goods (Figure 9.6). Kevlar 29 is found in protective apparel, cables, and cordage, and as a replacement for asbestos in brake linings and gaskets. Body-armor undervests of Kevlar 29 are relatively lightweight and bullet- and knife-resistant. Kevlar 49 has the highest tenacity of the aramids and is found as a plastic-reinforcement fiber for boat hulls, aircraft, aerospace uses, and other composite uses.

Nomex is used where resistance to heat and combustion with low smoke generation are required. Protective apparel, such as firefighters' and race-car drivers' suits, and flame-retardant interiors for aircraft are made of Nomex. Nomex Omega by DuPont includes an expanding air layer that helps insulate firefighters from heat. Hot-gas filtration systems and electrical insulation are constructed of Nomex. This heat-resistant fiber is also found in covers for laundry presses and ironing boards.

Hollow aramid fibers are used to produce fresh water from sea water through reverse osmosis. The fiber's thin, dense skin allows only water to pass through. Aramids are difficult to dye and have poor resistance to acids. Solution-dyed aramids are more common, but technology has been developed to dye aramid intense colors for high-visibility protective apparel. Composites of aramid fibers intermixed in resins are being investigated for use in civil-engineering structures like bridges and elevated highway-support structures.

Glass

Glass—a manufactured fiber in which the fiber-forming substance is glass.

—*Federal Trade Commission*

Glass is an incombustible textile fiber; it does not burn. This makes it especially suitable for end uses where the danger of fire is a problem—such as in draperies for public buildings. The problems of severe skin irritation from tiny broken fibers have limited the use of glass fibers in apparel.

The process of drawing out glass into hairlike strands dates back to ancient times. It is thought that the Phoenicians produced the first glass fiber. Glass fiber was first used commercially in the 1920s.

The raw materials for glass are sand, silica, and limestone, combined with additives of feldspar and boric acid. These materials are melted in large electric furnaces at 2,400°F. For filament yarns, each furnace has holes in the base of the melting chamber. Fine streams of glass flow through the holes and are carried through a hole in the floor to a winder in the room below. The winder revolves faster than the glass that comes from the furnace, thus stretching the fibers and reducing them in size before they harden. The round rodlike filaments are shown in Figure 9.7. For staple fibers, the glass flows out in thin streams from holes in the base of the furnace, and jets of high-pressure air or steam break the strands into fibers 8 to 10 inches long. They are collected on a revolving drum in a thin web, which is then formed into a sliver, or soft, untwisted yarn. Several types of glass fibers are produced. Table 9.5 summarizes the types and end uses for these fibers.

Table 9.5 Types of Glass Fiber

Type	Comments
A	Alkali-containing glass used in fibers
AR	Alkali-resistant glass used in reinforcing cement
C	Chemically resistant glass used in fibers
E	Almost universally accepted formulation used in many fibers and related products; high electrical resistance; used in glass-reinforced plastics
HS	Magnesium–aluminum–silica glass; high-strength
S	Similar in composition to HS glass; used in composites

Beta Fiberglas, by the Owens Corning Fiberglas Corporation, has one-sixth the denier of common glass fibers. The extremely fine filaments are resistant to breaking and abrasion. Beta Fiberglas has about half the strength of regular glass fiber, but its tenacity of 8.2 is still greater than that of most fibers. It is used in products like window-treatment fabrics, for which greater fiber flexibility is needed.

Owens Corning produces a bicomponent fiber, Miraflex®, of two forms of glass fused together into a single filament. As the fiber cools, the components cause the filament to twist in an irregular fashion along its length. The resulting fiber is soft, resilient, flexible, and form filling. It can be carded or needled to make a fiber batt used in home insulation and composites (Figure 9.8).

Glass has a tenacity of 9.6 g/d dry and 6.7 g/d wet. Glass has a low elongation of only 3 to 4 percent but excellent elasticity in this narrow range. Glass fibers are brittle, exhibit poor flex abrasion resistance, and break when bent. These fibers are very heavy, with a specific gravity of 2.48 to 2.69. The fibers are nonabsorbent and are resistant to sunlight and most chemicals. Glass is flameproof and melts at 2,400°F. Trade names include Fiberglas, Beta glass, Chemglass, J-M fiberglass, PPG fiberglass, and Vitron.

Machine washing of glass textiles is not recommended because it causes excessive fiber breakage. Tiny glass fiber bits in the washing machine will contaminate the next load and irritate the skin of people who use those textiles. Even hand washing may produce severe skin irritation. Care labels should disclose this possibility.

Glass textiles do not require frequent washing, however, because they resist soil; spots and stains can be wiped off with a damp cloth. No ironing is necessary. Items can be smoothed and hung to dry. Oils used in finishing may turn white fabrics gray, attract dirt and soil, and oxidize with age. Unfortunately, washing does not whiten the material, and dry cleaning is not recommended.

Glass fiber is used in interiors such as flame-retardant draperies. Here the fiber performs best if bending and abrasion from drafts, opening/closing the fabric, and abrasion from people and pets is minimized. The weight of the fabrics may require the use of special drapery rods.

Glass fiber has wide technical use where noise abatement, fire protection, temperature control (insulation), and air purification are needed. Glass is commonly used in insulation for buildings. Care should be exercised when working with glass because it has been identified as a possible carcinogen. Glass is common as a reinforcement fiber in molded plastics in boat, car, and airplane parts. Current research in civil engineering is evaluating glass fibers in resin as a repair material for highways and bridges. In addition, glass is found in ironing-board covers and space suits. Flame-resistant-glass mattress covers are produced for hotels, dormitories,

Figure 9.8 Miraflex®, bicomponent glass fiber.
SOURCE: Courtesy of Owens Corning.

and hospitals. Glass is used in geotextiles. Filters, fire blankets, and heat- and electrical-resistant tapes and braids are other technical products made of glass. Glass fibers are used to reinforce fabric used for printed circuits in electronics. A lightweight, durable, water-resistant material in fashion colors is used to support broken bones as they heal. Owens Corning is researching glass yarns suitable for apparel.

Optical fibers are very fine fibers of pure glass that use laser beams, rather than electricity, and thus are free from electrical interference. Optical fibers are found in communication and medical equipment and novelty lamps.

Metal and Metallic Fibers

Metallic—a manufactured fiber composed of metal, plastic-coated metal, metal-coated plastic, or a core completely covered by metal.

—*Federal Trade Commission*

Gold and silver have been used since ancient times as yarns for fabric decoration. More recently, aluminum yarns, aluminized plastic yarns, and aluminized nylon yarns have replaced gold and silver. **Metallic fibers** can be coated with transparent films to minimize tarnishing. A common film is Lurex polyester. Metal fibers are used to add a decorative touch to apparel and interiors.

Two processes are used to make these fibers. The *laminating process* seals a layer of aluminum between two layers of acetate or polyester film, which is then cut into strips for yarns (Figure 9.9). The film may be colorless so the aluminum foil shows through, or the film and/or the adhesive may be colored before the laminating process. The *metalizing process* vaporizes the aluminum under high pressure and deposits it on the polyester film. This process produces thinner, more flexible, more durable, and more comfortable fibers.

Fabric containing a large amount of metal can be embossed. Ironing is a problem when metallic film yarns are used because high temperature melts the plastic. The best way to remove wrinkles is to set the iron on its end and draw the edge of the fabric across the sole plate of the iron.

Stainless steel fibers were developed in 1960, and other metal fibers have also been made into fibers and yarns. Stainless steel has had the most extensive development.

The use of stainless steel as a textile fiber was an outgrowth of research for fibers to meet aerospace requirements. Superfine stainless steel filaments (3 to 15 micrometers) are a bundle of fine wires (0.002 inch) pickled in nitric acid and drawn to their final diameter. Metal yarns require special treatment to deaden yarn twist; otherwise, the yarns act like tiny coiled springs.

Stainless steel fibers are produced as both filament and staple. They can be used in complex yarns and can be either woven or knitted. Only 1 to 3 percent of the staple fiber is needed to blend with other fibers to reduce static permanently. Although it cannot be dyed, producers claim that small amounts will not affect the color of white fabrics.

Static is one of the annoying problems associated with carpets in terms of comfort and soiling. Stainless steel is used in some carpets to reduce static. Brunsmet, a stainless steel fiber from 2 to 3 inches long, can be mixed throughout any kind of spun yarn to make the yarn a good conductor. Only one or two fibers per tuft will carry the static from the face fiber to the backing. This kind of carpet yarn is used where static is a special problem, such as in rooms where sensitive computer equipment is kept. It is also suitable for upholstery, blankets, and work apparel. Stainless steel fibers are used for tire cord, wiring, missile nose cones, and in corrective heart surgery.

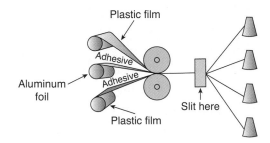

Figure 9.9 **Laminating layers to produce a metal yarn.**

Metal fibers of stainless steel, copper, and aluminum are blended with other fibers to produce static-free apparel worn in clean rooms in computer-production facilities and in other places where static creates a nuisance or hazardous conditions. Metals are much heavier than the organic materials that compose most fibers—the specific gravity of metal fibers is 7.88, as compared with 1.14 for nylon. They cannot bend without leaving permanent crease lines, are stiff or too springy, and do not have the hand associated with textiles. Reduction in the denier of the fiber improves its properties, but the finer fibers are more expensive. Metal fibers are used in technical products like wiring and cables (Figure 9.10). Metallic fibers are also used in cut-resistant gloves for butchers and meat cutters.

Modacrylic Fibers

Modacrylic fibers—manufactured fibers in which the fiber-forming substance is any long-chain synthetic polymer composed of less than 85 percent but at least 35 percent by weight acrylonitrile units except when the polymer qualifies as rubber.

—*Federal Trade Commission*

Modacrylic fibers are modified acrylics first produced in the United States in 1949. They are made from acrylonitrile, but a larger proportion of other polymers are added to make the copolymers.

Modacrylics were the first inherently flame-retardant synthetic fibers; they do not support combustion, are very difficult to ignite, are self-extinguishing, and do not drip. For these reasons, they are used in protective apparel and contract interior textiles.

Modacrylic is produced by polymerizing the components, dissolving the copolymer in acetone, pumping the solution into a column of warm air (dry-spun), and stretching while hot. S.E.F. (self-extinguishing flame) is one trade name.

The modacrylics are creamy white and are produced as staple or tow. Their cross section is dog-bone or irregularly shaped (Figure 9.11). Various deniers, lengths, crimp levels, and shrinkage potentials are available.

The chemicals used as copolymers include vinyl chloride (CH_2CHCl), vinylidene chloride (CH_2CCl_2), or vinylidene dicyanide (CH_2CCN_2).

Modacrylic has properties similar to acrylic, but modacrylic is flame-retardant. (See Chapter 8.) Furlike fabrics, wigs, hairpieces, and fleece-type pile fabrics are made of modacrylic fibers with different amounts of crimp and shrinkage potential. By mixing several fiber types it is possible to obtain furlike fabrics with fibers of different pile heights: long, polished fibers (guard hairs) and soft, highly crimped undercoat fibers (Figure 9.12). Fabrics are sheared, embossed, and printed to enhance their resemblance to real fur.

Modacrylic has an attractive appearance similar to that of acrylic. It can be made with a soft, matte luster to resemble wool or with a brighter luster to resemble the shiny guard hairs of fur.

Modacrylics are less durable than acrylics, but they have adequate durability for their end uses. The strength of modacrylics is similar to that of wool. Abrasion resistance is similar to acrylic. Elastic recovery is superior to that of acrylic.

Modacrylics are poor conductors of heat. Fabrics are soft, warm, and resilient, but have a tendency to pill. Their absorbency is low, varying from 2 to 4 percent moisture regain.

Modacrylics combine flame retardancy with a relatively low specific gravity (1.35). This means that protective apparel need not be uncomfortably heavy. Flame-retardant interior textiles, especially draperies, can be produced without great weight.

Modacrylic fibers exhibit moderate resiliency. In typical end uses, they do not wrinkle. They have moderate dimensional stability and high elastic recovery.

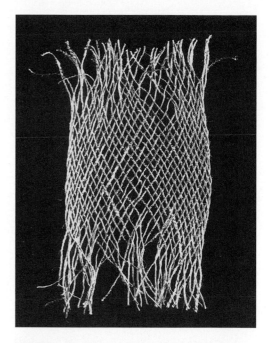

Figure 9.10 Copper braid used in wiring.

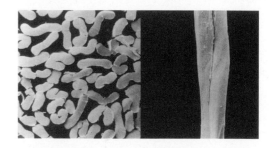

Figure 9.11 Photomicrographs of modacrylic: cross-sectional view (left), longitudinal view (right).
SOURCE: Courtesy of the British Textile Technology Group.

Figure 9.12 Furlike fabric of modacrylic. Note how the sleek guard hairs and the soft, fine underhairs simulate the appearance of fur.

Modacrylics pill more quickly, are more sensitive to heat, mat more readily, and are not as resilient as acrylics. Modacrylics tend to retain color well.

Modacrylics are resistant to acids, weak alkalis, and most organic solvents. They are resistant to mildew and moths. They have very good resistance to sunlight and very good flame resistance.

Modacrylics can be washed or dry-cleaned with special care. The heat-sensitive fibers shrink at 250°F and stiffen at temperatures over 300°F. If fabrics are machine-washed, use warm water and tumble dry at a low setting. The lowest iron setting should be used. Some fur-like fabrics are dry-cleanable; some require special care in dry cleaning (no steam, no tumble or tumble only on cold); and some should be cleaned by a furrier method.

Modacrylics are more sensitive to loss of appearance from improper care than the acrylics. The precautions regarding steam cleaning discussed with acrylics also apply to modacrylics.

Modacrylic is resistant to natural degradation. The concerns expressed for acrylic generally apply to modacrylic. Modacrylic has less of an impact on the environment than does acrylic, for two reasons. One, modacrylic is produced only using dry spinning, so concerns are limited to the dry-spinning process in which the solvent, acetone, is easy to reclaim and recycle. Two, modacrylic is used in small quantitites.

Modacrylics are used primarily in applications where environmental resistance is needed or where flame retardancy is necessary or required by law or building codes (see Chapter 21). End uses include outdoor fabrics, awnings, and marine applications; protective apparel (e.g., shirts and trousers for electric line personnel); interior textiles (e.g., upholstery, window-treatment fabrics, and blankets); and technical applications (e.g., filters). Because of its heat sensitivity, modacrylic is used to produce realistic fake furs and wigs or hairpieces that can be curled with a curling iron. Many modacrylics are mass-pigmented rather than dyed.

Novoloid

Novoloid—a manufactured fiber in which the fiber-forming substance contains at least 35 percent by weight of cross-linked novolac (a cross-linked phenolformaldehyde polymer).

—*Federal Trade Commission*

First commercially produced in 1972, **novoloid** shows outstanding flame resistance to the 2,500°C flame from an oxyacetylene torch. Rather than melt, burn, or fuse, the yarns carbonize.

Novoloid has an elasticity of 35 percent. It has good resistance to sunlight and is inert to acids and organic solvents but susceptible to highly alkaline substances. Novoloid has a tenacity of 1.5 to 2.5 g/d, a specific gravity of 1.27, and a regain of 6.0 percent. It is used for protective apparel and fabrics, chemical filters, gaskets, and packing materials. Fierce competition from other specialty fibers is shrinking its market.

▶ Learning Activity 2

Use Fabrics #10, 42, 59, and 88 from your swatch kit. Use the swatch set key to identify the fibers present in each of these fabrics. Identify an end use for each swatch. Describe the contribution that modacrylic, glass, spandex, and metallic fibers would contribute to a product.

PBI

PBI—a manufactured fiber in which the fiber-forming substance is a long-chain aromatic polymer having recurring imidazole groups as an integral part of the polymer chain.

—Federal Trade Commission

PBI is a condensation polymer that is dry-spun. Its specific gravity is 1.39; if the fiber has been stabilized, the specific gravity is 1.43. PBI has a tenacity of 2.6 to 3.1 g/d and a breaking elongation of 30 percent. PBI has a high moisture regain of 15 percent, but it is difficult to dye. It is usually mass-pigmented. PBI does not burn in air, melt, or drip and has very low shrinkage when exposed to flame. Even when charred, PBI fabrics remain strong, supple, and intact. Because of its heat resistance, it is ideal for use in heat-resistant protective apparel for firefighters, astronauts, military personnel, fuel handlers, race car drivers, welders, foundry workers, and hospital workers (Figure 9.13). PBI is used extensively in space and aerospace applications. The fiber is found in interiors textiles for aircraft, hospitals, and submarines and in flue-gas filters in coal-fired boilers and in reverse-osmosis membranes. Additional applications include semiconductors and electronics.

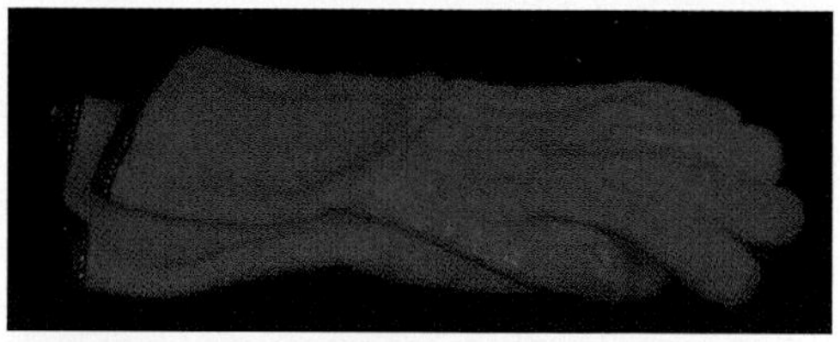

Figure 9.13 Heat-resistant gloves made from PBI.

Sulfar

Sulfar—a manufactured fiber in which the fiber-forming substance is a long-chain synthetic polysulfide in which at least 85 percent of the sulfide (—S—) linkages are attached directly to two aromatic rings.

—Federal Trade Commission

Sulfar is produced by melt spinning. It is gold in color. Sulfar has a tenacity of 3.0 to 3.5 g/d and a breaking elongation of 25 to 35 percent. It has excellent elasticity. Moisture regain is low (0.6 percent), and specific gravity is 1.37. Sulfar is highly resistant to acids and alkalis and is not soluble in any known solvent below 200°C (392°F). Sulfar is used in filtration fabrics, paper-making felts, electrolysis membranes, high-performance membranes, rubber reinforcement, electrical insulation, firefighting suits, and other protective apparel. Sulfar helps maintain a clean environment because of its use in incinerator filters in plants that generate electricity by burning garbage.

Aramid, glass, metal and metallic fibers, modacrylic, novoloid, PBI, sulfar, fluoropolymer, carbon, melamine, and PLA have special performance and safety characteristics. With their unique resistance to chemicals, heat, and flame, these fibers are used in technical textiles.

Saran

Saran—a manufactured fiber in which the fiber-forming substance is any long-chain synthetic polymer composed of at least 80 percent by weight of vinylidene chloride units (—CH_2CCl_2—).

—Federal Trade Commission

Saran is a vinylidene-chloride/vinyl-chloride copolymer developed in 1940. The raw material is melt-spun and stretched to orient the molecules. Both filament and staple forms are produced. Much of the filament fiber is produced as a monofilament for seat covers, furniture webbing, and screenings. Monofilaments may also be used in dolls' hair and wigs. The staple form is made straight, curled, or crimped. The curled form is unique in that the curl is inherent and closely resembles the curl of natural wool.

Saran has good weathering properties, chemical resistance, and stretch resistance. It is an unusually tough, durable fiber. Saran has a tenacity of 1.4 to 2.4 g/d, with no change when wet, an elongation of 15 to 30 percent with excellent recovery, and good resiliency. It is an off-white fiber with a slight yellowish tint.

Like the other melt-spun fibers, saran is perfectly round and smooth. It has a moisture regain of less than 0.1 percent. Saran absorbs little or no moisture, so it dries rapidly. It is difficult to dye; for this reason, mass pigmentation is used. Saran also has no static charge. It is heavy, with a specific gravity of 1.7. Saran does not support combustion. When exposed to flame it softens, then chars, and decomposes at 115°C (240°F). It has excellent size and shape retention and is resistant to acids, alkalis, and organic solvents. Exposure to sunlight causes light-colored objects to darken, but no strength loss occurs. Saran is immune to biological attack.

Saran fiber is being replaced by other fibers that cost less or that have a better combination of properties for specific end uses. Saran is used as an agricultural protective fabric to shade delicate plants such as tobacco and ginseng and is used in rugs, draperies, and upholstery. Saran is more widely used in films and plastics.

Vinyon

> Vinyon—a manufactured fiber in which the fiber-forming substance is any long-chain synthetic polymer composed of at least 85 percent by weight of vinyl chloride units ($-CH_2CHCl-$).
>
> —*Federal Trade Commission*

Commercial production of **vinyon** was begun in 1939. It is a copolymer of 86 percent vinyl chloride and 14 percent vinyl acetate. The raw material is dissolved in acetone and dry-spun.

Vinyon is white and somewhat translucent, with an irregular-, round-, dog-bone-, or dumbbell-shaped cross section. Vinyon is very sensitive to heat. It softens at 150 to 170°F, shrinks at 175°F, and should not be pressed or ironed. It is unaffected by moisture, chemically stable, resistant to insects and biological attack, a poor conductor of electricity, and flame-retardant. These properties make vinyon especially good as a bonding agent for rugs, papers, and nonwoven fabrics. The amorphous undrawn fibers have a tenacity of 0.7 to 1.0 g/d. These fibers have a warm, pleasant hand. Elongation ranges from 12 to 125 percent. Specific gravity ranges from 1.33 to 1.43. Moisture regain is 0.1 percent.

Imported vinyon is used for wigs, flame-retardant Christmas trees, filter pads, fishing lines and nets, and protective apparel. Some trade names of vinyon are Leavil, Teviron, and Viclon. Vinyon is used in film form, often labeled *vinyl*. It is used for rainwear, umbrellas, upholstery protectors in showrooms, and thousand of other applications.

Vinal

> Vinal—a manufactured fiber in which the fiber-forming substance is any long-chain synthetic polymer composed of at least 50 percent by weight of vinyl alcohol units ($-CH_2CHOH-$) and in which the total of the vinyl alcohol units and any one or more of the various acetal units is at least 85 percent by weight of the fiber.
>
> —*Federal Trade Commission*

No vinal fibers are produced in the United States. Modified **vinal** fibers are imported for use in some protective apparel because of their inherent flame-retardant properties. Vinal is made in Japan and Germany under the trade names of Kuralon, Mewlon, Solvron, Vilon, Vinol, and Vinylal.

When vinal fibers are extruded, they are water-soluble and must be cross-linked with formaldehyde to make them non-water-soluble. The fiber has a smooth, slightly grainy appearance with a U-shaped cross section. Vinal has a tenacity of 3.5 to 6.5 g/d, an elongation of 15 to 30 percent, and is 25 percent weaker when wet. The specific gravity of vinal is 1.26. It has a moisture regain of 5.0 percent. It does not support combustion but softens at 200°C (390°F) and melts at 220°C (425°F). It has good chemical resistance and is unaffected by alkalis and common solvents. Concentrated acids harm the fiber. Vinal has excellent resistance to biological attack. Mass pigmentation is used to color the fiber.

Technical uses for vinal include protective apparel, fishing nets, filter fabrics, tarpaulins, and brush bristles. In water-soluble forms, the fiber is used as a ground fabric to create laces and other sheer fabrics. Once the fabric has been produced, the vinal ground is dissolved and the sheer fabric remains.

Fluoropolymer

Fluoropolymer—a manufactured fiber containing at least 95 percent of a long-chain polymer synthesized from aliphatic fluorocarbon monomers.

—*Federal Trade Commission*

Polytetrafluoroethylene (PTFE) is the most common **fluoropolymer**. It is used as a coating for cookware, as a soil-resistant finish, and as a fiber with the trade name Teflon.

The monomer is polymerized under pressure and heat in the presence of a catalyst to achieve the following repeat unit: ($-CF_2-CF_2-$). **Emulsion spinning**, in which polymerization and extrusion occur simultaneously, is used (Figure 9.14). It has a tenacity of 1.6 g/d, with low elongation and good pliability. The fiber is heavy, with a specific gravity of 2.3, and it has unusually high resistance to heat and chemicals. It can withstand temperatures up to 260°C (500°F) without damage. It is resistant to sunlight, weathering, and aging. It also has an exceptionally low coefficient of friction and high resistance to deformation. It is tan in color but can be bleached white with sulfuric acid.

Gore-Tex is a trade name for fabrics that have a thin microporous film of PTFE applied to a fabric for use in outerwear. It is wind- and liquid/water-resistant but water-vapor-permeable. Gore-Tex can be dry-cleaned but needs to be rinsed well to prevent impairment of the film's functions. BlisterGuard is a sock made of cotton, wool, acrylic, nylon, or polyester with fluoropolymer in the heel, pad, and toe areas to reduce friction between the foot and the shoe. Teflon is used in hazardous material protective apparel. Fluorocarbon is used in filter fabrics (to reduce smokestack emissions), packing fabrics, gaskets, technical felts, covers for presses in commercial laundries, electrical tape, and as a layer of some protective fabrics.

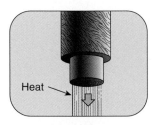

1. Polymer is dispersed as fine particles in a carrier.
2. Dispersed polymer is extruded through a spinneret and coalesced by heating.
3. Carrier is removed by heating or dissolving.

Expensive
Used only for those fibers that are insoluble
Carrier required

Figure 9.14   Emulsion spinning.

Carbon

Carbon is a fiber that is at least 96 percent pure carbon. It is made from precursor fibers such as rayon and polyacrylonitrile or from petroleum pitch. These fibers are heated to remove oxygen, nitrogen, and hydrogen. The fiber has exceptional heat resistance and does not ignite or melt. It maintains its full strength of 1.5 g/d after prolonged exposure to temperatures of more than 200°C. Carbon has a specific gravity of 1.4, a moisture regain of 10 percent, and an elongation of 10 percent. Carbon fibers have very low coefficients of thermal expansion, are chemically inert, and biocompatible. They also dissipate static quickly. Because of these properties and its comfortable hand, carbon is used in protective apparel, to reinforce lightweight metal components in golf clubs and bicycle bodies, in aerospace uses, in bone grafts, and as a substitute for asbestos in technical products (Figure 9.6). Civil engineers are evaluating carbon fibers in resins for use in repairing bridge and highway support columns. Carbon is also used as a coating of nylon for antistatic carpeting, upholstery, apparel, and technical brushes and belts. It is used in radar-transparent military aircraft communication satellites and rocket-motor nozzles.

A significant end use for carbon is in nanofibers and nanotubes. Carbon nanofibers and nanotubes have unusual properties: remarkable strength, high elasticity, low density, heat resistant, and large thermal and electrical conductivity. These nanomaterials have been described as having the strength of steel and the flexibility of a rubber band. Applications and potential applications include such smart textile end uses as mechanical relays and switches, thermal sensors, acoustic and pressure sensors, radiation detectors, and acceleration sensors.

Carbon or carbon black nanoparticles from coconut shells, bamboo, and other organic materials are used much like activated charcoal. When incorporated at the 5 to 20 percent level in nylon and polyester fibers, the carbon black nanoparticles provide cooling action, ultraviolet protection, odor absorption or resistance, and static resistance for textile products. These composite fibers also have improved abrasion resistance and tensile strength.

Table 9.6 compares selected properties of aramid, glass, PBI, sulfar, PTFE, and carbon.

Melamine

Melamine—a manufactured fiber in which the fiber-forming substance is a synthetic polymer composed of at least 50 percent by weight of a cross-linked melamine polymer.

—*Federal Trade Commission*

Melamine is produced by BASF as Basofil. It has a dry tenacity of 1.8 g/d, a 12 percent breaking elongation, 5 percent regain, a specific gravity of 1.4, fair abrasion resistance, and good to excellent resistance to ultraviolet light and chemicals except concentrated acids. Melamine is known for its heat stability, low flammability, and resistance to solvents. Its cost is moderate. It is used in products that require resistance to high temperatures and competes with meta-aramid, PBI, sulfar, and polyimide because of its lower cost. Melamine is available in white and dyeable forms. It is used in protective apparel, fiber-blocking fabric, and filters.

Table 9.6 Comparison of Selected Chemical-, Heat-, and Fire-Resistant Fibers: Aramid, Glass, PBI, Sulfar, PTFE, and Carbon

Fiber	Tenacity, g/d	Elongation, % Dry	Elasticity, %	Regain, %	Specific Gravity	Heat/Chemical Resistance
p-Aramid	21.5	4.0	100	3.5–7.0	1.44	Difficult to ignite, does not melt, decomposes at 900°F, resistant to dilute acids and bases, degraded by strong mineral acids, excellent solvent resistance
Glass	9.6	3.1	100	0	2.48–2.69	Does not burn, softens at 1,350°F, resists most acids and alkalis, unaffected by solvents
PBI	2.6–3.0	25–30	—	15	1.43	Does not ignite or melt, chars at 860°F, unaffected by most acids, alkalis, and solvents
Sulfar	3.0–3.5	35–45	100	0.6	1.37	Outstanding heat resistance, melts at 545°F, outstanding resistance to most acids, alkalis, and solvents
Fluoro-polymer	0.9–2.0	19–140	—	0	2.1	Extremely heat-resistant, melts at 1,550°F, most chemically resistant fiber known
Carbon	1.5	0.7	100	—	1.75–2.2	Does not melt, excellent resistance to hot, concentrated acids and alkalis, unaffected by solvents, degraded by strong oxidizers (chlorine bleach)

Other Special-Use Fibers

Polyimide (PI or PEI) from polyetherimide has a dry tenacity of 3.7 g/d, a 20 percent breaking elongation, 3 percent regain, a specific gravity of 1.41, good abrasion resistance, excellent resistance to heat, and good to excellent resistance to chemicals except alkalis. It is moderately high in cost. Because of its properties and its irregular cross section, it is used in filters for hot air or gas and corrosive liquids and in gaskets and seals, protective apparel, and fire-block seating (a layer between the upholstery and the padding to minimize flame spread).

Polyphenylene benzobisoxazole (PBO) is another high-temperature-resistant nonflammable polymer fiber based on repeating aromatic rings. It has a specific gravity of 1.5, a regain of 2 percent, and a breaking elongation of 3.5 percent. It has very good tensile strength and is used primarily as a reinforcing fiber in resins and for protective apparel.

Ceramic fibers are composed of metal oxide, metal carbide, metal nitride, or other mixtures. The fibers were developed because aerospace, metallurgical, nuclear, and chemical industries required fibers with better thermal resistance than glass fibers could give. These fibers are used where high strength, high thermal structural stability, and stiffness are required. Nanoparticles of clay (aluminosilicate) and metal oxides are used in composite fibers to add resistance to microbes, heat, electricity, chemicals, ultraviolet light, static, and flame for protective apparel and technical applications.

Polylactic acid (PLA) is a renewable product made from fermented cornstarch and melt-spun to produce polylactide. It is in a group known as biopolymers, meaning that the polymer is from completely renewable sources like plants. While PLA is currently made from cornstarch, other plants and plant components are additional potential sources for the starch starting material. PLA is a melt-spun fiber with a specific gravity of 1.25, low regain, good elasticity, and high tenacity. The producer claims that PLA has luster, drape, and hand similar to silk, quick drying properties, and good wrinkle resistance. It is available in staple and filament form. It also has good flame and ultraviolet resistance. Concerns relate to its colorfastness and dyeability, but research is addressing that problem. It is used in apparel, interior textiles as fiberfill, agricultural and landscaping applications, sanitary and medical products, filters, and food packaging materials. PLA is biodegradable.

▶ Learning Activity 3

Select three fibers that provide chemical, heat, or fire resistance and identify end uses for them. What are the end uses that you might come in contact with on a regular or daily basis or in an emergency situation?

▶ Learning Activity 4

Remove three to four fibers from each of the small self-sealing bags labeled Modacrylic, Spandex, Aramid, Glass, and Vinyon or three to four yarns from Fabrics #10 and 64 from your swatch kit. Following the procedures described in Chapter 3, examine the fibers using the microscope. Diagram what you see. Are there easily identifiable charateristics that would enable you to determine the specific fiber content? If yes, explain or describe them. If no, explain the factors in their production that make these fibers resemble each other.

key terms

Aramid   195
Carbon   203
Ceramic   205
Comfort stretch   190
Elastane   191
Elasterell-p   194
Elastoester   194
Elastomer   190
Emulsion spinning   203
Fluoropolymer   203
Glass   196
Gore-Tex   203

Grin-through   193
Lastol   194
Lastrile   191
Melamine   204
Metallic fibers   198
Modacrylic   199
Neoprene   191
Novoloid   200
PBI   201
Polyhenylene benzobisoxazole
   (PBO)   205
Polyimide (PI or PEI)   205

PLA   205
Power stretch   190
Rubber   190
Saran   201
Spandex   191
Stainless steel   198
Sulfar   201
Vinal   202
Vinyon   202

review questions

1. Compare the performance characteristics of rubber and spandex.

2. What are the differences and similarities between power and comfort stretch?

3. Explain why many woven fabrics include a small percentage of spandex.

4. What is the difference in serviceability between a pair of all-cotton slacks and a pair of 95 percent cotton/5 percent spandex slacks?

5. Explain why glass and metal are included as textile fibers.

6. Identify a fiber from this chapter that would be an appropriate choice for each end use listed below, and explain why that fiber was selected. (Some of these fibers may actually be used in blend form in the product.)
   a. Insulation for electrical wiring
   b. Support hosiery
   c. Theater costume for a performance of *King Lear*
   d. Apron for welder

e. Firefighting suit

f. Particle filter for smokestack

g. Support fiber in resin for auto-body repair

7. Compare and contrast the following pairs of fibers in terms of serviceability:

   a. Polyester and elastoester
   b. Spandex and nylon
   c. Nylon and aramid
   d. Glass and stainless steel
   e. Fluoropolymer and carbon

8. Explain why nanofibers and nanotubes are important end uses for carbon.

9. Select four fibers from the fibers with chemical, heat, and fire resistance and explain their role in sustainability and environmental quality.

10. Select four fibers not identified for Question 9 and identify technical end uses for these fibers. How do the fibers affect the quality of your life?

11. Besides rubber and spandex, name two other elastomeric fibers and explain how their properties differ from spandex. Identify an end use for each.

12. Explain how metal or metallic fibers are made. How does this process differ from the processes used to produce most manufactured or synthetic fibers?

section review questions

1. Differentiate among natural, regenerated, and synthetic fibers. Give an example of each.

2. Identify four characteristics for each fiber listed below that contribute to its importance in the textile complex:

   a. Acrylic
   b. Aramid
   c. Cotton
   d. Hemp
   e. Linen
   f. Lyocell
   g. Nylon
   h. Olefin
   i. PLA
   j. Polyester
   k. Ramie
   l. Rayon
   m. Silk
   n. Spandex
   o. Wool

3. Identify which of the fibers in Question 2 can be modified during fiber spinning to enhance performance.

4. Identify which of the fibers in Question 2 must be modified by finishing to enhance performance.

5. Identify which fiber from Question 2 is the best in terms of sustainability and explain why. Which fiber is the poorest in terms of sustainability? Explain why.

6. Explain how a fiber can be modified in the following ways:

   a. Fiber size
   b. Fiber shape
   c. Orientation and crystallinity
   d. Pilling
   e. Luster
   f. Solution dyeing
   g. Cross-dyeable
   h. Antistatic
   i. Sunlight resistance
   j. Flame resistance
   k. Antibacterial
   l. Fiber crimp

7. Describe four nanotechnology uses with textile fibers. How does nanotechnology change fiber performance?

Case Study

PBI and Its Expanding Markets*

A manufacturer of high-performance PBI fiber and polymer for heat- and flame-resistant protective apparel and other applications will be enlarging the plant and including new fiber spinning technology. Projected needs for current end uses, expanded research and development programs to identify new end uses, and global marketing programs demonstrate the need for the planned expansion. PBI is used for protective apparel for firefighting, military, and industrial safety. Other high-temperature applications include filtration, aerospace, and automotive industries.

DISCUSSION QUESTIONS

1. Why would a manufacturer of a high-performance fiber need a global marketing program?

2. In addition to the heat and flame resistance for which this fiber is known, what other performance characteristics would be desirable for protective apparel?

3. What are the performance categories in which PBI excels?

4. Which other fibers compete with PBI for similar markets?

*Anonymous, (2008, December 2). PBI to expand capacity, add jobs. *Textile World News* (www.textileworld.com).

suggested readings

Anonymous. (1995, April). Glass fibre makers go for target markets. *Technical Textiles International*, pp. 18–20.

Anonymous. (2008, December 2). PBI to expand capacity, add jobs. *Textile World News* (www.textileworld.com).

Anonymous. (2003, June). Specialty and performance fibres for industrial uses—2003. *Technical Textiles International*, pp. 22–27.

Butler, N. (1995, March). Specialty fibres to continue to flourish. *Technical Textiles International*, pp. 12–15.

Coffee, D. R., Serad, G. A., Hicks, H. L., & Montgomery, R. T. (1982). Properties and applications of Celanese PBI-polybenzimidazole fiber. *Textile Research Journal*, 52, pp. 466–472.

Fletcher, K. (2008). *Sustainable Fashion and Textiles: Design Journey*. London: Earthscan.

Foster, L. E. (Ed.). (2006). *Nanotechnology: Science, Innovation, and Opportunity*. Upper Saddle River, NJ: Prentice Hall.

Hethorn, J., & Ulasewicz, C. (2008). *Sustainable Fashion: Why Now?* New York: Fairchild Books.

Kirschner, E. N. (1997, July 28). Carbon fiber market revs up. *Chemical and Engineering News*, pp. 23–24.

Lunt, J. (2004). Ingeo PLA fibres: Chemistry, manufacture, and application. *Textiles Magazine*, (3), 15–16

Mukhopadhyay, S. K. (1993). High-performance fibres. *Textiles Progress*, 25 (3/4), pp. 1–71.

Qian, L. (2004). Nanotechnology in textiles: Recent developments and future prospects. *AATCC Review, 4*(5), 14–16.

Radhakrishnaiah, P. (2008, July/August). Extreme textiles. *Textile Horizons*, 16–17.

Reisfeld, A. (1997, September). The expanding world of high-tech textile products. *American Sportswear and Knitting Times*, pp. 36–39.

Roshan, P., & Roshan, S. P. (2005, January/February), Electrospinning: A breakthrough tecnology. *The Textile Journal*, 14–16.

Rozelle, W. N. (1997, January). Spandex: Miracle fiber now coming into its own. *Textile World*, pp. 80, 82, 84–87.

Smith, W. C. (1995, April). Hi-temperature fibers gain in performance, market. *Textile World*, pp. 31–32, 37–38.

10 Yarn Processing

11 Yarn Classification

YARNS

10

11

YARN
PROCESSING

CHAPTER OBJECTIVES

- To understand the processes used to produce yarns from filament and staple fibers.
- To recognize the different types and qualities of yarns.
- To relate yarn type to end-use performance.
- To relate yarn properties to processing method.
- To integrate fiber properties with yarn properties.
- To understand fiber blends and their effect on product performance.

10

Most apparel and interior fabrics are produced from yarns. "A **yarn** is a continuous strand of textile fibers, filaments, or materials in a form suitable for knitting, weaving, or otherwise intertwining to form a textile fabric" (American Society for Testing and Materials [ASTM]). This chapter explores the process of making a yarn from fibers or other starting materials. For filament yarns, this is a relatively quick and easy process. Spun yarns undergo a series of operations to make the fibers parallel and in the form of a yarn.

Yarn processing attracts a great deal of attention within the textile complex, but not much consumer interest. However, yarn type and quality affect product cost, quality, and performance. Thus, understanding yarn production will provide additional knowledge about products made from yarns.

Many changes continue to occur in the ways yarns are made. Efforts focus on improving productivity, decreasing costs, increasing uniformity and quality, solving problems, and developing new systems or approaches to deal with changes in other segments of the textile complex. For example, yarn-processing systems are modified for microfibers, and yarn characteristics are modified to cope with the greater speeds of fabrication equipment. In fact, yarns often limit fabric-production rates. Computer systems monitor yarn production and quality of yarns.

Filament Yarns

Filament yarns are made from manufactured fibers, except for the tiny percentage that is filament silk. Manufactured filament yarns are made by extruding a polymer solution through a spinneret and solidifying it in fiber form. Then the individual filaments are brought together with or without a slight twist (see Figure 8.3). The grouping of the filaments with the addition of twist creates the filament yarn. The spinning machine winds the yarn on a bobbin. The yarn is then rewound on spools or cones and is a finished product, unless additional treatments such as crimping, twisting, texturing, or finishing are required (see Figure 10.1).

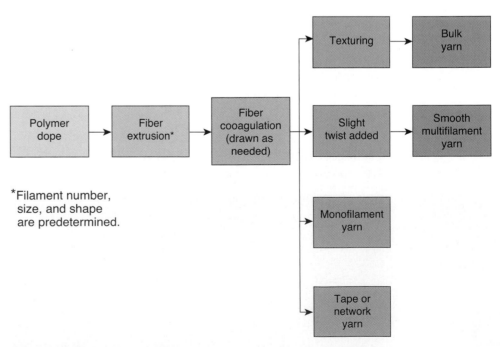

Figure 10.1 Production sequence for filament yarns.

Throwing, originally a process for twisting silk filaments, evolved into the twisting of manufactured fibers and then into texturing. Throwing provides the fabricator with the specific yarn needed for a particular product. Some fiber producers texture yarns as a final step in the fiber-spinning process; occasionally a trade name is associated with a textured filament yarn.

Smooth-Filament Yarn

Filament yarns are more expensive per pound than staple fibers; however, the cost of making tow into staple and then mechanically spinning it into yarn usually equalizes the final cost. The number of holes in the spinneret determines the number of filaments in the yarn.

Regular-, conventional-, or **smooth-filament yarns** are uniform as they come from the spinneret. Their smooth nature gives them more luster than spun yarns, but the luster varies with the amount of delusterant in the fiber and the amount of twist in the yarn. Maximum luster is obtained with bright filaments with little or no twist. Very-high-twist yarns, like crepe yarns, reduce filament luster. With thermoplastic fibers, the twist can be heat-set. Filament yarns generally have either high twist or low twist.

Filament yarns have no protruding ends, so they do not lint; the fibers are very parallel; they resist pilling; and fabrics made from them shed soil. Filaments of round cross section pack well into compact yarns that give little bulk, loft, or cover to fabric. Compact yarns are used in wind- and water-resistant fabrics. Compactness is a disadvantage in end uses in which bulk and absorbency are necessary for comfort. Nonround filaments create more open space for air and moisture permeability and produce greater cover.

Filament yarn strength depends on the strength of the individual fibers and the number of filaments in the yarn. The strength of filament fibers is usually greater than that of staple fibers. For polyester, staple tenacity is 3 to 5.5 g/d (grams per denier); filament tenacity is 5 to 8 g/d.

The strength of each filament is fully utilized. In order to break the yarn, all the filaments must be broken. Fine filaments make very sheer, strong fabrics possible. Filament yarns reach their maximum strength at a low twist—3 to 6 turns per inch (tpi)—then strength remains constant or decreases.

Fine-filament yarns are soft and supple, but not as abrasion-resistant as coarse filaments. For durability, fewer and coarser filaments in the yarn are most advantageous. Compare the difference in durability between a taffeta used for windbreakers and a taffeta used for backpacks. Both are probably nylon, but the windbreaker taffeta uses finer fibers in a finer yarn compared to the coarser fibers and larger yarn in the backpack taffeta. The windbreaker taffeta is resistant to wind and water, but flexible and comfortable to wear. The backpack taffeta is stiffer and less pliable, but stronger and more abrasion resistant.

Monofilament Yarns

Monofilament yarns are primarily for technical uses. These yarns consist of a single coarse-filament fiber. End uses include sewing thread, fishing line, fruit and vegetable bags, nets, and other woven or knitted fabrics for which low cost and high durability are most important. Metallic fibers are used as monofilament yarns for the sparkle they produce in apparel and interiors and for their ability to minimize static electricity in carpeting, clean-room apparel, and technical applications.

Tape and Network Yarns

Tape yarns are inexpensive yarns produced from extruded polymer films (Figure 10.2). Extrusion is the standard method of spinning fibers and some films. The split-fiber method is less expensive than the traditional fiber extrusion process and requires a minimal investment in

Smooth-filament yarns are uniform as they come from the spinneret. The fibers are parallel. There are no protruding ends, so they do not lint or pill. They give little bulk, loft, or cover to fabric. Fabrics made from them shed soil.

Figure 10.2   Tape and network yarns used in technical products.

equipment. Although some fiber polymers cannot be processed by the split-fiber method, polypropylene is often processed in this way because it is easy and inexpensive and produces strong yarns. Tape yarns are ribbonlike in appearance but can take on the more rounded appearance of traditional yarns.

Pellets of polypropylene with appropriate additives are melted and then extruded as a film 0.005 to 0.020 inch thick onto a chilled roll or cooled quickly by quenching in water. The film is slit into tapes approximately 0.1 inch wide and heat-stretched to orient the molecular chains. The stretching can be carried to a point at which the film fibrillates (splits into fibers), or the film is passed over needles to slit it. Twisting or other mechanical action completes the fibrillation.

Yarns as low as 250 denier have been made from split fibers. Tape yarns are coarse and usually used in carpet backing, rope, cord, fishnets, bagging, and interiors support fabrics for which ribbonlike yarn is needed.

Olefin films are slit into yarns that are used for the same textile products as split-fiber olefin. Slit-film-tape yarns are much more regular and may be thicker than fibrillated film-tape yarns. Tape yarns are slightly more expensive and their production is slower.

Network yarns are made of fibers that are connected in a network arrangement. They have a ribbonlike characteristic similar to tape yarns, but are bulkier and less dense. These yarns are produced by incorporating air into the polymer to create a foam. When the foam is extruded and stretched, tiny air cells rupture, forming an interconnected fibrous web. Although their strength is not as great as that of multifilament, monofilament, or tape yarns, these network yarns have interesting bulk and comfort characteristics. Uses include technical products in which bulk and low density are more important than high strength (see Figure 10.2).

Bulk Yarns

"A **bulk yarn** is one that has been processed to have greater covering power or apparent volume than that of a conventional yarn of equal linear density and of the same basic material with normal twist" (ASTM). Often these bulk yarns are referred to as **bulk-continuous-filament (BCF) yarns** or textured filament yarns. BCF yarns include any continuous-filament yarn whose smooth, straight fibers have been displaced from their closely packed, parallel position by the introduction of some form of crimp, curl, loop, or coil (Figure 10.3).

The characteristics of bulk yarns are quite different from those of smooth-filament yarns. Bulking gives filaments the aesthetic properties of spun yarns by altering the surface characteristics and creating space between the fibers. These yarns have an irregular surface, soft twist, and continuous nonparallel fibers that resist being pulled apart. Fabrics are more absorbent, more permeable to moisture, more breathable, and more comfortable, and they have better bulk, cover, and elasticity. Static buildup is lower. Bulk yarns do not pill or shed.

There are three classes of bulk yarns: bulky yarns, stretch yarns, and textured yarns. They will be discussed after the texturing processes are described.

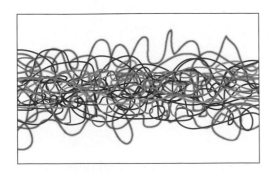

Figure 10.3   Typical bulk yarn.

▶ Learning Activity 1

Work in groups of two or three. Explain the process used to produce these filament yarns: monofilament, multifilament, and tape. Identify an end use for each type and explain why that yarn would be serviceable in that end use.

Texturing Filament Yarns The **texturing** processes discussed here are primarily mechanical methods used with thermoplastic fibers. Heat and chemical methods are used to achieve texture with bicomponent fibers.

False-Twist Process The *false-twist* spindle whirls at 600,000 revolutions per minute and generates such an intense sound that it adversely affects health and hearing. In the continuous process, the yarn is twisted, heat-set, and untwisted as it travels through the spindle (Figure 10.4). The filaments form a distorted helical coil. When the yarn is pulled at each end, the yarn stretches as the coils straighten out. This is one of the most important and cheapest methods used to add bulk and stretch to filament yarns.

Draw-Texturing In *draw-texturing*, unoriented filaments or partially oriented filaments (often referred to as partially oriented yarns—POY) are fed through the double-heater false-twist spinner, then stretched slightly and heat-set. Draw-texturing is a fast and inexpensive way to make textured bulk yarns.

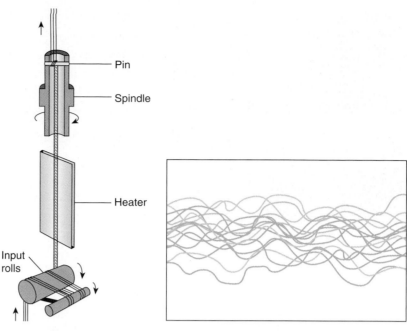

Figure 10.4 False-twist process (left), yarn (right).
SOURCE (left): Courtesy of Solutia Inc.

Stuffer Box The *stuffer box* produces a sawtooth crimp of considerable bulk. Straight-filament yarns are pushed into one end of a heated box (Figure 10.5) and then withdrawn at the other end in crimped form. The volume increase is 200 to 300 percent, with some elasticity. The stuffer box is a fast, inexpensive, and popular method for carpeting yarns.

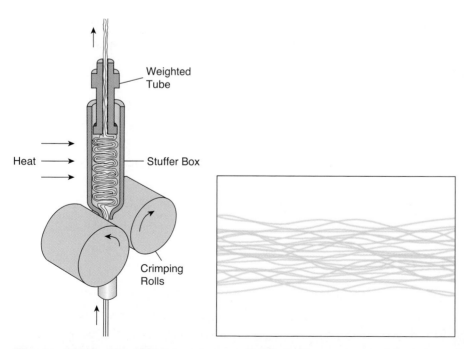

Figure 10.5 Stuffer box process (left), bulky yarn used in apparel (right).
SOURCE (left): Courtesy of Solutia Inc.

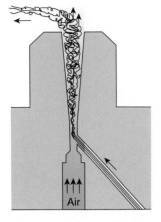

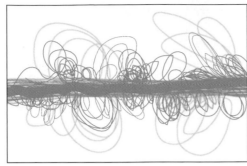

Figure 10.6 Air-jet process (left), bulky yarn (right).
SOURCE (left): Courtesy of Solutia Inc.

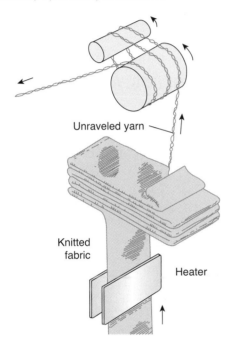

Unraveled yarn

Knitted fabric

Heater

Figure 10.7 Knit-deknit fabric is heat-set, then unraveled.

Bulky yarns are formed from inherently bulky manufactured fibers that are hollow along part or all of their length or from fibers that cannot be closely packed because of some fiber characteristic. **Stretch yarns** are thermoplastic filament or spun yarns with a high degree of potential elastic stretch, rapid recovery, and a high degree of yarn curl. **Textured or bulked yarns** are filament or spun yarns with notably greater apparent volume than a conventional yarn of similar filament count and linear density.

Air Jet Conventional filament yarns are fed over an air jet (Figure 10.6) at a faster rate than they are drawn off. The blast of air forces some of the filaments into very tiny loops; the velocity of the air affects the size of the loops. This is a slow, relatively costly, but versatile process. Volume increases with little or no stretch. *Air-jet* yarns maintain their size and bulk under tension because the straight areas bear the strain and the loops remain relatively unaffected.

Knit–Deknit In the *knit–deknit* process, a small-diameter tube is knit, heat-set, unraveled, and wound on cones (Figure 10.7). Crimp is varied by changing stitch size and tension. The gauge used to make a fabric must differ from that used in yarn texturing, or pinholes will form when texturing and knit gauges match.

Bulk Yarn Types "**Bulky yarns** are formed from inherently bulky manufactured fibers that are hollow along part or all of their length or from fibers that cannot be closely packed because of their cross-sectional shape, fiber alignment, stiffness, resilience, or natural crimp" (ASTM).

Bulky texturing processes can be used with any kind of filament fiber or spun yarn. The yarns have less stretch than either stretch or textured yarns. Bulky yarns are used in a wide array of products including carpeting, lingerie, sweaters, and shoelaces.

Stretch Yarns "**Stretch yarns** are thermoplastic filament or spun yarns with a high degree of potential elastic stretch (300 to 500 percent), rapid recovery, and a high degree of yarn curl" (ASTM). Stretch yarns have moderate bulk. Stretch yarns of nylon are used extensively in men's and women's hosiery, pantyhose, leotards, swimwear, leggings, football pants, and jerseys. Apparel manufacturers like stretch yarns because fewer sizes are needed since one-size items fit wearers of different sizes. Stretch yarns are not the same as yarns made with elastomeric fibers.

Textured Yarns "**Textured or bulked yarns** are filament or spun yarns with notably greater apparent volume than a conventional yarn of similar filament count and linear density" (ASTM). These yarns have much lower elastic stretch than stretch yarns, but greater stretch than bulky yarns. They are stable enough to present no unusual problems in subsequent processing or in consumer use. Fabrics made from these yarns maintain their original size and shape during wear and care.

Table 10.1 summarizes the three major types of bulk filament yarns.

Spun Yarns

Spun yarns are continuous strands of staple fibers held together in some way. Often, mechanical twist takes advantage of fiber irregularities and natural cohesiveness to bind the fibers together into one yarn. The process of producing yarns from staple fibers by twisting is an old one, but methods of producing spun yarns without twist are also used.

Table 10.1 Comparison of Bulk Yarns

Characteristic	Bulky Yarns	Stretch Yarns	Textured Yarns
Nature	Inherently bulky	High degree of yarn curl	High degree of bulk
Fiber type	May be hollow or crimped fibers	Any thermoplastic fiber	Fibers that develop crimp with moisture, heat, or chemical treatment
Stretch	Little stretch	300–500% stretch	Moderate amount of stretch
Characteristics	Sawtooth, single fiber loops	Torque and non-torque	Loopy, high bulk, crimped
Processes	Stuffer box, air jet, draw-texturing, friction texturing	False-twist, knit–deknit, draw-texturing, friction texturing	Air jet, flat-drawn textured, draw-texturing, friction texturing

▶ Learning Activity 2

Use Fabrics #5, 9, 42, 62, and 64 from your swatch kit and/or Yarns #4 and 5 from your yarn kit. Examine the yarns in each fabric and group them as smooth or textured filament and monofilament or multifilament. For the fabric swatches, are all the yarns in a fabric the same structure? (Some fabrics may include yarns of other types.) For the filament yarns, describe the relationship between the length or width of the fabric swatch and the length of the fiber. Describe the most noticeable differences between smooth and textured filament yarns. Examine the illustrations of texturing methods to identify the procedure most likely used for each of the textured yarns used in this activity.

Spun yarns have a fuzzy surface, greater amounts of twist compared to filament yarns, short fibers that pull apart, and partially parallel fibers. Spun yarns have protruding fiber ends that prevent close contact with the skin. A fabric made of spun yarn is more comfortable next to the skin than a fabric of smooth-filament yarn.

Many of the insulating characteristics of a fabric are due to the structure of the yarns used in that fabric. There is more space between fibers in a spun yarn than in a filament yarn. Spaces in a yarn trap air; yarns with more trapped air insulate better than yarns with less trapped air. A spun yarn with low twist has more air spaces than a spun yarn with a high twist and, thus, has better insulating characteristics. For that reason, most fabrics designed for warmth have lower-twist yarns. If wind resistance is desired, fabrics with high-twist compact yarns and a high count are more desirable because air permeability is reduced.

Carded yarns of short-staple fibers have more protruding fiber ends than combed yarns, which are made of long-staple fibers. Protruding ends contribute to greater comfort and warmth and produce dull luster, fuzzy appearance, shedding of lint from broken off fiber ends, and formation of surface pills. Fiber ends can be removed from the fabric's surface by singeing (see Chapter 16).

The strength of the individual staple fiber is less important in the strength of spun yarn than it is in filament yarns. The strength of spun yarn depends on the fibers' cohesiveness or clinging power and on the points of contact resulting from twist or other binding mechanisms used to produce the spun yarn. The greater the number of points of contact, the greater the resistance to fiber slippage within the yarn. Fibers with crimp or convolutions have a greater number of points of contact. The friction of one fiber against another also gives resistance to lengthwise fiber slippage. A fiber with a rough or irregular surface—wool scales, for example—creates more friction than a smooth fiber.

Spun yarns are continuous strands of staple fibers usually held together by twist. They have a fuzzy surface and protruding fiber ends, greater amounts of twist compared to filament yarns, short fibers that pull apart, and partially parallel fibers.

The mechanical spinning of staple fibers into yarns is one of the oldest manufacturing arts and has been described as an invention as significant as that of the wheel. The basic principles of spinning are the same now as they were when yarns were first made. Of course, advances in engineering and technology have increased the speed of spinning and the quantity of yarn produced.

Primitive spinning consisted of drawing out fibers held on a stick called a *distaff*, twisting them by the rotation of a spindle that could be spun like a top, and winding up the spun yarn (Figure 10.8). The spinning wheel was invented in India and was introduced to Europe in the 14th century. The factory system began in the 18th century, when James Hargreaves invented the spinning jenny that turns more than one spinning wheel at a time. Other inventions for improving the spinning process followed and led to the Industrial Revolution, when power machines took over hand processes and made mass production possible. Machines were developed for each separate step in the spinning process.

Spinning continues to evolve. Progress has been made in reducing the number of steps, automating the process, improving yarn quality, and making it faster, simpler, and more economical with higher production speeds and more user-friendly computerization. Spun-yarn processes are shown in Table 10.2.

Figure 10.8 Drop spindle (left), spinning wheel (right). Note the drop spindle at the wheel's base.

Processing Staple Fibers

Spinning may be done by several systems (cotton, woolen, worsted or long-staple, and flax), which are adapted to such fiber characteristics as length, cohesiveness, diameter, elasticity, and surface contour. These systems are used to process both natural and manufactured fibers as well as blends of these fibers. Because the cotton system is the most widely used system, it is discussed here in detail. Table 10.3 and Figure 10.9 summarize the steps in producing a spun yarn.

Opening Machine-picked cotton contains a high percentage of trash and dirt. The fibers have been compressed very tightly in a bale that may have been stored for many months. **Opening** loosens, cleans, and blends the fibers. Cotton varies from bale to bale, so blending the fibers from several bales achieves more uniform quality in the finished yarn. Manufacturers must produce yarns with consistent characteristics and performance so that basic fabrics do not differ by season or year.

Material removed from the bale of fiber in the opening step includes very short fibers, soil, plant debris, and other foreign matter. This waste may be discarded or purchased with the short

Table 10.2 Spun-Yarn Processes

From Staple Fiber	From Filament Tow
Conventional ring	Tow-to-top
Open-end	Tow-to-yarn
Airjet	High-bulk yarns
Direct	
Compact	
Vortex	
Twistless	
Self-twist	

Table 10.3 The Cotton System

Operation	Purpose
Opening	Loosens bales, blends and cleans fibers.
Carding	Cleans and aligns fibers, forms carded sliver.
Drawing	Parallels and blends fibers, forms drawn sliver.
Combing	Parallels and removes short fibers, forms combed sliver (for long-staple fibers only).
Roving	Inserts slight twist, forms roving.
Spinning	Reduces size, twists, winds finished yarn on bobbins.
Winding	Rewinds yarn to spools or cones.

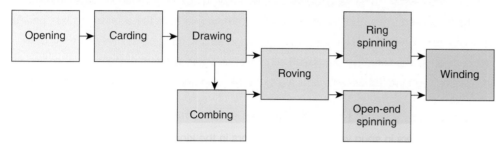

Figure 10.9 Production sequence for spun yarns.

fibers recycled into yarns, fiber batts, or other textile products. Recycling this waste improves spinners' bottom line since they do not have to pay landfill or hauling fees and are selling a secondary output from their facilities. Recycling these materials improves sustainability since new fibers do not have to be produced for the kinds of products made from these short fibers.

Carding **Carding** partially aligns the fibers and forms them into a thin web that is brought together as a soft, very weak rope of fibers called a *carded sliver* (Figure 10.10). A **sliver** is a ropelike strand of fibers. The carding machine consists of a revolving cylinder and an outer belt covered with fine, short wire teeth that remove trash and neps (entangled clumps of short, undeveloped or underdeveloped fibers).

Drawing **Drawing** increases the parallelism of the fibers and combines several carded or combed slivers into one *drawn sliver*. This blending operation contributes to greater yarn uniformity. Drawing is done by sets of rollers, with each set rolling faster than the preceding set (Figure 10.11). As slivers are combined, their size is reduced.

The drawing step is repeated once more for carded slivers. At this stage, fibers of different generic types often are combined into a blended drawn sliver. Because each fiber differs in its physical properties, conditions for the carding and initial drawing steps differ for each fiber in a blend. Blending during the drawing process also eliminates mixed wastes.

Combing If long-staple fibers are to be spun, another step is added to the process. **Combing** produces a yarn that is superior to a carded yarn in smoothness, fineness, evenness, and strength. Combing aligns fibers in a parallel arrangement. It also removes short fibers so that fibers in the *combed sliver* will be more uniform in length. The combing operation and long-staple fibers are

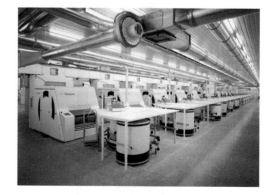

Figure 10.10 Carding.
SOURCE: Courtesy of Trützschler GmbH & Co. KG.

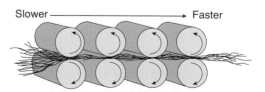

Figure 10.11 Drawing rolls.

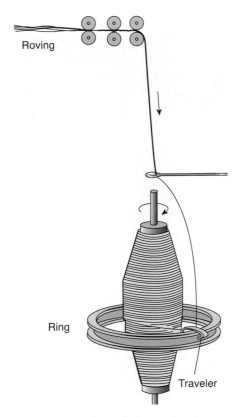

Figure 10.14 Ring spinning.

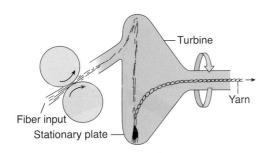

Figure 10.15 Open-end rotor spinning.

harsher hand and are weaker and more sensitive to abrasion, but more uniform and more opaque in appearance. While moderately thin yarns are possible, ring spinning is used to produce thinner yarns. Open-end yarns are preferred for toweling and other pile yarn fabrics, denim, sheeting, and base fabrics for laminated fabrics.

In the more commonly used rotor-air-jet spinning process, sliver is separated so that individual fibers are fed by an air stream and deposited on the inner surface of a high-speed rotor. As the fibers are drawn off, twist is inserted by the rotation of the rotor, making a yarn (Figure 10.15). Rotor-spun yarns have a higher twist at the center of the yarn.

Friction spinning, another type of open-end spinning, combines rotor and air techniques. The sliver is separated into fibers that are spread into carding or combing rolls and delivered by air to two cylinders rotating in the same direction, which pull the fibers into a yarn. The feed angle into the cylinder controls fiber alignment. Friction-spun yarns are more even, freer of lint and other debris, and loftier, but they are weaker as compared with conventional yarns. Friction spinning may be used to process very short waste staple fiber into yarns.

Alternate Spun-Yarn Processes

These processes simplify yarn spinning by eliminating some steps in ring spinning. They are more automatic and have higher production rates compared to ring spinning. Most processes eliminate one or more of these steps: drawing, roving, ring spinning, and rewinding. However, the two dominant spinning systems are ring and open-end spinning.

Air-Jet Spinning In **air-jet spinning**, a narrow sliver is fed into a machine with two nozzles facing in opposite directions. Each nozzle blows air against the sliver forcing the outermost fibers to wrap around the sliver, which produces a yarn. Air-jet yarns are less elastic, weaker, and rougher than either ring- or rotor-spun yarns.

Table 10.5 compares ring spinning, rotor spinning, and air-jet spinning. See Figure 10.16 to examine the similarities and differences of yarns produced by these three spinning methods.

Direct Spinning *Direct spinning* eliminates the roving and uses the ring-spinning device to insert twist. The sliver is fed directly to the spinning frame. These heavier yarns are used for pile fabrics and carpets.

Compact Spinning *Compact spinning* is a variation of ring spinning that condenses the roving before final twist insertion and creates a smoother compact or condensed yarn. Compact spun yarns are considered superior to ring spun yarns. Compact spun yarns are smaller, stronger with better elongation and reduced hairiness. Yarns with better fiber alignment and fewer defects are produced. Because of their smoothness and compact nature, these yarns create fewer problems with yarn breakage in weaving and better weaving efficiencies. While compact spinning is gaining in use, its popularity is limited because of its newness and higher technology demands for spinning equipment.

Vortex Spinning *Vortex spinning* produces a yarn that has an outer layer of fibers wrapped around a center of parallel fibers. While high speeds are possible, the sliver must have clean and strong fibers of uniform length. After the sliver has reached a desired fineness, high- speed or vortex air currents wrap the fibers around a hollow stationary spindle. Yarn twist develops as the fibers swirl around the spindle before they are pulled through the hollow center. Shorter fibers are removed in the process.

Table 10.5 Comparison of Ring-Spun, Rotor-Spun, and Air-Jet-Spun Yarns

Yarn Characteristic	Ring-Spun	Open-End Rotor-Spun	Air-Jet-Spun
Fiber Parallelism	High	Medium	High at yarn core, less at yarn edge
Fiber Orientation	All areas helical	Yarn core helical	Axial orientation in yarn core
Yarn structure	Compact	Less compact	Less compact
Insulation	Low	Moderate	Good
Yarn hairiness	High	Lower	Lower
Yarn stiffness	Low	More rigid	Depends on structure
Abrasion resistance	Medium	Low	High
Pilling propensity	Low	Pronounced	Less than rotor- and ring-spun
Yarn strength	Good	Low	Medium
Surface roughness	Low	Medium	Medium
Yarn size	Wide range	Not as fine as ring	Not as fine as ring, but finer than rotor
Yarn evenness	Least even	Most even	Less even than rotor
Comfort	Best	Moderate	Lowest
Thermal retention	Moderate	Moderate	Best
Hand (Softness)	Moderate	Low	High
Preferred for	Knits	Higher-weight apparel, interior textiles	Bedding, interior textiles

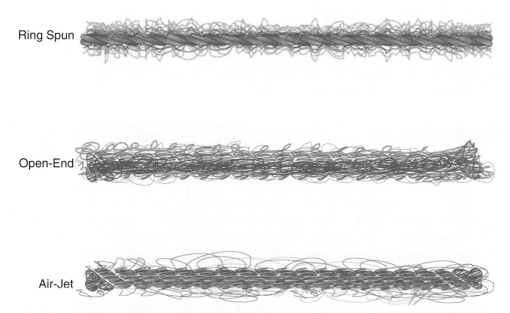

Ring Spun

Open-End

Air-Jet

Figure 10.16 Compare these three yarns: ring-spun (top), open-end spun (middle), and air-jet spun (bottom).

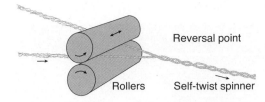

Figure 10.17 Self-twist spinning.

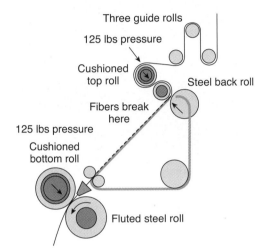

Figure 10.18 Direct spinning of yarn from filament tow.

Twistless Spinning *Twistless spinning* eliminates the twisting process. A roving is wetted, drawn out, sprayed with sizing or adhesive, wound on a package, and steamed to bond the fibers together. The yarns are ribbonlike in shape and stiff because of the sizing. They lack strength as individual yarns but gain strength in the fabric from the pressure within the components of the fabric. The absence of twist gives the yarns a soft hand, good luster, and opacity after the sizing is removed. The yarns are easy to dye and have good durability but are not suitable to very open fabric structures.

Self-Twist Spinning In *self-twist spinning*, two strands of roving are carried between two rollers, which draw out the roving and insert twist. The yarns have areas of S-twist and areas of Z-twist. When the two twisted yarns are brought together, they intermesh and entangle, and when pressure is released, the yarns ply over each other (Figure 10.17). This process can be used to combine staple strands, filament strands, or staple and filament strands.

Spinning Filament Tow into Spun Yarns

Filament tow of any manufactured fiber can be made into spun yarns by direct spinning without disrupting the continuity of the strand. The two systems are tow-to-top or tow-to-yarn.

Tow-to-Top (Sliver) System The **tow-to-top system** bypasses the opening, picking, and carding steps of conventional spinning. In this system, the filament tow is reduced to staple and formed into sliver (or top) by either diagonal cutting or break stretching. The sliver is made into regular-spun yarn by conventional spinning.

The diagonal-cutting stapler changes tow into staple of equal or variable lengths and forms it into a crimped sliver. In the break-stretch process, the tow is stretched and the fibers break at their weakest points without disrupting the strand's continuity. The resulting staple fibers vary in length.

Tow-to-Yarn System **Tow-to-yarn spinning** is done by a machine called a *direct spinner*. Light tow (4,400 denier) passes between two pairs of nip rolls. The second pair of nip rolls breaks the fibers at their weakest points. The resulting staple-fiber strand is drawn out to yarn size, twisted, and wound on a bobbin (Figure 10.18).

> ### ▶ Learning Activity 4
>
> Use Fabrics #39, 40, 42, and 53 from your swatch kit. Examine the yarns in each fabric and group them as carded/woolen or combed/worsted. Untwist yarns from each fabric and measure the fiber length. How do the fiber lengths compare between the carded/woolen and combed/worsted yarns? Describe the most noticeable differences between these two types of yarns.

> ### ▶ Learning Activity 5
>
> Compare the yarns and fabrics used in Learning Activities 2 and 4. Describe the differences between these major yarns types (filament and spun) in terms of fiber length, yarn appearance, hairiness, and uniformity.

High-bulk yarns are spun yarns with no stretch but significant bulk and loft.

High-Bulk Yarns

High-bulk yarns are spun yarns essentially free from stretch. Some of the staple fibers have assumed a relatively high random crimp caused by shrinkage of low-crimp fibers.

Some fibers can be produced with a *latent shrinkage potential* and retain their bulk indefinitely at room temperature. Latent-shrinkage fibers are achieved by heating, stretching, and then cooling while in the stretched condition. These heat-stretched fibers are called *high-shrinkage* fibers and are combined with non-shrinkage fibers in the same yarn, which is made into a product. Heat treatment of the product causes the high-shrinkage fibers to relax or shrink, forcing the non-shrinkage fibers to bulk (Figure 10.19). This makes high-bulk sweaters, knitting yarns, and other products. High-shrinkage fibers migrate to the center of the yarn. Thus, if fine-denier non-shrinkage fibers are combined with coarse-denier high-shrinkage fibers, the fine-denier fibers concentrate on the outer surface of the yarn. Regulating the heat stretching controls the bulk.

This high-bulk principle can be used to achieve interesting effects, such as guard hairs in synthetic furs and sculptured high–low carpets. Higher-density carpet pile or furlike fabrics can be made by using a high-shrinkage-type fiber for the ground yarns. When the yarns shrink, the fibers are brought much closer together.

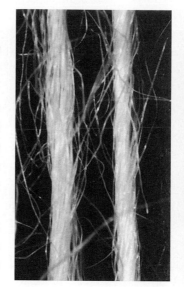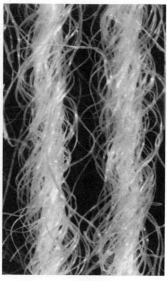

Figure 10.19 High-bulk yarn before (left) and after (right) steaming.

Fiber Blends

A **blend** is an intimate mixture of fibers of different generic type, composition, length, diameter, or color spun together into one yarn. In intimate blends, both fibers are present in the same yarn in planned proportions. Fiber types cannot be separated; they are next to each other throughout the yarn. When intimate blend yarns are untwisted and examined through a microscope, both fibers are visible in the viewing area.

Mixture refers to yarns of different generic types within a fabric. In a mixture, yarns of one generic type are used as one component of the fabric (e.g., the warp or the base structure yarn in knits) and yarns of another generic type are used as a second component of the fabric (e.g., the filling or as the pile component in velour). When these fabrics are unraveled, the fibers can be separated by placing all yarns of one component in one pile and all yarns of the second component in another pile.

In a **combination**, ply yarns are used. At least one strand of the ply yarn is of a different generic fiber type from the other strands of the ply yarn. For example, glitter and sparkle is incorporated in fabric by using a metallic monofilament as part of a plied fancy yarn.

Blends, mixtures, and combinations produce fabrics with properties that are different from those obtained with one fiber only. While this discussion relates to blends because they are the most common, it also applies to mixtures and combinations.

Blending is done for several reasons:

1. To produce fabrics with a better combination of performance characteristics. Although blends never perform as well in the areas of positive performance as fabrics of only one fiber, blends help compensate for poor performance. In end uses for which durability is important, nylon or polyester blended with cotton or wool increases strength and resistance to abrasion, while the comfort of wool or cotton is maintained. For example, 100-percent-cotton fabrics are not as durable as polyester/cotton blends, and polyester/cotton blends are less absorbent than 100-percent-cotton fabrics.

> A **blend** is an intimate mixture of fibers of different generic type, composition, length, diameter, or color spun together into one yarn. **Mixture** refers to yarns of different generic types combined to make a fabric. In a **combination**, ply yarns are used with at least one of the plies of a different generic fiber type than the other plies.

Table 10.6 Fiber Properties

Properties	Cotton	Rayon	Wool	Acetate	Nylon	Polyester	Acrylic	Olefin	Lyocell
Bulk and loft	1	1	4		1	1	4		1
Wrinkle recovery	1	1	4	3	3	4	3	3	1
Press (wet) retention	1	1	1	2	3	4			1
Absorbency	4	4	4	2	1	1	1	1	4
Static resistance	4	4	3	2	2	1	2	3	4
Resistance to pilling	4	4	2	4	2			3	2
Strength	3	2	2	2	4	4	2	4	4
Abrasion resistance	2	1	3	2	4	4	2	4	1
Stability	3	1	1	4	4	4	4	4	3
Resistance to heat	4	4	3	2	2	2	3	1	4

4, excellent; 3, good; 2, moderate; 1, low

Blending is done to produce fabrics with a better combination of performance characteristics; to improve processing efficiency and uniformity; to obtain better texture, hand or appearance; to reduce fiber cost; or to obtain unique effects.

2. To improve spinning, weaving, and finishing efficiency and to improve uniformity.
3. To obtain better texture, hand, or fabric appearance. A small amount of cashmere may be used to give a buttery or slick hand to wool fabrics, or a small amount of rayon may give luster and softness to a cotton fabric. Fibers with different shrinkage properties are blended to produce bulky, lofty fabrics or more realistic furlike fabrics.
4. To minimize fiber cost. Expensive fibers can be extended by blending them with less expensive fibers. Labeling requirements help protect consumers from unscrupulous labeling practices.
5. To obtain cross-dyed or unique color effects such as heather. Fibers with unlike dye affinity are blended together and dyed at a later stage in processing.

Blending is a complicated and expensive process, but the combination of properties it provides is permanent. Blends offer better serviceability of fabrics as well as improved appearance and hand.

Table 10.6 rates selected fiber properties. Note that each fiber is deficient in one or more important properties. Try different fiber combinations to see how a blend of two fibers might be used to produce a fabric with satisfactory performance in all properties.

Blend Levels

A blend of fibers that complement each other may give more satisfactory all-around performance than a fabric made from 100 percent of one fiber. For example, compare three fabrics, one of Fiber A, a second of Fiber B, and a third of a combination of Fibers A and B across five properties. A fabric made of 50 percent A and 50 percent B will have values for each property that are neither as high as possible nor as low as possible (Table 10.7). By blending the fibers, a fabric with intermediate values is obtained, but the values do not directly correspond to the fiber percentages.

Research by fiber manufacturers has determined the ideal percentage of each fiber for various products. It is difficult to generalize about percentages because they vary with fiber type, fabric construction, and end use. For example, a small amount of nylon (15 percent) improves the strength of wool, but 60 percent nylon is needed to improve the strength of rayon. For stability, 50 percent acrylic blended with wool in a woven fabric is satisfactory, but 75 percent acrylic is necessary in knitted fabrics.

Fiber producers have controlled blend levels fairly well by setting standards for fabrics identified with their trademarks. For example, a company that produces polyester may recommend

Table 10.7 Effect of Blending on Performance

| | KNOWN VALUES | | ACTUAL VALUES | |
Property	A	B	Predicted Values of 50/50 A and B	Actual Values of 50/50 A and B
1	12	4	8	9
2	9	12	10.5	11
3	15	2	8.5	6
4	7	9	8	8
5	12	8	10	10.5

a blend level of 65 percent polyester/35 percent cotton in lightweight or medium-weight fabrics, whereas 50 percent polyester/50 percent cotton is recommended for suit-weight fabrics.

By using specially designed fiber variants, it is possible to obtain desired performance and appearance in fabrics. For example, fading, shrinkage, and softening over time are desirable characteristics for denim jeans, but are undesirable in most other apparel. For this market, a polyester variant is available for blending with cotton that fades, softens, and shrinks uniformly.

Blending Methods

Blending of staple can be done at any stage prior to the spinning operation, including opening-picking, drawing, or roving. One of the disadvantages of direct spinning is that blending cannot be done before the sliver is formed.

The earlier the fibers are blended in processing, the better the blend. Figure 10.20 shows a cross section of yarns in which the fibers were blended in opening and in which the fibers were blended at the roving stage. Long, fine fibers tend to move to the center of a yarn, whereas coarse, short fibers migrate to the outside edge of a yarn (Figure 10.20c).

Fabrics are also produced that are mixtures of bulk-filament yarns and spun yarns. These fabrics may have filament yarns in only one direction and spun yarns in the other, or they may have different yarns in bands in the warp or filling to create a design in the fabric.

Blended-Filament Yarns

A **blended-filament yarn** has unlike filament fibers of different deniers or generic types blended together. This usually improves the performance and appearance of apparel and interior fabrics (Figure 10.21).

Fasciated or Rotofil Yarns These yarns combine coarse filaments for strength and fine broken filaments for softness to improve fabric texture and hand. The yarn has a low-twist staple fiber core wrapped with surface fibers to add integrity to the yarn. Air-jet spinning is used to produce these yarns.

▶ Learning Activity 6

Use Fabric #20 from your swatch kit. Determine the fibers present by examining the key for the swatch set. Predict the serviceability of this fabric based on its blend level. How would you expect the serviceability of this fabric to change if it were all cotton or all polyester?

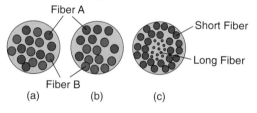

Figure 10.20 Cross section of yarn showing fiber location in blends: (a) blended at the opening stage, (b) blended at the roving stage, (c) blend of short and long fibers.

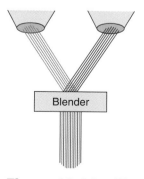

Figure 10.21 Blended-filament yarn. Different fibers are spun, then blended to form a yarn.

Case Study
Energy Use in Yarn Spinning*

Yarn spinning occurs in many countries where a constant and uniform power supply is not possible with the current infrastructure. When power supply brown-outs occur, the amount of power is decreased so that ring-spinning frames need to be shut off, operating speed reduced, or auxiliary power used. The power use by spinning mills is large. Power cost is second after raw material cost when calculating yarn cost. Most mills have diesel-fuel powered generators to produce power when brown-outs occur, but diesel-generated power is expensive. Even a slight increase in power costs can significantly impact profit. Research at one ring-spinning mill considered the cost of three options for maintaining production during brown-outs (from most expensive to least expensive): diesel-generated power; stop some frames and run others at normal speed; or run all frames at reduced speed. Cost savings are substantial and increase as yarn size decreases.

DISCUSSION QUESTIONS

1. Why would finer or smaller yarns produce a greater cost savings compared to coarser yarns?

2. How would an increase in yarn cost affect fabric and product price?

3. Why is profit a factor in considering yarn spinning costs?

4. What are the sustainability issues that might be factors in determining profit in a spinning mill?

*Anonymous. (2009, March 7). Optimize spinning profits during power cuts. www.fibre2fabric.com/news/yarn-news/newsdetails.aspx?news_id=69931

suggested readings

Alagirusamy, R., Fangueiro, R., Ogale, V., & Padaki, N. (2006). Hybrid yarns and textile preforming for thermoplastic composites. *Textile Progress, 38*(4), 1–71.

Anonymous. (2009, March 7). Optimize spinning profits during power cuts. www.fibre2fabric.com/news/yarnnews/newsdetails.aspx?news_id=69931

ASTM International. (2007). *Annual Book of ASTM Standards*, Vol. 7.01. West Conshohocken, PA: Author.

Becerir, B., & Omeroglu, S. (2007). Comparison of color values of plain cotton fabrics knitted from ring- and compact-spun yarns. *AATCC Review, 7*(7), 41–46.

Becerir, B., Omeroglu, S., & Alpay, H. R. (2006). Assessing color differences of cotton fabrics made from ring- and compact-spun yarns after abrasion. *AATCC Review, 6*(10), 37–41.

Douglas, K. (1995, February). Producing marketable quality ring- and rotor-spun yarns. *Textile World*, pp. 61–63.

Lawrence, C. A. (2003). *Fundamentals of Spun Yarn Technology*. New York: CRC Press.

Morris, B. (1991). Yarn texturing. *Textiles*, 1, pp. 10–13.

Nikolic, M., Cerkvenik, J., & Stjepanovic, Z. (1994). Influence of a spinning process on spun yarn quality and economy of yarn production. *International Journal of Clothing Science and Technology, 6*(4), pp. 34–40.

The polycotton story. (1994, Winter). *Textiles Magazine*, pp. 8–11.

Oxenham, W. (2004, January). Spinning. *Textile World, 154*(1), pp. 32–39.

Tortora, P. G., & Merkel, R. S. (1996). *Fairchild's Dictionary of Textiles*, 7th ed. New York: Fairchild Publications.

Wilson, D. K., & Kollu, T. (1991). The production of textured yarns by the false-twist technique. *Textile Progress, 21*(3), pp. 1–42.

YARN
CLASSIFICATION

CHAPTER OBJECTIVES

- To understand yarn classification based on appearance and structure.
- To identify and name the yarns in fabrics and products.
- To understand the relationships between yarn types and product performance.
- To integrate yarn selection with desired end-use performance.
- To relate yarn quality to product performance.

11

Table 11.2 Amount of Twist

Amount	Example	Characteristics
Low twist (2–3 tpi)	Filament yarns: 2–3 tpi*	Smooth or bulky; twist may be hard to see.
Napping twist (8–15 tpi)	Blanket warp: 12 tpi. Filling: 6–8 tpi	Bulky, soft, fuzzy, may be weak.
Average twist (15–30 tpi)	Percale warp: 25 tpi	Most common, smooth, regular, durable, comfortable. Produces smooth, regular fabrics.
	Filling: 20 tpi	
	Nylon hosiery: 25–30 tpi	
Voile twist (30–40 tpi)	Hard-twist singles: 35–40 tpi; plied with 16–18 tpi	Strong, fine yarns. Fabrics have harsher hand due to yarn twist.
Crepe twist (40–80 tpi)	Singles: 40–80 or more tpi; plied with 2–5 tpi	Lively yarns that kink and twist in fabrics with good drape and texture.

*Turns per inch.

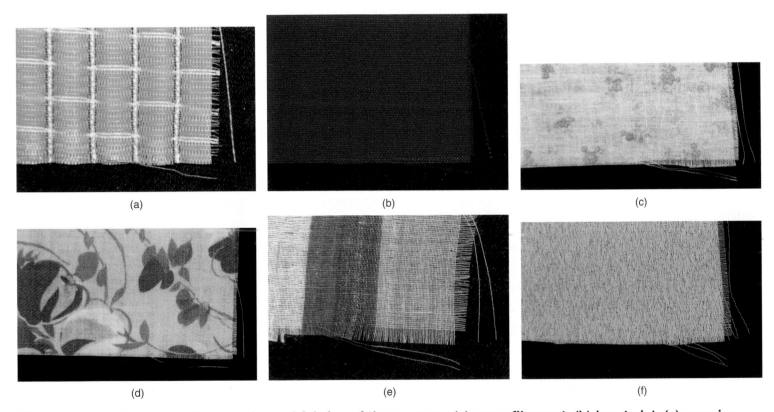

(a)   (b)   (c)

(d)   (e)   (f)

Figure 11.4 Examples of yarn twist and fabrics of these yarns: (a) monofilament, (b) low twist, (c) napping twist, (d) average twist, (e) voile twist, and (f) crepe twist.

Figure 11.5 Twist-on-twist two-ply yarn.

line (flax) yarns are made of long-staple fibers with a parallel arrangement. Carded, woolen, and tow (flax) yarns are made of short-staple fibers with a less parallel arrangement (Figure 11.4d).

Hard twist or **voile twist** yarns have a harsher hand and more turns per inch (Figure 11.4e). Yarn hardness results when twist brings the fibers closer together and compacts the yarn. This effect is more pronounced when a twist-on-twist ply yarn is used. **Twist-on-twist** means that the direction of twist in the single is the same as that of the plying twist, thus increasing the total amount of yarn twist (Figure 11.5). (See the discussion of voile in the section on lightweight sheer fabrics in Chapter 12.)

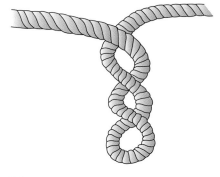

Figure 11.6 Crepe yarns knot, twist, or curl when removed from a fabric.

Crepe yarns have the highest number of turns per inch (40 to 80) inserted in the yarn (Figure 11.4f). These spun or filament yarns are also known as unbalanced yarns, since they twist and kink when removed from the fabric. These yarns are so lively that they must be twist-set, a yarn-finishing process, before they can be woven or knitted. To identify crepe yarns, test a yarn removed from the fabric by first pulling on the yarn and then letting one end go. A crepe twist yarn should resemble the shape illustrated in Figure 11.6. Most crepe fabrics have crepe yarns in the crosswise direction, although some are in the lengthwise direction and some have crepe yarns in both directions. Crepe fabrics are discussed in Chapters 12 and 13.

Increasing the amount of crepe yarn twist and alternating the direction of twist increases the amount of crinkle in a crepe fabric. For example, a fabric made of crepe twist yarns in a band of six S filling yarns followed by a band of six Z filling yarns produces a more prominent crinkle than bands of two S filling yarns followed by bands of two Z filling yarns.

Yarn Size

Yarn Number

Yarn size or fineness is referred to as **yarn number**. For filament yarns, it is expressed in terms of weight per unit length. For spun yarns, it is expressed in terms of length per unit weight. For spun yarns, the defined weights and lengths differ with fiber type. The cotton system is discussed here, since many yarns are numbered by the cotton system. It is an indirect or fixed-weight system: the finer the yarn, the larger the number. Thus, a fine yarn would be a 70 and a coarser yarn would be a 20. The yarn number or cotton count is based on the number of

Table 11.3 Cotton System

Fabric Examples (weight in oz/yd²)	Yarn Size		Number of Hanks Per Pound		Length of Yarn in One Pound (yards)	
	Warp	Filling	Warp	Filling	Warp	Filling
Sheer lawn (2.0)	70s*	100s	70	100	58,800	84,000
Print cloth (4.5)	30s	40s	30	40	25,200	33,600
Sailcloth (7.5)	13s	20s	13	20	10,920	16,800

*The "s" after the number means that the yarn is single.

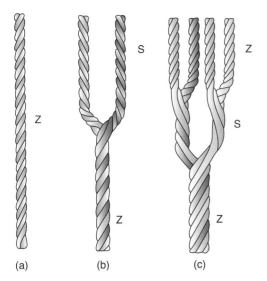

Figure 11.8 Parts of a yarn: (a) single yarn, (b) two-ply yarn, (c) cord yarn.

A **ply yarn** is made by a second twisting operation that combines two or more singles (Figure 11.8b). Each part of the yarn is called a *ply*. A machine called a *twister* twists the plies together. Most ply yarns are twisted in the direction opposite to that of the twist of the singles from which they are made. The first few revolutions tend to untwist the singles and straighten the fibers somewhat from their spiral position and soften the yarn slightly.

Plying increases yarn diameter, strength, uniformity, and quality. Ply yarns are sometimes used in the warp direction of woven fabrics to increase strength. Two-ply yarns are found in the best-quality men's broadcloth shirts. Ply yarns are frequently seen in knits and interior textiles. They are found in sewing thread and the string used to tie packages. When simple ply yarns are used only in the filling direction, they produce some fabric effect other than strength.

A **cord** is made by a third twisting operation, which twists ply yarns together (Figure 11.8c). Some types of sewing thread and some ropes belong to this group. Cord yarns are seldom used in apparel and interior fabrics, but are used in technical fabrics such as duck and canvas.

A **rope** is a heavy thick cord at least 2.5 cm or 1 inch or more in diameter consisting of strands of fiber, leather or wire that are twisted or braided together. The process of creating the rope by twisting or braiding is called *laying*. Some ropes have a core covered with a sheath. Ropes may be covered with a plastic film to protect interior components and increase their durability during use. Ropes are technical items where high performance is expected. Some ropes are made with special-use fibers like aramid. Ropes are used in a wide variety of uses including commercial and recreational fishing, farming and agricultural operations, logging, utility work, sailing vessels, tug and towing operations, shipping, and transportation.

Sewing and Embroidery Thread

Sewing thread is a yarn intended for stitching materials together using machine or hand processes. Sewing threads are available in a broad range of sizes and structures. Examples include ply, corded, cable, braided, textured-filament, smooth-filament, monofilament, and core-spun. Sewing thread is often finished with lubricant or wax so that it withstands the abrasion, stress, and manipulation required in high-speed machine sewing. Most sewing thread is S-twist. Many different fibers and fiber blends are used in sewing thread. The thread selected is based on the material or materials to be stitched together, the end use, cost, and the desired product performance. Thread size may be expressed as denier, tex, count, yarn number, or ticket number.

Embroidery thread is a yarn intended for stitching designs or patterns on the surface of a textile. It adds embellishment and value to textile products and is most often a two-ply Z-twist. Embroidery thread is available in a wide variety of luster, color, texture, fiber type, hand, and size. Thread is sized by titer or weight per unit length. Lower numbers describe coarser threads. For example, 12-weight thread is used for interiors while 60-weight is used for lighter weight apparel.

> A **rope** is a heavy thick cord at least 2.5 cm or 1 inch or more in diameter consisting of strands of fiber, leather or wire that are twisted or braided together. **Sewing thread** is a yarn intended for stitching materials together using machine or hand processes. **Embroidery thread** is a yarn intended for stitching designs or patterns on the surface of a textile.

► Learning Activity 5

Examine the textile products you have with you today. Describe the items that use sewing thread. If possible, examine the thread to determine its type and structure. Are all the sewing threads the same? Why might they differ in structure, size, and fiber content? Do any of your items have embroidery on them? If yes, describe the embroidery thread to determine its type. Are all the embroidery threads the same? How do they differ from the sewing threads?

Performance factors that affect embroidery thread include shrinkage during cleaning, bleeding, elongation during use, strength, and colorfastness to cleaning, light, and crocking. Metallic embroidery threads provide the highest luster, but are more expensive and less durable to washing.

Fancy Yarns

Fancy yarns are yarns that deliberately have unlike parts and that are irregular at intervals. The irregularities may be subtle or very obvious and the intervals may be regular or random.

Fancy yarns may be single, plied, or cord yarns. They may be spun, filament, or textured yarns—or any combination of yarn types. They are called *fancy yarns* or **novelty yarns** because they produce an interesting or novel effect in fabrics made from them. Their structure may be complex and consist of several yarn plies combined into one yarn.

Fancy yarns are classified according to their number of parts and named for the effect that dominates the fabric. Usually more common in interior fabrics than in apparel fabrics, fancy yarns also are used by artists and craftspeople to create interest in otherwise plain fabrics of many fiber types.

Fancy yarns are made on twisters with special attachments for producing different tensions and rates of delivery in the different plies. This produces loose, curled, twisted, or looped areas in the yarn. Slubs and flakes of short-staple fibers of different color are introduced into the yarn by special attachments. Knots or slubs are made at regular or random intervals as the machine operates.

Fancy or novelty yarns are used for a variety of purposes. Characteristics and performance vary widely by type and fiber content.

- Fancy yarns are usually plied yarns, but they seldom add strength to the fabric. Novelty yarns are often weak and sensitive to abrasion damage.

- When fancy yarns are used in one direction only, it is usually in the filling direction because it is more economical, with less waste. Filling yarns are subject to less strain and are easier to vary for design purposes.

- Fancy yarns add permanent interest to plain fabrics at a lower cost. Fabrics that include one or more fancy yarns are sometimes classified as **fancy fabrics,** which are fabrics that differ in appearance, pattern, or structure from plain fabrics.

- Fancy bulky yarns add crease resistance to a fabric, but they may make the fabric hard to handle in spreading, cutting, and sewing.

- The durability of fancy yarn fabrics depends on the size of the ply effect, how well it is held in the yarn, the fiber content of the various parts, and the firmness of the fabric structure. Generally speaking, the smaller the novelty effect, the more durable the fabric, since the yarns are less affected by abrasion and do not snag as readily.

- The quality and cost of fancy yarns are related to the quality of the fibers and plies from which the yarn is made, the manner in which the unique visual component is produced in the finished yarn, and the regularity of the yarn structure.

Figure 11.9 classifies the most common fancy yarns according to their usual single or ply structure.

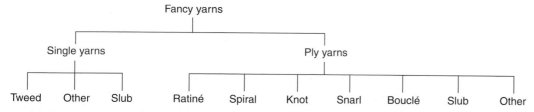

Figure 11.9 Classification of fancy yarns.

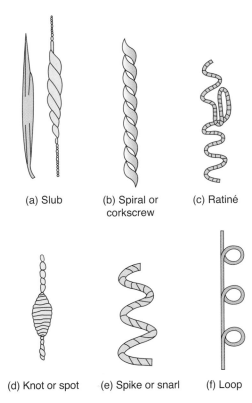

(a) Slub   (b) Spiral or corkscrew   (c) Ratiné

(d) Knot or spot   (e) Spike or snarl   (f) Loop

Figure 11.10 Effect ply for several fancy yarns.

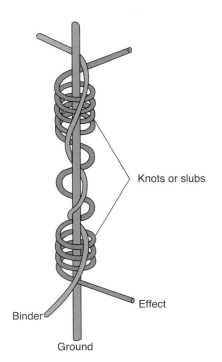

Knots or slubs

Binder   Effect

Ground

Figure 11.11 Fancy yarn, showing the three basic parts.

Tweed yarn is an example of a single, spun fancy yarn. Flecks of short colored fibers are twisted into the yarn to add interest. Some tweed yarns are two-ply yarns with each ply a different color. Tweeds are often made of wool because of its cohesiveness. Tweed yarns are found in apparel, upholstery, and draperies.

A **slub yarn** is a spun fancy yarn. This thick-and-thin yarn can be made in two ways: (1) the amount of twist in the yarn can be varied at regular intervals for a true slub yarn; (2) the thicker part of the yarn is twisted less and the thinner part of the yarn is twisted more. True slub yarns are found in shantung, drapery, and upholstery fabrics and in hand-knitting yarns and sweaters (Figure 11.10a). Intermittently spun flake or slub effects are made by incorporating soft, thick, elongated tufts of fiber into the yarn at regular intervals with a core or binder yarn. A slub yarn can be found as single or ply novelty yarns.

Spiral or corkscrew fancy **yarns** have two or more plies. The plies may differ in twist, size, type, and/or color. A two-ply fancy yarn may have one spun ply combined with a filament ply (Figure 11.10b). The two parts may be delivered to the twister at different rates of speed. A two-ply tweed yarn differs only in color while a spiral yarn differs in color and some other aspect, such as size or type. Spiral yarns are used in interiors and apparel.

Frequently, fancy yarns have three basic parts: (1) the ground, foundation, or core ply; (2) the effect or fancy ply; and (3) the binder ply. When a fancy yarn is examined, the first ply that can be unwound from the yarn is the **binder**. It holds the effect ply in place. The **effect ply** is primarily responsible for the appearance and the name of the yarn. The **ground ply** forms the foundation of the yarn. Figure 11.11 shows a three-ply novelty yarn. For clarity in the illustration, each ply appears to be a simple, single, monofilament (single-fiber) yarn. In actuality, each ply could be spun, filament, BCF, split film, or complex. Metallic components also may be used. For example, the ground may be a simple, single, filament yarn; the effect could be two-ply, with one ply a monofilament metallic yarn and the other ply a spun yarn; and the binder could be a simple, single, spun yarn. Each ply in two or more ply fancy yarns may have a different fiber content. Endless variations are possible.

The following are typical novelty ply yarns:

1. In **ratiné yarns**, the effect ply is twisted in a spiral arrangement around the ground ply. At intervals, a longer loop is thrown out, kinks back on itself, and is held in place by the binder (Figure 11.10c). These yarns are used primarily in interior textiles.

2. The **knot, spot, nub, or knop yarn** is made by twisting the effect ply many times in the same place (Figure 11.10d). Two effect plies of different colors may be used and the knots arranged so the colored spots alternate along the length of the yarn. A binder is added during the twisting operation. These yarns are used in apparel and interior textiles.

3. In **spike or snarl yarn**, the effect ply forms alternating open loops along both sides of the yarn (Figure 11.10e). These yarns are used in apparel and interior textiles.

4. **Loop, curl, or bouclé yarn** has closed loops at regular intervals along the yarn (Figure 11.10f). These yarns are used in fabrics to create a looped pile resembling caracul lambskin called *astrakhan cloth*. They are also used to give texture to other fabrics. Mohair, rayon, and acetate may be used for the effect ply in apparel and interior textiles.

5. **Metallic yarns** have been used for thousands of years. See Chapter 9 for processing and use information. Metallic yarns may be monofilament fibers or combined in ply yarns. Metallic fancy yarns are used primarily in apparel. However, some metallic-looking yarns are made from ultrafine plastic fibers of nylon or polyester split film made of many layers. These film yarns produce luminous and iridescent effects without the comfort problems of metallic monofilaments.

6. **Chenille yarn** is made by cutting a specially woven ladderlike fabric into warpwise strips (Figure 11.12). The cut ends of the softly twisted yarns loosen and form a fringe. Chenille or "caterpillar" yarn may be woven to produce pile on one side or on both sides

of a fabric. If the pile is to be on one side only, the yarn must be folded before it is woven. Chenille-type yarns can also be made by flocking or gluing short fibers on the surface of the yarn. Other chenille-type yarns are made by twisting the effect yarn around the core yarn, securing it in place with the binder, and cutting the effect so it forms a fringe or pile. Chenille yarns are used in interiors and apparel.

7. **Braided yarn** is made by braiding three or more fine yarns together to create one larger yarn (see Chapter 15). Braided yarns may be round or flat and uniform or irregular in structure. Eyelash yarn is usually a three-ply braided yarn made with short ends of one yarn protruding along the length of the yarn.

8. **Knit yarns** are narrow fabric yarns made by knitting (see Chapter 14). They may be a single narrow tube, a narrow tube wrapped with another yarn, a thick-and-thin tube, or a flat ribbonlike strand of yarn. Some knit yarns have an outer tube of fine yarn and an inner tube of heavier, opaque yarn.

9. **Stitched yarns** are narrow ribbon-like fabrics with one or more rows of stitched thread forming the basic structure of the yarn. Suede and ribbon-stitched yarns have a row of stitching on each side of the ribbon like yarn and a center of textured or smooth filament yarn. Other stitched yarns look like a simple spiral yarn. Many stitched yarns have stitched bands along each edge and periodically a bridge of filament yarn connecting the two bands. Sometimes these yarns are called train-track or windowpane yarns. These yarns may be folded to create a bouclé-like loop or cut into two separate yarns with a fringe along one side. Some yarns have multiple parallel lines of stitching with cross-bars arranged so that a checkerboard pattern is created.

While each novelty yarn type is described separately in this discussion, it is important to realize that any two or more simple or novelty yarns can be combined to create a novelty yarn. For example, a stitched yarn may be combined with a thick and thin yarn and wrapped with a metallic monofilament yarn to form a complex novelty yarn. Novelty yarn may also incorporate other details like sequins and beads. Figure 11.13 shows several novelty yarns ranging in structure from simple to complex.

Table 11.5 summarizes information about yarn appearance and performance. Use it to review the major yarns and compare their performance.

Composite Yarns

Composite yarns, regular in appearance along their length, have both staple-fiber and filament-fiber components. Composite yarns include covered yarns, core-spun yarns, filament-wrapped

Figure 11.12 Fabric from which chenille yarn is cut.

Fancy or novelty yarns are yarns that deliberately have unlike parts and that are irregular at intervals. They add interest and texture to fabric. They often have many parts and combine spun and filament components. Some of the many types include tweed, slub, spiral, bouclé, ratiné, chenille, knot, spike, metallic, braided, knit, and stitched yarns.

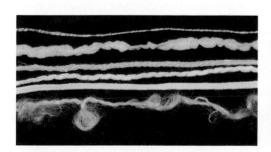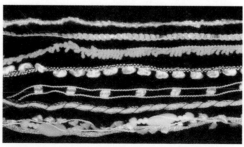

Figure 11.13 Novelty yarns. From top to bottom (left photo): braided yarn, nonwoven and stitched yarn, three-ply yarn (one ply is a flake yarn), braided yarn, warp knit yarn, and bouclé yarn. From top to bottom (right photo): ratiné yarn, filling knit and wrapped yarn, warp knit yarn, warp knit yarn, stitched yarn, three-ply yarn (braided yarn ply, filling knit yarn ply, and fine binder ply), and complex three-ply yarn (filling knit yarn ply, novelty flake ply, and stitched yarn ply).

Table 11.5 Performance of Yarns in Fabrics

Yarn Type	Aesthetics	Durability	Comfort	Care
Spun	Fabrics look like cotton or wool Fabrics lint and pill	Weaker than filament yarns of same fiber Ply yarns stronger than simple yarns Yarns are cohesive, so fabrics resist raveling and running	Warmer More absorbent because of larger surface area	Yarns do not snag readily Soil readily
Smooth-filament	Fabrics are smooth and lustrous Fabrics do not lint or pill readily	Stronger than spun yarns of same fiber Fabrics ravel and run readily Yarns may slip at seams and other areas of stress	Cooler Least absorbent but more likely to wick moisture	Yarns may snag Resist soiling
Bulk or textured-filament	Fabric luster is similar to spun-yarn fabrics Fabrics do not lint but may pill	Stronger than spun yarns of same fiber Yarns are moderately cohesive, so fabrics ravel and run like spun-yarn fabrics	Bulkier and warmer than smooth-filament yarns Moderately absorbent Stretch more than other yarns	Yarns likely to snag Soil more readily than smooth filament yarns
Fancy or novelty	Interesting texture Larger novelty effects are less durable than smaller novelty effects Fabrics lint and pill	Weaker than filament yarns Most resist raveling Less abrasion-resistant	Warmer More absorbent if one ply is a spun yarn	Yarns likely to snag Soil readily
Composite	Varies; larger yarns with spun or filament appearance	Related to process	May have stretch; larger than many other yarns	Large yarns may snag

▶ Learning Activity 6

Use Fabrics #5, 11, 12, 13, 14, 15, 29, 42, 53, 59, 63, and 86 from your swatch kit. Unravel a yarn from each direction of each fabric and determine their structure: simple or complex, single or ply; carded or combed; and staple or filament. Are the yarns for one fabric the same in both direction? Explain why they might be different. Identify an end use for each fabric. Describe how yarn structure and type influence fabric appearance and serviceability.

yarns, and molten-polymer yarns. The classification of composite yarns is shown in Figure 11.14. The quality of composite yarns is related to fiber and component ply quality, finished yarn structure, and yarn uniformity.

Covered yarns have a central yarn that is completely covered by fiber or another yarn. These yarns were developed to produce more comfortable rubber foundation garments and surgical hose. Stretch-covered yarns have a central core of one of the elastomeric fibers covered with at least one other yarn. Single-covered yarns have a single yarn wrapped around them. They are lighter, more resilient, and more economical than double-covered yarns and can be used in many woven and knit fabrics. Most ordinary elastic yarns are double-covered with two yarns to give them balance and better coverage. Fabrics made with these yarns are heavier

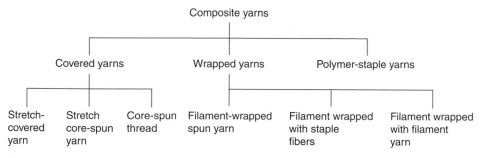

Figure 11.14 Classification of composite yarns.

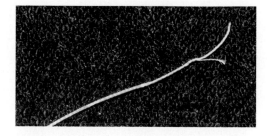

Figure 11.15 Covered stretch yarn.

> **Learning Activity 7**

Use Fabrics #42 and 44 from your swatch kit. Unravel a yarn from each direction and determine the structure of each yarn. Identify an end use for each fabric and describe how the serviceability might differ if simple, single yarns were used in both directions.

and thicker (Figure 11.15). Covered yarns are subject to "grin-through" (see Figure 9-4). Although these yarns usually include spandex, they should not be referred to as spandex yarns.

An alternate way of making a stretch yarn is to make a stretch **core-spun yarn** by spinning a sheath of staple fibers (roving) around a core. When working with elastomeric cores, the core is stretched while the sheath is spun around it so that the core is completely hidden. The sheath adds aesthetic properties to the yarn, and the core provides comfort stretch. Core-spun yarns in woven fabrics produce an elasticity more like that of the knits.

Polyester/cotton core-spun sewing thread has a sheath of high-quality cotton and a high-strength filament polyester core. The cotton sheath gives the thread excellent sewability, and the polyester core provides high strength and resistance to abrasion. Polyester/cotton thread provides the slight stretch that is necessary in knits.

Wrap-spun yarns have a core of staple fibers (often a twistless yarn) wrapped or bound by filament fibers. These yarns are economical and have good evenness, strength, appearance, and finishing properties.

In **fasciated yarns**, a grouping of filament fibers is wrapped with staple fibers. The yarns are combinations of coarse filaments for strength and fine stretch-broken filaments for softness (Figure 11.16). These yarns are quick to produce and give better texture and hand to fabrics. Another variation is a filament-wrapped filament yarn (Figure 11.17).

Yarns can be produced by pressing staple fibers of any length or generic class into a molten polymer stream. As the polymer solidifies, the fibers that are partially embedded become firmly attached and form a sheath of staple fiber. The resultant yarn is about two-thirds staple fiber and one-third coagulated polymer. The polymer, which is an extruded manufactured fiber, is a less expensive product than other melt-spun filaments.

Figure 11.16 Fasciated yarn.

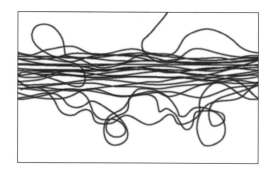

Figure 11.17 Filament-wrapped filament yarn.
SOURCE: Courtesy of Hercules, Inc.

Yarn Performance and Yarn Quality

Yarn characteristics and performance are identified and measured so that an appropriate yarn is used in the fabric and product. Standard test methods determine yarn size, twist, bulk, evenness, appearance, and performance. Yarn strength is determined by measuring the load that breaks a

Composite yarns, regular in appearance along their length, have both staple-fiber and filament-fiber components. These yarns include covered yarns, core-spun yarns, wrap spun yarns, and fasciated yarns.

Yarn quality is an important factor related to the quality of the resultant fabric and product and includes such factors as structure, strength, parallel fibers, uniformity of fiber length, amount of twist, and free of flaws or defects.

yarn and the percent of elongation at that load. Tolerances or variations allowed in a yarn of a given type are measured so that consistency in performance and appearance can be evaluated.

Yarn quality is an important factor related to the quality of the resultant fabric and product. *Yarn quality* refers to various factors such as yarn strength and thin spots in yarns that are weaker and likely to break when the yarn is under stress. These thin spots, or nips, create thin, weak areas in fabrics or unacceptable variations in fabric appearance. Yarns must be strong enough to withstand the stresses of looms and knitting machines. Strength demands on yarns depend on the structure of the fabric and its end use. Stress can be substantial during fabric production; yarn breaks are costly to repair and decrease fabric quality. Fabric producers demand high yarn quality and consistency of yarn characteristics at low prices. Yarn producers have responded to these demands by incorporating online systems to detect yarn defects and fix them as soon as they begin to develop in the spinning process.

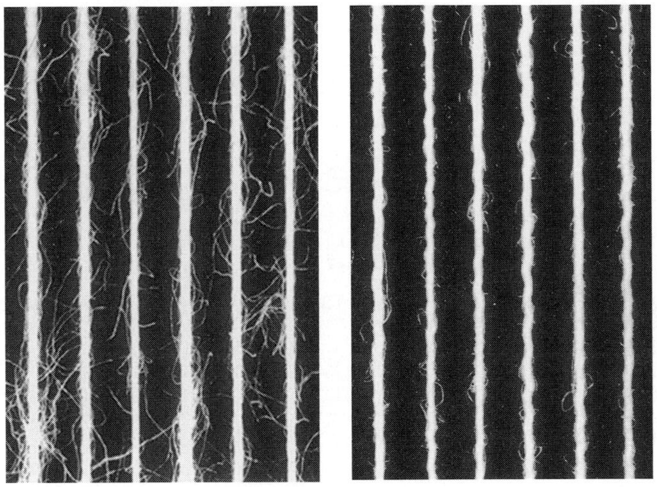

Many factors determine the quality of a yarn. Better-quality yarns have more parallel fibers, tighter twist, and are more regular than lower-quality yarns. High-quality yarns are strong enough to withstand additional processing (warping, weaving, knitting, etc.). High-quality yarns are regular in structure with few thin spots. They are relatively free of unacceptable neps and hairiness. A **nep** is a small knot of entangled fibers, which may be immature or dead and subsequently create problems by not accepting dye. Neps may create thick spots on yarns or uncolored flecks in finished fabrics. **Hairiness** describes excessive fiber ends on the yarn surface. Figure 11.18 shows differences in yarn hairiness due to spinning method. Hairy yarns may create problems in fabrication or in consumer use because they tend to be more sensitive to abrasion and pilling. Good-quality yarns facilitate subsequent dyeing and finishing steps. Their appearance and performance make the finished material suitable for the end use and target market. Yarn quality affects fabric quality, performance, and cost.

Figure 11.18 Yarn hairiness.
SOURCE: Courtesy of Textile World.

▶ Learning Activity 8

Make a list of the attributes of a high-quality yarn and a list of the attributes of a poorer quality yarn. Describe how serviceability might differ between identical products made with a high-quality yarn or a poor-quality yarn. Use your fabric swatch set to identify a fabric made with high-quality yarns and lower-quality yarns.

key terms

review questions

1. Describe the type of yarn (in terms of fiber length, yarn twist, yarn complexity, regularity, and size) that would likely be found in each of the following products. Explain the performance of each yarn selected.
   a. Percale sheeting in luxury hotel suite
   b. Muslin sheeting in budget motel room
   c. Tweed for a coat or blazer
   d. Carpet for family room
   e. Upholstery for antique formal settee
   f. Casual T-shirt
   g. Denim jeans
   h. Elastic wrap for sprained ankle
   i. Casement cloth for draperies in dentist's waiting room

2. What differences in fiber length and turns per inch would be expected between a low-twist yarn and an average-twist yarn?

3. What difference in performance would you expect between a 100 percent cotton shirt made with carded yarns and a 100 percent cotton shirt made with combed yarns? What are the major differences between these two yarns in terms of processing and structure?

4. Why is twist direction important for yarns?

5. What factor makes crepe yarns so lively?

6. Why are fancy or novelty yarns used? In what kinds of fabrics and for what uses are they most common?

7. How do fancy yarns change product serviceability? How do they enhance serviceability and how do they decrease serviceability?

8. What are the differences and similarities between the denier and tex systems?

9. Why is yarn size important? How does the serviceability of a fabric change if it were made using cotton system size 20s yarns versus cotton system 60s yarns?

10. What would be the differences in performance between a backpack made of a 400-denier yarn of 80 individual filament fibers and a backpack made of a 400-denier yarn made of 40 individual filament fibers?

11. What are the characteristics that differentiate between yarns of average quality and high quality?

section review questions

1. Describe the differences and similarities among these terms:
   a. Woolen, carded, combed, and worsted
   b. Sewing thread and two-ply yarn
   c. Covered yarn and core-spun yarn

2. Describe the visual clues that would help to differentiate these yarn pairs:
   a. Fine combed yarn and smooth filament yarn
   b. Woolen spun yarn and BCF yarn
   c. Carded yarn and novelty flake yarn
   d. Simple, single yarn and novelty, three-ply bouclé yarn

3. Explain the influences that yarn type, structure, and quality have on fabric serviceability.

4. From the following information about fibers and yarns, explain if the description is possible and how it would be achieved. If the description is not possible, explain why. Describe the serviceability of each product.
   a. Core-spun 95 percent cotton/5 percent spandex for casual slacks
   b. Filament cotton for a dressy shirt or blouse
   c. Carded spun rayon for a print skirt
   d. Bulk filament polyester for a casual top
   e. Carded acrylic for a sweater
   f. Filament nylon for a windproof jacket
   g. Combed silk for a jacket
   h. Combed 65 percent cotton/35 percent polyester for a work shirt
   i. Microdenier smooth filament polyester for a silky blouse
   j. Filament wool for a blanket
   k. Bouclé yarn consisting of 45 percent mohair, 39 percent wool, 15 percent nylon smooth filament, and 5 percent Lurex metallic monofilament for a knit hat

Case Study

Tweed Yarn*

Tweed refers to both a fabric type and a yarn structure. Tweed yarn can be made by introducing small bits of color into a yarn or by plying two yarns of different color together. Knitters and weavers like the textural and visual appearance that tweed yarns lend to their work. There are many varieties of tweed yarn available to hand knitters and weavers: 100 percent pure new wool (single ply), 70 percent merino wool/30 percent linen (5 ply), 60 percent cotton/40 percent wool (4 ply), 50 percent merino wool/25 percent alpaca/25 percent viscose rayon (2 ply), 65 percent wool/35 percent silk (2 ply), and 80 percent virgin wool/20 percent polyamide (nylon) (4 ply). Attributes for fabric will differ depending on the type of fabric produced and the yarn used.

DISCUSSION QUESTIONS

1. Describe the difference in structure among these yarns and suggest how the tweed component would be incorporated in each yarn.

2. Describe the serviceability expected for each yarn type, considering the fiber content and blend level.

3. How might yarn structure and size influence a knitter's or weaver's decision as to what to make from these yarns?

*Square, V. (2008). Tweed yarns. *Interweave Knits, 13*(4), 12–14.

suggested readings

Alagirusamy, R., Fangueiro, R., Ogale, V., & Padaki, N. (2006). Hybrid yarns and textile preforming for thermoplastic composites. *Textile Progress, 38*(4), 1–71.

ASTM International. (2007). *Annual Book of ASTM Standards*, Vol. 7.01. West Conshohocken, PA: Author.

Kadolph, S. J. (2007). *Quality Assurance for Textiles and Apparel*. 2nd ed. New York: Fairchild Publications.

Lawrence, C. A. (2003). *Fundamentals of Spun Yarn Technology*. New York: CRC Press.

Slit film extrusion of polypropylene yarns. (1990, May). *Textile Month*, pp. 53–54.

Square, V. (2008). Tweed yarns. *Interweave Knits*, *13*(4), 12–14.

Thiry, M. C. (2008). In stitches. *AATCC Review, 8*(11), 24–30.

Tortora, P. G., & Merkel, R. S. (1996). *Fairchild's Dictionary of Textiles*, 7th ed. New York: Fairchild Publications.

12 Weaving, Basic Weaves, and Fabrics

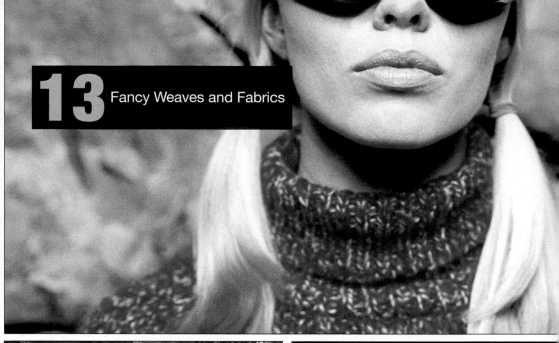

13 Fancy Weaves and Fabrics

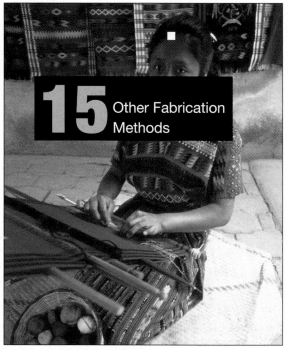

14 Knitting and Knit Fabrics

15 Other Fabrication Methods

FABRICATION

WEAVING, BASIC WEAVES, and FABRICS

CHAPTER OBJECTIVES

- To understand the loom, the process of weaving, and the three basic weaves.
- To identify fabrics made using the three basic weaves.
- To name basic woven fabrics.
- To predict performance of fabrics based on fabrication, yarn structure, and fiber.

12

A **fabric** is a pliable, planelike structure that can be made into two- or three-dimensional products that require some shaping and flexibility. Fabrics are used in apparel, interiors, and many technical products. The chapters in this section focus on methods used to produce fabrics, identification of fabric types based on their structure, and naming fabrics using current standard names. Not all fabrics will be discussed for each process. Many fabrics have applications too specialized for a basic book; others are no longer popular due to changes in fashion or lifestyles. Some fabrics are no longer commercially available due to changes in consumer expectations, lifestyle, or production cost. Some remain important, but their names have changed.

The fabric-forming process or fabrication method contributes to fabric appearance, texture, suitability for end use, performance, and cost. The process may determine the name of the fabric, like doublecloth, lace, double-knit, tricot, and felt. The cost in relation to fabrication process depends on the number of steps involved and the speed of production. If all other factors like fiber type, yarn structure, and fabric density are equal, the fewer the steps and the faster the process, the cheaper the fabric. Changes in fabrication have increased automation, enhanced quality, improved response to consumer demand, and advanced production flexibility so that a firm can produce a variety of fabrics with the equipment available.

Textile producers describe the shortest length of fabric they will produce to sell to another firm as the *minimum yardage*. Firms specialize in high-quality fabrics, special fabric types, or high-volume basic fabrics. Minimum yardage depends on the firm and its area of specialization. For example, 5,000 yards may be the minimum order for a basic fabric in a basic color, but 200 yards may be the minimum for a specialty-fabric producer.

Fabrics can be made from a wide variety of starting materials: solutions (films and foams), fibers (felts and fiberwebs or nonwovens), yarns (braids, knits, laces, and wovens), and fabrics (composite fabrics combining solutions, fibers, yarns, or fabrics to produce a fabric). The first three chapters of this section focus on fabrics made from yarns: woven and knitted fabrics. The final chapter focuses on all the other processes. Fabric names discussed in these chapters were selected because they are basic, commonly used fabrics. Many more named fabrics exist and can be found in the market. However, these other fabrics will not be discussed in this book. Several excellent resources are listed at the end of this chapter for additional information on fabrics not described in this book.

Determining the starting material used to make a fabric is the first step in identifying the fabric. Figure 12.1 is a flowchart to be used in determining fabric structure and name. This chart references some charts in this and other chapters that will help in identifying and naming a fabric.

Fabric Quality

Fabric quality is important to textile producers, designers, retailers, and consumers because it describes many characteristics: freedom from defects, uniform structure and appearance, and performance during production and in consumers' hands. Fabric quality influences product cost, suitability for a target market, aesthetic characteristics, and consumer appeal and satisfaction. Assessment of quality can be made by inspecting or examining fabric with the eyes or an instrument to identify visible irregularities, defects, or flaws (Figure 12.2). Computer-aided fabric evaluation (CAFE) systems speed this process and increase the accuracy of fabric inspection. **Defects** are assigned a point value based on their length or size. Fabric quality is graded by totaling the defect points of a piece of fabric. Producers have developed lists and examples of defects or flaws and guidelines for **fabric grading**. Manufacturers of cut and sewn

A **fabric** is a pliable, planelike structure that can be made into two- or three-dimensional products that require some shaping and flexibility. Fabric quality influences product cost, suitability for a target market, aesthetic characteristics, and consumer appeal and satisfaction. Fabric defects are assessed based on a grading system.

What is the component used to form the fabric?

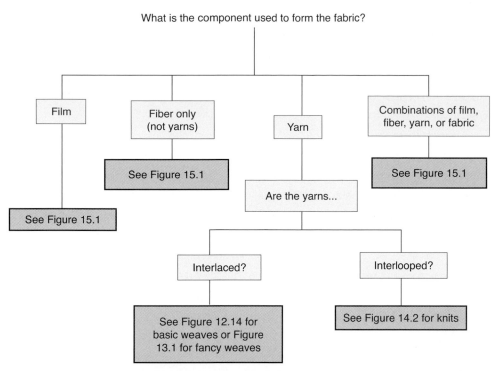

Figure 12.1 Fabric structure flow chart.

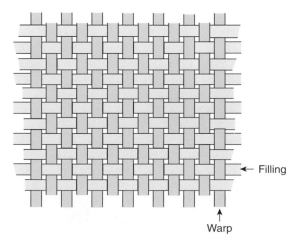

Figure 12.2 The defect in the center of this fabric decreases its quality and performance.

> ## ▶ Learning Activity 1

Describe the serviceability characteristics you desire in a pair of denim jeans or other pant fabric (woven, not knit, i.e., not sweat pants or exercise shorts). Which of these aspects of serviceability relate to fiber content and yarn structure and which relate to fabric structure? How would the manufacturer or retailer test the fabric to ensure that it meets your serviceability needs?

products determine the quality level suitable for their product line and target market and purchase fabric accordingly.

Another perspective of identifying fabric quality assesses fabric performance. Standard test methods have been developed by several professional organizations to aid in performance assessment so that fabric evaluation is consistent. Standard fabric performance tests assess abrasion resistance, strength, wrinkle resistance, shrinkage during laundering or dry cleaning, colorfastness to light or perspiration, snag resistance, flammability, water repellency, consistency of color throughout a length of fabric, soil resistance, and many other characteristics. Fewer manufacturers assess fabric quality from a performance perspective than by visual examination. Unfortunately, many consumer problems with textile products stem from minimal performance evaluation by manufacturers.

Woven Fabrics

With the exception of triaxial fabrics, all woven fabrics are made with two or more sets of yarns interlaced at right angles. Sometimes these fabrics are referred to as biaxial. They have two basic components: warp yarns and filling yarns (see Figure 12.3). The yarns in

← Filling

↑
Warp

Figure 12.3 Components of a woven fabric: warp and filling.

the lengthwise direction are **warp** yarns or *ends*, and the yarns in the crosswise direction are **filling** yarns, *weft*, or *picks*. The right-angle position of the warp to filling yarns produces greater fabric firmness and rigidity than yarn arrangements in knits, braids, or laces. Because of this structure, yarns can be raveled from adjacent sides. Woven fabrics vary in the ways the yarns interlace, the pattern formed by this interlacing, the number of yarns per inch, and the ratio of warp to filling yarns.

Woven fabrics are widely used, and weaving is one of the oldest and most widely used methods of making fabric. Some fabric names are based on an earlier end use (hopsacking used in bags for collecting hops; tobacco cloth as shade for tobacco plants; cheesecloth to wrap cheeses; and ticking in mattress covers, once called "ticks"); the town in which the fabric was woven originally (bedford cord from New Bedford, Massachusetts; calico from Calicut, India; chambray from Cambrai, France; and shantung from Shandong, China); or the person who originated or was associated with that fabric (batiste for Jean Baptiste, a linen weaver, and jacquard for Joseph Jacquard, who developed a loom for quickly weaving more intricate fabrics).

Woven fabrics used in apparel, interiors, and technical products have these characteristics:

- Two or more sets of yarns are interlaced at right angles to each other.
- Many different interlacing patterns give interest and texture to the fabric.
- Yarns can be raveled from adjacent sides.
- Fabrics have grain.
- Fabrics are relatively stable, with little stretch in warp or filling.

The Loom

Weaving is done on a machine called a **loom**. All the weaves that are known today have been made for thousands of years. The loom has undergone significant modifications, but the basic principles and operations remain the same. Warp yarns are held taut within the loom, and filling yarns are inserted and pushed into place to make the fabric.

In primitive and hand looms, the warp yarns are vertical or horizontal (Figure 12.4). Looms for hand weaving keep the warp yarns taut by attaching one beam to a tree or post and the other beam to a strap that fits around the weaver's hips, to another beam, or by using weights. Filling yarns are inserted by a shuttle batted between warp yarns—some raised and some lowered to create a space. To separate the warp yarns and weave faster, alternate warp yarns were attached to bars that raised these warp yarns. A toothed device similar to a fine comb pushed the filling yarns into place. Eventually, the bar developed into heddles and harnesses attached to foot pedals so the weaver could separate the warp yarns by stepping on the pedals, leaving the hands free for inserting the filling yarns.

During the Industrial Revolution, mass-production high-speed looms were developed. The modern loom consists of two beams, a warp beam and a cloth or fabric beam, holding the warp yarns between them (Figure 12.5). Warp yarns that are sufficient for the length, width, and density of the fabric to be woven are wound carefully onto a **warp beam**. The warp is raised and lowered by a harness-heddle arrangement. A **harness** is a frame to hold the heddles.

Figure 12.4   Hand looms: vertical (left) and horizontal (right).
SOURCE: Courtesy of Vesterheim Norwegian-American Museum, Decorah, Iowa (left), and Careyn Armitage (right).

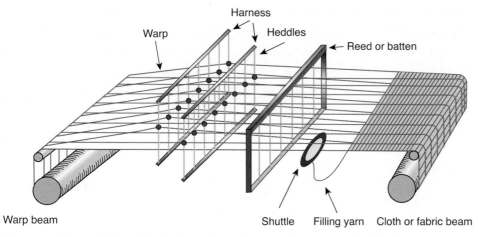

Figure 12.5 Simplified drawing of a two-harness shuttle loom.

The harness position, the number of harnesses, and the warp yarns that are controlled by each harness determine the weave or interlacing pattern. A **heddle** (headle) is a wire with a hole or eyelet in its center through which a warp yarn is threaded. There are as many heddles as there are warp yarns in the fabric, and the heddles are held in two or more harnesses. Each warp yarn passes through the eye of only one heddle. The selection of the specific heddle and harness is a major factor in determining the structure of the fabric. Figure 12.5 illustrates how a simple two-harness loom is used to raise one harness while the other harness remains in its original position. With this arrangement, the warp forms a **shed**, or space, through which the filling is inserted.

Devices of several types carry filling yarns through the shed. The name of the loom often refers to the device used to insert the filling yarn. Originally, these devices were fairly large, somewhat oval wooden **shuttles** with a bobbin of yarn in the center. In the automatic shuttle loom, a shuttle is thrown through the shed by picker sticks at both sides of the loom. These sticks bat the shuttle first to one side and then, after the shed has changed, back to the other side so quickly that the shuttle is a blur. Shuttle looms are limited to about 200 picks, or filling insertions, per minute. The noise of the picker sticks striking the shuttle is deafening. Looms with quieter and more efficient devices, called *shuttleless looms*, will be discussed later in this chapter.

A **reed**, or *batten*, beats or pushes the filling yarn into place to make the fabric firm. A reed is a set of wires in a frame; the spaces between the wires are called *dents*. Warp yarns are threaded through the dents in the reed. The spacing in the reed is related to the desired number of warp yarns per inch in the woven fabric. Reeds are available with a wide variety of spacings related to the density of the yarns in the finished fabric and the size of the yarns. For example, 20-dent reeds are used for low-density fabrics with coarse yarns; 80-dent reeds are used for higher-density fabrics with finer yarns. The way the reed beats the filling yarn in place helps determine the density of filling yarns and the grain characteristics of the finished fabric. Woven fabric is rolled onto the cloth, fabric, or take-up beam as it is produced.

Weaving consists of the following steps:

1. **Shedding**: raising one or more harnesses to separate the warp yarns and form a shed.
2. **Picking**: passing the shuttle through the shed to insert the filling.
3. **Beating up**: pushing the filling yarn into place in the fabric with the reed.
4. **Take-up**: winding finished fabric onto the fabric beam.

The most frequent type of commercial loom is a four-harness loom. This loom is extremely versatile and can be used to produce most basic woven fabrics. These fabrics comprise the greatest percentage of woven fabrics currently on the market and explain the popularity of the four-harness loom. Additional harnesses or other devices that control the position of the warp yarns are used to produce more intricate designs. However, generally six harnesses is the limit in terms of efficiency. Patterns that require more than six harnesses are made on looms that use other devices to control the warp yarns; these will be discussed later in this chapter.

Preparing for Weaving

Winding Yarns are repackaged so that they can be used to weave a fabric on a specific loom. This repackaging step is called **winding**. In this process, some spun yarns may be given more twist or combined with other singles to make ply yarns.

Creeling Yarn packages are placed on a large frame called a *creel*. The creel holds the yarn as it is wound onto a warp beam. To protect warp yarns from damage during weaving, they are treated with a sizing agent (while slashing is a preparation step for weaving, it is discussed with finishes in Chapter 16).

Warping or Dressing the Loom After the warp yarns are wound on the warp beam, each individual yarn is threaded through a heddle in a specific harness and through a dent in the reed before being attached to the cloth beam. Yarns must remain completely parallel from warp beam to cloth beam and not cross each other. If they do cross each other, excess abrasion or tension will occur that may cause warp yarns to break. In addition, depending on where yarns cross each other, a flaw in the fabric structure may occur.

The weave structure or pattern in the fabric is determined by three factors: (1) the order in which the warp yarns are threaded through the harness, (2) the combination of harnesses raised or lowered at a time, and (3) the sequence in which the harnesses are raised or lowered. In the simplest combination possible, warp yarn 1 is threaded through heddle 1 in harness 1. Warp yarn 2 is threaded through heddle 1 in harness 2. Warp yarn 3 is threaded through heddle 2 in harness 1. Warp yarn 4 is threaded through heddle 2 in harness 2. This pattern is followed until all warp yarns are threaded through the harnesses. Then warp yarn 1 is threaded through dent 1 in the reed. Warp yarn 2 is threaded through dent 2 in the reed. This pattern is followed until all warp yarns are threaded through the reed. After the yarns have been attached to the cloth beam, weaving can begin. To create the simplest weave, harness 1 is raised lifting all odd-numbered warp yarns. After the filling yarn is inserted, the harness lowers and the reed beats that yarn in place. Then harness 2 is raised lifting all even-numbered warp yarns. The second filling yarn is inserted and the reed beats that filling yarn in place. This sequence is repeated until the length of warp has been woven.

After weaving, the fabric is removed from the cloth or take-up beam, washed to remove the sizing, finished to specification, and wound on bolts or tubes for sale to manufacturers or consumers. (See Chapters 16–19.)

Loom Advancements

Loom advancements have centered on (1) devices to weave intricate designs; (2) computers and electronic monitoring systems to increase speed, patterning capabilities, and quality by repairing problems and keeping looms operating at top efficiency; (3) quicker and more efficient means of inserting filling yarns; (4) automatic devices to speed the take-up of woven cloth and let off or release more warp; and (5) devices that facilitate and speed up changing the warp.

Patterning Capabilities Devices that control the position (raised or lowered) of the warp yarns have included dobby, doup, lappet, and leno attachments and the jacquard loom. These have become so sophisticated that pictures can be woven in cloth (see Chapter 13). Warp yarns are individually controlled by microcomputers in some looms, referred to as electronic jacquards.

Computer Systems Computers and electronic devices are important in developing design tables for setting up "maximum weavability" properties, such as tightness and compactness in wind-repellent fabrics or tickings. CAD (computer-aided design) systems are used extensively to design fabric. Microcomputers control the operation of individual warp yarns to create the design. Quick style change (QSC) and electronic jacquards allow changes from one fabric style to another in a few minutes, as compared with the several hours or more required with traditional jacquard looms. With QSC, shorter minimum yardage orders are possible.

Automation of weave rooms uses computers and robotics to reduce fabric defects and improve weaving quality and efficiency. Automatic looms with multifunctional microcomputers permit high-speed filling insertion with minor adjustments of tension for both warp and filling yarns and taking up woven fabric. Computers detect incorrect filling insertions, remove the incorrect yarn, correct the problem, and restart the loom. All steps are done without the assistance of a human operator—weaverless weaving.

Loom Efficiency and Versatility Because of the noise and slower speeds, shuttle looms continue to be replaced with faster, quieter, more versatile shuttleless looms. However, shuttle looms still out number shuttleless looms, especially in developing countries. Many specialty and technical fabrics, such as fire hoses, circular industrial belts, and artificial blood vessels, cannot be produced on shuttleless looms. As old shuttle looms wear out, they are replaced with shuttleless looms.

Four types of shuttleless looms—air-jet, rapier, water-jet, and projectile—weave faster with less noise. In these looms, the filling yarns are measured, inserted, and cut, leaving a fringe along the side. These ends may make a fused selvage if the yarns are thermoplastic, or the ends may be tucked into the edge. Shuttleless looms are more common in developed countries and more versatile than shuttle looms. Many shuttleless looms can produce almost any basic weave or pattern in various yarn types and sizes with multiple colors at widths up to 160 inches. Most shuttleless looms are air-jet or rapier types. Water-jet and projectile looms are less common.

Air-Jet Loom In the **air-jet loom**, the filling yarn is premeasured and guided through a nozzle, where a narrow jet of air sends it through the shed. The loom can insert several thousand meters of yarn per minute and is suitable for any filling yarn that is not too bulky or heavy. Good warp preparation is required. Air-jet looms weave fabrics up to 400 centimeters (157 inches) in width and are the predominant looms used in weaving sheeting and denim. Energy consumption is high for air-jet looms, but engineering modifications are reducing energy use.

Rapier Loom The **rapier loom** weaves primarily spun yarns at up to 1,000 picks per minute. The double-rapier loom has one metal arm about the size of a thin fingernail clipper, called a *carrier* or *dummy shuttle*, on each side of the loom. A mechanism on one side of the loom measures and cuts the correct length of filling yarn to be drawn into the shed by the carriers. The two carriers enter the warp shed at the same time and meet in the center. The second

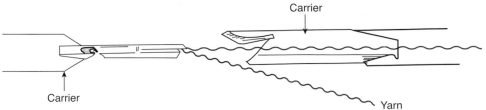

Figure 12.6 Carrier of a rapier shuttleless loom.

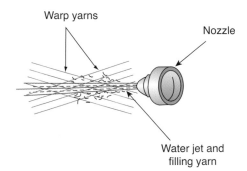

Figure 12.7 The water jet carries a filling yarn through the warp shed.

Figure 12.8 Circular loom used to weave bags.

SOURCE: Courtesy of Amoco Fabrics & Fibers Co.

carrier takes the yarn from the first carrier and pulls it across to the opposite side of the loom (Figure 12.6). This loom is widely used to produce basic cotton and worsted fabrics. Changes in engineering are reducing the length of the fringe along the selvages and reducing selvage waste by 50 percent.

Water-Jet Loom The **water-jet loom** uses a high-pressure jet of water to carry the filling yarn across the warp (Figure 12.7). Water-resistant sizing must be used for the warp. Water-jet looms are used only for hydrophobic nylon and polyester filament yarn fabrics. Excess water is removed from the loom by suction. The fabric is wet when it comes from the loom, so drying is an added cost. This loom produces fabrics without yarn streaks and is more compact, less noisy, and takes up less space than the conventional loom. It is a very fast loom, but limitations on fabric width are difficult to overcome.

Projectile Loom In the **projectile loom**, one projectile with grippers carries the yarn across the full width of the shed. The yarn may be inserted from one or both sides. This loom is also called the *missile* or *gripper loom* and is used to produce basic, specialty, and technical fabrics.

Multi-Width Loom In **multi-width looms**, additional warp beams allow two or more widths of fabric to be woven side by side. Because changing sheds is a time-consuming step in weaving, this loom makes optimal use of that time. Many basic fabrics are made on multi-width looms.

Multiple-Shed Loom In each of the looms discussed so far, one shed forms at a time. In **multiple-shed looms**, also called *multiphase looms*, more than one shed is formed at a time. In warp-wave looms, just before a yarn carrier enters one portion of the warp, a shed is formed; just after the carrier leaves that area, the shed changes. This action may occur simultaneously across the width of the warp several times. In weft-wave looms, several sheds form along the length of the warp yarns and open at the same time, one filling yarn is inserted into each shed, and then the sheds change.

As many as 16 to 20 filling carriers insert the precut filling in a continuous process instead of the intermittent process of single-shed weaving. Beating up and shedding arrangements are different. In this continuous-weaving process, the number of picks per minute (ppm) is much faster.

Circular Loom Most looms weave flat widths of fabric. **Circular looms** weave tubular fabric, such as pillowcases. The circular loom in Figure 12.8 weaves sacks of split-film polypropylene.

Triaxial Loom The **triaxial loom** weaves three sets of yarns, usually identical in size and twist, at 60-degree angles to each other (Figure 12.9). Two yarn sets are warp and the other set is filling. These fabrics can be produced more quickly than other weaves because there are fewer picks per inch, and the speed of weaving is based on the number of picks per minute. Triaxial fabrics are stable in horizontal, vertical, and bias directions. Biaxial fabrics (two sets of

> **Learning Activity 2**

In groups of two or three, discuss the different loom types and their advantages and disadvantages. What are the factors that drive loom developments? How does fabric quality relate to sustainability? Is loom type of importance in terms of fabric type, quality, or sustainability?

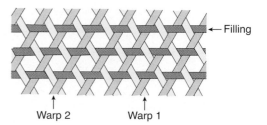

Figure 12.9 Triaxial weave pattern.

yarns at right angles to each other) are not stable on the bias. Triaxial fabrics are used for balloons, air structures, sailcloth, diaphragms, truck covers, and other technical products.

Environmental Concerns and Sustainability of Weaving Environmental concerns associated with weaving are related to the type of loom used to produce a fabric. For example, shuttle looms are incredibly noisy. Loom operators in shuttle weaving rooms wear hearing protectors to minimize hearing loss. Water-jet looms require clean water to carry the filling yarn across the fabric. This water is reclaimed and recycled. Fabrics produced with this loom must be dried before storage to reduce problems with mildew, and the amount of energy used in drying fabrics is great. Energy use varies significantly with the type of loom. For example, rapier looms use almost twice the energy of projectile looms, and air-jet looms use almost three times the energy of projectile looms. For this reason, shuttle and projectile looms are frequently used in parts of the world where electricity is irregular in strength or availability. Hand-operated looms, including backstrap looms, are often used to produce ethnic textiles and garments like patterned belts and shawls that are sold by the weavers to supplement family income.

Because of the demand for basic woven fabrics in the market, social abuses can occur in weaving mills. Employees may be expected to work excessive hours in uncomfortable conditions for low pay. Child workers may be paid less than adults for the same hours of work. During times of economic downturn, mills may close leaving workers with no source of income. However, during times of economic growth, mills do provide income for workers in the community.

Warp yarns are treated with sizing or lubricating compounds to minimize problems with abrasion in weaving. These compounds are removed after the fabric has been produced and are often reclaimed, but reclamation is not 100 percent efficient and residue disposal is required. Lint is a problem resulting from yarn abrasion during weaving and creates fabric quality and respiratory problems. Vacuum heads attached to flexible tubing move through weaving rooms to remove lint and minimize health, quality, and equipment problems. Finally, static electricity can build up in weaving when synthetic fibers are used. Humidity is controlled to minimize static charges that can create problems with loom operations and fabric quality.

The trend of producing better-quality fabric improves efficiency and lessens the environmental impact. Fewer fabric flaws mean less recutting of product pieces, fewer seconds from cut-and-sew production facilities, less waste for landfills, and lower energy use.

All woven fabrics are made with two or more sets of yarns interlaced at right angles. The two basic components are warp yarns in the lengthwise direction and filling yarns in the crosswise direction. Many types of woven fabrics exist. A loom is used to make all woven fabrics. Many types exist, but most commercial looms operate quickly and automatically to create the desired structure.

Characteristics of Woven Fabrics

All yarns in interior and apparel woven fabrics interlace at right angles to one another (Figure 12.10). An **interlacing** is the point at which a yarn changes its position from one side of the fabric to the other. When a yarn crosses over more than one yarn at a time, floats are formed and the fabric has fewer interlacings.

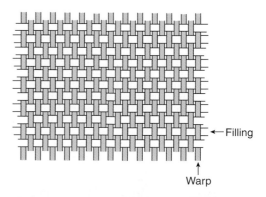

Figure 12.10 Warp and filling yarns in woven fabrics. Note that the yarns in this diagram interlace at 90-degree angles.

Warp and Filling

Warp and *filling yarns* have different demands placed on them and may differ in their structure or fiber type. Thus, a fabric may not have the same performance characteristics for warp and filling. The warp must withstand the high tensions of the loom and the abrasion of weaving, so the warp yarns are stronger and more uniform, with higher twist. Filling yarns are more often fancy or special-function yarns such as high-twist crepe yarns, low-twist napping yarns, or bouclé yarns.

Differentiating between warp and filling is possible by carefully examining the fabric and the lengthwise and crosswise yarns.

1. The selvage is always parallel to the lengthwise (warp) direction of all fabrics.
2. Most fabrics have lower elongation in the warp direction.
3. The warp yarns lie straighter and are more parallel in the fabric because of loom tension.
4. Fancy or special-function yarns are usually in the filling direction.
5. Fabric characteristics may differentiate between the warp and filling directions. For example, poplin has a filling rib and satin has warp floats.
6. Warp yarns tend to have higher twist and are smaller and more uniform in structure and appearance.
7. Fabric crimp is usually greater for filling yarns since they must curve over or under warp yarns due to the way the loom operates.
8. Warp yarn count tends to be higher than filling yarn count.
9. If yarn-dyed stripes are in one direction only, they tend to be in the warp direction.

Figure 12.11   Skewed fabric.

Grain

Grain refers to the geometry or position of warp yarns relative to filling yarns in the fabric. A fabric that is on-grain has warp yarns parallel to each other and perpendicular to the filling yarns that move straight across the fabric. Lengthwise grain is parallel to warp yarns. Crosswise grain is parallel to filling yarns. Fabrics are almost always woven on-grain. Handling, finishing, or stress due to yarn twist, weave, or other fabric aspects may cause fabrics to distort and become off-grain. Fabric quality has increased significantly, so it is rare to find fabrics as badly off-grain as those illustrated in Figures 12.11 and 12.12.

Off-grain fabrics create problems in production and use. During finishing, off-grain causes reruns or repeating finishing steps and lowers fabric quality. Products do not drape properly or hang evenly and printed designs are not straight. Figure 12.11 shows a design that has been printed off-grain—the print does not follow the yarns or a torn edge.

There are two kinds of off-grain. **Skew** occurs when the filling yarn is at an angle other than 90 degrees to the warp. It usually occurs in finishing when one side of the fabric travels ahead of the other (see Figure 12.11). **Bow** occurs when the filling yarns dip in the center of the fabric; it usually develops when the fabric center lags behind the two sides during finishing (Figure 12.12).

Fabrics should always be examined for grain. On-grain fabrics usually indicate high quality standards and minimize problems in matching designs or patterns in cutting and sewing.

Figure 12.12   Bowed fabric. Note the torn straight edge of the fabric and the slight curve of the printed red line.

Fabric Count

Fabric count, **count**, or **fabric density** is the number of warp and filling yarns per square inch (or per square centimeter in many parts of the world) of *gray goods* (fabric as it comes from the loom). Count may increase due to shrinkage during dyeing and finishing. Count is written with the warp number first, for example, 80×76 (read as "80 by 76"); or it may be written as the total of the two, or 156. Count is not synonymous with yarn number.

Count is an indication of the quality of the fabric—the higher the count, the better the quality for any fabric. Higher count also may mean less shrinkage and less raveling of seam edges. Catalogs and e-commerce sites may include count because the buyer must judge product quality from printed information rather than by examining the product.

Count can be determined with a fabric counter (Figure 12.13) or by hand. The number of yarns per inch or centimeter in each direction is counted. Count may vary depending on the end use or quality of fabric. Often it is listed as a total and may be described on labels as thread count, even though yarns, not threads, are counted. For example, two plain-weave fabrics often used in bedsheets are percale and muslin. Percale is a higher-quality fabric made of combed yarns in counts of 160, 180, 200, or more per inch. Muslin is a harder-wearing fabric designed for lower price points. It is usually made of carded yarns in counts of 112, 128, or 140 per inch. It is frequently used in bed linens for budget motels and hospitals. Higher numbers indicate better-quality, more expensive fabrics.

Figure 12.13   Fabric yarn counter.
SOURCE: Courtesy of Alfred Suter Co.

Balance

Balance is the ratio of warp yarns to filling yarns in a fabric. A balanced fabric has approximately one warp yarn for every filling yarn, or a ratio of 1:1 (read as "one to one"). An example of a balanced fabric is 78×78 print cloth. An unbalanced fabric has significantly more of one set of yarns than the other. A typical unbalanced fabric is broadcloth, with a count of 144×76 and a ratio of about 2:1. Although the numbers will vary depending on whether the count is based on inches or centimeters, the balance will remain the same regardless of the measurement system used.

Balance is helpful in recognizing and naming fabrics and in distinguishing the warp direction of a fabric. Balance plus count is helpful in predicting slippage. When the count is low, slippage is more likely in unbalanced fabrics than in balanced fabrics.

Balance can be determined by examining a fabric carefully. If the fabric can be raveled, unravel several yarns on adjacent edges and compare the density and size of yarn ends protruding from the fabric. In a balanced fabric, warp and filling yarns are nearly identical in size and frequency. In balanced fabrics, it may be difficult to differentiate between warp and filling yarns when the selvage is not present. In unbalanced fabrics, warp and filling yarn size or the density between warp and filling may be significantly different.

Selvages

A **selvage** is the lengthwise self-edge of a fabric. On conventional shuttle looms, it is formed when the filling yarn turns to go back across the fabric. The conventional loom makes the same kind of selvage on both sides of the fabric, but shuttleless looms have different selvages because the filling yarn is cut and the selvage looks like a fringe. In some fabrics, different yarns or interlacing patterns are used in the selvage.

Plain selvages are similar to the structure of the rest of the fabric. They do not shrink and can be used for seam edges. Tape selvages used in sheeting are made with larger or plied yarns for improved strength and abrasion resistance. They are wider than the plain selvage and may be of a different weave to maintain a flat edge. Split selvages are used when items such as towels are woven side by side, cut apart after weaving, and hemmed. Fused selvages are found in narrow fabrics of thermoplastic fibers cut from wide fabric, such as some ribbon.

Fabric Width

The loom determines the fabric width. Handwoven fabrics are narrow, often 27 to 36 inches wide because that is a comfortable reach for most weavers. Commercial fabric widths are wider because wide fabrics are more economical to weave and allow for more efficient use of fabric in products. Many basic fabrics, regardless of fiber type, exceed 60 inches in width. However, a few fabrics for the consumer market are available in traditional fabric widths related to fiber type: 45 or 60 inches for cotton fabrics, 54 to 60 inches for wool fabrics, and 40 to 45 inches for silk-type fabrics.

Fabric Weight

Fabric weight or *fabric mass* describes how much a fabric weighs for a given area or length of fabric. Fabric weight is important because it is used to identify fabric appropriateness for end use and in naming fabrics. Both length and area weight values are used in the global textile complex. For example, yards per pound or meters per kilogram may be used in the trade to identify current prices for basic fabrics, but fabric width is crucial in this system. Another system uses weight in ounces per square yard (oz/yd^2) or g/m^2 (grams per square meter).

Lightweight or *top-weight fabrics* are those that weigh less than 4.0 oz/yd^2. They are softer and more comfortable next to the skin and have better drape. Top-weight fabrics are used for shirts, blouses, dresses, apparel linings, bedsheets, curtains, sheer draperies, substrates for technical products, and backing fabrics for wall coverings and bonded and quilted fabrics.

Medium-weight fabrics weigh from 4.0 to 6.0 oz/yd^2. They are widely used for heavier and stiffer shirts, blouses, dresses, apparel linings, winter-weight bedsheets, draperies, upholstery, wall coverings, and table linens. Many medium-weight fabrics are used in quilted and bonded fabrics and as substrates for technical products.

Heavyweight fabrics also are described as *bottom-weight* or *suiting-weight* goods because they are used for apparel bottoms like pants and skirts and for suiting. They weigh more than 6.0 oz/yd^2. They are durable, stiff fabrics used for outerwear, work apparel, upholstery, draperies, bedspreads, and technical products.

Measures of fabric quality include freedom from defects, count, and weight.

▶ Learning Activity 3

Use Fabric #108 from your swatch kit. Identify the warp and filling yarns. Is your sample on grain? Using a pick glass or a magnifying glass and ruler, determine the count for the warp and filling directions of this fabric. Is it balanced? Is this sample lightweight, medium weight or heavyweight? How you can approximate fabric weight or weight category without using a balance? Why is it important to know the difference between the warp and filling directions of a fabric? How does that relate to serviceability?

▶ Learning Activity 4

Work in groups of two or three. Describe why such characteristics as grain, balance, count, and weight are important for textile products. Why would this information matter to consumers?

Assume you are buying fabric for a private label line to be produced by your company. Potential suppliers have sent you 4-yard samples of 5 fabrics that meet your basis requirements of fiber content, color, and fabric structure. Describe how you would determine which of these fabrics to buy for the private label merchandise.

Properties of Woven Fabrics

Fabric properties resulting from weaving variables are summarized in Table 12.1. The weave or interlacing pattern influences fabric properties as well as fabric appearance. Table 12.2 summarizes the various weaves. This chapter and Chapter 13 deal only with woven fabrics.

Table 12.1 Properties of Woven Fabrics

Fabric Characteristic	Properties
High count	Firm, strong, good cover and body, compact, stable, more rigid drape, wind- and water-repellent, less edge raveling.
Low count	Flexible, permeable, pliable, softer drape, higher shrinkage potential, more edge raveling.
Balanced	Less seam slippage, warp and filling wear more evenly.
Unbalanced (usually more warp)	Seam slippage with low count; surface yarns wear out first, leaving slits (common in upholstery fabrics). Add visual and tactile interest.
Floats	Lustrous, smooth, flexible, resilient, may ravel and snag, seam slippage with low count.

Table 12.2 Basic Weaves

Name	Interlacing Patterns	General Characteristics	Typical Fabrics	Chapter Reference
Plain $\frac{1}{1}$	Each warp interlaces with each filling.	Most interlacings. Balanced or unbalanced. Wrinkles. Ravels. Less absorbent.	Batiste Gingham Broadcloth Crash Cretonne Print cloth Glazed chintz	12
Basket $\frac{2}{1}$ $\frac{2}{2}$ $\frac{4}{4}$	Two or more yarns in warp, filling, or both directions woven as one in a plain weave.	Looks balanced. Fewer interlacings than plain weave. Looks flat. Wrinkles. Ravels more.	Oxford Monk's cloth Duck Sailcloth	12
Twill $\frac{2}{2}$ $\frac{3}{1}$	Warp yarns float over two or more filling yarns in a regular progression of one to the right or left.	Diagonal lines or wales. Fewer interlacings than plain weave. Wrinkles. Ravels more. More pliable than plain weave. High counts possible.	Serge Surah Denim Gabardine Herringbone Flannel	12

(*continued*)

Table 12.2 Basic Weaves (*continued*)

Name	Interlacing Patterns	General Characteristics	Typical Fabrics	Chapter Reference
Satin $\frac{4}{1}$ $\frac{1}{4}$	Warp yarns float over four or more filling yarns in a progression of two to the right or left.	Flat and lustrous surface. High counts possible. Fewer interlacings. Long floats may slip and snag. Ravels.	Satin Sateen Antique satin Peau de soie	12
Dobby	Many different interlacings. Used to create geometric patterns.	Simple patterns. Cord-type fabrics.	Shirting madras Huck toweling Waffle cloth	13
Extra yarn	Additional warp or filling yarn sets add texture, pattern, and interest.	Simple patterns with or without fringe.	Dotted swiss Eyelash Clipped dot	13
Piqué	Raised pattern area with dobby or jacquard technique.	Floats on back with or without stuffer yarns.	Piqué Bedford cord	13
Jacquard	Each warp yarn controlled individually. An infinite number of interlacings is possible.	Intricate patterns.	Damask Brocade Tapestry	13
Momie or crepe	An irregular interlacing of yarns. Floats of unequal lengths in no discernible pattern.	Rough-looking surface. Crepelike.	Granite cloth Moss crepe Sand crepe Bark cloth	13
Leno	A doup attachment on the loom crosses one warp yarn over a second warp yarn.	Meshlike fabric. Lower-count fabrics resist slippage.	Marquisette Sheer curtain fabrics	13
Double-cloth	Several possible patterns use three, four, or five sets of yarns.	Thick, stiff, durable, warm fabrics.	Doublecloth Suitings Coatings	13
Pile	Extra warp or filling yarns are woven in to give a cut or an uncut three-dimensional fabric.	Plush or looped surface. Warm. Wrinkles less. Pile may flatten.	Velvet Velveteen Corduroy Furlike fabrics Wilton rugs Terrycloth	13
Slack-tension	A variation of pile weave. Some warp yarns are under little tension in the loom to create texture or pile.	Crinkle stripes or pile surface. Absorbent. Non-wrinkling.	Seersucker Terrycloth Friezé	13
Tapestry	Discontinuous filling yarns create pattern.	Pattern created by difference in yarn color or texture.	Tapestry	13

Naming and Diagramming Woven Fabrics

Fabric names are based on many factors: fabric structure, fabric weight, yarn type, yarn balance, and finishes. Figure 12.14 is a flowchart that will help in determining fabric names for basic weaves. Basic weaves are those that are made on a loom without any modification. The remainder of this chapter focuses on basic woven structures and the standard fabrics made using these weaves. These fabrics are made of simple weaves that incorporate the same interlacing pattern throughout the fabric. Using the flowchart in Figure 12.14 should help in determining what to look for when trying to differentiate among fabrics and when naming a fabric. While the focus in this chapter is on the structure of the fabric, fancy or novelty yarns can be used with basic weaves to create fancy fabrics. However, most fabrics are made with single, simple spun or filament yarns.

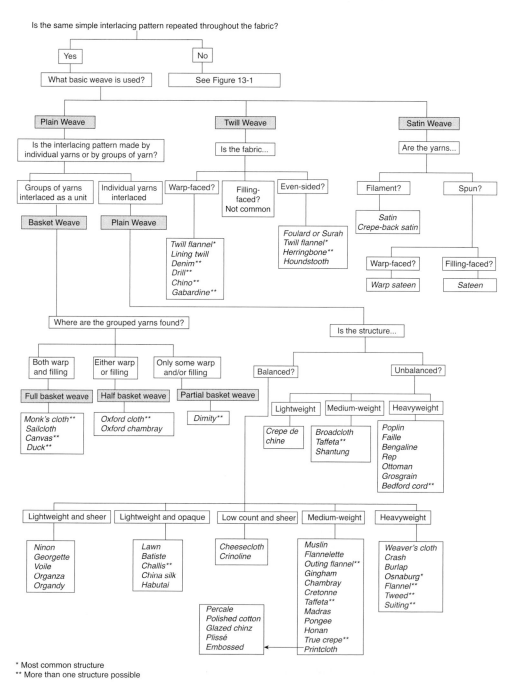

* Most common structure
** More than one structure possible

Figure 12.14 Basic woven fabric flowchart.

One convenient way of grouping fabrics is by fabric weight. Balanced-plain-weave fabrics will be discussed in five groups: lightweight sheer, lightweight opaque, low-count sheer, medium weight, and heavyweight. All of these categories could incorporate **narrow fabrics**, those that are no wider than 12 inches.

Lightweight Sheer Fabrics Lightweight sheer fabrics are very thin, weigh very little, and are transparent or semitransparent. High-count sheers are transparent as a result of the fineness of yarns. Fabric weight is less than 4.0 oz/yd². Most fabrics are used for lightweight apparel and curtains.

Filament-yarn sheers may be described in part by fiber content; for example, polyester sheer or nylon sheer. **Ninon** is a filament-yarn fabric that is widely used for sheer curtains. It is usually 100 percent polyester because of that fiber's resistance to sunlight, excellent resiliency, and easy washability. Although ninon is a plain weave, warp-yarn spacing is not uniform across the fabric. Pairs of warp yarns are spaced close to each other. The space between adjacent warp-yarn pairs is greater than the space between the two yarns in the pair. Ninon has medium body and hangs well.

Georgette and **chiffon** are made with filament yarns, the latter being smoother and more lustrous. In georgette, the direction of the crepe twist (S or Z) for warp and filling yarns alternates. For example, even-numbered warp and filling yarns may be S-twist and odd-numbered yarns may be Z-twist. Chiffon has smaller yarns with a hard, rather than a crepe, twist. Both fabrics can be a solid color or printed. Both are very lightweight, drape well, and are used in apparel. Both fabrics were originally made of silk but are now often made from manufactured filament yarns.

Voile is a sheer fabric made with high-twist or voile-twist spun yarns that are combed or worsted. It can be solid color or printed. Voile was originally a cotton or wool fabric, but it is now available in many fiber types.

Organdy is the sheerest cotton fabric made with combed yarns. Its sheerness and crispness are the result of an acid finish on lawn gray goods (see Chapter 17). Because of its stiffness and fiber content, it is very prone to wrinkling. **Organza** is the filament-yarn counterpart to organdy. It has good body and a crisp hand. These sheer fabrics are used for curtains and for summer-weight apparel. Both fabrics are available in solid colors or prints.

Lightweight Opaque Fabrics Lightweight opaque fabrics are very thin and light but are not as transparent as sheer fabrics. The distinction between the two groups of fabrics is not always pronounced. Fabric weight is less than 4.0 oz/yd². End uses include apparel and interior textiles.

Organdy (a sheer fabric), lawn, and batiste begin as the same gray goods. They differ from one another in the way they are finished. Lawn and batiste do not receive the acid finish and, thus, remain opaque. Better-quality fabrics are made of combed yarns. **Lawn** is often printed and is usually all cotton or cotton/polyester.

Batiste is the softest of the lightweight opaque fabrics. It is made of cotton, wool, polyester, or a blend. *Tissue ginghams* and *chambray* are similar in weight but are yarn-dyed.

China silk is similar to batiste, except that it is made from slightly irregular fine-filament yarns. It is a soft fabric that was originally made of silk and used for women's suit linings and matching blouses. **Habutai** is slightly heavier than China silk. The most common weight is 10 momme (see Chapter 5). Both fabrics can be dyed or printed.

Challis (shal'ee) tends to be heavier than the fabrics discussed so far and, depending on fiber content and fashion, it may be a medium-weight fabric. Challis is usually made with spun carded yarns and may be slightly napped so that a few fiber ends are raised to the surface.

A classic challis fabric is wool in a paisley print. It is soft and drapes well. Challis is usually printed and slightly napped and is frequently made from rayon.

Low-Count Sheer Fabrics Low-count sheer fabrics include *cheesecloth, crinoline, buckram, gauze,* and *bunting*. They are transparent because of open spaces between the yarns. They are made of carded yarns of size 28s and 30s in the warp and 39s and 42s in the filling. Count ranges from 10×12 to 48×44. These fabrics are neither strong nor durable, are seldom printed, and differ in the way they are finished. They are functional fabrics that may be used for decorative and technical purposes, or as shaping or support fabrics in apparel and interiors. Gauze is available in several weights and may have a wrinkled three-dimensional texture. (See the Glossary at the end of the book for more information about these fabrics.)

Medium-Weight Fabrics Medium-weight fabrics comprise the most widely used group of woven fabrics. These fabrics have medium-sized yarns and a medium count, with carded or combed yarns. They may be finished in different ways or woven from dyed yarns. They may be called *top-weight fabrics* because they are frequently used for blouses and shirts. Medium-weight fabrics are also used to produce many interior items, such as wall and window-treatment fabrics, bed and table linens, and some upholstery fabrics. Fabric weight ranges from 4.0 to 6.0 oz/yd².

The fabrics in this group are converted from a gray goods fabric called **print cloth**. Yarns can be carded or combed, depending on the desired count, quality, performance, and cost of the finished fabric. Yarn size ranges from 28s to 42s. Count ranges from 64×60 to 80×80. Figure 17.1 shows the variety of ways these fabrics can be finished. Chapter 17 will explain some of the differences in fabrics due to finishing. For example, two fabrics converted from print cloth are plissé and embossed.

Percale is a smooth, slightly crisp, printed or plain-colored fabric made of combed yarns. In percale bedsheets, counts of 160, 180, 200, 250, and 270 are available. Percale is called **calico** if it has a small, quaint, printed design; **chintz** if it has a printed design; and **cretonne** if it has a large-scale floral design. Some cretonne is coarser with slightly larger carded yarns. When a percale is given a highly glazed calender finish, it is called **polished cotton**. When chintz is glazed, it is called **glazed chintz**. Glazed chintz is made in solid colors as well as prints. These fabrics are often made with blends of cotton and polyester or rayon. They are used for shirts, dresses, blouses, pajamas, children's wear, matching curtains and bedspreads, upholstery, slipcovers, draperies, and wall coverings.

Any plain-woven, balanced fabric of carded yarns ranging in weight from lawn to heavy bedsheeting may be called **muslin**. It is usually available in counts of 112, 128, or 140. *Muslin* is also a name for a medium-weight fabric that is unbleached or white.

Napped fabrics may be of either medium weight or heavyweight. **Flannelette** can be found as both balanced- and unbalanced-plain-weave fabrics that are lightly napped on one side. It is available in several weights, ranging from 4.0 to 5.7 oz/yd². It is described as flannel and is used for sheets, blankets, and sleepwear. **Outing flannel** is heavier and stiffer than flannelette; it may be napped on one or both sides. It is used for shirts, dresses, lightweight jackets, and jacket linings. Some outing flannels are made with a twill weave. Both flannelette and outing flannel may be solid color, yarn-dyed, or printed.

Gingham is a yarn-dyed fabric in checks, plaids, or solids (Figure 12.16). **Chambray** may look like a solid color but is yarn-dyed with white filling and dyed-warp yarns; dyed warp of one color and dyed filling of another color, called iridescent chambray; or warp stripes of different colors.

Figure 12.16 Gingham fabrics: quality increases left to right.

Ginghams and chambrays are usually made of cotton or cotton blends. Better-quality fabrics are made with combed yarns. When they are made of another fiber, the fiber content is included in the name, for example, silk gingham. When filament yarns are used, these fabrics are given a crisp finish and called *taffeta*. In wool, similar fabrics are called *wool checks*, *plaids*, and *shepherd's checks*. **Madras**, or *Indian madras*, is usually all cotton and has a lower count than gingham.

Stripes, plaids, and checks present problems that do not occur in solid-colored fabrics. The design of ginghams may be up and down, right and left, or both. In order to match the seams of plaid materials, more time is needed to cut an item out, more attention must be given to the choice of design, and more care must be taken during production.

Imitations of yarn-dyed fabrics are made by printing. However, there is a technical face (front or right side) and a technical back (back or wrong side) to the print, whereas true yarn-dyed fabrics are the same on both sides. Lengthwise printed stripes are usually on-grain, but crosswise stripes may be off-grain.

Pongee is a filament-yarn, medium-weight fabric. It has a fine warp of uniform yarns with slub filling yarns that are irregular in size. It was originally silk with duppioni (slub) filling yarns, but is now made of a variety of fibers. **Honan** is similar to pongee, but it has slub yarns in both the warp and the filling.

Ripstop nylon or **ripstop taffeta** is a filament-yarn fabric with slightly larger warp and filling yarns appearing at regular intervals that create a grid within the fabric. The name of the fabric explains the purpose of these larger yarns—to stop rips in the fabric.

Plain-weave fabrics with crepe yarns in either warp or filling or in both warp and filling are known as **true crepe**. They can be of any weight but are most often medium weight or heavyweight. Because of their interesting texture and lively drape, these fabrics are frequently used by designers for apparel and interior textiles. In apparel, true crepes are found in several weights and are used in suits, coats, and dresses. In interiors, true crepes are common in upholstery, draperies, and wall coverings. True crepes are sometimes used in table linens.

Heavyweight Fabrics Heavyweight fabrics are also known as **suiting-weight** or **bottom-weight fabrics**. These fabrics weigh more than 6.0 oz/yd² and are heavy enough to tailor and drape well. Their filling yarns are usually larger than the warp yarns and have a slightly lower twist. Because of their weight, these fabrics are more durable and more resistant to wrinkling than are sheer or medium-weight fabrics, but they tend to ravel more because of the lower count.

Weaver's cloth is a general name for cotton suiting that is converted from gray goods called *coarse sheeting*. Cotton suiting is solid color or printed.

Homespun describes interior fabrics with slightly irregular yarns, a lower count, and a handwoven look.

Crash is made with yarns that have thick-and-thin areas, giving it an uneven nubby look. It is often linen or a manufactured fiber or fiber blend that looks like linen. The irregular surface shows wrinkles less than a plain surface does. *Butcher rayon* or **butcher cloth** is a similar fabric of 100 percent rayon or rayon/polyester. Heavier weights look like linen crash.

Burlap or **hessian** has a much lower count than crash. It is used in wall coverings. It has characteristic coarse, thick-and-thin yarns and is made of jute.

Osnaburg is a variable-weight fabric most often found in suiting weight. Like muslin, it may be unbleached or bleached. In general it is a lower-quality fabric than muslin, with a lower count. Bits of leaf and bark from the cotton plant produce a characteristic spotted appearance. It is a utility fabric used as a drapery lining, upholstery support fabric, or substrate for tufted upholstery fabric. When printed or dyed, it is used in upholstery, drapery, and apparel.

Flannel is a suiting fabric of woolen yarns that is napped. It is used for women's suits, slacks, skirts, and jackets. It may have a plain or twill weave.

Tweed is made from any fiber or blend of fibers and is always characterized by novelty yarns with nubs of different colors. *Harris tweed* is handwoven in the Outer Hebrides Islands and carries a certified registered trademark. *Donegal tweed* is handwoven in Donegal County, Ireland.

Tropical worsted suiting is made from long-fiber worsted yarns and typically weighs from 6 to 10 oz/yd^2. It is a wool-like fabric made for men's suits, intended for use in warmer weather. Blends are common.

Heavyweight balanced-plain-weave fabrics are often used in interiors such as wall coverings, upholstery, and draperies. Company-specific names are common.

Unbalanced Plain Weave In an **unbalanced plain weave**, there are significantly more yarns in one direction than the other. Increasing the number of warp yarns in a plain-woven fabric until the count is about twice that of the filling yarns creates a crosswise ridge called a

▶ Learning Activity 7

Identify two or more differences among each fabric in a grouping, such as lightweight sheer fabrics. How will this information help you in identifying these fabrics? Why is it important to be able to identify fabrics by name or to envision a fabric structure, drape, or appearance when hearing a fabric name? Select one fabric in each group and identify an end use for it. Determine an appropriate fiber content and yarn structure for the fabric and describe its serviceability based on fiber content, yarn structure, fabric structure, and weight.

▶ Learning Activity 8

Use Fabrics #16, 17, 18, 19, 20, 21, 24, 25, 26, 108, 110, 112, and 118 from your swatch kit. Name the weave used to produce each fabric. Unravel a warp and filling yarn from each sample. What are the similarities and differences among these fabrics in terms of weave, weight, and yarn type? Place the fabrics in order from lightest weight to heaviest weight. Can you detect a difference in weight among these samples? Count the number of yarns per inch for any two of these fabrics. Is the count balanced or unbalanced? Develop a list of the characteristics of this weave and its impact on fabric serviceability.

▶ Learning Activity 17

Examine the textile products you are wearing and have with you today. Which items are woven? What weaves are used for these fabrics? Use a magnifying or pick glass and name the weave used in each woven fabric. Describe your satisfaction with and the serviceability of one or more of the items based on fiber content, yarn type, and weave. Name these fabrics using Figure 12.14.

▶ Learning Activity 18

Create a table listing the three basic weaves: plain, twill, and satin. Identify the similarities and differences among the three. Describe how you would differentiate among them. List an example of a fabric made using each of these basic weaves. For each basic weave, list at least two alternate structures, i.e., for satin, you could list warp-faced and filling-faced. Explain the differences between or among the alternate structures and how they would influence product serviceability.

▶ Learning Activity 19

Work in groups of two. Identify the environmental issues associated with weaving. Is it a sustainable practice? Explain your response.

key terms

review questions

1. Describe how a loom produces a woven fabric.

2. Define these terms and explain how they relate to woven fabrics:
   a. Balance
   b. Bow
   c. Count
   d. Filling
   e. Float
   f. Grain
   g. Interlacing
   h. Off-grain
   i. Selvage
   j. Skew
   k. Wale
   l. Warp

3. Identify four ways to differentiate between warp and filling yarns.

4. Diagram the interlacing patterns for the three basic weaves. Use both the cross-section diagram and the checkerboard.

5. What criteria are used to determine the name of a fabric?

6. Identify the similarities and differences between these fabrics:
   a. Gingham and plissé
   b. Flannelette and challis
   c. Organdy and georgette
   d. Percale and broadcloth
   e. Herringbone and gabardine
   f. Denim and chambray
   g. Satin and sateen

7. Compare and contrast the characteristics of fabrics made from the three basic weaves.

8. Predict the performance of the following textile products:
   a. 100 percent olefin tweed upholstery with large-flake filling yarns and fine-filament warp yarns
   b. 50 percent cotton/50 percent polyester broadcloth shirt/blouse with combed yarns of similar size in both warp and filling
   c. 100 percent acetate antique satin drapery
   d. 100 percent nylon taffeta backpack with BCF yarns in the warp and filling
   e. 100 percent rayon challis skirt and blouse

FANCY WEAVES and
FABRICS

CHAPTER OBJECTIVES

- To understand the production of fancy woven fabrics.
- To identify the technique or process used to produce fancy woven fabrics.
- To integrate fabrication, yarn type, and fiber in predicting product performance.
- To relate advances in fabric production to market availability and cost.

13

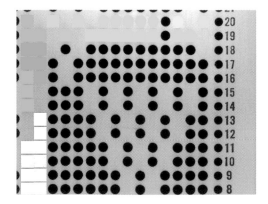

Figure 13.2 Pattern roll that controls warp shedding on a dobby loom.

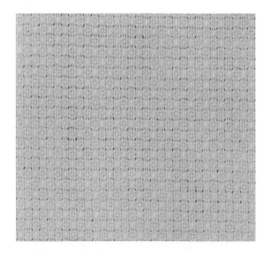

Figure 13.3 Dobby fabrics for use in apparel and interior textiles.

Figure 13.4 Huck-a-back.

> **Dobby weaves** are small-figured designs that require fewer than 25 different warp arrangements to complete one repeat of the design.

Dobby Weaves

Dobby weaves are small-figured designs that require fewer than 25 different warp arrangements to complete one repeat of the design. They are made on a loom with a dobby attachment—a **dobby loom**.

Two methods are used to create the pattern. In the older method, the weave pattern is controlled by a plastic tape with punched holes (Figure 13.2). These tapes resemble the rolls for a player piano. The holes control the position of each warp yarn in forming a shed. The newer method of creating a simple geometric pattern in the fabric uses a computer to control the position of the warp yarns. This system is faster, is compatible with several computer-aided design (CAD) systems, and allows for easy and quick pattern changes in the fabric.

Many designs made on either type of dobby loom are small geometric figures. There are many dobby fabrics; a few readily available and identifiable ones are discussed here. Figure 13.3 illustrates several generic patterned fabrics found in apparel and interior textiles.

Bird's-eye has a small diamond-shaped filling-float design with a dot in the center that resembles the eye of a bird. This design was originally used in white silk fabric for ecclesiastical vestments. At one time, a cotton version was widely used for kitchen and hand towels and diapers. **Huck or huck-a-back** has a pebbly surface made by filling floats. It is used primarily in roller, face, and medical-office towels (Figure 13.4).

Madras or *madras gingham* has small, satin-float designs on a ribbed or plain ground. **Waffle cloth** is made with a dobby attachment and has a three-dimensional honeycomb appearance. Waffle cloth is used for blankets, dish and bar cloths, upholstery, and apparel.

Extra-Yarn Weaves

Additional warp or filling yarns of different colors or types are woven into the fabric to create a pattern in an **extra-yarn weave**. When not used in the figure, the extra warp or filling yarns float across the back of the fabric and are usually cut away during finishing. In handwoven fabrics, the warp yarns are manipulated by hand and the extra yarns can be laid in where wanted by using small shuttles. But in power looms an automatic attachment must be used.

Extra-warp yarns are wound on a separate beam and threaded into separate heddles. The extra yarns interlace with the regular filling yarns to form a design and float behind the fabric until needed for the repeat. The floats are then clipped close to the design or clipped long enough to give an eyelash or fringed effect. Figure 13.5 shows a fabric before and after clipping.

Many of the fabrics that have small-dot designs are called *dotted swiss*. The dots may be extra-filling-yarn structural designs: clipped-dot designs or swivel-dot designs. Either side of these fabrics may be the fashion side. **Clipped-spot** or **clipped-dot designs** are made with low-twist filling yarns inserted by separate shuttles. By manipulating the shedding, the extra yarns interlace with some warp yarns and float across the back of others. A box loom uses a wire along the edge to prevent the extra yarns from being woven into the selvage. Clipped-dot fabrics have many yarn ends per dot.

Swivel-dot fabrics are made on a loom that has an attachment holding tiny shuttles. The fabric is woven so the shuttles and extra yarns are above the ground fabric. Each shuttle carrying the extra yarn wraps around the warp yarns in the ground fabric several times and then the yarn is carried along the surface to the next spot. The yarn is cut away between the spots (Figure 13.6). Swivel-dot fabrics have only two yarn ends per dot. Because of the slow production speed, swivel-dot fabrics in the United States are imported designer fabrics.

Dotted swiss may also be an applied design. (See Chapter 17 for more details.) Compare several different types of dotted swiss to determine their serviceability, quality, and cost.

Piqué Weaves

The word piqué (pee kay´) comes from the French word meaning "quilted," because the raised effect in these fabrics is similar to that in quilts. The **piqué** weave produces a fabric with ridges, called *wales* or *cords*, that are held up by floats on the back. The wales vary in width. *Wide-wale piqué* (0.25 inch) is woven with 20 or more warp yarns in the face of the wale with two warp yarns forming a valley in between. *Pinwale piqué* (0.05 inch) is a six-warp wale with two consecutive filling yarns floating across the back of the odd-numbered wales and then woven in the face of the even-numbered wales. The next two consecutive filling yarns alternate with the first two by floating across the back of the even-numbered wales. These long floats force the raised shape of the wale shown in Figure 13.7 in cross-section.

Stuffer yarns are laid under the ridges in better-quality piqué fabrics to emphasize the roundness, and their presence or absence is one way of determining quality. The stuffer yarns are not interlaced with the surface yarns of the fabric and may be easily removed when analyzing a swatch of fabric (Figure 13.8). Piqué fabrics are woven on either a dobby or a jacquard loom, depending on the complexity of the design.

Cords or wales usually run in the lengthwise direction. Cord fabrics have a definite technical face and technical back. With abrasion, the floats on the wrong side usually wear out first. Figure 13.8 shows the face and back of a piqué fabric. Piqué fabrics are more resistant to

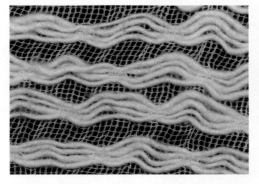
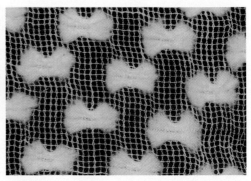

Figure 13.5 Fabric made with extra-warp yarns: face of fabric before clipping (left) and after clipping (right).

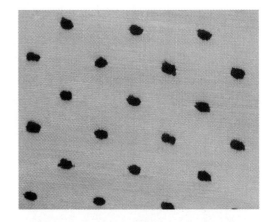

Figure 13.6 Dotted swiss made with extra filling yarns.

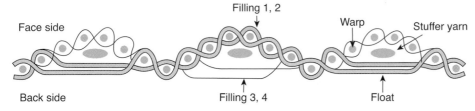

Figure 13.7 Six-warp pinwale piqué.

Face side — Filling 1, 2 — Warp — Stuffer yarn — Back side — Filling 3, 4 — Float

> **Learning Activity 2**

Use Fabrics #50 through 56 from your swatch kit. Name the weave used to produce each fabric. Unravel a warp and filling yarn from each sample. What are the similarities and differences among these fabrics in terms of weave, weight, and yarn type? Place the fabrics in order from lightest weight to heaviest weight. Develop a list of the characteristics of the weaves represented by this group of fabrics and the impact of fabric structure on serviceability. Select one fabric from this group and describe its quality.

Additional warp or filling yarns of different colors or types are woven into the fabric to create a pattern in an **extra-yarn weave**.

The **piqué** weave produces a fabric with ridges, called *wales* or *cords*, that are held up by floats on the back.

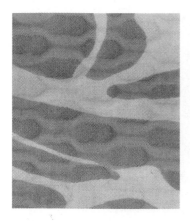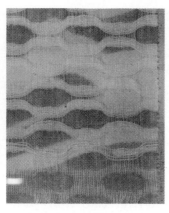

Figure 13.8 Piqué: face of fabric (left), back of fabric (right). Note stuffer yarns visible on the back and how the fabric flattens out at the bottom, where the stuffer yarns have been removed.

wrinkling and have more body than flat fabrics. Better-quality piqué fabrics are made with long-staple combed yarns and coarser carded stuffer yarns. Carded-yarn piqués are made without the stuffer yarn and are sometimes printed.

Fabrics in this group are called *piqué*, with the exception of bedford cord. **Bedford cord** is a heavy fabric with wide warp cords used for bedspreads, upholstery, window treatments, slacks, and uniforms. Its spun warp yarns are larger than the filling yarns. Lengthwise cords at intervals across the fabric are formed by extra filling yarns floating across the back, giving a raised effect. Stuffer yarns make a more pronounced cord, which may be the same size or alternately larger and smaller.

Bird's-eye piqué has a tiny design formed by the wavy arrangements of the cords and by the use of stuffer yarns. *Bull's-eye piqué* is similar to bird's-eye piqué but on a larger-scale. Both fabrics have crosswise rather than lengthwise cords and are used for apparel and interior textiles.

Jacquard Weaves

Large-figured designs that require more than 25 different arrangements of the warp yarns to complete one repeat design are **jacquard weaves**; they are woven on the **jacquard loom**. Two types of looms are used to produce jacquard weaves. In older looms, each warp is controlled independently by punched cards that form a continuous strip. The position of the warp yarns is controlled by rods. When the rods hit the cards, some go through the holes and raise the warp yarns; others remain down. In this manner the shed is formed for the passage of the filling yarn. Figure 13.9 shows a calendar woven with fine yarns on a jacquard loom. Note that this pattern does not repeat from top to bottom or from side to side. The repeat would be another picture.

The newer method for weaving these large patterns in fabric combines a computer with an air-jet loom and is called an *electronic jacquard loom* (Figure 13.10). The computer controls the position of the warp yarns and the insertion of different-colored filling yarns. The loom is fast, with weaving speeds of 600 picks per minute, compatible with several computer-aided design (CAD) systems, and allows for easy and quick pattern changes. Fabrics produced on these looms include fancy mattress ticking, upholstery, and apparel.

Fabrics made on a jacquard loom include damask, brocade, brocatelle, tapestry, and others (Figure 13.11). **Damask** has satin floats on a satin background; the floats in the design are opposite those in the ground. If the pattern is warp-faced, the ground is filling-faced. Damask patterns are subtle but visible because of slight differences in light reflected from the two areas. Damask can be made from any fiber and in many different weights for apparel and interiors.

Figure 13.9 Jacquard-woven calendar.

Large-figured designs that require more than 25 different arrangements of the warp yarns to complete one repeat design are **jacquard weaves.** Jacquard fabrics include brocade, brocatelle, and damask.

▶ Learning Activity 3

Compare the ground weave or basic fabric structure(s) used for dobby, extra yarn, and piqué weaves. Describe how these weaves compare to basic plain, twill, and satin weaves. What are the differences between the basic weaves and the fancy weaves? Why would these differences in fabric structure be of interest to professionals in the global textile complex or to consumers?

Use Fabrics #57 through 60 from your swatch kit. Name the weave used to produce each fabric. Unravel a warp and filling yarn from each sample. What are the similarities and differences among these fabrics in terms of weave, weight, and yarn type? Place the fabrics in order from lightest weight to heaviest weight. Develop a list of the characteristics of the weaves represented by this group of fabrics and the impact of fabric structure on serviceability. Select one fabric from this group and describe its quality.

► Learning Activity 5

Describe the differences and similarities among dobby, piqué, and jacquard weaves. Select one fabric from each weave that might be appropriate for an end use, identify the end use, and explain how the serviceability would be similar or different for each fabric.

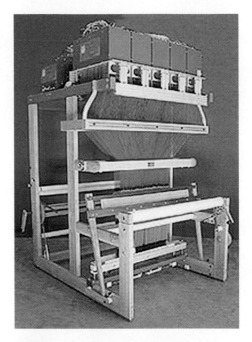

Figure 13.10 Electronic jacquard loom.
SOURCE: Courtesy of Bonas USA.

Damask is the flattest jacquard fabric and is often finished to maintain that flat look. Quality and durability are dependent on count. Low-count damask is not durable because the long floats rough up, snag, and shift during use.

Brocade has satin or twill floats on a plain, ribbed, twill, or satin background (Figure 13.12). Brocade differs from damask in that the floats in the design are more varied in length and are often of several colors.

Brocatelle fabrics are similar to brocade fabrics, except that they have a raised pattern. This fabric frequently is made with filament yarns, using a warp-faced pattern and filling-faced ground (Figure 13.11). Coarse cotton stuffer filling yarns help maintain the three-dimensional appearance of the fabric when used for upholstery.

Originally, tapestry was an intricate picture that was handwoven with discontinuous filling yarns. It was usually a wall hanging and was time-consuming to weave. Today's **jacquard tapestry** is mass-produced for upholstery, handbags, and the like. This tapestry is a complicated structure consisting of two or more sets of warp and two or more sets of filling interlaced so that the face warp is never woven into the back and the back filling does not show on the face. Upholstery tapestry is durable if warp and filling yarns are comparable. With lower-quality fabrics, fine yarns are combined with coarse yarns, and the resulting fabric is not durable.

Wilton rugs are figured-pile fabrics made on a jacquard loom. These rugs, once considered imitations of Oriental rugs, are so expensive to weave that the tufting industry has found a way to create similar figures through printing techniques.

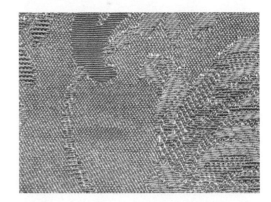

Figure 13.11 Jacquard brocatelle for upholstery.

Momie Weaves

Momie (mó-mee) is a weave that presents no wale or other distinct weave effect but gives the fabric the appearance of being sprinkled with small spots or seeds. The appearance resembles crepe made from yarns of high twist. Fabrics are made on a loom with a dobby attachment or electronic control. Some are variations of satin weave, with filling yarns forming the irregular floats. Some are even-sided and some have a decided warp effect. Momie weave is

Figure 13.12 Brocade: face (left) and back (right).

Momie (mó-mee) is a weave that presents no wale or other distinct weave effect but gives the fabric the appearance of being sprinkled with small spots or seeds. Many of these fabrics include crepe in the name even though they may not include crepe twist yarns.

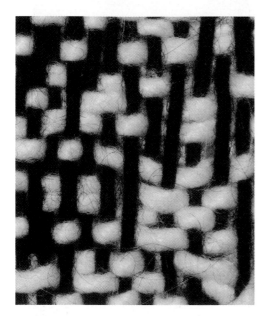

Figure 13.13   Momie weave.

Leno is a weave in which one or more warp yarns crosses over other warp yarns before the filling yarn is inserted. The leno weave is used to produce stable open fabrics. Marquisette is an example.

▶ **Learning Activity 6**

Compare the descriptions of jacquard and momie weaves. How do these weaves differ? What creates the different appearance between fabrics made using jacquard and momie?

also called **granite** or **crepe weave**. Any fiber can be used to make crepe-weave fabrics. An irregular interlacing pattern of crepe weave is shown in Figure 13.13. Momie fabrics are used for apparel and interior textiles.

Sand crepe is a medium-weight to heavyweight fabric of either spun or filament yarns. It has a repeat pattern of 16 warp and 16 filling yarns and originally required 16 harnesses. No float is greater than two yarns in length. Sand crepe is now made using electronic dobby or jacquard looms.

Granite cloth is made with a momie weave, based on the satin weave. It is an even-sided fabric with no long floats and no twill effect.

Moss crepe combines high-twist crepe yarns and momie weave. The yarns are plied yarns with one ply made of a crepe-twist single yarn. Regular yarns may alternate with the plied yarns, or they may be used in one direction while the plied yarns are used in the other direction. This fabric should be treated as a high-twist crepe fabric. Moss crepe is used in dresses and blouses.

Bark cloth is a heavyweight momie-weave fabric used primarily in interiors. The interlacing pattern uses spun yarns and creates a fabric with a rough texture resembling tree bark, hence the fabric's name. The fabric may be printed or solid. The rough texture adds visual interest and minimizes the appearance of soiling.

Leno Weaves

Leno is a weave in which the warp yarns do not lie parallel to each other. Warp yarns work in groups, usually pairs of two; one yarn of each pair is crossed over the other before the filling yarn is inserted, as shown in Figure 13.14.

Leno is made with a **doup attachment**, which may be used with a plain or a dobby loom. The attachment consists of a thin needle supported by two heddles. One yarn of each pair is threaded through an eye at the upper end of the needle, and the other yarn is drawn between the two heddles. Both yarns are threaded through the same dent in the reed. During weaving, when one of the two heddles is raised, the yarn that is threaded through the needle is drawn across to the left. When the other heddle is raised, the same yarn is drawn across to the right.

When looking at a leno fabric, one might think that the yarns were twisted fully around each other, but this is not true. Careful examination shows that they are crossed and that one yarn of the pair is always above the other.

Fabrics made by leno weave include **marquisette** (Figure 13.15), mosquito netting, agritextiles to shade delicate plants, and some bags for laundry, fruit, and vegetables. Polyester marquisettes are widely

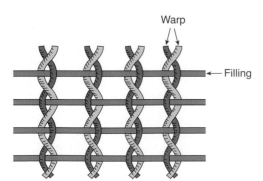

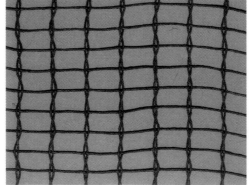

Figure 13.14   Leno weave: diagram (left) and fabric (right).

used for sheer curtains. Casement draperies are frequently made with leno weave and novelty yarns. Thermal blankets are sometimes made of leno weave. All these fabrics are characterized by open spaces between the yarns. The crossed-yarn arrangement gives greater firmness and strength than plain-weave fabrics of a similar low count and minimizes yarn slippage. Snagging may be a problem in use and care, however.

Chenille yarns (Chapter 11) are made using a leno weave. The fabric is produced with fine warp and low-twist filling. It is cut apart parallel to the warp, and the filling untwists to produce the fuzzy chenille yarn (see Figure 11.12).

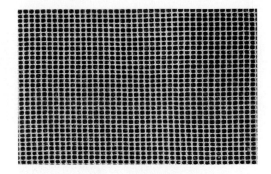

Figure 13.15   Marquisette.

Double Cloth

A single cloth, such as percale, is made from two sets of yarns: one set of warp yarns and one set of filling yarns. **Double cloth** is made from three or more sets of yarns. The two sides of double-cloth fabrics usually look different because of the fabrication method. Double cloths tend to be heavier and have more body than single cloths.

There are three types of woven double-cloth fabrics:

1. Double cloth—coat fabrics: melton and kersey.
2. Double weave—apparel and upholstery fabrics: matelassé and pocket weave.
3. Double-faced—blankets, double-satin ribbon, lining fabric, and silence cloth.

Double cloth is made with five sets of yarns: two fabrics woven one above the other on the same loom, with the fifth yarn (warp) interlacing with both layers (Figure 13.16). This technique is used to produce velvet (see the section "Pile Weaves" in this chapter). True double cloth can be separated by pulling out the yarns holding the two layers together. It can be used in reversible garments such as capes and skirts. Although it can be confusing, the term *double cloth* refers both to fabrics made with three or more yarn sets and to specific fabrics made with five yarn sets.

Double cloth is expensive to make because it requires special looms and the production rate is slower than for single fabrics. Double cloth is more pliable than single fabrics of the same weight because finer yarns can be used. The two specific fabrics that may be either true double cloth or single cloth are melton and kersey. Both of these heavyweight-wool coating fabrics are twill-weave fabrics that have been heavily finished so that it is difficult to identify the weave.

Melton has a smoother surface than kersey. **Kersey** is heavier than melton and has a shorter, more lustrous nap. Both fabrics are used in winter coats, overcoats, riding habits, and uniforms.

Spacer fabric is a three-dimensional technical fabric made by several methods. One type is a true double cloth used in technical products including interiors of buses, vehicle body components, and shaped airbags. The arrangement and length of the yarns connecting the two fabric layers determines the strength, thickness, and stiffness of the three-dimensional fabric.

Figure 13.16   Double cloth made with five sets of yarns.

Double Weaves

Double weave is made with four sets of yarns, creating two separate layers of fabric that periodically reverse position from top to bottom, thus interlocking the two layers of fabric. Between the interlocking points the two layers are completely separate, creating pockets in the fabric (Figure 13.17). Double-weave fabrics are also known as **pocket weave**, *pocket fabric*, or *pocket cloth*. Most commonly seen in high-quality upholstery fabrics, they offer unique design possibilities, heavy weight, and good durability.

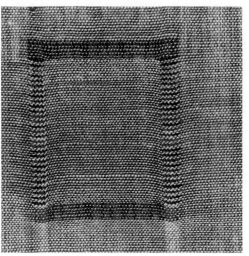

Figure 13.17 Double weave: face of fabric (left), back of fabric (right).

Matelassé is a double-cloth construction with either three or four sets of yarns woven on a jacquard or dobby loom. Two of the sets are the regular warp and filling yarns; the others are crepe or coarse cotton yarns. They are woven together so that the two sets crisscross, as shown in Figure 13.18. When the fabrics are finished, the crepe or cotton yarns shrink, giving the fabric a puckered appearance. Heavy cotton yarns sometimes are used as stuffer yarns beneath the fabric face to emphasize the three-dimensional appearance of the fabric. Matelassé is used in apparel and upholstery (Figure 13.19).

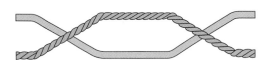

Figure 13.18 Interlacing of yarns between fabric surfaces of matelassé.

Double-Faced Fabrics

Double-faced fabrics are made with three sets of yarns: two warp and one filling or two sets of filling and one set of warp. Blankets, satin ribbons, interlinings, and silence cloth are made this way (Figure 13.20).

Blankets with each side a different color are usually double-faced fabrics. One set of warp yarns is used, with two sets of different-colored filling yarns. Sometimes designs are made by interchanging the colors from one side with the other. Double-faced blankets are usually wool and expensive.

Satin ribbons have a lustrous satin face on both sides of the ribbon and are used in lingerie and eveningwear. These ribbons have two sets of warp yarns that form the surface on each face of the ribbon. They are interlaced with one set of filling yarns.

A double-faced interlining fabric adds warmth to winter jackets and coats. The face of the fabric is a filament-yarn satin weave that slides easily over other apparel. The back of the fabric uses a third set of low-twist yarns that are heavily napped for warmth. Thus, the fabric functions as a combination of lining and interlining fabric.

Silence cloth is a heavy cotton fabric that has been napped on both sides. Available only in white, it is used under fine tablecloths to reduce the clatter of china and silverware while dining.

Figure 13.19 Matelassé: apparel weight.

Double cloth is made from three or more sets of yarns. Matelassé and pocket cloth are two examples.

Figure 13.20 Double-faced blanket: face (left) and back (right).

► **Learning Activity 7**

Use Fabrics #61 through 69 from your swatch kit. Name the weave used to produce each fabric. Unravel one or more warp and filling yarns from each sample. What are the similarities and differences among these fabrics in terms of weave, weight, and yarn type(s)? Place the fabrics in order from lightest weight to heaviest weight. Develop a list of the characteristics of the weaves represented by this group of fabrics and the impact of fabric structure on serviceability. Select one fabric from this group and describe its quality.

Pile Weaves

Woven-pile fabrics are three-dimensional structures made by weaving an extra set of warp or filling yarns into the ground yarns to make loops or cut ends on the surface (Figure 13.21). Pile comes from the Latin word *pilus*, meaning "hair." The pile is usually short—$\frac{1}{2}$ inch or less. Woven-pile fabric is less pliable than other pile fabrics. Sometimes when the fabric is folded, the rows of pile tufts permit the back to show, or "grin-through." As tuft density increases, grin-through decreases.

Pile fabrics can be both functional and beautiful. A high, thick pile adds warmth as either the shell or the lining of coats, jackets, gloves, and boots. High-count fabrics produce beautiful and durable carpets, upholstery, and bedspreads. Low-twist yarns produce absorbent towels and washcloths. Other uses for pile fabrics are stuffed toys, wigs, paint rollers, buffing and polishing cloths, and bed pads for bedridden patients. Interesting effects can be achieved by combinations of cut and uncut pile (Figure 13.21), pile of various heights, high- and low-twist yarns, areas of pile on a flat surface, flattening pile, or only partially flattening the pile.

In pile fabrics, the pile receives the surface abrasion and the base weave or ground receives the stress. A durable ground structure contributes significantly to a satisfactory pile fabric. A compact ground weave increases the resistance of a looped or uncut pile to snagging and of a cut pile to shedding and pulling out. A dense pile stands erect, resists crushing, and gives better cover. Care must be taken in cleaning and pressing to keep the pile erect. Cut pile may look better if dry-cleaned, but some pile fabrics—such as pinwale corduroy—can be washed, depending on the fiber content. Incorrect pressing may flatten the pile and result in a fabric that appears lighter in color. Special pressing aids—like needleboards—and steaming are used with pile fabrics.

Many pile fabrics are pressed during finishing so that the pile slants in one direction, giving an up-and-down look. When the pile is directed in the same way in all pieces of a product, the colors match. Otherwise, light will be reflected differently and the product will appear to be made of two or more colors of the fabric. (See Figure 17.16.)

Filling-Pile Fabrics

The pile in **filling-pile fabrics** is made by long filling floats on the surface that are cut after weaving (Figure 13.22). Filling-pile fabrics are always cut pile. Two sets of filling yarns and one set of warp are used. The ground fabric is made with one set of filling yarns and the warp yarn set. During weaving, the extra filling yarns float across the ground yarns, interlacing occasionally.

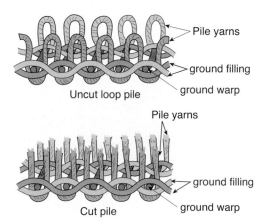

Figure 13.21   Cut pile and loop pile: woven-pile fabric.

Figure 13.22   Filling pile: cross section of weave in corduroy.

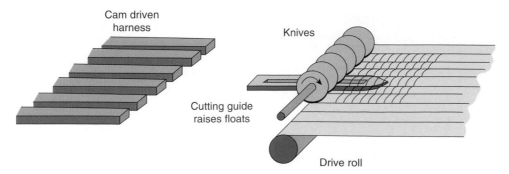

Figure 13.23 Process for cutting floats to make corduroy.

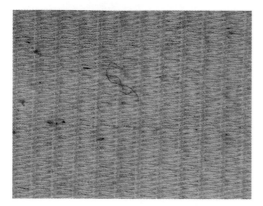 

Figure 13.24 Corduroy: gray goods (right) and cut and brushed open (left).

In **corduroy**, the floats are arranged in lengthwise rows; in **velveteen**, they are scattered over the base fabric.

Cutting is done by a special machine with guides that lift the individual floating yarns from the ground fabric and revolving knives that cut the floats (Figure 13.23). Gray-goods corduroy with uncut and cut floats is shown in Figure 13.24. For wide-wale corduroy, the guides and knives are set to cut all the floats in one operation. For narrow corduroy and velveteen, the rows are so close together that alternate rows are cut with each pass and two passes must be made.

After cutting, the surface is brushed crosswise and lengthwise to bloom open the yarn tuft, raise the pile, merge the separate pile tufts, and reduce pile pull-out due to abrasion. Finishing gives the fabric its final appearance.

Both velveteen and corduroy are made with long-staple combed cotton for the pile. In good-quality fabrics, long-staple cotton is used for the ground as well. Polyester/cotton blends are available with polyester in the ground yarns for strength. The ground weave may be either plain- or twill-weave. Twill ground weaves produce a higher count and a denser pile. Corduroy can be recognized by lengthwise wales. Velveteen has more body and less drapeability than velvet. The pile is not higher than $\frac{1}{8}$ inch. Both corduroy and velveteen are available in solid-color and printed fabrics. Table 13.2 describes characteristics of different types of corduroy.

Warp-Pile Fabrics

Warp-pile fabrics are made with two sets of warp yarns and one set of filling. One set of warp yarns and the one filling yarn form the ground fabric. The extra set of warp yarns forms the pile that can be cut or uncut. Several methods are used.

Table 13.2 Types of Corduroy

	Wales per Inch	Ounces per Square Yard	Characteristics and Uses
Featherwale	18–19	5±	Shallow pile, flexible, tops and bottoms
Pinwale	14–16	7±	Shallow pile, flexible, tops and bottoms
Midwale	11	10±	Outerwear and bottoms, upholstery
Wide wale	3–9	12±	Heavier and less flexible
			Most durable corduroy, coats, upholstery
Variable wale	Varies	Varies, but usually mid-range 7–10	Outerwear and bottoms, upholstery

Double-Cloth Method Two fabrics are woven, one above the other, with the extra set of warp yarns interlacing with both fabrics. There are two sheds, one above the other, and one filling yarn is inserted into each shed. The fabrics are cut apart while still on the loom by a traveling knife that passes back and forth across the loom. With the double-cloth method of weaving, the depth of the pile is determined by the space between the two fabrics. The interlacing pattern of the pile yarns determines their resistance to shedding, density, and durability (Figure 13.25). Pile with a W shape interlaces with more filling yarns, is more resistant to shedding, is less dense, and is more durable. Pile with a V shape interlaces with fewer filling yarns, is less resistant to shedding, is denser, and is less durable. When a fabric is unraveled, pile shape can be determined easily by placing it on a surface of a contrasting color.

Velvet is made of filament yarns with a pile height of $\frac{1}{16}$ inch or less. Velvet must be handled carefully so that no folds or creases flatten the pile.

Velvet and velveteen can be distinguished by fiber length: Velvet is usually made with filaments and velveteen with staple. To identify warp directions in these fabrics, ravel adjacent sides. In filling-pile fabrics, the pile is pushed out as individual tufts when a filling yarn is removed. But when a warp yarn is removed, the pile tufts cling to it and it looks a little like a woolly caterpillar (Figure 13.26). In warp-pile fabrics, the opposite occurs. Pile tufts cling to filling yarns. Another way to tell warp direction is to bend the fabric. In velveteen, the pile "breaks" into lengthwise rows because the filling tufts are interlaced with the warp yarns. In velvet, the pile breaks in crosswise rows because the warp tufts are interlaced with the ground-filling yarns. This technique works best with medium- to poor-quality fabrics.

Finishing is used to create other looks for velvet. **Crushed velvet** is made by mechanically twisting the wet cloth and randomly flattening the surface yarns in different directions. *Panné velvet* is an elegant fabric with the pile pressed flat by heavy pressure in one direction to give it high luster. If the pile is disturbed or brushed in the other direction, the smooth, lustrous look is destroyed. *Velour* is a warp-pile cotton fabric used primarily for upholstery and draperies. It has a deeper pile than velveteen and is heavier. *Plush* has the deepest pile—usually longer than $\frac{1}{4}$ inch.

Furlike fabrics may be finished by curling, shearing, sculpturing, or printing to resemble different kinds of real fur. (Most furlike fabrics are made by other processes; see Chapters 14 and 15.)

Warp
Filling
Warp

Figure 13.25 Warp pile: double-cloth method. W-interlacing (above), V-interlacing (below).

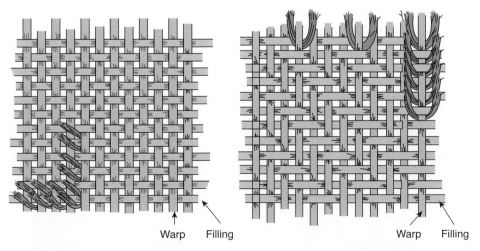

Warp   Filling   Warp   Filling

Figure 13.26 Comparison of filling pile and warp pile. Velvet: Warp-pile yarn is interlaced with ground filling (left). Velveteen: Filling-pile yarn is interlaced with ground warp (right).

Figure 13.27 Friezé is woven over wires.

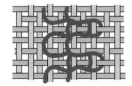

Figure 13.28 Warp pile: slack-tension method for terrycloth.

Woven-pile fabrics are three-dimensional structures made by weaving an extra set of warp or filling yarns into the ground yarns to make loops or cut ends on the surface. Filling pile fabrics include corduroy and velveteen. Warp pile fabrics include velvet, friezé, and terrycloth.

Over-Wire Method In the **over-wire method**, a single fabric is woven with wires placed across the width of the loom so that they are positioned above the ground warp and under the pile warp. For cut-pile fabrics, each wire has a hook at one end with a knife edge that cuts all the yarns looped over it as it is withdrawn. Uncut pile is produced using wires without hooks or waste picks of filling yarns. The wires are removed before the fabric is removed from the loom, and the waste picks are removed after the fabric is off the loom. Friezé, mohair-pile plush, and most woven-pile carpets and rugs are made in this way.

Friezé, an uncut or combination cut/uncut pile fabric, is an upholstery fabric that has fewer tufts per square inch than most other pile fabrics. The durability of friezé depends on the closeness of the weave (Figure 13.27).

Velvet can also be made by the over-wire method. Complex patterns using different-colored yarns and loops combined with cut pile result in a wide variety of fabrics for upholstery and apparel uses.

Slack-Tension Pile Method The pile in **terrycloth** is formed by a special weaving arrangement in which three picks or fillings are inserted and beaten up with one motion of the reed. After the second pick in a set is inserted, there is a let-off motion that causes the yarns on the warp-pile beam to slacken, while the yarns on the ground-pile beam are held at tension. The third pick is inserted, the reed moves forward all the way, and all three picks are beaten up firmly into place (Figure 13.28). These picks move along the ground warp and push the pile-warp yarns into loops. The loops can be on one side only or on both sides. Loop height is determined by the let-off motion of the warp-pile beam.

Quality is determined by the yarn type (carded or combed), the fiber (Pima, Egyptian, or regular cotton), and the number of filling yarns or picks used to create the weave. Common varieties include two- and three-pick terries. For example, a three-pick terrycloth, the highest quality, has two picks under the pile loop and one pick between loops. Figure 13.28 shows a three-pick terrycloth with closed loops on both sides of the fabric.

Terrycloth is used for kitchen and bath towels, beach robes, and sportswear. Each loop acts as a tiny sponge. Sheared loops are brushed to loosen and intermesh the fibers of adjacent yarns. The surface becomes more compact, less porous, and absorbs more slowly as compared with loop-pile terry. Institutional cotton/polyester terry towels have blended ground yarns and cotton pile; the pile yarns are for absorbency and the polyester ground yarns are for strength and durability, especially in selvages. Terrycloth towels for kitchen use are more likely to leave lint on glassware and dishes than glass toweling made in plain, twill, or dobby weaves. Glass toweling refers to the function—drying glasses—rather than the fiber content.

There is no up and down in terrycloth unless it is printed. Some friezés are made by this method. Another slack-tension fabric, *shagbark*, has widely spaced rows of occasional yarn loops.

▶ Learning Activity 8

Explain the differences and similarities between warp and filling pile weaves. Name one fabric of each type, identify an appropriate end use for each, and explain the serviceability based on fabric structure, pile yarn type (warp or filling), interlacing pattern (V or W), and fabric density.

Figure 13.29 Seersucker. Note that the yarns removed from the flat portion of the fabric are smaller and straighter. The yarns removed from the puckered area are larger and more crimped.

Slack-Tension Weaves

Two warp beams are used in a **slack-tension weave**. The yarns on one beam are held at regular tension and those on the other beam are held at slack tension. As the reed beats the filling yarn into place, the slack yarns crinkle or buckle to form a puckered stripe, and the regular-tensioned yarns form the flat stripe. Loop-pile fabrics, such as terrycloth, are made by a similar weave (see the previous section). **Seersucker** is a fabric made by slack-tension weave (Figure 13.29).

The yarns are wound onto the two warp beams in groups of 10 to 16 for a narrow stripe. The crinkle stripe may have slightly larger yarns to enhance the crinkle. The stripes are always in the warp direction and on-grain. Seersucker is produced by a limited number of manufacturers. It is a low-profit, high-cost item because of its slow weaving speed. Seersuckers are made in plain colors, stripes, plaids, checks, and prints. Seersucker is used in curtains, children's wear, and summer suiting, dresses, and sportswear.

> In a **slack-tension weave**, some of the warp yarns are held at regular tension and others are held at slack tension. As the reed pushes ahead, the slack tension warp slides forward creating either a textured band or loops. Seersucker and some terrycloth are made by the slack tension weave.

Tapestry Weave

A **tapestry weave** is a hand-produced, filling-faced, plain-weave fabric. The discontinuous filling yarns are arranged so that as the color in the weave changes, a pattern is created. Discontinuous filling means that one filling yarn rarely travels across the fabric from one side to the other. Each color of filling yarn moves back and forth in a plain-weave interlacing pattern as long as the design calls for that color; then another color is used. In tapestries, filling yarns are not always straight within the fabric and may interlace with the warp at an angle other than 90 degrees. If the color changes along a vertical line, slits can develop in the structure. Different methods of structuring the fabric can enhance or eliminate the slit, depending on the effect desired by the artist.

Two types of looms are used to create tapestries: horizontal and vertical. The differences between the looms relate to the size and end use of the tapestry. One-of-a-kind rugs, wall hangings, and fiber art pieces are made using this weave. Sometimes it is referred to as true tapestry to differentiate it from the jacquard-patterned tapestry. **True tapestries** usually have larger filling yarns than warp yarns. Warp yarns are covered completely by the filling. Although pictorial tapestries are common, there are many categories of tapestries based on the pattern and end use. Figure 13.30 shows a close-up of a tapestry.

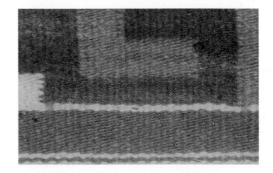

Figure 13.30 Close-up of a Navajo tapestry. Note how the yarns dovetail where the pattern changes color. This is one method used to avoid producing slits in a tapestry.

A **tapestry weave** is a hand-produced, filling-faced, plain-weave fabric with discontinuous filling yarns arranged so that as the color in the weave changes, a pattern is created.

Figure 13.31 Narrow fabrics (left to right): twill tape, grosgrain ribbon, bias tape, satin ribbon, rick-rack, and woven fancy ribbon.

Narrow fabrics include a diverse range of fabrics up to 12 inches wide made by a variety of techniques. Narrow fabrics are used for ribbon, trim, labels, tapes, belts, and webbing.

Narrow Fabrics

Narrow fabrics encompass a diverse range of products that are up to 12 inches wide and made by a variety of techniques. Woven narrow fabrics will be discussed here. Narrow fabrics include ribbons of all sorts, elastics, zipper tapes, window-blind tapes, couturier and manufacturer labels, hook and loop tapes such as Velcro™, pipings, carpet-edge tapes, trims, safety belts, and harnesses (Figure 13.31). Webbings are an important group of narrow fabrics used in packaging, cargo handling, furniture, and for animal control, like leashes or lead ropes for companion and show animals.

Narrow-fabric looms weave many fabrics side by side. Each fabric has its own shuttle but shares all other loom mechanisms. Plain, twill, satin, jacquard, and pile weaves are used. Many fabrics used in narrow form are woven wider and cut into strips. Cutting mechanisms include laser, ultrasonic or ultra-high frequency sound, or hot knives for converting thermoplastic wide fabrics into narrow strips and fusing the raw edges to reduce raveling.

Woven elastics are made using a variety of weaves. They are used in apparel for which tight fit and holding power are needed, such as in undergarments. They have better stability and rigidity than knit elastics and are less prone to riding up, but are more expensive.

▶ Learning Activity 10

Examine the textile products you are wearing and have with you today. (Be sure to look at labels, too.) Which items are woven? What weaves are used for these fabrics? Use a magnifying or pick glass to determine if any of these fabrics are fancy or structural design. Name these fabrics and/or weave. Describe your satisfaction with and the serviceability of one item based on fiber content, yarn type, and weave.

key terms

review questions

1. Explain why the fabrics in this chapter are referred to as fancy or structural design.

2. Summarize the structure of these weaves: dobby, extra yarn, piqué, jacquard, momie, leno, double cloth, pile, and slack-tension.

3. What performance differences would be expected among the weaves in Question 2?

4. Identify three features for each of the weaves in Question 2 that explain their use in weaving fabrics, that differentiate them from other weaves, or that contribute one or more serviceability functions to end products.

5. Name a fabric and end use for each of the weaves in Question 2. Explain why that fabric is appropriate for that end use.

6. Identify which of the fancy weaves discussed in this chapter make use of one or more of the basic weaves while creating the fancy or structural design.

7. For which of these fabrics can the pattern be removed without destroying the fabric? Explain your answer.

8. Explain why narrow fabrics are sometimes made as fancies. Name three end uses for fancy narrow fabrics.

9. Explain the differences between tapestry jacquard and tapestry weave.

10. What kind of information is conveyed by the following fabric names? Identify an appropriate end use for each of these fabrics.
   a. Bird's eye diaper
   b. Clipped spot
   c. Pinwale piqué
   d. Damask
   e. Brocatelle
   f. Sand crepe
   g. Leno
   h. Matelassé
   i. Corduroy
   j. Velvet
   k. Friezé
   l. Seersucker

Case Study
Damask for the Hospitality Industry*

Milliken & Company's new damask for the hospitality industry (table linens such as napkins and tablecloths for restaurants and dining facilities) combines a soft natural feel with performance and durability. The new high-luster design creates a bolder, more distinct pattern. The fabric is pill-resistant with good colorfastness to laundering and better durability than cotton or polyester/cotton blends. The fabric has finer yarns and an innovative fabric construction and is available in five patterns and eleven colors. The fabric is also stain resistant.

DISCUSSION QUESTIONS

1. Identify the fancy weave category in which damask is found.

2. Describe the characteristics of damask.

3. Why would elegant restaurants be interested in damask table linens?

4. Although the article did not indicate fiber content, identify two possibilities that are realistic given the easy care and durability required in the hospitality industry. Explain your choices.

5. How could traditional damask be modified in fiber, yarn, or fabric structure to produce high luster and bolder, more distinct patterns?

*Anonymous. (2007, June 11). Milliken defines innovative damask fabric for hospitality industry. *Business Wire*, record number 20070611005290.

KNITTING and KNIT FABRICS

CHAPTER OBJECTIVES

- To describe the differences between woven and knit fabrics.
- To differentiate between warp- and filling-knit fabrics.
- To distinguish between plain or basic knits and fancy knits.
- To understand the characteristics of warp- and filling-knit fabrics.
- To integrate fabrication, yarn type, and fiber with end use.
- To understand the versatility of knit fabrics for apparel, interior, and technical products.

14

311

only a row of loops is removed. Try unraveling a knit fabric and a woven fabric to compare this major distinction between the two structures. Compare the two unraveled fabrics in Figure 14.3. Table 14.1 compares knitting and weaving.

Knits can be classified by several factors: the machine on which the knit is made, the number of yarn sets in the knit, the type of stitch or stitches used, or the type of fabric produced. Categorizing knits by the number of yarn sets is a carryover from hand knitting. Some fabrics,

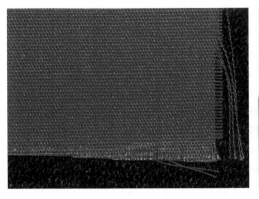

Figure 14.3 Woven fabrics can be unraveled by removing warp and filling yarns (left). Knit fabric can be unraveled by removing a course (right).

Table 14.1 Comparison of Knit and Woven Fabrics

Knitting	Weaving
Comfort and Appearance Retention	
Mobile, elastic fabric. Adapts easily to body movement. Good recovery from wrinkles. Air-permeable. Open spaces between yarns let winds and moisture penetrate. Bulky.	Stable to stress (unless made with stretch yarns). Less air and water permeable, especially if count is high. Bulk and wrinkle recovery vary with the weave.
Cover	
Porous, less opaque.	Provides maximum hiding power and cover.
Fabric Stability	
Less stable in use and care. Higher shrinkage unless heat-set.	More stable in use and care. Lower shrinkage.
Versatility	
Sheer to heavyweight fabrics. Plain and fancy knits with or without fancy yarns. Resembles many woven fabrics. Shaping of garments or garment parts possible.	Sheer to heavyweight fabrics. Plain and fancy weaves with or without fancy yarns. Shaping of garment parts much more difficult.
Economics	
Machines can be changed quickly to meet fashion needs. Process is less expensive but requires more expensive yarns. Faster process regardless of fabric width.	Machinery is less adaptable to rapid changes in fashion. Most economical method of producing a unit of cover. Wider looms weave more slowly.
Fabric Structure and Characteristics	
Series of interconnected loops made with one or more sets of yarns. Filling knits can be raveled from top or bottom depending on the knit type; warp knits cannot be raveled. May snag and run. May be bowed or skewed. Usually heavier because more yarn is used.	Two or more sets of yarns interlaced to form the fabric structure. Yarns are essentially straight in the fabric. Can be raveled from any cut edge. May snag and ravel. May be bowed or skewed. Usually lighter because less yarn is used.
Uses	
Apparel, interiors, and technical products.	Apparel, interiors, and technical products.

such as rib knits, are made with one set of yarns on a double-knit machine with two needle beds. Thus, rib knits could be categorized as a single-knit (one yarn set) or as a double-knit (machine type). In the textile complex and in this book, knits are most often categorized by the machine used to produce them.

Needles

Knitting is done by needles: **spring-beard**, **latch**, **double-latch**, or **compound** (Figure 14.4). These needles differ from hand knitting needles. Commercial knitting uses knitting machines with needles engineered to fit in the needle bar and be operated by the control mechanisms of the machine. Most filling knits are formed with the latch needle. The spring-beard needle may be used to produce fully fashioned garments, fleece, and fine yarn fabrics. A double-latch needle is used to make purl fabrics. The compound needle is used primarily in warp knitting.

Stitches

Needles manipulate the yarns to form **stitches** or loops. Stitch names are based on the way they are made. Stitches may be open or closed, depending on how the stitch is formed. Open stitches are most common in filling knitting. In warp knitting, open and closed stitches are found, depending on the design; they help in identifying the fabric, but have little effect on fabric performance.

Fabric Characteristics

Characteristics of knits differ significantly from those of woven fabrics. While both fabric types are made from yarns, knit characteristics are dependent on the type of knit and the stitches and yarn(s) that form the fabric. *Fabric density* is defined by counting the number of stitches, not yarns, in a specific direction. **Wales** are vertical columns of stitches in the knit fabric. **Courses** are the horizontal rows. In machine knitting, each wale is formed by a single needle. Wales and courses show clearly on filling-knit jersey (Figures 14.5 and 14.6). Follow the yarn path of Figures 14.5 and 14.6. Notice that a single yarn forms a stitch (a single wale) and a course (a row of stitches). Fabric density is often designated as wales by courses. For example, a T-shirt jersey might have 32 wales per inch and 44 courses per inch. This fabric would have a density of 32×44.

Gauge or **cut** indicates the fineness of the stitch; it is the number of needles in a specific distance on the needle bar and is often expressed as needles per inch (npi). Cut may be used in the textile complex to describe knit fabrics.

The higher the gauge, the finer the fabric. Finished fabrics may not have the same gauge as the knitting machine because of shrinkage or stretching during finishing. A fine-gauge filling-knitting machine may have 28 npi or more. A coarse one may have 13 npi or fewer.

It may be difficult to identify the technical face of the fabric. **Technical face** refers to the outer side of the fabric as knitted. This may not be the side used as the fashion side in a product. The **technical back** is the inner side of the fabric as it is knit and is used as the fashion side of such fabrics as fleece and knit terry. Identification of the technical face can be done in several ways. The technical face usually has a better finish. Finer and more expensive yarns are used on the face side. Floats on the face are shorter, finer, and less likely to snag. Fabric design is more obvious on the face side.

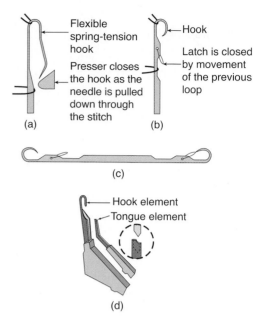

Figure 14.4   Knitting needles: (a) spring-beard needle, (b) latch needle, (c) double-latch needle, (d) compound needle.

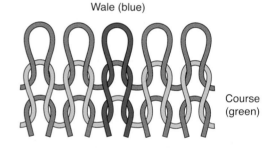

Figure 14.5   Wale and course as seen from the technical face of filling-knit jersey fabric.

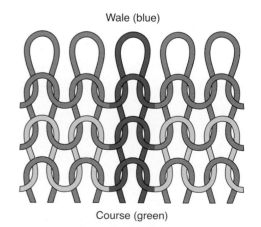

Figure 14.6   Wale and course as seen from the technical back of filling-knit jersey fabric.

Quality in knit fabrics is assessed in much the same way as for woven fabrics. (See Chapter 12.) Procedures focus on inspecting for flaws and assessing how the fabric performs in specific areas of interest. Characteristics that are used to define a high-quality knit fabric include a heavyweight for the fabric type, fiber content, and end use. Yarns are regular in appearance and may be combed or worsted, depending on the fiber. Pattern is incorporated into the fabric as part of its structure; fancy knit jacquard or raschel fabrics are of higher quality than printed or embossed fabrics. Skew is minimal. Garment parts can be shaped on the knitting machine rather than being cut and sewn.

Because of the unique interlooped structure of knits, they are more prone to such problems as snagging and sagging. Special procedures have been developed to assess these performance characteristics of knits. The next few paragraphs describe some procedures used to assess knit fabric performance.

Skew (an off-grain characteristic first discussed in Chapter 12) is also common with knits, especially circular knits, because of the way they are made (see the later discussion and Figure 14.10). In assessing skew, a fabric is placed flat on a surface and one course is followed across the fabric. A right angle is used to measure the difference between a straight course and a skewed course in the fabric.

Knitted fabrics have higher potential shrinkage than woven fabrics. The accepted standard is 5 percent for knits, whereas 2 percent is standard for wovens. However, ASTM performance specifications recommend maximum shrinkage for woven and knit products of 3 percent in both vertical and horizontal directions.

A knit's bulky structure provides many spaces to trap air for good insulation in still air, but a wind-repellent outer layer is needed to prevent chill winds from penetrating the open structure of the knit. On a warm, humid day, knits may be too warm because they conform to the body and insulate too well.

Knits are less likely to wrinkle during use, care, packing, or storage. Wrinkle recovery is related to the loop structure, but it is also strongly influenced by fiber and yarn type. *Snagging* is a serious problem with knit fabrics. When a yarn is snagged, it pulls out and stands away from the surface of the fabric. Shiners, or tight yarns, may form on either side of the snag. Finer yarns, smaller stitches, and higher yarn twist all reduce snagging. If snags are cut off (rather than being worked back into their original position), a run is likely in some knits, particularly in filling knits.

A **run** occurs when the stitches in a wale collapse or pull out. A run occurs in a stepwise fashion when one stitch after another in a wale collapses due to stress on the loop when a yarn is cut.

Environmental Concerns and Sustainability of Knitting

The process of knitting creates fewer environmental problems as compared with weaving. Chemicals to minimize abrasion on yarns or generation of static charges are less likely to be used with knits. Knitting machines operate with less vibration, lint, noise, and energy than shuttle

> ### ▶ Learning Activity 2

Consider the knit textile products you have owned. Have you experienced any of these problems: skew, snag, or run? Explain each of these problems as they relate to fabric structure and serviceability. How did the problem affect your satisfaction with the product? How could these problems be prevented during fabrication? Are there some problems that are inherent to knits? If yes, which ones and how do they relate to the knit structure? Do woven fabrics experience the same problems?

looms. However, because of the demand for knits in the market, social abuses do occur in knit facilities. Employees may be expected to work excessive hours in uncomfortable conditions for low pay. Some employees may be children who are paid less than adults for the same hours of work. Because of the relatively low cost of knitting machines, knitting mills are often concentrated in developing countries. During times of economic downturns, mills close leaving workers with no source of income. However, during times of economic growth, mills provide income for workers in the community.

Filling (or Weft) Knitting

Filling knitting can be done by hand or machine. In *hand knitting*, a yarn is cast (looped) onto one needle, another needle is inserted into the first stitch, the yarn is positioned around the needle, and by manipulating the needle a new stitch is formed while being transferred onto a second needle. The process is repeated over and over again until the product has been completed.

In *machine knitting*, many needles (one for each wale) are set into the needle bed of a knitting machine and the stitch is made in a series of steps. By the end of the final step, one needle has gone through a complete up-and-down motion, and a new stitch has been formed (Figure 14.7). In the *running* position, the needle moves up and the old stitch slides down the needle. In *clearing*, the needle reaches its highest position and the old stitch has dropped down to the needle's base. In *feeding*, the new yarn is caught by the needle's hook and the needle begins its downward stroke. In *knockover*, the old stitch is removed from the needle. The final step is *pulling*, when the new stitch is formed at the needle's hook and the needle is in its lowest position. These five steps are repeated in a continuous up-and-down motion to form a knit. Each needle in the knitting machine is at a slightly different stage in this process so that a wave or undulating motion appears to move across or around the machine. Each stitch is at a slightly

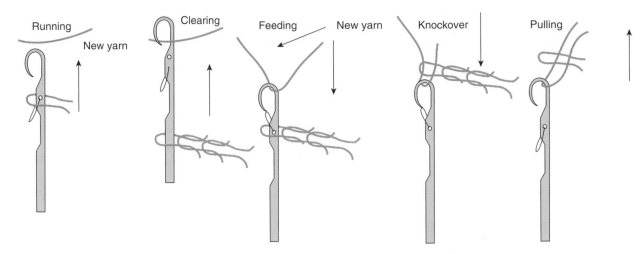

Running   New yarn   Clearing   Feeding   New yarn   Knockover   Pulling

Figure 14.7   Latch-needle knitting action. Arrows show the direction in which the needle is moving.

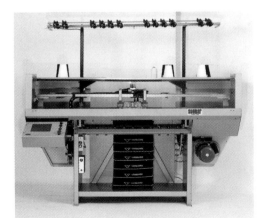

Figure 14.8   Flatbed knitting machine for fabric.
SOURCE: Courtesy of Stoll America Knitting Machinery, Inc.

different step in the process at any given time, but all the stitches in a course are formed by the same yarn, except for some fancy knits.

Knitting can be done on a flatbed machine in which the yarn is carried back and forth (Figure 14.8) or on a circular machine in which the yarn is carried in a spiral like the threads in a screw (Figure 14.9). Figure 14.10 shows yarn movement in fabrics knit using these two types of machines. In hand knitting, many kinds of stitches can be made by varying the way the yarn is placed around the needle (in front or behind) and by knitting stitches together, dropping stitches, or transferring stitches. Special devices are used to obtain these variations in machine knitting.

Machines Used in Filling Knitting

Machine knitting is done on single- and double-knit circular and flatbed machines. Production is faster with **circular machines**; they are described by the diameter of the fabric tube produced. Greater flexibility demands by the textile complex have resulted in machines that make a variety of tube diameters. Diameters can be changed with minimal down-time. New yarns can be fed into the structure at any point along the diameter. Yarn feeds normally range from three to four feeds per diameter inch. With a tube diameter of only 13 inches and three feeds per

Examine the knit products you are wearing today, including socks, tights, or hosiery. Which items are made on a flatbed machine and which are made on a circular machine? How can you tell what type of machine was used? What is the approximate diameter or circumference of the circular machine(s) used?

Figure 14.9 Circular knitting machine.
SOURCE: Courtesy of Vanguard Supreme.

diameter inch, there could be up to 39 courses between the point where a yarn began its circular pattern and the point where that same yarn began its second course around the fabric. High yarn feeds per diameter inch allow knitting machines to be very productive, but the resulting fabrics have significant skew, presenting potential problems in cutting, sewing, and consumer satisfaction. Circular machines are used to make yardage, sweater bodies, hosiery, and socks.

Flatbed machines knit a variety of fabric widths, usually at least 100 inches wide. These machines are slower than circular machines, but they produce less skew in the fabric and can fashion or shape garment or product parts.

Knitting machines may also be described by the type of fabric they produce, such as simple jersey, a more complex knit such as terrycloth, or fancy patterned knits using jacquard machines.

Filling-Knit Structures—Stitches

Filling-knit fabrics are classified by the four possible stitch types. Each stitch is controlled by the selection of cams, or guides, that control the motion of the needle. The first stitch is the **knit stitch**. This is the basic stitch used to produce the majority of filling-knit fabrics (Figure 14.11). These fabrics have greater crosswise and less lengthwise elongation. The sides of the stitches appear on the face of jersey; the back is comprised of the tops and bottoms of the stitches. Figure 14.11 illustrates the appearance of both sides of the fabric. When jerseys are printed, they are printed on the face, since that is the smoothest and most regular surface. However,

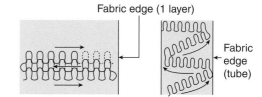

Figure 14.10 Yarn motion in flatbed knits (left) and circular knits (right).

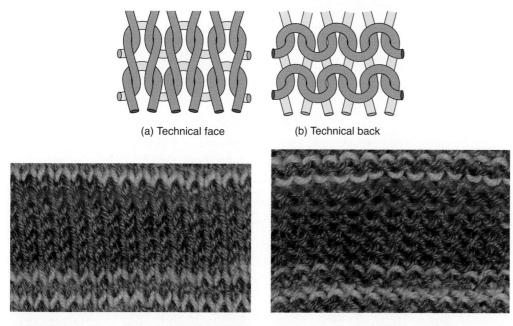

(a) Technical face   (b) Technical back

Figure 14.11 Jersey fabric diagram (top) and photograph (bottom). The blue part in the diagram indicates the yarn portions that can be seen from that view of the fabric.

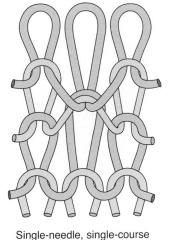

Single-needle, single-course
tuck stitch

Figure 14.12 Tuck-stitch diagram (left) and fabric (right).

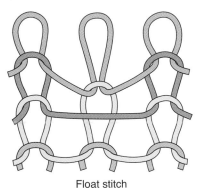

Float stitch

Figure 14.13 Float, or miss, stitch diagram (left). Jacquard jersey fabric (center and right). Note the pattern on the face (center) and the floats on the back (right)

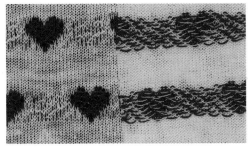

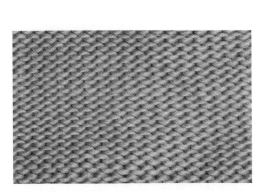

Figure 14.14 Purl stitch looks the same on both sides.

Examine the knit products you are wearing today. What kinds of knit stitches were used to create those fabrics? Are the stitches used to create a pattern in the fabric? How many repeats occur across or along the fabric? Is more than one color or type of yarn used? How does the structure of the fabric affect your satisfaction with the product?

many jerseys, especially the pile types, are used with the technical back as the fashion side because of the loop formation.

The **tuck stitch** is used to create a fancy knit, one with a pattern in the fabric. In the tuck stitch, the old stitch is not cleared from the needle. Thus, there are two stitches on the needle. Figure 14.12 shows how the tuck stitch looks in a fabric. In a knit fabric with tuck stitches, the fabric is thicker and slightly less likely to stretch crosswise than a basic-knit fabric with the same number of stitches. Tuck stitches create bubbles or puckers for visual interest. They may be in a pattern or added randomly to create texture. These fancy knits are usually referred to as jacquard jerseys.

The **float or miss stitch** is also used to create a fancy knit with a pattern in the fabric. In the float stitch, no new stitch is formed at the needle, while adjacent needles form new stitches. The float stitch is used when yarns of different colors knit in to create the design. Figure 14.13 shows how the float stitch looks in a fabric from the technical face and the technical back. A fancy knit fabric with float stitches is much less likely to stretch crosswise than a basic-knit fabric with the same number of stitches. In jacquard jerseys, float stitches are very common when several colors of yarn are used in the fabric. For example, if a fabric incorporates two or more colors in a pattern, float stitches are necessary, as one color comes to the face and the other floats in this area. A jacquard jersey made with different yarn colors combines tuck and float stitches in a course.

The **purl, or reverse, stitch** forms a fabric that looks on both sides like the technical back of a basic-knit fabric. The fabric is reversible (Figure 14.14). Purl-knit fabrics are slow and expensive to knit because they require special machines. Since the face and back of a purl fabric look like the back of a jersey, manufacturers often use the technical back of a jersey as the fashion side when a purl appearance is desired. These imitation "purl" fabrics pass casual inspection by consumers and are competitive in price with other knit structures, so the consumer does not pay more for this special look. An imitation purl fabric may be described as a reverse jersey.

Filling-Knit Fabrics

Single-Filling Knits **Single-filling knits** are made using a circular or flatbed machine with one set of needles. Single-knits can be plain or fancy and any pattern or weight. They are less stable than double-knits, tend to curl at the edges, and run readily, especially if made of filament yarns.

Single or Plain Jerseys

Single-jersey fabric is the simplest of the filling-knit structures. Wales—columns of stitches running lengthwise—may be easier to see on the face. Courses—rows of stitches running crosswise—may be easier to see on the back. Stretch a swatch of jersey crosswise and it curls to the back at the lengthwise edges. The ends curl toward the face. Yarns ravel crosswise because they run horizontally in the fabric. Cut edges or broken yarns may create problems with runs. Single jerseys made of spun yarns resist running because of fiber cohesiveness. The single-jersey structure, or plain knit, is widely used because it is the fastest filling knit to make and is made on the least complicated knitting machine.

Jersey is a plain, basic fabric of lightweight to heavyweight; it is usually knit on a circular jersey machine and sold in tubular form or cut and sold as flat goods. When tubular fabrics are pressed in finishing, the creases are off-grain and not parallel to wales so the fabric is skewed. Tubular fabric does not need to be cut and opened out when cutting out product parts, unless there is a specific reason for doing so. T-shirts with no side seams are made from circular knit jersey. Tube socks are another common circular knit product.

Figure 14.15 shows a T-shirt that was cut from tubular cotton jersey with yarn-dyed stripes. When purchased, the stripes and the side seams were parallel. After washing, the fabric assumed its normal position, causing the side seams to twist toward the front on one side and the back on the other side.

Heavier-weight jerseys are often used for simple solid-color or striped sweaters, tops, and skirts. Fancy and plied yarns add body, durability, warmth, cover, interest, or texture. **Stockinette** (or **stockinet**) is a heavier-knit jersey made with coarser spun yarns as compared with a regular jersey.

Lisle (pronounced lyle) is a high-quality jersey made of fine two-ply combed cotton yarns. It can be found in several weights, depending on its end use. Lisle is used for socks, undergarments, tops, skirts, and sweaters.

End uses for jersey include hosiery, underwear, shirts, T-shirts, dresses, and sweaters. Variations of plain knits are used to create fancy knits and are made by programming the machines to knit stitches together, to drop stitches, and to use colored yarns to form patterns or vertical stripes. Extra yarns or slivers are used to make pile fabrics like terrycloth, velour, and fake-fur fabrics.

Jacquard Jerseys

Fancy or figured single jerseys are made using a jacquard mechanism with electronic controls on circular jersey machines. Fancy jersey patterns are produced by combinations of knit, tuck, or float stitches; combinations of yarns that vary by color, structure, or texture; or incorporation of yarns in specific areas within the fabric, much like a true tapestry weave for woven fabrics. The maximum colors per row in a jacquard jersey is 42, allowing for a wide range of intricate patterns. Jacquard jerseys are the simplest of these fancy patterned fabrics. In a **jacquard jersey**, the pattern develops because of different stitch types, yarn texture or color, or a combination of variations in stitch type and yarn. Figure 14.13 shows the face and back of a jacquard jersey in which change of yarn color created the pattern.

Intarsia is a more complicated patterned single-knit fabric in which the yarn used to create a pattern in the fabric is knit into the fabric in that area only. Intarsia, the knit counterpart to a true tapestry weave, is made by knitting in colored yarns. True intarsia designs have a clear pattern on both the face and back with no pattern shadows, a characteristic of jacquard designs. These fancy fabrics have no extra weight, and the stretch is not impaired. Mock intarsia designs are made by knitting and float-knitting (float or miss stitch), which results in a heavier-weight fabric with floating yarns on the reverse side or shadow pattern. Floats reduce the elasticity of the fabric and may snag readily. Compare both fabrics in Figure 14.16.

Knits are made with four basic stitches. The **knit stitch** is the basic stitch used to produce the majority of filling-knit fabrics. The **tuck stitch** is used to create a fancy knit, one with a pattern in the fabric. In the tuck stitch, the old stitch is not cleared from the needle. Thus, there are two stitches on the needle. The **float** or **miss stitch** is also used to create a fancy knit with a pattern in the fabric. In the float stitch, no new stitch is formed at the needle, while adjacent needles form new stitches. The **purl**, or **reverse**, **stitch** forms a fabric that looks on both sides like the technical back of a basic-knit fabric.

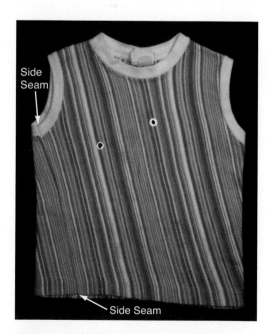

Figure 14.15 T-shirt showing skew of the circular knit jersey fabric. Note how the side seam twists toward the front of the shirt.

Figure 14.16   Compare these two fabrics: true intarsia, face (top left) and back (top right); mock intarsia, face (bottom left) and back (bottom right).

There are two types of filling knits. **Single-filling knits** are made using a circular or flatbed machine with one set of needles. Single-knits can be plain or fancy and any pattern or weight. Examples include jersey, intarsia, velour, and fleece. **Double-filling knits** are made using a machine with two beds of needles, with the second bed or set of needles located at a right angle to the first bed of needles. Examples include rib, interlock, double-knit, and purl.

Pile Jerseys **Pile jerseys** are made on a modified circular jersey machine. These fancy fabrics look like woven pile but are more pliable and stretchy. The pile surface may consist of (1) cut or uncut loops of yarn or (2) fibers (see the discussion of sliver knits later in this chapter). In velour and knit terrycloth, the fabric is made with two sets of yarns. One yarn set is spun yarns that will eventually form the pile surface of the finished fabric. The other set is a heat-sensitive bulk-continuous-filament (BCF) yarn that shrinks when heated. Both yarn sets are knit together to form a very loose jersey-type fabric. The fabric is heat-set and the BCF yarn shrinks creating a dense compact fabric with a spun yarn pile. Finishing produces the appropriate look.

Knit terrycloth is a loop pile fancy fabric used for beachwear, robes, and infant towels and washcloths. It is softer and more absorbent than woven terrycloth but does not hold its shape as well (Figure 14.17). **Velour** is a cut-pile fancy fashion fabric used in men's and women's wear and in robes. Velour is knit with loops that are cut open and sheared to an even pile height. When the yarn untwists in finishing, better cover is achieved (see Figure 14.17).

Sliver-pile knits are made on a special weft-knit, circular sliver-knitting machine. Figure 14.18 shows yarns used for the ground; the sliver furnishes the fibers for the deep pile. Sliver (pronounced slīˉ′ver) is an untwisted rope of fiber made by carding, drawing, or combing (Chapter 10). Fibers from the sliver and the ground yarns are knit into place as the stitch is formed. A denser pile can be obtained with sliver than with yarn because the amount of sliver is not limited by yarn size. **Fake fur** is made when the surface pile is heat-sensitive manufactured fibers that, after finishing, will resemble guard hairs for a more realistic look. Fake fur can be printed to resemble the furs of exotic protected species such as jaguar or leopard. Fibers are solution-dyed or fiber-dyed because piece-dyeing distorts the pile. Fake-fur fabrics are used for coat and jacket shells (the outer layer) and linings. Some sliver knits are used for casual upholstery fabrics and for bath rugs. These fancy furlike sliver knits are lighter weight, more pliable, more comfortable, less expensive, and easier to store than real fur.

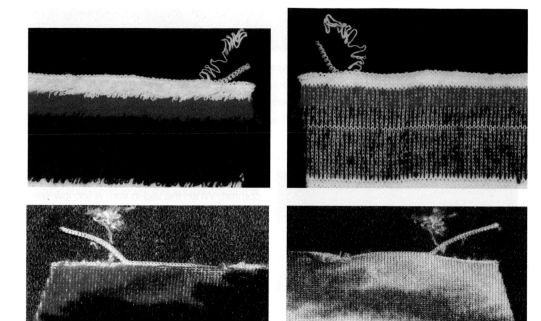

Figure 14.17 Pile-filling knit fabrics: knit terry, face (top left) and back (top right); velour, face (bottom left) and back (bottom right). Note the yarns raveled from each fabric and the side that forms the fashion side of the fabrics.

▶ Learning Activity 8

Examine the knit products you are wearing today. Name the fabric used in each product. Describe the serviceability of one product based on fiber content, yarn type, and fabric structure. Are you satisfied with the performance of this product? Why or why not?

Three-dimensional jersey **spacer fabric** for technical end uses is made by using a plush course with a ground yarn that forms the jersey structure. The fabric can be napped or sheared depending on the end use. Spacer fabrics are used in automobile upholstery and may expand into other applications where cushioning and protection are needed. Spacer fabrics that are circular filling knits are significantly less expensive compared to flat-bed warp knit spacer fabrics. Fabric thickness is limited to less than an inch for filling knit space fabrics.

Weft-Insertion Jerseys In **weft-insertion jersey**, another yarn is laid in a course as it is being knit. This additional yarn is not knit into stitches but is laid or inserted in the loops of the stitches as they are being formed. The laid-in yarn may increase the fancy fabric's crosswise stability, add visual interest if it is novelty or

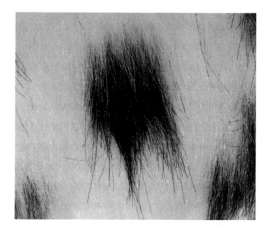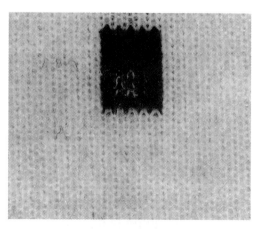

Figure 14.18 Sliver-knit furlike fabric: face (left) and back (right).

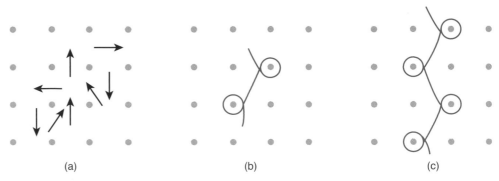

(a)   (b)   (c)

Figure 14.32 Guide-bar movements: (a) All steps of the guide-bar movement. (b) Yarn movement following the guide-bar movement. (c) Series of yarn loops creating the warp-knit fabric.

▶ Learning Activity 13

Use a piece of cardboard and sewing or push pins. Create a grid that is 4 pins wide by 4 pins deep. Select 3 yarns 6 to 12 inches long. Following the arrows in Figures 14.31 and 14.32 create the first series of loops demonstrated. Use the other two yarns and create parallel stitches to make a simple one bar tricot. Identify wales and courses for this sample. The sample will not hold together once the pins are removed unless you insert the new loops on each pin through the loop that was originally on the pin.

▶ Learning Activity 14

Compare the structure of filling and warp knits. Describe how the yarns move in both types of knits. Explain how fabric structure influences the serviceability of knits.

Machines Used in Warp Knitting

Warp knits are classified by the machine used to produce the fabric. Tricot machines use a single set of spring-beard or compound needles. Tricot-knitting machines with computer-controlled guide bars, electronic beam control, and computerized take-up are able to knit 2000 courses per minute. Raschel machines use one or two sets of vertically mounted latch needles. Jacquard raschel knitting machines with computer-controlled guide bars produce complex fancy fabrics for apparel, interior, and technical products. Several types of warp-knitting machines are listed in Table 14.3. Tricot and raschel machines account for more than 98 percent of all warp-knit goods.

Warp-Knit Fabrics

Tricot-Warp Knits The name **tricot** has been a generic name for all warp-knit fabric. Tricot comes from the French word *tricoter*, meaning to knit. It is the fabric produced on the tricot machine using the lock stitch.

The lock stitch is shown in Figure 14.33. The lock stitch is used in most tricots. The face of the fabric is formed of the vertical portion of loops; the back shows the horizontal portion of loops. The face has a much finer appearance than the back. Tricot does not ravel. Lock-knit tricots do not run. However, tricots may split or "zip" between wales. The fabric will curl just as filling-knit

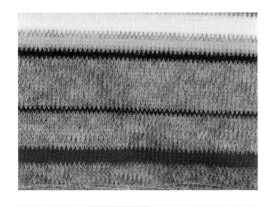

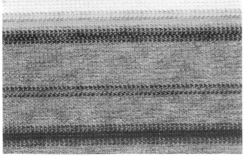

Figure 14.33 Two-bar tricot: technical face (top), technical back (bottom).

Table 14.3 Warp-Knitting Machines

Tricot	Raschel	Simplex	Milanese
Single bed	One or two needle beds	Two sets of needles	Flat—spring-beard needles
Spring-beard or compound needles	Latch needles	Spring-beard needles	Circular—latch needles
Fine gauge	Coarse gauge		
2–3–4 bars indicate number of warp-yarn sets	May have as many as 78 guide bars		Yarn travels diagonally from one side of material to the other
Simple fabric	Complex fancy fabric	Reversible, double-faced fabric with rib appearance	
High-speed, high-volume	Great design possibilities	Seldom used	Seldom used
Usually filament yarns	Spun or spun and filament yarns		
Wider fabric, 170 inches	Narrower fabric, 100 inches		
End Uses			
Plain, patterned, striped, brushed fabric	Sheer laces and nets	Gloves	Underwear
Underwear	Draperies		Outerwear
Outerwear	Power net		Gloves
Upholstery	Thermal cloth		
Technical uses	Outerwear		
	Upholstery		
	Technical uses		

▶ **Learning Activity 15**

Examine the knit products you are wearing today. Are any of these products warp knits? (Hint: You might have to use the restroom to check the structure of intimate apparel.) How can you tell if the fabrics are warp knits? Are you satisfied with the performance of these products? Why or why not?

jersey does. Tricot is more stable than filling knits. It has little elasticity in the lengthwise direction and some elasticity in the crosswise direction. Tricot is used for lingerie, sleepwear, shirts, blouses, uniforms, dresses, and automotive upholstery. Another stitch, the plain stitch, can be used to make tricot, but it runs and is seldom used except for inexpensive backings for quilts and bonded fabrics.

The tricot machine is the mainstay of the warp-knitting industry. It is a high-speed machine that can knit flat fabric up to 170 inches wide. The machine makes a plain-jersey stitch or can be modified to make many designs. Attachments are used to lay in yarns into a tricot structure.

Plain tricot is made on a machine that uses one set of needles and two guide bars. Filament yarns are used in either smooth or textured form. In the standard ranges of 15 to 40 denier, nylon tricot is lightweight (17.5 to 6.5 yards/pound), has exceptional strength and durability, and can be heat-set for dimensional stability. One of the unique features of nylon tricot is that the same piece of gray goods can be finished under different tensions to different widths and different appearances; for example, 168-inch gray goods can be finished at 98, 108, 120, 180, or 200 inches wide.

Fancy warp knit tricots include brushed or napped tricots, satin tricots, tricot net fabrics, and automotive tricot velvet. **Brushed or napped tricots** have fibers raised from the surface,

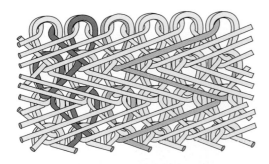

Figure 14.34 Warp-knit velour before napping: green and light blue yarns on the technical back will be broken during finishing.

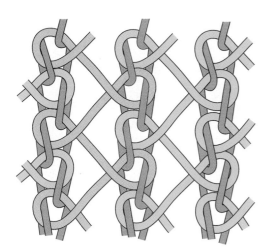

Figure 14.35 Raschel knit.

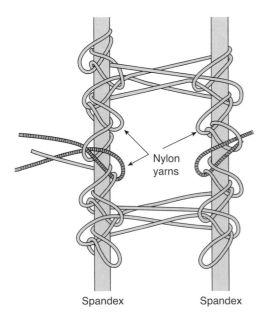

Figure 14.36 Raschel power-knit stitch.

making it feel like velvet. The knit stitches have long underlaps. One set of yarns is carried over three to five wales to form floats on the technical back; the second set of yarns, usually nylon to provide strength and durability, interloops with adjacent yarns. The long floats are broken when the fabric is brushed in finishing. The brushed side is used as the fashion side, even though it is the technical back (Figure 14.34). It is used in loungewear, women's wear, shoes, slacks, upholstery, and draperies.

Satin tricots are made in the same way as napped tricots except that the finishing produces high luster on the technical back. Satin tricots are usually 100 percent nylon or polyester, with long floats and used for lingerie and loungewear.

Tricot-net fabric can be made by skipping every other needle so only half as much yarn is used and open spaces are created in the fabric. **Tulle** (pronounced tool) is a hexagonal net used for veiling, support fabrics, and overlays for apparel. Tulle can be a confusing fabric since it can be made in several ways. Tricot-knit tulle is an inexpensive type of tulle.

Automotive tricot upholstery of a double-knit velvet is made in a manner similar to that of velvet. Two layers of fabric are warp knit face to face with a pile yarn connecting the two layers. The layers are separated when the pile yarn is cut. Pile height is approximately half the distance between the two layers.

Raschel-Warp Knits The raschel-warp-knitting machine has one or two needle beds with latch needles set in a vertical position with up to 78 guide bars. The fabric comes off the knitting frame almost vertically instead of horizontally as with the tricot machine. Raschel machines knit a wide variety of fancy fabrics, from gossamer-sheer nets and veilings to very heavy carpets. Raschel knits are used for such technical products as laundry bags, fish nets, dye nets, safety nets, and swimming pool covers. These knits are usually made with heavier yarns, have more elaborate design, or incorporate more open areas in the design.

Raschel fabrics have rows of chainlike loops called *pillars*, with laid-in yarns in various lapping configurations (Figure 14.35). These fabrics can be identified by raveling the laid-in yarn and noting that the fabric splits or comes apart lengthwise. Some window-treatment and outerwear fabrics are knitted on this machine, sometimes referred to as a raschel-crochet or crochet machine.

Carpets have been knitted since the early 1950s. Since production is faster, knitted carpets are cheaper to make than woven carpets. Another technique, tufting, is the most common method for producing carpet (see Chapter 15). Knitted carpets have two- or three-ply warps for lengthwise stability, laid-in crosswise yarns for body and crosswise stability, and pile yarns. Knitted carpets can be identified by looking for chains of stitches on the underside. They seldom have a secondary backing. These carpets are usually commercial or contract carpets.

Lace and curtain nets can be made at higher speed for low cost on raschel machines. Window-treatment nets of polyester with square, diamond, or hexagonal meshes are made on tricot machines. Light, delicate, and elaborate laces can be made quickly and inexpensively for apparel and interior textiles.

Knit meshes may be made using either tricot or raschel machines, depending on their complexity, yarn size, and end use. Raschel knitting is another way that tulle can be produced.

Thermal cloth has pockets knit in to trap heat from the body; it looks like woven waffle cloth and is used mainly for winter underwear and thermal blankets.

Power net is an elasticized fabric used for foundation garments and bathing suits. Nylon is used for the two-bar ground construction, and spandex or other elastomer is laid in by two other guide bars (Figure 14.36). Although sometimes referred to as spandex, these fabrics are blends of nylon and an elastomer.

► Learning Activity 16

Use Fabrics #87 through 92 from your swatch kit. Determine which of these fabrics is a tricot or raschel knit. Name each fabric and describe the characteristics that assisted you in naming them. (Figure 14.2 will be of assistance here.) Are you wearing any fabrics similar to these? If so, in what kind of products is this fabric used?

Warp knit **spacer fabric** has two fabric layers that are produced separately and joined with another yarn set. A wide variety of possibilities exist for the structure of the two fabrics, the joining yarn, and the thickness of the three-dimensional fabric. These fabrics are used in vehicle seat covers, interiors, seat heating systems, and mud flaps.

Insertion Warp Knits Insertion of yarns in the warp-knit structure is a relatively simple concept. Yarns are laid in the stitches during the knitting process but are not used to form any stitches. These laid-in yarns provide directional stability and can be in any direction or at an angle. Fabric characteristics can be engineered for desired properties. Yarns that are not appropriate for knitting can be used, such as extremely coarse, fine, or irregular yarns and yarns of fibers such as carbon and glass that have low flexibility. Insertion fabrics are used in aircraft and aerospace components, automotive parts, boat hulls, ballistic protective apparel, structural building elements, outerwear, interlinings for apparel, window treatments, and wall coverings.

Weft insertion is done by a warp-knitting machine with a weft-laying attachment. An attachment carries a single filling yarn to and fro across the machine, and this yarn is fed steadily into the needle zone of the machine. A firm selvage is formed on each side.

More complex attachments supply a sheet of filling yarns to a conveyor that travels to and fro across the machine. The yarns are then fed into the stitching area of the machine. A cutting device trims filling yarn "tails" from the selvages and a vacuum removes the tails.

Weft-insertion fabrics combine the best properties of both woven and knitted cloth, namely strength, comfort, cover without bulk, and weight. They are lighter weight than double-knits with more covering power. They have the increased crosswise stability of weaves but retain the comfort of knits.

In **warp-insertion warp knits**, the inserted yarn is caught in a vertical chain of stitching. The insertion of warp yarn into a knit structure gives the fabric the vertical stability of woven fabric while retaining the horizontal stretch of knit fabric. These fabrics are used for curtains, table linens, and other interior and technical uses.

Fabrics with both warp and weft insertion have characteristics very similar to woven fabrics, but at much lower costs and wider widths. They are frequently used as window-treatment fabrics (Figure 14.37). These fabrics can be confused with stitch-bonded fabrics (see Chapter 15). Careful examination will show that the warp-knit fabrics with inserted yarns have the fine-filament yarns knitting *around* the inserted yarns, not *through* them.

Minor Warp Knits

Simplex The **simplex machine** is similar to the tricot machine and uses spring-beard needles, two needle bars, and two guide bars. It produces a two-faced ribbed fabric somewhat like circular double-knits. End uses are primarily fashion gloves.

Milanese The **Milanese machine** produces diagonal warp-knit fabrics. The machine can use both spring-beard and latch needles. The fabric, similar to a two-bar tricot fabric, is made from

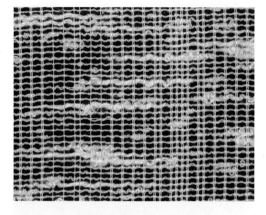

Figure 14.37 Warp-knit, weft-insertion casement fabric for windows.

There are two types of warp knits. Tricots use one or more yarn sets and guide bars to create basic warp knits. Tricot types include tricot (a simple, regular warp knit), brushed tricot, satin tricot, and tulle. **Raschel** knits have rows of chainlike loops called *pillars*, with laid-in yarns in various lapping configurations. Examples include raschel and lace.

Narrow knitted fabrics are made on a few needles on either filling- or warp-knitting machines. Narrow knit fabrics include knit elastics, trims, and edgings.

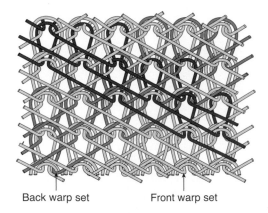

Back warp set   Front warp set

Figure 14.38   Milanese.

two sets of warp yarns, with one needle bar and one guide bar. The lapping movements take each warp yarn diagonally across the full width of the fabric, one set knitting from right to left and the other from left to right. The diagonal formation (Figure 14.38) is visible on the back of the fabric. The face has a very fine rib. The fabric is runproof and is used for gloves, lingerie, and outerwear.

Narrow Knitted Fabrics

Narrow knitted fabrics are made on a few needles on either filling- or warp-knitting machines. One of the more important types of narrow knitted fabrics is knit elastics. Knit elastics account for 35 to 40 percent of the narrow elastic market and are used in underwear, actionwear, slacks, fleece products, and hosiery. Hook and loop tape fasteners are warp-knit narrow fabrics. Other trim and knit elastics are shown in Figure 14.39.

Many narrow knitted fabrics of thermoplastic fiber are made on regular machines in wide widths and slit with hot knives to seal the edges. These are cheaper to produce and are satisfactory if properly heat sealed.

Figure 14.39   Narrow fabrics centre to right: raschel knit (2 samples), double-knit, and circular knit.

Warp Knits Versus Filling Knits

Warp and filling knits differ because techniques and machines used in their manufacture differ. These differences are summarized in Table 14.4.

> ▶ **Learning Activity 17**

Examine the textile products you are wearing or have with you today. Do any of these products include narrow knit fabrics? (Hint: You might have to use the restroom to check straps and bands of intimate apparel.) How you can you tell if the fabrics are knit? Where are narrow knit fabrics used? Are you satisfied with the performance of this product? Why or why not?

Table 14.4 Comparison of Filling and Warp Knits

Filling Knits	Warp Knits
Yarns run horizontally	Yarns run vertically
Loops joined one to another in the same course	Loops joined one to another in adjoining course
Loops connect horizontally	Loops connect diagonally
More design possibilities	Higher productivity
More open fabric	More compact fabric
Two-way stretch	Crosswise stretch, little lengthwise stretch
Run, most ravel	Most do not run or ravel
Hand or machine process	Machine process only
Flat or circular	Flat
Finished edges possible	Seldom have finished edges
Produced as shaped garments, garment pieces, or yardage	Produced as yardage only

key terms

review questions

1. Compare the characteristics of woven and knit fabrics.

2. Compare the characteristics of filling- and warp-knit fabrics.

3. Explain how these terms compare between woven and knit fabrics:
   a. Wale and warp
   b. Course and filling
   c. Count and gauge

4. What are the factors that are used in assessing quality of knit fabrics?

5. Describe the differences in appearance and performance between the following pairs of knit fabrics:
   a. Jersey and tricot
   b. Jacquard jersey and raschel
   c. Rib knit and interlock
   d. Fleece and velour
   e. Lace and tulle

6. Describe the performance that might be expected in the following products:
   a. 100 percent combed cotton filling-knit jersey T-shirt
   b. 100 percent modacrylic warp-insertion raschel casement drapery (smooth filament yarns and inserted thick-and-thin novelty yarns) for a public library

   c. 100 percent olefin raschel warp-knit contract carpet of BCF yarns for hallway of office building
   d. 80 percent nylon/20 percent spandex raschel-knit swimsuit

7. Compare the characteristics of a jersey and a tricot of similar quality.

8. Explain how pile knit fabrics are made.

9. Describe how knits that are to be brushed or napped are made. How do the yarns differ between the pile and the base or ground structure?

10. Explain why some knits are made with additional inserted yarns. How do the inserted yarns differ from the yarns used to create the base or ground structure? In what kinds of products are insertion knits used? How does the additional yarn alter serviceability and performance of the product?

11. How would the structure of a knit differ with each of these stitches? In what kinds of knit fabrics would these stitches be used?
    a. Knit stitch
    b. Tuck stitch
    c. Miss stitch
    d. Purl stitch

OTHER FABRICATION METHODS

CHAPTER OBJECTIVES

- To understand the production of film, foam, fiberweb and netlike structures, lace, braid, composite fabrics, leather, and fur.
- To recognize fabrics made using these techniques.
- To integrate the performance of these fabrics with end-use requirements.

15

339

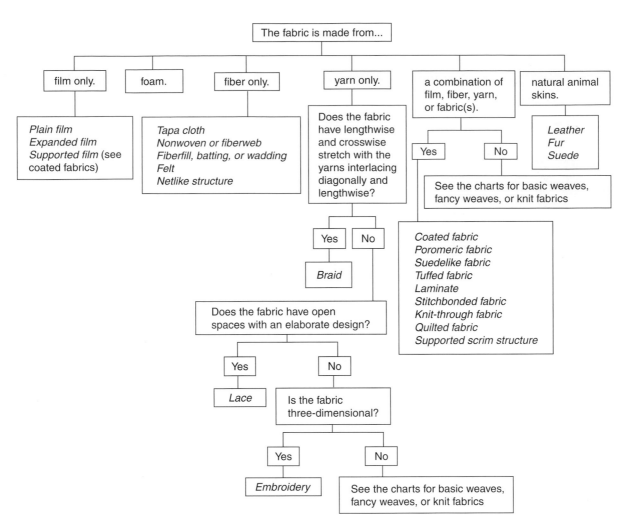

Figure 15.1 Flowchart for other fabrication methods.

There are many ways of producing fabric other than weaving and knitting. This chapter is organized according to the material from which these additional fabrics are made: solutions, fibers, yarns, or fabrics. Although many of these methods and fabrics do not fit the classic definition of a textile, they are included because they are used in textile products or as substitutes for textiles, they are made of the same chemicals as textiles, or they are made of textile components like fibers, yarns, and fabrics. These fabrics are important to the apparel, interiors, and technical markets. This discussion begins with the simplest process and component and moves to the most complex. Assessing the performance of these fabrics is often similar to the procedures used for woven or knit fabrics. Whenever special procedures are used, they will be discussed in the appropriate section. Figure 15.1 can be used to determine the fabric structure and name.

Fabrics From Solutions

Films

Films are made directly from a polymer solution by melt-extrusion or by casting the solution onto a hot drum. Film solutions are similar to fiber spinning solutions.

Most apparel and interior textile films are made from vinyl or polyurethane solutions (Table 15.1). The two types are similar in appearance, but they vary in their care requirements.

Table 15.1 Films Made from Solutions

Solution	Fiber	Film	End Uses for Film
Acetate	Acetate	Acetate	Photographic film, projection film
Polyamide	Nylon	Nylon	Cooking bags
Polyester	Polyester	Mylar*	Packaging, metallic yarns, novelty balloons
Polypropylene	Olefin		
Polyethylene		Polyethylene	Packaging, garment and shopping bags, squeeze bottles
Polyurethane	Spandex	Polyurethane	Leatherlike fabrics
Polyvinyl chloride	Vinyon	Vinyl	Packaging, garment bags, leatherlike fabrics for apparel and upholstery, seed tapes, water-soluble bags
Vinylidene chloride	Saran	Saran Wrap*	Packaging for food
Viscose (regenerated cellulose)	Rayon	Cellophane	Glitter weaving yarns—mostly in handwoven textiles

*Trade names.

Vinyl films are washable but become stiff and brittle when exposed to dry-cleaning solvents or cold temperatures. Urethane films are both washable and dry-cleanable. Urethane films remain soft in cold weather.

There are several structures of films. **Plain films** or *nonreinforced films* are firm, dense, and uniform. They are usually impermeable to air and water and have excellent soil and stain resistance and good recovery from deformation. Plain films such as latex, chloroprene, vinyl, and nitrile are used in disposable gloves for health-care workers because they provide a barrier for fluid-borne pathogens.

Expanded films are spongier, softer, and plumper because a blowing agent incorporates tiny air cells into the compound. They are not as strong or as abrasion-resistant as plain films. Expanded films are impermeable to air and water. Thousands of tiny pinholes, called *micropores*, punched in plain and expanded films permit air and water vapor, but not liquid water, to pass through the fabric, increasing their comfort characteristics. Nonporous films, used for inexpensive upholstery, are uncomfortable, especially in hot weather and in direct contact with skin.

Because plain films and expanded films are seldom durable enough to withstand normal use, they are usually attached to a woven, knit, or fiberweb support fabric or substrate. The end result is a supported, *coated*, or *reinforced* film. **Supported films** are composite fabrics and will be discussed later in this chapter. Supported films are more durable, more expensive, easier to sew, and less likely to crack and split than nonreinforced films.

Plastic films and coated fabrics are more waterproof than any other material. With finishing, they can be made to resemble almost any other textile (Figure 15.2). They vary in thickness from the very thin transparent film used to make sandwich bags to the heavy leatherette used to cover a dentist's chair. As compared with leather, films are uniform in appearance and quality, available in uniformly wide lengths, and much cheaper and easier to make into products.

This list briefly summarizes films:

- Solution is extruded through narrow slits into warm air or cast onto a revolving drum. Molding powders may be pressed between hot rolls.
- Films are waterproof, impermeable, stiff, low cost, resistant to soil, and nonfibrous.
- Films have poor drapeability and are weak unless supported by a fabric back.
- Films can be finished to look like many other fabrics or to have their own characteristic appearance.
- Films are used for shoes, shower curtains, upholstery, and bags.

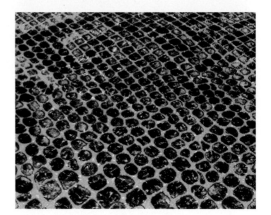

Figure 15.2 Film embossed and printed to resemble snakeskin.

Films are made directly from a polymer solution by melt-extrusion or by casting the solution onto a hot drum. Types of films include plain, expanded, and reinforced. Films are used for apparel, interior, and technical products.

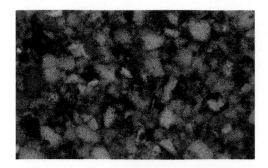

Figure 15.3   Foam carpet pad.

Foams are made by incorporating air into an elasticlike substance. Most foams are used to pad or shape textile products.

Foams

Foams are made by incorporating air into an elasticlike substance. Polyurethane is most common. Foams are known for their bulkiness and sponginess. They are used as carpet backings and underlays, furniture padding, and pillow forms and are laminated to fabric for apparel and interior textiles (Figure 15.3). Shredded foam is used to stuff accent pillows and toys.

Polyurethane foams are made with a wide range of physical properties, from very stiff to rubbery. The size of the air cells can be controlled. Polyurethane foam yellows when exposed to sunlight but does not lose its usefulness and durability. Foams are relatively weak and are not used by themselves. Reacting diisocyanate with a compound containing two or more hydroxyl groups and a suitable catalyst produces polyurethane foam. Chemicals and foaming agents are mixed thoroughly. After the foam is formed, it is cut into blocks 200 to 300 yards long, and strips of the desired thickness are cut from these blocks.

While foams have traditionally been based on petroleum-based products, soy-based foams are being used for some foam applications like intimate apparel. Soy-based foams are sustainable and do not yellow. They are also stable to light. Polyurethane based foams used in the automotive industry are being replaced by woven, knit, and nonwoven spacer fabrics. (See nonwovens in this chapter and Chapters 13 and 14.)

This list briefly summarizes foams:

- Foams are made by incorporating air into an elasticlike substance. Rubber and polyurethane are the most commonly used foams.
- Foams are lofty, springy, bulky material, too weak to be used without backing or covering.
- Polyurethane foams do not age well and discolor and lose elasticity when exposed to heat and light.
- Foams are used to shape and pad pillows, chair cushions, mattresses, carpet padding, and apparel, including shoulder pads and intimate apparel, and to add thickness and warmth in inexpensive outerwear as laminates (discussed later in this chapter).

Fabrics From Fibers

Some fabrics are made directly from fibers or fiber-forming solutions; thus, there is no processing of fibers into a yarn. These operations include very old and very new processes. The origins of felt and tapa cloth are lost in antiquity; netlike structures used to bag fruits and vegetables use new technologies; and composite fabrics are made by combining fibers with other materials to form fabrics.

Tapa cloth, the first fiberweb, is made from the fibrous inner bark of the fig or paper mulberry tree. It was used for clothing by people in many areas of the Pacific Islands and Central America. The cloth is made from the inner bark by soaking it to loosen the fibers, beating with a mallet, smoothing into a paperlike sheet, and decorating with block prints (Figure 15.4).

Nonwoven or Fiberweb Structures

Today, fabric made from fibers is a growing area of the textile industry. These fabrics usually have technical uses, but some are used in apparel and interior items. Research and development focusing on technical fabrics expands markets for fiber companies.

These fabrics are often referred to as **nonwovens** since they are not made from yarn. However, the term *nonwoven* creates confusion because knits are nonwovens as well.

Figure 15.4   Tapa cloth.

Nonwoven refers to a wide variety of fabric structures. In the textile complex, *nonwoven* refers to a fiberweb structure.

Increased usage of nonwovens is related to the cost of traditional textiles that include labor costs and fluctuating costs of natural fibers. Nonwovens are less expensive because some are produced during production of manufactured fibers and because of lower costs for unskilled labor to cut and sew these fabrics, and new technologies that produce made-to-order products inexpensively.

Nonwoven or **fiberweb structures** include all textile-sheet structures made from fibrous webs, bonded by mechanical fiber entanglement, by resin, by thermal fusion, or by forming chemical complexes. Fibers are the fundamental units of structure, arranged into a web and bonded so that the distances between fibers are several times greater than the fiber diameter. Nonwovens are more flexible than paper structures of similar construction.

The properties of nonwovens are controlled by the arrangement of the fibers in the web, the properties of the fibers used in the web, and the properties of any binders used.

Web Production Fiberwebs are quick and inexpensive to produce. Nonwoven fabrics of the same weight and fiber type as woven fabrics are often half the cost.

The basic steps include selecting the fibers, laying the fibers to make a web, and bonding the web together to make a fabric. Any fiber can be used to make the web. The fibers' inherent characteristics are reflected in the fabric: Filaments and strong staple fibers are used for strength and durability; cellulosics are used for absorbency; thermoplastics are used for spun-bonded webs.

Five techniques are used to form the web: dry-laid, wet-laid, spun-bonded, spun-lace, and melt-blown. Fiber orientation controls web characteristics and describes both fibers that are parallel in the web and with machine direction, the direction in which the supporting conveyor belt moves. Oriented webs have fibers parallel to each other. Webs in which the fibers are highly parallel to each other and to the machine direction are *oriented* in the lengthwise direction. Random webs have fibers that are not parallel to each other. Lengthwise-oriented webs have grain. Strength and drape are related to fiber orientation.

Dry-laid fiberwebs are made by carding or air-laying the fibers in either a random or an oriented arrangement. Air-laid webs can be made with very short fibers, especially important for recycling cotton waste from spinning mills. Carding is similar to the yarn process that produces a parallel arrangement of fibers. Webs can be cross-laid by stacking the carded web so that one layer is oriented lengthwise and the next layer crosswise to give added strength and pliability. *Cross-laid webs* do not have grain and can be cut more economically than woven or knitted fabrics. *Air-laid*, or *random, webs* are made by machines that disperse the fibers by air. While similar to the cross-laid web, this web has a random fiber arrangement. Oriented webs have good strength, low elongation, and low tear strength in the direction of orientation, but poor cross-orientation strength. Elongation and tear strength are higher in the cross-orientation direction. With random webs, strength is uniform in all directions. End uses for dry-laid fiberwebs include wipes, wicks, battery separators, backing for quilted fabrics, interlining, insulation, abrasive fabric bases, filters, and base fabric for laminating and coating.

Wet-laid fiberwebs are made from a slurry of short paper-process-length and textile-length fibers and water. The water is extracted and reclaimed, leaving a randomly oriented fiberweb. These webs are exceptionally uniform. Typical end uses for wet-laid fiberwebs include laminating and coating bases, filters, interlining, insulation, roofing substrates, adhesive carriers, wipes, and battery separators.

Figure 15.5 Spun-bonded filament fabric.

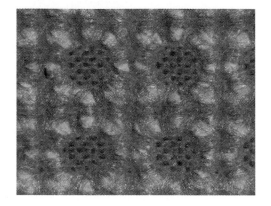

Figure 15.6 Hydroentangled or spun-lace fabric.

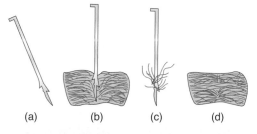

(a)　　　(b)　　　(c)　　　(d)

Figure 15.7 Needle-punch process: (a) barbed needle, (b) needle pulling fibers through web, (c) entangled fibers in a web cross section, (d) needle-punched web; (bottom) photo of fabric.

Spun-bonded or spun-laid webs are made immediately after melt-spun fibers are extruded from spinnerets. Fiber options include olefin, polyester, and nylon. The continuous hot filaments are laid down in a random fashion on a fast-moving conveyor belt in a semimelted state and fuse together at cross points. They may be further bonded by heat and pressure. Spun-bonded fiberwebs have high tensile and tear strength and low bulk (Figure 15.5). They are durable, lightweight, and have good air permeability. End uses for spun-bonded fiberwebs include hygiene products (diapers, feminine care), medical protective apparel, carpet backings, geotextiles, adhesive carriers, envelopes, tents and tarps, wall coverings, house-wrap vapor barriers, tags and labels, bags, filters, insulation, and roofing substrates. Spunbonding is the fastest and most economical way of producing nonwoven fabrics.

Hydroentangled or **spun-lace webs** are similar to spun-bonded webs except that jets of water are forced through the web, shattering the filaments into staple fibers and producing a wovenlike structure (Figure 15.6). When the drum that applies the water jets to the web is perforated in a design, the resulting web will incorporate that design. Spun-lace webs have greater elasticity and flexibility than spun-bonded webs. These webs are also known as water-needled fabrics. This technique makes products that are not possible with any other process. High-pressure jets of water from both sides entangle the fibers. The water is reclaimed, purified, and recycled. The degree of entanglement is controlled by the number and force of jets and the fiber type. Hydroentangled textiles are used in medical gowns and drapes, battery separators, interlinings, roofing substrates, filters, mattress pads, household wipes, wall coverings, window-treatment components, and protective apparel.

Melt-blown fiberwebs are made by extruding the polymer through a single orifice into a high-velocity heated-air stream that breaks the ultrafine fiber into short pieces. The fiber pieces are collected as a web on a moving conveyor belt and held together by fiber interlacing and thermal bonding. The fibers are not drawn so fiberweb strength is lower. Olefin and polyester are used to produce hospital/medical products, wipes, filters, sanitary applications, and battery separators.

The **spunmelt** process combines spun-bonded and melt-blown technology for applications where bicomponent or biconstituent webs are needed for barrier and filtration applications.

Fabric Production Webs have very little strength in the unbounded form. They become fabrics through mechanical needling or application of chemical compounds, adhesives, or heat.

In **needle punching** or needling, a dry-laid web passes over a needle loom as many times as is necessary to produce the desired strength and texture. A needle loom has barbed needles protruding 2 to 3 inches from the base (Figure 15.7). As the needles stitch up and down through the web, the barbs pull a few fibers through the web, interlocking them mechanically with other fibers. This process is a relatively inexpensive way to produce blankets, carpeting, and carpet backing. Fiber denier, fiber type, and product loft vary. Indoor/outdoor olefin needle-punched carpeting is used for patios, porches, pools, and putting greens because it is impervious to moisture. Needled carpet backings are used with some tufted carpets.

Needled fabrics can be made of a two-layer web with each layer a different color. Pulling colored fibers from the lower layer to the top surface creates geometric designs. Fibers pulled above the surface produce a pile fabric. Needle-punched fabrics are finished by pressing, steaming, calendering, dyeing, and embossing.

Thick needled spacer fabrics are also possible and competitive with foams for such applications as padding and cushioning automotive seats. While the nonwoven spacer fabric is less uniform in appearance, it has good air and water permeability and can be recycled easily. Other end uses for needled fabrics include cleaning wipes, medical/hygiene uses, insulation, protective apparel, shoulder pads, roofing substrates, paper machine felts, craft felts, floor and wall coverings, blankets, and carpet backing.

Other techniques include the use of a closed needle that penetrates the web, opens, grabs some fibers, and draws them back as a yarnlike structure to chain-stitch through the web. (See the stitch-through fabrics discussed later in this chapter.) Needle-punched fabrics are used for tennis-ball felts, blood filters, papermaking felt, speaker-cover fabrics, synthetic leathers, oil-absorbent pads, some ballistic vests, and insulator padding.

Chemical adhesives are used with dry-laid or wet-laid webs to bond the fibers together. Adhesives include vinyl acetate ethylene copolymers, styrene-butadiene copolymers, and acrylate polymers and copolymers. Most are water-based binders. Each one has characteristics that make it appropriate for certain applications. The adhesive is applied in a liquid, powder, or foam form. Heat and pressure are used to bond thermoplastic-fiber webs. Several techniques are used. In *area-bond calendering*, the fibers are heated and pressed to form a permeable film-like structure that is stiff, inextensible, and strong. In *point-bond calendering*, the heated fiber web passes between two calender rolls: one is engraved and the other is smooth. The engraved roller presses the web onto the smooth roller and the fibers adhere to each other. Characteristics relate to the size and density of the bond points. Fabrics are usually moderately bulky, elastic, and soft and are used for medical, sanitary, and filtration applications.

Nonwovens can be finished to meet customer needs. Options include coating, laminating, printing, flocking, dyeing, or finishing for special purposes such as being flame retardant, water repellent, antistatic, breathable, or absorbent.

Fiberfill Batting, wadding, and fiberfill are not fabrics, but they are important components in apparel for snowsuits, ski jackets, quilted robes, and coats and in interior textiles for quilts, comforters, furniture paddings, pillows, mattresses, and mattress pads.

Batting is made from new fiber, **wadding** is made from waste fiber, and **fiberfill** is a manufactured fiber staple made especially for use as a filler. Carded fibers are laid down to the desired thickness and may be covered with a sheet of nonwoven fabric.

Fiber density describes the weight or mass per unit volume. Fiber density is used to match components to end-use requirements for resiliency and weight. Resilient fabrics maintain their loft and incorporate more air space. When fibers stay crushed, the fabric becomes thinner and more compact, losing bulk, insulating power, and padding. **Shifting resistance** is important in maintaining a uniform fabric thickness. For instance, down comforters need to be shaken often because the filling shifts to the outer edges. Thermoplastic-fiber batts can be run through a needle-punch machine where hot needles melt the fiber areas that they touch, fusing them into a more stable batt known as a bonded web. The ability of a batt or fiberfill to insulate is based on the amount of still air trapped in a volume of fabric and the number of fibers present. In apparel there is a limit to fabric thickness because too much bulk restricts movement and limits styling. For this reason, microfibers are popular in low-profile fiberfills (Table 15.2). Several fiberfills are made from recycled polyester fibers.

> **Nonwoven** or **fiberweb structures** include all textile-sheet structures made from fibrous webs, bonded by mechanical fiber entanglement, by resin, by thermal fusion, or by forming chemical complexes. Fibers are the fundamental units of structure, arranged into a web and bonded so that the distances between fibers are several times greater than the fiber diameter. Fiberwebs are used for technical applications and to shape and support apparel and interior products. Types include dry-laid, wet-laid, spun-bonded, spun-lace, melt-blown, spun-melt, and needle-punched.

Table 15.2 Comparison of Properties of Commonly Used Battings

Fiber	Cost	Density	Resiliency	Shifting Resistance	Care
Down	High	Lightweight	Excellent	Poor	Dry-cleanable
Acetate	Low	1.30	Fair	Poor	Washable, dries more quickly than cotton
Polyester	Medium	1.30–1.38	Good	Good—can be bonded	Washable, quick-drying
Cotton	Low	1.52	Poor	Poor	Washable, slow-drying

Polyester fiberfills for apparel include high-loft varieties and hollow-fiber varieties with voids to increase loft and insulation while minimizing weight and microfiber varieties. Primaloft® is a microdenier polyester fiberfill by Albany International Research Company; it mimics down in weight and loft and is used in bedding.

Although not fibers, down and feathers are used as fiberfill. These fills are defined by the Federal Trade Commission in the Code of Federal Regulations. **Down** refers to the undercoating of waterfowl (ducks or geese) and relates to the fine, bulky underfeathers. Items labeled "100 percent down" must meet specific requirements for the down. Down-filled items must be 80 percent down or down fiber and may include up to 20 percent other feathers. Down is rated by its *loft capacity* or fill power—the volume one cubic ounce of down will fill. For example, 650 down is warmer and more expensive than 550 down. The range is generally 300 to 800.

Down is lightweight and warm. However, it has a tendency to shift, and when wet, it mats and loses its warmth. Challenges with down are maintaining its original loft and cleaning it. Some people are allergic to down and feathers. Down is used in apparel, bedding, and padding for pillows and soft furniture.

Figure 15.8 Fusible interlining. The coin under the web demonstrates its sheerness.

Fusible Nonwovens **Fusible nonwovens** contribute body and shape to garments as interfacing or interlinings in shirts, blouses, dresses, and outerwear.

A fusible is a fabric that has been coated with a heat-sealable, thermoplastic adhesive or a thin spider-web-like fabric of thermoplastic filaments (Figure 15.8). When placed on the back of a face fabric, the layers are bonded by heat and pressure.

Possible adhesives are polyethylene, hydrolyzed ethylene vinyl acetate, plasticized polyvinyl chloride, and polyamides. The adhesive is printed on the substrate so as to produce the desired hand in the end product.

Fusibles eliminate the need for stitching in some coat and suit lapels. Less skilled labor is required to produce garments and increase productivity. However, fusibles may generate problems involving differential shrinkage and separation of layers during care, bleed-through of adhesive to the face fabric, and unpredictable changes in hand and drape.

End Uses of Nonwovens Nonwovens are used for disposable goods, such as diapers and wipes, durable goods that are incorporated into other products, or used alone for draperies, furniture, mattresses, mattress pads, and some apparel (Table 15.3).

Table 15.3 Uses of Nonwovens

Durable	Type	Disposable	Type
Bedding and coated fabrics, mattress ticking, backings for quilting, dust cloths for box springs	Spun-bonded	Diapers, underpads, sanitary supplies	Dry-laid
	Needled, spunbonded, dry-laid		Dry-laid, melt-blown
Carpet backings, coated fabrics		Surgical packs and accessories	Dry- or wet-laid
Filters	Dry- or wet-laid		
Interfacings	Needled, dry-laid	Wipes and towels	Spun-bonded
Interlinings	Dry- and wet-laid, spun-bonded, hydroentangled, melt-blown	Packaging	Spunmelt
Draperies, upholstered furniture, backings, facings, dust covers, automotive, shoe parts, geotextiles, labels, backings for wall coverings, leatherlike fabrics, craft felts			

To summarize, nonwovens are

- Produced by bonding and/or interlocking fibers by mechanical, chemical, or thermal, or combinations of these processes.
- Cheaper than woven or knitted fabrics and widely used for disposable or durable items, and some have grain.
- Used for apparel, interior, and technical purposes.

Felt

True **felt** is a mat or web of wool, or mostly wool, fibers held together by the interlocking of the wool scales. Felting is one of the oldest methods of making fabric. Early peoples made felt by washing wool fleece, spreading out the wet wool, and beating it until it had matted and shrunk into fabriclike form. In modern factories, layers of wool or wool blends are built up until the desired thickness is attained and then heat, soap, and vibration are used to mat the fibers together. Finishing processes for felt resemble those for woven fabrics. Most craft felts are not true felt because they do not include wool. They are usually wet- or dry-laid nonwoven fiberwebs.

Felts do not have grain and do not ravel. They are stiff, less pliable, and weaker than other structures. The quality of felt depends on the quality of the fibers used.

Felt has many technical and some apparel uses. It is used for padding, soundproofing, insulation, filtering, polishing, and wicking.

Felt is not used for fitted apparel because it lacks the flexibility and elasticity of fabrics made from yarns. However, it is widely used in products such as hats, slippers, applied design, and pennants. Because felt does not fray, it needs no seam finish. Colored felt letters or decorations on apparel may fade in washing and should be removed before washing or the garments should be dry-cleaned.

The following are characteristics of felt:

- Wool fibers are carded (and combed), laid down in a thick batt, sprayed with water, and agitated, causing the fibers to entangle (Figure 15.9).
- Felt has no grain; it does not fray or ravel.
- Felt has poor pliability, strength, and stretch recovery.
- Felt is used in apparel accessories, crafts, and technical matting.

Netlike Structures

Netlike structures include all textile structures formed by extruding one or more fiber-forming polymers as a film or a network of ligaments or strands. In the *fibrillated-net process*, the extruded and noncoagulated film is embossed as it passes through a pair of heated and engraved rollers that form a pattern on the fabric. When the film is stretched biaxially, slits occur, creating a netlike structure. In the *extruded-net process*, the spinneret consists of two rotating dies.

Figure 15.9   Felt.

True **felt** is a mat or web of wool, or mostly wool, fibers held together by the interlocking of the wool scales. Felt is used for apparel, interior, craft, and technical products.

▶ Learning Activity 1

Examine the textile products you are wearing and have with you today. Which items include films, foams, fiberwebs/nonwovens, fiberfill, felt, or netlike structures? Describe your satisfaction with and the serviceability of one of each of these items based on fiber content, yarn type, and fabric structure. Identify the fabrication method, end use, and serviceability of the items. Explain why these fabrication methods were used.

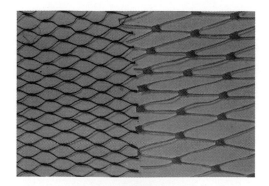

Figure 15.10 Netlike structures.

Netlike structures include all textile structures formed by extruding one or more fiber-forming polymers as a film or a network of ligaments or strands. Netlike structures are used for technical products.

► **Learning Activity 2**

Use Fabrics #94 through 99 from your swatch kit. List the textile components used to produce these fabrics, the fabrication method used, and an appropriate application for each. Examine the key for the swatch kit and describe the serviceability that you would predict for each swatch based on application, fiber content, and fabrication method.

► **Learning Activity 3**

Film, foam, tapa cloth, fiberweb, fiberfill, felt, and netlike structures differ from woven and knit fabrics in what fundamental way(s)? Identify the basic structural unit for these fabrics and describe how the fabrication method of these simpler structures affects serviceability.

When the polymer is extruded, the fibers form single strands that interconnect when holes in the two rotating dies coincide. The process produces tubular nets used for packaging fruits and vegetables, agricultural nets, bird nets, and plastic fencing for snow and hazards (Figure 15.10).

Fabrics From Yarns

Braids

Braids are narrow fabrics in which yarns interlace lengthwise and diagonally (Figure 15.11). They have good elongation characteristics and are very pliable, curving around edges nicely. They are used for trims, shoelaces, and coverings on components in technical products such as wiring and hoses for liquids like gasoline and water. Sennit is a type of hand-made braid using basketry, fibrous inner bark, or related materials. Three-dimensional braids are made with two or more sets of yarns. Their shape is controlled by an internal mandrel.

Figure 15.11 Braids.

The characteristics of braid include the following:

- Yarns are interlaced both diagonally and lengthwise.
- Braid is stretchy and easily shaped.
- Flat or three-dimensional braid is used for trim and technical products.

Lace

Lace is an openwork fabric with complex patterns or figures, handmade or machine-made using several fabrication methods. Most commercial lace is made using raschel knitting machines or special lace machines. Yarns may be twisted around each other to create open areas. Lace is classified according to the way it is made and its appearance.

► **Learning Activity 4**

Explain the differences and similarities in structural component and fabrication method between braids and tricot knits. How do the yarns move in braids and knits? How does fabrication method affect serviceability for these two structures?

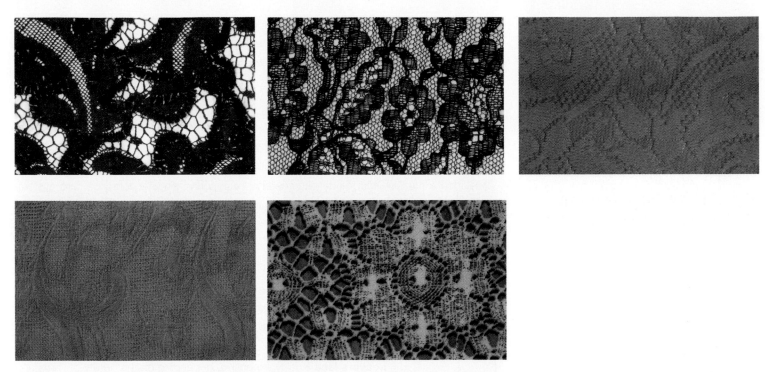

Figure 15.12 Lace and lacelike fabrics: cordonnet or re-embroidered lace made on Leavers lace machine (upper left), raschel warp-knit lace (upper center), double-knit lace (upper right), woven lace (lower left), and Imitation lace (cotton printed with a lacelike design) (bottom center).

It is difficult to determine the machine used to make a fine lace fabric without the aid of a microscope. Some imitation lacelike fabrics are made by printing or flocking (Figure 15.12). The quality of lace is based on the fineness of yarns, number of yarns per square inch or closeness of the ground, and intricacy of the design.

Lace was important in fashion between the 16th and the 19th centuries, and all countries in Europe developed lace industries. Lace remains important today as a trim or accessory in apparel and interiors. Lace names often reflect the town in which the lace was originally made. For example, the best-quality needlepoint lace was made in Venice in the 16th century—hence the name *Venetian lace*. Alençon and Valenciennes laces are made in French towns.

Handmade Lace Handmade lace remains a prestige textile. With the contemporary interest in crafts, many of the old lace-making techniques are experiencing renewed interest. Handmade lace is used for wall hangings, belts, bags, shawls, afghans, bedspreads, and tablecloths. Handmade laces include needlepoint, bobbin, crochet, and Battenberg.

Needlepoint lace is made by drawing a pattern on paper, laying down yarns over the pattern, and stitching over the yarns with needle and thread. The thread network forming the ground is called *reseau* or *brides*. The solid part of the pattern is *toile*. Needlepoint designs may include birds, flowers, and vases.

Bobbin lace is made on a pillow. The pattern is drawn on paper and pins are inserted at various points. Yarns on bobbins are plaited around the pins to form the lace (Figure 15.13).

Crocheted lace is made by hand with a crochet hook. Examples are Irish lace and Syrian lace.

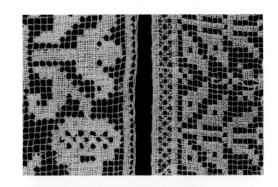

Figure 15.13 Bobbin lace: handmade (left), machine-made (right).

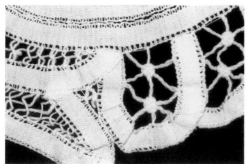

Figure 15.14 Close-up view of a Battenberg lace tablecloth.

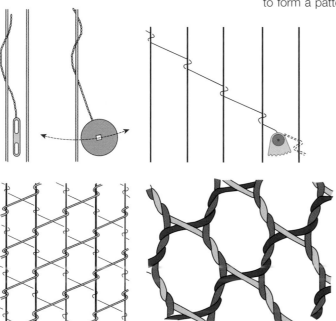

Figure 15.15 Brass bobbins (upper left) carry the thread and twist around warp yarns (upper right and lower left) to form the lace fabric (lower right).

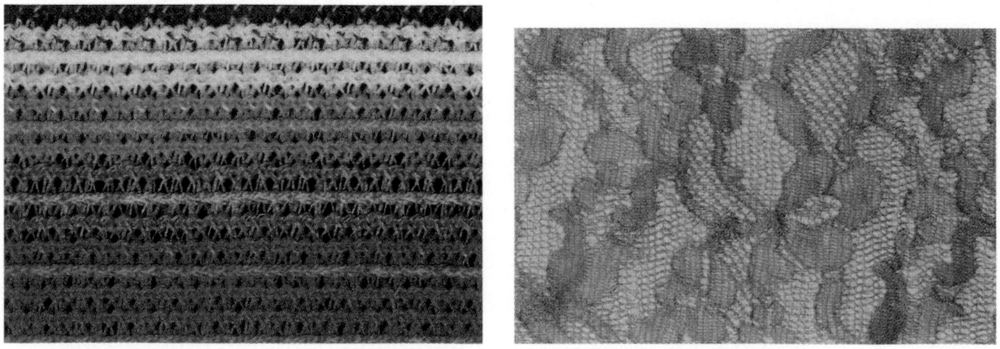

Figure 15.16 Raschel crochet (top), raschel lace (bottom).

Battenberg lace is handmade with loops of woven tape attached by yarn brides in patterns (Figure 15.14). Making Battenberg lace was a common hobby in the United States in the early 20th century. Contemporary pieces are imported from Asia, especially China, for apparel and interior accessories.

Machine-Made Lace In 1802 in England, Robert Brown perfected a machine that made nets on which lace motifs could be worked by hand. In 1808 John Heathcoat made the first true lace machine by developing brass bobbins to make bobbinet. In 1813, John Leavers developed a machine that made patterns and background simultaneously. A card system, similar to the technique used on card jacquard looms, made it possible to produce intricate designs with the Leavers machine.

The warp yarns and oscillating brass bobbins of the Leavers machine are set in frames called *carriages*. The carriages move back and forth while the bobbins swing around the warp to form a pattern. These bobbins, holding 60 to 300 yards of yarn, are thin enough to swing between adjacent warp yarns and twist themselves around one warp before moving to another yarn (Figure 15.15). The Leavers machine may have as many as 20 bobbins per inch. Tulle can also be made on a Leavers lace machine.

Leavers lace is fairly expensive, depending on the quality of yarns and the intricacy of the design. **Cordonnet**, or **re-embroidered**, **lace** has a yarn or cord outlining the design (see Figure 15.12).

Raschel-knitting machines (see Chapter 14) make patterned laces that resemble Leavers lace. **Raschel laces** are produced at much higher speeds and thus are less expensive. Filament yarns are used to make coarser laces for tablecloths, draperies, and casement fabrics (Figure 15.16).

Care of Lace Because lace has open spaces, it can easily snag and tear. Fragile laces should be washed by hand-squeezing suds through the fabric rather than rubbing. Some laces can be put into a protective bag and machine-washed or dry-cleaned.

Embroidery

Embroidery is the only technique in which yarn can be arranged in almost any direction. While embroidery is usually considered an aesthetic or surface design (see Chapter 17), embroidery is used to create technical textiles. Embroidery is used to create smart textile structures with high performance and small mass using aramid, carbon, PBO, glass, and other special-use fibers. A ground material of acetate or polyvinyl alcohol is used and embroidery cords, yarns, or fibers are arranged in a three dimensional-structure. Padding and shaping may be needed to achieve the end product. The item may include shape memory components that shrink when heated or wetted to create the three-dimensional shape. Often the shape is coated with resin after construction and dissolution

▶ Learning Activity 5

Examine the textile products you are wearing and have with you today. Which items include braid and lace? Describe your satisfaction with and the serviceability of one of each of these items based on fiber content, yarn type, and fabric structure. Identify the fabrication method, end use, and serviceability of the items. Explain why these fabrication methods were used.

▶ Learning Activity 6

Explain the differences in structure, appearance, and serviceability between spun-lace and lace.

▶ Learning Activity 7

Use Fabrics #68, 90, 91, and 92 from your swatch kit. List the fabrication method used to produce each fabric and an appropriate application for each. Examine the key for the swatch kit and describe the serviceability that you would predict for each swatch based on application, fiber content, and fabrication method. Name each of these fabrics.

Braids are narrow fabrics in which yarns interlace lengthwise and diagonally. **Lace** is an openwork fabric with complex patterns or figures. **Embroidery** is the only technique in which yarn can be arranged in almost any direction. Braids are used for trim for apparel and interior products and for technical products.

by water or solvent of the ground material. Embroidered textiles are used for mechanical engineering applications and medical implants and wound dressings.

Composite Fabrics

Composite fabrics are fabrics that combine several primary and/or secondary structures, at least one of which is a recognized textile structure, into a single structure. This broad category includes diverse possibilities. Composites can be flat two-dimensional structures or shaped three-dimensional structures. Composites include coated fabrics, poromeric fabrics, suedelike fabrics, flocked fabrics, tufted-pile fabrics, laminates, stitch-bonded fabrics, quilted fabrics, supported-scrim structures, and fiber-reinforced materials. Composites are found in such end uses as boating, automotive, aerospace, communication satellites, sporting goods, toys, appliances, furniture, swimming pools, construction components, structures such as stadiums and airports, and equipment used by industry, the military, and the energy industry.

Coated Fabrics

A **coated fabric** combines a textile fabric with a polymer film. The woven, knit, or nonwoven fabric substrate provides strength and elongation control. The coating or film protects from environmental factors, such as water, chemicals, oil, and abrasion. Commonly used films include rubber and synthetic elastomers such as polyvinyl chloride (PVC), neoprene, and polyurethane. PVC-coated fabrics are most common and are used in window shades, book covers, upholstery, wall coverings, apparel, and shoe liners and uppers. Neoprene is used for protective

Composite fabrics are fabrics that combine several primary and/or secondary structures, at least one of which is a recognized textile structure, into a single structure. Composites include coated fabrics, poromeric fabrics, suedelike fabrics, flocked fabrics, tufted-pile fabrics, laminates, stitch-bonded fabrics, quilted fabrics, supported-scrim structures, and fiber-reinforced materials. Composite fabrics are used for apparel, interior, and technical products.

apparel such as chemical gloves and wetsuits. Most polyurethane-coated fabrics are used in shoe uppers and apparel. Heavy polyurethane-coated fabrics are used in tarpaulins.

The coating is added to the fabric substrate by several methods. Most common is *lamination*, in which a prepared film is adhered to fabric with adhesive or heated to slightly melt the back of the film before pressing the layers together. In *calendering*, the viscous polymer is mixed with filler, stabilizing agent, pigment, and plasticizer to control the coating layer's opacity, hand, color, and environmental resistance. The mixture is applied to preheated fabric by passing the fabric and the mixture between two large metal cylinders, or calenders, spaced close together. A third method is *coating*, in which a more fluid compound is applied by knife or roll. The degree that the mixture penetrates into the fabric substrate is controlled by allowing the mixture to solidify or gel slightly before contacting the substrate. Composite sails for racing yachts combine polyester film with aramid or high-strength olefin to reinforce scrim and polyester woven fabric.

Several other methods of coating are also used. In the *rotary screen technique*, the coating is applied to the fabric through a rotating open screen in contact with the fabric. A smoothing blade smoothes out the coating compound producing a continuous surface. This technique is used for lightweight upholstery fabrics where flame retardancy is required or air permeability is desired. In the *slot die technique*, the solution is extruded over the substrate's full width at the desired thickness. The *foam technique,* for thermal drapery fabrics and blackout curtains, applies the coating as a foam. In the *spray technique*, a thin solution is sprayed onto the surface of the substrate. Under heat or pressure, the solution flows over the surface and forms a continuous layer. In *transfer coating*, the coating compound is applied to release paper, dried, and then applied to the substrate. Transfer coating is used only when no other technique can be used.

Coated fabrics, also referred to as supported films, can be printed or embossed. They may resemble real leather and may be sold as "vegetarian" leather. They are used for apparel, shoe uppers and liners, upholstery, vinyl car tops, floor and wall coverings, window shades, bandages, acoustical barriers, filters, soft-sided luggage, awnings, pond and ditch liners, and air-supported structures and domes.

Coated fabrics are impermeable to water in liquid and vapor forms. As apparel, they feel hot and clammy. When used in upholstery, coated fabric sticks to exposed skin. In architectural applications, they provide lightweight roofs for structures and allow for open spaces without the need for heavy support columns.

Coated fabrics can be modified in several ways to improve comfort. One method punches tiny holes in the fabric. In another method, coated fabrics incorporate a nonporous hydrophilic membrane or film. Sympatex, by Akzo, incorporates a hydrophilic polyester film and is washable or dry-cleanable. (Another method uses a microporous film, which will be discussed in the next section.) Sympatex can be laminated to an outer shell, a lining fabric, or a lightweight insert fabric, such as tricot or fiberweb, for use in skiwear. Stomatex, by MicroThermal Systems, adds thermal comfort and breathability to protective and extreme sports apparel by using a closed-cell foam layer of neoprene or polyethylene. A series of tiny convex domes are vented with a microporous opening at the apex of each dome. As the wearer moves, a pumping action is created that releases excess moisture in a controlled fashion.

A fabric calender coated with a very thin flexible polymer film filled with conductive pigments is used to create heatable apparel, bedding, and in technical products to produce heated seats in automobiles, safety and military apparel, and plant covers and blankets for sick or injured animals in agricultural applications.

Table 15.4 End Uses for Films and Coated Fabrics

Air-supported roofings	Tablecloths and placemats
Self-lined draperies	Umbrellas
Hospital-bed coverings	Upholstery
Hose container for fuel and water	Waterproof apparel: mittens, raincoats, and boots
Inflatable floodgates	Wetsuits
Leatherlike coats and jackets	Chemical protective apparel and gloves
Shower curtains	

Figure 15.17 Coated fabrics.

A summary of coated fabrics includes these aspects:

- Coated fabrics are produced by applying semiliquid materials (neoprene, polyvinyl chloride, and polyurethane) to a fabric substrate (Figure 15.17).
- Coated fabrics are stronger and more stable than unsupported films.
- Coated fabrics are used for upholstery, luggage and bags, and apparel (Table 15.4).

A **coated fabric** combines a textile fabric with a polymer film. Coated fabrics are used for apparel, interior, and technical products.

Poromeric Fabrics

Poromeric, or *microporous*, **fabrics** incorporate films, but they are categorized separately because the film is very thin and microporous. These two major distinctions determine many characteristics of the resulting fabric. The poromeric, or membrane, layer is stretched in both directions and annealed to impart micropores in the fabric that are small enough to allow water vapor, but not liquid water, to pass through. A water-vapor droplet is 250,000 times smaller than a liquid-water droplet. Hence, poromeric fabrics are water vapor–permeable and much more comfortable in apparel.

Poromeric films are made from polytetrafluoroethylene (Gore-Tex) (Figure 15.18), polyester, or polyurethane. These smart textiles are waterproof, windproof, and breathable. They keep out liquid moisture but allow perspiration to evaporate. The film can be applied to a wide variety of fabrics and fibers. It is used in protective and comfortable apparel for active sportswear and rugged outdoorwear such as hunting apparel. Other uses include tents, sleeping bags, medical products, filters, coatings for wires and cables, and protective apparel. Other poromeric fabrics include warp knits with a polyurethane membrane, and Entrant and Breathe-Tex, which have polyurethane membranes. Several of these fabrics are used in the medical field because they present a barrier to bodily fluids that might carry pathogens.

Smart poromeric fabrics with medical applications incorporate an outer protective layer, a polymer matrix with drug microspheres, and a rate-limiting membrane that controls the release of the drug into the skin. The membrane is worn next to the skin. Types of drugs included in these textiles include hormones, pain-control medications, nausea control medication, and medication to ease the stress of quitting smoking.

The enhanced performance of poromeric fabrics is reflected in their price. Fabrics that are both comfortable and waterproof incorporate expensive components and processes.

Figure 15.18 Gore-Tex fabric: backing, polytetrafluoroethylene film, face, and poromeric fabric (left to right).

Suedelike Fabrics

Because of the beautiful texture and hand of suede and the problems encountered in its care, **suedelike fabrics** have been developed. These fabrics are needle-punched fabrics made from microdenier fibers combined with a resin coating and nonfibrous polyurethane. The

Poromeric, or *microporous*, fabrics incorporate very thin, microporous films. Poromeric fabrics are smart textiles used for apparel and technical products.

Table 15.5 Leather, Suede, and Imitations

Construction Technique	Characteristics	Trade Name
Composite fabric—polyester fibers and polyurethane mixed, cast on drum, napped or embossed	Washable, dry-cleanable	Ultrasuede
	Looks like leather or suede	Ultraleather
Composite fabric	Easy care	None
	Looks like suede	
Woven cotton/polyester substrate, surface coating of polyurethane	Dry-cleanable, washable	None
100% polyester-pile fabric with suedelike finish	Dry-cleanable, washable	None
Flocked cotton	Least expensive and least effective imitation	None
	Flock may wear off at edges	
Leather (cow, pig, lamb, or other animal)	Natural product, irregular in nature, available in a wide variety of finishes, cleanability may not be good	None
Suede (cow, pig, lamb, or other animal)	Natural product, irregular in nature, cleanability may not be good	None

microdenier fibers are arranged in a manner that reproduces the microscopic structure of natural suedes. The fabric is dyed and finished. The process was developed by Toray Industries in Japan. Ultrasuede and Ultraleather are used in apparel and interiors. Ultrasuede is made of microfine polyester needle punched, impregnated with a binder, and treated to create the soft and flexible hand. Ultraleather is 100 percent polyurethane with a knit back of 70 percent rayon and 30 percent nylon. The embossed fabric is lightweight, soft, and water-repellent with a comfort stretch. Ultrasuede may be backed with a woven fabric when used for upholstery.

Suedelike and leatherlike fabrics are used in apparel, upholstery, wall coverings, and accessories. These fabrics are made in various ways (Table 15.5). The process can be summarized as follows:

- Fibers and polyurethane solution are mixed together, cast on a drum or forced through a slit to make the fabric, and then napped on both sides.
- The fabric looks and feels like suede but is uniform in thickness, appearance, and quality; it is sold by the yard or meter.
- The fabric is machine-washable and dry-cleanable.

> **Suedelike fabrics** are needle-punched fabrics made from microdenier fibers combined with a resin coating and nonfibrous polyurethane. Suedelike fabrics are used for apparel and interiors.

Flocked Fabrics

In **flocking**, a fine natural or synthetic surface fiber is applied after a base fabric has been produced. Flocking can be localized to imitate extra yarn weaves (see Chapter 17) or all over to imitate pile fabrics.

Flock fibers are very short, straight (not crimped) fibers attached to a fabric surface by an adhesive to create an inexpensive pile. Flocking decorated walls as early as the 14th century, when short silk fibers were applied to freshly painted walls. Flock can be applied to such base materials as fabric, foam, wood, metal, and concrete, or it can be applied to an adhesive film and laminated to a base fabric. Aqueous-based acrylic, nylon, or polyester adhesives have good flexibility, durability, drape, hand, no color, and no odor.

The two methods of applying the flock fibers are mechanical and electrostatic. In both processes the flock is placed in an erect position and oven-dried. Table 15.6 compares the two

Table 15.6 Flocking Process

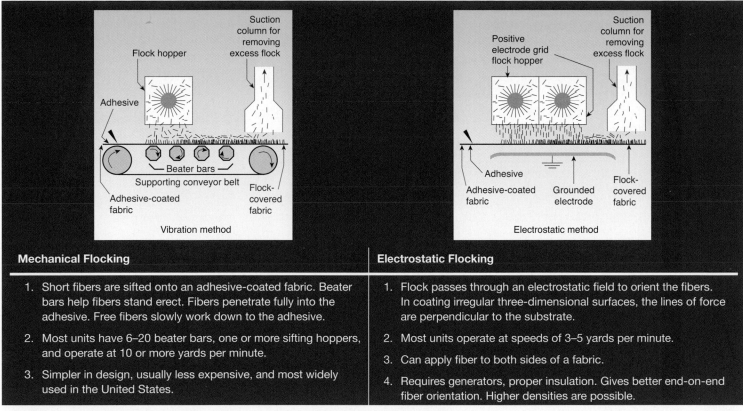

Mechanical Flocking	Electrostatic Flocking
1. Short fibers are sifted onto an adhesive-coated fabric. Beater bars help fibers stand erect. Fibers penetrate fully into the adhesive. Free fibers slowly work down to the adhesive.	1. Flock passes through an electrostatic field to orient the fibers. In coating irregular three-dimensional surfaces, the lines of force are perpendicular to the substrate.
2. Most units have 6–20 beater bars, one or more sifting hoppers, and operate at 10 or more yards per minute.	2. Most units operate at speeds of 3–5 yards per minute.
3. Simpler in design, usually less expensive, and most widely used in the United States.	3. Can apply fiber to both sides of a fabric.
	4. Requires generators, proper insulation. Gives better end-on-end fiber orientation. Higher densities are possible.

SOURCE: Courtesy of the Fibers Division of Monsanto Chemical Co., a unit of Monsanto Co.

methods. Overall flocking, or area flocking, can be done by either method. A rotating screen is used to deposit the flock. As the fiber length increases, the denier also must increase so that the fiber will remain erect in the fabric. Fibers that are cut square at the ends anchor more firmly in the adhesive (Figure 15.19). Examine Tables 15.7 and 15.8 to compare flocking with other methods used to produce fabrics with a pile or imitation pile surface.

Rayon fibers are inexpensive and easy to cut and are used for wall coverings, toys, and garments. Cotton is used in packaging and greeting cards. Nylon for upholstery and blankets has excellent abrasion resistance and durability. Acrylics, polyesters, and olefins are used for weather stripping, sealing applications, and automotive squeak and rattle controls in window channels and dashboards. Polyester and olefin fibers are also used for flocked marine surfaces (boat hulls, docks, and ballast tanks) to protect against barnacles, mussels, and other marine life. Flocking is a sustainable alternative to paints containing heavy metals that had been used for this purpose, but are banned in some countries.

Figure 15.19 Flock with square-cut ends is attached more firmly.

▶ Learning Activity 8

Examine the textile products you are wearing and have with you today. Which items include these composite fabrics: coated, poromeric, suedelike, or flocked? List the textile components used to produce these fabrics and the fabrication method used. Describe your satisfaction with and the serviceability of one of each of these items based on fabric structure. Explain why these fabrication methods were used.

Table 15.7 Look-Alike Pile Fabrics

FURLIKE FABRICS—USED FOR COAT AND JACKET SHELLS, LININGS, BED PADS, AND ACCENT RUGS

	Woven-Warp Pile	Sliver Knit	Tufted
Fibers used	Cotton ground	Cotton or acrylic ground	Cheesecloth or sheeting substrate of cotton or cotton/polyester
	Wool, acrylic, rayon, polyester pile	Acrylic pile	Acrylic or nylon pile
Cost	Most expensive	Variable	Least expensive
Characteristics	Pile firmly held in place	Most widely used	Mostly used for sheepskin-type goods
	Tendency to grin-through in low-count fabrics	Dense surface possible	Blooming of yarns and shrinkage of ground hold tufts in place
		Fur-like with underfibers and guard hairs	

CARPETS

	Woven-Warp Pile	Knit: Filling or Raschel	Chenille Yarns	Tufted	Flocked
Types and kinds	Wilton	Laid-in pile yarn	Usually woven to order	Most widely used	Not very durable
	Axminster Velvet	Raschel knits		Variety of textures	
				Backing holds tufts	Limited pile height
Cost	Most expensive	Expensive	Expensive	Inexpensive to moderate in cost	Inexpensive

VELOUR

	Woven-Warp Pile	Filling Knit—Jersey	Warp Knit
Fiber content	Cotton, wool, acrylic, blends	Cotton, polyester	Nylon, acetate
Characteristics	Heavy fabric, durable, drapeable	Medium weight, soft	Medium weight to heavyweight
End uses	Upholstery, draperies	Robes, shirts, casual apparel	Robes, nightwear

VELVET

	Woven-Warp Pile	Tufted	Flocked
Fibers	Rayon, nylon, cotton, acetate, polyester	Nylon, olefin	Nylon
Characteristics	Filament—formal, pile flattens	Pile not held as firmly as woven, less expensive	Least expensive
	Durability related to fiber and pile density		
End uses	Apparel	Upholstery	Upholstery, draperies, bedspreads, wall coverings
	Upholstery		

TERRYCLOTH

	Slack-Tension Weave	Filling Knit—Jersey
Characteristics	Usually cotton	All fibers
	Holds its shape	Soft, stretchy
		Cotton does not hold its shape well
		Very pliable
End uses	Towels, washcloths, robes	Baby towels and washcloths, bed sheets
		Baby sleepers, adult sportswear, socks

Table 15.8 Comparison of Pile Fabrics

Method	Types and Kinds	Fabrics—End Uses	Identification
Weaving	Filling floats cut and brushed up	Velveteen, corduroy	Filling pile
	Made as double cloth and cut apart	Velvet, velour	Warp pile
	Overwire	Friezé, Wilton and velvet carpets	Warp pile
	Slack tension	Terrycloth, friezé	Warp pile
Knitting	Filling knit: laid-in yarn or sliver knit	Velour, terry, fake fur, fleece	Stretchy—rows of knit stitches on back
	Warp knit: laid-in yarn or pile loops		More stable
Tufting	Yarns punched into substrate	Rugs and carpets	Rows of machine stitches on wrong side
		Robes, bedspreads	
		Upholstery	
		Fake furs	
Flocking	Fibers anchored to substrate	Blankets, jackets, upholstery	Stiff fiber surface
		Applied fabric designs	
Chenille yarns	Pile yarns made by lenoweave	Upholstery	Ravel and examine novelty yarn
	Chenille yarns woven or knitted into fabric	Outerwear fabric	

▶ Learning Activity 9

Use Fabrics #100 through 102 from your swatch kit. List the textile components used to produce these fabrics, the fabrication method used, and an appropriate application for each. Examine the key for the swatch kit and describe the serviceability that you would predict for each swatch based on application, fiber content, and fabrication method.

Flocking has two safety and sustainability issues. Fiber dust may create a potential fire hazard. In addition, a lung disease nicknamed "flock worker's lung" may be related to tiny airborne fiber particles found in many flocking facilities. To address these issues, producers use vacuuming systems and require that workers wear respirators and masks for certain processes.

Tufted-Pile Fabrics

Tufting is a process of making pile fabrics by stitching extra yarns into a fabric base or substrate. The ground fabric ranges from thin sheeting or nonwoven to heavy burlap or coarse warp knit; it may be woven, knitted, or nonwoven. Tufting developed as a handcraft when early settlers worked candlewicks into bedspreads to add texture and create designs. The making of candlewick bedspreads and hooked rugs grew into a cottage industry. In the 1930s, machinery was developed to convert the hand technique to mass production (Figure 15.20). Carpets, rugs, bedspreads, and robes are produced in many patterns and colors at low cost.

Tufting is done by a series of needles (Figures 15.21 and 15.22), each carrying a yarn from a spool held in a creel. The substrate is in a horizontal position, and the needles all come down at once and go through the fabric to a predetermined depth, much as a sewing machine needle goes through fabric. For each needle, a hook moves forward to hold the loop as the needle is retracted. In loop-pile fabrics, the loop remains when the hook is removed. For cut-loop pile,

In **flocking,** a fine natural or synthetic surface fiber is applied after a base fabric has been produced. **Flocking** can be localized to imitate extra yarn weaves or all-over to imitate pile fabrics. Flocking is used to create upholstery, wall coverings, and technical products.

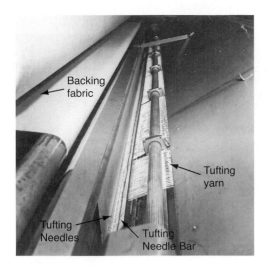

Figure 15.20 Needle area of commercial tufting machine.

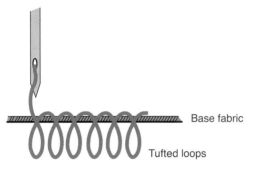

Figure 15.21 Tufting.

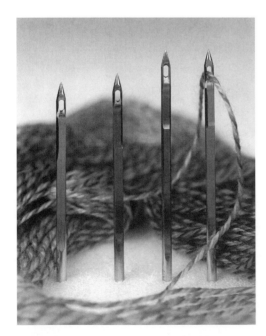

Figure 15.22 Tufting needles and yarn.

a knife incorporated with the hook moves forward as the needles are retracted to cut the loop. The fabric moves forward slightly, and the needles form another row of tufts.

With cut loops, the yarn ends or tufts are held in place by blooming or untwisting the yarn, by shrinkage of the ground fabric in finishing, or by applying a coating on the back of the ground fabric. **Tuft density** refers to the number of tufts per square inch (needles/inch × stitches/inch = tuft density). Any pile fabric with low pile density is subject to grin-through, a problem of the ground structure showing through the pile. This problem is obvious when the fabric is bent or rolled and is common with carpet, especially on stairs.

Thousands of patterns are computerized and can be created quickly and easily by changing yarn color or type, tuft depth, and tuft type (cut or uncut). The popularity of carpets in homes, businesses, and technical facilities is because of the low cost of tufted carpets.

Tufting is an inexpensive method to make pile fabrics because it is extremely fast and involves less labor and time to create new designs. Furlike tufted fabrics can be used for shells or linings of coats and jackets, but there are few other tufted apparel fabrics. Tufted bed-sized blankets can be made in less than two minutes. Tufted upholstery fabric is made in both cut and uncut pile and is widely available. The back is coated to hold the yarns in place.

Carpeting of room-width size was first made by tufting in 1950; today tufting is the most widely used method of producing carpets. A tufting machine can produce more than 650 square yards of carpeting per hour, as compared with an Axminster loom, which weaves about 14 square yards per hour. Tufted carpets are shaped to fit a space and are easily removed and replaced.

Gauge refers to the distance in inches between the tufting needles. In general, carpets for home or lower-traffic areas differ in gauge from carpets for commercial, technical, and high-traffic areas. Typical gauges for commercial carpets range from $\frac{5}{32}$ inch (0.16 inch) to $\frac{1}{16}$ inch (0.063 inch). Tufting specifications also include stitches per inch and pile height.

Variations in texture are possible by varying loop height and combining cut and uncut tufts. Tweed textures use different-colored plies in the tufting yarns. Special dyeing and printing techniques produce colored patterns or figures in which the color penetrates the tufts completely. A latex coating applied to the back of the carpet holds the tufts in place (Figure 15.23). *Face weight* refers to the mass or weight of the tuft yarns used in the carpet. In general, the higher the face weight, the more expensive and durable the carpet. Face weights of 25 oz/yd² or more are common for commercial carpets.

One can predict carpet performance based on five factors: color, design, density, pile texture, and fiber. *Color* is an important factor in hiding soil. *Design* describes how colors are blended and also relates to hiding soil. *Density* refers to the number of tufts per unit area. The denser the carpet, the better it is at resisting soiling and compacting. *Pile texture* describes the tuft-loop structure and yarn type used, also factors in resisting soiling and compacting. *Fiber* addresses the performance of the fibers used in the carpet pile yarns. Carpet fibers are specifically engineered for soil and static resistance.

▶ Learning Activity 10

Explain why tufted carpets are so common. Describe how knit and woven carpets compare to tufted carpets for each of the reasons you listed. Do you have carpets or rugs where you live? What type are they? Describe the serviceability of one carpet or rug and explain your degree of satisfaction with that item.

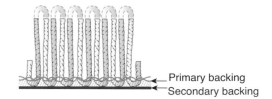

Figure 15.23 Tufted carpet. Tufts are punched through primary backing. Secondary backing is bonded to primary backing to lock pile in place.

Primary backing
Secondary backing

> ## ► Learning Activity 11

Use Fabric #103 from your swatch kit. Explain how the structure of this fabric is similar to and different from that of tufted carpet. Describe an end use for this fabric and explain its serviceability based on fabric structure, yarn type(s), and fiber content. (Use the fabric key to determine fiber content.)

Tables 15.7 and 15.8 compare the different methods of producing pile fabrics. Tufted fabrics can be summarized as follows:

- Yarns carried by needles are forced through a fabric substrate and formed into cut or uncut loops.
- Tufted fabrics are cheaper than woven or knitted pile fabrics.
- Tufted fabrics are used in carpets and rugs, upholstery, coat linings, and bedspreads.

Laminates

Laminates are fabrics in which two layers of fabric are combined into one with an adhesive or foam. *Laminate* usually refers to a fabric in which an adhesive was used. *Bonded* usually refers to a fabric in which a foam was used. However, the two terms are used interchangeably.

Introduced in 1958, bonding was originally a way to deplete inventories of tender (weak) or lightweight fabrics. Shoddy operators, not interested in quality, bought two hot rolls discarded by finishers and were in business. The fabric often was stretched during lamination. Consequently, many problems were associated with early laminated fabrics: layers that separated (delaminated) or shrank unevenly, and blotchy colors caused by adhesive bleed-through to the technical face. These problems gave laminated fabrics a poor reputation. However, current laminates have good performance and quality. Some advantages and limitations are listed in Table 15.9.

> **Tufting** is a process of making pile fabrics by stitching extra yarns into a fabric base or substrate. The ground fabric ranges from thin sheeting or nonwoven to heavy burlap or coarse warp knit; it may be woven, knitted, or nonwoven. Tufting is used to create carpet, upholstery, and technical products.

Laminating Process Random nonwovens or acetate or nylon tricot are used as the backing fabric for knits because they give when the face fabric is stretched and they are low cost. Using a different color for the backing can be a decorative feature in bonded laces. Three methods of bonding are used (Figure 15.24).

Table 15.9 Laminated Fabrics

Advantages	Limitations
Less costly fabrics are upgraded.	Top-quality fabrics are not bonded.
Self-lining gives comfort.	Backing does not prevent bagging, so a lining may be needed.
Stabilized if good quality.	Uneven shrinkage possible.*
Reduces time in sewing.	May be bonded off-grain.
Interfacings may be eliminated.	May delaminate.*
Underlinings, stay-stitching, and seam finishing are not needed.	Stiff and boardy layered areas (hems, seams, etc.).
	Do not hold sharp creases.

*These are the two major problems.

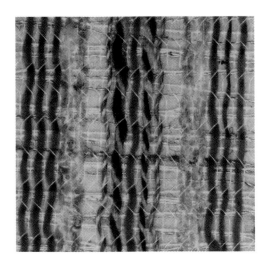

Figure 15.26 Malimo fabrics: drapery and casement fabric.

structure. Knitting fibers or knitting yarns around laid (not woven) warp and filling yarns is the second method. To make these knit-through fabrics, needles are used to create interconnected loops from yarns or fibers to stabilize the structure. These fabrics look like wovens, but careful examination shows that the lengthwise and crosswise yarns are not interlaced.

Araknit is a knit-through fiberweb fabric used as a coating substrate. Arachne and Mali-watt are fabrics made by warp-knitting yarns through a fiberweb structure. These knit-through fabrics are produced at high speeds and are used for interior (upholstery, blankets, and window treatments) and technical uses (insulation and interlining). Malimo uses warp or filling (or both) laid-in yarns with warp-knitting yarns (Figure 15.26). These fabrics are produced at very high speeds and are used for tablecloths, window-treatment fabrics, vegetable bags, dishcloths, and outerwear. These fabrics can be confused with warp-knit insertion fabrics (see Chapter 14). Careful examination will show that the knit-through fabrics have the fine filament yarns knitted *through* the inserted yarns, not *around* them.

Some knit-through fabrics use split-polymer films from recycled bottles. These fabrics are used in the carpet, geotextile, and bale-wrap industries.

Quilted Fabrics **Quilted fabrics** are composite fabrics consisting of three layers: face fabric, fiberfill or batting, and backing fabric. Three layers are stitch-bonded with thread, chemical adhesive, or fusion by ultra-high-frequency sound, often in a pattern. The area physically bonded is a tiny percentage of the fabric's surface so that the quilt's desired high loft and bulky appearance are not sacrificed.

Most quilted fabric is made by stitching with thread. The thread and quilting stitch type are good indicators of the quality and durability of the finished fabric. A durable quilt combines a lock stitch with a durable thread. Twistless nylon-monofilament thread may be used because of its strength and abrasion resistance. Because it is transparent, it disappears in the colors of the face fabric.

Almost any thread can be used, but those designed for quilting have different performance characteristics as compared with regular sewing thread. Quilting threads must be durable. The disadvantage of thread stitches in quilting is that when the threads break from abrasion or snagging, the loose ends are unsightly and the fiberfill may shift.

Any fabric can be used for the shell or covering. A fashion fabric is used on one side. If the article is reversible or needs to be durable or beautiful on both sides, two fashion fabrics are used. If the fabric is to be lined or used as upholstery or a bedspread, the underlayer is often an inexpensive fabric such as cheesecloth, tricot, or nonwoven. The batting may be foam, cotton, down, or fiberfill. Fiberfill is a manufactured fiber modified to maintain loft.

Quilting is done in straight or curved lines. In upholstery, quilts, comforters, and bedspreads, the stitching may outline printed figures. This is an expensive process in which the machine quilting is guided by hand. Fabric beauty and fashion appeal are important for all end uses. For ski jackets and snowsuits, a closely woven water- and wind-repellent fabric is desirable; for comforters, resistance to slipping off the bed is important; for upholstery, durability and resistance to soil are important.

Chemical-adhesive quilts are rare. Chemical adhesives are applied in a pattern, but these fabrics are not as appealing or as durable as those produced by other quilting methods.

Ultrasonic quilting requires thermoplastic fibers. Heat generated by ultra-high-frequency sound or ultrasonic vibrations melts thermoplastic fibers, fusing several layers. Figure 15.27 shows a Pinsonic Thermal Joining Machine that heat-seals thermoplastic materials by ultrasonic vibrations. The machine quilts seven times as quickly as conventional quilting machines. This process is used on some mattress pads and lower-priced bedspreads because it eliminates the problem of broken threads. However, the outer layer may tear along the quilting lines. Figure 15.28 shows a Pinsonic fabric.

Quilted fabrics can be summarized as follows:

- One or two fabrics and fiberfill, wadding, batting, or foam are stitched together by machine or by hand or are welded by sonic vibrations.
- Quilted fabrics are bulky, warm, and decorative.
- Quilted fabrics are used in ski jackets, robes, comforters, quilts, and upholstery.

Supported-Scrim Structures

Supported-scrim structures include foam-and-fiber blankets and outwear that combine a lightweight nylon scrim and a loose warp-knit fabric between two thin layers of polyurethane foam. Short nylon-flock fiber is adhered to the surface. These blankets are attractive, durable, easy care, and inexpensive. Vellux is a trade name.

Figure 15.27   Pinsonic Thermal Joining Machine (left) and close-up (right).
Source: Courtesy of Branson Ultrasonics Corp.

▶ Learning Activity 12

Explain the differences and similarities among doublecloth, doubleknit, and quilted fabrics. Be sure to address market availability, complexity of structure, components used to create them, and number of layers.

▶ Learning Activity 13

Examine the textile products you are wearing and have with you today. Which items are laminated or stitch-bonded? List the textile components used to produce these fabrics and the fabrication method used. Describe your satisfaction with and the serviceability of one of each of these items based on fabric structure. Explain why these fabrication methods were used.

▶ Learning Activity 14

Use Fabrics #104 through 107 from your swatch kit. List the textile components used to produce these fabrics, the fabrication method used, and an appropriate application for each. Examine the key for the swatch kit and describe the serviceability that you would predict for each swatch based on application, fiber content, and fabrication method.

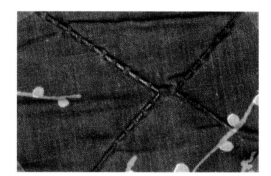

Figure 15.28   Bedspread. Two layers of fabric and fiberfill batt joined by a Pinsonic Thermal Joining Machine.

Quilted fabrics are composite fabrics consisting of three layers: face fabric, fiberfill or batting, and backing fabric. They are used for apparel, interior, and technical products.

Case Study
Leather*

By 2011, the 206 leather tanneries (employing 30,000 people and part of the global leather industry) in the tannery district of Dhaka, the capital city of Bangladesh, are expected to either shut down or move to another location in the city. Tanners dump untreated waste into drains and ditches that lead to the main river flowing through the city. Barefoot and unprotected workers handle chemicals. They live next to contaminated streams, ponds, and canals. Chemicals used in tanneries include lime, sodium sulfide, sodium hydrosulfite, sulfuric acid, caustic soda, arsenic sulfide, calcium hydrosulfide, and chromium compounds

Bangladesh exports approximately $250 million of leather and $170 million of footwear annually. Because most of the leather exported is shipped to the United States and Europe, foreign pressure is demanding

changes in tannery operations. Many companies insist that suppliers meet Western environmental standards rather than those of their home countries. Safer chemicals are available for leather tanning: a more benign form of chromium, detergents free of a compound suspected of being endocrine disrupters, and formaldehyde-free compounds. The new tannery district will have effluent treatment facilities and incentives to introduce comprehensive safety equipment and practices. Housing will be provided for workers, but not for their families. Although it is hoped that the move will take place by 2011, many are skeptical and expect that less than one-third of the tanneries will move. Without government financial support, most tanneries will not be able to afford to move their heavy equipment.

Cost estimates for the move are approximately $35 million.

DISCUSSION QUESTIONS

1. Locate Bangladesh on the world map. Why are the conditions of leather tannery workers of interest?

2. Search the Web for the chemical names for lime and caustic soda. Search the Web for these and the other chemicals mentioned to determine the hazards associated with direct contact with them or with dumping them in water systems. What are the short- and long-term hazards associated with these chemicals?

3. What would be an appropriate list of safety apparel for tannery workers?

4. How would you define socially responsible leather?

*Tremblay, J. F. (2009, February 2). Leather from another era. *Chemical and Engineering News, 87*(5), 18–21.

suggested readings

Anand, S. (1996, September). Nonwovens in medical and health care products. Part 1. Fabric formation. *Technical Textiles International*, pp. 22–28.

Atlaş, S., & Pamul, G. (2007). Ultrasonic energy in the textile industry. *AATCC Review, 7*(6), 29–31.

Bertrand, D. (2005, January/February). High performance coated fabrics. *The Textile Journal*, 18–21.

Brown, S. G. (1994, July/August). The making and coloration of leather. *Journal of the Society of Dyers and Colourists*, 10, pp. 213–214.

Crabtree, A. (1999, March). Hot-melt adhesives for textile laminates. *Technical Textiles International*, pp. 11–14.

Earnshaw, P. (1999). *A Dictionary of Lace*. New York: Dover Publications.

Ford, J. E. (1991). Nonwovens. *Textiles*, 4, pp. 17–21.

Humphries, M. (2009). *Fabric Glossary*, 4th ed. Upper Saddle River, NJ: Prentice Hall.

Isaacs, M. (2005). Nonwoven fabrics wipe out the doldrums. *AATCC Review, 5*(9), 14–17.

Landmann, A. (1994, July/August). The effect of "natural" defects on leather dyeing. *Journal of the Society of Dyers and Colourists*, 10, pp. 217–219.

Magic membrane for all-weather clothing. (1995, January). *Textile Month*, pp. 20–22.

Mansfield, R. G. (2003, January). Combining nonwovens by lamination and other methods. *Textile World*, pp. 22–25.

Mohamed, M. H. (1990, November/December). Three-dimensional textiles. *American Scientist*, 78, pp. 530–541.

Ondovcsik, M. (1999, February). Riding the wave. *America's Textiles International*, pp. 40–43.

Pamuk, G., & Çeken, F. (2008). Recyclable spacer fabrics for automotives. *AATCC Review 8*(8), 32–36.

Pourdeyhimi, B. (2004, February). Nonwovens. *Textile World*, pp. 40–44.

Pourdeyhimi, B. (2008, January/February). Nonwovens technology: Implications for the nonwovens industry. *Textile World, 158*(1), 49–55.

Rupp, J. (2008, March/April). Drylaid nonwovens. *Textile World, 158*(2), 32–34

Rupp, J. (2008, May/June). Spunbond & meltblown nonwovens. *Textile World, 158*(3), 34–38.

Rupp, J. (2008, July/August). Spunlaced or hydroentangled nonwovens. *Textile World, 158*(4), 36–39.

Rupp, J. (2008, September/October). Needlepunched nonwovens. *Textile World, 158*(5), 37–41.

Sutton, K. D. (1998, August and November). Spec smarts. *Interiors*, pp. 47 and 58.

Tao, X. (Ed.), (2001). *Smart Fibres, Fabrics, and Clothing*. Cambridge, England: Woodhead Publishing.

Thiry, M. C. (2006). Not just one thing or the other. *AATCC Review, 6*(8), 7–11.

Tortora, P. G., & Merkel, R. S. (1996). *Fairchild's Dictionary of Textiles*, 7th ed. New York: Fairchild Publications.

Tremblay, J. F. (2009, February 2). Leather from another era. *Chemical and Engineering News, 87*(5), 18–21.

Tullo, A. H. (2004, August 30). Composite materials. *Chemical and Engineering News*, pp. 34–39.

Ward, D. (1996, March). Domotex growing despite industry's mixed fortunes. *Textile World*, pp. 8–11.

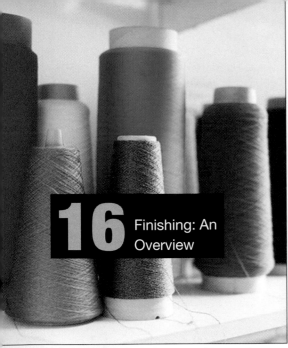

17 Aesthetic Finishes

16 Finishing: An Overview

19 Dyeing and Printing

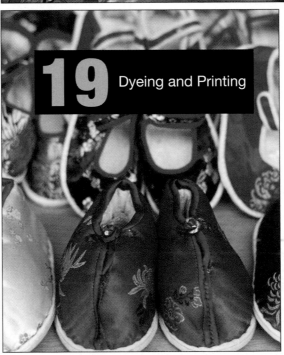

18 Special-Purpose Finishes

FINISHING

 16

 17

 18

 19

FINISHING: An OVERVIEW

CHAPTER OBJECTIVES

- To understand the general steps and sequence involved in fabric finishing.
- To understand how finishing affects fabric cost, quality, performance, and appearance.
- To relate finishing to fabric quality, end-use suitability, and product performance.

16

The four chapters in this section focus on converting a fabric from a raw form to the form consumers expect. Finishing enhances fabric performance and appearance.

A **finish** is any process that is done to fiber, yarn, or fabric either before or after fabrication to change the *appearance* (what is seen), the *hand* (what is felt), or the *performance* (what the fabric does). All finishing processes add to the cost of the end product and to the time it takes to produce the item.

While this section focuses on finishing, it is helpful to start with a summary of the process that is followed in producing a fabric from the fiber stage to the finished fabric stage for most fabrics for apparel and interiors. The sequence normally followed in textile processing is involved. Several steps may be repeated. A common sequence is fiber processing followed by yarn processing. Fabrication (producing a fabric) usually follows some preparation steps. In preparation, the yarn or fabric is made ready for additional steps in processing. Bleaching is almost always done before dyeing. Coloration usually is done before finishing and reworking (repairing). Figure 16.1 shows a typical sequence used to produce a fabric.

Finishing may be done in the mill where the fabric is produced, or it may be done in a separate facility by highly specialized companies called *converters*. **Converters** perform a service for mills by finishing goods to order, in which case they are paid for their services and never own the fabric; or they buy fabric from a mill, finish it according to their needs, and sell it, sometimes under their trade name.

Vertically integrated firms are an important part of the textile complex and direct and control every step of processing for fabrics used in their products, from opening bales of raw fiber

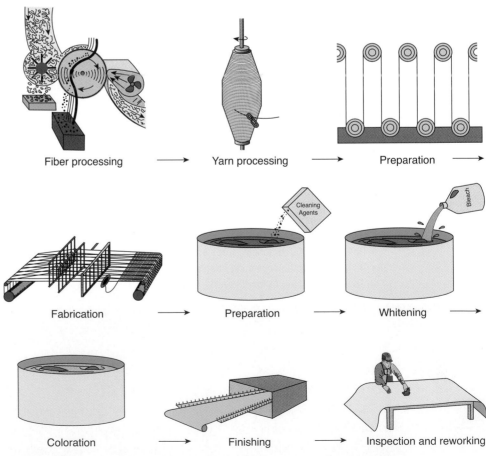

Fiber processing ⟶ Yarn processing ⟶ Preparation ⟶

Fabrication ⟶ Preparation ⟶ Whitening ⟶

Coloration ⟶ Finishing ⟶ Inspection and reworking

Figure 16.1 Typical production sequence for textile fabrics.

to cutting and sewing finished products. Vertical firms convert or finish fabrics in facilities they own and operate.

Finishes can be classified by how long they are effective. A **permanent finish**, such as mercerization, lasts the life of the item. A **durable finish**, such as wrinkle resistance, may last for the life of the product, but its effectiveness diminishes with use or age. These finishes require some effort by the user as the fabric ages. With wrinkle-resistant finishes, older items may require some ironing. A **temporary finish**, such as simple calendering, lasts until the item is washed or dry-cleaned. A **renewable finish**, such as some water-repellent finishes, can be applied by consumers or reapplied by dry cleaners. Dyeing, printing, embossing, and several other finishes are easy to recognize because they are visible. Other finishes—such as wrinkle resistance—are not visible but affect fabric performance. Consumers have difficulty understanding the higher costs for fabrics with such invisible finishes as wrinkle- and soil-resistance. Improved performance is a benefit for all finishes. The improved performance resulting from finishing adds to the inherent value and the cost of the product.

Many similar finishing processes are used on a range of fabric types. However, because of their importance and greater likelihood of being finished, the emphasis here will be on woven and knitted fabrics. The major differences that exist between finishing woven or knitted fabrics occur in the way the fabric is handled and moved. Most woven fabrics have little stretch. Knits and fabrics with elastomers have a much greater potential for stretch; hence precautions need to be taken to minimize stretching during finishing. Pile fabrics are handled so that finishing does not flatten the pile.

Gray (grey, greige, or loom state) **goods** are fabrics (regardless of color) that have been produced but have received no wet- or dry-finishing operations. Some gray-goods fabrics have names, such as print cloth and soft-filled sheeting, that describe only the gray goods. Other gray-goods names, such as lawn, broadcloth, and sateen, are also used as names for the finished fabric.

Converted, or finished, goods have received wet- or dry-finishing treatments such as bleaching, dyeing, or embossing. Some converted goods retain the gray-goods name. Others, such as madras gingham, are named for the place of origin; still others, such as silence cloth, are named for the end use. Figure 16.2 shows a print-cloth gray goods and the various looks of the fabric with different finishing procedures. **Mill-finished** fabrics are sold and used without further finishing. Some may be sized before they are sold.

Finishing textiles uses tremendous amounts of water. When used in finishing, water must be clean and neutral without inorganic or organic contaminants that may interfere with finishing and lower the quality of finished fabric. In some parts of the world, sufficient good-quality water for finishing is hard to acquire. Regulations defining the quality of water being discharged into water systems are becoming more stringent. Before discharge, water often needs mechanical filtration, chemical treatment, and reverse osmosis to remove finishing chemicals and dyes. Heat exchangers recover energy from hot water. Significant research is occurring worldwide to reduce water use in textile processing. Finishing operations need to know the amount of water used to reduce it and cut costs, meet environmental regulations, and satisfy buyers' expectations for socially responsible finishing. Conserving water, reducing energy use, and reusing water are important concerns in finishing. Recycling water is a challenge in geographic regions with a ready supply of water and of growing importance where water is not as readily available.

For years, **water-bath finishing** was standard because water is a good, readily available, and inexpensive solvent. In water-bath finishing, the finishing chemical is placed in a water solution and padded onto the fabric by immersing the fabric in the solution and squeezing out excess

Figure 16.2 Print-cloth: gray goods as produced, bleached, piece-dyed, and printed (from left to right).

different bales of cotton will be blended to ensure that fabric performance and quality will be consistent from season to season and from year to year. However, since the properties of these two fibers differ significantly, the processing is separate until well into the yarn-production process; for blends, fibers are often combined at the drawing or roving stage. Once the fibers are blended, the appropriate amount of twist is added to the yarns. In general, warp yarns have a slightly higher twist to facilitate the weaving process. After the yarns have been spun, they are wound on bobbins and shipped to the mill to be processed into fabric. Yarn processing is discussed in Chapter 10.

Yarn Preparation

Preparation involves several steps. The first step involves the yarns and will be discussed before the fabrication step.

Sizing In **sizing** (also known as slashing), warp yarns are treated before being threaded into the loom for weaving. These yarns are usually wound onto a creel and then coated with a mixture of natural starches, synthetic resins (polyvinyl alcohol or polyacrylamide), and other ingredients so that they resist the abrasion and tension of weaving. Natural starch and its derivatives are most common and the predominant ingredient in most sizings because of low cost, availability, and renewability factors. However, environmental issues related to their use involve non- or low-treatment of wastewater in some countries and the challenges in recycling them. Other sizings are used because of demands from new spinning and weaving technologies. Sizing uses large quantities of chemicals, energy, and water in the process. Research focusing on reducing, improving, or eliminating warp sizing should decrease cost and sustainability issues related to this process. However, sizeless weaving requires greater improvements in yarn quality and loom mechanisms and settings than currently exist. Research has contributed to smaller particle dimensions of the sizing and lower amounts of sizing applied to warp yarns.

Sizing adds a protective coating to the yarn to obtain optimal weaving efficiency, increase yarn rigidity, and decrease yarn hairiness, factors of importance with the faster shuttleless looms. If the sizing is not uniformly applied, warp streak defects may appear on the woven fabric (Figure 16.3). The sizing may contain a starch, metal-to-fiber lubricant, preservative, defoamer, or a combination of these ingredients. Recipes vary by fiber type. For the cotton/polyester-blend fabric, the sizing is probably a mixture of a starch and a lubricant or polyvinyl alcohol. The filling yarns generally receive little, if any, treatment prior to weaving. The sizing must be removed after weaving in order for dyes and finishes to bond with the fibers.

> In **sizing** (also known as slashing), warp yarns are treated before being threaded into the loom for weaving.

Fabrication

Fabrication normally follows sizing. In the fabrication step, the fabric is woven, knitted, or created in some other manner. At the mill, the cotton/polyester yarns are repackaged into the appropriate-size unit for weaving. Warp yarns are threaded through the heddles in the harnesses and the spaces in the reed after sizing. Filling yarns are packaged for the specific type of loom to be used in weaving. Since shuttleless looms are common in the global textile complex, let's assume that this fabric will be made on such a loom. The filling-yarn length is measured during weaving, and the yarns are cut so that only the length needed for one insertion or pick is available at any time. The filling yarn is inserted in a shed that has every other warp yarn raised

Figure 16.3 Warp streaks result from irregular application of sizing on denim: face (left) and back (right).

to create a plain weave. When the length of warp yarns has been woven, the fabric is removed from the loom and transported to the finishing plant for further treatment. For a more detailed discussion of weaving, see Chapter 12.

If yarns break during weaving, fabric defects occur. Figure 16.4 shows defects in denim that occurred when filling or warp yarns broke.

Fabric Preparation

Preparation or pretreatment of fabric is an important step in dyeing and finishing. Fabrics that are properly prepared dye well. Fabrics that are not properly prepared do not dye well or finish poorly. Key preparation steps include desizing, scouring, bleaching, mercerization, and heat setting. These steps focus on improving absorbency, reducing shrinkage, removing impurities, and whitening. Research efforts related to preparation usually focus on improving equipment design, process efficiencies, and chemical and effluent awareness. Because of its impurities, cotton requires more preparation than any other fiber—a significant factor regarding sustainability.

Other dimensions of finishing will be discussed in this section to explain factors that influence fabric quality and freedom from defects that might occur during finishing.

Handling **Handling** refers to the physical form of the fabric during finishing. The components that influence how a fabric will be handled are its width, length, and fabrication. The choices made with regard to handling influence cost, quality, and minimums. **Minimums** describe the smallest quantity of a fabric a buyer can purchase from a mill. Firms that allow for shorter minimums tend to charge higher prices because the cost per yard of finishing short pieces or short runs of fabrics is higher. **Run** describes the quantity of fabric receiving the same processing at the same time. In general, as the length of a run increases, the cost per yard

Figure 16.4 Yarns that break during weaving create fabric flaws: warp yarn break (top) and filling yarn break (bottom).

Figure 16.5 Rope marks on denim: face (top) and back (bottom). These long, irregular marks are caused by abrasion during finishing when the fabric is in rope or tubular form.

decreases. Thus, in general, it is cheaper for a mill to work with a longer piece of fabric than to work with several shorter pieces of fabric.

In terms of fabric width, one option is **open-width finishing**, during which the fabric is held out to its full width. Open-width finishing is often done with the fabric mounted on a tenter frame. Tentering will be discussed later in this chapter.

In a second option, the fabric is allowed to roll and fold in on itself to form a tube or rope. This form of finishing is known as **rope or tubular finishing**. Heavier-weight woven fabrics are usually finished at open width because of the likelihood of creases and wrinkles or tube marks being set in fabric finished in rope form (Figure 16.5). Fabrics for prints or whites can be finished in tube form because rope marks will be removed or hidden during bleaching or printing. However, lighter-weight woven fabrics, especially polyester/cellulose blends, give better results if finished in open-width form. Knit fabrics are usually finished in tube form because of the difficulties in controlling the knit structure in open-width form.

Tube finishing is more economical, but it may create problems with penetration of finishes and dyes into interior portions of the rope or tube. Creasing and wrinkling occur more readily when fabrics are finished in tube form, and some machine-induced creases, wrinkles, and marks are permanent. New techniques and use of different processing chemicals minimize problems with tubular finishing.

A second component of handling refers to whether the fabric is handled in a batch or a continuous process. In **batch processing** a relatively short length of fabric, say several hundred yards, is processed as a unit at one time in one machine. The entire quantity of fabric is immersed in a solution at the same time. **Continuous processing** works with longer pieces of fabric that move in and out of a solution. Continuous processing is more economical but requires larger quantities of fabric to achieve its full potential for minimizing costs per yard. In addition, the size of the finishing equipment requires fairly long pieces of fabric in order to engage all parts of the equipment. It is not as sustainable as batch processing because it consumes huge quantities of water and energy. Because the heavyweight blend fabric used as the example in this chapter is a commodity fabric, continuous open-width processing will be used. However, batch processes are not necessarily sustainable since entire treatment baths may be discarded after each run.

Singeing **Singeing** burns any fiber ends projecting from the surface of the fabric. These protruding ends cause roughness, dullness, and pilling and interfere with finishing. Singeing may be the first finishing operation for smooth-finished cotton or cotton-blend fabrics and for clear-finished wool fabrics. The fabric is passed between two gas flame bars or hot plates to singe it on both sides in one step. Fabrics containing heat-sensitive fibers such as cotton/polyester blends must be singed carefully and often are singed after dyeing because the melted ends of the polyester may cause unevenness in color. Singeing is one way to minimize

> ## ▶ Learning Activity 1

As a product manager for a private label line for shirts and tops, you are discussing fabric options with the product development team. Define these terms: minimum, run, batch process, continuous process, open-width, and tubular finishing. Explain why these terms might be important in determining fabric purchases for private label merchandise.

pilling. Singeing is used to give a smooth surface to fabrics that will be printed so that the print remains sharp and clear with crisp and distinct edges of the print pattern. Even a slightly fuzzy surface would produce a hazy or blurred print.

Desizing

In **desizing**, the sizing added to the warp yarns is removed. Desizing is needed with wovens, but not with knits. (Remember, only woven fabrics have warp yarns, which usually require sizing before weaving.) Desizing is necessary so that dyes and finishes will bond to both warp and filling yarns. For desizing to be effective, the finisher needs to know the sizing agent used to select the best means of desizing.

Physical, biological (or bio), or chemical desizing may be done, depending on the sizing agents and fiber content. Although sizing is present only on the warp yarns, the entire fabric is treated since the warp and filling yarns cannot be separated. In cotton-blend fabrics, a combination of physical desizing (agitation) and biological desizing using an amylase enzyme may be used to destroy the starch.

Desizing is another significant step in terms of energy and water use. Desizing is a large source of wastewater pollutants. Bio desizing with enzymes, also known as enzyme desizing, is gaining in popularity since it saves water, energy, and time. But it is more expensive and slower compared to chemical desizing. Combining bio desizing with ultrasonic energy may speed the process without affecting sustainability of this process.

Cleaning

All gray goods must undergo **cleaning** to be made ready to accept any finish. Warp sizing residue left on gray goods after desizing must be removed because it makes the fabric stiff and interferes with the absorption of liquids. Fabrics that are soiled during fabrication and storage also must be cleaned. Warp sizing, dirt, and oil are removed by a washing process. Terms used to describe cleaning vary with fiber content. *Degumming* of silk usually is done in boiling water with detergent, although acid degumming and enzyme degumming are also used. *Scouring*, also know as *kier boiling* or *boiling-off,* of cotton is done in an alkaline solution at high temperature and under pressure in large vessels called *kiers*. *Scouring* of wool is a gentler washing process under less alkaline conditions.

Scouring

Scouring is a general term referring to removal of foreign matter or soil from the fabric prior to finishing or dyeing. The specific procedure is related to the fiber content. The foreign matter involved may be processing oils, starch, natural waxes, pectins, proteins, minerals, soils, and tints or color added to aid in fiber identification during production. Foreign matter must be removed to achieve good absorbency, which is necessary for good dyeing and finishing. Scouring usually involves the use of detergents and alkaline solutions. It may be repeated during finishing to remove excess chemicals or soil.

Alkaline souring is widely used, but it is not considered a sustainable practice because of the high temperatures, quantities of water and scouring chemicals used, and the content and pH of the wastewater. For example, scouring wastewater contains alkalis, fats, oils, waxes, lint, and wetting agents.

Bio-scouring or enzyme scouring uses pectinase enzymes and is more sustainable. In some facilities bio-desizing is combined with bio-scouring in one step, further increasing savings, reducing time and energy use, and decreasing waste water treatment. Ultrasonic scouring is an alternate to chemical scouring and may be combined with bio-scouring.

Singeing burns any fiber ends projecting from the surface of the fabric. These protruding ends cause roughness, dullness, and pilling and interfere with finishing.

In **desizing**, the sizing added to the warp yarns is removed. Desizing is necessary so that dyes and finishes will bond to both warp and filling yarns.

Scouring is a general term referring to removal of foreign matter or soil from the fabric prior to finishing or dyeing.

Bio-polishing is the use of a cellulase enzyme treatment to remove surface fuzz from spun yarns of cellulose or cellulose blends.

Figure 16.6 Unbleached (bottom) and bleached fabric (top).

Bleaching is the process of whitening fibers, yarns, or fabrics by removing irregular natural color. **Optical brighteners** are also used to whiten off-white fabrics.

Bio-polishing **Bio-polishing** is the use of a cellulase enzyme treatment to remove surface fuzz from spun yarns of cellulose or cellulose blends. The process is most often applied to cotton or cotton/polyester-blend fabrics. Bio-polishing is a permanent finish. The finished fabric has a soft, smooth appearance with very little surface fuzz. Protruding fiber ends that make up the fuzz in most spun-yarn fabrics are destroyed by the enzyme treatment. By removing the fiber ends, the potential for fabric pilling during use is decreased. Colors look brighter because the fabric's smooth surface does not scatter the light as much as a fuzzy surface would. Although the surface properties and appearance of the fabric are improved, a slight decrease of 3 to 10 percent in tensile strength usually occurs. Some products may be marketed with a hang-tag indicating that they have been bio-polished. This process may be used instead of singeing.

Whitening

Bleaching **Bleaching** is the process of whitening fibers, yarns, or fabrics by removing irregular natural color (Figure 16.6). Most bleaches are oxidizing agents; the actual bleaching is done by active oxygen. A few bleaches are reducing agents and are used to strip color from poorly dyed fabrics. Bleaches may be either acidic or alkaline in nature. The goals of bleaching are uniform removal of hydrophobic fabric impurities and a high, uniform degree of fabric whiteness in order to achieve clear uniform colors when dyeing, especially for pale colors.

The same bleach is not suitable for all fibers. Because chemical reactions differ between fibers, bleaches are selected with regard to fiber content. Synthetic fibers rarely need bleaching since fiber whiteness can be controlled during spinning.

Any bleach damages fibers. Since damage occurs more rapidly at higher temperatures and concentrations, these two factors are carefully controlled. Bleaches clean and whiten gray goods. Natural fibers have an off-white color because they contain impurities. These impurities are easily removed from cotton, so most cotton gray goods are bleached without damage. Bleaching may be omitted with wool because it has good affinity for dyes and other finishes even when not bleached. Ultrasonic energy can be combined with conventional bleaching to speed the process and improve whiteness, especially with fine fibers.

Peroxide bleaches are common commercial bleaches for cellulose and protein goods. Hydrogen peroxide is an oxidizing bleach most often used on cotton. Peroxide bleaches best at high temperatures in alkaline solutions. These bleaching conditions make it possible to bleach cellulose gray goods as the final step in the kier boil. However, fiber damage occurs if the process is not closely controlled. In the peroxide cold-bleach procedure, the fabric is soaked for several hours. This procedure is common with cotton-knits and wool to preserve a soft hand. Peroxide bleaching is not as sustainable as alternate procedures because of the high temperatures and high use of energy, water, and additional chemical agents needed such as salt and stabilizers.

Peracetic acid bleaching is a more sustainable alternative because of the cooler temperatures, lower energy and water use, and minimal fiber damage. It is used for nylon, cotton, and flax that will be dyed medium or dark colors.

Optical Brighteners **Optical brighteners** are also used to whiten off-white fabrics. These fluorescent whitening compounds are not bleaches. They soak into the fiber and mask yellow by absorbing energy in the ultraviolet region of the spectrum and re-emitting it as visible light. Optical brighteners work best when used with bleach rather than as a substitute for it. They are also added to the spinning solution of some manufactured fibers to optically brighten them, since bleach may not be effective on these fibers. Optical brighteners can be used with delustered and nondelustered fibers without affecting fiber luster.

Alternate Preparation Steps

Mercerization **Mercerization** is the process of treating a cellulosic fabric or yarn with an alkali (caustic soda, also known as sodium hydroxide or lye). Although Native Americans used wood ash (lye) to strengthen plant fibers, modern mercerizing was discovered in 1853 by John Mercer, a calico printer. He noticed that cotton fabric shrank and became stronger, more lustrous, and more absorbent after filtering the caustic soda used in dyeing. Mercerization was little used until 1897 when H. Lowe discovered that fabrics under tension became lustrous and silky.

Mercerization is used on large lengths of cotton, linen, and some HWM rayon and lyocell fabrics. It increases luster, softness, strength, and affinity for dyes and waterborne finishes. Cotton yarn, fabric, and sewing thread are mercerized. Plissé effects are achieved with cotton fabrics (see Chapter 17). Systems are becoming available to handle shorter lengths of fabric.

Yarn mercerization is a continuous process in which the yarn under tension passes through a series of boxes with guide rolls and squeeze rolls, a boil-out wash, and a final wash (Figure 16.7).

Fabric mercerization is done on a frame that contains rollers for saturating the fabric; a tenter frame for tensioning the fabric both crosswise and lengthwise while wet; and boxes for washing, neutralizing the caustic soda with dilute sulfuric acid, scouring, and rinsing. In **tension mercerization**, the fabric or yarn being mercerized is held under tension. The concentration of the sodium hydroxide solution is high enough that the fiber swells. Because the fibers are under tension during swelling, they become rounder in cross section and more rodlike, and the number of convolutions decreases (Figure 16.8). The smoother fiber reflects more light. A small percentage of cotton, primarily long-staple cotton yarns and fabrics, is mercerized for the luster increase.

Mercerization increases absorbency because the caustic soda causes a rearrangement of the molecules, making more of the hydroxyl groups available to absorb water and waterborne substances. Moisture regain improves to approximately 11 percent. Dyes enter the fiber more readily and have better colorfastness. For the same reason, mercerized fabrics take resin finishes better.

Mercerized cotton fibers are stronger because in the swollen fiber the molecules are more oriented. When stress is applied, the end-to-end molecular attraction is harder to rupture than in the more spiral fibril arrangement. The increase in fiber strength is approximately 30 percent.

In **slack mercerization**, cotton fabric is dipped, at low tension, into a weaker caustic soda solution for a shorter time before neutralizing and washing. As the fabric shrinks, yarn

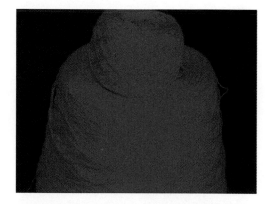

Figure 16.7 Regular cotton yarn (bottom) and mercerized cotton (top).

Figure 16.8 Photomicrographs of mercerized cotton: cross-sectional view (left), longitudinal view (right).
SOURCE: Courtesy of the British Textile Technology Group.

A neighbor has just gotten involved in quilting and wants to know the advantages or disadvantages of mercerized quilting thread over regular sewing thread. What will you tell the neighbor?

Mercerization is the process of treating a cellulosic fabric or yarn with an alkali to make cellulosic fabrics stronger, more lustrous, and more absorbent.

crimp increases. Straightening the crimp when stress is applied produces stretch. In addition, slack mercerization increases fiber absorbency and improves dyeability.

Sodium hydroxide is a strong alkali with a high pH. It requires careful handling and can cause severe tissue burns. Solutions containing sodium hydroxide or rinses after mercerization require neutralization of the high pH and treatment to remove sodium salts.

Ammoniating Finishes An **ammoniating finish** is an alternative to mercerization used on cotton and rayon. Yarns or fabrics are treated with a weak ammonium solution at high temperatures, passed through hot water, stretched, and dried in hot air. The finish is similar to mercerization but is less expensive. Liquid ammonia is complex to process and dangerous to handle. However, safer and more workable systems are available. The ammonia swells the fiber less than sodium hydroxide. Ammonia-treated or ammoniated fabrics have good luster and dyeability, but less than mercerized fabrics. Ammonia-treated fabrics have good crease recovery with less loss of strength and abrasion resistance and may not need to be treated to be wrinkle-resistant. Ammonia-treated fabrics are softer than mercerized fabrics. These fabrics have an increase in tensile strength of 40 percent and an increase in elongation two to three times that of untreated cotton. These fabrics are less sensitive to thermal degradation. Sanforized and Permafix are trade names for easy-care cotton fabrics. Liquid ammonia treatments are a common substitute for mercerization of cotton sewing threads.

An **ammoniating finish** is an alternative to mercerization in which yarns or fabrics are treated with a weak ammonium solution.

Coloration

Color is normally added to the fabric at this stage. Properly prepared goods are critical to the quality of the dye or print. Dyeing and printing are discussed in detail in Chapter 19.

Finishing

Special-Purpose Finishes *Special-purpose finishes* that might be appropriate for the cotton/polyester-blend fabric include wrinkle-resistant, soil-release, and fabric-softening finishes. They usually follow dyeing to avoid interfering with fiber dye absorption. These finishes are discussed in Chapter 18.

Drying

Because of the frequent wetting of textiles in finishing, **drying** also is frequent, especially with cellulosics, to minimize mildew and weight. In drying, hot air is blown past the textile in a large convection oven to remove the water quickly by evaporation. Fabrics in convection ovens are usually tentered. Some dryers combine hot air and radio frequency technology that agitates water molecules and speeds drying, Other less efficient means of drying fabrics include contact with hot metal rollers (conduction drying) and use of infrared lamps, or microwaves (irradiation).

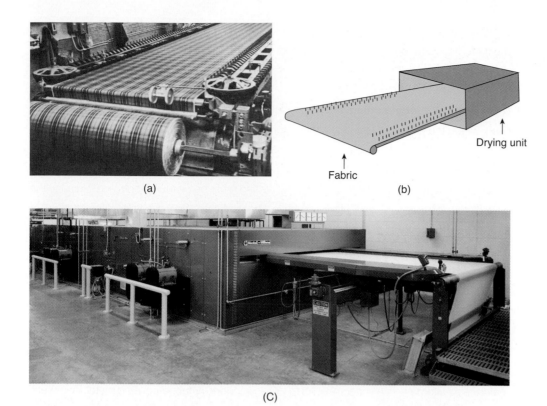

(a)

Fabric

Drying unit

(b)

(C)

Figure 16.9 Tenter frames: (a) clip tenter, (b) drawing of pin-tenter frame, (c) modern tentering line.
SOURCE: Courtesy of Marshall & Williams Co.

Computers and software reduces the risk of poor or overdrying that will create problems in other processes. Drying should not create wrinkles or creases. Overdrying of cotton can create problems in dyeing. Some dryers combine heat exchangers, cooling exchangers, and condensers for increased efficiency and energy recovery.

Tentering **Tentering**, an important finishing operation, applies crosswise and lengthwise tension to fabric while it dries. Its purpose is to produce fabric that meets specifications for width and width uniformity, and warp and filling count. Tenter frames are either pin tenters or clip tenters (Figure 16.9). The mechanisms on the two sides move around like a caterpillar tractor wheel, holding the fabric selvage by a series of pins or clips. More tension can be exerted by the clip tenter. The pin tenter is used for stretch and knit fabrics that are tentered at slower speeds to reduce fabric stretching. To minimize lengthwise shrinkage or to minimize stretching of knits, overfeeding is used. In overfeeding, the fabric is fed into the tentering frame faster than the frame moves. The marks of the pins or the clips may appear along the selvage (Figure 16.10).

Tentering is an important finishing step in determining fabric quality. If the filling yarns are not exactly perpendicular to the warp yarns, the fabric is off-grain. When the filling yarn does not cross each warp yarn at a 90-degree angle, the fabric exhibits *skew*. When the center of the fabric moves at a slower speed than the two edges, the fabric exhibits *bow* (see Chapter 12). Both off-grain problems can be eliminated by proper tentering. Most tentering frames have electronic sensors to reduce off-grain problems. Fabric may go through a tentering frame several times during finishing. When a fabric is tentered off-grain, it will be printed off-grain. Tentering is usually the last opportunity to correct any fabric variations that develop during finishing.

Figure 16.10 Fabric selvages of clip tentering (left) and pin tentering (right). Clip tentering rarely leaves easily visible marks. Pin tentering almost always leaves telltale holes along the edge.

Tentering applies crosswise and lengthwise tension to fabric while it dries. In **heat setting**, the fabric is placed on a tenter frame and passed through an oven, where the exposure time and temperature are carefully controlled based on fiber content and resins used.

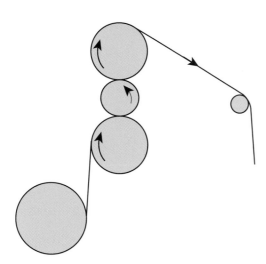

Figure 16.11 Calender machine.

Calendering is a mechanical finishing operation performed by a series of rollers between which the fabric passes. Types include simple, friction, moiré, schreiner, and embossing.

Reworking includes inspecting fabric for defects or flaws and repairing problems wherever possible.

Loop Drying
Fabrics with a soft finish, towels, and stretchy fabrics such as knits are not dried on the tenter frame but on a *loop dryer* without tension. Many rayon fabrics are dried on loop dryers because of their lower wet strength and soft hand.

Heat Setting
In **heat setting**, the fabric is placed on a tenter frame and passed through an oven, where the exposure time and temperature are carefully controlled based on fiber content and resins used. A cotton/polyester fabric would require heat setting if it had been given a wrinkle-resistant or soil-release finish or if the percentage of polyester was 50 percent or more to achieve a degree of shrinkage control. Heat setting must be carefully controlled because the heat history of polyester and other synthetic fibers affects their dyeability. Heat setting of synthetics can set yarn twist, weave crimp, and wrinkle resistance.

Calendering
Calendering is a mechanical finishing operation performed by a series of rollers between which the fabric passes. The types of calendering include simple, friction, moiré, schreiner, and embossing. Each type produces a different finish. Simple calendering will be discussed here; the others will be discussed in Chapter 17.

The *simple calender* produces a smooth, flat, ironed finish on the fabric. The fabric is slightly damp before it enters the calender. Calenders have from two to seven rollers. Hard-metal rollers alternate with softer rollers of foam, solid paper, or fabric-covered metal. Two metal rollers never run against each other. The metal rolls are heated. The fabric travels through the calender at the same speed as the rollers rotate, so they exert pressure to smooth out the wrinkles and give a slight sheen (Figure 16.11).

Reworking

Reworking includes inspecting fabric for defects or flaws and repairing problems wherever possible.

Inspecting
Fabric inspection is done by moving fabrics over an inverted frame in good light. Fabric inspectors mark flaws in the fabric and record its quality at the same time. Flaws may be marked on the fabric, usually on the selvage, so that subsequent cutting and sewing operators can avoid working with and adding value to product parts that incorporate flaws. Computers and electronic sensors help assess fabric quality. Fabric quality is a complex area that takes into account the number of flaws, their severity, and their length or size. Mills and buyers work together to define quality levels acceptable to both parties.

Repairing
When economically feasible, **repairing** corrects flaws marked by inspectors. Broken yarns are clipped, snagged yarns are worked into the fabric, and defects are marked so that adjustments can be made when fabrics are sold. The fabric is then wound on bolts or cylinders, ready for shipment.

Routine Finishing Steps for Wool Fabrics
Crabbing

Crabbing is a finishing process used to set wool fabrics. Fabrics are immersed first in hot water, and then in cold water, and passed between rollers as in simple calendering.

Decating

Decating produces a smooth, wrinkle-free finish and lofty hand on woolen and worsted fabrics and on blends of wool and manufactured fibers. The process is comparable to steam ironing. A high degree of luster can be developed by the decating process because of the smoothness of the surface. The dry fabric is wound under tension on a perforated cylinder. Steam is forced through the fabric. Moisture and heat relax tensions and remove wrinkles. The yarns are set and fixed in this position by cold air. For a more permanent set, dry decating is done in a pressure boiler. Wet decating often precedes napping or other finishes to remove wrinkles that have been acquired in scouring. Wet decating as a final finish gives a more permanent set to the yarns than does dry decating. Decating may also be used with wool blends of rayon and other manufactured fibers or knits.

Carbonizing

Carbonizing, the treatment of wool yarns or fabrics with sulfuric acid, destroys plant matter in the fabric and allows for more level dyeing. Recycled wool is carbonized to remove any cellulose that may have been used in the original fabric. Carbonizing, a preparation finish for wool, gives better texture to all-wool fabrics, but the process requires high temperatures and strong acid. The process can damage wool fibers causing subsequent problems in dyeing and finishing wool. The acid must be neutralized to avoid problems in dyeing or in consumer use. High temperatures require more energy use and increase the cost of finishing wool. Bio-scouring of wool to remove plant matter is a more sustainable alternate to carbonizing because it can be done at lower temperatures and less wastewater treatment is needed.

Pressing

Pressing is the term used with wool or wool blends. In pressing, the fabric is placed between metal plates that steam and press the fabric.

Finishing steps for wool include crabbing, decating, carbonizing, and pressing.

▶ Learning Activity 4

Use Fabrics #108, 109, and 126 from your swatch kit. Explain the differences and similarities among the three 100 percent cotton fabrics. Describe the serviceability of each based on fiber content, yarn type, fabrication method, and finish. How has finishing changed the serviceability of these fabrics?

▶ Learning Activity 5

Select one of the textiles you are wearing today and list the finishes in the most likely sequence that were probably used to finish this fabric. Describe their impact on the quality and performance of the product. How would this sequence change if the fabric were made of wool or silk?

Environmental Concerns and Sustainability of Finishing

Finishing transforms a harsh and unattractive fabric into an attractive one. Unfortunately, the environmental impact of this transformation can be significant. Almost every step in finishing a fabric has an impact on the environment. The textile complex is acutely aware of the situation and has become proactive to safeguard the environment. Many environmental concerns and issues of sustainability were discussed with specific finishes. Finishing facilities incorporate systems for air-pollution control, pollution prevention, and hazardous-waste disposal. These systems minimize discharge into any part of the environment (air, land, or water).

Gaining interest within the textile complex are pollution prevention and pollution reduction. Possibilities being investigated include closed-loop systems, reclaiming or reusing chemicals, recycling water, using new technologies like plasma treatment, and using less hazardous chemicals like enzymes. Factors that are influencing these changes include costs, regulations and laws, liability lawsuits, and public awareness.

Finishing uses significant quantities of water and energy. Forty years ago, it was not unusual for a large finishing facility to use millions of gallons of water daily. Water use has decreased, but it continues to be used to dissolve chemicals and to remove waste and soil from the system. The quality of the water supply is a growing concern. Foam finishing and other less water-intensive processes are increasing in importance. Better and more efficient means of extracting water from fabrics prior to drying and heat-recovery systems minimize energy use.

Finishing uses quantities of potentially hazardous chemicals. There are restrictions on the discharge of waste with high biological oxygen demand (BOD), such as sizing agents, and high chemical oxygen demand (COD), such as chlorine-containing compounds. Hazardous, toxic, and carcinogenic finishing chemicals are being replaced with less hazardous, nontoxic, and noncarcinogenic chemicals. Biodegradable finishes are becoming more common. Many companies are phasing out chemicals used as ingredients in some finishes because they are not sustainable. Such chemicals being phased out include some wetting agents, detergent additives, and softening compounds.

In addition, changes in technology and good operating practices ensuring that fabrics are finished correctly limit excess use of chemicals, water, and energy; minimize environmental impact; and improve sustainability. Many finishers have treatment facilities on-site so that they can reclaim and reuse chemicals and remove contaminants before discharging waste to municipal systems. Membrane technology and reverse osmosis provide effective means of producing high-quality discharge by separating salts, metals, organic compounds, and other contaminants before water leaves the finishing plant's treatment facility.

▶ Learning Activity 6

Describe the environmental impact of finishing one of the textile products you are wearing today. How much of the appeal of this product is due to its finish(es)? How likely would its purchase have been if the fabric had not been finished?

key terms

review questions

1. Describe the differences among permanent finish, durable finish, temporary finish, and renewable finish.

2. Why are yarns finished before fabrication? What finishes are used on yarns? Of these yarn finishes, which are designed to facilitate other processes and which will be present when items are purchased by consumers?

3. Why are fabrics finished before dyeing or printing? How does the quality of finishing affect the quality of the dye or print?

4. At what stage is bleaching normally done? Why is it done at that time?

5. What problems can occur if tentering is improperly done? How does this affect fabric quality?

6. What differences may occur in finished fabrics between open-width and tubular or rope finishing?

7. Describe a finishing routine for these fabrics. Explain how the finishing routine differs because of fiber content or fabric structure from that of a cotton/polyester bottom weight plain-weave fabric.
   a. Acetate velvet
   b. Cotton knit velour
   c. Polyester crepe de chine
   d. Upholstery weight wool pocket cloth
   e. Silk brocade

8. Explain how tentering can affect fabric quality. How can improper tentering create bow or skew in fabrics?

9. Explain why finishing is done for almost all fabrics.

10. How does finishing add value to textile fabrics?

11. How has finishing been modified to be more sustainable? What kinds of chemicals are becoming more common in finishing? How do these chemicals reduce the environmental impact of finishing?

Case Study
Finishing Linen Fabric*

Linen, one of the bast fibers known for its strength, comfort, and easily identifiable look, is experiencing renewed interest because of its sustainability. It is prone to wrinkling, shrinkage, and poor abrasion resistance. Liquid ammonia finishing can compensate for some of linen's negative characteristics. Treated linen has less shrinkage and improved abrasion resistance and appearance after washing. Treated fabrics, especially heavier ones, have noticeably fewer wrinkles after washing, but show only slight improvements in wrinkle performance during wear.

DISCUSSION QUESTIONS

1. Why is linen experiencing renewed interest? What is it about linen's production that makes it sustainable?

2. Name two heavier weight and two lighter weight fabrics that are often linen. Why would liquid ammonia treatment have a greater impact on the wrinkling of heavier weight fabrics?

3. Explain how this treatment might affect consumer satisfaction with a linen suit or a linen blouse.

4. How might the care labels differ between two identical linen garments where one has been given the liquid ammonia treatment and the other one did not receive that treatment?

*Csiszár, E., Dornyi, B., Somlai, P., & Bors, A. (2006). Liquid ammonia treatment of linen fabrics. *AATCC Review, 6*(7), 43–48.

suggested readings

Atlaş, S., & Pamul, G. (2007). Ultrasonic energy in the textile industry. *AATCC Review, 7*(6), 29–31.

Csiszár, E., Dornyi, B., Somlai, P., & Bors, A. (2006). Liquid ammonia treatment of linen fabrics. *AATCC Review, 6*(7), 43–48.

Etters, J. N., & Annis, P. A. (1998, May). Textile enzyme use: A developing technology. *American Dyestuff Reporter*, pp. 18–23.

Fulmer, T. D. (1992, November). Cotton preparation is crucial. *America's Textiles International*, pp. 52, 53, 55.

Gebhart, G. (1995, September). Comparing mercerizing concepts: Chain versus chainless systems. *American Dyestuff Reporter*, pp. 76–78, 80, 82, 84.

Goswami, B. C., Anandjiwala, R. D., & Hall, D. M. (2004). *Textile Sizing*. New York: Marcel Dekker.

Gouveia, I. C., Fiadeiro, J. M., & Queiroz, J. A. (2008). Enzymatic wool treatment: Preliminary evaluation of *Trichoderma reesei* cellulases and *Aspergillus aculeatus* pectinases and hemicellulases. *AATCC Review, 8*(10), 38–44.

Isaacs, M. (1999, September). Tenterframes: Finishing plant workhorses. *Textile World*, pp. 110, 112–115.

Kuilderd, H., & Wu, G. (2008). Simultaneous desizing and scouring with enzymes. *AATCC Review, 8*(6), 33–36.

Perkins, W. S. (1996, January). Advances made in bleaching practice. *America's Textiles International*, pp. 92–94.

Perkins, W. S. (1996, February). The two sides of warp sizing. *America's Textiles International*, pp. 79–80.

Preša, P., & Tavčer, P. F. (2008). Pretreated cotton fiber characterization. *AATCC Review, 8*(11), 37–43.

Sawhney, A. P. S., Sachinvala, N. D., Calamari, T. A., Dumitras, P. G., Bologa, M. K., & Singh, K. V. (2005). Approaches for reducing or eliminating warp sizing in weaving: An interim report. *AATCC Review, 5*(9), 23–26.

Thiry, M. C. (2006). A thirsty industry. *AATCC Review, 6*(7), 21–24.

Thiry, M. C. (2006). Do you believe in magic? *AATCC Review, 6*(4), 21–26.

Thiry, M. C. (2008). Half-dyed: The importance of preparation. *AATCC Review, 8*(9), 24–31.

Thomas, H. (1994, April). The current state of weaving preparation. *America's Textiles International*, pp. 71–73.

Wang, Y. (Ed.), (2006). *Recycling in Textiles*. Cambridge, England: Woodhead.

Zein, K. (1994, July). Teamwork needed to combat environmental problems. *Textile Month*, pp. 9–13.

AESTHETIC FINISHES

CHAPTER OBJECTIVES

- To understand how finishes alter aesthetic aspects of fabrics.
- To recognize the value added to fabrics and products by aesthetic finishes.
- To know the ways that aesthetic finishes can be applied to fabrics.
- To predict the performance of textiles with aesthetic finishes.
- To differentiate between applied designs and structural designs and their implications for quality and performance.

17

Aesthetic finishes change the appearance and/or hand of fabrics. The finished fabric's name may reflect the change in appearance or the technique. For example, eyelet embroidery, ciré satin, and organdy are made by aesthetic finishes. Figure 17.1 shows several fabrics that were converted from print cloth: percale (printed), chintz (waxed and friction calendered), plissé (caustic-soda print), and embossed cotton (embossed calendered). This fabric also could be flocked, embroidered, or surface-coated.

Aesthetic finishes are an **applied design**. This means they are applied to a fabric with the express purpose of altering some visual, textural, hand, or other aesthetic dimension of the fabric. They are quicker and less expensive than incorporating the design as the fabric is produced (*structural design*). Sometimes applied designs are also referred to as **surface design**, meaning that the finish is applied to the surface of the textile. Many of these finishes are used for both apparel and interior textiles. Table 17.1 compares structural and applied designs.

Aesthetic finishes can be grouped by the change produced in the fabric: luster, drape, texture, and hand. The process, its effect, and the relationship of the finish to the fabric name will be explained for each group. Some aesthetic finishes determine or influence the name of a fabric. Other finishes give certain fabrics their traditional luster, drape, texture, or hand. Fabrics that have received aesthetic finishes are shown in Figure 17.2.

Many of these finishes are **additive finishes** where a finishing chemical is added to the fabric to produce texture (body, stiffness, softness), luster, embossed designs, and abrasion resistance in the fabric. Some are **subtractive finishes**: Something is removed from the fabric during finishing. Some finishes are mechanical where the fabric is mechanically distorted or altered with heat or pressure; other finishes are chemical where the fabric is chemically changed. Finish permanence depends on the process, the fiber content, and the type of finish itself.

> **Aesthetic finishes** change the appearance and/or hand of fabrics. They are an **applied or surface design**. They are applied to a fabric to alter some visual, textural, hand, or other aesthetic dimension of the fabric. They are quicker and less expensive than *structural design*. In **additive finishes**, a finishing chemical is added to the fabric to produce texture, luster, embossed designs, and abrasion resistance in the fabric. In **subtractive finishes**, something is removed from the fabric during finishing. Finish permanence depends on the process, the fiber content, and the type of finish itself.

Figure 17.1 Fabric converted from print cloth: gray goods (upper left), screen-printed (upper center), waxed and friction-calendered (upper right), printed with caustic soda (bottom left), embossed (bottom center), piece-dyed and flocked (bottom right).

Table 17.1 Comparison of Structural and Applied Designs

Structural Designs	Applied Designs
Usually more expensive	Usually less expensive
Decisions made earlier in the process; more time-consuming	Decisions made later in the process; less time-consuming
Permanent design	Permanent, durable, or temporary design
Often on-grain (knits and some wovens may be skewed)	Figures may be off-grain
Fabric not damaged by process	May tender or weaken fabric
	Process may damage fabric
Kinds and Types	
Novelty or fancy yarns (in any fabrication)	Printed
Woven—jacquard, dobby, extra yarn, swivel dot, lappet designs, piqué, double cloth, or any fabric made with novelty or fancy yarns	Flocked
	Tufted
	Embroidered
	Burned out
	Embossed
Knitted—jacquard single-knits, jacquard double-knits, or any fabric made with novelty or fancy yarns	Plissé
	Napped
	Emerized
Lace	Abrasive or chemical wash
Typical Fabrics	
Huck, damask, brocade, tapestry, shirting madras, piqué, dotted swiss, matelassé	Flock dotted swiss, embroidered, burned out, glazed chintz, moiré taffeta, embossed, frosted, suede

Sustainability issues associated with aesthetic finishes relate to use of chemicals, energy use for the process, and processing of waste. As with routine finishes, efforts to make these finishes more sustainable focus on controlling energy use, recycling chemicals, reducing water use, treating waste, and substituting sustainable chemicals and processes.

The **padding machine** applies dyes and finishing chemicals in either liquid or paste form to fabric (Figure 17.3). Padding is done by passing the fabric through the solution, under a guide roll, and between two padding rolls. The type of roll depends on the finish to be applied. Rolls exert tons of pressure on the fabric, forcing the finish into the fiber or yarn to ensure good penetration. Excess liquid is squeezed off. The fabric is then steamed, cleaned, and dried.

▶ Learning Activity 1

Work in groups of three or four to answer these questions:
1. How do aesthetic finishes add value to textiles?
2. What are the interactions between fashion and aesthetic finishes?
3. How do aesthetic finishes affect product serviceability?
4. Are aesthetic finishes sustainable? Why or why not?

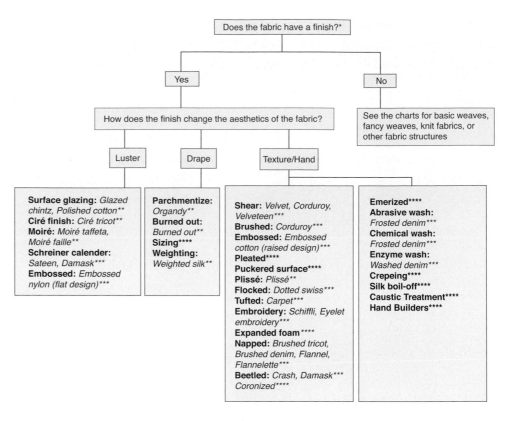

Figure 17.2 Flowchart of fabrics with aesthetic finishes.

The flowchart shows:

Does the fabric have a finish?*
- **Yes** → How does the finish change the aesthetics of the fabric?
- **No** → See the charts for basic weaves, fancy weaves, knit fabrics, or other fabric structures

Branches from "How does the finish change the aesthetics of the fabric?":

Luster
- **Surface glazing:** *Glazed chintz, Polished cotton***
- **Ciré finish:** *Ciré tricot***
- **Moiré:** *Moiré taffeta, Moiré faille***
- **Schreiner calender:** *Sateen, Damask****
- **Embossed:** *Embossed nylon (flat design)****

Drape
- **Parchmentize:** *Organdy***
- **Burned out:** *Burned out***
- **Sizing******
- **Weighting:** *Weighted silk***

Texture/Hand
- **Shear:** *Velvet, Corduroy, Velveteen****
- **Brushed:** *Corduroy****
- **Embossed:** *Embossed cotton (raised design)****
- **Pleated******
- **Puckered surface******
- **Plissé:** *Plissé***
- **Flocked:** *Dotted swiss****
- **Tufted:** *Carpet****
- **Embroidery:** *Schiffli, Eyelet embroidery****
- **Expanded foam******
- **Napped:** *Brushed tricot, Brushed denim, Flannel, Flannelette****
- **Beetled:** *Crash, Damask**** *Coronized*****

- **Emerized******
- **Abrasive wash:** *Frosted denim****
- **Chemical wash:** *Frosted denim****
- **Enzyme wash:** *Washed denim****
- **Crepeing******
- **Silk boil-off******
- **Caustic Treatment******
- **Hand Builders******

* Only some finishes create a visual or tactile change in the fabric
** Fabric name influenced by this finish
*** Examples of fabrics with this finish
**** Finish is not used to determine a fabric name

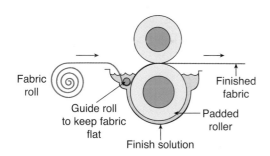

Figure 17.3 Padding machine.

(Labels: Fabric roll; Guide roll to keep fabric flat; Finish solution; Padded roller; Finished fabric)

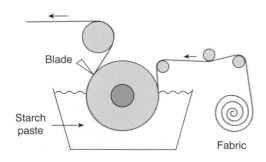

Figure 17.4 Backfilling machine.

(Labels: Blade; Starch paste; Fabric)

The **backfilling machine** is a variation of the padding machine. It applies the finish to one side only, usually to the back of the fabric (Figure 17.4). Padding and backfilling machines that use less water in the process are becoming increasingly common.

Luster

Luster finishes produce a change in a fabric's light reflectance. Most of these finishes increase light reflectance and improve the fabric's luster or shine. The increase in luster may be over the entire fabric—as in the glazed, ciré, and schreiner finishes—or it may be a localized increase in luster—as in the moiré and embossed finishes. These finishes are done by calendering—passing the fabric between two cylinders that exert pressure on the fabric. Different calenders produce different effects on the fabric: glazed, ciré, moiré, schreiner, and embossed.

Glazed

Glazed chintz and polished cotton are two fabrics that receive surface glazing. A **friction calender** produces a highly **glazed surface**. If the fabric is first saturated with starch and waxes, the finish is temporary. If resin finishes are used, the glaze is durable. The fabric is passed through the finishing solution and partially dried. It is then calendered. The speed of the metal roller is greater than the speed of the fabric, and the roller polishes or glazes the surface (see Figure 17.1). Glazed chintz and polished cotton are used for apparel, lightweight upholstery, window treatments, and bedspreads. Because of consumer expectations and sustainability issues, wax and starch are less commonly used while resins, modified to decrease environmental impact, are more commonly used because they produce a more durable aesthetic change.

Ciré

A **ciré finish** is similar to a glazed finish, except that the metal roll is hot to produce greater luster on the fabric's surface. When thermoplastic (heat-sensitive) fibers are used, the fiber surface that comes in contact with the metal roll melts and flattens slightly, producing a highly polished fabric. Ciré is a taffeta, satin, or tricot fabric hot-friction-calendered to give a high gloss, or "wet" look for apparel and accessories.

Plasticize

A **plasticize finish** is a very thin layer of polymer added to a dyed fabric. Often applied to heavier-weight fabrics, this finish adds a more pronounced glaze and slicker hand to the fabric's surface. As an added bonus, the fabric is also soil-resistant and water-repellent. Plasticize fabrics are most often used for apparel.

Moiré

Moiré fabrics have a wood grain or watermarked appearance and are used for somewhat formal looks for apparel and interior textiles, especially upholstery and wall and window coverings. Two techniques are used to produce a **moiré** pattern on fabric. In *true moiré*, two layers of an unbalanced plain-weave rib fabric such as taffeta or faille are placed face to face so that the ribs of the top layer are slightly off-grain in relation to the underlayer. The two layers are stitched or held together along the selvage and are then fed into a smooth heated-metal-roll calender. Pressure of 8 to 10 tons causes the rib pattern of the top layer to press into the bottom layer and vice versa. Flattened areas in the ribs reflect more light and contrast with unflattened areas. This procedure can be modified to produce patterned moiré designs other than the traditional watermarked one.

In the second technique, an embossed-metal roll is used. The embossed roll has a moiré pattern engraved on it. When the roll passes over a ribbed fabric, the ribs are flattened in areas and a moiré pattern is created. If the fabric is thermoplastic and the roll is heated, the finish is permanent (Figure 17.5). The pattern of the embossed roll determines the pattern achieved. The repeat of the pattern is related to the diameter of the embossed roll.

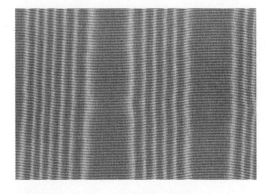

Figure 17.5   Moiré taffeta.

Schreiner

Fabrics with a schreiner finish have a softer luster than most of the other luster finishes. The **schreiner calender** (Figure 17.6) has a metal roller engraved with 200 to 300 fine diagonal lines per inch that are visible only under a magnifying glass. (These lines should not be confused with yarn twist.) Unless resins and thermoplastic fibers are used, this finish is temporary and removed by the first washing. This finish scatters light rays and produces a deep-seated luster rather than a shine. It also flattens the yarns to reduce the space between them and increase smoothness and cover. It can upgrade a lower-quality fabric. A schreiner finish is used on cotton sateen for apparel, upholstery, wall and window coverings, and table damask to make them more lustrous and on nylon tricot for apparel to increase its cover.

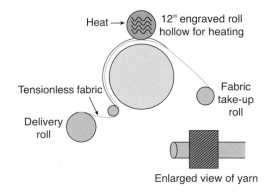

Figure 17.6   Schreiner calender machine for tricot.

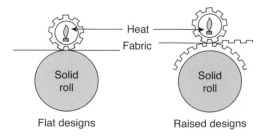

Figure 17.7   Embossing process.

Figure 17.8   Embossing rolls.
SOURCE: Courtesy of Lee Lun.

Embossed

Embossed fabrics for apparel and interiors are created using an embossing calender that produces either flat or raised designs on the fabric. Embossing is an important finish with heat-sensitive fibers because it produces a durable, washable embossed pattern. Fabrics made of solution-dyed fibers can be embossed directly off the loom and sold.

The embossing calender consists of a heated, hollow engraved-metal roll and a solid roll twice the size of the engraved roll (Figure 17.7). The fabric is drawn between the two rollers and is embossed with the design. Embossing can be done to both flat and pile fabrics.

The process differs for the production of flat and raised designs. Raised embossed designs will be discussed later in this chapter in the section on texture. Flat embossed designs are the simplest to produce. A metal, foam, or plastic roll engraved in deep relief (Figure 17.8) revolves against a smooth roll. The hot engraved areas of the roll produce a glazed pattern on the fabric. Embossed brocades are an example of this type of design. The effect can be seen as a difference in luster, but the fabric's texture does not change. Embossing will be discussed again later in this chapter when the process creates a three-dimensional fabric texture.

Drape

Drape finishes change the way a fabric falls or hangs over a three-dimensional shape. These finishes make the fabric stiffer or more flexible. They usually add a chemical compound to the fabric (*additive finish*) or dissolve a portion of the fibers present (*subtractive finish*).

Transparent and Crisp

Transparent or parchment effects in cotton fabrics for apparel are produced by treatment with sulfuric acid; this is called **parchmentizing**. Since acid dissolves cotton, this subtractive process must be very carefully controlled. Split-second timing is necessary to prevent **tendering** (weakening) of the fabric. Several effects are possible: all-over, localized, or plissé.

Because *all-over parchmentizing* produces a transparent effect, sheer combed lawn is used. The lawn is singed, desized, bleached, and mercerized. The fabric is then dyed or printed with colors that resist acid damage. The fabric is immersed in the acid solution and the fiber surface is partially dissolved. This surface rehardens as a cellulosic film, and when dry, it is permanently crisp and transparent. After the acid treatment, the fabric is neutralized in a weak alkali, washed, calendered to improve surface gloss, and perhaps mercerized again to improve transparency. This all-over treatment produces organdy.

In *localized parchmentizing*, if the design is a small figure with a large transparent area, an acid-resistant substance is printed on the figures and the fabric is run through the acid bath. The acid-resistant areas retain their original opacity and contrast sharply with the transparent background (Figure 17.9). If a small transparent design is desired, the acid is printed on in a paste form and then quickly washed off.

Burned-Out

Burned-out effects are produced by printing a chemical solvent on a blend fabric made of different generic fibers, such as rayon and polyester. One fiber, usually the more solvent-sensitive fiber, is dissolved, leaving sheer areas (Figure 17.10). Frequently, fabrics are specifically made so that they can be burned out later during finishing. Fiber combinations are usually either rayon and polyester or nylon and silk. Rayon is the fiber dissolved in the first example while silk is dissolved in the second example. Both rayon and silk are more sensitive to the solvents used than the nylon or polyester, the other fiber, in the fabric. Fabrics with this finish can be flat or pile weaves and include burned-out satin and velvet for apparel and window treatments. This finish is also known as *etched* or *devoré* because part of the fibers are removed by this subtractive finish. After the solvent has removed one of the fibers in the desired areas, the fabric is washed. The wastewater must be treated before discharge. Some solvents are reclaimed and reused; others are not.

Sizing

In **sizing**, or **starching**, the fabric is immersed in a mixture containing waxes, oils, glycerine, and softeners to add or control fabric body. For added weight, talc, clay, or chalk may be used, but they are often used with lower-quality fabrics. Gelatin is used on rayon because it gives a clear finish that enhances rayon's natural luster. Sizing adds stiffness, weight, and body to fabric. Its permanence is related to the type of sizing and method of application. If the sizing is resin-based and heat-set, it will be permanent. If the sizing is water-soluble, it will be removed during washing or it may create problems for consumers. Gelatin, for example, may create water spots on rayon that are difficult to remove if condensation or other water drops onto the fabric. Sizing is most often used to add body to apparel fabrics.

Weighting

Weighting is another technique used to add weight and body to apparel fabric. A metallic salt, a mineral weighting compound such as tin phosphate silicate, or plant-based compounds are used. Some salts bond with the fiber and are durable; other salts produce temporary surface coating. Mineral weighted silk was common once but is rare today; these silks are sensitive to light damage and do not age well. Plant and metallic salts add fiber volume, luster, and hand.

Figure 17.9 Localized parchmentizing (acid finish) yields a transparent background.

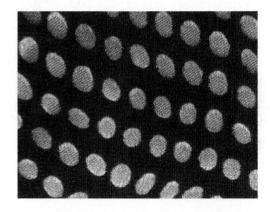

Figure 17.10 Burned-out design.

Drape finishes change the way a fabric falls or hangs over a three-dimensional shape. Types include parchmentizing, burned out, sizing, and weighting.

▶ Learning Activity 3

Explain how the finishes in this section affect fabric drape. Are these finished additive or subtractive? How might each finish influence serviceability for finished fabrics or products?

Texture and Hand

Texture and hand finishes modify fabric texture, add components that greatly alter a fabric's original texture, or alter the feel of a fabric.

Embossed

Some *embossed fabrics* have a three-dimensional raised design or pattern. The embossed design is permanent if the fiber is thermoplastic or if a resin is used and heat-set. To create raised, or relief designs, a more complicated routine is used. Two rolls are used: one hard and one soft to create the relief design. The two rolls fit together so that the fabric is forced to take on the shape of the relief design of the rollers. In heat embossing, the temperature is adjusted based on the fiber content of the fabric. The fabric is passed between the rolls to create permanent three-dimensional designs that can be seen and felt. In dry embossing, the process is the same, but the design is temporary or durable rather than permanent. Three-dimensional embossed textiles are used for both apparel and interiors.

Pleated

A **pleated fabric** is made using a variation of embossing. Pleating is a highly specialized operation done by either the paper-pattern technique or the machine process.

The *paper-pattern technique* is a more costly hand process, but it produces a wider variety of pleated designs. Partially completed garment components, such as hemmed skirt panels, are placed in a pattern mold by hand. Another pattern mold is placed on top so that the fabric is pleated between the pleating papers. The three layers are rolled into a cone shape, sealed, and heat-set in a curing oven.

The *machine-pleating or running process* is less expensive. Blades pleat the fabric as it is inserted between two heated rolls in the machine. A paper backing is used under the pleated fabric, and paper tape holds the pleats in place. After leaving the heated-roll machine, the pleats are set in an aging unit. Stitching the pleats in place produces permanent three-dimensional effects in apparel, upholstery, wall coverings, window treatments, and lampshades. Pleated fabric without stitching is used in similar products, but the pleats soften with use.

Puckered Surface

Puckered surfaces are created by partially dissolving the surface of a nylon or polyester fabric. Sculptured and "damasque" effects are made by printing phenol on the fabric to partially dissolve or swell it. As the fabric dries, it shrinks and creates a puckered surface, used primarily in apparel.

Plissé

Plissé is converted from either lawn or print-cloth gray goods by printing an alkali, sodium hydroxide (caustic soda), onto the apparel fabric in the form of stripes or designs. The alkali shrinks the fabric in the treated areas. As this shrinkage occurs, the untreated stripes pucker. Shrinkage causes a slight difference in count between the two stripes. The treated or flat stripe is denser. The upper portion of the fabric in Figure 17.11 shows the fabric before finishing, and the lower portion shows the crinkle produced by the caustic-soda treatment. This piece of goods is defective because the roller failed to print the chemical in the upper area.

The crinkle stripes can be narrow, as shown in Figure 17.11, or wide. In piece-dyed fabrics, the flat treated area may be a deeper color than the puckered area. The texture change is permanent but can be flattened somewhat by steam and pressure. The fabric must be neutralized after finishing and the sodium hydroxide washed off. Research focusing on recycling the sodium hydroxide is underway. Wastewater with sodium hydroxide requires treatment before being discharged into natural or municipal water systems.

Seersucker, plissé, and embossed fabrics can be similar in appearance and price range. Table 17.2 compares these and other similar fabrics.

Figure 17.11 Plissé, showing treated (bottom portion) and untreated (upper portion) areas.

Flocked

In a flocked fabric, a fine natural or synthetic surface fiber is applied after a base fabric has been produced. **Flocking** can be localized to imitate extra yarn weaves or all-over to imitate pile fabrics (see Chapters 13 and 15). When flocking is localized, only small areas of the fabric appear

Table 17.2 Comparison of Crepelike Fabrics

Crepe Yarns, Natural or Manufactured	Crepe Yarns, Thermoplastic	Bulky Yarn	Weave	Finish
Permanent texture	Permanent texture	Permanent texture	Texture does not flatten during use	Texture may flatten after washing
Flattens during use, but restored with water or high humidity	Retains appearance during use and care	Does not flatten or need ironing		
High potential shrinkage	Low potential shrinkage	Low potential shrinkage	Lower potential shrinkage	Lower potential shrinkage
Good drapeability	Good drapeability	Less drapeable	Less drapeable	Less drapeable
Stretches	Moderate stretch	Low stretch	Low stretch	Low stretch
Resilient, recovers from wrinkles	Resilient	Does not wrinkle	Rough surface hides wrinkles	Rough surface hides wrinkles
Dry cleaning preferable	Easy care	Easy care	Fiber and finish determine care	Fiber and finish determine care
Typical fabrics:	Typical fabrics:	Typical fabrics:	Typical fabrics:	Typical fabrics:
Wool crepe	Chiffon	Silky synthetics	Sand crepe	Plissé
Crepe de chine	Georgette		Granite cloth	Embossed
Matelassé			Seersucker	
Chiffon				
Georgette				
Silk crepe				

> ## ▶ Learning Activity 5

Compare Fabrics #74, 111, and 115. How do these three fabrics compare or differ in terms of structure? Which ones are applied designs and which ones are structural? Based on fiber content (see the fabric key), yarn type, fabric structure, and finish, explain the serviceability of these three fabrics. In what kinds of products would you expect to see these fabrics?

to have pile yarns, but the imitation pile is applied to the surface. An adhesive holds the very short, straight fibers in place. Area flocking can be done using either mechnical or electrostatic methods. Area and all-over flocking is used to create inexpensive pile upholstery and wall and window coverings. Area flocking is more commonly used to add pattern and interest to apparel. All-over flocking is seldom used for apparel. See Table 15.6 to compare flocking methods and Tables 15.7 and 15.8 to compare flocking with other methods used to produce fabrics with a pile or imitation pile surface.

Embroidered

Figure 17.12 Embroidered linen (right), printed to look like embroidery (left).

Embroidered fabrics for apparel and interiors are decorated by hand or by machine with a surface-applied thread. Machine embroidery uses compact zigzag stitches of various lengths. Two machines are used for embroidery: the shuttle and the multihead. The *shuttle embroidery* machine produces all-over embroidered fabrics such as eyelet (Figure 17.12). *Schiffli embroidery* describes earlier machines that used punched cardboard rolls to produce all-over embroidered fabrics. Contemporary shuttle embroidery machines use computers to control the pattern.

Multihead embroidery creates flat embroidery or pile embroidery. *Multihead* machines have several sewing heads combined in one machine operated simultaneously by the same computer system (Figure 17.13). Multihead machines are extremely versatile and can work with a variety of threads, ribbons, or bead/sequin strands. They can incorporate one or more colors of threads to create elaborate or simple designs in small or large scale. They create designs and emblems that are sewn to products such as letter jackets, hats, and shirts, or they are used to stitch crests, logos, and other designs on finished items (Figure 17.14).

Embroidered figures are very durable, often outlasting the ground fabric. The fabric is more expensive than the same fabric unembroidered. Like other applied designs, the figure may or may not be on-grain.

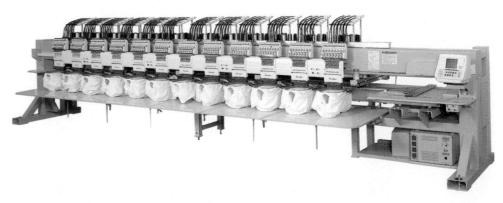

Figure 17.13 Multihead embroidery machine.
SOURCE: Courtesy of Barudan America, Inc.

Eyelet is an embroidery fabric with small round holes cut in the fabric, with stitching completely around the holes. The closeness and amount of stitching, as well as the quality of the background fabric, vary tremendously.

Ajouré is an embroidery technique in which open areas are created within a figure or pattern. Ajouré embroidery is often made by embroidering on a base or ground structure. Once the embroidery is complete, the base or ground structure is dissolved leaving a stable, open finished component ready to be used as is or applied to another material.

Fabrics and products with hand embroidery and beading are also available. In these cases, the stitching is done by individuals by hand with needle and thread. While hand embroiderers can create one-of-a-kind products, most often they are paid by the piece to meet mass merchandise demands. Embroiderers often work at home as a component of a cottage industry. While this allows families to work together, income is based on the number of items produced. Abuses can occur when companies gather embroiderers together in more factorylike settings expecting long hours of work, providing poor working conditions, or rewarding efforts with low pay.

Figure 17.14 Multihead embroidered design.

Expanded Foam

Another technique to create surface texture for apparel uses **expanded foam**. A colored compound printed on the fabric expands during processing to give a three-dimensional texture to the fabric. These foams are durable but create problems with pressing. Some do not age well, with the foam yellowing or disintegrating with age.

Sheared

A sheared fabric is a pile or napped fabric in which the surface has been cut to remove loose fiber or yarn ends, knots, and similar irregularities or surface flaws. **Shearing**, a finish done by a machine similar to a lawn mower, controls the length of the pile or nap. It may create a smooth surface or a patterned or sculptured effect by flattening portions of the pile with an engraved roller, shearing off the areas that remain erect, and steaming the fabric to raise the flattened and now taller portions. Most pile fabrics and many napped fabrics, including cut-pile carpet, are sheared. At one time, the fiber ends from shearing were discarded as waste, but today they are gathered together and sold to parts of the textile complex that work with very short, mixed content fiber.

Figure 17.15 When the nap in corduroy does not match, two pieces may look as if they are different colors.

Brushed

After shearing, the fabric surface usually is brushed to clean off the fiber ends. When **brushing** is combined with steaming, the nap or pile is set so that it slants in one direction, producing an up-and-down direction for pile and nap fabrics such as corduroy (Figure 17.15).

Napped

Nap is a layer of fiber ends raised from the ground weave of the fabric by a mechanical brushing action. Napped fabrics are literally "made" by finishing. Figure 17.16 shows a fabric before and after napping.

Napping is less expensive than many other ways of producing a three-dimensional fabric. Originally a hand operation using several teasels or dried plant burrs to gently brush up fiber ends, napping is done using pile rollers covered by a heavy fabric in which bent wires are

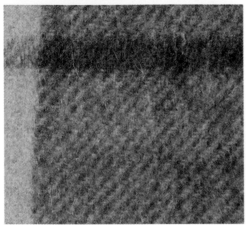

Figure 17.16 Fabric before and after napping.

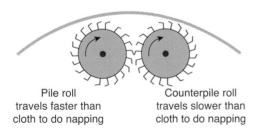

Pile roll travels faster than cloth to do napping   Counterpile roll travels slower than cloth to do napping

Figure 17.17 Napping rolls.

Napping is less expensive than many other ways of producing a three-dimensional fabric.

embedded (Figure 17.17). Napping machines may be single-action or double-action. Fewer rollers are used in the single-action machine. The bent wires point in the direction in which the fabric travels. Several identical rollers are mounted on a single large drum or cylinder that rotates in the same direction as the fabric. The pile rolls must travel faster than the fabric to raise any nap.

In the double-action napping machine, every other roll is a counterpile roll, with wires that point in the direction opposite that of the pile roll. The counterpile roll travels more slowly than the fabric to produce a nap. When the pile rolls at slower speed and the counterpile rolls at faster speed, a "tucking" action occurs that pushes the raised fibers back into the fabric and smooths the surface.

Napping produces a fabric with appealing characteristics. A napped surface combined with soft-twist filling yarns increases the air volume. The fabric is soft and attractive and is a good insulator. A dense mat of fiber ends on the surface imparts a degree of water repellency.

The amount of nap does not indicate fabric quality. The amount may vary from the slight fuzz of flannel to the thick nap of imitation fur. A short compact nap on a fabric with firm yarns and a closely woven ground wears best. Stick a pin in the nap and lift the fabric; a durable nap will hold the weight of the fabric. Hold the fabric up to the light and examine it. Move the nap aside and examine the ground weave. A napped surface will cover defects or a sleazy construction. Rub the fabric between your fingers and then shake it to see if short fibers drop out. Thick nap may contain very short fibers or flock. Rub the napped surface to see if it is loose or likely to pill.

Napped fabrics are made from gray goods in which the filling yarns are made of low-twist staple (not filament) fibers (see Chapter 11 for information about yarn twist). This difference in yarn structure makes it easy to identify the lengthwise and crosswise grain of the fabric.

Fabrics can be napped on either or both sides. The nap may have an upright position, or it may be "laid down" or "brushed." A heavy nap sometimes weakens the yarns in the fabric.

Yarns of either long- or short-staple fibers are used in napped fabrics. Worsted flannels are made of long-staple wool. The short-staple yarns used in woolen flannels have more fiber ends per inch, which produce a heavier nap. In wool blankets, which may be heavily napped for maximum loft, a fine-core ply adds strength to the yarn.

Napped fabrics may be plain or twill weave, or knit. More filling yarn is exposed on the surface in a twill or a filling-faced twill, and a heavier nap can be raised on twill fabrics. Napped knit fabrics are used for soft and flexible items and may be given woven pile fabric names such as velvet, velour, or fleece. Almost all napped fabric is used for apparel.

Flannel is an all-wool napped fabric made in dress, suit, or coat weights. It may be made with either worsted or woolen yarns, which may be yarn-dyed. Worsted flannels are firmly woven with a very short nap. They wear well, are easy to press, and hold a press well. Woolen flannels are fuzzier, less firmly woven fabrics. Because napping causes some weakening of the fabric, 15 to 20 percent nylon or polyester may be blended with the wool to improve the strength. Fleece is a coat-weight fabric with a long brushed nap or a short clipped nap.

Cotton flannels flatten under pressure and do not insulate as well as wool because cotton is less resilient. The shorter cotton fibers shed more lint. These fabrics are used in robes, nightwear, and baby clothes. *Flannelette* is a plain-weave fabric that is converted from a gray-goods fabric called *soft-filled sheeting*. It has a short nap on one side only and is often printed. Small pills will form on the nap, and the fabric is subject to abrasion. *Suede* and *duvetyn* are converted from the same gray goods but are sheared close to the ground to make a smooth, flat surface. Of the two, duvetyn is lighter weight. *Outing flannel* is a yarn-dyed, white, or printed fabric that is similar in fabric weight and nap length to flannelette but is napped on both sides. Since the warp yarns in these fabrics are standard yarns, it is easy to identify fabric grain.

Crepeing

Crepeing is a special compacting process to produce a fabric with a soft hand. In crepeing, the fabric is fed into the machine by a special blade at a faster rate than it is removed from the machine. Crepeing can create an all-over texture or a localized plissé effect and add comfort stretch with soft drape to apparel fabrics.

Fulled

Fulling of wool fabrics for apparel and upholstery fabrics improves their appearance, hand, thickness, softness, body, and cover. Fabrics are fulled by moisture, heat, and friction in a very mild, carefully controlled felting process. Fulled fabric is denser and more compact in both warp and filling directions (Figure 17.18). Almost all woven wool fabrics and many knit wool fabrics are fulled. Some are lightly fulled while others are heavily fulled. Boiled wool is a heavily fulled jersey.

Beetled

Beetling is a finish originally used on linen and fabrics resembling linen. As the fabric revolved slowly over a wooden drum, it was pounded with wooden hammers until the yarns flattened into an oval, not round, cross section. The weave appeared tighter than it really was. The greater surface area increased fabric luster, absorbency, and smoothness.

A contemporary method of producing a beetled fabric uses high pressure, resin, and thermoplastic fibers. In this case, the pressure flattens the yarns into the oval shape associated with beetled fabrics. The heat and resin result in a permanent flattening of the yarns. This finish is used on damask, crash, and other linenlike fabrics for apparel and interiors.

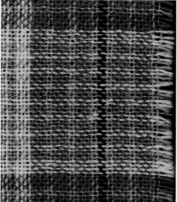

Figure 17.18 Wool fabric before (left) and after (right) fulling.

> ▶ **Learning Activity 8**

Use Fabrics #1, 2 and 39 from your swatch kit. Name the fabric based on its structure and finish. Use the key from the swatch kit to identify the fiber content. Based on your knowledge of fibers and aesthetic finishes, predict which of these finishes are permanent, durable, or temporary. How could temporary finishes be made durable or permanent? Name an end use for each fabric and predict its serviceability for that end use based on fiber content, yarn structure, fabric structure, and finish. Why is this finish used for linen fabrics and damask?

Coronized

Coronizing is a process for heat setting, dyeing, and finishing glass fiber in one continuous operation. Since the flexibility of glass is low, the yarns resist bending around one another in a woven fabric. Heat setting at a temperature of 1,100°F softens the yarns so that they bend and assume yarn crimp. Coronized fabrics have greater wrinkle resistance and softer draping qualities and are used for window treatments.

Emerizing, Sueding, or Sanding

Emerizing, sueding, sanding, or *peach skin* is a process used on fine silk-like fabrics of natural or manufactured fibers for apparel and some interior uses. The different terms describe different starting plain- or twill-weave fabrics and different surface effects produced by the process. It may be applied to polyester microfiber fabrics to improve their hand and comfort. The finish is usually applied to washed fabrics before they are heat-set or dyed. The fabric moves at a speed of 15 to 20 meters per minute under two or more rollers with fine emery paper on the first roller to more abrasive paper on each successive roller. The process abrades the surface, causing fibrils to split from the fibers, producing a soft hand and sueded texture on the fabric. Too much abrasion or too coarse an abrasive rips or tears the fabric. Too little abrasion may generate sufficient heat to produce a harsh hand with thermoplastic fibers. The process damages the fabric and can decrease its tensile strength by as much as 60 percent. After treatment, the fabrics are heat-set and washed to remove the dust. Dyeing follows. These fabrics need to be handled carefully. Machine washing may abrade the fibrils and destroy the look of the fabric. Peach-skin finishes can be applied to silk, nylon, polyester, and cotton blended with nylon or polyester.

Abrasive, Chemical, or Enzyme Washes

Abrasive, chemical, and enzyme washes are processes that were used originally on denim garments and go in and out of fashion under such names as acid, frosted, pepper, and enzyme wash. These finishes are modified for application to other fabrications and fibers. The washing process alters the surface of the fabric and damages it to some degree. This look is popular for apparel and interiors.

Manufacturers can do the washing at a sewing facility in an area known as the laundry. These processes require special equipment and knowledge and cannot be duplicated in the home. Some consumers have attempted to duplicate these finishes at home, resulting in expensive washing-machine repair or replacement.

The sustainability among these processes differs depending on the look desired and chemicals used. When enzymes are used, the impact is reduced compared to alkalines, oxidizing compounds, bleaches, and other chemicals. Enzymes are easier to process in waste-water, use less energy and chemicals in finishing, and require less energy. Alternate procedures with better sustainability are discussed with each wash where such an alternate exists.

Abrasive Wash

With **abrasive washes**, pumice or other abrasive material is saturated with a chemical and tumbled with the fabric or garment for a predetermined time related to the desired change in hand and appearance. The abrasive material is removed, and the chemical is neutralized in a bath. With fabrics such as cotton, abrasion is controlled by the cycle length and the style and type of abradant used. With lighter-weight fabrics like silk, abrasion results from tumbling against other fabrics in the chamber. Fabrics finished in this manner are described by a variety of terms, including stone-washed denim; sanded, sand- or mud-washed silk; and sand-washed nylon.

Chemical Wash

In a **chemical wash**, a special chemical is added to the wash solution to alter the fiber's surface. Chemicals include alkalis, oxidizing agents, bleaches, and others that are specific to the fiber being treated. These chemicals partially destroy the fiber and create irregularities, pits, pores, or other surface aberrations. This technique is used to produce fashion denims, comfort polyesters, and washed silks. Sometimes a chemical name is attached, such as acid wash, even though acid is not or rarely used in the process.

Bleaches are used to strip color from fabric or products to create fashion looks. Sodium hypochlorite is used in the majority of bleaching treatments of denim fabrics and products. Un-fortunately, this process releases adsorbable chlorinated organic compounds in the waste-water, requiring expensive treatment before the water is released into natural or municipal water systems. Alternate chlorine-free bleaching agents are possible, but the results are grayer and not as clear. Other options include **ozonation** or treating cotton fabrics with ozone, which breaks down easily and is currently used to remove color from dye wastewater.

Enzyme Washes

Enzyme washes are similar to chemical washes except that they use cellulase, an enzyme that dissolves part of the cellulose molecule. The process has a permanent effect on the surface of the fabric, producing a softer hand. The enzyme removes surface fuzz, reduces pilling with use or care, decreases fabric weight, and reduces strength loss by less than 10 percent (Figure 17.19). Cellulase and other enzymes produced by the fermentation of molds are naturally occurring proteins used to degrade the surface fuzz. Relatively small concentrations of these sustainable and biodegradable enzymes are used with little negative environmental effect as compared with that of chemical washes. After treatment with the enzyme, mechanical action removes the weakened fiber ends. In some instances, abrasive stones are combined with the enzyme for mechanical abrasion. Enzyme washes, also known as bio-polishing or bio-finishing, increase productivity with fewer seconds. They increase moisture absorption and dyeability. Some yarns are also enzyme treated.

Figure 17.19   Enzyme-polished cotton fibers: original fibers (left) and bio-polished fibers (right).
SOURCE: Reprinted with permission from the *Canadian Textile Journal*, Vol. 109, No. 10, December 1992.

▶ Learning Activity 9

Use Fabric #8 from your swatch kit. Name the fabric based on its structure and finish. Use the key from the swatch kit to identify the fiber content. Based on your knowledge of fibers and aesthetic finishes, predict if the finish is permanent, durable, or temporary. Name an end use for this fabric and predict its serviceability for that end use based on fiber content, yarn structure, fabric structure, and finish.

Silk Boil-Off

Sericin comprises about 30 percent of a silk fabric's weight. The **boil-off** process removes the sericin and creates a looser, more mobile fabric structure. Options include using an alkaline solution, enzymes, ultrasonic vibrations, plasma treatment, or sodium salts. If the fabric is in a relaxed state when the sericin is removed, the warp yarns take on a high degree of fabric crimp. This crimp and the looser fabric structure together create the liveliness and suppleness of silk, a suppleness that has been compared with the action of the coil-spring "Slinky" toy. While used primarily for apparel fabrics, some silk window treatment fabrics also receive a boil-off treatment to enhance their texture.

The properties are quite different when the boil-off is done under tension. The fabric crimp is much less, and the response of the fabric is duller, more like that of a flat spring. This explains some of the differences between qualities of silk fabric.

In some areas where silk is produced, the wastewater from the boil-off process is not always treated before discharge. However, socially responsible companies are demanding that suppliers treat wastewater before it is discharged.

Caustic Treatment

To create a synthetic apparel fabric with a hand and texture like silk, **caustic treatment** is used. Finishing starts with heat setting to stabilize the fabric to a controlled width, remove any wrinkles, and impart resistance to wrinkling. The next step is a caustic-soda (alkali) treatment to dissolve a small amount of the fiber, usually 5 to 18 percent. Similar to the degumming of silk, this step gives the fabric structure greater mobility, with a slight loss in tensile strength and abrasion resistance. The fabric is more hydrophilic and more comfortable. In all remaining finishing, the fabric is completely relaxed to achieve maximum fabric crimp. Figure 17.20 shows the effect of

With **abrasive washes**, pumice or other abrasive material is saturated with a chemical and tumbled with the fabric or garment for a predetermined time related to the desired change in hand and appearance. In a **chemical wash**, a special chemical is added to the wash solution to alter the fiber's surface. **Enzyme washes** are similar to chemical washes except that they use cellulase, an enzyme that dissolves part of the cellulose molecule.

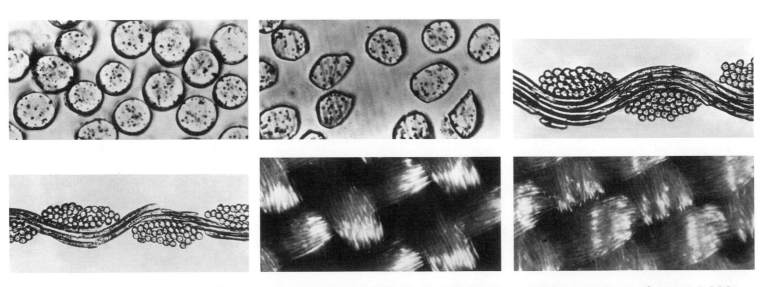

Figure 17.20 Photomicrographs showing the effect of heat-caustic treatment. Fiber cross sections at 1,000×: original polyester (upper left) and treated polyester (upper center), fabric cross section at 200×: original polyester (upper right) and treated polyester (bottom left), and fabric surface at 50×: original polyester (bottom center) and treated polyester (bottom right).

SOURCE: Courtesy of E. I. du Pont de Nemours & Company.

the alkali treatment on a fabric made of a circular cross-section polyester. With the microfibers, caustic treatment is not as necessary. As with any treatment using caustic sodium hydroxide, sustainability concerns relate to wastewater treatment and recycling of the chemical.

Hand Builders

Hand builders are compounds, such as silicone softeners and cellulase enzyme, that soften fabric hand. These hand builders are used primarily for apparel and bedding. These compounds produce a dryer hand as compared with compounds previously used. Better wrinkle resistance and improved durability occur with some of the silicone softeners. Because of health and environmental issues related to some silicone softeners, use of enzymes as softening agents is increasing in popularity.

Texture and hand finishes modify fabric texture, add components that greatly alter a fabric's original texture, or alter the feel of a fabric. Types include embossed, pleated, puckered, plissé, flocked, embroidered, expanded foam, sheared, brushed, napped, creped, fulled, beetled, coronized, emerized, washed, boiled-off, caustic treated, and hand-built fabrics.

▶ Learning Activity 10

Examine the textile products you are wearing or have with you today. Do any of these items have applied design? If yes, which ones? How can you be sure it is an applied design and not a structural design? Which of the items with an applied design have an additive finish and which have a subtractive finish? For each of the applied designs with you today, name the fabric, identify the fiber content (or make your best guess if no labels are present), and name the aesthetic finish used. Select one of the products and describe your satisfaction with that product.

▶ Learning Activity 11

You are part of a creative team developing a new line for casual summer sportswear. Identify an appropriate list of five aesthetic finishes that might be used in this line. Explain the process used for each of the finishes, the value each finish would add to a product, and how that finish would reflect current fashion.

▶ Learning Activity 12

Work in groups of two. Select three finishes—each one from a different main type—and discuss the sustainability of each of the finishes you selected. Consider the finishes applied to fashion denim items. How have these processes been modified to make them more sustainable?

key terms

review questions

1. Explain the differences between embossed and plissé in terms of process and fabric.

2. Explain the changes in serviceability of a fabric after it has been napped.

3. What is the purpose of shearing? What kinds of fabrics are generally sheared?

4. Describe the manner in which each fabric of these pairs was produced. Which are applied designs and which are structural?
   a. Swivel dotted swiss and flocked dotted swiss
   b. Extra yarn eyelash fabric and burned out
   c. Plissé and seersucker
   d. Flocked velvet and true velvet
   e. Velveteen and napped denim
   f. Damask and embossed cotton
   g. Piqué and puckered surface nylon

5. Predict the serviceability of each fabric listed in question 4.

6. Which of these finishes would be permanent, and which would diminish with time or use? Why?
   a. Heat-embossed nylon tricot
   b. Pressure-embossed cotton
   c. Burned-out rayon/polyester sheer drapery
   d. Fulled wool gabardine
   e. Water-soluble sizing on 100 percent cotton print cloth
   f. 65 percent polyester/35 percent cotton glazed chintz upholstery (resin compound)
   g. Caustic-treated 100 percent polyester crepe de chine

7. Which of the fabrics described in question 6 are additive and which are subtractive finishes? How is the aesthetic change in the fabric achieved?

8. How do the finishes in this chapter add value to textiles and textile products?

9. Explain the difference in structure and process among woven pile fabrics, knit pile fabrics, flocked fabrics, tufted fabrics, and napped fabrics. How would these differences influence product serviceability? What do these fabrics have in common?

10. How do the abrasive and chemical wash finishes affect product durability?

Case Study

Embroidery Exhibit*

Hand embroidery is an ancient and widely pursued art form. Seventeenth-century England was the site of one of embroidery's golden ages, in spite of it being a tumultuous time in England with two civil wars, beheading of a king, plague, the Great Fire of London, and formation of a constitutional monarchy. In spite of all that tumult or perhaps because of it, embroidery was used to embellish all kinds of textiles, including royal regalia, jewelry, apparel, gloves, caps, purses, trays, and embroidered satin panels on the sides and tops of small cabinets. Embroidery is valued for its structure and design elements. Real gold and silver embroidery thread, glass beads, appliqué (small pieces of fabric stitched on the surface), raised work (areas stitched to a backing and stuffed from the back), and ribbons were used in addition to colored embroidery thread. Embroidery merges two components, fabric and thread, stitch by stitch. Often the entire surface was embellished with embroidery so that none of the support fabric could be seen. Some embroiderers were professionals; others were amateurs. Most worked from existing images or professionally designed patterns called blackwork. Both men and women did embroidery, but most embroiderers were women. Floral, biblical, and mythological motifs were popular. Quality of the embroidery is based on stitch types, uniformity and fineness of the stitches, and the pattern or motif.

DISCUSSION QUESTIONS

1. Do you embroider? If yes, what kinds of embroidery do you do? What types of motifs and stitches do you usually use in your embroidery? What types of items do you embroider?

2. Do you own any textile product that has been embroidered? If yes, what type of item is it? Do you know where it was done or who did the embroidery? Was the embroidery done by hand or by machine? How can you tell?

3. What kind of value does embroidery add to textiles?

4. What are the factors that would be used to determine quality of machine embroidery? How do those factors relate to quality characteristics of hand embroidery?

*Smith, R. (2008, December 19). Seeing history in the eye of a needle. *The New York Times*, 27.

suggested readings

Cegerra, J. (1996, November). The state of the art in textile biotechnology. *Journal of the Society of Dyers and Colourists*, 112, pp. 326–329.

Creswell, F. (1994, October/November). Finishing fabrics in the nineties. *Canadian Textile Journal*, pp. 28–29.

Franck, R. R. (Ed.), (2001). *Silk, Mohair, Cashmere and Other Luxury Fibres*. Cambridge, England: Woodhead.

Goldstein, H. G. (1993). Mechanical and chemical finishing of microfabrics. *Textile Chemist and Colorist*, 25(2), pp. 16–21.

Goswami, B. C., Anandjiwala, R. D., & Hall, D. M. (2004). *Textile Sizing*. New York: Marcel Dekker.

Lacasse, K., & Baumann, W. (2004). *Textile Chemicals: Environmental Data and Facts*. New York: Springer-Verlag.

McCurry, J. W. (1999, February). Flocking: A niche of niches. *Textile World*, pp. 91–92, 94.

Morgan, N. (1997, June). Environmentally friendly finishing using enzymes. *Technical Textiles International*, pp. 12–14.

Özdemir, D., Duran, K., Bahtiyari, M. I., Perincek, S., & Körlü, A. E., (2008). Ozone bleaching of denim fabrics. *AATCC Review, 8*(9), 40–44.

Schindler, W. D., & Hauser, P. J. (2004). *Chemical Finishing of Textiles*. Cambridge, England: Woodhead.

Smith, R. (2008, December 19). Seeing history in the eye of a needle. *The New York Times*, 27.

Taylor, M. (1993). What is moiré? *Textiles*, 1, p. 14.

Thiry, M. C. (2008). Half-dyed: The importance of preparation. *AATCC Review, 8*(9), 24–31.

Waddell, R. B. (2002). Bioscouring of cotton: Commercial applications of alkaline stable pectinase. *AATCC Review, 2*(4), 28–30.

Wang, Y. (Ed.), (2006). *Recycling in Textiles*. Cambridge, England: Woodhead.

SPECIAL-PURPOSE FINISHES

CHAPTER OBJECTIVES

- To recognize how special-purpose finishes influence fabric performance and consumer satisfaction.
- To understand how special-purpose finishes are applied.
- To understand the value that special-purpose finishes add to textile products.
- To relate special-purpose finishes to fabric, yarn, and fiber types and end use.

18

Special-purpose finishes are chemical finishes that are applied to fabrics to enhance performance for specific end uses. They add value and cost to textiles.

Special-purpose finishes or **functional finishes** are **chemical finishes** that are applied to fabrics to enhance performance for specific end uses. Although these finishes usually do not alter the appearance of fabrics, they address some consumer problem or performance deficiency with textile products or enhance fabric suitability for a specific purpose. New techniques and new applications are appearing frequently. Many of these finishes incorporate nanotechnology; some make use of smart textile technology so that the finish responds to environmental stimuli. This chapter is organized by performance categories.

Special-purpose finishes add to product cost and to product value. Yet, their impact on performance may be difficult for consumers to recognize. The effect of some finishes may be invisible or beyond consumer perception, especially at point of purchase. Even during use, assessment is difficult. For example, how does one assess the effectiveness of a soil-resistant finish if the fabric stays cleaner longer? Unfortunately, for some finishes, improved performance in one area means a loss of performance in another.

Many functional finishes are topical—a chemical compound is added to the surface of the fabric, but it may not penetrate to the interior of fibers or yarns. Finishes applied in liquid form often are referred to as **wet processes**. Although finishing traditionally has been done to fabrics, it is not uncommon to find garments that are wet-processed, especially to satisfy demand for quick response.

Wet processing of textiles is an area of great concern because of its impact on the environment and water, chemical, and energy use. Many textile researchers are investigating alternate procedures, chemicals, and technology to reduce problems and make finishing textiles more sustainable.

Nanotechnology is one alternative to traditional wet process finishing of textiles. Nanofinishing allows for significantly smaller amounts of chemicals to produce the desired result with few adverse effects, Nanoparticles are transparent and have very small mass with large surface area. While finishing has not moved completely to nanotechnology processes, significant progress has occurred in the past few years. Nanofinishes can be added during dyeing or finishing, by spray coating, or electrostatic methods.

Stabilization: Shrinkage Control

A fabric is stable when it retains its original size and shape during use and care. Unstable fabrics shrink or stretch, usually as a result of cleaning. *Shrinkage*, the more serious and more frequent problem, is the reduction in size of a product. Shrinkage is reported as a percentage of the original length and width dimension, for example, 2.5 percent warp and 1.5 percent filling.

Shrinkage potential is introduced in spinning, fabrication, and finishing. Yarns are under tension during spinning and slashing. Fabrics are under tension during fabrication. In wet finishing, fabrics may be pulled through machines in long continuous pieces and may be dried

> ## ▶ Learning Activity 1

Work in groups of two or three. Describe the kinds of problems or performance issues you have had with textile products. Discuss how the material performance issues could be resolved or reduced by finishes. Scan this chapter and select one or two of the performance issues to determine how a finish is designed to reduce or remove the problems discussed.

and set under excessive tension, which leaves the fabric with high potential shrinkage. Shrinkage occurs when tensions are released by moisture and heat, as in laundering or steam pressing. Predicting lengthwise and crosswise shrinkage is difficult. Many factors contribute to shrinkage: fiber type, blend level, yarn process, fabrication type, and number and type of finishes. Some manufacturers of sewn products try to address this problem during pattern-making by oversizing patterns, but these efforts are inaccurate at best.

Shrinkage is a plus in the processing of some fabrics, as in fulling or shrinkage of crepe yarn in matelassé. But it is a problem for manufacturers and consumers when it changes product dimensions.

The two major types of shrinkage of interest here are relaxation shrinkage and progressive shrinkage. **Relaxation shrinkage** occurs during washing, steam pressing, or dry cleaning. Most relaxation shrinkage occurs during the first care cycle. However, many manufacturers and retailers test for shrinkage through three or more cleaning cycles because **progressive shrinkage** often continues at smaller rates for several additional care cycles. If the care is mild in the first cycle and more severe in later cycles, the product may shrink more during these later cycles. For example, for items dried flat in the first cycle and machine-dried later, shrinkage will be more severe with machine drying. Relaxation shrinkage can be eliminated by mechanical-control methods or heat. Chemical-control methods are used to prevent progressive shrinkage. The following list groups fibers by the kind of shrinkage they normally exhibit:

- Cotton, flax, lyocell, and HWM rayon exhibit relaxation shrinkage and little progressive shrinkage.
- Regular rayon exhibits high relaxation shrinkage and moderate progressive shrinkage.
- Wool exhibits moderate relaxation shrinkage and high progressive shrinkage.
- Other properly heat-set manufactured fibers exhibit relaxation shrinkage and no progressive shrinkage.

Relaxation Shrinkage and Finishes

Knit Fabrics Knit fabrics shrink because the stitches may elongate lengthwise from 10 to 35 percent in knitting and wet finishing (Figure 18.1). During laundering, the stitches return to their normal shape and the item becomes shorter and wider.

Shrinkage of knits can be minimized in finishing by overfeeding the fabric between sets of rollers to induce lengthwise shrinkage or by using loop drying (see Chapter 16). Heat setting of thermoplastic fibers or blends with at least 50 percent thermoplastic fibers also stabilizes knits.

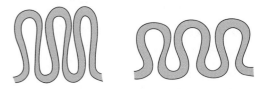

Figure 18.1 Knit stitches: after finishing (left), as produced (right).

Woven Fabrics Woven fabrics shrink when wetting relaxes the strains of yarn production, weaving, preparation finishes, and wet finishing. The warp yarns are under tension while they are on the loom, and the filling is inserted as a straight yarn. The filling takes on crimp as it is beaten back into the fabric, but the warp stays straight (Figure 18.2). When the fabric is thoroughly wet and allowed to relax, the yarns readjust themselves and the warp yarns take on some crimp, shortening the fabric in the warp direction (Figure 18.2). With the exception of crepe fabrics, less change occurs in the filling direction.

In **compressive shrinkage**, a thick felt blanket is used to maximize shrinkage. The moist fabric adhering to the blanket's surface is passed around a feed-in roll that feeds the fabric in slightly faster than it is taken off. The rubber belt and pressure roll hold the fabric tight against the rubber cylinder and compress it. The

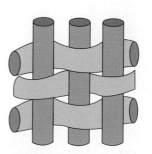

Figure 18.2 Position of the warp (blue yarns) on the loom (left), after the fabric relaxes (right).

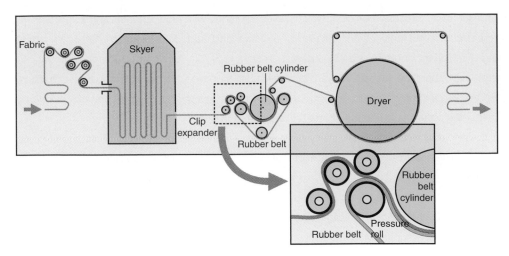

Figure 18.3 The compressive-shrinkage process. The box shows a close-up of the area where compressive shrinkage occurs.
SOURCE: Courtesy of the Sanforized Company.

Figure 18.4 Comparison of wrinkling and shrinkage of thermoplastic fiber fabrics: heat-set (fabric 1) and not heat-set (fabrics 2 and 3).

fabric then passes against a heated dryer cylinder to dry and set it with a smooth finish. The count will increase, and the fabric will be improved after compressing (Figure 18.3). Compressive shrinkage is used on many woven fabrics, but is not effective with rayon. Because of its high swelling and wet elongation, rayon will not hold a compressive-shrinkage treatment.

However, even with a compressive-shrinkage finish, improper laundering may shrink fabrics. Tumble drying also may compress yarns beyond their normal shrinkage.

London shrunk was developed in the 18th century as a relaxation finish for wool fabrics to remove production strains. A wet wool or cotton blanket is placed on a long platform, a layer of fine worsted fabric is spread on it, and alternate layers of blanket and fabric are built up. Weight is placed on the top for about 12 hours to force the moisture from the blankets into the wool. The fabric is hung to dry naturally. When dry, the fabric is layered with special pressboards. Preheated metal plates are inserted at intervals and on the top and bottom of the stack. This setup of fabric, boards, and plates is kept under pressure for hours.

The label "Genuine London Process" or similar wording is licensed by the Parrot Group of companies to garment makers all over the world. The permanent-set finish Si-Ro-Set for washable, wrinkle-free wool fabrics is applied to some London-shrunk fabrics during processing.

Progressive Shrinkage and Finishes

Thermoplastic Fibers Thermoplastic fibers are stabilized by **heat setting**, a process in which fabrics are heated to temperatures at or above their **glass transition temperature** (T_g: the temperature at which the amorphous regions of a fiber are easy to distort) and then cooled. The glass transition temperature is lower than the melting point of a fiber, and it differs for each fiber type. When properly heat-set, fabrics have no progressive shrinkage and little relaxation shrinkage (Figure 18.4).

Figure 18.5 While originally the same size, the wool sock (top) has dramatically altered in size and shape from the nylon sock (bottom).

Wool Fibers Washable wool is important in apparel and some interior textiles and in blends with washable fibers. Wool must be finished to retain its original size and surface texture during laundering. Figure 18.5 illustrates the shrinkage of wool.

To prevent felting shrinkage, a finish must alter or mask the scale structure and reduce the differential-friction effect that prevents wool fibers from returning to their original position in fabric. The effectiveness of felting-shrinkage treatments depends on the kind and amount of finish used and on the yarn and fabric construction. Worsteds need less finish than woolens. Low-count fabrics and low-twist yarns need more finish to produce good washability. Treated-wool fabrics may be machine-washable, but care should be taken to use warm (not hot) water, gentle agitation, and a short agitation period. Hand washing is preferred, because soil is easy to remove from wool, and hand washing ensures a lower temperature and less agitation. Machine washing may produce a fuzzy or slightly pilled surface.

Two methods are used to smooth off the free edges of the wool scales: surface coating and halogenation treatment. **Surface coating** with a polyamide solution (a very thin, microscopic film applied to fiber surfaces) enables the fibers to move back and forth without entangling. In addition to controlling shrinkage, the coating minimizes pilling and fuzzing (a problem with washable wool), gives the fabrics better wash-and-wear properties, and increases resistance to abrasion. Total Easy Care Wool is promoted as having the same attributes (hand, comfort, and resiliency) as untreated wool while being able to be washed repeatedly without shrinkage.

Halogenation treatments, primarily with chlorine, partially dissolve the fiber scales and reduce felting shrinkage. These finishes cost little, can be applied to large batches of small items such as wool socks, do not require padding or curing equipment, and are fairly effective. The process damages the fibers and must be carefully monitored to minimize damage. The scales are more resistant to damage than the interior of the fiber and should not be completely removed or the fabric will feel harsh and rough and be lighter weight and less durable. To maintain the strength of the fabric, nylon fiber is often blended with wool. Halogenation is especially good for hand-washable items. A process combining chlorination and resin makes wool knits machine-washable and machine-dryable. Shrinkage is less than 3 percent in length and 1 percent in width, and goods retain their loft and resiliency. Superwash is the trade name of fabric or knitting yarn that has undergone halogenation treatment.

Both surface coating and halogenation alter the hand of wool and affect moisture absorbency. The processes produce fabric that is washable, but hand washing is preferred to machine washing.

Because chlorine is an environmental hazard, its use is being restricted. Alternative chemicals including oxidizing agents and enzymes are becoming more important.

Rayon Fibers Shrinkage of regular rayon relates to the handling of wet fabric during finishing. Since wet fabric stretches easily, overstretching may occur. If fabric dries in this stretched condition, it will have high potential shrinkage. It will shrink when wet again and dried without tension. But laboratory or home testing is required to determine this.

Shrinkage-control treatments for rayon reduce fiber swelling and make it resistant to distortion. Resins form cross links that prevent swelling and keep the fiber from stretching. The

▶ Learning Activity 2

Poll your friends, coworkers, neighbors, or family members regarding problems they have encountered with shrinkage. Develop a table identifying the kinds of textile products, fiber content (if known), and comments about shrinkage. Summarize your results and relate them to the discussion of shrinkage and stabilization or shrinkage control. Is there more than one type of shrinkage involved? What was the general consumer reaction to the problem of shrinkage?

resin also fills up spaces in the amorphous areas of the fiber, reducing absorbency. Aldehyde resin are superior to other resins because they do not weaken the fabric, do not retain chlorine, and have excellent wash-fastness. Treated rayons are machine-washable if the wash cycle is short. When HWM rayon is resin-treated, it is for durable-press purposes because its shrinkage is controlled by relaxation shrinkage-control methods.

Shape-Retention Finishes

Even though care of contemporary textiles is time-consuming, imagine the time and physical effort that were required 75 years ago. Almost every item of apparel and bedding needed ironing! With thermoplastic fibers, **shape-retention finishes**, and modern washers and dryers, easy-care textiles are the norm. Now, it is only occasionally that items need the extra effort of ironing.

Theory of Wrinkle Recovery

Wrinkles occur when fabrics are crushed during use and care (creases and pleats made by pressing are desirable style features, however). Wrinkle recovery depends on **cross links**, which hold adjacent molecular chains together and pull them back into position after the fiber is bent, thus preventing wrinkles. Fibers with strong intermolecular bonds have good molecular memory and resist wrinkling and creasing. Fibers with weak bonds wrinkle and crease readily.

The cellulosic fibers lack strong natural cross links. Molecular chains are held together by weak hydrogen bonds that break with the stress of bending or the introduction of water molecules within the fiber's amorphous regions. New bonds hold the fiber in this bent position and form a wrinkle. Resin cross links give fibers a "memory" and good wrinkle recovery (Figure 18.6).

Resin finishes were first used in England in 1920 and in the United States in 1940 on rayon, cotton, and linen fabrics. Urea formaldehyde was the first resin used to prevent wrinkles; significant improvements in resins have occurred since then. Although these early resin-treated fabrics were smooth and wrinkle-resistant, problems included low abrasion resistance, tear strength, yellowing, chlorine retention from bleach, hand, affinity for oily soils, static, pilling, odor, frosting, dye migration because of high curing temperatures, and construction problems with seam pucker or alterations.

Resin is a general term used to describe the organic chemical compounds used to apply durable-press and crease-resistant finishes to cellulosic fibers. Formaldehyde resin use is restricted because it is a possible carcinogen, so other resins are used. Modified glyoxal-based reactants slightly decrease formaldehyde release. Polycarboxylic acid derivatives produce fabrics with better abrasion resistance, good durable-press performance, and low shrinkage. While performance problems continue, they are less pronounced with these resins. Because these resins are more expensive, many durable-press finishes include some DMDHEU (dimethyloldihydroxyethylene urea) in the process. Research into recycling chemicals used in durable-press finishing has found some potential for reusing old baths by adding fresh ingredients, but the percentage of the old bath and its age determine the effectiveness of the finish.

Durable Press

Durable press describes items that retain their shape and a pressed appearance even after many uses, washings, and tumble dryings. The terms *durable press*, *wrinkle-free*, and *permanent press* are used interchangeably, but *durable* is a more realistic term because the

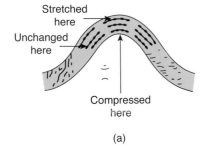

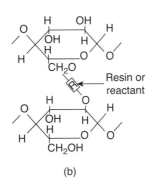

Figure 18.6 (a) Effect on internal structure when fiber is bent and (b) resin cross link.

finish's effectiveness decreases with age. Older items may require some touch-up ironing to meet appearance standards. The term *wrinkle-free* is misleading because many almost new products require some touch-up ironing to meet consumer standards. Other terms are *wrinkle-resistant*, *anticreasing*, and *crease retention*. Most often, the fabric is cotton, rayon, linen, lyocell, or a blend of one or more of these fibers with polyester.

Several processes for durable-press items and fabrics are outlined here. Differences include when the chemical is applied and the stage at which cutting, sewing, and pressing take place. In the **precured** and **postcured processes**, the finish is applied to fabric (Figure 18.7). In the **immersion**, **metered-addition**, and **vapor-phase processes**, the finish is applied to garments or products (Figure 18.8). The immersion process is also known as the *garment* or *product dip process*. Table 18.1 summarizes these processes.

Problems continue to be associated with resin finishes. Blends of cotton/polyester use less resin than 100 percent cotton. The high strength and abrasion resistance of polyester make these fabrics much more durable. Cotton pretreated with liquid ammonia or mercerized under tension reduces loss of strength due to the finish. Organic or silicone softeners and well-controlled tension during curing are effective at reducing strength loss due to resin finishes. Polymer sizing added to the yarns before curing increases abrasion resistance. Although most

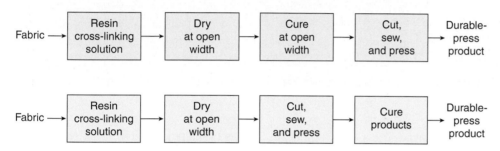

Figure 18.7 Shape-retention finishes: precured process (top) and postcured process (bottom).

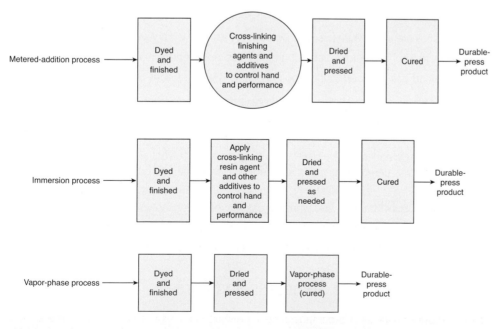

Figure 18.8 Shape-retention finishes: metered-addition process (top), immersion process (center), and vapor-phase process (bottom).

Table 18.1 Durable-Press Finishes

	Precure	Postcure	Immersion	Metered Addition	Vapor Phase
Applied to	Fabric	Fabric	Product	Product	Product
Stage of Curing	Fabric	Product	Product	Product	Product
			Untreated fabric	Untreated fabric	Untreated fabric
Advantages	Dimensionally stable	Dimensionally stable	No premature setting	No premature setting	No premature setting
	Lowest-cost process	Crease retention	Wet-finished goods used	Wet-finished goods used	Wet-finished goods used
		Minimal seam puckering	Control performance, hand, aesthetics	Control performance, hand, aesthetics	Control performance, hand, aesthetics
			Greater flexibility	Greater flexibility	Greater flexibility
				Wet-on-wet processing possible	Uses less chemicals
Disadvantages	No permanent creases	Higher costs	Higher costs	Higher costs	Higher costs
	Puckered seams	May set prematurely	Process control difficult	Process control difficult	Process control difficult
	Strength loss Abrasion-sensitive	Overfinished areas	Fabric preparation critical	Fabric preparation critical	Fabric preparation critical
Uses	Shirting, draperies	Skirts, slacks, other items with set-in creases or pleats	Apparel of 100% cotton	Apparel and interiors of 100% cotton	Cotton and other natural-fiber products

Wrinkle recovery depends on **cross links**, which hold adjacent molecular chains together and pull them back into position after the fiber is bent, thus preventing wrinkles. Fibers with strong intermolecular bonds have good molecular memory and resist wrinkling and creasing. Fibers with weak bonds wrinkle and crease readily. Several processes are used to add **durable-press** finishes to help items retain their shape and a pressed appearance even after many uses, washings, and tumble dryings. The processes differ by when the finish is added, when it is cured, end use, advantages, and side effects.

curing uses forced-air convection ovens, microwave ovens produce a more uniform cure for lighter-weight fabrics such as shirtings. Continuing research on durable press finishing with alternate chemicals and processes focuses on improving the finish's sustainability and reducing losses in other performance areas.

Durable-Press Wool Wool has good resiliency when it is dry, but its durable-press characteristics are poor when it is wet. *Durable-press wool* is achieved with combination resin treatments to impart durable-press characteristics and control wool's excessive shrinkage. Several procedures are used, but the one described here is typical. Si-Ro-Set is a trade name.

1. Flat fabric is treated with a durable-press resin and steamed for a few minutes.
2. The item is made up, sprayed with more durable-press resin, and pressed to achieve a permanent-crease effect.
3. Shrink-resistance resin is mixed with a dry-cleaning solvent and the item is dry-cleaned. The item is cured for several days before it can be laundered.

Durable-Press Silk Since silk wrinkles easily when wet, polycarboxylic acid is used to produce durable-press or wrinkle-resistant silk. The finish is durable to laundering but produces a 20 percent loss in strength, increase in stiffness, and decrease in whiteness.

Quality Performance Standards and Care

Because performance standards had not been developed during the wash-and-wear era, there was wide variation in fabric performance. To avoid problems with consumer confidence, the **quality performance standards** for durable press were developed by professionals.

Consider the degree of wrinkles present when you remove your laundry from the dryer, clothesline, or drying rack. Based on the fiber content and presence or absence of wrinkles, which items have probably been treated to be durable press and which have not? What kinds of trends do you see in terms of product categories with and without treatment? Do you own an iron? How often do you use it? What kinds of items do you regularly press, if any? Discuss frequency and type of ironing with an older relative or neighbor and their practices at approximately your age. What are the differences, if any, between your practices and theirs? How does this relate to durable-press finishing?

> **Learning Activity 4**

Use Fabrics #30, 34, and 108 from your swatch kit. For each fabric, crumple it in your hand and hold it for three seconds. Release and flatten out the fabric. Is it wrinkled? Compare the results for all three fabrics. Can you determine which of the three has a durable-press finish? Describe the kinds of problems associated with durable-press finishes. How might these side effects of the finish affect consumer satisfaction with a textile product?

Registered trade names indicate to the consumer that the product has met standards related to performance, hand, and minimal odor.

General care guidelines for durable-press items include the following:

* Wash items frequently because resins have a strong affinity for oil and grease so that soil penetrates deeply and builds up.
* Pretreat stains, collars, and cuffs. Use a spot-removal agent on grease spots.
* Keep wash loads small to minimize wrinkling.
* Avoid setting in wrinkles with heat. Keep washing and drying temperatures cool.
* Remove items promptly when dry.

Appearance-Retention Finishes

Soil- and Stain-Release Finishes

Soil- and stain-release finishes reduce the degree of soiling of the fabric by repelling the soil or by preventing formation of bonds between soil and fabric. They improve a fabric's performance in resisting soil, releasing soil, and retaining whiteness by resisting redeposition of soil from the wash water. Finished fabrics are easier to clean than those without such finishes. Fluorochemicals and silicon-based compounds are durable and effective soil-resistant finishes. These finishes may only be durable enough to last through 20 to 30 washings. The lack of permanence is due to the finish's surface application. These finishes are also known as *soil-repellent*, *stain-resistant*, and *antisoil* or *antistain finishes*.

Soil-release finishes were developed as a reaction to the tendency of durable-press items to pick up and hold oily stains and spots. Soil-release finishes either attract water to permit soil

> **Soil- and stain-release finishes** reduce the degree of soiling of the fabric by repelling the soil or by preventing formation of bonds between soil and fabric.

to be lifted off the fabric or coat the fibers to prevent soil from penetrating the coating and bonding with the fiber.

Many cotton/polyester blends are treated to be durable-press. Untreated cotton is hydrophilic and releases oily soil when laundered. A resin finish, however, is hydrophobic and does not release the oily soil. Since polyester is hydrophobic and oleophilic, it must be spot-treated to remove oily soil from areas such as shirt collars. When the polyester is coated with resin, as it is in durable press, its oil affinity is increased. Finer fibers soil more readily than coarse fibers, and soil can penetrate low-twist yarns more easily than high-twist yarns. Soil-release finishes make the surface less attractive to oil and more easily wetted—more hydrophilic.

Soil-release finishes are mechanically or chemically bonded to the surface. Many are organic silicone or fluorocarbon substances. Soil-release finishes include Scotchgard and Scotch Release by 3M, Visa by Milliken, and Teflon by DuPont. Soil-resistant, stain-repellent fabrics use nanofibers attached to individual fibers. The hand and comfort of the fabric are not affected and liquids roll off the surface. Solid soils do not bond with the fibers so that staining is minimal. Fluorocarbon compounds can be reclaimed by an ion exchange process and reused.

Soil resistance for carpets is especially important given their wide use and exposure to soil. The process for carpets is a three-part program that combines a special carpet fiber (larger denier, modified cross section, and antistatic modification) with a fluorocarbon stain-repellent finish and a compound to block the dye sites on the fibers. When the dye sites are blocked, the fibers no longer accept color from stains. These blockers concentrate near the fiber's surface, the area most susceptible to staining. They are most effective against the coloring agents (acid dyes) found in food and beverages and are not effective against other staining agents. The stain-resistant treatments are not easily wetted by oil or water but may yellow with exposure to heat, ultraviolet light, or high relative humidity. Ultraviolet light may also destroy the stain blocker part of this program. A side benefit is that these carpets are more resistant to fading when exposed to ozone.

There are several companies that can be hired by design firms or consumers to add a chemically protective soil- and stain-resistant finish on site to products such as carpeting, upholstery, and wall coverings. The firms provide a follow-up service as needed, a cleaning kit, and care instructions. There are also soil-resistant finishes a consumer can apply on site. However, research has shown that some of these finishes may actually increase soiling.

Abrasion-Resistant Finishes

Abrasion-resistant finishes are thermoplastic acrylic resins that fix fibers more firmly into the yarns so they do not break off as readily. They are used on lining fabrics, especially for pockets, waistbands, and other areas that receive significant abrasion. The resin may increase wet soiling of the fabric. Blending nylon or polyester with cotton or rayon produces better abrasion resistance compared to finishes, but blends may cost more than finished fabric.

Abrasion-resistant finishes are thermoplastic acrylic resins that fix fibers more firmly into the yarns so they do not break off as readily.

> ▶ **Learning Activity 5**

Work with a partner and identify the advantages and disadvantages of soil- and stain-resistant clothing. Identify an apparel product that would have a soil- and stain-repellent finish and explain how you would market it to consumers.

Antislip Finishes

Antislip finishes are used on low-count, smooth-surfaced woven fabrics and some sheer, open knits like women's hosiery to prevent the movement of yarns within the fabric. When fabrics are treated with resins, stretched, and dried under tension, yarns are bonded at their interlacing points. Antislip finishes reduce seam slippage and fraying. Seam slippage occurs when yarns near the seam slide away from the stitching line. Thus, in areas next to seams, only one set of yarns is seen. Slippage is especially noticeable where warp and filling yarns differ in color. Areas that have experienced seam slippage have poor abrasion resistance and an unacceptable appearance. In some cases, seams can ravel completely. Antislip finishes are also called *slip-resistant*, *anti-ladder*, or *nonslip* finishes. The most effective and durable finishes are resins of urea or melamine formaldehyde.

Antislip finishes are used on low-count, smooth-surfaced woven fabrics and some sheer, open knits like women's hosiery to prevent the movement of yarns within the fabric.

Fume-Fading-Resistant Finishes

Fume-fading-resistant finishes are used on dye–fiber combinations that are susceptible to fading when exposed to atmospheric fumes or pollutants. The most common problem is with acetate dyed with disperse dyes. Of course, this problem disappears with mass pigmentation. However, in cases in which mass pigmentation is not economical, fume-fading-resistant finishes of tertiary amines and borax are used. The finish is also known as *antifume-fading finish* and *atmospheric-fading protective finish*. They are used primarily for interiors, especially draperies.

Fume-fading-resistant finishes are used on dye–fiber combinations that are susceptible to fading when exposed to atmospheric fumes or pollutants.

Surface or Back Coatings

Metallic, **plastic**, or **foam coatings** are used on the backs of fabrics to reduce heat transfer, alter fabric appearance, lock yarns in place, control porosity, and minimize air and water permeability. Metallic or aluminum coatings are used on apparel and window-treatment fabrics. A very thin layer of aluminum is bonded to the back of drapery fabric for greater heat retention or lower heat transfer. In apparel, these coatings are found in winter coats for cold climates and specialized protective apparel for extreme temperature conditions such as firefighters' uniforms and spacesuits. Some of these finishes will be discussed in the section on comfort.

Plastic coatings reduce fabric soiling and give a leatherlike look to fabrics. (See "Coated Fabrics" in Chapter 15.) Metallic and plastic coatings may crack and peel. In order to increase the life of these fabrics, follow care instructions.

Acrylic-foam back coatings, common on drapery fabrics, minimize air movement through the draperies, give a greater comfort factor by increasing the thickness of the fabric, and improve opacity, thereby minimizing the need for a separate lining. Draperies with a foam-back coating may be sold as self-lined draperies (Figure 18.9).

Latex or polyurethane back coatings are used on tufted fabrics for interior uses. Tufted carpet and tufted upholstery use back coating to lock tufted yarns in place and to add dimensional stability to fabric. Back coatings also add durability to low-count upholstery fabrics, but they may create problems with comfort because of their low air and moisture permeability. Outgassing of fumes from the back coating can also create environmental problems.

These coatings may have poor resistance to aging. They separate, peel, flake off, or experience a change in hand with age or exposure to environmental conditions such as heat or light. Acrylic-foam backing on draperies may become tacky or sticky, and stick to itself when the drapes are opened.

Back coating is also used as a means of delivering water-based polymers for finishes such as flame retardancy.

Figure 18.9 Window-treatment fabric with acrylic-foam coating: face (left) and back (right).

Metallic, **plastic**, or **foam coatings** are used on the backs of fabrics to reduce heat transfer, alter fabric appearance, lock yarns in place, control porosity, and minimize air and water permeability.

► **Learning Activity 6**

Use Fabric #63 from your swatch kit. Describe the purpose of the back coating on this fabric. Identify an end use for this fabric. Describe the serviceability of this fabric and explain how the back coating alters serviceability.

Light-Stabilizing Finishes

Light-stabilizing finishes apply light-stabilizing or ultraviolet-absorbing compounds to fabrics to minimize damage from light exposure, especially important for interior and technical products. Products that are exposed to sunlight or interior lighting that has a high percentage of ultraviolet light may require this finish. Artificial-light sources that may contribute to fading include the fluorescent lights found in many office buildings and retail establishments. Products that require light stabilizers include tarpaulin and awning fabrics, tents, sewing thread for outdoor products, outdoor furniture, car interiors, window treatments, and some carpeting and upholstery.

> **Light-stabilizing finishes** apply light-stabilizing or ultraviolet-absorbing compounds to fabrics to minimize damage from light exposure.

Pilling-Resistant Finishes

Pilling-resistant finishes minimize the formation of tiny balls of fiber bits on a fabric's surface. The fabric is exposed to short-wavelength ultraviolet radiation and then immersed in a mild oxidation solution. Surface fiber ends are weakened and much less likely to form pills. This finish, Siroflash, is used on wool and cotton blends. Siroflash also works well as a finish to prepare wool for printing.

> **Pilling-resistant finishes** minimize the formation of tiny balls of fiber bits on a fabric's surface.

Anti-Yellowing Finishes

Because so many textile products are produced far from their intended market, they can spend months in transit or storage. Most often textiles are packaged or wrapped in plastic to avoid soiling or mildew. Unfortunately, this can also mean interactions with the chemicals in the plastics so that pale or white textiles develop a yellowish discoloration. This *storage yellowing* as it is known often occurs where the textile and the plastic wrap come in contact. The yellow develops because of a colorless additive in the plastic (butyl hydroxytoluene or BHT) that reacts with nitrogen oxides from vehicle exhaust in humid, warm climates. These conditions and chemicals produce a yellow dye. **Anti-yellowing finishes** prevent the nitrogen oxides from combining with the BHT so that the yellow dye does not develop.

> **Anti-yellowing finishes** prevent the nitrogen oxides from combining with the BHT so that the yellow dye does not develop.

► **Learning Activity 7**

Explain how pills develop on fabric. Describe three ways that pills can be prevented or their frequency reduced. (Hint: You might want to review information in Chapters 3, 6, and 16.) Describe items that you have that pill. How could the pilling have been prevented or reduced for each of these items? How does pilling affect your satisfaction with these textile products?

Comfort-Related Finishes

Water-Repellent Finishes

A **water-repellent finish** on a fabric resists wetting, but if the water strikes with enough force, it will penetrate the fabric (Figure 18.10). A **waterproof fabric** will not wet regardless of the amount of time it is exposed to water or the force with which the water strikes the fabric. Waterproof fabrics are almost always films or coated fabrics. Waterproof, water-repellent, and microporous fabrics are compared in Table 18.2. (The Federal Trade Commission recommends using *durable* and *renewable* in describing water-repellent fabrics.) Water-repellent composite fabrics that incorporate a film or membrane were discussed in Chapter 15. Surface coatings were discussed early in this chapter.

Water repellency depends on surface tension and fabric penetrability. It is achieved by a combination of dense fabric structure and finish. Calendering flattens yarns making the spaces between them smaller so it is harder for liquid water to penetrate the fabric. Chemical finishes fill in the spaces between fibers and yarns. Compounds that make fabric water-repellent include fluorocarbons, wax emulsions, metallic soaps, and surface-active agents. These chemicals are applied in a water-based solution to fabrics with a very high warp count and small regular yarns. A different option, plasma treatment, uses ionized vapor to modify the fiber's surface and allows for a more effective and uniform finish. Some fluoropolymer waterproof finishes are applied using this technique.

Outerwear often incorporates three layers: an outer waterproof layer, a middle insulating layer (or layers), and an inner or internal wicking

A **water-repellent finish** on a fabric resists wetting, but if the water strikes with enough force, it will penetrate the fabric. A **waterproof fabric** will not wet regardless of the amount of time it is exposed to water or the force with which the water strikes the fabric.

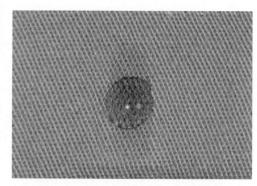

Figure 18.10 Fabric before and after treatment with a water-repellent finish. Notice how the water soaks into the untreated fabric (left) and beads up on the finished fabric (right).

Table 18.2 Comparison of Waterproof and Water-Repellent Fabrics

Waterproof Fabrics	Water-Repellent Fabrics	Water-Repellent Microporous Fabrics
Films or low-count fabrics with a film coating	High-count fabrics	Composite fabrics
	Finish coats yarns but does not block space between yarns.	
Characteristics		
No water can penetrate	Heavy rain will penetrate	Liquid water and wind will not penetrate
Films may stiffen in cold weather	Fabric is pliable, similar to untreated fabric	Fabric is pliable
Cheaper to produce	Fabric "breathes" and is comfortable for rainwear	Expensive to produce
		"Fabric breathes," but pores may stretch or fill with soil
Permanent	Durable or renewable finish	Permanent

> ► **Learning Activity 8**

Use Fabrics #35 and 110 from your swatch kit. Take an eyedropper and drop 1 or 2 drops of water on each fabric. Describe what happened. Wait 30 seconds to see if the drop is being absorbed or if the fabrics are getting wet. Use the end of the eyedropper to work the drop of water into the fabrics. Explain what is happening and why. How do water- and stain-resistant finishes compare?

layer. The outer layer is sometimes called a "hard shell" if waterproofing was achieved with a coating that produced a stiff coat or jacket. "Soft shell" coats and jackets use finishing technology to achieve a durable (not permanent) water repellent (DWR) finish that is less wind resistant. Soft shells protect from light rain and snow and are used for active wear for skiing, bicycling, jogging, and related activities. Material usage in inner layers differs depending on the demands of various body parts. For example, underarm areas need better wicking to remove perspiration while the mid-back area needs more thermal insulation.

Fluorocarbons are popular for improving both water and oil repellency. Water repellency decreases significantly with washing but recovers with heat treatment. See the earlier discussion on soil- and stain-resistant finishes for more detail.

Wax emulsions and *metallic soaps* coat the yarns but do not fill the interstices, or spaces, between the yarns. These finishes are removed in cleaning but can be renewed.

Surface-active agents have molecules with one end that is water-repellent and one end that reacts with the hydroxyl (OH) groups of cellulose. After these agents are applied, heat bonds the finish to the fabric. This finish is permanent to washing and dry cleaning.

Silicone is the most commonly used water repellent chemical. Combined with durable-press chemicals, it produces finishes that are durable and fabrics with good drape, soft hand, and stain resistance.

Some water-repellent finishes hold greasy stains more tenaciously than untreated fabrics. However, some water-repellent finishes, such as the trade-name finishes Scotchgard and Teflon, impart resistance to both oil-borne and water-borne stains. Syl-mer is a silicone finish that resists water-borne stains. Teflon and Fybrite are trade names for fluorocarbon finishes. Nanowhiskers (0.0001 the size of regular fibers) attached to nylon and polyester fibers absorb and wick moisture, improve comfort, and reduce static buildup.

Highly water-repellent fabrics using the lotus effect can be achieved with nanoparticles, nanospheres, or nanowhiskers. The lotus effect is a biomimicry or bionic finish based on the lotus leaf's ability to repel moisture due to nanoparticles of wax on the leaf's surface. This self-cleaning and water-repelling effect is expected to be available on smart textiles in a few years.

Although not a finish, microporous composite fabrics also produce a water-repellent effect. See Chapter 15 for more details.

Moisture Management Finishes

Moisture management finishes remove sweat from the skin's surface and help cool the body. These smart finishes are applied to athletic apparel, sportswear, leisurewear, work apparel, socks, and interlinings for shoes. **Moisture transport** is a measure of the speed with which perspiration is drawn from the skin's surface to the fabric's surface so it can evaporate, cool the body, and keep the wearer dry. While manufactured fibers may have modified cross sections with multilobal lateral cuts to improve moisture management, finishes are also used to improve comfort.

One of the challenges is to produce a fabric that resists wetting or penetration by liquid while allowing air and water vapor to flow through the fabric. Air permeability and water vapor transport are two key factors in comfort in water-repellent textiles. Air permeability allows body heat to dissipate and keep the wearer from getting too warm while water vapor transport allows perspiration to evaporate, keep the wearer dry, and reduce or eliminate clamminess.

Moisture management finishes remove sweat from the skin's surface and help cool the body.

Porosity-Control Finishes

Porosity-control or **air-impermeable finishes** are used to limit penetration of the fabric by air. These finishes are used for technical air filters and use low-density foam as a back coating.

Porosity-control or **air-impermeable finishes** are used to limit penetration of the fabric by air.

Water-Absorbent Finishes

Water-absorbent finishes increase the moisture absorbency of fabric and its drying time. These finishes are different from the water-repellent and moisture management finishes. Water-absorbent finishes may facilitate dyeing. The durability of absorbent finishes is fair. They are applied as surface coatings on synthetic fabrics to be used for towels, diapers, underwear, and sportswear. On nylon, a solution of nylon 8 is used; on polyesters, the finish changes the molecular structure of the fiber surface so that moisture is broken up into smaller particles that wick more readily; on cellulosics, the finish makes them absorb more moisture. Fiber modifications and different fabric structures may be more effective than some finishes. Visa and Zelcon are trade names. Hydrolon is a trade name for a polymer finish applied to nylon, polyester, and acrylic that improves surface wicking. Capilene is a finish that wicks perspiration from base layers to the outer layers of garments.

Water-absorbent finishes increase the moisture absorbency of fabric.

Ultraviolet-Absorbent Finishes

Ultraviolet-absorbent finishes incorporate chemical compounds or nanoparticles that absorb energy in the ultraviolet region of the electromagnetic spectrum. Because of the ever-increasing incidence of skin cancer, photosensitivity-based illnesses, and accelerated aging of skin (wrinkles and desiccated appearance), apparel is an important means of reducing exposure to ultraviolet radiation. Fabrics can be treated with ultraviolet inhibitors during dyeing that absorb energy in this region.

Ultraviolet-absorbent finishes incorporate chemical compounds or nanoparticles that absorb energy in the ultraviolet region of the electromagnetic spectrum.

These finishes are also referred to as *sunprotective* and *ultraviolet* or *UV blockers*. Many dyes and fluorescent whitening agents also absorb ultraviolet energy. The darker the color of a fabric, the more ultraviolet energy it will absorb and the more protection it will provide. Fabrics with ultraviolet absorbent finishes or modifications may be promoted with an *ultraviolet-protection factor* (*UPF*). Higher UPF ratings are better than lower ratings. Ratings are identified as good (15–24); very good (25–39); and excellent (40–50+).

Other ways of improving the sun-protective factors of fabric include using thicker and denser fabrics and manufactured fibers modified to be sunlight-resistant or modified with sunlight blockers. Protection from ultraviolet radiation is related to fiber content: polyester offers the most protection followed by nylon, wool, silk, cotton and rayon (in that order). Wet or stretched fabrics offer less protection. Use detergents with optical brightening or fluorescent whitening agents when doing the laundry to improve fabric ability to block damaging ultraviolet radiation. Other commercial compounds can be added to the wash water to improve absorption of ultraviolet radiation.

Antistatic Finishes

Antistatic finishes are important in both the production and use of the fabrics. Static buildup causes fabrics to cling to machinery in factories and to people, attract dust and lint, and produce sparks and shocks.

Static buildup on natural-fiber fabrics is controlled by increasing humidity and using lubricants, but these controls were inadequate with thermoplastic fibers. Antistatic finishes work by (1) improving the surface conductivity so that excess electrons move to the atmosphere or ground; (2) attracting water molecules to increase fiber conductivity; or (3) neutralizing electrostatic charge by developing a charge opposite to that on the fiber. The most effective finishes combine all three effects. Most finishes use quaternary ammonium compounds, which are not durable and must be reapplied after cleaning. Washing aids such as fabric softeners help control static. Chemical finishes can feel soapy or oily and cause allergic reactions for some people. An alternate to a chemical finish is nanoparticles that make textiles more conductive. Because the nanoparticles work with moisture in the atmosphere, static problems can develop when the air is dry.

Incorporating antistatic substances into the fibers produces the best static control. Most manufactured fibers are produced in antistatic form, especially for rugs, carpets, lingerie, and uniforms (see Chapter 6). Some trade names of antistatic nylon variants are Ultron, Antron, Staticgard, and Anso.

> **Antistatic finishes** improve the surface conductivity so that excess electrons move to the atmosphere or ground; attract water molecules to increase fiber conductivity; or neutralize electrostatic charge by developing a charge opposite to that on the fiber.

Fabric Softeners

Fabric softeners or **hand builders** improve the hand of harsh textiles that develops from resin finishes or heat setting of synthetics. Consumer demand for softer fabrics and finishes and more pleasant fabric hand is increasing. Softener types include anionic, cationic, and nonionic. *Anionic softeners* are usually sulfonated, negatively charged fatty acids and oils that must be padded onto fibers because they lack fiber affinity. Anionic softeners often are used commercially on cellulosic fibers and silk. *Cationic softeners*, most often used in domestic washing, have good fiber affinity. They tend to yellow with age and may build up if used frequently, reducing fabric absorbency. Cationic softeners that contain quaternary ammonium compounds may confer some incidental antimicrobial properties. *Nonionic softeners* are padded onto the fabric. These commercial softeners are usually a complex alcohol.

Silicone softeners produce a dryer hand as compared with that of the other compounds listed here. Better wrinkle resistance and durability occur when these softeners are combined with durable-press finishes. Some fabric softeners include menthol to help cool the body. These finishes are more durable to wear and cleaning than those with menthol microcapsules.

> **Fabric softeners** or **hand builders** improve the hand of harsh textiles that develop from resin finishes or heat setting of synthetics.

Phase-Change and Temperature Regulation Finishes

Phase-change finishes minimize heat flow through a fabric. They insulate against very hot or very cold temperature extremes. Phase change finishes are types of smart textiles since they absorb or release heat in response to environmental stimuli.

Several hundred phase-change chemicals exist. Only a few are used in textile finishes because they operate in a temperature range compatible with the human body. These phase change materials (PCM) have the ability to absorb or release heat in a relatively narrow temperature range as they undergo phase change. As the chemicals change phase from solid to liquid, they absorb heat and cool the body. As they change phase from liquid to solid, they release heat and warm the body. The time span of these phase changes is relatively brief—approximately 20 minutes. They are used on active sportswear. Aside from the heat aspects, phase-change chemicals also contribute antistatic characteristics, water absorbency, resiliency, soil release, and pilling resistance.

The phase-change chemical is microencapsulated and applied in a thin coat (0.002 inch) onto a hydroentangled nonwoven fabric (Figure 18.11). The insulation properties are not affected by compression, washing, or moisture. The chemicals change phase at temperatures very close to skin temperature. This finish is used in gloves, boots, socks, garment liners, sleeping bags, ski and winter wear, wetsuits, underwear, jackets, blankets and other bedding, and hats. Outlast® is a trade name of a PCM finish.

Other finishes that help regulate body temperature use nanotechnology. Ceramic nanoparticle coatings applied to the surface of a fabric help keep wearers warm. Ceramic coatings add a slightly yellow tint, reflect external heat, absorb contact heat, block ultraviolet light, are stable to heat, and insulate from electricity. They are used in military, automotive and technical products.

Figure 18.11 **Microencapsulated phase-change thermal finish.**
SOURCE: Courtesy of Gateway Technologies, Inc.

Phase-change finishes minimize heat flow through a fabric. They insulate against very hot or very cold temperature extremes.

Biological-Control Finishes

Insect- and Moth-Control Finishes

Moths and carpet beetles damage protein fibers such as wool. In addition, insects may damage other fibers if soil is present. More than 100 species of insects and spiders, including silverfish, crickets, and cockroaches, have been known to damage textiles. In most cases, an insect-infestation problem develops when there is soil as a food source and under proper environmental conditions. Manufactured fibers are not immune, but natural fibers are more likely to be damaged by insects.

Insect- and **moth-control finishes** are also known as *fumigants, insecticides, insect-repellent finishes*, and other terms that imply resistance to a specific insect pest, such as silverfish or moths. Both moths and carpet beetles damage 100 percent wool and blends of wool and other fibers. Although they can digest only the wool, the insects eat through the other fibers.

Insect- and **moth-control finishes** provide resistance to specific insect pests.

The damage is done by the larvae, not the adults. Clothes moths are small, about 1/4 inch long. The larvae shun bright sunlight and live in the dark. Thus, it is necessary to clean often under sofas and furniture cushions, in the creases of chairs, and apparel stored in dark closets.

Most wool interior fabrics are treated with a moth-control or mothproofing agent. Approximately 70 percent of mothproofing agents are used by the carpet industry; wool and wool blend carpets obtain the "Wool Mark" standard of quality. If information to that effect is not on the label, check into it.

Traditionally, mothproofing used a chemical, often Permethrin, at the scouring or dyeing stage. Because excess chemical would be flushed into nearby water systems, killing invertebrates, methods of applying Permethrin via foam processes are preferred.

Permethrin repels and kills spiders, ticks, mosquitoes, and other crawling and flying insects. It is also applied to tents of all kinds and canvas used in fold-down camping trailers and hunting blinds. Expel, by Graniteville, is odorless and resistant to washing, heat, and ultraviolet light.

Means of controlling insect damage are listed below:

1. *Cold storage* decreases insect activity so that damage is much less likely to occur. Museums use freezing to control insect problems in storage areas because the extreme conditions kill the insects. This technique is generally not practical for consumer use.
2. *Odors* can repel insects. Paradichlorobenzene and naphthalene (mothballs) are used in storage. These insecticides are poisons and should be used with caution and only when absolutely necessary.
3. *Stomach poisons* such as fluorides and silicofluorides are finishes for dry-cleanable wool.
4. *Contact poisons* such as DDT are very effective, but DDT is banned in the United States and many other parts of the world.
5. *Chemical additives* in the dye bath permanently change the fiber, making it unpalatable to the larvae. Surface and on-site applications may yellow carpet fiber or cause color loss.

Mold- and Mildew-Control Finishes

Mold and *mildew* grow on and damage cellulosic and protein textiles, but the problem is far more common on cellulosics. They also grow on, but do not damage, thermoplastic fibers. **Mold-** and **mildew-control finishes**, also known as *fungicides* or *mildew-preventive finishes,* prevent this growth.

Prevention is the best solution to the problem because cures are often impossible. Mildew occurs when the microorganism feeds on the fiber surface, creating tiny pits and craters. The color associated with mildew is due to shadows from the pits. To prevent mold or mildew, keep textiles clean and dry. Keep soiled items dry, and wash them as soon as possible. Frequent sunning and airing should be done during periods of high humidity. Use an electric light and dehumidifiers in dark, humid storage places.

If mildew occurs, wash the article immediately. Mild stains can be removed by bleaching. Mold and mildew growth is prevented by many compounds. Salicylanilide is used on cellulosic fibers and wool.

Mold- and **mildew-control finishes** prevent the growth of mold, mildew or other compounds that damage cellulosic fabrics. **Rot-proof finishes** are used primarily on technical products that are used outdoors to improve their durability and longevity.

▶ Learning Activity 11

Identify two textile products that might have an insect control finish. Explain why these finishes are used. Describe how an insect control finish might work. Are there any safety or health concerns for the wearer or user of textiles treated with these finishes?

Rot-Proof Finishes

Rot-proof finishes are used primarily on technical products that are used outdoors to improve their durability and longevity. Textiles rot when they are exposed to moist, warm conditions for several days or more. Soil microbes secrete enzymes that disintegrate the textile. Cellulosic textiles are most susceptible to rotting, but protein fibers will rot under certain conditions. Finishing agents N-methylol and glyoxal impart rot resistance to cotton canvas for tents, tarpaulins, awnings, lawn and deck furniture, and other outdoor applications. Because so many synthetic fibers are used for these technical applications today, rot-proof finishes are decreasing in use.

Antimicrobial Finishes

Antimicrobial finishes inhibit the growth of microbes, reduce or prevent odor, prevent decay and damage from perspiration, control the spread of disease, and reduce the risk of infection following injury. Antimicrobial finishes are also known as *antibacterial*, *bacteriostatic*, *germicidal*, *permafresh*, *antiodor*, or *antiseptic finishes*. There are two types of finishes: leachable (not bonded to the fiber) and nonleachable (bonded to the fiber or used as additives during fiber production). Leachable finishes are removed by water. Nonleachable finishes are fast to repeated washings. Ideally, both types should be safe for consumers and producers, be easy to apply, and not adversely affect the fabric.

These finishes are used in apparel that comes in contact with the skin, shoe linings, hospital linens, contract carpeting, medical textiles, pillow covers, bed pads, towels, shower curtains, handkerchiefs, and air filters. The chemicals are surface reactants such as quaternary ammonium or silicone compounds, diphenyl ether, chitosan (a natural polymer), or silver-based compounds. Liquid solutions incorporating the active ingredient are applied by padding, exhaust, or spraying. The chemicals are added to the spinning solution of manufactured fibers for use in wall coverings and upholstery. Diaper services may add an antimicrobial finish, such as Sanitized®, with each laundering.

The processes include chemical treatment, gas treatment, irradiation treatment, and addition of nanoparticles. Chemical antimicrobial finishes may cause yellowing and fading on nylon—a major problem for carpets. Ethylene oxide gas treatment is used in some cases. Since it is a hazardous material, it is being replaced with *irradiation sterilization*, also known as *electron-beam sterilization*. This treatment is cheaper, simpler, safer, and ideal for medical products such as bandages, sutures, and surgical gloves. Since the beam penetrates thermoplastic and foil packaging, items are packaged and then treated to maintain the sterile environment until the package is opened. Silver nanoparticles are applied to fabrics during dyeing. Use of silver nanoparticles may be regulated because of their release during laundering and accumulation in bio-solids in water treatment facilities.

> **Antimicrobial finishes** inhibit the growth of microbes, reduce or prevent odor, prevent decay and damage from perspiration, control the spread of disease, and reduce the risk of infection following injury.

▶ Learning Activity 12

Identify five textile products that might have an antibacterial finish. Be sure your list includes apparel, interior, and technical products. Are there concerns about use of these finishes?

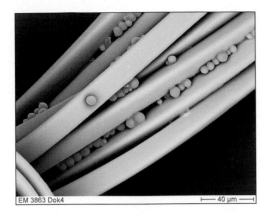

Figure 18.12 Microencapsulated fragrance on textile fibers.

SOURCE: Courtesy of Cognis.

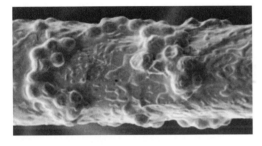

Figure 18.13 Microencapsulated insect-repellent finish.

SOURCE: Reprinted with permission from Nelson, G. (1991). Microencapsulates in textile coloration and finishing. *Review of Progress in Coloration*, 21, pp. 72–85. Published by the Society of Dyers and Colourists, Bradford, UK.

Microencapsulated finishes incorporate a material in a tiny capsule form. Contents of the capsule determine the overall effect of the finish.

> ### ▶ Learning Activity 13
>
> Work with a partner. Make a list of six chemicals that are used in microcapsule form on textiles. List a purpose and an end use for each of the chemicals. Compare your list with another team. Select one end use on your list and describe the serviceability of the finish. Are these finishes temporary, durable, or permanent?

Microencapsulated Finishes

Microencapsulated finishes, a smart textile finish, incorporate a water-soluble or other material in a tiny capsule form. The capsules are between 5 and 50 microns and may contain fragrance, insect repellents, disinfectants, cleaning agents, cooling chemicals like menthol, warming chemicals like capsaicin, body lotions, oils to relief stress, deodorants, activated charcoal, or other materials. Phase change materials in microcapsule form were discussed earlier in this chapter. The microcapsules are sprayed onto a fabric and held in place with a polyvinyl alcohol or acrylic binder. The finished fabric may be durable for up to 10 washings for some products. They cause no skin irritation. Unfortunately, once the microcapsules have been ruptured and released their content, they cannot be refilled or replenished.

End uses for microcapsules with fragrance include ribbons, handkerchiefs, scarves, curtains, upholstery, bedding, hosiery, sweaters, ties, and T-shirts (Figure 18.12). Normal physical forces during wear rupture the capsules and release the fragrance. Synthetic and natural insect-repellent microcapsules have been used in outdoor and military apparel, in bedding to control dust mites, and in tents. Extra repellent can be released by squeezing the fabric. Cooling or warming chemical microcapsules are used in sportswear, underwear, and socks. Lotions and oils are used in hosiery, lingerie, bedding, and gloves (Figure 18.13). Mothproofing microcapsules are applied to wool carpet. Microcapsules containing bactericidal agents are applied to hospital gowns and bed linens, protective apparel worn in the pharmaceutical and food industries, socks, underwear, and activewear. Activated charcoal and nanoparticles are used as deodorant finishes to absorb body odor and for gym wear and hunters' apparel. Other deodorant nanoparticles are being engineered to absorb specific odors such as cigarette smoke and will be effective longer than activated charcoal that absorbs all odors.

Safety-Related Finishes

Flame-Retardant Finishes

Each year a large number of fatalities and injuries result from fires associated with flammable fabrics. The financial losses from such fires are estimated to be in the millions of dollars. Five common causes of these fires are smoking in bed, starting fires with flammable liquids, children playing with matches and lighters, burning trash, and being trapped in a burning structure.

Fabrics that burn quickly are sheer or lightweight fabrics and napped, pile, or tufted surfaces. Some items made from these fabrics ignite quickly, burn intensely, and are difficult to extinguish. "Torch" sweaters (a sweater that presents a fire hazard), fringed cowboy chaps, and chenille berets are examples of some apparel items that catch fire and cause tragic accidents. Hazardous style features include long full sleeves, flared skirts, ruffles, frills, and flowing hems.

Many terms are used when discussing the ability of a fabric to resist ignition, burn more slowly than normal, or self-extinguish once the source of ignition has been removed from the fabric. The following definitions are from ASTM, an international organization that develops standards:

- **Fire retardance**: The resistance to combustion of a material when tested under specified conditions.
- **Flame resistance**: The property of a material whereby flaming combustion is prevented, terminated, or inhibited following application of a flaming or nonflaming source of ignition, with or without subsequent removal of the ignition source.
- **Flammability**: Those characteristics of a material that pertain to its relative ease of ignition and relative ability to sustain combustion.

Fabrics are made flame-resistant by using inherently flame-resistant fibers or fiber variants that have been made flame-resistant by adding compounds to the spinning solution or by applying flame-retardant finishes to the fabrics.

The burning characteristics of fibers are listed in Table 3.6. Fibers that are inherently flame-resistant include aramid, PBI, and sulfar. Flame-retardant additives are used in the spinning solution of some acetates, nylons, polyesters, and rayons.

Flame-retardant (FR) finishes function in a variety of ways. The finish may function by blocking the flame's access to fuel and hindering further flame propagation. A foam-containing, flame-extinguishing gas may be produced, which extinguishes the flame, or the solid may be modified so that the products of combustion are not volatile or require excess heat to continue the fire, thus extinguishing the flame.

Flame-retardant chemicals may include compounds that contain halogens such as bromine, phosphorus, or antimony. Regulations requiring registration and assessment of these and other finishing chemicals on the environment are becoming more common. (See Chapter 21.)

Flame-retardant finishes are used on cotton, rayon, nylon, and polyester fabrics. Flame-retardant finishes must be durable (able to withstand 50 washings), nontoxic, and noncarcinogenic. Ideally, they should not change the hand and texture of fabrics or have an unpleasant odor. Most finishes are not visible, and they add significantly to the cost of the item, so the consumer is asked to pay for something that cannot be seen.

Flame-retardant finishes can be classified as durable and nondurable. Durable finishes are specific to fiber type and are usually phosphate compounds or salts, halogenated organic compounds, or inorganic salts.

Flame-retardant finishes are less expensive than flame-resistant fibers or fiber variants. Knitted or woven gray goods are given a topical flame-retardant finish when necessary, a more economical process for fabric producers.

In general flame-retardant finishes require the addition of a fairly large amount of finish to the fabric. **Add-on** describes the percentage by weight of solids left on a fabric after finishing and drying. Normal rates for flame retardant cellulosics range from 5 to 30 percent of the fabric's weight. For polyester, the normal rates are 1 to 10 percent of the fabric's weight. The range of add-on is related to the specific chemical used, the product's performance expectations, and the cost of the finish.

The finishes for cotton are of two general types. The first is the ammonium cure, which provides excellent flame-retardance protection with minimal strength loss; it is most often used on apparel. However, it requires the use of special equipment, so the investment in capital is great. The second type uses conventional finishing equipment and a resin. The resin results in greater strength loss and is therefore used more commonly for window treatments.

Flame-retardant (FR) finishes may block a flame's access to fuel and hindering further flame propagation; may produce foam-containing, flame-extinguishing gas to extinguish the flame; or may modify the compound so that the products of combustion are not volatile or require excess heat to continue the fire, thus extinguishing the flame.

Use Fabric #69 from your swatch kit. Explain why flame-retardant finishes are important for upholstery. What other kinds of end uses often have flame-retardant finishes? Describe two other ways that a fabric may be made flame retardant.

Cost, durability, and care of FR finishes are the greatest problems for the consumer. The cost of research and development for fibers and finishes, testing of fabrics and products, and liability insurance result in higher costs for apparel and interior textiles. Because the items look no different, the consumer may think the item is overpriced. Government standards limit consumer choices. For example, even people who do not smoke in bed pay a higher price for mattresses because only mattresses that pass safety standards can be sold in interstate commerce. The safety component is present regardless of consumer preferences.

Most of the topical finishes require special care in laundering to preserve the flame resistance. Labels should be followed carefully: do not bleach, do not use soap, and do not use hot water. Excess soil can block the effectiveness of a finish, so frequent cleaning may be required.

Flame-retardant-treated fabrics are more expensive. The fabric may be stiffer, weaker, and less abrasion-resistant than unfinished fabric. Consumers may develop a false sense of security; even though the finish makes the fabric flame retardant and slower to ignite and burn, it will not prevent the fabric from igniting or burning when conditions are right.

Liquid-Barrier Finishes

Liquid-barrier finishes protect the wearer from liquids penetrating through a fabric. These finishes are important to health-care professionals because of the presence of viral and bacterial pathogens in body fluids. Agricultural and chemical workers also require liquid-barrier protection because of the toxic and hazardous liquids with which they work. It is difficult to develop finishes that combine the degree of protection and comfort required. Often these finishes are very thin, impermeable films applied to the fabric face or back.

Antipesticide protective finishes protect from pesticides penetrating through the fabric and aid in pesticide removal during washing.

Light-Reflecting Finishes

Light-reflecting finishes are used on fabrics to increase the visibility of its wearers in low-light conditions. Two types are painted or printed on the fabric's surface: fluorescent dyes and small glass retroreflective materials. Fluorescent dyes will be discussed in more detail in Chapters 19 and 20. Small glass retroreflective spheres or prisms are used on apparel (Figure 18.14). The glass surface alters the angle of reflected light and makes objects more visible. Bonding agents are used with the retroreflective finish. These finishes are expensive and durable to a limited number of washings and are used most often on trim for footwear and actionwear. Occasionally, these finishes are used on fabric for social events because of the effect with black light.

> **Liquid-barrier finishes** protect the wearer from liquids penetrating through a fabric. They are most often used for specific occupations such as health care or farming to protect from hazardous liquids or fluid-borne pathogens.

> **Light-reflecting finishes** are used on fabrics to increase the visibility of its wearers in low-light conditions.

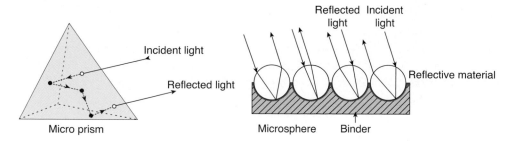

Figure 18.14 Retroreflective materials increase the visibility of the wearer at night.

▶ **Learning Activity 15**

Special-purpose finishes enhance product performance but are usually difficult to see. In some cases, the effect of the finish is difficult to perceive. Select one of the finishes from this chapter and explain how it could be promoted and marketed to enhance sales.

key terms

18

review questions

1. Explain how stabilization finishes work for these products:
   a. 100 percent wool sweater
   b. 65 percent cotton/35 percent polyester upholstery of glazed chintz
   c. 100 percent acetate antique satin draperies
   d. 100 percent cotton flannelette bedsheets

2. How do the differences among the stabilization finishes relate to fiber structure and characteristics?

3. Describe the differences in process and product performance for methods used to apply durable press to a fabric or a product.

4. Describe some of the problems associated with fabrics or products with durable press finishes.

5. Compare and contrast water-repellent and stain-repellent/soil-release finishes.

6. For what end uses are metallic, plastic, and foam coatings used? What purpose do they serve?

7. Explain how these finishes enhance comfort:
   a. Water-repellent
   b. Fabric softener
   c. Antistatic
   d. Phase-change

8. For what fibers and products are moth-control finishes likely to be used? How do they function?

9. How can flame retardancy be achieved with fabrics?

10. Explain how these finishes affect fabric properties such as comfort, care, durability, and appearance:
    a. Halogenated wool
    b. Antistatic nylon
    c. Durable-press cotton
    d. Flame-retardant rayon

11. Explain how nanotechnology is used in finishing textiles. In what kind of end uses is this technology used?

12. Explain how smart textiles relate to special purpose finishes.

13. Describe how and why fragrance is added to textiles.

14. Identify an appropriate finish and explain how it enhances the safety of these products:
    a. Carpet for a movie theatre lobby
    b. Hazardous material clean-up coveralls
    c. Child's pajamas
    d. Trim on bicycling shorts
    e. Welder's pants

15. Explain the differences and similarities among these finishes:
    a. Water absorbent and water repellent
    b. Soil resistant and water repellent
    c. Fume fading resistant and anti-yellowing
    d. Light stabilizing and ultraviolet absorbent
    e. Surface coating and water repellent
    f. Fabric softener and antistatic
    g. Insect-control and antimicrobial

Case Study
Fragrance and Textiles*

Fragrance, scent, and aroma describe pleasant smells while odor, stink, or stench describe unpleasant smells. Unpleasant smells can originate with perspiration, urine, mold, bacteria, gasoline, food, tobacco smoke, and plants. Fragrance can be incorporated in textiles by adding substances in the fiber or yarn or by using nanotechnology and microencapsulation. Odor can be masked by fragrances or by odor-absorbing compounds attached to fibers.

Individuals differ in their sense of smell and tolerance or comfort level for scents.

Consumers want textiles that control or neutralize odor, emit a pleasing fragrance, or suggest "freshness" for such things as travel, casts, and bandages.

DISCUSSION QUESTIONS

1. Identify four textile products or end uses where odor control might be important or necessary.

2. Identify four textile products or end uses where fragrance might be desirable.

3. How might a company market textiles with odor control or fragrance?

4. What are some of the concerns consumers might have about textiles with odor control or fragrance?

5. What would be an ideal fragrance for a textile product that would appeal to other students? Adults? Individuals of different ethnic groups or from different geographic regions? Will one scent satisfy all users?

6. How would appropriate scents be selected and screened for textile products?

7. What are some of the issues that product developers would have to address when preparing to add fragrance to textiles?

*Thiry, M. C. (2007). A pleasing scent. AATCC Review, 7(7), 18–25.

suggested readings

Anton-Katzenbach, S. (2008). Keep cool or get hot. *AATCC Review, 8*(6), 28–31.

Davies, B. (1999, June). Buoyant prospects for flame retardant cellulosic fabrics. *Technical Textiles International*, pp. 19–22.

Havich, M. (1999, September). Don't be afraid of the dark. *America's Textiles International*, p. 86.

Holme, I. (2004). Microencapsulation: The changing face of finishing. *Textiles Magazine,* (4), 7–10.

Hyde, T, (2006, June). Simple proven technology for the control of bad odours. *Technical Textiles International*, 25–26.

Johnson, A. S., Gupta, B. S., & Tomasino, C. (1994, June). Topical treatments of nylon carpets: Fluorochemicals and stainblockers. *American Dyestuff Reporter*, pp. 17–21, 39.

Lacasse, K., & Baumann, W. (2004). *Textile Chemicals: Environmental Data and Facts*, New York: Springer-Verlag.

Leigh, I. (1998, February). Foam textile backcoatings. *Technical Textiles International*, pp. 18–21.

Lo, L. Y., Li, Y., Yuen, C. W. M., & Yeung, K. W. (2007). Understanding wrinkle resistance (Part I). *AATCC Review, 7*(11), 28–31.

Lo, L. Y., Li, Y., Yuen, C. W. M., & Yeung, K. W. (2007). Understanding wrinkle resistance (Part II). *AATCC Review, 7*(12), 25–28.

Mansfield, R. G. (2004, March). Phase change materials. *Textile World, 154*(3), pp. 36–38.

Meirowitz, R. (2003). Water proosistance. *AATCC Review*, 3(3), pp. 19–22.

Menezes, E., & Choudhari, M. (2007). Special finishes and effects. *AATCC Review, 7*(3), 29–32.

Payne, J. (1997, February). From medical textiles to smell-free socks. *Journal of the Society of Dyers and Colourists*, 113, pp. 48–50.

Perkins, W. S. (2000). Functional finishes and high performance textiles. *TCC & ADR*, 32(4), pp. 24–27.

Powell, C. S. (1998, September). Phosphorus-based flame retardants for textiles. *American Dyestuff Reporter*, pp. 51–53.

Purwar, R., & Joshi, M. (2004, March). Recent developments in antimicrobial finishing of textiles—A review. *AATCC Review*, 4(3), pp. 22–26.

Ramaratnam, K., Iyer, S. K., Kinnan, M. K., Chumanov, G., Brown, P., & Luzinov, I. (2008), Unltrahydrophobic textiles: Lotus approach. *AATCC Review, 8*(1), 42–47.

Schindler, W. D., & Hauser, P. J. (2004). *Chemical Finishing of Textiles*. Cambridge, England: Woodhead.

Stipe, M. (1997, November). Easy care wool promoted by the wool bureau. *American Sportswear and Knitting Times*, p. 45.

Thiry, M. C. (2007). A pleasing scent. *AATCC Review, 7*(7), 18–25.

Thiry, M. C. (2007). Lightening on a small scale. *AATCC Review, 7*(11), 18–23.

Thiry, M. C. (2007). Small scale—Huge potential. *AATCC Review, 7*(6), 22–26.

Thiry, M. C. (2006). Special effects, special finishes. *AATCC Review, 6*(11), 21–25.

Thiry, M. C. (2005). The sunnier side of textiles. *AATCC Review, 5*(8), 18–22.

Thiry, M. C. (2006). Wet and dry. *AATCC Review, 6*(6), 26–31.

Yang, C. Q. (1999, May). Durable press garment finishing without formaldehyde. *American Dyestuff Reporter*, pp. 13–17.

DYEING AND PRINTING

CHAPTER OBJECTIVES

- To understand the theory and processes of dyeing and printing textiles.
- To relate quality and performance to the materials and processes used in dyeing or printing.
- To identify the stages of dyeing and types of printing.
- To relate dyeing and printing to the performance of textile products.
- To identify problems related to dyed and printed textiles and textile products.
- To understand the basics of color matching.

Color is one of the most significant factors in the appeal and marketability of textile products. Consider the array of color when scanning the merchandise in a specialty apparel store. Each season has a fashion palette and a wide range of color available to appeal to consumer taste. Determining how the color is applied and what colorants are used is challenging.

The manner in which color is added to a textile and the chemical nature of the colorant contribute to a product's appearance, performance, rate of response to fashion change, quality, and cost. **Colorant** is a general term describing materials that are used to add color to a fabric. Colorants are either dyes or pigments and will be discussed later in this chapter. Information about the colorants and process is combined with other data including fiber content, other materials used in the product, and product assembly processes to identify appropriate care label instructions. For example, a plaid shirt made of dyed yarns will look different, cost more, and be of different quality than a shirt made from fabric printed to look like a plaid. A red T-shirt dyed with a reactive dye has different care requirements than a shirt dyed with a direct dye. Selection of materials appropriate for a textile product involves application of basic principles of dyeing and printing and understanding how these factors affect a textile product's appearance, performance, response to fashion change, quality, and cost.

Manufacturers select colorants and dyeing or printing processes based on their capabilities, knowledge, and market demands. Manufacturer capabilities include the type and size of equipment, laws and regulations, air and water quality requirements, and the colorants used. Type and size of equipment determines the amount of textile materials a manufacturing facility can color at one time and the type of material they work with. For example, some manufacturers only dye cotton yarn or fiber while others only dye wool yarn or fiber. Some manufacturers only dye warp yarns for denim. Some manufacturers only dye fabric and still others only screen print fabric. Laws and regulations affecting dyeing and printing or marketability of dyed or printed textile products vary country by country. In some parts of the world the focus is on water treatment and air quality. In other parts of the world, the kinds of colorants used may also be addressed by laws and regulations.

This chapter discusses the characteristics of color and focuses on identification (when color was added to the product), process (how color was added to the product), serviceability (how color affects product performance), sustainability (chemicals, water use, and environmental issues), and problem solving (what kind of problems can develop because of color). While many processes and processes are included, some are of minor importance. Others are mainstays in the industry and represent the vast majority of colored textiles. Watch for these distinctions.

Although some consumers try home dyeing, they are usually not happy with the process because it is difficult to predict the final color, achieve a fast color, produce uniform and level color, and clean up the mess after dyeing. Commercial dyeing is much more successful because it uses specialized equipment and dyes or pigments not available to the consumer. In addition, dyers and printers have a great deal of training and experience that minimize problems with the process and finished product.

The goal of adding color to textiles is to produce an appealing, level, fast color on a product at a reasonable price, with good performance characteristics and with minimal environmental impact. **Level** describes a color that looks the same throughout the product. Level color has the same hue, value, and intensity in all areas. There are no lighter or darker areas. **Colorfastness** refers to dyes and prints that do not shift hue or fade when exposed to light and other environmental factors and that do not move onto other fabrics or material during storage, processing, use, or care. Poor colorfastness can create problems in production, storage, and use. Figure 19.1 shows color migration that occurred during storage. Colorfastness is

Figure 19.1 Color migration that occurred during storage.

Coloration is evaluated based on its levelness, color match to a predetermined color, and colorfastness. Level describes a color that looks the same throughout the product. Colorfastness refers to dyes and prints that do not shift hue or fade when exposed to light and other environmental factors and that do not move onto other fabrics or material during storage, processing, use, or care.

evaluated for conditions that a fabric may experience in finishing in textile mills, heating and pressing in production facilities, storage in warehouses and distribution centers, and use and care by consumers.

Color has always been important in textiles. Until 1856, plants, insects, and minerals were the sources for natural dyes and pigments. When William Henry Perkin discovered mauve, the first synthetic dye, a new industry—synthetic dyeing—came into being. Europe was the center for synthetic dyes until World War I interrupted trade with Germany and a dye industry developed in the United States and other parts of the world. Today there are hundreds of colorants or coloring agents from which to choose.

While consumers are not aware of the challenges involved in achieving a particular color in a uniform manner on a textile product, they have high expectations for the product. They expect that the color will remain vivid and uniform throughout the life of the product and that it will not create problems in use, care, or storage. It is remarkable that dyed and printed textiles generate as few complaints from consumers as they do, since achieving uniform and fast color is such a difficult challenge. Slight differences in fabric due to minor irregularities in fiber, yarn, fabric, or finishing can result in subtle color variations that can be readily apparent in finished products when seams join parts cut from different bolts.

Adding color to a textile product is an involved process. Fiber chemistry plays an important role. Differences in the chemical compositions of fibers were discussed in Chapters 3 through 9. These differences can be seen in various properties and performance characteristics. A match between the chemistry of the dye and that of the fiber is needed in order for the color to be permanent. Any colored textile product may be exposed to such potential color degradants as detergent, perspiration, dry-cleaning solvents, sunlight, air or water pollutants, makeup, and personal care products. To achieve a fast color, the dye must be permanently attached to or trapped within the fiber by using a combination of heat, pressure, and chemical assistants. Since access to the fiber's internal regions is critical, crystallinity, chemical finishes, and fabric and yarn structure are factors that influence the success of dyeing.

Color Theory and Practice

Color theory is a complex phenomenon that combines the physics of light, the chemistry of colored objects, the biology of the eye, the behavioral sciences in terms of social and cultural meaning of color, and aesthetics—the appreciation of what one sees. These elements interact

in either solutions or pastes. Dye pastes are used for printing. Fabrics printed with dyes can often be distinguished from fabrics printed with pigments because the dyes tend to penetrate a bit more within and between yarns so more color or a discernable pattern is seen on the reverse side of the fabric.

A **fluorescent dye** absorbs light at one wavelength and re-emits that energy at another. Fluorescent dyes are used for many applications. In detergents and preparation finishing, they make whites appear whiter and mask the yellowing of fibers. Fluorescent dyes are used in apparel to increase the wearer's visibility at night, in costumes and protective apparel to produce intense glow-in-the-dark effects, and in some medical procedures.

A **dye process** describes the environment created for the introduction of dye by hot water, steam, or dry heat. Chemical additives such as salt or acid are used to regulate penetration of the dye into the fiber. A knowledge of fiber–dye interactions, methods of dyeing, and equipment produces a better understanding of color behavior.

The stage at which color is applied has little to do with fastness but has a great deal to do with dye penetration. It is governed by fabric design, quality level, and cost. In order for a fabric to be colored, the dye must penetrate the fiber and either be combined chemically with it or be locked inside it. Fibers that dye easily are absorbent and have chemical sites in their molecular structure that react with the dye molecules. The dye reacts with the surface molecules first. Moisture and heat swell the fibers, causing polymer chains to move farther apart so that sites in the fiber's interior are exposed to react with the dye. During cooling and drying the chains move back together, trapping the dye in the fiber. Wool dyed with an acid dye is a good example of a fiber that is absorbent and has many sites that chemically react with the dye to color the fiber.

The thermoplastic fibers can be difficult to dye because their absorbency is low. However, most of these fibers are modified to accept different classes of dyes. This makes it possible to achieve different color effects or a good solid color in blends of unlike fibers by piece-dyeing.

Dyes are classified or grouped by chemical composition or method of application. Table 19.1 is a resource for future use that lists major dye classes along with some of their characteristics and end uses. No one dye is fast to everything. Dyes within a class are not equally

Table 19.1 Classification of Fiber Dyes

Dyes	Fiber Types and End Uses	Characteristics
Acid (Anionic)		
Complete color range.	Major dye class used on wool, silk, and nylon.	Bright colors.
	Modified rayon, acrylic, and polyester.	Vary in lightfastness.
		May have poor washfastness.

Table 19.1 Classification of Fiber Dyes (*continued*)

Dyes	Fiber Types and End Uses	Characteristics
Azoic (Naphthol and Rapidogens) Complete color range. Moderate cost.	Minor dye class used primarily on cotton and some polyester.	Bright shades. Good to excellent lightfastness and washfastness. Poor crocking resistance.
Cationic (Basic) Used with mordant on fibers other than silk, wool, and acrylic. Complete color range.	Minor dye class used on acrylics, modified polyester and nylon, direct prints on acetate, and discharge prints on cotton.	Fast colors on acrylics. May bleed and crock. On natural fibers, poor fastness to light, washing, perspiration.
Developed, Direct Complete color range.	Primarily cellulose fibers. Discharge prints.	Duller colors than acid or basic. Good to excellent lightfastness. Fair washfastness.
Direct (Substantive) Commercially significant dye class. Complete color range.	Major dye class used on cellulose fibers.	Good colorfastness to light. May have poor washfastness, especially with hot water.
Disperse Commercially significant dye class. Dye particles disperse in water. Good color range.	Developed for acetate, major dye class used on most synthetic fibers.	Fair to excellent lightfastness and washfastness. Blues and violets on acetate fume fade.
Fluorescent Brighteners Specific types for most common fibers.	Used on textiles and in detergents. Used to achieve intensely bright colors.	Mask yellowing and off-whiteness that occur naturally or develop with age and soil.
Mordant Fair color range.	Major dye class used on same fibers as listed for acid dyes.	Good to excellent lightfastness and washfastness. Duller than acid dyes.
Natural or Vegetable Derived from plant, animal, or mineral sources. Earliest dyes used.	Minor dye class; used to dye some apparel and interior textiles. Primarily used on natural fibers.	Fastness varies. Limited colors and availability.
Reactive or Fiber-Reactive Combines chemically with fiber.	Most important dye class used on cotton and cellulose fibers; also used on wool, silk, and nylon.	Bright shades. Good lightfastness and washfastness. Sensitive to chlorine bleach.
Sulfur Insoluble in water. Complete color range except for red.	Minor dye class, used primarily for heavyweight cotton.	Dull colors. Poor to excellent lightfastness and washfastness. Sensitive to chlorine bleach. May tender stored goods.
Vat Insoluble in water. Incomplete color range.	Primarily for cotton work clothes, sportswear, prints, drapery fabrics. Some use on cotton/polyester blends.	Good to excellent lightfastness and washfastness.

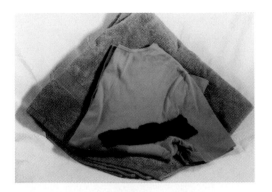

Figure 19.9 Product-dyed/garment-dyed items: towel, shirt, socks.

apparel and interiors industries, with an emphasis on quick response to retail and consumer demands (Figure 19.9).

Methods of Dyeing

The method chosen for dyeing depends on fiber content, fabric weight, type of dye, and degree of penetration required in the finished product. In mass production, time is money, so processes in which the goods travel quickly through a machine are used whenever possible.

Many methods and processes are used in dyeing. The methods tend to involve one of three ways of combining the dye bath with the textile: The textile is circulated in a dye bath; dye bath is circulated around the textile; or both textile and dye bath are circulated together.

Batch Dyeing

Batch dyeing is also known as exhaust dyeing. In this process, the textile is circulated through the dye bath. Batch dyeing can be used for textiles in any stage of production from fiber to product but tends to be used for smaller lots or shorter yardages. The process has good flexibility in terms of color selection, and the cost is low, especially if done close to the product stage. Temperature can be controlled for the dye–fiber combination. Equipment used includes the beck, pad, and jig.

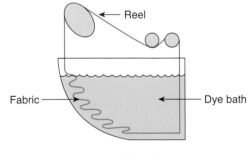

Figure 19.10 Winch dyeing.

Beck, Reel, or Winch Dyeing The oldest type of piece dyeing is *beck*, *reel*, or **winch dyeing** (Figure 19.10). The fabric, in a loose rope sewn together at the ends, is lifted in and out of the dye bath by a reel. Most of the fabric is immersed in the dye bath except for the few yards around the reel. Penetration of dye into the fiber is obtained by continued immersion of slack fabrics rather than by pressure on the wet fabrics under tension, as is done in some other processes. This method is used on lightweight fabrics that cannot withstand the tension of the other methods, and on heavy fabrics, especially woolens.

In beck dyeing, a pressurized liquor ratio of 5:1 or 4:1 is used. **Liquor ratio** refers to the weight of solution as compared with the weight of the textile to be dyed. Thus, liquor ratios of 5:1 have five times as much liquid as the textile by weight. Beck dyeing is generally used for fabric lengths ranging from 50 to 100 meters in rope or full width forms. It is simple, versatile, and low cost. Fabrics are subjected to low warp tension, and bulking of yarns occurs. Beck dyeing uses large amounts of water, chemicals, and energy. It also causes abrasion, creasing, and distortion of some fabrics when they are dyed in rope form.

Jig Dyeing **Jig dyeing** uses a stationary dye bath with two rolls above the bath. The fabric is carried around the rolls in open width and rolled back and forth through the dye bath at regular intervals. It is on rollers for the remaining time. Level dyeing is a challenge with this process. Acetate, rayon, and nylon are usually jig-dyed (Figure 19.11).

In jig dyeing, much larger runs of fabric at open width are used; several thousand meters is common. The way the fabric is moved in the process creates great warp tension. Fabrics that may crease in rope form are dyed in this manner, such as carpet, some twills, and some satins.

Pad Dyeing In **pad dyeing**, the fabric is run through the dye bath in open width and then between squeeze or nip rollers that force the dye into the fabric with pressure (Figure 19.12). Because the pad box holds a very small amount of dye bath or dye liquor, this is an economical way to piece-dye. The fabric runs through the machine at a rapid rate, 30 to 300 meters a minute. Pad-steam processes are common methods of dyeing fabric.

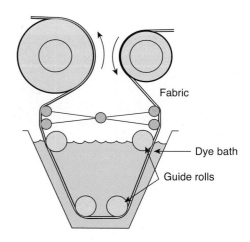

Figure 19.11   Jig dyeing.

Package Dyeing

In **package dyeing**, the dye bath is forced through the textile. Normally, the textile is in the yarn stage and wound on a perforated core of stainless steel, plastic, or paper and placed on a perforated spindle in a pressurized machine. This technique is also used for some fiber and fabric dyeing. In beam dyeing, the yarn or fabric is wound on perforated beams. This method is practical for fabrics whose warp is one color and filling another. In skein dyeing, the yarn skeins are hung in the machine and the dye circulates around the hanging skeins. Package dyeing is used primarily for bulky yarns such as acrylic and wool for knits and carpet. Liquor ratios are high to ensure uniformity of the dyeing, usually ranging from 10:1 to 4:1 (depending on the process, dye–fiber combination, and quality desired).

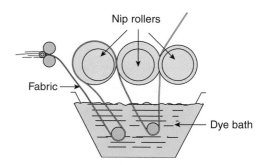

Figure 19.12   Pad dyeing.

Combination Dyeing

In combination dyeing, both the textile and the dye bath are circulated. Techniques include jet dyeing, paddle machines, rotary drums, tumblers, and continuous dyeing.

Jet Dyeing **Jet dyeing** is similar to beck dyeing. Here, the fabric is processed as a continuous loop. The technique is especially useful for delicate polyester fabrics; but, depending on the machine, almost any weight, structure, or fiber type can be used. It involves vigorous agitation of the dye bath and the textile. Because of its rapid speed (200 to 800 meters per minute), fabric wrinkling is minimal. Low warp tension helps develop bulk and fullness. High temperatures result in rapid dyeing, increased efficiency of dyes and chemicals, good fastness characteristics, and lower use of energy. However, equipment and maintenance costs are high, foaming can be a problem, and fabric abrasion can be a problem.

Paddle Machines, Rotary Drums, or Tumblers *Paddle machines* and *rotary drums* are used primarily for product dyeing (Figure 19.13). Both the dye bath and the product are circulated by a paddle or by rotation of the drum. *Tumblers* are similar to rotary drums except that they tilt forward for easier loading and unloading. Tumblers are used in product dyeing and in abrasive or chemical washes.

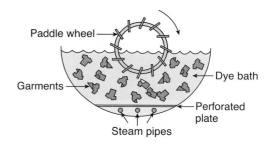

Figure 19.13   Paddle dyeing.

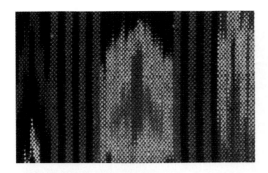

Figure 19.16 Ikat.

Computer-aided design (CAD), computer-aided manufacturing (CAM), and inexpensive and powerful personal computer system have revolutionized the design and preprinting process. The design is created on-screen or scanned in and manipulated in scale or pattern and recolored as desired. CAD allows designers to quickly create coordinating prints for apparel and interior uses by selecting a portion of the original design and copying it.

Different colorways, variations in scale, or changes in pattern detail can be examined in seconds with a few simple commands. The term **colorways** describes the different color options available for a fabric. Some fabrics are produced in one color combination only, but most are available in several colorways.

A paper or fabric copy of the design is printed using a color printer. With improvements in the capabilities of color printers, inks, and textile fabrics prepared for ink-jet printers, rapid development of samples significantly decreases development and preproduction time. This time-saving process keeps product development costs down.

Screens are created and sample yardage is printed, if necessary, or bulk production occurs immediately. Computer systems are also used to engrave the screens, predict color matches, and prepare print pastes for bulk production. These systems make it possible to create designs and convert them into fabrics in a few hours or days rather than months. Computer use increases automation of the process and decreases costs associated with labor, raw materials, and inventory.

Wet prints use a thick liquid paste; *dry prints* use a powder. In **foam prints**, the colorant is dispersed in a foam. The foam is applied to the fabric and then collapses. The small amount of liquid limits color migration. Foam printing has less environmental impact than some other printing methods.

Table 19.4 lists the various methods of creating printed designs. Table 19.5 summarizes the characteristics of the various printing methods.

> **Printing** is used to add color in localized areas only. In **direct printing**, color is applied directly to the fabric in the pattern and location desired in the finished fabric. The most common printing method is screen printing.

Direct Printing

In **direct printing**, color is applied directly to the fabric in the pattern and location desired in the finished fabric. Direct printing is a common method of printing a design on a fabric because it is easy and economical.

Block Printing **Block printing** is a hand process; it is probably the oldest technique for decorating textiles. It is seldom done commercially because it is expensive and slow. A pattern is carved on a block. The block is dipped in a shallow pan of dye paste and stamped on the fabric

Table 19.4 Printing Processes

Direct	Discharge	Screen	Others
Block	Discharge	Flat	Digital
Direct-roller*		Rotary*	Heat transfer
Warp			Electrostatic
			Differential
			Foil printing
			Stencil

*Major printing processes.

Table 19.5 Methods of Printing

Stage	Name	Advantages	Disadvantages	Identifying Features
Direct print on fabric	Block print	Handmade craft. Used to produce unique, one-of-a-kind items.	Expensive process. Slow. Pattern alignment difficult.	Irregular depth of color. Repeat blocks may be out of alignment. One to several colors in pattern.
Direct print on fabric	Roller print	Multiple colors. Less expensive method. Versatile in colors, pattern, and scale. Duplex prints possible.	Number of colors limited by equipment. Creating engraved rollers expensive. Out-of-register prints. Scale limited by size of roller.	From 1 to 16 colors in pattern. Scale of repeat can vary. Second most common printing method.
Direct print on yarn	Warp print	Soft edge to pattern. Unique look.	Expensive process. Not quick response.	Hazy, irregular pattern edges that become more distinct when filling removed. Minor process.
Dyed fabric printed with discharge paste	Discharge print	Cost dependent on design.	Discharge paste may tender fabric. Limited to patterns with few colors and dark ground.	Patterned areas show ground color on back; usually white or one to two colors with dark ground.
Print fabric or product with resist screens	Screen print	Fine detail possible. Many colors possible with overprinting. Inexpensive process. Quick response. Applicable to fabric and product. Minimal downtime. Quick colorway changes. Hand or commercial process. Can imitate many other techniques.	Registration of screens critical to process. Change of fabric hand can be a problem. Separate screen for each color of print. Quality of screen related to quality of fabric. Out-of-register, if careless.	Most common printing method.
Fabric and carpet	Digital print	Inexpensive. Quick response. Minimal downtime. Quick colorway changes. Mass customization possible.	Currently commercially limited to carpet. Fineness of detail limited. Fastness and fabric hand problems.	Most common method of printing carpet. Widely used in textile design and development of samples.

(continued)

Table 19.5 Methods of Printing (*continued*)

Stage	Name	Advantages	Disadvantages	Identifying Features
Print paper, transfer to fabric/product	Heat- transfer print or sublimation-transfer print	Unique designs possible.	Production speed and fabric width limitations.	Sharp print on face; little, if any, transfer to fabric back.
			Image-quality and color matching issues.	
		Quick response.	Disposal of waste paper.	
		Minimal downtime.	Limited to sublimable disperse dyes and synthetic fibers.	
		Detailed designs possible.	Storage conditions may cause dye transfer.	
		Minimal environmental impact from dyes.		
		Inexpensive.		
		Low capital and space needs.		
Powdered dye applied to fabric	Electrostatic print	No washdown needed.	Powder difficult to control.	Printed face, unprinted back.
				Minor process.
		Minimal environmental impact from dyes.	Limited to synthetic fibers and disperse dyes.	
		Inexpensive.		
Dye applied to carpet fibers with different dye affinities	Differential print	Unique looks possible.	Limited to carpet.	Carpet with less precise patterns.
Adhesive applied to fabric, heat-transfer printed	Foil print	Quick response.	Difficult to control design.	Metallic film design.
		Metallic film designs possible.	Detailed and time-consuming process.	Minor process.
		Combine with screen or heat-transfer printing for multicolor patterns.	Expensive.	
	Stencil print	Hand process.	Expensive.	Most often simple patterns.
				Minor or hand process.
		Unique look.	Easily duplicated with other processes.	
			Color may be irregular.	

(Figure 19.17). More than one color print is possible, but a separate block is needed for each color. Extra time and attention are needed to align blocks correctly. Slight irregularities in color register or positioning are clues to block prints, but these can be duplicated by other techniques.

Direct-Roller Printing **Direct-roller printing** was developed in 1783, about the time all textile operations were becoming mechanized. Figure 19.18 shows the essential parts of the printing machine. The fabric is drawn around a metal or high-density foam cylinder during printing. Each engraved printing roller is etched with the design for each color in the print. A different printing roller applies each color. There are as many different rollers as there are colors in the fabric. Furnisher rollers revolve in a small color trough, pick up the dye paste, and deposit it on the rollers. The fabric to be printed, a rubberized blanket, and an unfinished-back fabric pass between the cylinder and the engraved rollers. The blanket gives a good surface for sharp printing; the gray goods protect the blanket and absorb excess dye. Roller printing, once the most common printing method, has been almost completely replaced by screen printing.

A **duplex print** is a roller print with a pattern on both sides of the fabric (Figure 19.19). Both sides of the fabric may be printed at the same time or the face and back may be printed in two separate steps.

Warp Printing

In **warp printing**, the warp yarns are printed before weaving. This technique gives a hazy pattern, softer than other prints. To identify it, ravel adjacent sides. The color design is in only on the warp yarns. Filling yarns are white or solid color. Imitations have splotchy color on both warp and filling yarns. Warp printing is usually done on taffeta, satin ribbons, or cotton fabric, and on upholstery or drapery fabric (Figure 19.20). Since the practice is time-consuming and expensive, it is not common.

Discharge Printing

Discharge prints are piece-dyed fabrics in which the design is made by removing color from selected fabric areas (Figure 19.21). Discharge printing is usually done on dark backgrounds. The fabric is first piece-dyed by an appropriate method. A discharge paste containing chemicals to remove the color is printed on the fabric using roller or screen techniques. Dyes that are not harmed by the discharge chemicals can be added as part of the paste if color is desired in the discharge areas. The fabric is then steamed to develop the design, as either a white or a colored area. Discharge printing produces better dye penetration compared to roller or screen printing because it is difficult to get good, rich dark colors except by piece dyeing.

Discharge prints can be detected by examining the back of the fabric. The background color may not be completely removed, especially around pattern edges. For discharge printing to work, background colors must use dyes that can be removed by strong alkalis. Unfortunately, the discharge chemical or bleach may cause tendering or weakening of the fabric in the areas where the color was discharged.

Screen Printing

Screen Printing

Screen printing is an incredibly versatile, yet simple process. A mesh screen is coated with a compound that seals all openings in the screen and prevents the pigment or dye paste from moving through the screen, except in the areas to be printed according to the design. A separate screen is used for each color. The paste is forced through the openings within the screen by a squeegee. Patterns can have up to 32 colors in them. Figures 19.22 and 19.23 show a close-up and a screen used in screen printing.

Figure 19.17 Block printing.

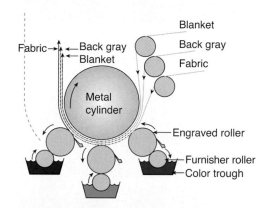

Figure 19.18 Direct-roller printing. This diagram shows the setup for a three-color print.

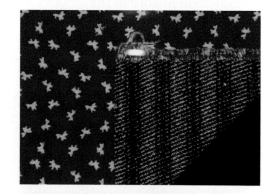

Figure 19.19 Duplex print.

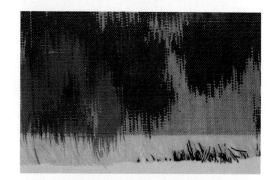

Figure 19.20 Warp-printed fabric. Note the difference in yarn appearance and clarity of design between woven and raveled areas.

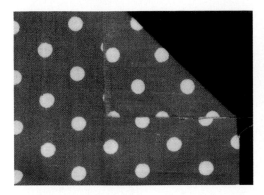

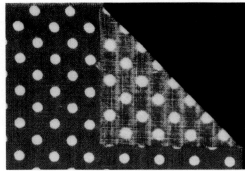

Figure 19.21 Discharge print (left), direct print (right).

Figure 19.22 Close-up of a screen used in screen printing. Note the white area where the paste is forced through the screen.
SOURCE: Courtesy of Kimberly Baxter Packwood.

Figure 19.23 Screen used in flatbed screen printing.
SOURCE: Courtesy of Kimberly Baxter Packwood.

Flatbed screen printing is done commercially for lengths from 500 to 1,000 meters and often is used for designs larger than the circumference of the rolls used for roller printing. Approximately 18 percent of print fabrics worldwide are flatbed screen prints.

In the hand process, the fabric to be printed is placed on a long table. Two people position the screen on the fabric, apply the color paste, move the screen to a new position, and repeat the process until all the fabric is printed with that color. Then they repeat the process for each color until all the colors have been applied. For screen-printing products, a similar process is used, but the equipment is specifically adapted to the type of product.

In the automatic-screen batch process, the fabric to be printed is placed on a conveyor belt. A series of flat screens are positioned above the belt and are lowered automatically. Careful positioning of the screen is required to be sure print edges match. On screen-printed yardage, small color squares or blocks along the selvage aid in print alignment and help identify a screen print. Color is applied, and the fabric is moved automatically and fed continuously into ovens to be dried.

Rotary screen printing is much more common and done with cylindrical nickel metal mesh screens that operate in much the same way as the flat screens, except that the operation is continuous rather than the step-by-step or batch process as is the case for flat screen printing. Rotary screen printing is more economical for pieces of fabric at least 1,000 meters long. These printers are fast—up to 100 meters per minute when printing with pigment inks and 40–80 meters per minute when printing with dye paste. Pigment inks are used more frequently in the United States; dye pastes are used more frequently in Europe and Asia. Rotary screens are much cheaper than the rollers used in roller printing (Figure 19.24).

Screen printing can print regular inks and pastes in patterns, but it can also be used to add special effects such as glitter, texture, sparkle, foam, and half-tones. While production of the metal mesh screens is expensive, high production speeds and large fabric runs make it economical. Pattern repeats are related to the diameter of the cylindrical screen. Flatbed screens allow for larger repeats, especially popular for interior textiles.

Screen printing is useful for printing almost any size design on fabrics. The majority of printed fabrics in the market are screen prints. **Differential printing** describes screen printing on carpets tufted with yarns that have different dye affinities.

▶ Learning Activity 12

Work in teams of two. One member of the team will explain to his or her partner how screen printing is done from the development of the screen through the application of color. The other member of the team will explain the differences and similarities between flatbed and rotary screen printing. It might be helpful to use Fabrics #16 or 43 from your swatch kit during this discussion.

Other Printing Methods

Digital Printing In **digital (ink-jet) printing**, microdrops of colored liquid ink are applied through tiny nozzles onto the fabric surface at precise points. Computers control the specific color ink jet, amount of ink, and location of the microdrops. Digital printers operate with four, eight, or more basic colors. A four color system would include yellow, magenta, cyan, and black. Systems with more colors include additional colors or variations of intensity of the basic four colors. The more colors available in a digital printer, the fewer the challenges in mixing colors for textiles and the greater the flexibility in creating designs.

There are several types of digital printers, including continuous ink jet (CIJ) and drop on demand (DOD). High numbers of separate, tiny nozzles are used for each color. Development and refinement of ink-jet printers for textiles is a slow process because of the technical limitations of nozzles and the different types of inks and pastes. These printers are used to print carpet (Figure 19.25), samples, prototypes, and limited commercial or production fabrics, usually less than 500 meters in length. Digital printing has had a pronounced impact on small-lot, custom printing and samples by textile designers (Figure 19.26). *Proofing* is the printing of strike-offs or samples to check the pattern, color, and design. It allows the print facility to get customer approval before preparing equipment for commercial or full-scale production and significantly speeds up the production process.

Its very slow production speed (only a few meters per minute) as compared with other commercial printing methods is a limitation. Image resolution and crispness can also be problems. Limitations in color reproduction, color matching, fabric width, fastness of the print inks and pastes, and changes in fabric hand are also concerns with ink-jet-printed fabrics. Besides the strike-off and custom applications, other benefits of digital printing include the ability to use large numbers of colors, application to a wide range of substrates, excellent reproduction of images (especially continuous-tone images), unlimited repeat size, and ability to print engineered designs that cross seam lines.

Digital printing is being used to create smart fabrics. Nanoparticles with conductive properties are printed onto fabrics. Changes in the environment and heat and pressure application to specific spots of a touchpad will allow the wearer to control such potential aspects as comfort, communication and entertainment devices, and global positioning systems or to provide monitoring of such health and medical conditions as activity, respiration, and heart rate.

Heat-Transfer Printing In **heat-transfer printing**, designs are transferred to fabric from specially printed paper by heat and pressure (Figure 19.27). The paper is printed by one of several paper-printing techniques: gravure, flexograph, offset, or converted rotary screen. The fabric, yarn, or item is placed on a plastic frame and padded with a special solution. Paper is placed over the fabric and then covered with a silicone-rubber sheet. These layers are compressed under high pressure at high temperatures for a few seconds so that the print sublimes and migrates from the paper to the fabric. In sublimation, a solid evaporates and recondenses as a solid in a new location. High pressure ensures that the edges of the print are sharp and clear.

The advantages of heat-transfer printing are better penetration and clarity of design, lower production costs, and elimination of some chemical waste. However, disposal of waste paper is a problem. Transfer printing can be done on three-dimensional fabrics such as circular knits without splitting them and on three-dimensional products such as garments. Although other

Figure 19.24   Screen used in rotary screen printing.
SOURCE: Courtesy of Stork Prints B.V.

Figure 19.25   Jet-dyed carpet.

Figure 19.26 Ink-jet or digital print fabric.

Figure 19.27 Heat-transfer printing: Design on paper (left) is transferred by heat to fabric (center). Design on paper is lighter after printing (right).

> ▶ **Learning Activity 13**

Use Fabrics #16, 17, 43, 46, 75, 125, and 126 from your swatch kit. Identify the printing method used to apply color to each of these fabrics. Explain the visual clues you used in that identification. Which of these samples represent more than one coloration method? How can you tell? Select two of the samples and use the fabric key to determine fiber content. Explain the serviceabilty of these two fabrics based on fiber content, yarn structure, fabrication method, finish(es), and coloration method.

> ▶ **Learning Activity 14**

Examine the textile products you are wearing and have with you today. Determine which of these products have been printed. You might want to check product labels, too. Identify the printing method used for each printed product. Explain how the print influenced your decision to purchase the item.

options exist, synthetic fibers and disperse dyes are the most common combination on the market. Heat-transfer or sublimatic printing is used for apparel, drapery fabrics, upholstery, shower curtains, and floor coverings.

Electrostatic Printing **Electrostatic printing** is similar to electrostatic flocking. A prepared screen is covered with powdered dye mixed with a carrier that has dielectric properties. The screen is positioned about $\frac{1}{2}$ inch above the fabric. When passed through an electric field, the dye powder is pulled onto the material, where it is fixed by heat.

Foil Printing In **foil printing**, an adhesive is applied to the fabric by a flatbed or rotary screen. The fabric is dyed and partially cured. The foil combines a thin polyester film with a heat-sensitive release coating, a very thin layer of aluminum, and a clear or tinted lacquer. The metallic foil is heated on a heat-transfer press and foil bonds only where the adhesive pattern exists on the fabric.

Stencil Printing In **stencil printing**, a separate pattern is cut from a special waxed paper or thin metal sheet for each color. Color, in a thick solution or paste, is applied by hand with a brush or sprayed with an air gun. Stenciling is done on limited yardage.

Recent Developments in Dyeing and Printing

Recent advances in commercial coloration include using dyes with different environmental sensitivities to create novel effects on textiles, such as photosensitive or photochromic dyes in selected pattern areas and embroidery thread so that hue changes occur or color develops with exposure to ultraviolet light or sunlight. When removed from sunlight, the fabric returns to its original color. Heat-sensitive dyes combined with another dye cause dramatic color changes, such as purple to bright blue, when exposed to body heat. Incorporating tiny liquid crystals in a surface coating creates patterns that change color as temperature changes.

A small amount of metal nanoparticles have been used to color natural and synthetic fibers. The fabric is soaked in a special solution, dried, then dipped in a salt solution of the metal and dried. Chromium produces a golden sheen, while gold gives a purple cast.

Some techniques combine dyeing and printing, such as yarn-dyed denim that is printed or overdyed. In overdyed denims, the yarn-dyed fabric is dyed another color after an abrasive or chemical wash (see Chapter 17).

Other developments in coloration relate to changes in the textile processes, including technological advances and computer applications in dyeing and printing. The shift away from large runs of the same color or print continues. Speeds of 100 meters per minute do not contribute to extremely high quality or intricate prints. As quality increases in importance, production speeds and length of standard runs decrease. For example, in the 1950s and 1960s standard runs were 100,000 yards. By the 1980s, standard runs were less than 10,000 yards. In the 1990s, standard runs as short as 250 yards became more common. In spite of these changes, costs continue to be higher for shorter runs.

Specialization of fabric or design continues. The textile complex is strongly committed to minimal seconds, strict color control, and decreased dead time. Dead time is the time the equipment is not operating because of changing equipment components, like screens, or changing colors for different patterns. Dead time in screen printing has decreased to less than 30 minutes for most systems and patterns.

Efficient use of dyes, chemicals, and water or other solvents is another concern. For example, with reactive dyes, standard utilization rates were 60 to 80 percent. New reactive dyes with utilization rates of 80 percent or more are available. Solvent dyeing systems that are required for aramid require high recovery rates, such as 98 percent, to be economically feasible. Solvent dyeing has great potential, especially with increasing water costs and water-quality standards. With solvent dyeing, geographic regions with limited availability of water could become involved in dyeing.

Computer monitoring of dyeing and printing processes decreases the environmental impact as manufacturers recognize the direct costs of inefficient use of materials and energy and incorporate closed-loop recycling of chemicals, solvents, water, and energy. Dye chemists use computers to calculate formulas to match swatches submitted by designers and monitor dyeing or printing processes so color is consistent. Computers automatically register each color in a print so that edges match.

Digital printing is being used to create smart textiles. Soft-structured sensors are being created by printing conducting polymers with metallic nanoparticles and other compounds onto fabrics. Sensors of this type are used to monitor joints and for other medical sensor end uses and have the potential for personal electronic entertainment and communication applications.

In an effort to reduce the energy use in dyeing, ultrasonic applications are being investigated. For cotton, nylon, silk, polyester, and PLA, ultrasonics have been found to have a positive impact in one or more of the following areas: dyeing time, dyeing temperature, dyeing efficacy, and the amount of dyes and other chemicals needed in the dyebath. In some cases, ultrasonics improved colorfastness to washing.

Color Problems

Good colorfastness of dyed and printed fabrics is expected, but it is not always achieved. *Colorfastness* refers to resistance to change in any color characteristic or to transferring color to another object. When considering all the variables connected with dyeing and printing and the hostile environment in which fabrics are used, it is amazing how well most colored fabrics perform.

The factors that influence colorfastness are

1. Chemical nature of fibers
2. Chemical nature of dyes and pigments
3. Penetration of dyes into the fabric
4. Fixation of dyes or pigments on or in the fibers

The coloring agents must resist washing, dry cleaning, bleaching, and spot and stain removal with all of the variables of time, temperature, and cleaning chemicals used. Colorants must resist light, perspiration, abrasion, fumes, and other use and environmental factors. Dyes for products like car interiors and outdoor furniture must be stable to ultraviolet light. Upholstery, toweling, carpeting, and bedding may experience color problems from exposure to acne medication, bleaches, acids, and alkalis. These color-damaging agents are found in a host of materials with which interior textiles are likely to come in contact, such as vomit, drain and toilet cleaners, spray room deodorizers, urine, plant food or fertilizers, insecticides, furniture polish, and disinfectants and germicides found in bathroom cleaners.

If the color is not fast in the fabric as purchased, it is not possible to make it fast. Salt and vinegar are used as exhaust agents for household dyes, but research does not support the theory that they will "set" color. If the dye could not be set using the knowledge of the dye chemist, the specialized equipment available in the dyehouse, and the carefully selected dyeing chemicals, the consumer will not be able to accomplish this task at home with salt, vinegar, or any other common household ingredient identified on some improper care labels.

Color loss occurs through bleeding, crocking, and migration or through chemical changes in the dye. **Bleeding** is color loss in water. In bleeding, other fibers present in the wash load may pick up the color. **Crocking** is color loss from rubbing or abrasion. In crocking, some color may be transferred to the abradant. For example, tight-fitting dark denim jeans may color the wearer's thighs or white leather upholstery. **Migration** is shifting of color to the surrounding area or to an adjacent surface (Figure 19.1). An example of migration occurs with some red-and-white striped fabrics when the white closest to the red takes on a pinkish cast. Figure 19.28 shows a hat whose sewing thread was not fast to washing. Atmospheric gases (fume fading), perspiration, and sunlight may cause fading as a result of a chemical change in the dye (Figure 19.29).

Certain vat and sulfur dyes **tender**, or destroy, cotton fabric. Green, red, blue, and yellow vat dyes and black, yellow, and orange sulfur dyes have been the chief offenders. Manufacturers can correct the problem by thoroughly oxidizing the dye within the fiber or after-treating the fabric to neutralize the chemical causing tendering. The damage is increased by moisture and sunlight, a problem for draperies. Damage may not be evident until the draperies are cleaned, and then slits or holes occur (Figures 19.30 and 19.31). Sunlight, air pollution, and acidic

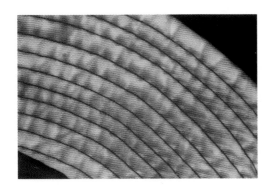

Figure 19.28 Bleeding of sewing thread on a hat.

Figure 19.29 Fume fading: navy blue dress fading to pink.

Consider textile products that you own or have owned that have failed because of color-fastness issues. Describe the problem that occurred and identify that problem by name. (See Table 19.6.) How did the problem influence your satisfaction with the product?

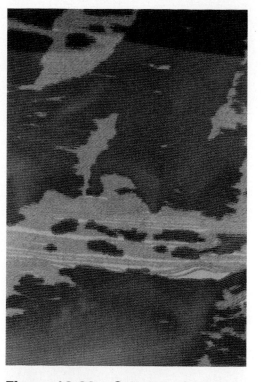

Figure 19.30 Cotton-and-rayon drapery fabric. After washing, damaged areas of the fabric had disappeared as a result of fiber swelling in water and abrasion from the washer.

atmospheric gases, as well as dyes, cause fabric damage. Some reactive dyed cotton fabrics also demonstrate weak or tender areas.

Frosting occurs when the colored portion of fibers or yarns are abraded (Figure 19.32) as is common with denim where the large indigo dye molecule does not penetrate into the center of cotton fibers. Frosting occurs with blends and with durable-press garments that have been union-dyed. During wear, the surface is abraded and becomes lighter in color, while the unabraded or more durable area maintains its color.

The movement of yarns during use may cause undyed fibers to work their way to the surface. Color streaks may result from uneven removal of sizing before the dye is applied. The best way to check the dye penetration in heavy fabrics is to examine the fabric. If possible, ravel a yarn to see if it is the same color throughout. With finished products, look at the edge of seams. For roller prints, look at the reverse side. The more color on the back, the better the dye penetration.

A defect in printed fabrics occurs when two colors of a print overlap each other or do not meet. This defect is referred to as **out-of-register** (Figure 19.33). Computer registering of screens and rollers during printing has significantly reduced this problem.

Printed fabrics may be printed off-grain. **Off-grain prints** create problems because the fabric cannot be both straight with the print and cut on-grain. If cut off-grain, the fabric tends to assume its normal position when washed, causing twisted seams and uneven hemlines. If cut on-grain, the print will not be straight. In an all-over design this may not be important, but in large checks and plaids or designs with crosswise lines, matching at seams becomes impossible and slanting lines across the fabric are not pleasing. Off-grain prints are created by incorrect fabric finishing. The gray goods are started into the tentering machine crooked or the mechanism for moving the fabric does not work properly so that the two selvages move at slightly different speeds, or the fabric is not properly supported in the center of its width. The off-grain problem can be corrected at the mill before printing.

Other problems related to dyeing and printing are concerns of the producer and manufacturer. These are problems related to the consistency of the color throughout the width and length of the fabric or from dye lot to dye lot. Manufacturers of apparel and interior textile items require a fabric that is consistent in color. The color needs to be the same from side to side (selvage to selvage), side to center (selvage to center), and end to end (from one end of the roll of fabric to the other). If the color is not consistent, the producer will have problems with off-shade or with product parts not matching in color. When several rolls of the same color fabric are required, all rolls must be consistent in color. Color-matching equipment, like a colorimeter, is used to assess color uniformity within or among fabric rolls.

Color loss occurs through bleeding, crocking, and migration or through chemical changes in the dye. Other problems include fabric tendering, frosting, and prints that are out-of-register or off-grain.

Figure 19.33 Printed fabric: out-of-register (left), in register (right).

The fastness of the dye often determines the method of care that should be used. The consumer must depend on the label, but some knowledge of color problems that occur in use and care will allow for more intelligent choices. Table 19.6 summarizes these basic color problems.

Environmental Concerns and Sustainability of Dyeing and Printing

Dyeing and printing textiles can have a significant impact on the environment from the production of dyes and pigments; water and other chemical use; discharge of dyes, pigments, and other chemicals into water systems; air pollution; and energy consumption. Components that contribute to water quality problems include color, salt, acids, and heavy metals. Some materials create problems because of high biological oxygen demand (BOD); others have high chemical oxygen demand (COD). High BOD and COD materials create environments that are hostile to aquatic plants and animals and may create problems with future use of the water. Color in water creates problems with photosynthesis of aquatic plant life.

Most textiles are colored in one manner or another because consumers demand color. One option to decrease environmental impact is to use fewer dyed or printed textiles. White textiles create problems with the use and disposal of chemical bleaches. Even though consumers purchase beige and off-white goods, they will probably continue to demand a broader range of colors. Another option is to use color-grown textiles, such as the naturally colored cottons and wools. However, a full color spectrum is not available and these natural colors tend to be low in intensity.

Another alternative is to greatly expand the current use of natural dyes in commercially available fabric and products (Figure 19.34). In order to compete with synthetic dyes and pigments, natural dyes must be economical, consistent in quality, and available in quantity. Mordants used with natural dyes must be restricted to those that have little, if any, impact on the environment. Examples of commercial natural dyes from Earthues, A Natural Color Company include indigo, madder, cochineal, cutch, and osage. Natural dyes are used on cotton, wool, silk, and some synthetic fabrics for apparel and interior uses.

Color in water systems in very dilute concentrations can be detected by the unaided eye. Unfortunately, color is very difficult to remove by traditional waste (sludge) treatment facilities.

Figure 19.31 Tendering of cotton draperies caused by sulfur dye, atmospheric moisture, and heat.

Figure 19.32 Denim jeans: loss of surface color.

Table 19.6 Color Problems

Problem	Component	Description	Cause
Bleeding	Fiber	Dye loss in water that may color other items in water.	Poor fiber–dye bond, poor washfastness. Poor washdown (excess dye on fabric).
Crocking	Fiber	Color transfers to other fabrics, skin, etc.	Dye only on fiber surface.
Migration	Fiber	Color moves to other areas or materials.	Poor fiber–dye bond; dye migrates.
Fume fading	Disperse dye (most common)	Fading or hue shift when exposed to some atmospheric pollutants.	Dye sensitive to pollutants.
Poor fastness to sunlight, perspiration, etc.	Dye	Fading or hue shift when exposed to the degrading factor.	Energy in sunlight degrades dye. Chemical reaction of dye with perspiration, deodorant chemicals, or bacterial enzymes.
Tendering	Fiber	Fabric becomes weak and sensitive to abrasion.	Dye–fiber interaction.
Frosting	Fiber	With abrasion, white areas appear on fabric, seams, or hems.	Poor dye penetration into fiber. As colored portion of fiber is abraded away, uncolored portion shows through. Also seen in blends where one fiber is more abrasion-resistant.
Out-of-register	Fabric	Edges of print do not match.	Poor alignment of screens or rollers in printing.
Off-grain	Fabric	Fabric printed off-grain.	Fabric not tentered properly and defect not detected before printing.
Off-shade	Fabric	Products, components, thread, other materials, or coordinating fabrics don't match in color or don't meet color specifications.	Evaluation of color match under different lights, chemical composition requires dyes from different classes, poor control of bath or paste.

Alternatives for treating color in water systems include use of hyperfiltration, electrochemical methods, ozonation, and chemical coagulation. Reconstitution and reuse of textile dyeing water is another possibility being investigated.

Limiting the use of salt and other chemicals is another option. For example, current reactive dyes use large amounts of salt, but some new reactive dyes use significantly less salt and have higher fixation rates. Lower-sulfide sulfur dyes are replacing higher-sulfide sulfur dyes. Use of heavy metals in dyes, catalysts, or after-treatments is restricted. Dye producers are developing dyes that incorporate iron rather than chromium because iron is more environmentally safe. Dyes and pigments with low environmental impact will continue to be a major thrust in preparing goods with consumer appeal. Biodegradable dyes are also becoming more readily available.

Liquid carbon dioxide or supercritical carbon dioxide can be used as the carrier rather than water for dyeing polyester and high-performance fibers. Liquid carbon dioxide dyeing increases dye-fixation rates, decreases energy use, and decreases treatment of waste. In addition, this process does not require use of salt or other dye-bath chemicals, and drying is not needed. The process is quick and efficient, with good leveling. Carbon dioxide can be recycled and is readily available, nontoxic, and economical.

20 Care of Textile Products

21 Legal, Sustainability, and Environmental Issues

SILK MATERIALS

22 Career Exploration

OTHER ISSUES
RELATED to
TEXTILES

SECTION VI

Care describes the cleaning procedures used to remove soil and return products to new or nearly new condition and appropriate storage for textile products. Care is an important consideration for most apparel and interior textiles as well as many technical textiles. The ability to clean textile products makes them reusable and sustainable. However, care also can be the route through which product problems and serviceability issues become apparent. For example, a new striped shirt of white and an intense color may fit, be attractive, comfortable, and appropriate to wear with several other apparel items in the closet. After a day or two of wearing, the shirt needs to be cleaned and made usable again. If the shirt is washed and all stains and odor are removed, it does not shrink or wrinkle, and the colors do not bleed or fade, the consumer is satisfied. However, if the stains or odor are not removed, if the shirt shrinks or wrinkles severely, or if the colors bleed, then the consumer is not satisfied with the performance of the shirt.

Because there are so many variables that affect cleaning, many countries require care labels in most apparel and some interior textile products. These laws and regulations identify the kinds of information required, define terms and symbols, and identify appropriate locations for the care labels. Table 20.1 provides definitions and shows the care symbols for several common terms used on care labels. (For the entire list of terms, see Appendix E. For the entire set of care symbols, see Figure 21.2.)

> Care describes the cleaning procedures used to remove soil and return products to new or nearly new condition and appropriate storage for textile products. The ability to clean textile products makes them reusable and sustainable.

Table 20.1 Terms Commonly Found on Care Labels

Machine wash—A process by which soil may be removed from products through the use of water, detergent, agitation, and a machine designed for this purpose. When no temperature is given, hot water up to 150°F (66°C) can be used.

a. Warm—Initial water temperature setting 90 to 110°F (32 to 43°C) (hand comfortable).

b. Cold—Initial water temperature setting same as cold water tap up to 85°F (29°C).

c. Delicate cycle or gentle cycle—Slow agitation and reduced time.

d. Durable-press cycle or permanent-press cycle—Cool-down rinse or cold rinse before reduced spinning.

e. Separately—Alone.

f. With like colors—With colors of similar hue and intensity.

Hand wash—A process by which soil may be manually removed from products through the use of water, detergent, and gentle squeezing action. When no temperature is given, hot water up to 150°F (66°C) can be used.

Tumble dry—Use machine dryer. When no temperature setting is given, machine-drying at a hot setting may be used.

a. Remove promptly—When items are dry, remove immediately to prevent wrinkling.

b. Dry flat—Lay out horizontally for drying.

c. Block to dry—Reshape to original dimensions while drying.

Iron—Ironing is needed. When no temperature is given, the highest temperature setting may be used. (See Figure 20.1.)

a. Warm iron—Medium temperature setting.

b. Cool iron—Lowest temperature setting.

Bleach when needed—All bleaches may be used when necessary.

No bleach or do not bleach—No bleaches may be used.

Wash or dry-clean, any normal method—Can be machine-washed in hot water, can be machine-dried at a high setting, can be ironed at a hot setting, can be bleached with any bleaches, and can be dry-cleaned with any commercially available solvent.

Dry-clean—A process by which soil may be removed from products or specimens in a machine that uses any common organic solvent located in any commercial establishment. The process may include moisture, hot tumble drying, and restoration by steam-press or steam-air finishing.

Professionally dry-clean—Use the dry-cleaning process, but modified to ensure optimal results either by a dry-cleaning attendant or through the use of a dry-cleaning machine that permits such modifications or both.

SOURCE: Web site of Federal Trade Commission (April 14, 2009). http://ecfr.gpoaccess.gov/cgi/t/text/text, 16 CFR Part 423, Appendix A.

▶ Learning Activity 1

Examine the care labels present in the textile items you are wearing or have with you to-day. Find the terms from your product's labels in Table 20.1 or Appendix E. Read through these terms. Did you find anything new or surprising in the definitions that you did not know in terms of cleaning these items? Will you use this new information the next time you clean any of these items? How might an understanding of the definitions help consumers in cleaning their textiles? Do you think most consumers are aware of the specific details in these definitions?

▶ Learning Activity 2

Work in teams of two. Assume that the two of you are part of a creative team for a company that produces a private label line of casual all-cotton shirts for men and boys. What aspects of cleaning should be considered when determining care label information? How could the performance specific to each term or symbol that will be used on the care label be assessed? If you do not require that this assessment be made, what kinds of problems, complaints, or repercussions might develop if the care labels are not correct? Would this omission cost your company money or profit? Why or why not?

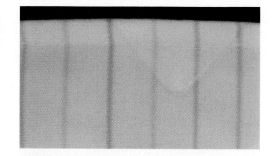

Figure 20.1 No temperature setting was included on the care label. When ironed at the highest setting, the polyester melted.

Because care labels are required, it is the responsibility of the creative team, manufacturer, or supplier to determine appropriate care information and affix the correct label on a product. Determination of appropriate care is based on an assessment of the materials used in the product and the performance of these materials in standard test methods. However, not all care labels for all products are based on material performance testing. Many labels are based solely on the fiber content, color, or use of other materials in products.

Many textile items combine materials that simply are not compatible. For example, color that bleeds from the trim to the base fabric combines incompatible materials. There is little the consumer can do to reduce this problem or prevent it from occurring. Consumers' expectations for quality and performance of textiles are ever increasing. Consumers demand more and expect more from textile products. An appropriate and accurate care label for all textile products is one area where these expectations are evident. However, even though care labels are required, many consumers do not read them before cleaning the item or only read labels for unusual items or items that have unusual stains.

Factors Related to Cleaning

To understand **care**, discussion of soils and soiling, the interaction between detergent and solvent, and the additives that improve soil removal and the appearance of the cleaned item provide useful information for making appropriate cleaning decisions.

Soil and Soil Removal

Soil is any substance not intended to be on a textile. Soils can be classified into several categories based on its type and how it is held on the fabric. Soils such as gum, mud, or wax are held on the fabric mechanically and can be removed mechanically by scraping or agitation. Sometimes

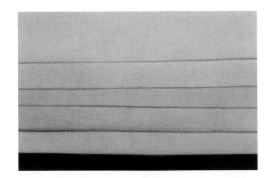

Figure 20.2 Effect of water temperature on cleaning: 140°F, 120°F, 100°F, 80°F, and 60°F (top to bottom).
SOURCE: Courtesy of Maytag Corp.

Soil is any substance not intended to be on a textile. Soil is classified by its type and how it is held on the fabric.

Figure 20.3 Notice the difference in surface tension between the shape of the water drop (left) and the water with detergent (right).

A **soap** or **detergent** molecule includes an organic "tail" that has an affinity for organic soils and a polar "head" that has an affinity for the solvent. The two parts of the soap or detergent molecule dislodge the soil. Agitation breaks it into very tiny globules that are held in suspension until they are rinsed away.

removal of these soils is most effective if it is allowed to cool or dry before removal is attempted. Care should be taken since excessive agitation or vigorous scraping can abrade fabrics.

Lint and dust soils are held on the fabric by electrostatic forces. When this force is neutralized, the soil is removed. Because water is such an excellent conductor of electricity, immersing the fabric in water, as is done in laundering, neutralizes any static charge on the fabric's surface.

Water-soluble soils, such as coffee and other beverages, are absorbed into hydrophilic fibers. When the fabric is immersed in water, the soil is dissolved. Organic soils such as grease and oily food can be absorbed by oleophilic fibers and require the chemical action of a detergent, an organic solvent (such as is used in dry cleaning), heat, or thermal energy to be removed. Removing organic soils using a cold water wash is especially difficult since these compounds are often solids at cold temperatures. The warmer the water, the more likely organic soils, especially oil and grease stains, will liquefy and be easier to remove.

Of course, many soils are mixtures and are removed by a combination of thermal, mechanical, and chemical actions. If one aspect of removal is decreased, another aspect must be increased in order to maintain the degree of soil removal. For example, if the water temperature is decreased, either more detergent or more agitation will be required for the cleaning process to be as effective. As temperature decreases, cleaning power, even when cycles are repeated, decreases (Figure 20.2).

Detergency

Detergency refers to the manner in which the soap or detergent removes soil. Adding soap or synthetic detergent to solvent lowers the surface tension of the solvent, allowing things to wet more quickly. The solvent does not bead up but spreads over and wets the surface (Figure 20.3). A **soap** or **detergent** molecule includes an organic "tail" that has an affinity for organic soils and a polar "head" that has an affinity for the solvent. As a result of its nature, the two parts of the soap or detergent molecule literally dislodge the soil. Agitation breaks the soil into very tiny globules that are held in suspension until they are rinsed away (Figure 20.4). If hot solvent and agitation are used, oily soils soften and break into small globules.

Because of the different functions of each ingredient in detergents, the amount of detergent needs to be sufficient to clean. Recommendations, based on research, for the proper amount of detergent to use are included on detergent labels. Many detergents are sold with a measuring device in the container or engineered within the lid or cap for liquid detergents. If too much detergent is used, it may build up on textiles or be wasted and flushed down the drain. If too little detergent is used, soil will remain on the textiles.

▶ Learning Activity 3

Take a very clean glass or beaker. Be sure it is well rinsed so no detergent residue remains. Fill it about $\frac{2}{3}$ full of water and place it on the table or counter. Carefully place a thumbtack (point side up) or a needle on the surface of the water. If the container is clean, the thumbtack or needle should float. Without disturbing the container, look closely and describe what you see. Now, fill a separate container about $\frac{2}{3}$ full of water and add a drop or two of soap or detergent (dish or laundry). Stir the water so that the detergent or soap is dissolved. Take one or two drops of the soapy water and add it to the water that is floating the thumbtack or needle. Explain what happens and why it happened.

Detergent or soap is needed to remove most soils. Alternative laundry products (disks, globes, and doughnuts of plastic or ceramic materials) claim to replace detergents. Research has demonstrated that these laundry gimmicks are no more effective than water used alone in cleaning soil from fabric.

Solvents

A **solvent** is a liquid that dissolves other materials. Solvents dissolve common soils such as salt from perspiration or body oils. The most common and widely used solvent is water. Other cleaning solvents include organic liquids such as perchloroethylene. The choice of a particular solvent is based on the soil types present, the cost and availability of the solvent, and the textile product's characteristics. The basic care methods of washing and dry cleaning differ by the solvents and equipment used.

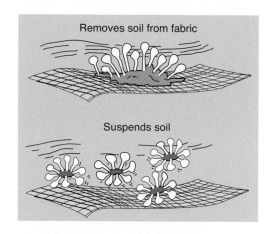

Figure 20.4 Mechanism of soil removal: Detergent surrounds soil and lifts it off the fabric.

Water **Water** is used as the solvent in washing because it is cheap, readily available, nontoxic, and requires no special equipment. Hardness, temperature, and volume are water characteristics that affect cleaning. *Water hardness* refers to the type and amount of mineral contaminants present. Water that contains mineral salts is known as hard water. The more mineral salts dissolved in water, the harder it is. Hard water makes cleaning more difficult and can accumulate as deposits in pipes and faucets (Figure 20.5). In softening the water, the minerals are removed, or *sequestered* (bonded to another molecule). Water is usually softened by adding a water-softening agent, such as sodium hexametaphosphate, to the water or by using an ion-exchange resin in a water softener.

Water temperature determines the effectiveness of the cleaning additives used and in removing some soils. Some additives are more effective at certain temperatures. The following water-temperature ranges are identified by the Federal Trade Commission in the Care Labeling Rule: Cold water is 85°F (29°C) or less, or the initial water temperature from a cold water tap; warm water is 90 to 110°F (32 to 43°C), or hand comfortable; and hot water is up to 150°F (66°C). However, these temperatures rarely correspond to actual home water temperatures.

The temperature of the water in the washing machine is dependent on many factors. Warm and hot water temperature is dependent to the temperature at which the water heater is set, the distance between the water heater and the washer, the air temperature of the room, the temperature of the washer, the temperature of the cold water, and the mix level established by the washer manufacturer. Mix level describes the percentage of hot and cold water combined to achieve "warm" water. The temperature of water entering the house can vary widely depending on the geographic location and season. In some areas in the warmer months, water from the cold water tap may be 75°F (24°C). In other areas during the winter months, it might be 38°F (3°C).

In an effort to reduce energy use in laundry and reduce scalding burn injuries from hot water, consumers are encouraged to lower the temperature of water heaters and use colder wash water.

Detergents were originally formulated for use in hot water. However, sustainability, environmental, regulatory, and cost issues have driven the development of cold water detergents. These detergents include a mix of ingredients specifically selected because of their effectiveness in cooler water. The surfactants in cold water detergents are based on enzyme chemistry. However, the ability of washing to remove bacteria and other microbes is temperature dependent. Hotter water is more effective at killing microbes; colder water is less effective. For more discussion on cold water detergents, see the next section on surfactants.

Figure 20.5 Water hardness deposits on faucet.

Water volume is controlled to allow for agitation, to remove and keep soil suspended, and to avoid wrinkling items in the load. Actual water volume relates to the amount of fabric present in the machine. Water use for laundry is phenomenal. Older machines might use 50 gallons (189 liters) of water per wash cycle. While newer machines are designed to use less water and energy, the water use is still significant.

Other Solvents Organic solvents are used in dry cleaning, spot removal or spotting agents, and carriers for other spotting materials. Perchloroethylene, also known as perc or PCE, is the solvent most often used in dry cleaning. Trichloro-trifluoroethane (also known as CFC 113), a high-flash-point hydrocarbon known as DF 2000, and glycol ether are other organic solvents used in commercial dry-cleaning plants in many countries. These solvents dissolve oils, greases, and other stubborn stains that are difficult to remove in water-based systems.

Perc and CFC 113 have been popular dry-cleaning solvents because they create fewer problems with fabric shrinkage, do not affect water-soluble dyes, and are nonflammable. Both solvents are hazardous to the environment. CFC 113 is being phased out of use because of its detrimental effect on the ozone layer. Perc is carefully regulated as a possible carcinogen and identified as contributing to forest decline. Significant changes in dry cleaning equipment and standard operating procedures have greatly reduced the amount of perc used. Current usage is approximately 16 percent of what it was in 1990.

Research has identified some solvents that equal or exceed perc's effectiveness in some areas of cleaning, but no one solvent is consistently equal to perc in all areas. Most of these alternate solvents have less environmental impact compared to perc. These other solvents include hydrocarbons with high flash points, polypropylene glycol ethers, silicones, and liquid carbon dioxide. Hydrocarbons are used as solvents in some stain-removal compounds and by some dry cleaners as their primary solvent in cleaning. Hydrocarbons include such solvents as EcoSolv,® which is biodegradable and virtually odorless. Polypropylene glycol (PG) ethers are used under the tradenames Rynex® and Impress.® The PG solvents are not considered hazardous chemicals. A silicone-based solvent is another alternative to perc that works well in removing soil and odor. A siloxane compound called D5 is used by some dry cleaners. Unfortunately, these alternate solvents cannot be used in machines designed for perc so switching solvents is an expensive proposition for dry cleaners. Most cleaners are small business owners and do not consider switching solvents until they need to replace dry-cleaning machines.

When liquid carbon dioxide is used, special cleaning additives, special cleaning machines, and high pressure are needed. The machines needed for liquid carbon dioxide are almost twice as expensive as those used with perc. The process is effective at cleaning and does not subject items to the high temperatures used to remove perc in traditional systems.

Laundering

Laundering is the most common means of cleaning consumer textiles. Table 20.2 summarizes the care required for generic fibers. While fibers are a significant factor in determining appropriate care, other factors also influence care labels. The care appropriate for a textile product depends on its dyes or pigments, fabrication, finish, product construction, other materials (such as trims, support materials, linings, buttons, etc.), type of soil, and extent of soiling. This section focuses on additives and methods.

A **solvent** is a liquid that dissolves other materials. Water is most commonly used. Dry cleaning uses organic solvents.

Table 20.2 Suggested Care of Textile Products by Fiber Type

Fiber Group	Cleaning Method	Water Temperature	Chlorine Bleach Use	Dryer Temperature	Iron Temperature	Storage Considerations
Acetate	Dry clean*	Warm	Yes	Low	Very low	Avoid contact with nail polish remover
Acrylic	Launder	Warm	Yes	Warm	Medium	—
Cotton	Launder	Hot	Yes	Hot	High	Store dry to prevent mildew
Cotton/Polyester/DP	Launder	Hot	Yes	Warm	Medium	—
Flax	Launder	Hot	Yes	Hot Do not press in sharp creases	High	—
Lyocell	Dry-clean or launder	Warm	Yes	Warm	High	Minimize agitation
Metallic	Launder	Warm	Yes	Warm	Low	—
Nylon	Launder	Hot	Yes	Warm	Low	—
Olefin	Launder	Warm	Yes	Warm	Very low	—
PLA	Launder	Hot	Yes	Warm	Low	—
Polyester	Launder	Hot	Yes	Warm	Low	—
Rayon (including bamboo)	Launder	Hot	Yes	Hot	High	Store dry to prevent mildew
Silk	Dry-clean*	Warm	No	Warm	Medium	—
Spandex	Launder	Warm	No	Warm	Very low	—
Wool	Dry-clean*	Warm	No	Warm	Medium, with steam	Protect from moths and carpet beetles; do not store in plastic bags

*Or hand-wash, avoiding excessive agitation and stretching.

▶ Learning Activity 4

Work in groups of two. Identify the cleaning method recommended for the fibers listed in Table 20.2. For those fibers where dry cleaning is recommended, identify why that recommendation is made. What will happen if products made from these fibers are washed?

Synthetic Detergents and Soaps

Synthetic detergents and soaps are used to remove and suspend soils, minimize the effects of hard water, and alter the surface tension of water and other solvents.

Synthetic Detergents *Synthetic detergents* are mixtures of many ingredients. The recipe depends on the type of detergent. Detergent formulas differ from region to region of one country and from country to country. The differences are related to the type of soil, water conditions, regulations, and laws. In this text the term *detergent* will be used to refer to the box, tablet, or bottle of general cleaning compound.

Some detergents are promoted as being nontoxic, phosphate-free, and biodegradable, and made from renewable resources. Other detergents promote their lack of perfumes and dyes. Still others promote the convenience of using an all-in-one detergent that combines cleaning, bleaching, and fabric softening. Many detergent ingredients are based on synthetic compounds while others are derived from plant-based materials. Approximately 35 percent of the compounds used in a typical laundry detergent originate from renewable resources. More concentrated detergents use less packaging and require less energy to transport them from the manufacturing site to the store and to the consumer's home.

Surfactants are organic compounds that are soluble in hard water and, unlike soap, do not form an insoluble curd. They are vigorous soil-removal agents and are frequently sulfonated, linear, long-chain fatty acids. Surfactants include nonionic, anionic, and cationic types. Non-ionic surfactants, such as ethers of ethylene oxide, are used in liquids and recommended for use in cold or warm water because they are effective at cooler temperatures. Anionic surfactants are good at removing oily soils and clay-soil suspension and function best in hotter water. These surfactants are usually biodegradable linear alkyl sulfonates (LAS) in powder or liquid form. Liquid anionic and nonionic surfactants are used in liquid detergents. Some liquid detergents are combinations of both anionic and nonionic surfactants; others include only one type of surfactant. Cationic surfactants are used primarily in liquid form in disinfectants, fabric softeners, and compounds to clean hard surfaces, like toilets and floors.

Cold water detergents include anionic and nonionic surfactants. New cold water surfactants include enzymes that attack protein-based and carbohydrate-based soils. These new surfactants are effective on oily soils in cold water. These new surfactants make cold water detergents as effective as earlier detergents were in warm water.

Builders soften water; add alkalinity to the solution, since a pH of 8 to 10 is best for maximum cleaning efficiency; emulsify oils and greases; and minimize soil redeposition. Builders are not present in large quantities in most detergents.

Builders include phosphates (sodium tripolyphosphate), carbonates (sodium carbonate), citrates (sodium citrate), and silicates (sodium silicate). Phosphate builders offer the best performance over the widest range of laundering conditions, but they have been replaced in the United States because of their role in water pollution. However, researchers have found that phosphates may have the lowest life-cycle costs and are urging reevaluation of phosphate bans. Although carbonate builders do not contribute to water pollution, they are found in some powder detergents and combine with hard-water minerals to form water-insoluble precipitates that may harm the washing machine, fabric, and zippers (Figure 20.6).

Citrate builders, used in liquid detergents, are weaker at softening hard water. Sodium silicate functions as a builder when present in large concentrations, but it is usually present in small concentrations because it is a corrosion inhibitor. Zeolites, insoluble ion-exchange compounds, are used in most heavy-duty detergents, but are being reevaluated for sustainability and environmental impact. New biodegradable builders are being used in Europe.

Enzymes in detergents remove fuzz resulting from the abrasion of cellulosic fibers. Since cotton or cotton blends comprise up to 80 percent of the fabrics in a normal load, this ingredient has a profound effect on home laundering. Enzymes prevent the formation of pills and keep textile products looking newer longer. By removing fuzz, enzymes also minimize physical entrapment of soil in worn areas of fibers. Use of biodegradable enzymes may slightly decrease the product's life because a tiny portion of the fibers is destroyed with each laundering. Other types of enzymes are used to remove specific food stains, but these are usually present only in stain removal aids.

Other ingredients are designed to enhance the textile product's appearance. **Antifading agents** maintain original color intensity by minimizing color bleed in the wash. **Dye-transfer inhibitors**

Figure 20.6 Residue forms on fabrics laundered with carbonate builders in hard water.

▶ Learning Activity 5

Work in groups of three or four. Make a list describing an ideal laundry detergent. Review the ingredients commonly found in laundry detergent and identify the ingredients your detergent should include. Is your detergent a liquid or powder?

usually contain borax compounds to prevent any dye that bleeds in the wash from redepositing on lighter-colored products (Figure 20.7).

Antiredeposition agents, such as sodium carboxymethylcellulose or organic polymers, minimize fabric picking up soil from the wash water. **Perfumes** are designed to mask the chemical smell of detergents and to add a "clean" smell to the wash. Perfume-free detergents usually incorporate a compound that masks or absorbs the odor of the other ingredients. **Dyes** make the detergent look better and function as bluing. Detergent manufacturers have replaced some of the dyes used with food-grade and more benign dyes. Perfume-free and dye-free formulations are available.

Fluorescent whitening agents are also known as *fluorescent brightening agents*, *optical whitening agents*, and *optical brightening agents*. These compounds are low-grade or weak dyes that fluoresce or absorb light at one wavelength and reemit the energy at another wavelength. Thus, it is possible to have whites that are "whiter than white." These ingredients do not contribute to soil removal; they mask soil and make yellow or dingy fabrics look white.

Other ingredients that may be found in detergents include *fabric softeners* and *bleaches* (to be discussed later in this chapter), processing aids that keep powders from caking and liquids from separating, suds-control agents, and foam-control agents. New bleaches that are activated by catalysts are surprisingly effective at low concentrations when included as one of several ingredients in a laundry detergent. *Processing aids* include sodium sulfate in powders, and water, alcohol, and propylene glycol in liquids. *Alcohol* dissolves some ingredients of the detergent, assists in stain removal, and acts as an antifreeze during shipping in colder climates. *Opacifiers* give a rich, creamy appearance to some liquid detergents. A **soil-release polymer**, present in some detergents, is deposited on the fabric in the first wash, soil binds with it in use, and the soil is released in the wash. *Ultraviolet (UV) absorbers* and *antibacterial compounds* are incorporated in some specialty detergents.

Soaps *Soaps* are salts of linear, long-chain fatty acids produced from naturally occurring animal or vegetable oils or fats. Soaps react with hard-water minerals and produce insoluble curds that form a greasy, gray film on textiles and a ring on tubs or sinks. Because this curd is lighter than water, it floats on the surface (Figure 20.8). Soaps are effective in removing oily or greasy stains, but they are not vigorous soil-removal agents and have been replaced by synthetic detergents in almost all applications, except for hand soaps and some hair shampoos.

Other Additives

Other additives used in laundering textiles include bleaches, fabric softeners, water softeners, disinfectants, presoaks, pretreatments, starches or sizing, and bluing. Some are seldom used today.

Bleach Most **bleaches** are oxidizing agents. The bleaching is done by active oxygen. Bleaches may be either acid or alkaline. They are usually unstable, especially in the presence of moisture. Bleaches that are old or have been improperly stored lose their oxidizing power.

Figure 20.7 Color-transfer inhibitors would minimize the stains on this multifiber test fabric laundered with a fabric sample that bleeds. Darker stripes in the test fabric indicate greater color transfer during washing.

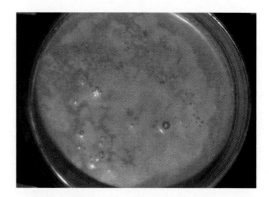

Figure 20.8 Soap curd is lighter than water and floats on the surface.

Synthetic detergents and soaps are used to remove and suspend soils, minimize the effects of hard water, and alter the surface tension of water and other solvents. Synthetic detergents are liquid or powder mixtures of ingredients. Each ingredient is designed to contribute one or more functions to cleaning. Other additives include bleach, fabric and water softeners, disinfectants, and stain removers.

Figure 20.9 Adding bleach directly to the wash water can bleach color as the areas of color loss on this shirt demonstrate.

Any bleach will cause damage, and because damage occurs more rapidly at higher temperatures and concentrations, these factors should be carefully controlled. Because fibers vary in their chemical composition, the choice of bleach should reflect fiber content.

Liquid chlorine bleach is a common household bleach. It is a cheap and efficient bleach for cellulosic fibers. The bleaching is done by hypochlorous acid, which is liberated during the bleaching process. Because acid weakens cellulosic fibers, the bleach must be diluted before coming in contact with textiles and thoroughly rinsed out (Figure 20.9). Chlorine bleaches will cause yellowing on protein and thermoplastic fibers. As effective bactericidal agents (disinfectants), they are also used for sterilizing or disinfecting fabrics.

Powdered-oxygen bleaches, also known as all-fabric or color-safe bleaches, may be used on all fibers and colored fabrics and in cold, warm, and hot water. They include catalysts that activate the powder bleaches, making them more effective in cooler water temperatures. Their bleaching effect is much milder than that of chlorine bleaches. These bleaches include sodium perborate and sodium percarbonate. Powdered sodium perborate combines with water and forms hydrogen peroxide. It is a safe bleach for home use with all fibers. However, since perborates are harmful to plant life, sodium percarbonate is a safer and equally effective alternative. Powder bleaches are recommended for regular use to maintain a fabric's original whiteness rather than as a whitener for discolored fabrics. Bleach may be an additional ingredient found in powder detergents—often marketed as color-safe detergents with bleach—and are effective in this role. However, color-safe bleaches are not as effective at removing stains as are chlorine bleaches. In addition, color-safe bleaches do not disinfect.

Acid bleaches, such as oxalic acid and potassium permanganate, have limited use. Citric acid and lemon juice, also acid bleaches, are used as rust-spot removers.

Fabric Softener **Fabric softeners** coat the fabric to increase its electrical conductivity, minimize static charges, and decrease fabric stiffness. Some softeners incorporate compounds to minimize wrinkling during washing and drying. The types of fabric softeners include those added to the final rinse, those present in detergent, and those used in the dryer. Many fabric softeners are cationic compounds that form insoluble precipitates with anionic surfactants, the cleaning compound found in many detergents. This means that the anionic surfactant must be rinsed off the fabric before the softener is added or the formulation changed so that the softener and surfactant are compatible and effective. Nonionic softeners do not create the compatibility problem seen with cationic softeners, but they are not as effective at softening fabrics.

The instructions for any fabric softener need to be followed or problems may result. For example, fabric-softener dryer sheets should be added to a cold dryer. If they are added to a warm or hot dryer, oil from the fabric softener may spot synthetic items. Fabric softeners may build up on fabrics in a greasy layer, resulting in less absorbent fabrics. Instead of using a fabric softener with every washing, using it every other time or every third time may be sufficient and reduce buildup.

Water Softener **Water softeners** are used as separate ingredients that can be added to increase detergent efficiency if the water is especially hard. If a water softener is used, a nonprecipitating type is recommended to avoid buildup of precipitates on washer parts and textiles.

Disinfectant **Disinfectants** include pine oil, phenolics, chlorine bleach, and coal-tar derivatives. These items are used occasionally to disinfect sickroom apparel and bed and bath linens. Any product with an EPA (Environmental Protection Agency) registration number on the label has met EPA requirements for disinfectants. Not all disinfectants with these ingredients will meet EPA requirements, so be sure to check the label.

Presoak **Enzymatic presoaks** are used to remove tough stains. These additives contain enzymes—such as protease (for protein stains), lipase (for fat stains), and amylase (for carbohydrate stains)—that aid in the removal of specific soils. Enzymatic presoaks require more time to work than most other additives. A presoak of one-half hour or longer, even overnight, is recommended. Presoaks also include a surfactant to improve performance. These additives are not safe with protein fibers such as silk, wool, and specialty wools.

Pretreatment **Pretreatments** are used to remove difficult stains. They usually are added directly to the stain shortly before the item is laundered. Pretreatment products contain a solvent and a surfactant.

Starch or Sizing **Starch** or *sizing* is used after washing to add body and stiffness to fabrics. Laundry starch is seldom used today, but spray starches and sizings to be applied during ironing are available.

Bluing **Bluing** is a weak blue dye that masks yellowing in fabrics. Bluing is seldom used by itself but it may be present in detergents as a dye. Use of fluorescent whitening agents in detergents may make it unnecessary to add bluing.

Special Products There are many specialty products for cleaning for a variety of textile items. Products available in the fabric-care section of stores are designed for home use.

Compounds for cleaning items containing down minimize clumping of down and damage by alkaline detergents. Some manufacturers' care labels suggest placing tennis balls or other objects in the dryer with down-filled items to minimize clumping. These items may cause problems: The rubber in the ball may not be sufficiently resistant to heat, dye may transfer, and balls may become wedged between the baffles and the bulkhead, creating expensive repair problems. Stopping the dryer periodically and shaking the item vigorously reduces clumping.

Special soaps and detergents for hand washing of wool and other items work in cooler water and remove body and other light soils and perspiration. Read and follow label instructions. Long soak periods can cause problems with some dyes. Some detergents are formulated to remove baby formula and diaper-accident soils.

Compounds in powder or spray form remove stains from carpet and home or car upholstery and neutralize odor on textiles. Other products retard the soiling of leather, upholstery, carpet, and outdoor textiles. Antistatic sprays minimize problems with static soiling from dust and lint. Still other sprays are available to remove odor from a variety of textile products, including upholstery, draperies, car interiors, carpets, and apparel. They incorporate ring-shaped organic chemicals, cyclodextrins, that capture odor. These organic chemicals are renewable and many are based on corn-derived carbohydrates. Some of these fabric fresheners also claim to remove allergens from the air. Other fabric fresheners are based on zinc compounds that react with nitrogen and sulfur compounds that are frequently the source of unpleasant odors.

Specific laundry aids for removing grease and rust stains should be used with caution because they may damage fibers or may cause minor chemical burns when they come in contact with the skin.

Laundry aids to absorb excess dye and color from soil include pieces of cotton terrycloth that has been saturated with a polymer to remove color from the wash solution. The fabric with dye absorber is washed with any item that might bleed in the wash.

Compounds to freshen horizontal or front-loading washing machines should be used once a month to prevent growth of odor-forming bacteria.

With the increasing concern for health, sustainability, and environmental protection, some laundry compounds include all-natural ingredients. Others are free of perfume and dye. Another product incorporates compounds to remove dust mite matter from textiles—especially important to consumers who are allergic to dust mites.

Sorting

Before cleaning, consumers should **sort** the items to be washed in order to minimize problems and remove soil as efficiently as possible. Sort by color, type of garment (for example, separate work garments from delicate items), type of soil, recommended care method, and propensity of fabrics to lint. Closed zippers and buttons will not snag other items in the wash. Pockets should be checked for pens, tissues, and other items that may create problems during washing. Also check items for stains, holes, or tears and treat or repair as needed.

Washing Machines

Most contemporary washing machines allow for easy use by providing predetermined wash cycles for today's textiles. Consumers can select wash and rinse water temperatures, agitation speeds, and time. But spin speed, type of agitation, number of deep rinses, and other factors are usually determined by the washing-machine producer. Instruction booklets for each machine help the consumer understand more of the science of laundering; the machine's performance will be enhanced if these instructions are followed. Wash-cycle information for textiles is provided on care labels and should be followed to minimize dissatisfaction with laundry performance.

Traditional washing machines load from the top and include an agitator that occupies significant space in the tub and reduces the cleaning capacity of the machine. These machines have the tub and agitator in a vertical position. Vertical axis machines use an agitator to provide the physical energy needed to remove soil from textiles. They agitate textiles in a pool of water with detergent and other additives. Consumers expect to see a certain amount of suds if they open the machine during operation. These machines are efficient at cleaning, but consume significant amounts of water and energy with every load. Their cleaning cycles are relatively short. They remove water during a spin cycle in which the tub rotates at 600 to 700 rpm (revolutions per minute) to pull water out of the textiles. Estimates are that vertical axis machines use approximately 90 percent of the energy for heating water and from 35 to 50 gallons (132 to 189 liters) of water per load.

Washing machines are designed for efficient and convenient cleaning. Machine design has changed as a result of government mandates related to water and energy use. Dryers remove solvent from textiles.

Because of this high energy and water consumption, the federal government required laundry equipment manufacturers to change machine design to reduce energy and water use. The U.S. Department of Energy requires machines to meet a modified energy factor (MEF) of 1.26 or better (the higher the number, the better the energy efficiency). Water factor (WF) requirements will be 9.5 by 2011 for home washing machines. Energy Star, a joint program by the U.S. Environmental Protection Agency (EPA) and the U.S. Department of Energy (DOE), is a voluntary labeling program that identifies and promotes energy-efficient appliances, equipment, lighting, and other home devices. Washers and dryers that meet the qualifications carry an Energy Star label.

Horizontal axis machines, common in Asia and Europe for years, are now common in the United States as well. Sometimes these machines are referred to as front-loaders, but some horizontal axis machines also load from the top. Horizontal axis machines clean by rotating textile products in a manner similar to that used in dryers. The items are dropped in or tumbled through a shallow pool of water with detergent and other additives many times during the wash cycle. The impact from hitting or tumbling through the water provides the physical energy needed for cleaning. Textile shrinkage is less with horizontal axis machines, but abrasion can increase. Dye transfer or bleeding is more likely to occur. Wrinkling is more pronounced. If consumers hang items to dry, ironing may be needed to remove wrinkles. Savings are approximately 40 percent for water, 65 percent for energy, and 30 percent for drying, since extraction is more efficient in the spin cycle. Cleaning cycles are longer, but cleaning is more efficient.

Horizontal axis machines have a larger capacity since there is no internal agitator in the tub. Consumers cannot open the machine mid-cycle as can be done with vertical axis machines. Once the cycle has started, the last-minute item cannot be added. Most machines have several dispensers to add bleach, fabric softeners, and other compounds that are added at some point during the wash cycle. Because these machines are horizontal, the doors must seal tight to prevent water leakage and mid-cycle opening of the door. Because of this, these machines need to be cleaned approximately every month or a musty, mildew odor develops. Vertical axis machines dry out between uses; horizontal axis machines are much less likely to dry out.

Horizontal washers will also have an effect on fabric finishing. Durable finishes are designed to last through a certain number of wash and dry cycles, but the standards were established with vertical axis machines that used greater amounts of water per cycle and a different type of agitation. These changes in washing machines may be most noticeable on fabrics with surface finishes. In addition, the lower volume of rinse water increases the likelihood of biofilms developing on textiles. A *biofilm* is an aggregate of microorganisms that adhere to textile surfaces and may create problems with odor and mold, mildew, or fungus growth. When heat and humidity, such as may occur during wearing, are introduced, odor may develop. Hot water, steam and chlorine bleach are effective disinfectants. To counteract the development of biofilms, antimicrobial finishes may become more common.

Special cleaning compounds for horizontal axis machines are available. Specially formulated high-efficiency (HE) detergents should be used in a horizontal-axis machine. These HE detergents provide the correct level of sudsing for horizontal axis machines. Horizontal axis machines are sensitive to sudsing. Most of these machines have suds warning devices because too many suds can damage the machine. In addition, HE detergents incorporate compounds that keep soil in suspension. Remember, with these machines, less water is used, but the same or greater amounts of textiles can be cleaned in one load. Hence, chemicals that are more efficient at keeping soils in solution are needed or textiles will accumulate soil from the wash water. Finally, HE detergents incorporate compounds that disperse detergent more quickly.

Again, this ingredient is needed because of the lower water usage in horizontal axis machines. Fabric softeners specially formulated for horizontal axis machines are not yet on the market.

Steam washers are available for home use, but the steam is used only in selected cycles to help wet fabrics more completely. Steam is used to boost cleaning, improve detergent action, and remove oil and other challenging stains. During the rinse, steam kills microorganism, sterilizes fabrics, and removes wrinkles that form during use or washing. Some washers heat the water to generate steam. Others use a separate heating unit to create the steam that is delivered to the tub by a nozzle. Steam washers use less energy and less water than conventional washers.

Drying

Drying removes the solvent from the textile. The drying procedure usually is specified on the care label. In machine drying, the textiles are tumbled in a rotating drum. Heated air is circulated through the drum. It heats the water remaining on the textiles from washing. This water evaporates and the moisture-laden air is vented out of the dryer. Figure 20.10 shows a drawing of a dryer.

Machine-drying is considered the most severe method because of the abrasion and agitation. Fabrics tumble against the rotating cylinder and other items in the dryer. If zippers, heavy or harsh fabrics, or rough trims are present, fragile items can be damaged.

Other drying options use less energy, but may require more individual effort and time. Items that are hung to dry can be hung out in the weather or inside a home, apartment, or other building. In line drying, items are hung outside to dry in the weather. Wind speed, humidity levels, and sunlight intensity have a significant impact on the speed of drying. Strong winds and dust or other atmospheric pollutants can damage textiles that are hung to dry. Dew or rain can rewet

1. Drying Chamber
2. Lint Screen
3. Fan
4. Motor
5. Dryer Vent
6. Heating Element
7. Door

Figure 20.10   **Parts and air flow for a clothes dryer.**

> ► **Learning Activity 7**

Describe how you clean the textile items you own (apparel, interior textiles, accessories, and other items like bags, etc.). Be sure to include such dimensions as sorting, drying, spot or stain removal, and ironing. Describe your degree of satisfaction with the outcomes of a normal cleaning process. Are there any problems you normally experience? What are they? Did anyone train you as to how to clean textiles? Who? Do you continue to follow those practices or have you changed some or most of what you do? Why?

dry items requiring more time for drying. In addition, line drying in areas with bird and insect populations may result in some clean items being soiled during drying. Strong sunlight can fade items while they dry. While fading is usually not apparent immediately, it can accumulate over time. Line drying also may be too severe for some items because wet fabrics are extremely heavy and are likely to stretch or tear. This is especially a problem for wool, rayon, and other fibers that are weaker when wet.

Items can also be hung to dry inside on drying racks or lines. Inside drying can increase humidity levels, especially in humid regions or humid seasons. Finding a space where items can dry without interfering with family or household activities can be difficult. It is a challenge to find a space to dry large items like bedding. It may require more time to dry items indoors. Drying items in this manner is much less likely to result in damage compared to drying in the wind and soiling during drying rarely occurs.

Drying flat is the least severe method because the fabric is under little stress. Special drying racks and sweater drying hammocks are available. However, drying flat requires the most time and area for drying. This method is recommended only for items that cannot be tumble dried or hung to dry. Combination dryers are available that incorporate hanging, flat, and tumble drying in separate chambers in the dryer.

Steam dryers are available. They do not actually use steam to dry. Several cycle options exist. Steam dryers use heat to dry much like a regular dryer. However, steam dryers do use steam to more effectively remove wrinkles. Steam also softens, deodorizes, and sanitizes fabrics. Some dryers add a fine mist of water that is heated to steam by the dryer. Others generate steam in a small unit and deliver the steam to the textiles. Steam dryers can be used to freshen textiles between uses. Products should be checked for stains before freshening or the process might set the stain. Fabric softener sheets should not be used with a steam dryer since they are more likely to stain.

Vent-free dryers do not exhaust moisture-saturated air outdoors. They use a closed circuit in which air inside the dryer is heated and circulated among the wet items. The hot air absorbs moisture and passes through a heat exchanger, where the water is condensed and drained off. The air is reheated and the process continues until the items are dry.

Commercial Laundering

Commercial laundries include several types: businesses that wash apparel and some interior textiles for individual consumers, businesses that wash uniforms for companies where uniforms are required, and businesses that operate an in-house laundry such as in the medical field. Often uniforms are leased in a full-service package, meaning that the lease includes weekly laundering.

Commercial laundering places high demands on the textiles, the equipment, and the chemicals used in cleaning. Textiles may be washed more than 100 times and are expected to withstand the heavy wear that results from washing and drying in commercial machines. The wash and dry units used in commercial laundering resemble home washers and dryers, except that they are much larger, are equipped with heavier motors and belts, and have fewer cycle options. Factors similar to those driving the home laundry and dry-cleaning industries are affecting commercial laundering: energy efficiency, reducing water use, and selecting chemicals with the least environmental impact or best sustainability options.

Dry Cleaning

In **dry cleaning**, solvents other than water are used to remove soil from textiles. The solvents include the following: perchloroethylene (perc), petroleum solvent (Stoddard's solvent), silicon-based solvent, carbon dioxide–based solvent, and fluorocarbon solvent. Of these, perc is most common. However, because of concerns regarding the toxicity and environmental impact of perc and fluorocarbon, new replacement solvents are available. Because of cost and regulations associated with perc and fluorocarbon, dry cleaners are gradually switching to other solvents or cleaning systems. If asked, most dry cleaners will identify the solvent they use. Some items are labeled dry clean only because of the fiber content, dyes that bleed in washing, leather or fur trim, fragile components like beads or open lace, support materials that would lose their body and stiffness after wetting with water, or water soluble finishes on the fabric or fiber like sericin on silk. Washing by hand or machine would damage the item or destroy the look or drape of the item. Many machine-washable items may be dry-cleaned. The reverse is also true: many items labeled dry clean can be hand or machine washed with no adverse effects.

The International Fabricare Institute (IFI), a professional organization, trains and educates dry cleaners, has developed a fair-claims adjustment guide for use in consumer complaints, and provides an evaluation service when problems develop. Members display an IFI plaque in their business.

When items are brought to the dry cleaner, they are identified with a tag that includes special instructions, the owner's identification number, and the number of pieces in the group. Items are inspected. Because a solvent is used, stains that are water-soluble and other hard-to-remove spots are treated at the spot board before cleaning. Customers who identify stains for the dry cleaner make cleaning easier and ultimately improve their satisfaction with the cleaned product. About one-fourth of the items taken to a dry cleaning business will be cleaned in water rather than solvent. Many stains and odors, including perspiration, require wet cleaning to be removed.

After treatment at the spotting board, items are placed in a dry-cleaning unit to be tumbled with a charged solvent (solvent, detergent, and a small percentage of water) (Figure 20.11). After tumbling, solvent is reclaimed in the dry-to-dry unit or in a separate reclaimer unit. These units serves the same function as a dryer in laundering, except that the solvent is passed through a refrigeration unit, condensed and filtered to be used again. Because so much solvent is lost in transfer, reclaimers are being replaced with dry-to-dry units. Use of dry-to-dry units, more efficient equipment, and better management practices have reduced perc consumption substantially. Solvents are reclaimed to minimize environmental impact and lower costs. Filtering and distilling remove soil, color, odor, and other residue and allow the solvent to be reused many times.

After the items are dry, they go to the pressing area, where steam and special steam-air forms give a finished appearance to the item. For example, pants are pressed with a topper that

In **dry cleaning**, solvents other than water are used to remove soil from textiles. Special equipment is used to reclaim and reuse organic solvents. Special techniques are needed for such items as leather and fur.

Figure 20.11   Dry-cleaning unit.

presses the top part of the pants. Each leg is pressed separately with a press. Jackets, shirts, and blouses are finished with a suzie, a steam-body torso form (Figure 20.12). After pressing, items are placed on hangers or shirt boards and the group is reassembled to wait for pick-up by the owner. More than 3 billion wire hangers (approximately 195 million pounds of steel) are discarded and end up in landfills annually in the United States. Many dry cleaners will reuse hangers and shirt boards if they are clean and in good condition. Check with the dry cleaner before assuming they will reuse these items. New environmentally friendly hangers that are durable for approximately two months of use are made from 100 percent recycled and recyclable paper.

Many dry cleaners also will replace buttons; make minor repairs to items; replace sizing, water repellency, and other finishes; add permanent creases to pants; and clean fur and leather. Some dry cleaners can also clean and sanitize feather pillows and clean and press draperies. Many dry cleaners offer a combination service for wedding dresses that includes cleaning the gown, preparing it for storage, and providing a special box for storage. Although this service is appealing, it may not completely protect the gown from aging, and the dry cleaner may not use archival materials in the box or packing materials. Some specialty gowns with lots of bead and sequin trim may require a special expensive and time-consuming cleaning process.

Other unique items such as quilts, old laces, sheer fabrics, embroidery, historic or vintage apparel and furnishing textiles, and other fragile items also require special care. Dry cleaners may refuse to work with some of these items if the dyes are not fast (a problem that may occur with pieced quilts and embroideries) or if the fabric is fragile, as it is with many vintage items. Dry cleaners that work with unique or historic items may require a signed disclaimer form because of their fragile nature or use of incompatible materials.

Figure 20.12 Pressing equipment: pants press (top), inflatable "suzie" for steaming blouses and shirts (bottom).

Dry Cleaning of Leather and Fur

Products made of leather and fur, and those that contain these materials, should be cleaned by specialists because of their complex and special requirements. **Leather** and **fur (furrier) dry cleaning** must remove soil without damaging the dye or finish and restore oils that cleaning removes. This is a complex and expensive process. Wide variations in hides or skins and processing create potential problems for the consumer and dry cleaner. Frequently, the leather/fur cleaner is required to redye or refinish the item to restore it to a form that will satisfy the customer. Because of this additional processing, leather and fur cleaning is expensive. Most dry cleaners do not clean these items themselves but send them to a specialist.

Dry cleaners frequently see problems with leather dyes that are not fast to dry cleaning. This is especially common with high-fashion items and items that combine leather trim with woven or knit fabrics. The problem is more common with apparel because apparel items are more likely to have leather trim. However, interior textiles made of leather or trimmed in leather may also present problems in dry cleaning.

Home Solvent Cleaning

A product for freshening dry-clean-only items is available in a kit that includes a stain-removal solution, a bag for use in a home dryer, and a solvent-treated moist cloth. Consumers should pretreat stains and test items for colorfastness before cleaning them. The moistened cloth is placed in the bag with the garments. The bag is then placed in an otherwise empty dryer with an outside vent. Heat from the dryer activates the solvent, which removes light soil and some

Work in groups of two or three. Explain the differences and similarities between washing and dry cleaning. Do any of the group members have any items that require dry cleaning? Do any of the group members have any leather or fur items? Have they been dry cleaned? Has anyone in the group tried home solvent cleaning or had any item professionally wet cleaned? Describe the individual's degree of satisfaction with the outcomes of these cleaning processes. What kinds of items were dry cleaned? Why were they dry cleaned? What component of the item mandated dry cleaning? Would hand or gentle machine washing be effective and safe for that item? What care is listed on the care label for these items?

odor. Items should be removed promptly and hung to minimize wrinkling. The product works best with lightly soiled items and items that do not require special care or pressing, such as simple slacks and skirts and wool sweaters. The kit is not as effective as commercial dry cleaning, but it reduces the number of times many products will need dry cleaning. Tradenames include Dryel,® Custom Cleaner,® and FreshCare.®

Professional Wet Cleaning

Professional wet cleaning is a commercial alternative to dry cleaning for items labeled "dry clean only." This process is more complex than home laundering and requires training in selecting and using the proper technique.

Almost every type of dry-cleanable fabric can be wet-cleaned, provided there is careful control of temperature, mechanical action, moisture levels, soap, and other cleaning additives. Before cleaning, products are sorted by fabric type, not color; they are checked for the presence of water-soluble dyes; and stains are treated. The process is labor-intensive and uses controlled applications of heat, steam, and natural soaps to clean textiles and pressing techniques to restore the item's appearance. Even though water is used, these computer-controlled wet-cleaning and drying machines differ from home washing machines and dryers. The item may not be fully immersed in water during the process. The cleaner selects from steam cleaning, spot removing, hand washing, gentle machine washing, tumble drying, and vacuuming. Microwave drying reduces shrinkage during drying. The method selected depends on the item and fabric type, degree of soiling, and condition. Research has found that approximately 80 percent of the items labeled "dry clean only" can be wet-cleaned successfully.

Consumers report that wet cleaning offers essentially the same cleaning potential as dry cleaning and appreciate the lack of solvent odor on wet-cleaned items. Consumers also are pleased with the short-term effects on general cleanliness, shrinkage or stretching, and overall appearance; however, some shrinkage, wrinkling, and color loss may occur.

Because the process uses less expensive equipment, less capital is needed to open a plant. Wet cleaning makes significant use of water and energy during the cleaning process, but there are fewer risks in terms of flammability, health problems, and environmental contamination that are associated with traditional dry-cleaning solvents. To clean 100 items, wet cleaning uses only one-fourth to one-third the electricity and approximately 1.4 times more natural gas/steam and 1.2 times more water than dry cleaning. Discharge from wet-cleaners has not created problems in water-treatment facilities.

Professional wet cleaning is a commercial alternative to dry cleaning for items labeled dry clean only.

Storage

Storage is another important aspect to consider for textile products. Most textile materials are placed in storage during one or more stages of their production. With quick response and just-in-time initiatives expected of producers and distribution centers, the amount of storage time in the production sequence has decreased for many items. Nevertheless, storage continues to generate concerns regarding the potential for damage that may occur. The conditions under which textile materials and products are stored may influence their appearance, quality, and performance. For example, natural fibers are stored from the time they are harvested until they are cleaned and processed into yarns. If storage conditions are poor, the fibers develop mildew problems, become infested with insects, or discolor. Incorrect storage of finished fabrics or products may result in permanently set wrinkles, discoloration from contact with other materials and dye or print transfer, and damage from insects, mold, or heat. Storage concerns also relate to conditions in transportation and shipping, especially with so many items being produced offshore.

Most products should never be stored in direct contact with raw wood, raw wood products, wood finishes, brown paper, newspaper, or cardboard. Raw wood and wood pulp papers and cardboard produce acid as they age. Cellulosic fibers are degraded by acid, and brown or yellow stains may develop as a result of exposure to the wood (Figure 20.13). Plastic bags from dry cleaners are provided as a service to avoid soiling freshly cleaned items during transport. These bags often incorporate phenolic antioxidants and are not intended for storage. They should be discarded immediately after the product is brought into the house. Items stored in dry-cleaning bags may discolor because of the materials in the bag; build up static and attract dust; or trap moisture, creating an ideal environment for mildew. For more information regarding storage, see the appropriate fiber chapter.

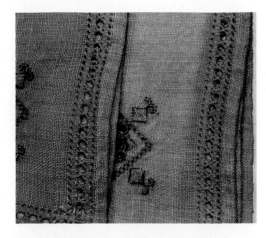

Figure 20.13 Yellowed cotton napkin stored next to wooden drawer bottom for several years.

> Most textile products should never be stored in direct contact with raw wood, raw wood products, wood finishes, brown paper, newspaper, or cardboard because of the problems these materials cause with fibers, dyes, or finishes.

Other Cleaning Methods

This section discusses methods of cleaning carpets and upholstery. The challenges of cleaning carpet and upholstery is that almost always the textile is cleaned in situ or on-site. Selection of cleaning compounds is based on the type of reside that is left since rinsing cannot occur. Selection of the type of cleaning method is based on the degree of soil, fabric structure (loop pile, cut pile, or no pile), and convenience. Most of these methods clean only the surface and are considered light or surface cleaning methods because they do not clean to the base of the pile or fabric structure. As with other textiles, it may not be possible to completely clean interior textiles that have become heavily soiled. While the myth is not true, many consumers continue to postpone cleaning for fear that cleaning will make the carpet or upholstery soil more quickly. Table 20.3 lists upholstery cleaning codes.

Table 20.3 Upholstery Cleaning Codes

W	Use water-based upholstery cleaner only.
S	Use solvent-based upholstery cleaner only.
WS	Can use either water- or solvent-based upholstery cleaner.
X	Do not clean with either water- or solvent-based upholstery cleaner; use vacuuming or light brushing only.

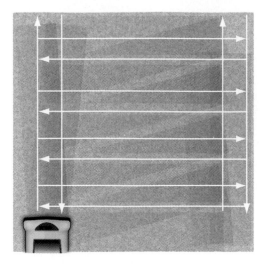

Figure 20.14 Recommended pattern for vacuuming carpets and rugs.

Vacuuming

Vacuuming uses suction to pull particulate soil, such as dust, lint and dirt, from carpeting, upholstered furniture, and wall and window coverings. It is the most common and important method of cleaning carpets. Vacuuming removes soil that has not adhered to the fibers. Large particles such as small rocks and paper clips may not be removed by vacuuming and may need to be swept or picked up by hand. Since vacuuming removes only particulate soil, other types of soil must be removed by other means. For industrial and commercial carpets, the vacuum cleaner must have a heavy-duty rating so that it cleans deeply into the surface pile and can withstand frequent, heavy use. Most home vacuum cleaners are not of this type.

Regular vacuuming is recommended so that soil does not work deep into the pile of the carpet. In many applications, this means daily vacuuming. For vacuuming to be most effective, the vacuum should pass over the carpet in several directions so that soil protected by yarns or fibers in one direction is exposed and removed when the vacuum approaches from another direction (Figure 20.14).

On any carpet, spots and stains should be treated as soon as possible after soiling. Carpet manufacturers provide a list of recommended cleaning compounds for specific stains. If carpets accumulate oily soils or airborne dust and dirt that is not removed with regular vacuuming, corrective action should be taken. A variety of procedures are discussed in this chapter. However, before attempting any of these other methods, a thorough vacuuming should be done first to remove surface soil and separate and loosen packed pile.

Wet Cleaning

Wet cleaning or **shampooing** of carpets is a method that uses water-based detergents in foam form and extended drying times. The cleaning solution generates high levels of foam to reduce wetting of the carpet yarns and eliminate wetting of the carpet backing and padding. The foam is worked into the pile with rotating brushes. A lubricating agent is incorporated in the cleaning solution to reduce damage to the carpet yarns and fibers from the rotating brushes. A thorough wet vacuuming follows to remove the soil-laden solution. Some carpets may require several days before they are completely dry. The solution also often includes an optical brightener to enhance the clean appearance of the carpet. Ingredients are selected so that the residue dries without being sticky, which would attract soil and lint.

Two types of machines are used: a cylindrical foam machine and a rotary shampoo machine. The cylindrical foam machine includes an air compressor that creates the foam before it is applied to the carpet. A revolving cylindrical brush applies the foam to the carpet and provides the agitation. This method is not as effective at removing particulate soil, so it is essential to thoroughly vacuum carpet before and after shampooing.

The rotary shampoo machine is the same kind of machine as used for cleaning and polishing hard floor surfaces. This machine sprays the cleaning solution onto the carpet. The rotary brush whips the solution into a foam and agitates the carpet surface. Many carpet manufacturers do not recommend this type of cleaning because of the potential for damage to the carpet, especially cut pile carpets which are common in residential applications. Overwetting is more common with this machine with potential staining from carpet backing or padding, shrinkage, and odor.

Testing the cleaning solution on an inconspicuous area of the carpet is recommended before the entire surface is cleaned in this manner. This process is also known as the *rotary brush method*.

Cleaning solutions may not be completely removed, resulting in brown stains appearing on the surface of the pile. Brush action may permanently distort the pile. Detergents should be selected that prevent dulling of the carpet's surface, minimize rapid resoiling, avoid creating problems with static electricity, and disinfect. After wet cleaning, problems with static electricity may develop if a water-based antistatic agent was originally applied to the carpet and not restored after wet cleaning. If compounds containing chlorine, such as bleach, are added to the shampoo, a yellow discoloration may appear on the carpet. This problem is common in communities where chlorine is used to treat the water. Shampooing is not as effective at cleaning as several other methods.

A variation of this method is carbonated cleaning or the bonnet method that uses carbonated water, supposedly to improve the cleaning efficiency of the process. The bonnet machine is a modification of the hard floor spray buffing machine.

Dry-Foam Cleaning

Dry-foam cleaning or *aerosol cleaning* of carpet is done by hand with a foam sprayed onto the carpet or by employing a machine that deposits a detergent solution as a foam on the carpet just ahead of an agitating brush. The brush works the solution into the carpet, loosens soil particles, and suspends them in the foam, and the vacuum removes the soil. Since application of the foam, agitation, and vacuuming is almost simultaneous, complete wetting of the carpet is avoided. Dry-foam cleaning does not remove deeply embedded soil because the solution works more on the surface. Dry-foam processes allow the carpet to be used soon after cleaning, often within the hour. This process is also used to clean upholstery.

Hot-Water Extraction

In the **hot-water extraction** method a fine spray of hot-water–detergent solution is injected into the carpet. To be most effective, water temperature should be between 150°F (66°C) and 200°F (93°C). The solution is under pressure and wets the carpet quickly but is removed almost immediately by a powerful vacuum. Vacuuming removes both the water and the soil.

Several types of equipment exist. All are based two options: a portable unit or a truck-mounted system. A machine sprays the cleaning solution into the carpet, a powerful vacuum removes the soiled solution, and a holding tank contains the soiled water. Truck-mounted systems are more effective at cleaning and reduce the potential for indoor air that contains excess humidity and tiny dirt particles. If a truck-mounted system is used, the truck runs in neutral to power the system so it must be parked to avoid exhaust fumes from entering the building. All-electric systems are available without the exhaust problems. Because of the hot water used in this process, scalding injuries may occur if a hose breaks or detaches.

Overwetting of the carpet sometimes occurs if an area is treated too slowly. To minimize rapid resoiling, the detergent must be completely removed. Since no brushes are used in this process, pile distortion is minimized. This process is sometimes referred to as warm water extraction. Although sometimes also referred to as steam cleaning, no steam is used in the process. This method is recommended by almost all carpet manufacturers because it provides deep cleaning to the base of the pile or fabric structure with minimal pile distortion or damage.

Advantages of hot water extraction are that the high cleaning temperatures kill bacteria, dust mites, mold, fungus, and other organisms. If properly done, there is little or no residue. The high pressure and powerful vacuum clean more effectively than other methods.

Many interior textiles have different cleaning needs because they must be cleaned in situ. **Vacuuming** uses suction to pull particulate soil from the textile. **Wet cleaning** uses water-based detergents in foam form and requires extended drying times. In **dry-foam cleaning**, a foam is sprayed onto the carpet and worked in by an agitating brush. The soil is removed by vacuuming. In the **hot-water extraction** method a fine spray of hot-water–detergent solution is injected into the carpet and removed almost immediately by a powerful vacuum. In **absorbent powder cleaning**, a dry powder is sprinkled on the surface, worked in, and removed by vacuuming. **Ultrasonic cleaning** requires that the textile be taken to a special cleaning facility. High-frequency sound waves attract the soil and remove it from the carpet fibers.

► **Learning Activity 9**

Work in groups of three or four. Explain the processes used for cleaning carpeting and upholstery. Has anyone in the group tried to clean carpeting or upholstery, including spot or stain removal? Describe the process used and the degree of satisfaction with the end result.

Absorbent Powder Cleaning

Absorbent powder cleaning, also known as powder cleaning, uses absorbent powders combining detergents, water, and solvents. The dry powder is sprinkled on the surface of the carpet or upholstery and brushed or otherwise worked into the pile or fabric. The powder combines with the soil and holds it in suspension until it is removed by vacuuming. The powder should remain in contact with the fabric's surface for a brief time before being removed by vacuuming. The method is fast and requires no time for drying, but removes surface soil only. Pile distortion is related to the vigor with which the powder is worked into the pile. With cleaning compounds that have extremely fine particles, it may be difficult to remove all of the compound. If white powder appears on shoes or pant cuffs, too much was used or removal was not complete. This method is also known as dry extraction cleaning, absorbent powder cleaning, or absorbent compound cleaning. It is also used to clean upholstery.

Ultrasonic Cleaning

Ultrasonic cleaning requires that the rug or carpet be removed from the use site and taken to a special cleaning facility. High-frequency sound waves attract the soil and remove it from the carpet fibers. At present, this method is not used on carpets that cannot be removed from the location. Ultrasonic cleaning in conjunction with water-based and solvent-and-water-based systems is being investigated as an alternative to solvent dry cleaning.

Conservation Practices

Vintage and collectible textiles in private and museum collections require different methods of handling, cleaning, and storage because many are one-of-a-kind, irreplaceable items. **Conservation** makes use of special techniques that require training, specialized equipment, and mild chemicals.

These special textiles are analyzed in detail before cleaning to determine fiber content, type of other materials present, condition, and colorfastness of all colors and materials to water and detergent. Cleaning may include any or all of these steps: hand removal of particulate soil and lint, carefully controlled vacuuming, supported immersion soak in a solution of warm water and mild detergent, and flat drying. The goal of cleaning in conservation is not the same as in the other processes discussed in this chapter. Conservation cleaning removes harmful materials from the textile, but stains and soil may remain once cleaning has been completed. Harsh and potentially damaging spot-removal agents and bleach are rarely used in conservation cleaning because they threaten the integrity of the item.

Proper storage is especially important for these textiles since they will spend most of their time there. Techniques that protect items from light, dust, insects, abrasion, tension, environmental pollution, and changes in temperature and humidity are used. Materials that neutralize damaging by-products of aging and provide protection from the surrounding environment support and cushion each item individually.

Environmental Concerns and Sustainability of Cleaning

The environmental impact of cleaning textile products is profound and multidimensional. The newer dry-cleaning solvents that have replaced highly flammable ones have been linked to cancer and environmental hazards. In addition, ground contamination by dry-cleaning solvents leads to contamination of water systems. Several communities have experienced problems with perc contamination of water because of accidental or deliberate spills resulting in modifications of the way dry cleaners handle perc. Cleaners also have changed the handling of all items cleaned with any solvent and are converting to dry-to-dry equipment to minimize the loss of solvent by evaporation.

Phosphate builders in laundry detergents have been largely replaced in the United States and Europe because of their suspected contribution to accelerated eutrophication of ponds and lakes; but some research indicates that these builders may have the least impact on the environment as compared with other builders when one also considers the costs and efficiency of water treatment. Phosphate builders are rarely restricted or banned in other cleaning compounds, such as bathroom cleansers and dishwashing detergents. Bans on phosphates in detergents have had little effect on the problems with water systems that the bans were designed to address.

In the 1960s, detergent manufacturers voluntarily switched to biodegradable surfactants. Manufacturers have changed formulations of detergents to concentrated forms for liquids and powders that require less packaging and reduce transportation costs. Recycled plastic and paper packaging is used. Refillable containers decrease the use of packaging materials even more. Some ingredients in the new formulations are multifunctional, decreasing the number of ingredients and reducing the environmental impact of producing many different ingredients.

Concerns related to compounds from palm-oil derivatives used in many organic laundry detergents relate to destruction of rain forests in Indonesia, Malaysia, and elsewhere to develop palm tree plantations. Laundry detergents raise sustainability concerns because of the amount used. After use, detergent is discarded into water treatment systems or, in some parts of the world, dumped into surface water systems without treatment. Some large retailers have identified detergent ingredients that are "chemicals of concern" that they would like to see phased out over the next few years. One such chemical is nonylphenol ethoxylate (NPE), which is known to break down into more toxic compounds that disrupt the endocrine systems of fish and shellfish.

▶ Learning Activity 10

Examine the labels for detergents and other laundry aids or listen to commercials promoting these products. What kinds of claims are made? Based on your experiences with these products, do you find the claims valid? Why or why not? Is there information on labels describing ingredients used in these products? Is there a way you can determine this information?

Detergent manufacturers are developing products that have a lower carbon footprint during manufacturing and from packaging, distribution, and use. Some companies require that 99 percent of the ingredients be based on plants or minerals, be biodegradable, nontoxic to fish and other aquatic life, and formulated without animal testing. One problem with biodegradable compounds is that they can begin degrading before they are used. Preservatives are used to eliminate that problem, but that also decreases the biodegradation of the detergent after use.

Life cycle analysis of cotton textiles has demonstrated that up to three-fourths of the energy consumed during the life of the product is consumed in laundering the item.

key terms

review questions

1. Define detergency, and explain what happens when a soiled textile product is cleaned.

2. Explain what happens when soap is used in hard water.

3. Why is water used in laundering and many other methods of cleaning?

4. Use a thermometer and measure the water temperature of the wash water. How does this temperature relate to the temperature you selected? How will that difference affect the cleaning process?

5. Explain the differences and similarities between vertical and horizontal axis washing machines. What kinds of differences might consumers see in terms of their textile products?

6. You are a member of a product development team for a retailer who sells private label merchandise. A supplier wants to use a dry-clean-only label for an all-cotton shirt. What factors might make this label appropriate for such a product? Would such a label affect sales for an all-cotton shirt? Why or why not?

7. Briefly explain the most appropriate process for the following items:

   a. Blue geometric print all-cotton sheeting after one week of normal use

   b. Dark blue, all-polyester hotel front desk staff jacket and slacks after one week of normal use (worn for two eight-hour shifts)

   c. Two-year old's blue denim shorts stained with chocolate ice cream and diaper accident

   d. White T-shirt with branded logo worn for a casual game of volleyball on a warm spring day with grass stains

   e. Beige silk blouse with red wine stain

   f. Cotton/polyester dress slacks worn all day at the office

   g. Black knit cotton pants with barbecue sauce stain on one knee

8. Compare the similarities and differences between dry cleaning and laundering.

9. Identify the ingredients, and their function, that may be present in your favorite laundry detergent.

10. What ingredients have been incorporated in one container to make doing the laundry easier and more convenient?

11. How does carpet or upholstery cleaning differ from laundering? What factors should be considered when selecting a cleaning method?

12. How have environmental and sustainability issues changed the manner in which textile products are cleaned?

13. What textile problems can develop during storage?

14. How should cleaning of a vintage or historic textile item be done? What are the concerns that should be considered before cleaning is attempted?

Case Study
Dryer Sheets*

Dryer sheets were invented in the late 1960s by a chemist who wanted to save his wife extra trips to the ground floor laundry room from their apartment. He sold his patent to Procter & Gamble who soon commercialized his idea. There are numerous brands of dryer sheets on the market today. All are designed to soften clothes, prevent static cling, and deliver a fresh scent. Most of the dryer sheets are a nonwoven polyester coated with softening agents based on fatty acids, fatty alcohols, or similar compounds. A naturally occurring calcium clay is also used to control how the softener melts in the dryer. The softeners have high melting points so they don't feel sticky to touch, effectively transfer to textiles in the dryer, but don't come off the dryer sheet too quickly to reduce leaving streaks on textiles. The softener gives the fabric a slippery surface, which feels soft to the touch. The slippery surface also increases fibers' surface conductivity and reduces static buildup. Fragrance molecules are added to the softener coating. Since fragrance is highly volatile (evaporates quickly, especially with heat), it may be encapsulated to slow down evaporation.

DISCUSSION QUESTIONS

1. Do you use dryer sheets? Why or why not? How satisfied are you with the results?

2. Explain why the sheets are made of polyester.

3. Examine a dryer sheet and determine what kind of nonwoven process was used to make the fabric.

4. Why are the dryer sheets nonwoven? What are the advantages or disadvantages of using a nonwoven for this application?

5. Do you know of any other uses consumers make of dryer sheets? If yes, what are some other uses?

*Wang, L. (2008). Dryer sheets. *Chemical and Engineering News*, 86 (15), 44.

suggested readings

American Association of Textile Chemists and Colorists. (2008). *Technical Manual*, 83. Research Triangle Park, NC: Author.

Eckman, A. L. (2004). The dirt on drycleaning. *AATCC Review*, 4(3), pp. 9–11.

Lumley, A. C., & Gatewood, B. M. (1998). Effectiveness of selected laundry disks in removing soil and stains from cotton and polyester. *Textile Chemist and Colorist*, 30(12), pp. 31–35.

McCoy, M. (2007). A new kind of clean. *Chemical and Engineering News*, 85(11), pp. 29–31.

McCoy, M. (2007). Going green. *Chemical and Engineering News*, 85(5), pp. 13–19.

McCoy, M. (2008). Greener cleaners. *Chemical and Engineering News*, 86(3), pp. 15–23.

McCoy, M. (2006). Soaps and detergents. *Chemical and Engineering News*, 83(5), pp. 13–19.

McCoy, M. (2009). The greening game. *Chemical and Engineering News*, 87(4), pp. 13–19.

Moe, K. D. (2000). With bleach detergents: How they work. *Textile Chemist and Colorist and American Dyestuff Reporter*, 32(8), pp. 79–81.

Perkins, W. S. (1998, August). Surfactants—A primer. *America's Textiles International*, pp. 51–54.

Reznikoff, S. C. (1989). *Specifications of Commercial Interiors*. New York: Whitney Library of Design.

Ridgley, H. (2003). Cleaning up the dry cleaning business. *National Wildlife*, 41(5), pp. 16–17.

Thiry, M. C. (2008). It's a new laundry day. *AATCC*, 8(3), 22–28.

Wang, L. (2008). Dryer sheets. *Chemical and Engineering News*, 86(15), 44.

LEGAL,
SUSTAINABILITY, and
ENVIRONMENTAL
ISSUES

CHAPTER OBJECTIVES

- To understand laws and regulations related to textiles and textile products.
- To understand legal requirements for labeling textiles and textile products.
- To understand professional and consumer rights and responsibilities in terms of legal and environmental concerns.
- To recognize how textiles and textile products affect the environment.
- To realize efforts within the global textile complex to make the production, use, care, and disposal of textiles and textile products more sustainable.

21

The global textile complex is affected by regulations and laws related to fair trade practices, information labeling, worker and consumer safety, and environmental protection. Laws and regulations will continue to affect the global textile complex in the areas of general operations, label requirements, environmental issues, design aspects, and health and safety concerns. This chapter focuses on the pertinent laws and regulations, sustainability, and environmental issues. It is beneficial to understand how these issues affect textile products and to recognize where professional responsibilities imply legal and social responsibilities.

Labeling Laws and Care Regulations

This chapter discusses laws and regulations that relate to producing safe products and providing the consumer with product information. It does not include laws and regulations regarding import/export and other trade practices. Some international laws and regulations will be addressed when they have far-reaching implications. Many countries have similar laws or regulations that differ in specific details.

Because of the financial and public relations implications of failure to comply, professionals need to understand and abide by all laws and regulations related to label requirements for textiles and textile products in any country in which they work. Many regulations and laws relating to textiles and textile products focus on providing the ultimate consumers with information so that they are better prepared to make decisions regarding purchase, use, and care of textile products (Figure 21.1). In the U.S., the interpretation and enforcement of these laws and regulations are the responsibility of the **Federal Trade Commission (FTC).** The activities of the FTC are designed to protect the ultimate consumer and legitimate domestic segments of the global textile complex. The FTC is responsible for preventing unfair or deceptive trade practices, for example, the marketing of a rayon/polyester blend crash in such a way that suggests it was made of flax, implied by the use of the term *linen*. Trade and business publications frequently carry articles describing current efforts of the FTC to prevent unfair or deceptive trade practices in the United States. Many other countries have similar laws and regulations to protect their business and consumers.

The first four laws and regulations deal with "truth-in-fabrics." For these to be beneficial, the consumer must have some knowledge about fibers and fabrics.

Figure 21.1   Garment labels.

Silk Regulation, 1932

Silk may be weighted (treated with a solution of metallic salts) to increase a fabric's weight and hand and improve its dyeability. However, weighted silk is not as durable and wrinkle-resistant as regular silk. Because of these problems, the FTC ruled in 1932 that anything labeled **pure silk** or **pure dye silk** could contain no more than 15 percent weighting for black and no more than 10 percent for all other colors. Anything exceeding these levels is weighted silk. At present, very little silk on the market is weighted. However, museum collections have many weighted silk items that are disintegrating.

Wool Products Labeling Act, 1939 (Amended)

Wool may be blended with less expensive fibers to reduce fabric cost or to extend its use. The **Wool Products Labeling Act** of 1939 (amended) protects consumers as well as producers, manufacturers, and distributors from the unrevealed presence of substitutes and mixtures and informs consumers of the source of the wool fiber. This act applies to any textile product containing wool, except carpets, rugs, mats, and upholstery. The law requires that the label describe the fiber content in terms of percentage and the fiber source. Fiber produced from sheep, lamb, angora goat, cashmere goat, camel, alpaca, llama, and vicuña can be referred to as wool. Further details relating to fiber size also apply to fine wool and cashmere, primarily because of problems with items claiming to include higher quality or more expensive fibers than were evident with analysis.

The term *fur fiber* can be used for the fiber from any other animal. The name of the manufacturer or the registered identification number of the manufacturer also must be on the label. The registered number is designated WPL or RN. **WPL** refers to the wool product label number, and **RN** to the registered number. Finally, the act requires that the label list the name of the country where the product was manufactured or processed. These labels must be sewn into the item; their location is designated in the act. The act does not state or imply anything regarding fiber quality used in the product, except for fine wools and cashmere. Consumers must rely on their knowledge to determine the quality and suitability of the product.

The terms that appear on the labels of wool items are defined by the FTC as follows:

1. Wool—new wool or wool fibers reclaimed from knit scraps, broken thread, and noils. (Noils are short fibers combed out in the production of worsted wool yarns.)
2. Recycled wool—scraps of new woven or felted fabrics that are garnetted or shredded back to the fibrous state and used again in the manufacture of woolens.
3. Virgin wool—wool that has never been processed in any way; thus knit clips and broken yarns cannot be labeled "virgin wool."

Fur Products Labeling Act, 1952 (Amended)

The **Fur Products Labeling Act (FPLA)** applies to furs—items of animal origin with the hair/fiber attached. The act requires that the animal's true English language name be used on labels for wearing apparel and that dyed furs be so labeled. The country of origin must be listed. The presence of used, damaged, or scrap fur must be identified. The act has been amended to identify animals by name and has expanded the list of modifications to the natural fur to include tip dyeing, pointing (coloring the tips of the guard hairs), and other means of artificially altering the color or appearance of the fur. This law does not provide for a quality designation.

The law protects consumers from buying economical furs sold under names implying expensive furs. For example, prior to this law, rabbit was sold under such highly imaginative and blatantly false names as lapin, chinchilette, ermaline, northern seal, marmink, Australian seal, Belgian beaver, and Baltic leopard. "Hudson seal" was muskrat plucked and dyed to look like seal.

Textile Fiber Products Identification Act, 1960 (Amended)

The **Textile Fiber Products Identification Act (TFPIA)** protects consumers and producers from unfair competition resulting from the unrevealed presence of substitute materials in textile products. This act was needed because several new fibers were introduced in the 1950s and 1960s that made it very difficult for consumers to know what they were purchasing. The TFPIA covers all fibers except those already covered by the Wool Products Labeling Act, with certain other exceptions.

The list of manufactured fiber generic names in Table 6.1 was established by the FTC in cooperation with fiber producers. This list is updated whenever a new generic fiber name is approved. A **generic name** is the name of a family of fibers all having similar chemical composition. (Definitions of these generic names are included with the discussion of each fiber.)

The TFPIA does not require that the label be sewn into the item, but that the information be available at the point of sale. Hangtags or printed packaging materials like those used for some apparel or bedding may list fiber content. Hangtags may combine fiber-content information as required by TFPIA with such promotional information as suggested price, size, style number, trade name, or trademark. Since hangtags are removed before use and often discarded or lost, manufacturers combine fiber-content information with such other required information as care instructions and manufacturer identification information and sew it into the item as a permanent label (see Figure 21.1).

The following information is required, in English, on the label of most textile items, including apparel, outer coverings of furniture and mattresses/box springs, bedding, and toweling.

1. The percentage of each natural or manufactured fiber present must be listed in the order of predominance by weight and correct within a tolerance of 3 percent. Thus, if a label states 50 percent cotton, the cotton content can be no less than 47 percent and no more than 53 percent.

    If a fiber or fibers represent less than 5 percent by weight of the item, the fiber cannot be named unless it has a clearly established and definite function. In those cases, the generic name, percentage by weight, and functional significance must be listed. For example, a garment that has a small amount of spandex may have a label that reads "96% Nylon, 4% Spandex for elasticity."

2. The name of the manufacturer or the company's registered WPL or RN number must be stated. Often the company's registered number is listed with the letters and the number.

3. The first time a trademark appears in the required information, it must appear in immediate conjunction with the generic name and in type or lettering of equal size and conspicuousness. When the trademark is used elsewhere on the label, the generic name must accompany it in legible and conspicuous type the first time it appears. Trademarks are not required information.

4. The name of the country where the product was processed or manufactured must be stated, such as "Made in USA." Country of origin is identified as the country where the item was assembled. That can be very confusing since the law allows labels to identify when products have been made of components assembled elsewhere. For example, jeans may be labeled "Made in USA" if they were completely assembled in the United States from domestic fabric. If the most labor-intensive parts were assembled in Jamaica, the jeans would be labeled "Made in USA of imported components" or "Made in USA of components made in Jamaica." For fabrics, country of origin refers specifically to the country where the fabric was finished. Jeans made in the United States from imported fabric would be labeled "Made in USA of imported fabric."

Guidelines and restrictions of a similar, but slightly less restrictive nature to those for labels also apply to advertising in terms of generic names, percentages, and use of trademarks or trade names. Again, the intent is to provide accurate information to the consumer to assist in purchase and use decisions.

The truth-in-fabrics laws and regulations are intended to provide consumers with accurate information about the fibers used in textile products. Specific laws and regulations address silk, wool, fur fiber, and manufactured fibers. Fibers are defined and information regarding labeling is included.

▶ Learning Activity 1

Work with a partner. Discuss how or if you use fiber content information when deciding to purchase textile products. Talk to friends, neighbors, and family members to see if they use fiber content information in making decisions to purchase textile products. Have you or any of the people you talked with experienced problems with a textile product because the fiber content was not what you thought it was? What kinds of problems did you experience? Has your behavior related to textile product purchases changed as a result of your expanding knowledge of textiles? If yes, how has it changed?

Permanent Care Labeling Regulation, 1972 (Amended)

The **Care Labeling Regulation** requires manufacturers or importers of textile wearing apparel and certain fabrics to provide an accurate, permanently attached and legible label or tag that contains regular-care information and instructions (about washing, drying, ironing, bleaching, warnings, and dry cleaning). The regulation specifies label location by product type. For example, most shirt and blouse labels should be attached at the center back neckline. Pants and trouser labels should be at the center back waistband.

The regulation was developed because of consumer complaints regarding care instructions. Revisions of the rule have required more specific, detailed information concerning only one care method for a product. Labels use common and carefully defined words (see Appendix E) or standard symbols (Figure 21.2) that have a standard meaning. When products are produced offshore and sold in the United States, they must meet U.S. **care-labeling requirements**. When a label identifies washing, it must state the washing method, water temperature, drying

The **Care Labeling Regulation** requires manufacturers or importers of textile wearing apparel and certain fabrics to provide an accurate, permanently attached and legible label or tag that contains regular-care information and instructions. Specific terms are defined in the regulation.

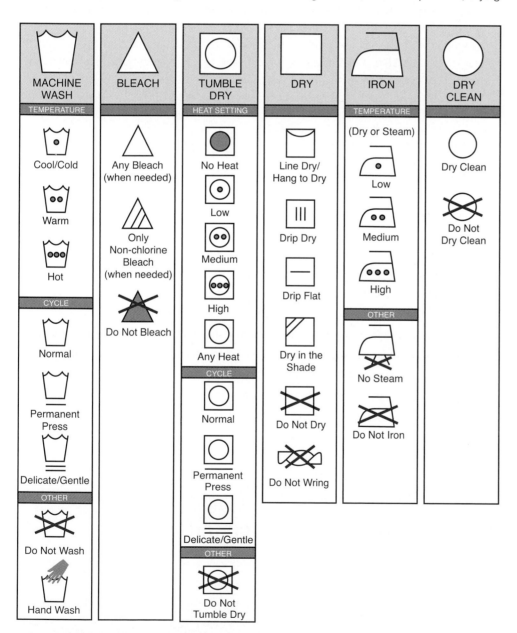

Figure 21.2 Care symbols.

SOURCE: Courtesy of the Soap and Detergent Association.

method, drying temperature, and ironing temperature, when ironing is necessary. Procedures to be avoided must be identified, such as "Only nonchlorine bleach, when necessary." If multiple care methods are appropriate for that product, the manufacturer is not required to list them on the label. If the care-label instructions are followed and some problem develops during care, the manufacturer is liable. However, if the care-label instructions are not followed, the manufacturer is not liable for any problems caused by improper care.

The rule applies to most apparel. It does not apply to leather, suede, fur garments, ties, belts, and other apparel not used to cover or protect a part of the body. Some apparel items, such as reversible garments, are required only to have removable, not permanent, care labels. For piece goods, the information must be supplied on the end of the bolt, but neither the manufacturer nor the retailer is required to provide a label to be sewn to the finished product. The rule does not apply to remnants. Although interior textiles are not required to have care labels, voluntary care labels appear on most sheets, towels, and other items.

The Federal Trade Commission and the International Fabricare Institute (IFI) work together to identify problems with compliance with the labeling regulation and to minimize future problems with inadequate and incorrect care labels. The IFI had found that many problems encountered in cleaning are due to faulty or misleading care labels.

Laws and Regulations Related to Safety

Laws and regulations addressing safety of textile products require that selected textile products meet a predetermined level of performance in terms of flammability. The procedure for flammability testing and a pass/fail scale identifying acceptable performance are included in these laws and regulations. Federal regulations often are referred to by the designation **CFR (Code of Federal Regulations)**, with the identifying numbers indicating the product category into which they fall (Table 21.1). Various governmental agencies are responsible for the enforcement

Table 21.1 Federal Standards Implementing the Flammable Fabrics Act

Item	Requirements	Test Method
Flammability of clothing, Title 16 CFR 1610	Articles of wearing apparel except interlining fabrics, certain hats, gloves, footwear.	Fabric placed in a small holder at a 45-degree angle exposed to flame for 1 second will not burn the length of the sample in less than 3.5 seconds for smooth fabrics or 4.0 seconds for napped.
Flammability of vinyl plastic film, Title 16 CFR 1611	Vinyl plastic film for wearing apparel.	A piece of film placed in a holder at a 45-degree angle will not burn faster than 1.2 inches per second.
Large carpets and rugs, Title 16 CFR 1630	Carpets greater than 6 feet in any dimension and a surface area greater than 24 square feet. Excludes vinyl or asphalt tile and linoleum. All items must meet standards.	"Pill" test. Carpet specimens exposed to methenamine tablet placed in the center of each specimen do not char more than 3 inches in any direction.
Small carpets and rugs, Title 16 CFR 1631	Carpets with no dimension greater than 6 feet and a surface area no greater than 24 square feet. Product may be sold if it does not meet standards but must be labeled: Flammable. (Fails U.S. Department of Commerce Standard FF2–70.)	Same as for large carpets and rugs.
Children's sleepwear, sizes 0–6X, Title 16 CFR 1615	Any item of wearing apparel intended to be worn for sleeping (nightgowns, pajamas, or other) up to and including size 6X. Excludes diapers and underwear. All items must meet requirements as produced and after 50 washings and dryings.	"Vertical Forced Ignition" test. Each of five fabrics is suspended vertically in holders in a cabinet and exposed to a gas flame along the bottom edge for 3 seconds. Specimens cannot have average char length of more than 7 inches.
Mattresses (and mattress pads), Title 16 CFR 1632	Ticking filled with a resilient material intended for sleeping upon, including mattress pads. Excludes pillows, box springs, sleeping bags, and upholstered furniture. All items must meet standards.	"Cigarette" test. A minimum of 9 cigarettes allowed to burn on smooth top, edge, and quilted locations of bare mattress. Char length must not exceed 2 inches in any direction from any cigarette. Tests also conducted with 9 cigarettes placed between two sheets on the mattress surface.
Children's sleepwear, sizes 7–14, Title 16 CFR 1616	Similar to 16 CFD 1615 except for size. All items must meet standards.	Similar to 16 CFR 1615.

of these safety standards, including the **Consumer Product Safety Commission** (**CPSC**, a subdivision of the FTC) and the Department of Transportation. These performance requirements may be identified as part of federal, state, or local building codes for interior textiles for public-use areas. However, when more stringent requirements are identified, these must be met by any textile product used in a structure.

Flammable Fabrics Act, 1953, and Its Amendment

Congress enacted the first national law dealing with flammable fabrics following several deaths from fire involving apparel. The **Flammable Fabrics Act** prohibits the marketing of dangerously flammable material, including all wearing apparel, regardless of fiber content or construction. One purpose of the law was to develop standards and tests to separate dangerously flammable fabrics from normally combustible ones.

Later, the act was amended to cover a broader range of apparel and interior textiles. The Consumer Product Safety Commission has broad jurisdiction over consumer safety including the Flammable Fabrics Act. Federal standards that regulate the flammability of textile products are shown in Table 21.1. These standards and/or test methods are subject to future modifications, depending on further research and evaluation.

Selected textile products must meet predetermined levels of performance related to flammability.

Figure 21.3 UFAC label.

SOURCE: Courtesy of the Upholstered Furniture Action Council.

It takes considerable time to develop a standard. First, facts must be collected to indicate a need. Then a notice is published in the Federal Register identifying a need for a standard. Interested persons are asked to respond. Test methods are developed and published in a second notice. A final notice, including details of the standard and test method, is published with the effective date of compliance. One year is usually allowed so that merchandise that does not meet the standard can be sold or otherwise disposed of and new merchandise can be altered as necessary to meet the standard.

Each year, the CPSC recalls dangerously flammable textile items that do not meet performance requirements. Sweatshirts, skirts, and jackets made from a fleece-type fabric and lined rayon, and imported rayon/cotton chiffon skirts are items that have been recalled.

Mandatory standards have been issued for children's sleepwear, sizes 0 to 6X and 7 to 14, large and small carpets and rugs, and mattresses and mattress pads. The **Upholstered Furniture Action Council (UFAC)** has issued voluntary standards for upholstered furniture. Figure 21.3 shows a UFAC label.

Some cities and states have established standards for additional textile items. Various product sectors have adopted voluntary standards for items such as tents, blankets, and career apparel for people who work near open flame.

Assessment of Textile Flammability Because of space restrictions, summaries of procedures and pass/fail scales are given here rather than full specifications. The textile product category determines the procedure and pass/fail scale used to assess performance. These procedures are described briefly because flammability is the only performance category specifically identified by federal law because it deals with human safety.

For large and small carpets and rugs, the methenamine pill test is required by CFR 1630. In this procedure, a 9-inch-diameter piece of carpet is placed in the bottom of an enclosed cube (open on the top) and held in place by a metal template with an 8-inch-diameter opening. The methenamine pill is placed in the center of the carpet sample and ignited. Samples that burn to within 1 inch of the metal template fail. Seven of the eight samples must pass for the carpet or rug to pass the test (Figure 21.4).

The Steiner tunnel test is required by many state codes and some federal agencies to assess carpet and rug flammability. In this procedure, a much larger sample (24 feet long, 20 inches wide) is placed on the ceiling of a tunnel. A double gas jet burns for 10 minutes as an air draft pulls the flame into the tunnel for a distance of approximately 4 feet. The distance the carpet sample burns is used to assess the flame-spread rating. Flame-spread ratings are

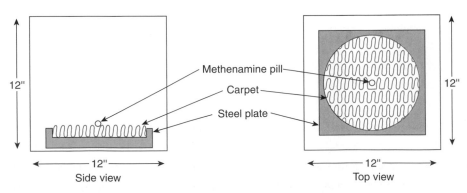

Figure 21.4 The methenamine pill test for carpets.

based on a 100-point rating scale, where 0 represents materials that will not burn and 100 represents the flammability of red oak flooring (classification A, flame spread 1 to 25; B, flame spread 26 to 75; C, flame spread 76 to 200).

The flooring radiant panel test is another procedure used by many federal agencies to assess carpet and rug flammability. In this procedure, a sample 39 inches long by 8 inches wide is mounted horizontally, preheated, and ignited. The burn distance is measured and converted into a flame-spread index. Higher numbers indicate greater resistance to flame spread and therefore greater safety.

Children's sleepwear testing requires that the fabric meet minimum flammability performance standards after 50 care cycles in order for products to be sold. The procedures are similar for 16 CFR 1615 and 16 CFR 1616. In both cases, the fabric is suspended vertically in a draft-free cabinet and exposed to an ignition flame for 3 seconds. Pass/fail ratings are based on burn time and burn length.

Regular apparel covered by 16 CFR 1610 is tested at a 45-degree angle (Figure 21.5). With an ignition time of 1 second, ignition is not necessarily guaranteed. Based on burning behavior, fabrics are classified as Class 1 (fabrics suitable for apparel, with a flame-spread time greater than 7 seconds), Class 2 (fabrics suitable for apparel, with intermediate flame spread), and Class 3 (fabrics unsuitable for apparel, with flame spreads of less than 3.5 seconds). There are distinctions within the class ratings for brushed-surface fabrics that are not included in this discussion.

Because of the concern about the flammability of upholstered furniture used by consumers, the Upholstered Furniture Action Council has developed a voluntary flame-retardant upholstery standard. Two categories of ignition propensity are identified. Class I, the safer category, indicates no ignition occurred in the fabric classification test and char lengths were less than 1.75 inches. Class II identifies fabrics that ignited in the fabric classification test. A hangtag is used to indicate the flammability rating.

In addition to the voluntary UFAC program, interior textiles are regulated by several federal departments and agencies. The Department of Health, Education, and Welfare sets fire-safety standards for health-care facilities.

Several states are considering including in their fire codes California's standards to limit fires related to upholstered furniture, especially the incorporation of a **fire block** layer in upholstered furniture and mattresses to minimize their flammability.

Federal Insecticide, Fungicide, and Rodenticide Act (FIFRA)

The **Federal Insecticide, Fungicide, and Rodenticide Act (FIFRA)**, administered by the Environmental Protection Agency (EPA), may apply to textile products that incorporate antibacterial or antimicrobial agents such as fiber additives or finishes. This act requires that product labels provide information regarding content and safety precautions (Figure 21.6). Nanosilver antimicrobial finishes may be included within the purview of this act.

Figure 21.5 The 45-degree angle tester for apparel.
SOURCE: Courtesy of SDL Atlas LLC.

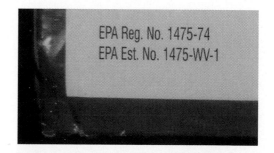

Figure 21.6 EPA Registration numbers required for the FIFRA label on a box of mothballs.

legal, sustainability, and environmental issues **513**

Consumer Product Safety Improvement Act (CPSIA)

The **Consumer Product Safety Improvement Act (CPSIA)**, also known as HR 4040, of 2008 includes components that may have far-reaching impact for entrepreneurs, resale shops, and nonprofit organizations that produce or sell children's items. The act is designed to reduce children's exposure to such toxic chemicals as lead and phthalates, which have been prevalent in many children's toys in the past few years. CPSIA requires that all consumer goods that will be used by children, except those that are naturally free of these chemicals, must be tested.. Textiles are excluded from the testing requirement, except those that include silk screen or transfer prints because some inks may contain lead. Plastic items made with polyvinyl chloride, such as baby bibs, must be tested.

Other Label Information

Mandatory and Voluntary Labeling Programs

Mandatory labeling describes acceptable and legal commercial practices for companies to follow. The law requires that the information be available and accurate, but requirements do not extend beyond that. Mandatory labeling includes care labels and fiber-content information as specified in several laws.

Voluntary practices and labeling programs are often used in marketing textile products. Voluntary programs include certification, licensing, and warranty programs, and such branding dimensions as trademarks and trade names. In many cases, a voluntary program also implies a quality-control program, since products must meet company performance and quality specifications.

Warranties can be implied or written. Implied warranties indicate that the product is suitable for the purpose for which it was marketed. For example, an implied warranty for a raincoat suggests that it will not shrink significantly when wet. The written warranties offered for some apparel and interior textiles are legally binding and imply performance at a predetermined level.

Licensing describes the situation in which one company legally uses another company's trademarks and expertise to make, use, and/or sell a product. Licensing agreements usually are restricted to specific geographic areas. For example, Company A has a licensing agreement with Company B to produce and sell in the United States a print featuring one of Company B's cartoon characters. Company A cannot sell the print outside the United States, nor can it incorporate another character in the print without negotiating another licensing agreement with Company B.

Certification programs describe agreements between fiber and fabric producers regarding product performance and trade names or trademarks. A fabric manufacturer must demonstrate that a fabric meets specified end-use performance requirements as identified by the fiber producer before the end product can be certified. For example, pillows marketed with a company's certification mark first must be tested to verify that the pillows meet its end-use specifications.

A textile may be given a **trade name** or **trademark** that distinguishes it from another textile that is made and sold by other producers. A producer may adopt a single trade name, word, or symbol, which may be used to cover all (or a large group) of the fibers made by that company. Trade names are often protected by quality-control programs.

Mandatory labeling describes acceptable and legal commercial practices for companies to follow. Voluntary programs include certification, licensing, and warranty programs, and trademarks and trade names. Implied warranties indicate that the product is suitable for the purpose for which it was marketed. The written warranties offered for some apparel and interior textiles are legally binding and imply performance at a predetermined level. Licensing describes the situation in which one company legally uses another company's trademarks and expertise to make, use, and/or sell a product. **Certification programs** describe agreements between fiber and fabric producers regarding product performance and trade names or trademarks.

The producer assumes the responsibility for promoting the product. The company must sell not only to its customers, the manufacturers and retailers, but also to their customer's customer—the consumer. Trademarks and trade names are used for fibers, finishes, yarns, and fabrics.

Codes

Codes are systematic bodies of laws or regulations that enforce adequate standards of practice and uniformity of work. Building codes generally provide minimum levels of performance and ensure safety for people who live, work, shop, or otherwise use these buildings. All too often codes are developed following a tragedy that results in great loss of life, such as night club or hotel fires. Federal, state, and local city or county codes for interiors often include in their purview such textile products as upholstery, wall and floor coverings, and window-treatment fabrics. Frequently, codes deal with fire prevention and control the flammability of textiles used in interiors.

> Codes are systematic bodies of laws or regulations that enforce adequate standards of practice and uniformity of work. Torts address behaviors that interfere with personal rights.

Most fire-prevention regulations are based on occupancy classification (business, apartment, industrial, mercantile, health care, educational, etc.); fuel-load classification (museum, office building, retail shop, paint shop, warehouse, mobile home, underground structure, etc.); occupancy load (number of people); and type of occupancy (adults, children, elderly, or physically disabled). Unfortunately, building codes from the various agencies and government groups are not uniform. For example, federal agencies have adopted the Unified Building Code (UBC) and all standards and codes of the National Fire Protection Association (NFPA) and the American National Standards Institute (ANSI). However, county, city, and state codes often reflect situations that may be unique to their locale, such as codes for high-rise apartment and office buildings.

The jurisdiction of codes depends on several factors, briefly discussed here. In general, federal codes are applicable to federal buildings or those built with federal funds, such as hospitals. State codes apply to state-owned buildings such as schools, state hospitals, and public buildings where large crowds are common. City and county codes often are incorporated in zoning ordinances. If two codes are applicable in a specific situation, the more stringent code prevails. Designers are expected to ensure that the textile products they select meet the specified code requirements. This may mean that products be tested following the standard procedure specified in the code and that adequate performance records be kept.

In addition to knowing code requirements, designers should check with insurance company representatives early in the design process, since their decisions may significantly affect insurance rates for interiors. Designers must know that some finishes and fabrication methods may interfere with inherently flame-retardant fiber characteristics. All products, including those made from inherently flame-retardant fibers, should be tested to ensure that they meet code requirements. For example, the toxicity rule for the state of New York requires that companies register their products with the state if they wish to sell in New York. This rule has fire–gas toxicity ratings for carpets and for curtains, draperies, and wall coverings. The registration system removes the requirement of having each fabric individually tested at a substantial cost per fabric.

Codes applicable to upholstery fabrics include those listed for window-treatment fabrics. The procedures listed in these codes assess flammability by several methods. However, all regulate the length of time allowed for self-extinguishment of the flame and afterglow. The methods also identify the maximum allowable length or area of fabric that may burn or char during the test. Samples tested include pieces of fabric, mockups of the upholstery and padding, and full-scale tests that use a real piece of upholstered furniture.

Wall coverings are rated for flammability, durability, and stain resistance and, depending on the applicable code, may need to meet any or all requirements. Window treatments usually are not regulated by codes, but those that cover more than 10 percent of the wall area may be considered an interior finish. The codes most often cited for window-treatment fabrics are those of the cities of Boston and New York, the state of California, and the commonwealth of Massachusetts.

The NFPA 701 Small Scale Test and the NFPA 702 Large Scale Test are used to assess the flammability of curtains, draperies, upholstery, and wall coverings. In these procedures, the sample is ignited, and afterflame and length of char for both warp and filling directions are measured. The length of afterflame cannot exceed 2 seconds. In the large-scale test, dripping also is assessed. In the small-scale test, length of permissible char depends on fabric weight; in the large-scale test, it cannot exceed 10 inches, or 35 inches if the fabric is folded.

Interior textiles in airplanes and motor vehicles are regulated by the Federal Aviation Administration and the Department of Transportation, respectively. Flame retardancy is mandated for all textiles used in these interiors, including seat cushions and backs, seat belts, and interior roof, side, and wall panels. The standard extends to other items to augment the crashworthiness and emergency evacuation equipment of airplanes.

Tort

Torts address behaviors that interfere with personal rights. Torts generally are categorized as either negligence or intentional torts. Negligence torts include substandard performance with regard to legal and regulatory requirements and contracts. Acceptable levels of performance are described as professional standards of care and usually are identified in professional codes of ethics. An example of substandard performance could include a product manager's failure to verify that a fabric meets appropriate flame-retardance requirements.

Intentional torts are wrongful acts performed in a deliberate fashion and may include deliberate misrepresentation and strict liability. For example, deliberate misrepresentation would include knowingly labeling a rayon/polyester crash as "all-linen crash." Strict liability generally applies to the physical harm caused to a user or consumer if a product is defective and unreasonably dangerous. Strict liability, which holds people liable even in circumstances in which they were not negligent, applies to manufacturers, suppliers, retailers, and others.

Consumer Recourse

When consumers purchase products, they enter into an implied contract. They expect the product to perform and to meet their needs. In most cases, textile products perform satisfactorily. However, at times, products do not meet the consumer's expectations. Reasons for textile failure include improper care labels, improper dyeing or finishing, and improper use by consumers.

Problems with care labels are a great concern to both consumers and businesses. When care-label instructions are followed and the result is disastrous, consumers expect to be compensated for their loss. Many stores take returns of this nature; however, some do not. In these cases, the consumer can complain to the manufacturer or the Federal Trade Commission, since incorrect care labels are prohibited by the Care Label Regulation. Other reasons for product failure include poor design, improper selection of dyes or finishes, inappropriate combination of materials in a product, improper fabric processing, or poor fabric selection for an end use. In all cases, manufacturers should be informed of the problem either by direct notification or by returning the item to the place of purchase. The address of the regional office of the Federal Trade Commission is in most telephone directories. Consumers should write to or call the FTC and include the manufacturer's name or RN/WPL number. The FTC can then identify the manufacturer and provide the consumer with the address for direct correspondence.

Textile and apparel professionals usually take a stronger position when products result in consumer complaints. Frequently, the professional is responsible for dealing with the unhappy consumer or for some production process. In either case, the professional's responsibility is to identify the source of the problem and suggest a solution that will satisfy both the consumer and the company.

▶ Learning Activity 6

Work in groups of three or four. Define code and tort and discuss their legal implications. If you work for a business that unknowingly violates a code, law, regulation, copyright, or trademark and the violation is discovered, how might that information be used in a civil lawsuit addressing unfair business practices? How might that information be used if the violation resulted in personal injury or death? What might be the penalty for individual employees of a firm that committed such a violation?

▶ Learning Activity 7

Consider a recent textile product failure you have experienced. Describe the failure and determine if the failure was because of your behavior or due to an error in product development, material production, labeling, or construction. (For example, an item that shrinks excessively when cleaned following the care label instructions may have been improperly finished.) Describe how you would proceed to get recourse from the retailer and/or producer. Have you ever returned something because of product failure? Were you satisfied with your interaction with the store or producer? Why or why not?

Sustainability Issues

Sustainability describes practices and policies that reduce environmental pollution, do not exploit people or natural resources in meeting the lifestyle needs of the present, and do not compromise the future. Sustainability has broad-reaching implications. It encompasses many areas including human rights, energy use, materials use, production, consumption, disposal, and recycling. It addresses both current practices and future implications. Materials and products are made from recyclable materials and renewable resources and do not pollute the environment at any stage of production or processing. Materials are biodegradable. Workers and animals are treated with dignity and respect.

Full life cycle analysis is becoming more important. **Life cycle analysis** examines the way the production, use, care, and disposal of a product affects the environment and the people involved with the product. This means that the assessment include everything from the raw materials through the treatment of waste generated during production or processing as well as impacts from consumer use, cleaning, and disposal or recycling of the product. Human rights assessment within production facilities, animal welfare, and cultural impacts may also be included in the assessment.

Professionals frequently deal with sustainability issues. Although an in-depth exploration of all elements regarding sustainability is not possible here, several concerns and efforts within the global textile complex are included to assist in developing awareness and a knowledge base.

Consumers can influence what is available in the market by their demand for **green,** eco, environmentally friendly, recycled, or sustainable **products**. However, these terms are not well defined or understood. Some products are evaluated by recognized certification organizations to verify their environmental claims. Table 21.2 summarizes several certification organizations and standards focusing on textiles and related products.

Consumer practices also have a significant environmental impact. Consider the diaper dilemma. A conservative estimate is that each baby will use 5,000 diapers in his or her first 30 months, with an annual total of 19 billion diapers in the United States alone. Many babies in the United States wear only disposables from birth through toilet training. Reusable fabric diapers may leak, require special handling, and use significant amounts of water and laundry additives in cleaning. Disposable diapers are easy to use, convenient, and readily available. But they make up at least 2 percent of landfill material and must be disposed of properly to avoid fecal contamination of ground water.

Consumers and professionals are faced with many difficult choices when it comes to textile products. Environmental correctness is another dimension in the decision-making matrix. Which of two shirting fabrics is better—polyester or cotton? While the choice may seem obvious, the polyester shirt is made from recycled beverage bottles, and the 100 percent cotton shirt is made from cotton produced using current large-scale farming practices.

Identifying the complete environmental ramifications of the production, distribution, use, care, and disposal of textile products is a complex and multidimensional problem. Many assumptions made by consumers are far too simplistic. For example, assuming that all natural fibers are better for the environment as compared with any synthetic fiber ignores many environmental issues related to land use, current farming or harvesting practices, fiber-processing needs, finishing and dyeing practices, use and care of the product by consumers, and disposal or recycling of the product once the consumer is finished with it. A full life cycle analysis of a product is an involved process. Unfortunately, much of the information is conflicting, misleading, or missing so that the total picture is not clear.

Table 21.2 Sustainability and Related Certification Organizations and Standards

Name	Description	Impact
Oeko-Tex Standard 100 and Standard 1000	European certification standard for acceptable limits for extract pH, heavy-metal content, colorfastness, carcinogenic and sensitizing dyes, pesticides, emissions of volatile substances, and other textile aspects with environmental or user hazards.	Widespread changes in production and materials.
Scientific Certification Systems	Multidisciplinary scientific organization verifies environmental claims; provides detailed environmental profile for products and packaging based on life cycle analysis.	Product certification.
Global Organic Textile Standards (GOTS)	Standards developed by an international group of certification bodies to certify from field to final product.	Provide for two labels: organic or made with X% organic.
ISO 1400	ISO (International Organization for Standardization) standards address environmental management in the global market and is a primary requirement for doing business in many regions and industries.	Product certification.
Bluesign	A practice-oriented standard that implements resources related to environment, health, and safety for products.	Includes all textile processes.
Nordic Swan Ecolabel	Identifies products that have a positive effect on the environment; examines factors throughout the lifecycle from raw material, production, distribution, use, and waste disposal. Considers use of natural resources, energy, air and water emissions, and generation of noise and waste.	Widespread product impact, but few are textiles.
Green Seal Product Standards	Independent, nonprofit organization that protects the environment by promoting production and sale of environmentally responsible consumer products.	Life cycle analysis of products.
Global Reporting Initiative (GRI) Social Performance Indicators	International organization that focuses on suppliers, products and services and reports on workplace and human rights.	Employees and communities.
Life Cycle Assessment (LCA)	Evaluates and discloses environmental claims regarding sustainable, green, or environmentally preferred products.	Addresses life cycle analysis of product.
SMART (The Institute for Market Transformation to Sustainability)	Rating system that examines multiple dimensions of environmental, social, and economic benefits over the supply chain; business benefits; and life cycle analysis.	Includes textiles, interiors, and apparel products.
GreenBlue	A for-profit consultant company that works with suppliers, designers, and retailers to make product design ecologically and socially sound; includes Clean Gredients (cleaning products) and Sustainable Packaging Coalition (packaging materials).	Manufacturers of cleaning compounds and packaging materials.
Global Recycling Standards (GRS)	A three-tiered certification system based on the amount of recycled content in any specific product; includes environmental processing criteria and raw materials.	Bronze, gold, and silver levels.
Cradle to Cradle Certificate	Ecological certificate for product materials, focuses on environmental and human health, recyclability or compostability; includes approved ingredient category; combines science and design to move beyond sustainability to adopt eco-effective strategies to use only healthy materials and design so fibers become nutrients for future textiles; modeled after natural systems with a closed loop of production, use, recovery, and reproduction.	Applicable to textiles and textile products. Includes designing for disassembly and reuse.

Retailers work with suppliers to reduce use of environmentally harmful materials and processes, to decrease energy use, to improve workers' rights, to improve communities in which production facilities are located, to reduce negative impacts on human health, to reduce use of packaging materials, and to improve recycling of materials. Corporate environmental policies require that suppliers meet their standards. Engineers visit textile facilities to ensure that standard practices related to the work environment, handling and use of chemicals, wastewater treatment, and recycling programs meet the firm's expectations. All environmentally conscious companies face stiff competition from companies who ignore these issues and the related expenses. Social and environmental responsibilities are gaining the interest of governments, producers, and consumers worldwide.

Professionals deal with these kinds of problems on a daily basis. Although an in-depth exploration of all elements regarding sustainability is not possible here, several concerns and efforts within the global textile complex are included to assist in developing awareness.

Environmental Issues

Environmental issues affect production of fiber, yarn, fabric, finishes, dyes, and pigments; distribution of components or finished goods; product use and cleaning, and waste and product disposal. These areas concern producers, retailers, consumers, and others. Many industries have realized that environmental challenges are important part of doing business in the global market.

In the United States, two federal agencies work to protect the environment and create safe working conditions. The **Environmental Protection Agency (EPA)** enforces and regulates air, water, and noise pollution and waste disposal. The **Occupational Safety and Health Administration (OSHA)** develops and enforces standards for safety and educational training programs for workers. Individual states and other countries have environmental and worker safety divisions. Some countries have adopted environmental standards that are more severe than those of the United States.

The global textile complex is often identified as one of the most polluting industries. Many segments, especially fiber producers, dyers and finishers, have modified processes, researched new chemicals, and implemented processing changes to decrease the environmental impact. At one time, the textile complex discharged great quantities of water contaminated with dyes, finishing chemicals, cleaning compounds, wax and lanolin removed from natural fibers, and compounds used to produce manufactured and synthetic fibers into rivers, streams, and lakes. Estimates are that 85 percent of the water used in producing textiles was used in dyeing and finishing. Emissions into the air included excess heat, fly ash, carbon dioxide, formaldehyde, and sulfurous and nitrous compounds that contribute to acid rain. Excess packaging, discarded cardboard and paper goods, empty metal drums, and hazardous and toxic chemicals were deposited in landfills. Other environmental problems once included high-intensity noise in spinning and weaving rooms and dust and airborne debris in opening and spinning areas. The processing of textiles from raw materials into finished products used large amounts of water and energy. However, the global textile complex has reduced energy use and environmental impact and improved its perception by the public. Efforts to reduce the environmental impact of the global textile complex continue. Research using ultrasonic systems, enzymes, foam finishing, and nanotechnology in finishing is being driven by sensitivity to reducing costs, improving product performance, enhancing sustainability, and decreasing environmental impact.

The components of wastewater and its processing in a **water treatment** facility address water quality. The presence and level of polluting materials in wastewater, regardless of the source—manufacturing facility, athletic complex, school, park, lawn, home, or office—is assessed in several ways. Surface water systems are frequently contaminated with chemicals and other materials. Often this is a natural process that develops because of the plants and animals that live in or near the water. The contaminants in the water are broken down, usually by microorganisms that occur in the natural environment. However, when the contaminants in the water, whether from nature or human activity, become excessive, water quality problems develop. **Biological oxygen demand (BOD)** describes the amount of oxygen necessary for the decomposition of organic wastes in the water. **Chemical oxygen demand (COD)** describes the amount of oxygen necessary to reduce a soluble organic compound to carbon dioxide and water. A high BOD or COD indicates such a large amount of contamination that fish and other aquatic life might die. Wastewater is treated to speed up natural purification processes and to reduce contaminants that might interfere with these natural processes.

Treating wastewater requires several steps. In preliminary treatment, large debris such as wood and sand is physically removed by screening or slowing the water to allow the heavy materials to settle out. In primary settling, the water spends several quiet hours in large tanks, where most of the suspended solids (raw sludge) settle to the bottom. Bottom scrapers remove the sludge while skimmers collect oil and grease from the surface. Microorganisms in oxygen-rich trickling filters or activated sludge tanks accelerate the natural decay of waste. Four to twelve hours later, in final clarification, the microorganisms are removed from the wastewater by settling or straining.

Wastewater from fiber processing, dyeing, and finishing receives additional processing to remove salts, dyes or pigments, other organic compounds, heavy metals, and finishing chemicals. Carbon adsorption removes organic compounds, color, and chlorine; ultrafiltration reduces turbidity; reverse osmosis and electrodialysis remove dissolved solids; oxidation and ozonation remove color; and demineralization removes salts (Figure 21.7). With membrane technology, latex from carpet manufacturing, salt from dyeing, and sizing materials from weaving and finishing can be recovered and recycled.

Figure 21.7 Hollow fiber membranes filter contaminants and microorganisms during water treatment.
SOURCE: Courtesy of Siemens Water Technologies.

Environmental Laws and Regulations

More than a dozen significant laws and regulations have been passed since the establishment of the Environmental Protection Agency. Environmental concerns include air and water quality, pollution prevention, and resource recovery.

More than a dozen significant laws and regulations have been passed since the establishment of the Environmental Protection Agency. This discussion focuses on those that have had the greatest impact on textile processes.

The **Pollution Prevention Act** (1990) addresses waste minimization (Figure 21.8). Efforts focus on source reduction, environmentally sound recycling, treatment of toxic chemicals, and disposal of waste materials in registered toxic-dump landfills. Source reduction minimizes waste by substituting less hazardous or less harmful materials when possible and emphasizes product reformulation, process modification, improved cleaning standards and practices, and environmentally sound, closed-loop recycling. Companies are required to maintain a toxic-release inventory to help improve practices from both cost and environmental perspectives.

The **Clean Air Act** (1970) focuses on air quality and addresses acid rain, toxic air emissions, and ozone. Acid rain is produced when water droplets in the air combine with air pollutants such as sulfur dioxide and nitrous oxides. Textile production and finishing use large quantities of hot water and steam. Stack emissions can be minimized by limiting fly ash from coal-burning units, sulfur dioxide and nitrous oxide (by-products of burning fuels that contribute to acid rain), and fume emissions from processes. The EPA is the authority responsible for establishing restrictions and enforcing policy related to this act.

The **Clean Water Act** (1972) is concerned with toxic contamination of ground or surface water. Modifications to the handling of wastewater ensure that discharge meets or exceeds current standards. The EPA is the authority that establishes surface water quality standards and enforces them.

The **Resource Conservation and Recovery Act** (1976) (RCRA) regulates solid- and hazardous-waste disposal from generation to final disposal, including transportation, treatment, and storage of hazardous materials. The EPA determines which wastes pose a human health or environmental hazard from "cradle to grave" or production to disposal.

In the European Union (EU), a comprehensive piece of legislation, **REACH** (Registration, Evaluation, Authorization, and Restriction of Chemicals), became effective in 2007. It has

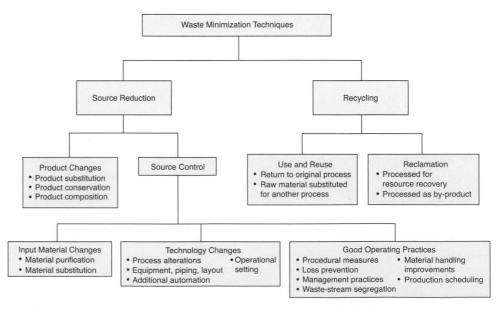

Figure 21.8 **Waste minimization within the global textile complex.**
SOURCE: Courtesy of *Textile World.*

significant implications for other geographic regions that are part of the global textile complex. REACH affects every industry importing or producing chemicals in the EU. REACH is intended to protect the environment and human health. Companies are required to prove that chemicals are environmentally safe and provide safety information for users and, in some cases, consumers.

REACH incorporates several components for every chemical used. Registration occurs before manufacturing or importing chemicals. Information about each chemical, risk management, and a safety report are required. Evaluation allows the regulatory agency to determine if the information provided is complete, if more information or testing is needed, and if restrictions or authorization requirements should be imposed. Authorization is required for chemicals deemed to be of very high concern because of their human health or environmental risk. Chemical restriction applies to chemicals that present an unacceptable risk.

Evaluation, record keeping, and communication are essential components of REACH. Companies need to know the chemical history of each chemical produced or imported. It is expected that some special finishes and dyes will disappear from the EU as REACH becomes fully implemented. While the impact on retailers is expected to be minimal, it may be difficult to achieve specific colors. More production may move offshore. Several other countries will likely develop similar legislation in the near future.

Efforts within the Global Textile Complex

Figure 21.9 shows a textile-processing material balance model that identifies what happens to substances used to process raw materials into finished textile products. Any substance that is used in the process leaves the system as either a component of a finished product or as waste. Waste from a plant should be treated before being discharged into the air or water or onto the land.

The global textile complex has reduced the amount of waste generated in textile processing by significant percentages by changing methods and materials so that a facility generates less waste. Jet-dyeing machines use less water. Continuous dyeing, which used huge quantities of water, dyes, and chemicals, has been partially replaced with beck dyeing, which uses

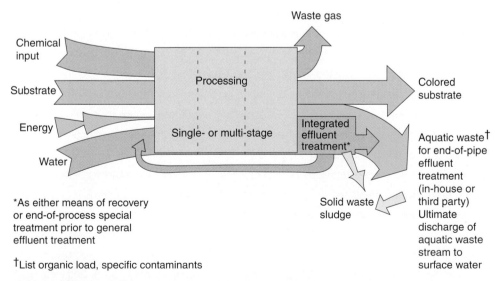

*As either means of recovery or end-of-process special treatment prior to general effluent treatment

†List organic load, specific contaminants

Figure 21.9 Dyeing process balance sheet.

SOURCE: Reprinted with permission from Nelson, G. (1991). Microencapsulates in textile coloration and finishing. *Review of Progress in Coloration,* 21, pp. 72–85. Published by the Society of Dyers and Colourists, Bradford, UK.

smaller quantities of these materials. Water usage has decreased and water quality discharged from production facilities has improved. Energy use has decreased.

Low-impact dyes and pigments are more commonly used. New sulfur dyes eliminate sulfide wastes, metal-free dyes replace metal-complex dyes, direct dyes use less salt, acid and mordant dyes use iron rather than chromium, reactive dyes have greater use efficiencies, and more disperse dyes work in water-based systems. Reactive dyes have been developed that use a tiny fraction of the salt compared to earlier reactive dyes. Pigment inks are often water-based rather than solvent-based, and many are formaldehyde free. The metal content of pigment inks has decreased. Digital printing offers great potential for sustainable printing since this process wastes nothing: no fabric is printed except what is used in products and virtually no solvent is used.

By focusing on improving the quality of fabrics, doing things right the first time also means less use of stripping agents to remove color and less redyeing of fabrics that were not dyed correctly the first time. Thus, a better quality of goods is produced with less waste.

Environmental Health and Safety

The EPA issues permissible exposure levels for hundreds of chemicals that are known to be or are likely to be human carcinogens. OSHA sets standards for air quality in the workplace, including a formaldehyde standard. **Formaldehyde** has been identified as a carcinogen and had been used in some durable-press treatments, leather finishing, and dyeing applications. Exposure limits included in the standard relate to a permissible exposure limit (PEL), a short-term exposure limit (STEL), and an action level (AL) for workers. Off-gassing (releasing fumes or gases from a material into the air) formaldehyde at levels of 0.1 ppm or more creates problems with indoor air quality and may adversely affect the health of those working or living in that environment.

Another chemical on the EPA list is perchloroethylene (perc), one of the solvents most commonly used in dry cleaning. Regulations at federal and state levels restrict the use and disposal of perc with detailed record-keeping requirements. Changes in standard dry cleaning practices and new dry-to-dry units have substantially decreased workplace and environmental problems with perc.

Indoor air quality has become a major concern. Indoor air pollution develops from many sources that may emit volatile organic compounds (VOCs), including textile products. Carpeting, carpet padding, fabrics used in interiors and apparel, latex backcoatings, finishes, and dyes on textiles have been identified as contributing to this problem. Buildings with poor ventilation and indoor air pollution may have sick building syndrome, in which occupants experience a variety of health problems. Textile manufacturers have changed production materials and methods to reduce off-gassing problems.

Health hazards involved in textile production relate to reducing noise and dust levels in fiber- and yarn-processing areas and in weaving rooms. Toxic and hazardous chemicals have been replaced with less toxic and less hazardous chemicals or by limiting human exposure when the use of alternative chemicals is not feasible. Safety devices have been incorporated into equipment at the design stage or added to older equipment to minimize risk in the workplace.

Multiple chemical sensitivity is a chronic problem for some people. Carpet and installation materials (glues, pads, etc.), fabric finishes, dyes, components in inks used on printed textiles, and cleaning compounds contribute to the problem. Some products incorporate no bleaches, finishes, or dyes.

Disposal and Recycling

Concern for the environment also extends to disposal of textiles. Currently, very few textiles are **recycled**, although the percentage is increasing with awareness and changes in technology. Recycling facilities may refuse textiles because of the numbers of generic fibers present, the small quantities of materials in each item, and the difficulties of shredding these items. Textiles tangle shredders and cause malfunctions or excess wear.

Normally easily biodegradable items such as newsprint, natural fiber textiles, and grass do not degrade under landfill conditions. Most communities require recycling of newspaper, junk mail, cans, clear glass bottles, plastic materials of specific types, and yard waste so that landfill space is reserved for hazardous materials. At present, textile products are not included in the list of products that must be recycled. Many consumers recycle apparel and interior textiles by donating items to organizations. Member firms of the Council for Textile Recycling divert 93 percent of the 2.5 billion pounds of postconsumer textile product waste from landfills to used clothing dealers, exporters, rag graders, and various parts of the global textile complex for use in recycled products.

Textile products use a significant amount of packaging materials. Sustainable packaging includes minimizing use of materials, use of recycled materials (hangtags, plastic wraps, and cardboard), and use of quickly degradable materials. Some firms have decreased the amount and number of types of packaging materials for consumer products. This decreases the costs of materials and labor for packaging and the weight of packaged goods. It also decreases the amount of packaging with which the consumer must deal. For example, shirts once packaged with six straight pins, tissue paper, cardboard flat and collar stands, and plastic bags are now packaged with only one plastic bag and two straight pins.

A significant quantity of the chemicals used in producing manufactured and synthetic fibers are recycled. For example, membrane filtration systems allow for the recovery and reuse of sizing from warp yarns. Not only does this process reuse a chemical, but it also minimizes the processing needed to purify water discharge from the plant. In the manufacture of lyocell, the solvent is recycled and reused numerous times.

Revising production methods to limit the variety of fiber types present in such products as carpets facilitates their recycling when discarded. Recycling nylon 6, made from a single monomer, is a simpler process than that required for recycling other fibers that are copolymers. Polyester fibers are made by recycling plastic beverage bottles (Figure 21.10). Other recycled synthetic fibers are used in fiberfill, carpeting, sleeping bags, hazard fences, apparel, and other textile products. Most fiberglass insulation used in buildings and homes is 30 to 40 percent recycled glass. Recycling synthetic fibers decreases the use of landfill space, saves petroleum for other uses, uses less energy, and eliminates harmful air emissions.

Denim scrap is recycled into yarn, pencils, paper, paper money, stationery, sludge for compost to improve garden soil, denim fabric of 50 percent reprocessed and 50 percent new fiber, and handwoven rugs (Figure 21.11). Textile waste fiber is used in nonwoven products for furniture, wiping cloths, coating substrates, filters, geotextiles, floor coverings, car interiors, floor mats, mattresses, and shoulder pads. Waste cotton fiber is recycled and used in apparel, interior textiles, and technical products such as mop yarns and in other materials for the absorbent trade. Figure 21.12 shows numerous options for postconsumer recycled textiles.

Materials used to protect textiles during shipping are being recycled. Fabric rolls are wrapped in reusable polyethylene wrap. Many firms have decreased the use of cardboard tubes and plastic wraps while not compromising fabric condition or quality. Many firms use recycled or recyclable tubes and wraps for fabric and finished products.

Figure 21.10 A T-shirt made from recycled polyester fibers.

Figure 21.11 Recycling denim: pencils made from scraps, and a rag rug.

Case Study
Floor Coverings*

Rugs and carpets can trap significant amounts of allergens (chemicals and other materials such as pet dander and dust mites that cause an allergic reaction). Some materials used in carpets and rugs produce VOCs that can give some people headaches and respiratory problems. It is more challenging to remove allergens from larger and thicker pile carpets and rugs compared to smaller or no-pile ones. Frequent cleaning of carpets and rugs with a vacuum cleaner equipped with a HEPA filter and an annual professional cleaning help address the problem.

Carpets and rugs with the Green Label or Green Label Plus from the Carpet and Rug Institute are certified to have low VOC emissions. To reduce the problem with VOC emissions verify that adhesives used in applying the carpet or rug do not emit VOCs,

DISCUSSION QUESTIONS

1. Why are allergens a concern regarding air quality?
2. What kinds of materials are sources of VOCs?
3. How do VOCs contribute to air quality problems?
4. What other certification programs or organizations assess green claims for products?
5. Do you own or use any textile products that are certified by at least one of these organizations? Why did you purchase the item? Are you satisfied with its performance? Will you purchase more such items? Why or why not?

*Roehrig, E. (2009, March). Could your rug make you sick? *Health, 23*(2), p. 104.

suggested readings

Ben-Shabat, H. (2007). Green is the new black. *Textiles, 34*(4), pp. 17–18.

Braungart, M. (2006). Cradle to cradle. *Textiles, 33*(1), pp. 8–11.

Domina, T., & Koch, K. (1997). The textile waste life cycle. *Clothing and Textile Research Journal, 15*(2), pp. 96–102.

Elliott, E. J. (1996, February). Recycling: Saving money and the environment. *Textile World*, pp. 72–74.

Environmental stewardship. (2001, February). *America's Textiles International*, pp. 31–33.

Esty, D. C., & Winston, A. S. (2006). *Green to Gold: How Smart Companies Use Environmental Strategy to Innovate, Create, Value, and Build Competitive Advantage.* New Haven, NJ: Yale University Press.

Fletcher, K. (2008). *Sustainable Fashion and Textiles: Design Journey.* London: Earthscan.

Gale, M. E., Shin, J., & Bide, M. (2000). Textiles and the environment from AATCC. *Textile Chemist and Colorist and American Dyestuff Reporter, 32*(1), pp. 28–31.

Geisberger, A. (1997, July/August). Azo dyes and the law—An open debate. *Journal of the Society of Dyers and Colourists,* 113, pp. 197–200.

Gross, E. (1999, September). Home textiles listen to the eco movement. *Textile World*, pp. 81–82, 84, 86, 88.

Harmon, S. K. (1994). *The Codes Guidebook for Interiors.* New York: Wiley.

Hethorn, J., & Ulasewicz, C. (2008). *Sustainable Fashion: Why Now?* New York: Fairchild Books.

Leonard, C. (2007). What dye would you like to go with your organic cotton? *AATCC Review, 7*(05), pp. 28.

Lewis, P. (2009). Better safe than sorry? *The Crafts Report, 35*(395), pp. 42–43.

Lloyd, J. (2007). REACH: Threat or opportunity? *Textiles, 34*(3), pp. 14–16.

Maxwell, D. (2007). On the road to sustainability. *Textiles, 34*(4), pp. 10–12.

McCoy, M. (2008). Converging pathways. *Chemical and Engineering News, 86*(33), pp. 47–56.

McDonough, W., & Braungart, M. (2002). *Cradle to Cradle: Remaking the Way We Make Things*. New York: North Point Press.

Pullen, J. (1995, March). D-13 textile and apparel care labeling standards. *ASTM Standardization News*, pp. 42–47.

Reznikoff, S. C. (1989). *Specifications for Commercial Interiors*. New York: Watson-Guptill.

Roehrig, E. (2009, March). Could your rug make you sick? *Health, 23*(2), p. 104.

Textile laws and regulations can be viewed on the Federal Trade Commission website (www.ftc.gov/) and by searching for the law or regulation by name.

Thiry, M. C. (2008). Ecological edict. *AATCC Review, 8*(1), pp. 24–29.

Thiry, M. C. (2007). If the environment is important. *AATCC Review, 7*(5), pp. 20–28.

Thiry, M. C. (2006). Thirsty industry. *AATCC Review, 6*(7), pp. 21–24.

Tortora, P. G., & Merkel, R. S. (1996). *Fairchild's Dictionary of Textiles*, 7th ed. New York: Fairchild Publications.

Wang, Y. (Ed.). (2006). *Recycling in Textiles*. Cambridge, England: Woodhead.

CAREER
EXPLORATION

CHAPTER OBJECTIVES

- To understand how textile knowledge is used by professionals.
- To recognize the need to communicate textiles information quickly and accurately to other professionals and consumers.
- To be aware of the diverse career options requiring a knowledge of textiles.

22

Since the science of textiles has been explored in some depth, it may be helpful to know how this information is used in various careers. General terms and sample job titles are used, since each company, firm, or agency may be organized differently. Essential abilities for most positions in the global textile complex include good communication and teamwork skills, correct use of terms when communicating with others, application of knowledge, analysis of information, problem solving and critical thinking skills, creativity, organizational and time management skills, and computer application skills. The specific knowledge and approach will depend on the portion of the supply chain in which the firm is focused (Figure 22.1). For example, the handling and marketing of a fabric being sold to a manufacturer differs from that of a fabric being sold to an individual consumer.

Each section in this chapter includes a general discussion of skills and knowledge, positions/job titles, and responsibilities. Although this chapter explores many career possibilities, it is not complete. The goal is to demonstrate the range of positions available and to explain how a knowledge of textiles will help in obtaining a position and career advancement. Because it becomes dated so quickly, salary information is not included. There are many websites that include information about positions and careers. These sites usually include requirements, responsibilities, performance expectations, and salary and benefits information. Many entry-level positions include assistant, associate, or trainee as part of the position title. Examples include associate designer, visual merchandising assistant, or management trainee. A range of positions are included: entry, mid-level, and upper level. In many cases, the difference between entry and mid-level has to do with the number of projects one person manages or supervises

> Essential abilities for most positions in the global textile complex include good communication and teamwork skills, correct use of terms when communicating with others, application of knowledge, analysis of information, problem-solving and critical-thinking skills, creativity, organizational and time management skills, and computer application skills.

▶ Learning Activity 1

Work in groups of three or four. Identify a job or leadership position you have held. Describe the skills and knowledge you used in the position. Explain two things that you learned about working with people in that position that will apply in most team situations.

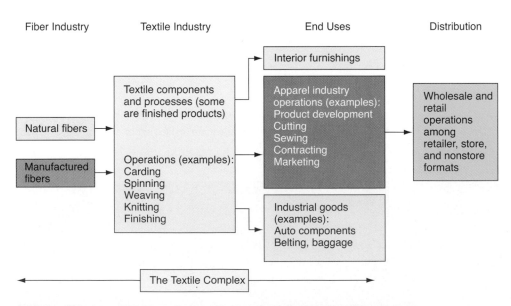

Figure 22.1 The supply chain for the global textile complex.

SOURCE: Modified from K. G. Dickerson (1999), *Textiles and Apparel in the Global Economy.* Upper Saddle River, NJ: Merrill.

and the level of independence under which he or she makes decisions. With very few exceptions, the position describes responsibilities within a team. Other team members have different titles and responsibilities. Frequent interactions with team members enable each person to accomplish the responsibilities inherent in the position.

Sourcing

Materials and production **sourcing** deals with identifying the supplier for the materials or services needed. Sourcing positions require some professional and international experience. Sourcing specialists need to understand textiles, textile products, production, marketing, performance and quality evaluation, and products or services. The ability to write and understand product/service specifications is critical. Sourcing specialists must have good communication skills in English and other languages and a global perspective. Sourcing specialists need strong analytical and decision-making skills. They are detail oriented and have good problem-solving skills. They offer logistical support and ensure that suppliers meet company standards. Some position titles include product preparation analyst, supplier performance supervisor, and operations specialist. Sourcing production involves contractor selection and management of products throughout production. Fabric and trim buyers find producers who can meet fabric and trim requirements and negotiate color, cost, and logistics.

Mical is a knit production assistant sourcing manager for a retailer who produces private label merchandise. "I help develop and execute our sourcing plan for all knit categories. I work with my supervisor to identify new suppliers so that our sourcing needs are met. This includes prelim costs, social compliance, factory assessment, logistics, and delivery/financial details. I'm part of a cross-functional team with development where we take things from concept to line adoption. One of our biggest issues is sourcing fabric. We work together to achieve a good product mix. Part of our job is to negotiate prices and determine strategies for replenishment for products that are selling through. We work hard at establishing and maintaining good relationships with our suppliers. You really have to have a diplomat's mindset to do this job. There is a lot of networking and negotiation involved. I like to travel and experience new things, which is really good for this job. It is demanding, but I like the analytical and problem-solving parts of the job. I'm amazed at how much I have to rely on my old textbooks. I can't remember everything and they really help me do my job!"

Production specialists may be responsible for follow-up to ensure that the contract will be met, that items are shipped on time, and that shipping occurs as contracted. With offshore production, sourcing specialists must be familiar with import/export requirements and regulations. Trade specialists, trade advisors, or customs brokers work with customs officials to minimize problems or to solve them as they develop. A sourcing agent is a specialist who works in a specific country and is an essential individual for international full-package sourcing. The agent deals with all aspects of sourcing offshore, including materials sourcing, production, and import/export issues. Some companies use domestic sourcing firms to place their product with contractors. Other firms do direct sourcing—placing their products without using agents. A retailer's production manager would investigate companies who produce items similar to what is needed, evaluate countries, factories, and agents, and analyze their ability to meet production deadlines. The sourcing specialist usually recommends one or more companies with whom the firm should negotiate for sample runs or contract terms.

Product Development

Product development specialists must have extensive product knowledge. Developing new fabrics, especially high-performance fabrics, and products gives the manufacturer a competitive edge in the market. Product developers work with target-market and consumer-expectation information provided by marketing. Product development is a major activity both in manufacturing and in vertically integrated retail firms. **Prototypes** (original product samples) are developed in a time-consuming process that may involve large numbers of people. Prototypes are evaluated by combining **performance testing** with **product testing**. In performance or textile testing, materials are tested in a specialized laboratory for essential aspects of performance such as tensile strength, abrasion resistance, washability, and comfort. Lab testing uses standard test methods and specialized testing equipment so that results are reliable, precise, and accurate.

Forecasting colors and trends is a significant factor in product development and design of fashion merchandise. Color and trend forecasting is big business and influences a wide range of behaviors and consumer goods including apparel, interiors, cosmetics, cars, magazines, accessories, athletic gear, and sporting goods. Forecasters and analysts may work for independent consultant companies who sell the service to designers and retailers or they may be part of a creative or product development team in the corporate headquarters of a design or retail company.

In product or field testing, identical products are used by consumers to assess how the product performs and how they react to it. A field or prototype test manager or analyst manages testing, including recruiting subjects to participate in the test, verifying that the prototype(s) being tested are complete and correct, identifying the extent and dimensions of the test, developing the questionnaires or survey instruments, analyzing the data, and reporting the results. The analyst is often one member of the design or product development team and guides them as prototypes are refined based on field tests. Testing may occur several times as the prototype is modified based on analyses of cost, consumer reaction, and performance. Fabrics are tested and performance specifications are used for material selection. Testing and quality assurance evaluations are often done in the country where the product is purchased. Positions with similar responsibilities may be described as manager of product integrity, product comparisons analyst, and manager of material testing.

Quality assurance specialists evaluate materials and products for adherence to company specifications and standards. Jaycee, a quality assurance assistant, manages a component of product testing for a large department store chain. Her job includes supervising testing of

Prototypes are original product samples and are evaluated by combining performance testing with product testing.

materials, product components, and products. "I spend a lot of time looking at numbers and talking to product development team members about materials. Some team members don't know much about textiles so discussions about material performance can be slow when a team has a new member. First, I have to explain why my results matter and then I have to explain what the numbers mean. They catch on pretty fast so that helps. My lab data helps us make good products and produce repeat customers. We always have to keep the bottom line in mind. When our global trade people [sourcing] find a new supplier, it can be a challenge until we learn how to work together. Solving problems and making a difference is what I like about my job."

Product development involves analyzing trends in color and style, taking the garment from the rough sketch to the consumer, defining fit, and determining product cost. In many companies, product development teams consist of one or more creative designers, product development managers, merchandisers, technical designers, and fit specialists. Product development does not cease once the product is on the market. Follow-up studies assess consumer acceptance of the product. Modifications help products remain competitive.

Some product development teams include fabric managers, fabric specialists, trim developers, fabric researchers, or fabric development specialists. These individuals require expertise in textile science. They research and develop fabrics and trims for specific end uses and meet quality and performance requirements. They act as liaisons with merchandising, production, and design. Fabric managers travel to suppliers as needed.

A merchandise evaluation engineer evaluates product performance based on company standards and customer expectations. The engineer also evaluates competitors' products to ensure that the company's products are competitive in performance and price. Engineers work with suppliers to ensure that product quality expectations are understood.

Product managers work with buyers and overseas agents to ensure that products meet design criteria and the company's business plan. Charlie is a product manager for a diverse corporation that includes hardgoods and softgoods in their product line. "I manage products in the sporting goods and tools area and work with branded products—our own private label. I manage the process between buyer and manufacturer—facilitating lab dips, price, product specs, and materials. I am more of an expert on the merchandise than the buyer or the production people. The buyers buy. They hold the check and know how much to buy and when to buy. I make sure they buy the best product available. If we go directly to the factory, we have more control over the specs, color, and changes we want in the product. I'm good at what I do. I increase our margin quite a bit. I watch trends and keep an eye on what is happening in Europe and Asia. I love traveling and my job lets me do that."

Production

Production deals with manufacturing the textile or the textile product. There are positions at all levels of the production–distribution chain wherever product development and production occur. There is a great demand for production managers who enjoy traveling and working internationally. Position titles are production managers or production supervisors. These positions require a combination of people skills and knowledge of the materials with which the facility works, as well as how the equipment works with or processes the materials. Obviously, essential knowledge includes understanding textile properties such as ease of handling, melting point of thermoplastic fibers, elongation potential of knits, and sewability or compatability of materials and components. Problem-solving and critical-thinking skills are frequently applied so that products and materials meet specifications, cost requirements, and shipping deadlines. Responsibilities include managing work flow and assessing and revising production processes, equipment, or procedures. Production managers ensure efficient, appropriate, and safe working conditions.

Design

Designers research fashion trends and understand current style. They create the concept, idea, or **design** for a product or select the components for a room setting. They are innovators who work in a high-stress, fast-paced industry. They need to have a strong knowledge of design, materials, and product development processes. Two common career paths for design are creative and technical. Designers need to understand the sewability of materials and fabrics. Designers work at all levels and may work with such components as yarns, fabrics, or patterns for prints, or apparel items, interior textile items, rooms, or other settings. **Creative designers** focus on specific product types, price points, and target markets. They forecast trends, create colorways, develop line concepts, and coordinate product lines. Decisions regarding silhouette, fabric, and finishing are design decisions. Designers identify what will sell, what will satisfy the consumer, what is within the company's mission and scope, and what is within the target market's price range. The use of computers in design is common, and designers need experience working with systems and software appropriate to their specialization in securing a position or advancing within a firm. Beginning positions in design include design assistant or assistant designer.

Samuel is a designer. "Silk has always been an absolute passion of mine! It is a natural choice for wedding gowns. My delicate, ornate gowns are featured in bridal publications and upscale bridal boutiques throughout North America. I do one theme collection a year. We produce the finest quality dress with perfect fit using top-of-the-line fabrics, beadings, and embroideries. Trunk shows are the key tool for bringing in new business. For a trunk show, I am in a salon for three days. I work with the customer to find the dress for her dream wedding. I use only silk from Italy, Korea, and China—organza, taffeta, georgette, duchess satin, charmeuse, and chiffon. The lace is from France. I have solid relationships with a number of distributors overseas. My broker in Taiwan translates all order information and design specifications to the design teams in the three Chinese factories we use. There is a lot of back and forth as design details get worked out. I travel to the factories at least once a year. The only colors I use are white and off-white, but getting colors to match can be quite an undertaking. Figuring out price is another undertaking. I pay the staff, me, marketing and website design consultants, factory costs, fabric costs, customs fees, broker fees, shipping costs, and miscellaneous expenses. I design the gowns and figure out the cost per gown and the cost of running the business. I use those numbers to determine what to charge the store. In the couture wedding industry, we have built a reputation based on quality."

Technical designers step in at different stages in design and product development. They need to understand the performance of the textiles with which they work and select the appropriate materials to produce the expectations of the finished product. Tech designers determine material and product specifications and oversee execution. They need experience with product data management. Technical designers ensure that designs meet the appropriate laws, regulations, and codes. They interpret the designer's intentions and analyze construction methods for performance, quality, and cost. They analyze lab dips, strike-offs, and product test results. They develop specifications and standards for samples and production and work with suppliers to see that components, materials, and products meet specifications and perform at the prescribed level. They manage product development from adoption to production. Technical designers use their textiles knowledge to assess the quality of contract purchases and identify possible sources of problems in production. For example, solving the problems related to seam puckering in a tightly woven fabric may involve examining the size of the sewing thread, stitch type, thread tension, and handling of materials to determine the cause and resolve it. Tech designers work with creativity teams, buyers, and sourcing specialists to ensure that design concepts are executed on time and at cost. Some tech designers function as development managers or color analysts.

Pat is a patternmaker/technical designer and a member of a product development team for a company that produces outwear. "Working with the designer to create the pattern is the best and the worst part of my job. Sometimes we are on the same page about the design and sometimes we aren't. I create the pattern using CAD and have to interpret the designer's rough sketches. Sometimes I make the profile too skinny and sometimes too poofy. I supervise the sewers who make the garments, correct my patterns based on the designer's comments, and work with the designer and technical designers in fitting garments on models. Once the team is happy with the profile and fit, I make production patterns for all appropriate sizes."

Most design work means problem solving and satisfying the company's target market while making a profit. Design positions may be found in product-development areas in manufacturing firms and retail businesses. Knitwear design is a rapidly growing area and requires an even greater understanding of materials and their performance. This is especially important in terms of pattern making, since elasticity and elongation vary with the type of knit and fiber content.

Design positions are also available in the entertainment field, but they are difficult to obtain. Designers create the set or stage. A designer may spend several years as an assistant. *Stylist* is the term used to describe the person who works with a photographer to take images of textile products for catalogs, promotional materials, advertisements, and websites. Stylists also work in television, film, and commercial shoots to convey the production's image.

Print or textile designers develop prints and structural design fabrics for both woven and knit fabrics for apparel and interiors. An understanding of trends, fiber content and fabric structure, production processes, and graphic design are essential in this area. Creativity and good visual acuity are critical. CAD systems are used to create the design, modify it, develop colorways, and create patterns to complete assortments. Textile designers most often use digital printing to proof their designs.

Tim is a textile designer for a mass merchandiser. "I create production prints that can be produced with minimal revisions and reworking of prototypes or samples and that fit within pricing parameters of a product category. I manage the print evaluation process and approve final prints. Creating manufacture-ready CAD files for product development packages and providing guidance to designers, product development, and suppliers is a big part of my job. My boss expects me to keep current on new printing processes and technologies so that we maintain a competitive edge. I help ensure brand integrity and brand quality across product categories. I work with fabric teams to ensure that prints and materials are a good match. I also often help designers create product presentations for management. I really like the design part of my job. I spend a lot of time listening to people talk about prints and colors. The hardest thing for me was understanding business strategies, but now I see how that all works together. I love doing what I'm doing!"

The **artist** or craftsperson creates one-of-a-kind items (Figure 22.2). Most artists specialize in one medium or type of object such as weaving large tapestries for public buildings or office spaces. Another artist may specialize in creating wearable art, using such techniques as weaving, screen printing, and quilting. The artist must select appropriate materials and be

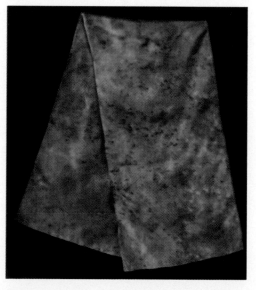

Figure 22.2   Naturally dyed silk.

sufficiently adept to produce the piece. Becoming a self-employed artist requires tremendous effort, talent, and discipline.

Interior designers may work for a design firm, as part of an architectural firm, or with a retailer who specializes in furniture, carpeting, or interior components such as lighting, kitchen/bath, or window/wall coverings. Support teams often include customer service coordinators, interior designers, and project managers. Contract interior designers meet with architects, conduct on-site visits to ensure correct installation of carpet and wall coverings and verify that installation is on schedule, coordinate with suppliers and contractors to facilitate shipping and installation, visit showrooms, design interiors, and educate clients and architects.

Merchandising

Working in the retail setting as a merchandise buyer or manager is an exciting career goal. Merchandisers are expected to predict styles and trends, understand the needs of their target market, anticipate customer demand, ensure that merchandise is in stock, understand data, take risks, and make sound decisions quickly. Merchandisers plan lines and make the final decision on items to be included in a line based on budget, price point, and other factors. However, many positions in **merchandising** exist beyond the retail setting. There are buying positions in companies throughout the global textile complex. For example, yarn companies buy fiber. Weavers and knitters buy yarn. Converters, dyers, and finishers buy dyes and chemicals to finish fabrics. Sewing facilities buy fabric, trim, thread, support materials, zippers, buttons, and wood and metal for furniture frames used in producing the finished item. Product coordinators track components, deadlines, and activities so that the finished product is available on schedule. Merchandising specialists represent manufacturers in retail stores and ensure good product placement and appealing visual merchandising of their products. Multichannel marketing includes mail order, kiosk, direct, home shopping networks, and e-commerce. Just as with other merchandising positions, these relate to buying or developing merchandise to be presented to the consumer. Production of catalogs or Web sites and product presentation are other important positions where a knowledge of textile terminology is essential since accurate product descriptions and clear images inform the consumer.

Managers work at different levels: departments, divisions, stores, or regions. Their goals are to maximize sales and profit for the company and ensure customer satisfaction with the merchandise and shopping experience. Store managers direct merchandising, operational, and human resource functions within a single store. They ensure store security; assist in recruiting, training, and hiring store employees; and work with local political, educational, and law enforcement officials and agencies. They deal with dissatisfied customers and employees and resolve conflicts.

Allocator or planner is usually an entry-level position for buyers. Allocators manage purchase orders from the initial contract through the life cycle of the product, including replenishment or reorders and consolidation of nonselling merchandise to other stores or sales venues. They manage store inventory levels based on store size, season, and sales. They review sales data to ensure that stock levels meet sales trends. They work with spreadsheets and analyze data. Allocators decide which store receives which merchandise and work to get the right merchandise in the store at the best time to ensure sales. They track sales, promote merchandise within the store, keep track of inventory, and work with staff to help them know the merchandise. **Visual merchandisers** deal with how the merchandise is presented to the customer. They need to know how textiles drape and interact with store lighting to attract customers. In **direct marketing**, the

nonstore retailer sells merchandise such as cosmetics, interior decorating items, kitchen supplies, and some apparel directly to the consumer through in-home parties and telephone sales.

Store managers are responsible for meeting sales goals and ensuring that staff are trained to sell. They must have an in-depth knowledge of all aspects of their merchandise. They implement business and selling strategies from the corporate office, including visual directives for maximizing sales. They support special events such as collection previews and client events. They are expected to maintain a floor presence to assist customers, build rapport with customers and staff, and monitor interactions between staff and customers. They are expected to quickly resolve any issues that develop. Store managers monitor store expenses and maintain budgets while identifying ways to reduce costs. They build and maintain good communications within the store, between the store and the mall office, with the corporate office, and with other stores.

Merchandise managers analyze product trends and sales and use that information to develop sales strategies. They review financial goals and redefine product assortments based on their analyses. They work with creative teams so that new products are added or current products are redesigned to meet projected needs. They conduct competitive analyses and search out trend inspiration by searching other stores and evaluating product assortments, quality, pricing merchandising strategies, and business opportunities. They are often members of cross-functional teams representing merchandising, design/product development, and production.

Margarite is a sales supervisor for a women's specialty store. "My job is busy! I guide my staff to meet their personal goals so that the store meets its sales goals. I work with my associates to develop their selling skills and provide customer service to ensure sales. We build clientele and use individual client books. Associates contact clients when merchandise that meets their needs arrives in the store. When problems develop with merchandise or between associates and clients, I resolve the complaint quickly and ensure that the client is satisfied with the solution. It is important that we maintain repeat clientele and that they come to us for their fashion needs! We provide an alterations service and ship articles—part of my after-hours supervision. I help the store manager with risk management (theft), security, and inventory management. I train associates and help them meet our grooming and image requirements. Keeping the selling area neat, organized, and well stocked is another one of my jobs. I also help implement and maintain merchandising visual directives from the main office. I help with receiving and shipping, including the paperwork—my least favorite part of the job! Finally, I check work schedules for hours and attendance. My days are full and busy, but never boring!"

Buyers work with vendors and the distribution center to ensure timely delivery of merchandise. They manage and project markdowns, analyze sales performance, understand the target market by individual stores, can plan margins and open to buy, and communicate regularly with stores and vendors. Strong math skills, knowledge of the merchandise, and good communication and decision-making skills are essential job skills.

Other positions related to merchandising include managing loss prevention. These individuals implement policies and programs to reduce store shortage related to shoplifting, theft, and damage.

Visual merchandisers or visual coordinators implement visual merchandising strategies and guidelines for stores. Often this includes training associates to dress mannequins or forms, light merchandise effectively, and install fixtures. Developing a consistent visual brand with a variety of merchandise throughout the year requires creative thinking and problem solving. Visual merchandisers have to seek out product information to develop appropriate presentations. Visual merchandisers often direct in-store marketing and update this on a regular basis, sometimes weekly. They often work with computer-simulated stores to create the setting and develop a guide so that stores can implement it. They work with cross-functional teams from concept to in-store placement of merchandise. Visual merchandising involves attention to detail, a good eye for color, positive interactions with team members, and travel. Communicating successful visual merchandising strategies to supervisors is a difficult, but essential part of the job.

Marketing

Marketing positions in areas as diverse as advertising, marketing research, journalism, and display require people with an understanding of what motivates consumers to buy. Marketing specialists develop the presentation of the product and create its image. These professionals must understand their target market fully so that they can help the consumer become aware of their product, recognize its usefulness or desirability, and purchase the product. Managing websites and development of materials for e-commerce sites involves product promotion, public relations, understanding brand image, and the ability to communicate a brand image. Knowledge of a product's special features or design aspects will assist in marketing it. Textile knowledge may help market products by promoting performance and product quality. Other firms focus on product serviceability and highlight their product testing programs and performance ratings. Still other firms focus on the high-fashion aspects of their products. A knowledge of textiles provides an understanding of the product and an expanded vocabulary useful in marketing the product.

Producers of textile products use sales reps to market the product line to retailers. Often this presentation takes place in a company showroom located at headquarters or in a merchandise center where similar merchandise lines are grouped together. Showroom managers and staff explain the company's line to retail buyers, apparel designers, or interior designers. Sales reps must be self-starters and enjoy traveling. Sales reps may represent several companies, product lines, or product types that complement each other. For example, one sales rep may carry a women's dress line, a coordinates line aimed at the same target market, and jewelry that could be worn with either of these two lines. Another rep may represent three companies: upholstered furniture, accent rugs, and household accessories. Fabric reps specialize in selling fabric to producers, interior or apparel design firms, or consumer fabric stores. Rep positions are seldom starting positions and are often paid on commission.

Fashion and event coordinators or managers promote fashion shows, trunk shows, and other fashion events for retailers, malls, designers, apparel marts or centers, or the entertainment industry. Some also are freelance entrepreneurs.

Entrepreneurs

Entrepreneurship is the starting of a new business venture. **Entrepreneurs** identify a need within the community or develop a creative approach that would fit a niche and differentiate a new small business from other similar businesses in the community. Entrepreneurs are creative thinkers. They should do a feasibility analysis and business plan and identify how their business is innovative and creative. They need to develop a competitive business strategy and analyze current and future needs. Entrepreneurs and small-business owners often handle every part of running a business: identifying the target market and product mix, sourcing materials and supplies, promoting and selling the merchandise or service, hiring staff, dealing with financial arrangements and budgets, and maintaining the store or facilities.

Government

Governments are some of the world's largest consumers of textile products and employ many people with a knowledge of textiles. Purchasing officers locate producers of specific textile products and verify that items meet government requirements and performance by testing and examining samples. The performance of these items is evaluated by textile-testing engineers using specific test methods and standards. Because of the large number of textile items purchased, sourcing specialists are in demand. **Customs officials** and inspectors ensure that all imported goods meet the appropriate requirements in terms of authenticity and labeling requirements, and are free from insects and disease organisms. For example, wool from certain countries may be checked for anthrax, a highly contagious disease in sheep. Counterfeit items are confiscated and destroyed. Government employees may develop, enforce, or interpret standards, laws, and regulations and work within the global textile complex and for business so that current guidelines and standards are met. Research and development positions in government research facilities focus on textile products such as military uniforms, apparel for adverse weather conditions, spacesuits, interiors for space vehicles and submarines, and suits that offer protection from biological and chemical warfare.

Other Career Areas

The careers in this section either require further education or are more limited in terms of the number of positions available.

Fashion writers and editors work for publishers who provide written information about the fashion industry. Fashion writers develop the written materials while editors coordinate written works and verify that content, style, and format is appropriate for the audience. While fashion writers and editors have tremendous impact on fashion of apparel and interiors, there are relatively few of these positions available. Most writers and editors are employed by fashion and general-interest magazines, trade publications, and a few newspapers. There are also freelance writers and editors.

Education positions can be formal, such as university/college or secondary school educator, or informal, such as consumer education specialist in extension. In the formal setting, an advanced degree or periodic additional coursework may be necessary. Many colleges and universities require a Ph.D. College/university faculty members teach specific classes related to their area of specialization and often do research, engage in scholarship, create artistic works, or judge design competitions. A secondary teacher may be involved in several areas, including family and child development, food and nutrition, at-risk programs, and sex education. Secondary teachers may have additional responsibilities including advising a student group or club.

In the informal setting, professionals have a wide variety of possible job descriptions. Some positions involve educating other employees of the company so that they better understand the consumer. For example, some **consumer education specialists** may help engineers understand problems consumers have with automatic washers and dryers. Trade associations and businesses employ people with a background in education and textiles to write brochures describing the product, develop educational materials such as brochures, write instructional books on the proper use of a specific machine, or produce teaching aids such as CDs. Specialists may teach workshops to consumers or sales representatives and deal with consumers who have questions about the use of the product or complaints about a product. An understanding of textiles is essential for these positions.

Case Study

The Resume*

Job opportunities exist regardless of the overall economic outlook. A resume is an influential way to secure interviews that can develop into job offers. Human resource managers may receive 50 or more resumes for each open position, spending less than one minute appraising each resume. This means that your resume needs to convey the value you will bring to a potential employer quickly and clearly. Resume should be tailored for each position and explain how your skills can help the company. You need to match your skills and experience with a company's goals and objectives and by researching a company and determine what they need and what you can bring to the job.

A resume should incorporate four basic elements: an objective that defines your expertise and skills and demonstrates how you might fit with a company; a summary statement describing a few key skills and accomplishments; a key word list of relevant skills and competencies; and a list of your achievements using action verbs rather than a list of job titles. Be careful about what you include. Make sure it is error-free. Try reading it bottom to top. Seek assistance from your campus career center, career days, e-job fairs, open houses, and so on.

DISCUSSION QUESTIONS

1. Explain how you would research a company. Why is it necessary to research a company?

2. What are the sources of information available to you for researching companies and identifying available positions?

3. Identify experiences that you could include on a resume. Based on those experiences, what would be the best way to describe those experiences in terms of skills and competencies that would convince an employer to invite you for an interview?

4. What kinds of action verbs would best describe your skills and competencies?

5. Why is a separate resume needed for each type of position?

*Marasco, C. A. (2009). Make your resume work for you. *Chemical and Engineering News, 87*(8), 71–72.

suggested readings

Anonymous. (2007). *Ferguson's Careers in Focus: Fashion*, 3rd ed. New York: Ferguson.

Azoulay, J. F. (2004). Global sourcing, global trade. *AATCC Review*, 4(11), pp. 34–37.

Bolles, R. N. (2009). *What Color Is Your Parachute? 2009*. Berkeley, CA: Ten Speed Press.

Eckman, A. L. (2004). Mastering the supply chain. *AATCC Review*, 4(5), pp. 33–36.

Marasco, C. A. (2009). Make your resume work for you. *Chemical and Engineering News, 87*(8), 71–72.

Paulins, V. A., & Hillery, J. L. (2005). *Careers! Professional Development for Retailing and Apparel Merchandising*. New York: Fairchild Publications.

U.S. Department of Labor. *Occupational Outlook Handbook*. Washington, DC: Bureau of Labor Statistics. (updated annually)

Fiber Names in Other Languages

English	Chinese	French	German	Italian	Korean	Japanese	Spanish
acetate	—	acetate/acétate	Acetate faser	acetato	*	sakusan	acetato
acrylic	—	acrylique	Acryl nachgestellf	—	*	akuriru	acrilico
cotton	mianhua	coton/cottonade	Baumwolle	cotone	myun	momen	algodón
linen	mah bou	lin/linge	Leinen	tela di lino	ma	asa or asa/amanuno	lino/lilo de lino
nylon	nilong	nylon	Nylon	nàilon	*	nairon	nilón
olefin	—	—	—	—	*	ourehin	olefina
polyester	huaxian	—	Polyester	poliestere	*	*	poliestero
ramie	—	—	—	—	mo shi	ramii	rame
rayon	—	rayonne	Reyon, Kunstseide	ràion	*	reyon	rayón
silk	sichou	soie	Seide	seta	kyun	kina	seda
wool	yangmao	laine	Wolle	lana	mo	keito	lana

*English term used.

Fibers No Longer Produced in the United States

Anidex—A manufactured fiber in which the fiber-forming substance is any long-chain synthetic polymer composed of at least 50 percent by weight of one or more esters of a monohydric alcohol and acrylic acid (CH_2—CH—COOH).*

Azlon—A manufactured fiber in which the fiber-forming substance is composed of any regenerated naturally occurring proteins.*

Lastrile—A type of rubber fiber that is made from a diene and at least 10 percent but no more than 50 percent by weight of acrylonitrile.

Nytril—A manufactured fiber containing at least 85 percent of a long-chain polymer of vinylidene dinitrile (—$CH_2C(CN)_2$—), in which the vinylidene dinitrile content is no less than every other unit in the polymer chain.*

Triacetate—A type of acetate in which not less than 92 percent of the hydroxyl groups are acetylated.

Vinal—A manufactured fiber in which the fiber-forming substance is any long-chain synthetic polymer composed of at least 50 percent by weight of vinyl alcohol units (—CH_2—CHOH—) and in which the total of the vinyl alcohol units and any one or more of the various acetal units is at least 85 percent by weight of the fiber.*

Vinyon—A manufactured fiber in which the fiber-forming substance is any long-chain synthetic polymer composed of at least 85 percent by weight of vinyl chloride units (—CH_2—CHCl—).*

*Federal Trade Commission definition.

Wool

Australian Me

MAPP (Merind

Sportwool

Fabrics

Composite

Bion (and all r

Darlexx Super

Hydroflex by (

Hydroweave k

Stomatex by !

Xalt by Burling

Fiberfill

Thermolite by

Thinsulate by

Imitation Le

Belleseime, S

Hydrasuede b

Ultraleather, U

Other

Bluesign by S

Cryon by Con

Dry Inside Per

Earthile by Cc

Green Line by

Poromeric

Entrant, Entra

Event by BHA

Goretex (and

Spunbonde

Typar by Reer

Tyvek by DuP(

Warp Knit

Hydric by Hafi

Rentex Fabric

Velcro by Velc

Weft or Filli

Artic Fleece, (

GreenSpun by

OuterBounds

Polartec (and

Selected Trade Names

Fibers

Acetate

Celanese, Celstar, MicroSafe by Celanese Acetate

Chromspun, Estron by Voridian Company

Acrylic

BioFresh, CFF fibrillated fiber, Conductrol, Creslan, MicroSupreme, WeatherBloc by Sterling Fibers, Inc.

Aramid

Kevlar, Nomex by DuPont

Cotton

FoxFibre by Natural Cotton Colours Inc.

Lyocell

Tencel by Lenzing Fibers Corp.

Nylon

Akwadyne by Cekal Specialties

Anso (and all related names), Caprolan, Dry Step, Hydrofil, Royalbrite, Shimmereen, Silky Touch, SpectraTrilene, Ultra Micro Touch, Ultra Touch, Zefsport, Zeftron (and all related names) by Allied-Signal Performance Fibers

Antron (and all related names), Cordura, DSDN, DuPontXTI, Fiberloc, MicroSupplex, Natrelle BCF, SolarMax, Stainmaster (and all related names), Supplex, Tactel, Tactesse by Invista Inc.

DyeNAMIX, Ultron (and all related names), Wear Dated (and all related names) by Solutia Inc.

Meryl (and all related names) by Nylstar, Inc.

Nylon 6 by Beaulieu of America, Inc.

Stay Gard by Berkley, Inc.

Wellon, Wellstrand by Wellman, Inc.

Olefin

Biobarrier, Typar by Reemay, Inc.

CoolVisions by FiberVisions

Essera, Impressa, Innova, Marqesa, Trace by American Fibers & Yarn Co.

Polyloom by TC Thiolon

Spectra Guard, Spectra 1000 (and all related Spectra fibers) by Honeywell, Inc.

Tyvec by DuPont Performance Materials

A Guide to Stain Removal*

Precautions

- Items labeled dry clean only should be taken to the dry cleaners as soon after staining as possible so that they can use their spot removal chemicals to remove the stain. Dry cleaners are not successful at removing all stains.
- Items made of natural or synthetic rubber or vinyl are damaged by most dry-cleaning solvents.
- Items of olefin are damaged by perc (perchloroethylene).
- Items with some kinds of sequins, beading, and metallic components are damaged by dry-cleaning solvents.
- Items of leather, suede, or fur should be taken to a dry cleaner for professional treatment.

General Procedures for Removing Stains from Washable Fabrics

- Blot excess liquid with a clean white towel (paper or fabric) or other white fabric. Colored fabric may leave a stain.
- Wait until mud has dried, and wax has cooled. Remove by gently scraping or chipping the residue with a dull knife or spatula. Brush or shake off small particles.
- Avoid rubbing stained areas with fabric or paper towels that leave lint.
- Avoid rubbing a stain with bar soap. It may set the stain.
- Heavily stained and soiled items should be washed separately.
- Avoid heat, hot water, or ironing for protein (milk, blood, or egg) or unknown stains since heat can set stains.
- Check for stains before laundering items. Pretreat as needed (see following page). Before machine drying, check stained items to ensure that the stain has been removed.

Spot Treating Stains

Spot treating keeps the stain confined to a small area.

Supplies needed:

Absorbent fabric, paper toweling or sponges (white or neutral color; nonlinting)

Dry-cleaning solvent, spot remover, or spray pretreatment

- Place the white fabric or towels on the working surface to avoid stain transfer to the counter or table top.
- Place the stained area of the item face down on the white fabric or towel.
- Dampen another piece of white fabric with the solvent.

- Pat the stain from the back with the dampened price of white fabric. Start at the outside edge and work towards the center of the stain. This keeps the stain from spreading.
- As the white fabric picks up the stain, refold it so that you are using a clean area.
- Repeat until all evidence of the stain is gone.
- Launder to remove all of the solvent.

Pretreating Stains Before Washing

Supplies needed:

Absorbent fabric, paper toweling or sponges (white or neutral color; nonlinting)

Detergent (heavy-duty liquids work best)

Bleach (hydrogen peroxide, powder color-safe bleach, liquid chlorine bleach)

Pretreatment compounds (aerosol sprays, pump-type sprays, sticks, pens, gels)

Odor-reducing or odor-absorbing materials (activated charcoal, spray compounds, baking soda, or calcium carbonate)

Stain-removal chemicals (rubbing or isopropyl alcohol, ammonia or ammonium hydroxide, color remover or sodium hydrosulfite, enzyme presoak, lemon juice (citric acid) and salt, acetone (found in some nail polish removers), rust removers (hydrofluoric or oxalic acid), white vinegar)

Stain Removal Safety Precautions

- Store these chemicals out of reach of children or pets. Store them away from food.
- Read and follow all label directions.
- Use in a well-ventilated room.
- NEVER combine hydrofluoric or oxalic acid with powder or liquid bleach of any kind.
- Do not use solvents near an open flame or electrical outlet.
- Seal containers immediately after use.
- Never mix any of these compounds together since some combinations form toxic fumes.

Stain Removal

Stain Type	Examples	Process
Protein	Milk products, baby food, blood, cheese, mud, pudding, egg, urine, feces, vomit, school paste, white glue	Soak in cold water for 15 to 30 minutes. Wash in warm or cold water, rinse, and inspect. If stain remains, soak for 30 more minutes, rewash. If not removed after this wash, bleach.
Tannin	Red wine, beer, fruit, coffee, cologne, felt-tip watercolor pens, carbonated drinks, tea, vegetable and fruit juice, washable ink	Use detergent, not bar soap, and hot water. Set-in tannin stains may require bleaching.
Oil-based	Cooking oil or fat, hand or body lotion, car or hair oil, car door grease, salad dressing, sunscreen, mayonnaise, body oil	Pretreat with a heavy-duty liquid detergent or pretreatment compound. Work into the oily stain and wash using warm or hot water depending on the care label instructions. Use the amount of detergent recommended for a regular load, rinse, and inspect before machine drying. Repeat if the stain remains.

(*Continued*)

Stain Removal (*continued*)

Stain Type	Examples	Process
Dye	Berry or flower stains, color bleed from washing, grass, ink, powder drink mix, mustard, tempera paint	These are difficult to remove. Pretreat with heavy-duty laundry detergent, rinse thoroughly. Soak in a dilute solution of color-safe bleach. If the stain remains, check if the fabric can be bleached with a liquid chlorine. If it can, soak for 15 minutes in a dilute solution of liquid chlorine bleach. If the stain is not removed at this point, it is permanent.
Combination I	Permanent ink, eye makeup, candle wax, crayon, tar, furniture polish, livestock paint, pine resin, shoe polish	Sponge with dry cleaning solvent, then rub with heavy-duty liquid detergent. Use color-safe bleach, wash in warm water, and rinse. Check for stain removal before machine drying. If stain remains, repeat process before machine drying. Use liquid chlorine bleach for tough dye stains if fabrics are safe for this bleach.
Combination II	Calomine lotion, tomato or barbecue sauce, chocolate, face cosmetics, gravy, hair spray	Rub heavy-duty liquid detergent into stain before washing. Use color-safe bleach, wash in warm water, and rinse. Check for stain removal before machine drying. If stain remains, repeat process before machine drying. Use liquid chlorine bleach for tough dye stains if fabrics are safe for this bleach.
Chewing gum		Use ice to harden the gum. Crack or scrape off excess. Use pretreatment compound. Rub with heavy-duty liquid detergent. Rinse. Repeat, if necessary. Wash.
Deodorant		Apply liquid detergent, wash in warm water.
Fingernail polish		Do not use nail polish remover on acetate. Take to a dry cleaner and identify the stain. For other common apparel fibers, use nail polish remover and spot treatment method (check to ensure dyes are colorfast to nail polish remover).
Lead pencil		Use art gum eraser to lift off excess, but avoid hard rubbing. For delicate fabrics, use spot treatment method. For more durable fabrics, use pretreatment compounds and heavy-duty liquid detergent. Rinse and wash.
Mildew		Shake or brush item outdoors. Pretreat dark stains with heavy-duty liquid detergent. Wash with heavy-duty liquid detergent. Bleach as safe for fabric.
Odor		Treat with odor absorbing spray.
Paint, latex		Treat while wet. Soak in cold water, wash in cold water with heavy-duty detergent. Dried paint is almost impossible to remove.
Paint, oil-based		Treat while wet. Use thinner recommended for paint. Spot treat paint until it is soft and can be flushed away in heavy-duty detergent wash.
Perspiration		Use liquid detergent or soak in warm water with presoak 15 to 30 minutes. Wash.
Rust		The only treatments effective are either oxalic acid crystals or hydrofluoric acid (extremely toxic and can damage the finish on washers).
Smoke, soot		Shake off excess outdoors. Wash in machine using heavy-duty liquid detergent, one cup of water conditioner, and 0.5 cup color-safe bleach. Hang to dry or dry flat. Check for odor of smoke. Repeat as necessary. Multiple washes may be needed.
Urine		Rinse in cold water and wash.
Water spots		Wash. For dry clean only items, water spots may not be removed.

For Unknown Stains

- Use odor, location, and color to help identify the stain.
- Use the least destructive method first and gradually move to higher risk methods: cold water, warm water and spot treatment, liquid detergent and warm or hot water, color-safe bleach, and finally liquid chlorine bleach.

Ineffective Remedies

Remedy	Potential Problem
Dishwasher detergent	Intended for very hot water, highly alkaline, contains bleach. May fade colors and damage some fibers or finishes.
Ironing candle wax between paper towels	Ironing will drive stain deeper into fibers.
Milk on washable ink	Does not work and adds protein stain.
Salt to make dyes fast	Ineffective, unless large quantities are used with every wash and rinse.
Shampoo	Laundry detergents are as effective and less expensive. Some compounds in shampoo may stain fabric and are more difficult to rinse out.
White vinegar	The acid in vinegar may weaken cellulosic fibers and silk and cause color change.

*Adapted from Stone, J. *Quick 'n Easy Stain Removal*, Cooperative Extension Service, Iowa State University, Ames, IA 50011.

Circular loom—is a type of loom in which the warp yarns form a full circle to weave tubular fabric.

Ciré finish—is a process in which a thermoplastic fabric is calendered with one roll hot enough to slightly melt and flatten the fiber surfaces.

Clean Air Act—is the federal law that focuses on air quality.

Cleaned wool—(*See* Scoured wool.)

Cleaning—is the process of removing soil from fabric; it is also a step in preparing fabrics for additional finishing steps.

Clean Water Act—is the federal law that focuses on surface-water and groundwater quality.

Clipped-dot fabric—is an extra-yarn fabric made with extra filling yarns inserted so that they interlace with some warp yarns and float across some filling yarns. Part of the float may be cut away in finishing, leaving a fringe to add fabric texture.

Clip spot—refers to a fabric in which design is created with an additional yarn that interlaces with the ground fabric in spots and floats along the technical back of the fabric. The floats are removed by shearing.

Cloque (klō-kay´) fabric—is a general term used to refer to any fabric with a puckered or blistered effect.

Cloth—is a generic term referring to all textile fabrics.

Cluny (klu´-ne´)—is a coarse, strong bobbin lace.

Coated fabric—is a multiplex fabric with a thin plastic film combined with a woven, knit, or fiberweb fabric.

COD—(*See* Chemical oxygen demand.)

Code of Federal Regulations—is the document published each work day in which changes in federal laws and regulations are announced.

Codes—are systematic bodies of laws or regulations that often focus on safety or health areas.

Cohesiveness—refers to the ability of fibers to cling together, which is especially important in yarn spinning.

Coir—is the fiber obtained from the fibrous mass between the outer shell and the husk of the coconut.

Colorant—is a general term describing materials that are used to add color to a fabric.

Colorfastness—refers to a colorant that does not shift hue, fade, or migrate when exposed to certain conditions.

Color-grown cotton—(*See* Naturally colored cotton.)

Color match—describes when a color standard and a lab dip are within acceptable tolerances.

Color measurement—is the process of assigning numerical values to a color to assist in color matching and shade sorting.

Color problems—refer to any aspect that creates difficulty for consumers, producers, or manufacturers due to dyes, pigments, or techniques used in coloring the fabric. See specific color problems: bleeding, frosting, fume fading, migration.

Color scavenger—describes a tendency of nylon to pick up color from soil or dyes that bleed when fabrics are wet.

Color standard—is a large sample of fabric or digital information that represents the desired color.

Color theory—describes a complex phenomenon combining the physics of light, the chemistry of colored objects, the biology of the eye, the behavioral sciences in terms of what colors mean to society or the individual, and the aesthetics of appreciating what one sees.

Color-transfer inhibitors—are present in some detergents to prevent any dye that bleeds in the wash from redepositing on lighter-colored products.

Colorway—refers to various color options available in one fabric.

Combed yarn—is a uniform spun yarn with long-staple fibers and few protruding fiber ends.

Combination—refers to a fabric of two or more generically different fiber types in which ply yarns consist of strands of each generic type.

Combing—is an additional step in the production of smooth, fine, uniform spun yarns made of long-staple fibers.

Comfort—describes the way a textile product affects heat, air, and moisture transfer and the way the body interacts with the textile product.

Comfort stretch—refers to the ability of a fiber or fabric to elongate slightly as the body moves and to recover a significant portion of that elongation when the stretching force is removed.

Composite fabric—is a fabric that combines several primary and/or secondary structures such as fiberweb and film, yarn and base fabric, or two layers of fabric.

Composite fiber—is any fiber that incorporates nanoparticles.

Composite yarn—is regular in appearance along its length; it is made with both staple- and filament-fiber components.

Compound needle—is a type of needle used in warp knitting.

Compressibility—is resistance to crushing.

Compressional resiliency—describes the ability of a fabric or pile to return to its original thickness after compression. (*See also* Loft.)

Compressive shrinkage process—refers to finishing that removes stress from weaving and earlier finishing.

Confinement—refers to a color, pattern, or fabric that is restricted by contract to one firm or producer.

Conservation—refers to special handling, storage, cleaning, and display techniques used for textiles that are valued for their age, history, or type.

Consumer Product Safety Commission—is the federal agency responsible for ensuring the safety of products used by consumers.

Consumer Product Safety Improvement Act (CPSIA)—is an act designed to remove lead and phthalate compounds from items used or worn by children under 12 years of age.

Continuous dyeing—is a process in which large pieces of fabric are colored in ranges with separate compartments for wetting-out, dyeing, after-treatment, washing, and rinsing.

Continuous processing—describes working with long pieces of fabric that move in and out of solution.

Conventional cotton—describes cotton grown and processed by regular mainstream practices.

Conventional spinning—(*See* Ring spinning.)

Converted goods—(*See* Finished goods.)

Converters—refer to firms that finish fabrics.

Convolutions—are ribbonlike twists along a cotton fiber.

Copolymer—refers to a polymer composed of more than one type of mer.

Cord—consists of two or more ply yarns held together by twist or some other means.

Cordonnet lace—is a type of lace in which heavier yarns emphasize certain elements in the design.

Corduroy—is a filling-yarn pile fabric. The pile is created by long-filling floats that are cut and brushed in finishing. The ground weave may be a plain or a twill weave.

Core-spun yarn—is made with a central sheath of fibers completely covered by other fibers spun around it.

Coronizing—is a finish specific to fiberglass to assist in yarn production and printing.

Cortex—is the main part of wool fibers; it contains two cell types.

Cost—is the amount paid to acquire, use, maintain, and dispose of a product.

Cotton—refers to several fibers belonging to the genus *Gossypium* used to produce commercial and craft textile products.

Cottonize—describes the process of cutting ramie, linen, hemp, and other fibers into shorter fibers to facilitate blending with cotton or processing on equipment designed for cotton.

Count—refers to yarns per inch in warp and filling directions in woven fabrics.

Course—refers to the yarn's path in a filling-knit fabric as it moves across the fabric.

Cover—is the ability to occupy space for concealment or protection.

Covered yarn—has a central ply that is completely wrapped by another ply.

Covert—was first made in England to meet a demand for a fabric that would not catch on brambles or branches during fox hunts. This tightly woven fabric is made from a two-ply yarn, one cotton and one wool. Because the cotton and wool did not take the same dye, the fabric had a mottled appearance. Cotton covert is always mottled. It may be made with ply yarns, one ply white and the other colored. It is a twill, of the same weight as denim, and used primarily for work pants, overalls, and service coats. Wool covert is made from woolen or worsted yarns. It may be mottled or solid color of suit or coat weight. It may be slightly napped or have a clear finish. The mottled effect is obtained by using two different-colored plies or by blending different-colored fibers.

Crabbing—is a process used to set wool fabrics.

Cradle to cradle—is an environmentally intelligent design framework that examines the overall impact of the production, use, care, disposal, and recycle potential of products from economic, industrial, and social perspectives.

Crash—is a medium-weight to heavyweight plain-weave fabric made from slub or irregular yarns to create an irregular surface.

Crease-retention finish—(*See* Durable press.)

Creel—is a rack of spools or cones of yarn arranged so that the individual yarns can be removed without tangling or a rack on which warp yarns are wound.

Creep—is delayed or gradual recovery from elongation or strain.

Crepe (krā-p)—refers to any fabric with a puckered, crinkled, or grainy surface. It can be made with crepe yarns, a crepe weave, or such finishes as embossed or plissé. Fabric examples include chiffon, crepe-back satin, georgette, and crepe de Chine. For more information, see these fabric names.

Crepe-back satin or Satin-back crepe—is a reversible satin-weave fabric in which the filling yarns have a crepe twist. The technical face has satin floats, and the technical back resembles crepe.

Crepe de chine (krā-p-duh-sheen)—is a lightweight, opaque, plain-weave, filament-yarn fabric with a medium luster. Silk crepe de chine usually is made with crepe yarns.

Crepeing—is a compacting process that softens fabric hand.

Crepe twist—refers to a yarn with extremely high twist and great liveliness.

Crepe weave—(*See* Momie weave.)

Crepe yarn—refers to a yarn with crepe or very high twist.

Cretonne (kreh´-tahn)—is a plain-weave fabric similar to chintz, but with a dull finish and a large-scale floral design.

Crimp—is a two- or three-dimensional aspect in which fibers or yarns twist or bend back and forth or around their axis.

Crinoline (krihn´-uh-lihn)—is a stiff, spun-yarn, plain-weave fabric similar to cheesecloth, used in book bindings, hats, and stiffening for apparel.

Crocheted lace—is lace done by hand with a crochet hook.

Crocking—describes a color problem in which abrasion transfers color to the abradant.

Cross dyeing—describes a special method of dyeing fiber blends in which each fiber type is dyed a different color.

Cross links—are temporary or permanent bonds that connect adjacent molecular chains.

Crushed velvet—is a warp-pile fabric in which the pile yarns are crushed in a random pattern by mechanically twisting the fabric when it is wet.

Crystalline—describes molecular chains that are parallel to each other in a fiber or in regions within a fiber.

Cuprammonium rayon—is a rayon produced in Europe by the cuprammonium process.

Cut—refers to needles per inch in knitting machines; it is another term for gauge.

Cuticle—is a waxlike film covering the outermost layer of a cotton fiber.

Damask (dam´-ask)—is a reversible, flat jacquard-woven fabric with a satin weave in both the pattern and the ground. It can be one color or two. In two-color damasks, the color reverses on the opposite side. It is used in apparel and interior textiles.

Darned lace—has a chain stitch outlining the design on a mesh background. The needle carries another yarn around the yarns in the mesh. The mesh is square in filet lace and rectangular in antique lace.

Dead time—refers to time that a machine is not operating because of changing settings on the equipment so that another fabric can be processed.

Decating—is a process that produces a smooth, wrinkle-free surface on wool fabrics. It is also known as decatizing.

Decitex (dek´-ah-teks) or dtex (de¯´-teks)—is used to identify yarn or fiber size and is equal to 10 tex.

Decortication—is a process used to remove ramie or any bast fiber from the plant stem.

Defects—are flaws in fabrics that are assigned a point value based on their length or size.

Degree of polymerization—refers to the number of small molecules (monomers) connected to form a polymer.

Delustered fiber—describes a fiber with dull luster resulting from the incorporation of a white pigment within the fiber.

Denier (den´-yehr)—describes yarn or fiber size and is defined as weight in grams for 9000 meters of fiber or yarn.

Denier per filament (dpf)—is a way of describing fiber size. Dpf is calculated by dividing the yarn size in denier by the number of filaments.

Denim—is a cotton or cotton/polyester blend, twill-weave, yarn-dyed fabric. Usually the warp is colored and the filling is white. It is often a left-hand twill with a blue (indigo) warp and white filling for use in apparel in a variety of weights.

Density—is the weight in grams per cubic centimeter of an object.

Dents—refer to the spaces within the reed that help to establish warp-yarn density in the woven fabric.

Desizing—is the physical or biological process in which warp sizing is removed after weaving.

Detergency—refers to the chemical action of a soap or detergent in removing soil from a textile.

Detergent—is a chemical compound specially formulated to remove soil or other material from textiles.

Developed dyes—are a dye class used primarily with cellulosics. (*See also* Direct dyes.)

Differential printing—is a screen-printing process on carpets.

Digital printing—refers to the adaptation of paper ink-jet methods to textile printing.

Dimensional stability—is the ability to retain a given size and shape through use and care; also refers to a finish that minimizes fabric shrinkage or growth in use or during care.

Dimity (dim´-ih-te¯)—is a sheer, lightweight fabric with warp cords created by using heavier-warp yarns at a regular distance, grouping warp yarns together, or using a basket variation with two or more warp yarns woven as one. It may be printed or piece-dyed and of combed-cotton yarns. Barred dimity has heavier or double yarns periodically in both the warp and the filling.

Direct dyes—are a class of dye used primarily with cellulosics. (*See also* Developed dyes.)

Direct printing—describes a process in which the color is applied to its final location as a paste or powder.

Direct-roller printing—is a process in which a pattern is engraved on rollers. The roller picks up a colored paste and transfers the paste to the fabric as it passes under the roller. One roller is used for each color in the pattern.

Direct spinning—is a yarn-spinning process that eliminates the roving step.

Discharge printing—describes a process in which color is removed from piece-dyed fabric in specific locations.

Disinfectants—are compounds used in cleaning to kill microorganisms.

Disperse dyes—are a dye class used primarily with manufactured and synthetic fibers.

Dobby loom—is a loom with a punched-tape attachment or microcomputer control used to control warp-yarn position and create dobby-weave fabrics.

Dobby weave—is a small-figured woven-in design in which fewer than 25 different warp-yarn arrangements are required to create one design repeat.

Dope—refers to the chemical solution extruded as a fiber.

Dotted swiss—is a sheer, lightweight or medium-weight plain-weave fabric with small dots created at regular intervals with extra yarns, through either a swivel or clip-spot weave. Look-alike fabrics are made by flocking, printing, or using an expanded-foam print.

Double cloth—is a fabric made by weaving two fabrics with five sets of yarns: two sets of warp, two sets of filling, and one set that connects the two fabrics.

Double-faced fabric—is made with three sets of yarns: two warp and one filling, or two filling and one warp.

Double-filling knit—is made on a machine with two sets of needles in two needle beds.

Double-knit—is a general term used to refer to any filling-knit fabric made on two needle beds.

Double-knit jersey—is a fabric made on a rib-gait double-knitting machine. Both sides look like the technical face of a single jersey.

Double weave—is a fabric made by weaving two fabrics with four sets of yarns (two sets of warp and two sets of filling yarns) on the same loom. The two fabrics are connected by periodically reversing the positions of the two fabrics from top to bottom. Double weave is also known as pocket cloth or pocket weave.

Double-width loom—is a loom that weaves two widths of fabric side by side.

Doup attachment—is the device used on looms to create the leno weave, in which warp yarns cross over each other to create an open, stable woven structure.

Down—refers to the undercoating of waterfowl and relates to the fine, bulky underfeathers.

Drape—is the manner in which a fabric falls or hangs over a three-dimensional form.

Drawing—describes a fiber-finishing step in which a manufactured fiber is elongated after spinning to alter the molecular arrangement within the fiber, increasing crystallinity and orientation and resulting in a change in specific performance properties.

Draw-texturing—is a yarn-texturing process in which oriented or partially oriented filaments are stretched slightly and heat-set.

Drill—is a strong, medium-weight to heavyweight, warp-faced, twill-weave fabric. It is usually a left-handed twill and piece-dyed.

Dry cleaning—describes a fabric-cleaning process that uses an organic solvent rather than water.

Dry-foam cleaning—is a cleaning technique for furnishings. A foam is worked into the textile, and the soiled foam is removed by vacuuming.

Drying—is the process of removing liquid water or other solvent from a textile so that it feels dry to the touch.

Dry-laid fiberweb—is a layer of oriented or random fibers laid down by carding or air layering.

Dry spinning—is a fiber-forming process in which a solution of polymer dissolved in a solvent is extruded; the fiber coagulates as the solvent evaporates.

Duchesse (du¯-shes´)—is a bobbin lace with a fine net ground and raised pattern.

Duck—is a strong, heavy plain- or basket-weave fabric available in a variety of weights and qualities. It is similar to canvas.

Duplex printing—describes a printing process in which both sides of the fabric are printed.

Duppioni silk—is a naturally thick and thin silk resulting from two caterpillars having formed one cocoon.

Durability—describes how a product withstands use or the length of time the product is considered suitable for the use for which it was purchased.

Durable finish—lasts for the life of the product, but the performance diminishes with time.

Durable press—describes a finish that maintains a fabric's smooth, flat, unwrinkled appearance during use, care, and storage.

Duvetyn (doov´-eh-te¯n)—is a woven suede imitation that is lighter weight and drapeable. It has a soft, velvetlike surface made by napping, shearing, and brushing.

Dye—is an organic compound with high color strength capable of forming a bond of some type with fibers.

Dyeability—is the fiber's receptivity to coloration by dyes or its dye affinity.

Dyeing—is the process of combining a fiber with a dye and achieving a bond of some type.

Dye process—refers to the method of applying colorant to a textile.

Dye-transfer inhibitors—are compounds often found in detergents that prevent any dye that bleeds in the wash from redepositing on other fabrics.

Eco (e¯´-ko) products—(*See* Green products.)

Effect ply—is the ply of a fancy yarn that creates visual or tactile interest.

Egyptian cotton—(*See* Pima cotton.)

Elasterell-p—is a generic subclass of a stretch polyester.

Elasticity—is the ability of a strained material to recover its original size and shape immediately after removing stress.

Elastic recovery—is the ability of fibers to recover from strain.

Elastoester—is a manufactured fiber in which the fiber-forming substance is composed of at least 50 percent by weight of aliphatic polyether and at least 35 percent by weight of polyester.

Elastomer—is a natural or synthetic polymer that, at room temperature, can be stretched repeatedly to at least twice its original length and that, after removal of the tensile load, will immediately and forcibly return to approximately its original length.

Electrical conductivity—is the ability to transfer electrical charges.

Electrospinning—is a technique used to produce nanofibers in which the fiber is forced through a tiny spinneret opening into an electric field.

Electrostatic printing—is a type of printing with a dye powder.

Elongation—is the ability of a fiber to be stretched, extended, or lengthened.

Embossed—refers to a finish in which a localized surface glazing of thermoplastic fibers is achieved or a three-dimensional effect is created to imitate a more elaborate fabric structure.

Embossed fabrics—are created by applying a design with heated engraved calenders. Often print cloths are embossed to imitate seersucker, crepe, or other structural-design fabrics.

Embroidered—refers to stitching flat surface yarns to a fabric to create a pattern.

Embroidery thread—is a yarn intended for stitching designs or patterns on the surface of a textile.

Emerizing—is a surface-abrasion finish applied to alter a fabric's appearance, hand, and drape.

Emulsion spinning—is a fiber-extrusion method in which polymerization and extrusion occur simultaneously.

Environmental concerns—refer to the effect on the environment of the production, use, care, and disposal of textiles and textile products.

Environmental Protection Agency (EPA)—is the federal agency responsible for issues related to the quality of the natural environment.

Enzyme—is a biological chemical compound that reduces complex organic compounds to simpler compounds.

Enzyme wash—is a fabric finish that uses cellulase enzyme to remove surface fuzz from cellulosic fabrics.

Etched—(*See* Burned-out.)

Even-sided twill—is a type of twill weave. The fabric's technical face is formed by equal amounts of warp and filling yarns.

Expanded film—is a film with tiny air cells incorporated into the solution.

Expanded foam—is a permanent surface texture or pattern created on fabric by printing.

Extra-yarn weave—is made with extra yarns of a different color or type from the ground yarns that are used to create a pattern in the fabric.

Extrusion—is the process of forcing the dope or spinning solution through the openings in a spinneret to form a fiber.

Eyelet embroidery—is a type of embroidered fabric with a thread pattern around and connecting small holes in the fabric.

Fabric—is a planar substance constructed from solutions, fibers, yarns, fabrics, or any combination of these.

Fabrication—refers to the method used to produce a fabric.

Fabric crimp—refers to bends caused by distortion of yarns in a fabric.

Fabric grading—refers to the process of inspecting fabrics and assigning grade or quality levels based on the number, size, and kinds of defects present.

Fabric inspection—describes the process of examining a fabric for irregularities, defects, flaws, or other appearance problems.

Fabric quality—refers to a fabric's freedom from defects, uniform structure and appearance related to the fabric type, and performance during production and in consumer use. Fabric quality is graded by totaling defect points within a piece of fabric.

Fabric softener—is a compound used in finishing and cleaning to improve fabric hand.

Fabric weight—describes fabric mass or how much a fabric weighs for a given area or length of fabric; it is described as oz/yd^2 or g/m^2. Another way to express fabric weight is yards/pound.

Face weight—refers to the mass or weight of the tuft yarns used in a carpet or pile fabric.

Faille (pronounced file)—is a medium-weight to heavyweight, unbalanced plain-weave fabric with filament yarns and warp-faced, flat ribs created by using heavier filling yarns. It has a light luster.

Fake fur—(*See* Sliver-pile knit.)

False-twist process—is a method of texturing filament yarns by twisting the yarn, heat-setting it, and untwisting it.

Fancy fabric—is a fabric that differs in appearance, pattern, or structure from plain fabrics.

Fancy weave—refers to any weaving method, other than plain, twill, or satin weave, used to create a fabric with a surface texture or pattern resulting from the interlacing pattern.

Fancy yarn—describes a yarn with an irregular or unusual appearance as compared with simple basic yarns.

Fasciated yarn—is a yarn made with a filament grouping of fibers wrapped with staple fibers.

Fashioning—is the process of adding or dropping stitches during knitting to shape garment parts. (*See also* Full fashioning.)

Federal Insecticide, Fungicide, and Rodenticide Act (FIFRA)—is the federal law that requires that products containing insecticides, fungicides, and rodenticides provide label information regarding content and safety precautions.

Federal Trade Commission (FTC)—is the federal agency that enforces interstate and international trade regulations.

Felt—is a fiberweb fabric of at least 70 percent wool made by interlocking the scales of the wool fibers through the use of heat, moisture, and agitation.

Feltability—refers to the ability of fibers to mat together.

Felting—refers to a method of producing a fabric directly from wool fibers by interlocking the fibers' scales.

Fiber—is any substance, natural or manufactured, with a high length-to-width ratio and with suitable characteristics for being processed into a fabric.

Fiber additives—are compounds added to manufactured fiber dope to improve appearance or performance.

Fiber blend—refers to an intimate mixture of two or more generic fiber types in the yarns of a fabric. It is usually used to refer to the presence of more than one generic fiber in a fabric.

Fiber crimp—refers to waves, bends, twists, coils, or curls along the length of the fiber.

Fiber density—describes fiber weight or mass per unit volume.

Fiber dyeing—is the addition of color, generally as dyes, to textiles while they are in fiber form. It also refers to adding pigment to fiber solutions before fibers are extruded.

Fiberfill—is a lofty, weak structure of fibers designed to be incorporated as the center layer in a quilted fabric.

Fiber modifications—are changes in the parent manufactured fiber to improve performance relative to a specific end use.

Fiber spinning—is the process of producing a manufactured fiber from a solution.

Fiberweb—refers to a fabric made directly from fibers.

Fibrillation—refers to the longitudinal shattering of some fibers into fibrils or tiny fibers when exposed to abrasion.

Fibroin—is the protein of silk fibers.

Filament—refers to fibers that are extremely long (length measured in miles or kilometers) or yarns made of these fibers.

Filament tow—is an intermediate stage in the production of staple manufactured fibers when manufactured fibers are produced in large bundles in filament length and crimped prior to cutting or breaking into staple fibers.

Filament yarn—is a yarn made from filament fibers; smooth or bulky types are possible.

Filling—refers to the yarns perpendicular to the selvage that interlace with warp yarns in a woven fabric.

Filling-faced twill—is a type of twill weave in which the majority of the fabric's technical face is formed by filling yarns.

Filling knitting or Weft knitting—is a process in which one yarn or yarn set is carried back and forth or around and under needles to form a fabric.

Filling-pile fabric—is a fabric in which the pile is created by extra filling yarns.

Filling sateen—is a spun-yarn satin-weave fabric in which filling yarns form the fabric's technical face.

Film—is a fabric made directly from a polymer solution in a dense, firm sheet form.

Finish—is any process used to convert unfinished gray goods into a completed fabric.

Finished goods—are fabrics that have completed the production process and are ready to be made into apparel or furnishings.

Fire-block seating—is a layer of flame-retardant material between the upholstery and the padding of furniture to minimize flame spread.

Fire retardance—is the resistance to combustion of a material when tested under specific conditions.

Flame resistance—is the property of a fabric whereby burning is prevented, terminated, or inhibited following application of an ignition source.

Flame-resistant fiber or finish—is any finish or fiber modification that is designed to reduce the flammability of a textile.

Flame-retardant finish—is a finish that makes a fabric resistant to combustion when tested under specific conditions.

Flammability—describes the characteristics of a fabric that pertain to its relative ease of ignition and ability to sustain combustion.

Flammable Fabrics Act—is a federal act that prohibits the marketing of dangerously flammable textile products.

Flannel—is a lightweight to heavyweight plain- or twill-weave fabric with a napped surface.

Flannelette—is a lightweight to medium-weight plain-weave cotton or cotton-blend fabric lightly napped on one side.

Flatbed machine—refers to a knitting machine that makes a flat width of fabric.

Flat-screen printing—is a resist printing method. For each color, a flat screen is treated so that print paste passes through openings to create a design on the fabric.

Flax—is the bast fiber (often called linen) produced by the flax plant.

Fleece—is a type of weft-insertion knit fabric.

Flexibility—is the ability of a fiber to bend repeatedly without breaking.

Float—is the portion of a yarn that is on the surface or back of fabric.

Float stitch or Miss stitch—is a type of knit stitch in which yarn lengths float past but do not interloop with the previous stitch. It is used to create a more stable structure or a pattern in the fabric.

Floats—are formed when a yarn in one direction, such as warp, crosses over more than one yarn at a time in the other direction, such as filling.

Flocking—refers to the bonding of very short surface fibers onto a fabric to produce an imitation-pile appearance.

Fluorescent dyes—are a dye class used primarily to create or maintain white fibers and are found in some laundry detergents.

Fluorescent whitening agent—is a compound used to mask the natural color of fibers, yellowing from aging, or other colors resulting from soil.

Fluoropolymer—is a manufactured fiber containing at least 95 percent of a long-chain polymer synthesized from aliphatic fluorocarbon polymers.

Foam—refers to a mixture of air and liquid used in the application of finishes, dyes, or pigments; it also refers to a textile product in which a high percentage of air is mixed with the polymer to form a bulky, lofty material.

Foam coating—is a back coating of acrylic foam on lightweight drapery fabrics to block air flow, minimize heat transfer, and finish the back side of the fabric.

Foam finishing—refers to processes in which the chemical is suspended in a foam.

Foam-flame process—uses foam partially melted by heat to adhere two layers of fabric together to create a laminate.

Foam printing—is a type of printing in which the colorant is suspended in foam prior to application.

Foil printing—is a printing process in which a special adhesive is screen-printed onto fabric, an aluminum-coated polyester film is pressed onto the fabric, and the foil adheres only to areas with the adhesive.

Formaldehyde—is a restricted hazardous chemical that is used in finishing and dyeing textiles.

Foulard (foo´-lahrd)—is a soft, lightweight, filament-yarn twill-weave fabric. It is woven in a twill weave and piece-dyed or printed.

French terry—is a weft-insertion filling knit, but the fabric is not napped.

Friction calendering—is a type of calendering in which one cylinder rotates more quickly than the other, shining or polishing the fabric surface; it is used to produce polished cotton with or without a resin.

Friezé (fre¯´-zay or fre¯z)—is a strong, durable, heavy-warp-yarn pile fabric. The pile is made by the over-wire method to create a closed-loop pile.

Frosting—is a problem with color retention related to a dye's inability to penetrate deeply in the fiber. Abrasion removes the colored portion and reveals the uncolored portion. It also refers to a chemical or abrasive finish that deliberately produces this whitish cast on fabrics.

Full fashioning—is the process of shaping knit garments during the knitting process by adding or decreasing stitches. (*See also* Fashioning.)

Fulling—is a finish of woven or knitted wool fabrics that produces a tighter, more compact fabric by a carefully controlled felting process.

Fume fading—is a color-retention problem. Colors alter when exposed to gases, fumes, or other atmospheric pollutants.

Fume-fading-resistant finish—refers to a finish designed to minimize the effect of atmospheric pollutants on dyes.

Functional finish—(*See* Special-purpose finish.)

Fur—is any animal skin or hide to which the hair is attached and that has been processed to protect the hide from rotting.

Fur cleaning—is a specialized process of removing soil from fur so that the hide does not lose its color or suppleness and the hair is not damaged.

Fur Products Labeling Act—regulates the labeling of fur products to protect the consumer from unscrupulous trade practices.

Fusible nonwoven—is a type of fiberweb with a chemical adhesive on its technical back.

Gabardine (gaberdine)—is a tightly woven, medium-weight to heavyweight, steep- or regular-angle twill-weave fabric with a pronounced wale. The fabric can be wool, a wool blend, or synthetic fibers that resemble wool. Gabardine can also be 100 percent texturized polyester or a cotton/polyester blend.

Gaiting—describes the arrangement of needles in a double-knitting machine. (*See also* Interlock Gaiting and Rib Gaiting.)

Garment dyeing—(*See* Product dyeing.)

Garment or product dip process—(*See* Immersion process.)

Garnetted—is a term for shredding wool yarns or fabrics to produce wool fibers for recycling.

Gauge (ga¯j)—refers to needles per inch in the machines used in making knits or tufted fabrics.

Gauze (gawz)—is a sheer, lightweight, low-count plain- or leno-weave balanced fabric made of spun yarns. It is often cotton or rayon or a blend of these fibers. Indian gauze has a crinkled look and is available in a variety of fabric weights.

Gel spinning—is a spinning method in which the dissolved polyethylene polymer forms a viscous gel in the solvent, followed by extrusion through the spinneret, solvent extraction, and fiber drawing.

Generic group—refers to fibers with similar chemical composition.

Generic name—refers to the family of manufactured or synthetic fibers that have similar chemical composition.

Georgette—is a sheer, lightweight plain-weave or momie-weave fabric made with fine-crepe yarns. It is livelier and less lustrous than chiffon.

Geotextiles—are textile materials used in contact with the soil in technical applications.

Gin—is a mechanical device used to separate cotton fibers from the seeds.

Gingham—is a yarn-dyed plain-weave fabric that is available in a variety of weights and qualities. It may be balanced or unbalanced and of combed or carded yarns. If two colors of yarn are used, the fabric is called *check* or *checked gingham*. If three or more colors are used, the fabric is referred to as *plaid gingham*.

Glass—is a manufactured fiber in which the fiber-forming substance is glass.

Glass transition temperature (Tg)—refers to the temperature at which amorphous regions of fibers are easily distorted. It is used in heatsetting fabrics.

Glazed—refers to a fabric that has been treated with a friction calender to polish the surface.

Glazed chintz—(*See* Chintz.)

Glazing—is a flattening of the cross section of heat-sensitive fibers or yarns resulting from exposure to high temperatures.

Globalization—refers to companies purchasing from and/or selling to multiple sites in the world.

Glucose—is the basic monomer of cellulose.

Gore-Tex—is a poromeric multiplex fabric combining fluoropolymer film with fabric to produce a water-impermeable but comfortable fabric. It is produced by W. L. Gore & Associates.

Grading wool—refers to judging a wool fleece for its fineness and length.

Graft polymer—is a type of copolymer; another type of mer is attached to the backbone polymer chain.

Grain—refers to the natural surface characteristic of leather and is related to the species of animal. It also describes the relationship of warp to filling yarns in a woven fabric.

Grain-sueded (or nubuck) leather—is leather that has been napped on the grain side of the skin or hide.

Granite cloth—is a wool momie-weave fabric. The term may be used for any momie-weave fabric.

Gray goods or Grey goods or Greige goods—is a general term used to describe any unfinished woven or knitted fabric.

Grease wool—(*See* Raw wool.)

Green cotton—describes cotton fabric that has been washed with mild natural-based soap, but it has not been bleached or treated with other chemicals, except possibly natural dyes.

Green products—are those sold with claims, valid or not, that they have been produced using systems that have minimal environmental impact.

Grin-through—occurs when some elastomeric fibers break and the broken ends or loops of broken fibers appear on the fabric's surface. In pile and tufted fabrics, it describes where the base structure shows through the pile surface.

Grosgrain (grow´-grain)—is a tightly woven, firm warp-faced fabric with heavy, round filling ribs created by a high warp count and coarse filling yarns. Grosgrain can be woven as a narrow ribbon or a full-width fabric.

Ground ply—is the ply of a fancy yarn that forms the foundation for the effect ply.

Guanaco—is the fiber produced by the South American guanaco.

Habutai—is a soft, lightweight silk fabric, heavier than China silk.

Hackling—is a process of separating bast fiber bundles into individual fibers and removing short irregular fibers.

Hairiness—describes excessive fiber ends on a yarn's surface that may create problems in fabrication or in consumer use because they are more sensitive to abrasion and pilling.

Halogenation—is a finish for wool that partially dissolves fiber scales in order to produce a washable fabric.

Hand—is the way a fiber feels to the sense of touch.

Hand builders—are compounds that soften a fabric's hand.

Handkerchief linen—is similar in luster and count to batiste, but it is linen or linenlike, with greater body.

Handling—refers to the physical form of the fabric in terms of length and width during finishing.

Handmade lace—includes several types of lace made by people.

Hard twist—is a high amount of yarn twist in the range of 30 to 40 tpi, which produces a harsher fabric hand.

Harness—is the part of the loom that forms the weave by controlling the up or down position of warp yarns.

Heat conductivity—is the ability to conduct heat away from the body.

Heat retention—is the ability of a fiber to retain heat or to insulate.

Heat sensitivity—is the ability to soften, melt, or shrink when subjected to heat. (*See also* Thermoplastic.)

Heat setting—describes the process of producing fiber, yarn, or fabric stability through the use of heat.

Heat-transfer printing—describes a process of adding color to fabric by using heat to cause a pattern printed on paper to transfer to the fabric.

Heddle—is a rigid wire in the loom through which a warp yarn is threaded and held in place in a harness.

Hemp—is a bast fiber produced by *Cannabis sativa*.

Henequen—is a smooth, straight, yellow leaf fiber similar to sisal.

Herringbone—is a broken twill-weave fabric created by changing the direction of the twill wale from right to left and back again. This creates a chevron pattern of stripes that may or may not be equally prominent. Herringbone fabrics are made in a variety of weights, patterns, and fiber types.

Hessian—(*See* Burlap.)

High-bulk yarn—is a bulk yarn with little or no stretch.

High-tenacity fibers—are fibers that have been modified in the spinning process to increase fiber strength.

High-wet-modulus rayon—is a modification of rayon with better performance characteristics.

Hollow fibers—are fibers that contain air space in their interiors.

Home fashions—(*See* Interior textiles.)

Homespun—is a coarse plain-weave fabric with a handwoven look.

Homopolymer—refers to a polymer composed of a single type of mer.

Honan (ho¯´-nahn)—was originally of Chinese silk but is now made of any filament fiber. It is similar to pongee, but it has slub yarns in both warp and filling.

Hopsacking—is a coarse, loose-suiting, or bottom-weight basket-weave fabric often made of low-grade cotton.

Hot-melt lamination—is a method of combining outer fabric, adhesive, and liner fabric into a composite fabric with the use of heat and pressure.

Hot-water extraction—is a cleaning technique for furnishings in which a hot water–detergent solution is injected into the textile and the soiled solution is removed by vacuuming.

Houndstooth—is a medium-weight to heavyweight, yarn-dyed twill-weave fabric in which the interlacing and color pattern create a unique pointed-check or houndstooth shape.

Huck or Huck-a-back—is a medium-weight to heavyweight fabric made on a dobby loom to create a honeycomb or bird's-eye pattern. Often the filling yarns are more loosely twisted to increase fabric absorbency.

Hydroentangled web—is a layer of fibers in which jets of water are forced through the web after extrusion to entangle the fibers.

Hydrogen bonds—are attractions between positive hydrogen atoms of one molecule and negative oxygen or nitrogen atoms in another molecule.

Hydrophilic—describes fibers with high moisture absorbency or regain.

Hydrophobic—describes fibers with low moisture absorbency or regain.

Hygroscopic—describes fibers with high moisture absorbency or regain and the ability to remain dry to the touch.

Ikat—is a resist printing method; yarns are treated to resist dye in certain areas, dyed, and woven into a fabric.

Immersion process—is a process for creating durable-press items in which the finished item is immersed in a finishing agent mixed with appropriate additives to control for hand and performance, pressed, and cured.

Industrial textiles—include a broad range of materials used in technical non-apparel and non-furnishing uses.

Ink-jet printing—is another name for digital printing.

Insect- and moth-control finish—uses chemical compounds to reduce a fabric's attraction to insects, including moths.

Inspection—describes the finishing step in which fabric quality is assessed.

Intarsia—is a type of filling-knit fabric in which yarns that appear on the surface of the fabric are discontinuous. Intarsia is a knit counterpart to a true tapestry weave.

Intelligent or interactive textiles—(*See* Smart textiles.)

Interior textiles, interior furnishings or home fashions—describe textiles and textile products used in the home and other building interiors for functions such as absorbency or to add comfort and visual interest.

Interlacing—is the point at which a yarn changes its position from one side of the fabric to the other.

Interlock—is a firm double-filling knit. The two needle beds knit two interlocked 1×1 rib fabrics. Both sides of the fabric look like the face side of jersey.

Interlock gaiting—refers to a double-needle-bed arrangement. Needles in one bed are directly opposite needles in the other bed. It is used to produce interlock and other double-knits.

Isotactic—refers to the same type of spatial arrangement of side groups attached to the backbone chain throughout the polymer.

Jacquard double-knit—is a patterned fabric made on a double-knitting machine.

Jacquard jersey—is a jersey knit with a pattern that uses a combination of knit, tuck, or miss stitches.

Jacquard loom—is a loom with warp yarns individually controlled by punched cards or a microcomputer used to create jacquard fabrics.

Jacquard weave—refers to large-figured designs that require more than 25 different arrangements of the warp yarns to complete one repeat design.

Jean—is a warp-faced twill of carded yarns. It is lighter weight than drill, and it has finer yarns but a higher warp-yarn count.

Jersey—is a single-filling-knit fabric with no distinct rib. Jersey can have any fiber content and be knit flat or circular.

Jet dyeing—is a process in which the fabric is in a continuous loop when dyed.

Jet printing—is the application of color to fabric by spraying dye through tiny nozzles to create the pattern.

Jig dyeing—is a process for dyeing fabric in open-width form.

Jute—is a bast fiber used to produce burlap and other technical fabrics.

Kapok—is the fiber removed from the seeds of the Java kapok or silk cotton tree.

Kenaf—is a bast fiber removed from the kenaf plant.

Keratin—is the protein found in animal fibers.

Kersey—is a very heavy, thick, boardy wool coating fabric that has been so heavily fulled and felted that it is difficult to see the twill weave. Kersey, heavier than melton, may be either a single or a double cloth.

Knit-deknit process—is a filament yarn texturing process in which a yarn is knit into a fabric, heat-set, and unknit.

Knit stitch—is the basic stitch that forms the majority of knit fabrics.

Knitted terrycloth—is a filling-knit fabric with a loop pile.

Knit-through fabric or Sew-knit fabric—includes several types of composite fabric made by knitting a fine yarn through a thin fiberweb or by knitting fibers or yarns to lock laid yarns in place.

Knitting—refers to the production of fabric by interlooping yarns.

Knit yarns—are narrow fabric yarns made by knitting.

Knot, Spot, Nub, or Knop yarn—is a fancy yarn. The effect ply is twisted many times around the ground ply in the same place.

Lab dip—is a sample that is sent to the creative team to determine when a color match has been achieved.

Labeling requirements—refer to information required by law or regulation that must be available to the consumer at the point of purchase.

Lace—is an openwork fabric with yarns that are twisted around each other to form complex patterns or figures. Lace is handmade or machine-made by a variety of fabrication methods, including weaving, knitting, crocheting, and knotting.

Lacoste—is a double-knit fabric made with a combination of knit and tuck stitches to create a meshlike appearance. It is often 100 percent cotton or a cotton/polyester blend.

Lamb's wool—is wool removed from animals less than seven months old.

Lamé (lah-may´)—is any fabric containing metal or metallic yarns as a conspicuous feature.

Laminated fabric—describes a composite fabric created by adhering two layers of fabrics with a thin foam.

Laminates—are composite fabrics in which two layers of fabric are adhered by foam or adhesive.

Lastol—is a generic subclass of an elastic olefin.

Lastrile—is a synthetic rubber in which the fiber-forming substance is a copolymer of acrylonitrile and a diene composed of not more than 50 percent but at least 10 percent by weight of acrylonitrile units.

Latch needle—is a type of needle used in knitting fabrics from coarse yarns.

Lawn—is a fine, opaque, lightweight plain-weave fabric usually made of combed-cotton or cotton-blend yarns. The fabric may be bleached, dyed, or printed.

Leaf fiber—refers to fiber removed from the leaves of a plant.

Leather—is processed from the skins or hides of mammals, birds, reptiles, or fish so that it does not rot.

Leather cleaning—is a specialized process of removing soil from treated animal hides so that color and suppleness are not lost.

Leavers lace—is a type of machine-made lace in which bobbins move back and forth and around warp yarns to create the fabric's open pattern.

Leno (le¯´-no¯)—refers to any leno-weave fabric in which two warp yarns are crossed over each other and held in place by a filling yarn. This requires a doup attachment on the loom.

Level—refers to a colorant that is uniform throughout the fabric or product.

Licensing—describes the situation in which one company legally uses another company's trademarks and expertise to make, use, and/or sell a product.

Life cycle analysis—examines the way the production, use, care, and disposal of a product affects the environment and the people involved with the product.

Light-reflecting finishes—incorporate fluorescent dyes or small glass retroreflective spheres or prisms to enhance fabric visibility in low-light conditions.

Light resistance—is a finish or fiber modification to minimize the degradative effects of sunlight on fiber or dye.

Light-stabilizing finishes—incorporate light-stabilizing or ultraviolet-absorbing compounds to minimize damage from light exposure.

Line—refers to long, combed, and better-quality flax fibers.

Linen—(See Flax.)

Lining twill—is an opaque, lightweight warp-faced twill of filament yarns. It may be printed.

Lint—refers to usable cotton fibers removed in the ginning process. It also refers to fiber debris that creates pills on fabrics or accumulates in dryer lint traps.

Linters—are very short cotton fibers that remain attached to the cotton seed after ginning.

Liquid-barrier finish—protects fabrics from liquids penetrating through them.

Liquor ratio—refers to the weight of water or other solvent as compared with the weight of fabric in a solution.

Lisle (pronounced lyle)—is a high-quality jersey made of fine two-ply combed-cotton yarns.

Llama—is the fiber produced by the South American llama.

Loft—is the ability to spring back to original thickness after being compressed. (See also Compressional resiliency.)

London shrunk—is a relaxation finishing process for wool fabrics.

Loom—is the machine used to make woven fabrics.

Loop yarn, curl yarn, or bouclé yarn—is a fancy yarn. The effect ply forms closed loops at regular intervals along the length of the yarn.

Looping machine—is used to join knit garment parts in a way that the join is hidden.

Low-elongation fibers—are used in blends with weaker fibers to increase fabric strength and abrasion resistance.

Low-pilling fibers—have been engineered to have a lower flex life, thus decreasing pill formation.

Low twist—is a very small amount of twist used in filament yarns that keeps fibers together in processing and fabrication.

Lumen—is a hollow central canal through which nutrients travel as a cotton fiber develops in the plant.

Luster—refers to the way light is reflected from the fiber or fabric surface.

Luster finish—is a fabric treatment that changes the light reflectance characteristics of the fabric.

Lyocell (li¯´-o¯-sel)—is a manufactured fiber composed of solvent-spun cellulose.

Madras (mad´-ras) gingham or Madras shirting—is a lightweight to medium-weight dobby-weave fabric in which the pattern is usually confined to vertical stripes.

Maltese lace—is a bobbin lace with a Maltese cross in the pattern.

Man-made fibers—(See Manufactured fibers.)

Manufactured fibers—are made from chemical compounds produced in manufacturing facilities. The material's original form is not recognizable as a fiber.

Manufactured regenerated fibers—are produced in fiber form from naturally occurring polymers.

Marquisette (mahr-kui-zet´)—is a sheer, lightweight leno-weave fabric, usually made of filament yarns.

Mass pigmentation—(See Solution dyeing.)

Matelassé (mat-luh-sa¯´)—is a double-cloth fabric woven to create a three-dimensional texture with a puckered or almost quilted look. Matelassés are made on jacquard or dobby looms, often with crepe yarns or coarse cotton yarns. When finished, the shrinkage of the crepe yarn or the coarse cotton yarn creates the puckered appearance. It is used in apparel as well as in furnishings.

Mechlin (mek´-lihn) lace—is a bobbin lace with a small hexagonal mesh and very fine yarns.

Medulla—is an airy, honeycombed core present in some wool fibers.

Melamine—is a manufactured fiber in which the fiber-forming substance is a synthetic polymer composed of at least 50 percent by weight of a cross-linked melamine polymer.

Melt-blown fiberweb—is made by extruding the polymer into a high-velocity air stream that breaks the fiber into short pieces that are held together by thermal bonding and fiber interlacing.

Melton—is a heavyweight plain- or twill-weave coating fabric made from wool. It is lighter than kersey and has a smooth surface that is napped and then closely sheared. It may be either a single or a double cloth.

Melt spinning—is the process of producing fibers by melting polymer chips and extruding the melt (the molten polymer) in fiber form. Coagulation occurs by cooling.

Mercerization—is a finish in which sodium hydroxide is used to increase cotton's absorbency, luster, and strength. (See also Slack mercerization and Tension mercerization.)

Merino—is a sheep breed that produces superior-quality wool.

Metallic coating—is a surface application of a thin layer of metal, usually aluminum, primarily to minimize heat transfer through the fabric or to add a metallic luster to the fabric.

Metallic fibers—are manufactured fibers composed of metal, plastic-coated metal, metal-coated plastic, or a core completely covered by metal.

Metallic yarn—is a yarn made with at least one metal monofilament fiber.

Metamerism (meh-tam´-uhr-izm)—describes when two items match in color under one light source, but not under another light source.

Metered-addition process—is a durable-press process in which finished goods are sprayed with a controlled amount of the finishing agent mixed with additives that control hand and performance, tumbled to distribute the finish evenly, pressed, and cured.

Microdenier—refers to a fiber of less than 1.0 denier per filament.

Microencapsulated finishes—incorporate a water-soluble material in a tiny capsule form, which may contain fragrance, insect repellents, disinfectants, cleaning agents, or other materials.

Migration—describes a color problem in which the dye shifts from the area where it was applied to adjacent areas of the same fabric or a fabric in close proximity.

Milanese machine—uses two sets of yarns, one needle bed, and one guide bar to knit milanese fabrics.

Mildew control—describes a finish that inhibits the growth of mold or mildew.

Mildew resistance—is resistance to the growth of mold, mildew, or fungus.

Mill-finished—describes a fabric finished by the same company that produced the fabric, a type of vertical integration within the textile industry.

Milling—(See Fulling.)

Minimum or Minimum yardage—refers to the shortest length of fabric a textile firm will produce or sell to another firm.

Mixed-denier filament bundling—combines fibers of several denier sizes, such as microfibers (0.5 dpf) with macro or regular denier (2.0 dpf) fibers, in one yarn.

Mixture—is a fiber blend. Yarns of one generic type are present in one fabric area (i.e., the warp) and yarns of another generic type are present in another fabric area (i.e., the filling).

Modacrylic—is a manufactured fiber in which the fiber-forming substance is any long-chain synthetic polymer composed of less than 85 percent but at least 35 percent by weight acrylonitrile units except when the polymer qualifies as rubber.

Modulus—is the resistance to stress/strain to which a fiber is exposed.

Mohair—is the hair fiber produced by the Angora goat.

Moiré (mwah-ra¯´) calendering—describes a finish that produces a watermarked or wood-grain texture on rib or unbalanced plain-weave fabrics like taffeta.

Moiré pattern—is a wood-grain or watermarked pattern produced on some unbalanced plain-weave fabrics by finishing.

Moisture management finishes—remove sweat from the skin's surface and help cool the body.

Moisture transport—is a measure of the speed with which perspiration is drawn from the skin's surface to the fabric's surface.

Moisture vapor transport rate (MVTR)—measures how quickly moisture vapor moves from the side of the fabric next to the body to the fabric's exterior side.

Mold control—(See Mildew control.)

Moleskin—is a napped, heavy, strong fabric often made in a satin weave. The nap is suedelike.

Momie weave—is a class of weaves with no wale or other distinct weave effect, resulting from an irregular interlacing pattern.

Momme or Momie or Mommie (mum´me)—is a standard way to describe the weight of silk fabrics and is abbreviated mm; one momme weighs 3.75 grams.

Monk's cloth—is a heavyweight, coarse, loosely woven basket-weave fabric usually in a 2×2 or 4×4 arrangement made of softly spun two-ply yarns in oatmeal color.

Monofilament yarn—is a filament yarn consisting of a single fiber.

Mordant dyes—are a class of dyes that require the use of a metal salt (mordant) to bond with the fiber.

Moss crepe—combines a momie weave with crepe-twist yarns.

Moth resistance—describes a finish in which the wool fabric is treated to be unpalatable or harmful to insects; resistance to insect damage.

Multicellular fibers—are fibers with a modified cross section that encloses air cells within the fiber.

Multihead embroidery—refers to the machine that creates several identical designs or emblems simultaneously.

Multiple-shed weaving—is a type of loom in which the filling yarn is inserted in a series of sheds that form as the filling yarn moves across the fabric. It is also known as multi-phase weaving.

Multiplex fabric—describes fabrics that combine fibers, yarns, fabrics, or a combination of these into one fabric; it is another term for a composite fabric.

Multiprocess wet cleaning—(See Professional wet cleaning.)

Muslin—is a firm, medium-weight to heavyweight plain-weave cotton fabric made in a variety of qualities.

Nanofiber—is a fiber with a cross section measuring less than 1,000 nm (nanometers).

Nanoparticle—is any particle with one or more dimensions measured in nanometers.

Nap—refers to fiber ends on the fabric's surface due to finishing.

Napping—is a finish in which fiber ends are brushed to the surface to produce a softer hand.

Napping twist—is a small amount of twist used to produce lofty spun yarns for fabrics that will be napped.

Narrow fabric—describes any fabric up to 12 inches wide.

Natural bicomponent fiber—contains the two types of cortex cells; wool fiber is an example.

Natural dyes—are a dye class produced by plants and other natural sources used primarily with natural fibers.

Natural fibers—are grown or developed in nature in recognizable fiber form.

Naturally colored cotton—is cotton grown in colors of brown, tan, yellow, green, rust, and so on.

Natural protein fiber—is a fiber of animal or insect origin.

Needlepoint lace—includes Alençon, which has a hexagonal mesh, and rosepoint and Venetian point, which have an irregular mesh.

Needle punching—is a fiberweb made by passing barbed needles through a fiberweb to entangle the fibers.

Neoprene—describes a composite fabric combining a film of polychloroprene with a woven, knitted, or fiberweb fabric.

Nep—is a small knot of entangled fibers. The fibers may be immature or dead and create problems in dyeing.

Net—is a general term used to refer to any open-construction fabric, whether it is created by weaving, knitting, knotting, or other methods.

Netlike structure—includes all fabric structures formed by extruding one or more polymers as film that is embossed and partially slit or by extruding a network of ligaments or strands.

Network yarn—is a yarn made from fibers that are connected at points along their length.

Ninon (nee´-nohn)—is a sheer, slightly crisp, lightweight plain-weave fabric made of filament yarns. The warp yarns are grouped in pairs, but ninon is not a basket-weave fabric.

Nodes—are irregular crosswise markings present in many bast fibers.

Nonreinforced film—(See Plain film.)

Nonwoven—is a general term for fabrics directly made from fibers.

Novelty yarn—is another term for a fancy yarn.

Novoloid—is a manufactured fiber in which the fiber-forming substance contains at least 35 percent by weight of cross-linked novolac.

Nylon—is a manufactured fiber in which the fiber-forming substance is any long-chain synthetic polyamide in which less than 85 percent of the amide linkages are attached directly to two aromatic rings.

Occupational Safety and Health Administration (OSHA)—is the federal agency that enforces laws and regulations that ensure safety in the workplace.

Off-grain—refers to a fabric in which the warp and filling yarns do not cross each other at a 90-degree angle.

Off-grain print—describes a fabric defect in which the print pattern does not line up with the fabric grain.

Off-shade—describes when one fabric or portion of a product does not precisely match the color of another fabric or portion of a product.

Olefin—is a manufactured fiber in which the fiber-forming substance is any long-chain synthetic polymer composed of at least 85 percent by weight of ethylene, propylene, or other olefin units except amorphous (noncrystalline) polyolefins qualifying as rubber.

Oleophilic—refers to fibers that have a high affinity or attraction for oil.

Open-end rotor spinning—is a spun yarn process that eliminates roving and twisting.

Opening—is an initial step in the production of spun yarns that loosens fibers from bale form and cleans and blends the fibers.

Open-width finishing—refers to holding the fabric out to its full width during finishing.

Optical brighteners—are chemical compounds used to produce a white appearance.

Organdy—is a transparent, crisp, lightweight plain-weave fabric made of cotton-spun yarns. The fabric has been parchmentized or treated with acid to create the crisp, wiry hand.

Organic cotton—describes cotton produced following state fiber-certification standards on land where organic farming practices have been used for at least 3 years.

Organza—is a transparent, crisp, lightweight plain-weave fabric made of filament yarns.

Orientation—refers to the alignment of the fiber's polymers with its longitudinal axis.

Osnaburg (osnaberg)—is a coarse, bottom-weight, low-count cotton fabric characterized by uneven yarns that include bits of plant debris.

Ottoman—is a firm, plain-weave, unbalanced fabric with large and small ribs made by adjacent filling yarns of different sizes that are completely covered by the warp.

Outing flannel—is a medium-weight, napped, plain- or twill-weave spun-yarn fabric. It may be napped on one or both sides. It is heavier and stiffer than flannelette.

Out-of-register—is a problem with some printed fabrics. The edges of a print do not match as the designer intended.

Over-wire method—is one technique used to create pile fabrics such as friezé.

Oxford chambray—is an oxford cloth made with yarn-dyed warp yarns and white, or sometimes yarn-dyed, filling yarns.

Oxford cloth—is a lightweight to medium-weight fabric with a 2×1 half-basket weave.

Ozonation—is treating fabrics with ozone to remove color for fashion looks.

Package dyeing—is a process for dyeing yarn cones or other textiles in which the dye bath is forced through the textile.

Padding machine—passes the fabric through a solution, under a guide roll, and between two padding rolls to evenly distribute a finish across the fabric.

Pad dyeing—is a process for dyeing fabric in open-width form where dye is forced into the fiber by nip or squeeze rollers.

Panné velvet—is a warp-pile fabric in which the pile yarns are pressed flat in the same direction.

Parchmentizing—is an acid finish for cotton fabrics that produces a thinner fabric with a crisper hand than the original fabric; it is used to produce organdy.

Parent fiber—is the simplest form of a manufactured fiber that has not been modified in any way.

PBI—is a manufactured fiber in which the fiber-forming substance is a long-chain aromatic polymer having recurring imidazole groups as an integral part of the polymer chain.

PBO—is a special-use fiber made of polyphenylene benzobisoxazole.

Peau de soie (po¯´-deh-swah)—is a very smooth, heavy, semidull satin-weave fabric of silk, acetate, or other manufactured fibers. It often has satin floats on both sides of the fabric.

Percale—is a balanced, plain-weave, medium-weight piece-dyed or printed fabric finished from better-quality print cloths.

Performance—is the manner in which a textile, textile component, or textile product responds when something is done to it or when it is exposed to some mechanical or environmental element that might adversely affect it.

Performance fibers—are fiber modifications that provide comfort and improve human performance for products such as active sportswear.

Performance testing—refers to subjecting a textile to selected procedures and determining how the textile reacts.

Perfume—is a compound added to some detergents to mask an unattractive odor with one that is more pleasant.

Permanent finish—describes a finish whose effectiveness will not diminish with time or use.

Phase-change finish—is a chemical compound that changes physical state (solid or liquid) as it absorbs or loses heat.

Picking—is the step in weaving in which the filling yarn is inserted in the shed.

Pick-up—is the amount of liquid or chemical a fabric absorbs during finishing.

Piece dyeing—describes adding color to a textile when it is in fabric form. (See also Cross dyeing and Union dyeing.)

Pigment—is a colorant that is insoluble and must be attached to the fiber with the use of a binding agent.

Pile jersey—is a filling knit made with two sets of yarns, in which one set forms the base structure and the other set forms the pile.

Pile weave—is a three-dimensional structure made by weaving an extra set of warp or filling yarns with the ground yarns so that loops or cut-yarn ends create a pile.

Pilling—is the formation of tiny balls of fiber ends and lint on the surface of the fabric.

Pilling-resistant finish—is any finish designed to minimize the formation of pills on a fabric.

Pima cotton—is a type of extra-long-staple cotton.

Piña—is a leaf fiber obtained from the pineapple plant.

Pinsonic quilting—is the production of a composite fabric by using ultra-high-frequency sound to heat-seal face fabric, fiberfill, and backing fabric together in localized areas.

Piqué (pee-kay´)—is a fabric made on a dobby or jacquard loom with carded or combed yarns. Some piqués are made in a variety of patterns. Some have filling cords. Most have three or more sets of yarns.

PLA—is a renewable fiber made from fermented cornstarch and melt-spun.

Plain film—consists of the polymer solution in sheet form with no supporting layer.

Plain weave—is the simplest weave structure in which two sets of yarns at right angles to each other pass alternately over and under each other to form the maximum number of interlacings.

Plasma treatment—uses highly ionized gas to change the surface nature of textiles with thin, inexpensive functional coatings.

Plastic coating—is the surface application of a thin film to a fabric for increased luster and water repellency or to minimize yarn slippage.

Plasticize finish—is a very thin layer of polymer added to a dyed fabric to create a shiny synthetic surface.

Pleated fabric—is a special type of embossed fabric in which pleats are formed during finishing and heat-set into the fabric.

Pleating calender—is a special type of embossing calendering that produces three-dimensional pleats in the fabric.

Plissé (plih-sa¯´)—is a fabric usually finished from cotton-print cloth by printing on a caustic-soda (sodium hydroxide) paste that shrinks the fabric and creates a three-dimensional effect. The stripe that is printed is usually darker in piece-dyed goods because the sodium hydroxide increases the dye absorbency.

Plush—is a woven warp-pile fabric with a deep pile.

Ply yarn—consists of two or more strands of fibers held together by twist or some other mechanism.

Pocket weave—(See Double weave.)

Point paper—is a type of paper used to diagram warp knits.

Polished cotton—is a balanced, medium-weight plain-weave fabric that has been given a glazed-calender finish.

Pollution fading—(*See* Fume fading.)

Pollution Prevention Act—is the federal law that focuses on waste minimization.

Polyamide—is a generic term for polymers containing an amide group and is a term used for nylon in some countries.

Polyester—is a manufactured fiber in which the fiber-forming substance is any long-chain synthetic polymer composed of at least 85 percent by weight of an ester of a substituted aromatic carboxylic acid, including but not restricted to substituted terephthalate units or substituted hydroxybenzoate units.

Polyethylene—is a type of olefin made from polymerizing ethylene.

Polyimide—is a special-use fiber made from polyetherimide.

Polymer—is a very large molecule made by connecting many small molecules, or monomers, together.

Polymerization—is the process of connecting many small molecules (monomers) to produce one very large molecule, called a *polymer*.

Polypropylene—is a type of olefin made from polymerizing propylene.

Polytetrafluoroethylene—is the polymer found in fluoropolymer fibers.

Pongee (pahn-jee´)—is a medium-weight, balanced plain-weave fabric with a fine regular warp and an irregular filling. Originally from tussah or wild silk, pongee now describes a fabric that has fine warp yarns and irregular filling yarns.

Poplin—is a medium-weight to heavyweight, unbalanced, plain-weave spun-yarn fabric that is usually piece-dyed. The filling yarns are coarser than the warp yarns. Poplin has a more pronounced rib than broadcloth.

Poromeric fabric—incorporates a thin film that is microporous in nature.

Porosity-control finish—is a finish that minimizes airflow through a fabric.

Postcured process—is a durable-press process in which the fabric is saturated with the cross-linking solution, cut and sewn into a product, and cured.

Powder cleaners—are dry, absorbent powders that combine detergent and solvent and are applied to the textile in dry form, worked in, and removed by vacuuming.

Power net—is a raschel-warp knit in which an inlaid spandex fiber or yarn produces high elongation and elasticity.

Power stretch—refers to the ability of a fiber or fabric to exhibit high retractive forces that mold, support, or shape the body.

Precured process—is a durable-press process in which the fabric is saturated with the cross-linking solution, cured, cut, and sewn into a product.

Preparation—refers to a series of steps to get yarns ready for weaving or dyeing or fabrics ready for dyeing, printing, or finishing.

Pressing—is a finishing process used with wool or wool blends in which the fabric is placed between metal plates that steam and press it.

Pretreatment—includes a variety of chemicals that make it easier to remove stains during cleaning.

Primary fiber bundle—refers to naturally occurring groupings of individual bast fibers that are difficult to separate completely and that contribute to the natural thick-and-thin appearance of yarns made from bast fibers.

Print cloth—is a general term used to describe unfinished, medium-weight, balanced plain-weave cotton or cotton-blend fabrics. These fabrics can be finished as percale, embossed cotton, plissé, chintz, cretonne, or polished cotton.

Printing—is the localized application of color to the surface of the fabric or yarn. (*See also* Direct printing, Resist printing, Roller printing, and Screen printing.)

Producer coloring—(*See* Solution dyeing.)

Product development—is the design and engineering of a product so that it has the desired serviceability characteristics, appeals to the target market, can be made within an acceptable time frame for a reasonable cost, and can be sold at a profit.

Product dyeing—refers to the process of adding color to the textile after it has been cut and sewn into the final product.

Product testing—refers to consumers using textile products and evaluating how the products perform.

Professional wet cleaning—is a commercial alternative to dry cleaning that uses carefully controlled wet processes to clean textiles that cannot be machine-washed.

Progressive shrinkage—is shrinkage that occurs through several care cycles.

Projectile loom or Gripper loom—is a type of loom in which the filling yarn is inserted in the shed with a small metal projectile or gripper.

Prototype—is an original sample product used to assess fit, design, construction, and production decisions.

Puckered surface—is created on nylon and polyester fabrics by printing them with a chemical that causes the fibers to shrink slightly when dry.

Pure silk and Pure dye silk—describe 100 percent silk fabrics that do not contain any metallic weighting compounds or where the metallic weighting compounds are within the minimums set by the 1932 federal silk regulation.

Purl gaiting—is a special type of needle arrangement for knitting machines that make purl knits.

Purl knit—is made on a special type of double-knitting machine that can produce plain jersey knits, rib knits, and purl knits.

Purl stitch or Reverse stitch—is a stitch that looks the same on both sides of the fabric.

Qiviut—is the fine underwool fiber obtained from the musk ox.

QSC—(*See* Quick Style Change.)

Quality—refers to the sum total of product characteristics, including appearance, appropriateness for the end use, performance and interactions of materials in the product, consistency among identical products, and freedom from defects in construction or materials.

Quick Style Change (QSC)—describes changes in looms and loom control mechanisms to facilitate a rapid change for a loom from one structural design fabric to another.

Quilted fabric—is a composite fabric consisting of a face or fashion fabric, a layer of fiberfill or batting, and a backing fabric. The three layers may be connected with heat (pinsonic quilting) or thread (regular quilting).

Ramie—is a fiber removed from a perennial shrub grown in hot, humid climates.

Rapier loom—is a type of loom in which the filling yarn is inserted in the shed using a rigid or flexible rod or steel tape.

Raschel (rah-shel´) knit—is a general term for patterned warp-knit fabric made with coarser yarns than other warp-knit fabrics.

Raschel lace—is a type of lace made using warp knitting.

Ratiné yarn—is a fancy yarn. The effect ply is twisted in a spiral arrangement around the ground ply, with an occasional longer loop.

Raw wool—is wool as it is removed from the animal with soil, suint, and other impurities present.

Raw silk—is silk that has not been processed to remove the sericin.

Rayon—is a manufactured fiber composed of regenerated cellulose in which substituents have replaced not more than 15 percent of the hydrogens of the hydroxyl groups.

REACH—(Registration, Evaluation, Authorization, and Restriction of Chemicals) is a comprehensive chemical law related to environmental quality and human health that applies to the European Union.

Reactive dyes—are a dye class used primarily with natural fibers and rayon.

Reclining twill—is a shallow twill with a wale angle of 35 degrees or less.

Recycled wool—is wool that has been processed into fabrics, garnetted, and processed into another fabric.

Recycling—is the process of using materials more than one time before they are disposed of when they can no longer be reused in any form.

Reed—is the part of the loom through which warp yarns are threaded and that is used to push filling yarns into place after they have been inserted in the shed.

Reeling—refers to the process of removing silk fibers from several cocoons and winding them onto a reel.

Reembroidered lace—(*See* Cordonnet lace.)

Regular twill—is a twill with a wale angle of approximately 45 degrees.

Relaxation shrinkage—refers to loss of dimensions resulting from tensions introduced during fabric production or finishing.

Renewable finish—is a finish that can be replaced by consumers, dry cleaners, or other firms when its effectiveness has been decreased or destroyed.

Rep—is another term for an unbalanced plain weave.

Repairing—is a finishing step in which minor flaws in fabrics are corrected.

Resiliency—is the ability to return to original shape after bending, twisting, compressing, or a combination of these deformations.

Resist printing—refers to a coloration process in which a portion of the yarn or fabric is treated so dyes will not be absorbed during dyeing; it includes screen printing, ikat, and batik.

Resource Conservation and Recovery Act—is the federal law that regulates solid and hazardous materials from their generation to final disposal.

Retting—is the process of bacterial rotting or decomposing the pectin in plant stems in order to remove bast fibers.

Reworking—refers to inspecting fabric and repeating steps in finishing that were done incorrectly to achieve appropriate performance.

Rib—is a ridge formed in the fabric when the balance is something other than 1:1 or when the size of one yarn set is significantly greater than the size of the other yarn set in the fabric. It also refers to double-knit structures when one stitch is made on one bed and the next stitch is made on the other bed.

Rib gaiting—refers to the double-needle-bed arrangement. Needles in one bed are directly opposite the spaces in the other bed. It is used to produce rib knits and other double-knits.

Ring spinning—is a process for producing spun yarns. A series of operations removes fibers from a bale, removes debris, makes the fibers parallel, draws them into a fine strand, and adds twist to hold them together.

Rippling—is the process of removing seeds by pulling a plant through a machine in order to obtain a bast fiber.

RN number—refers to the manufacturer's identification number assigned to the firm, as allowed for in the Textile Fiber Products Identification Act.

Roller printing—is the application of color in localized areas through the use of engraved rollers.

Rope—is a heavy thick cord at least 2.5 cm or one inch or more in diameter consisting of strands of fiber, leather, or wire that are twisted or braided together.

Rope finishing—refers to allowing the fabric to roll and fold in on itself and form a tube or rope during finishing.

Rotary-screen printing—is a resist printing method. A cylindrical screen is treated so that print paste passes through openings to create a design on the fabric. One screen is used for each color in the pattern.

Rot-proof finish—is a finish that improves the longevity of fabrics used outdoors.

Roving—is a step in the production of some spun yarns. The drawn sliver is reduced in size, fibers are made more parallel, and a small amount of twist is inserted.

Rubber—is a manufactured fiber in which the fiber-forming substance is comprised of natural or synthetic rubber.

Run—describes a quantity of fabric receiving the same processing at the same time. For knits, it also refers to the collapse of a wale.

Safety—describes the ability of a textile or textile product to protect the body from harm.

Sailcloth—is a bottom-weight, half-basket-weave (2×1), unbalanced fabric of spun- or textured-filament yarns that can be piece-dyed or printed.

Sand crepe—is a momie-weave fabric with a repeat pattern of 16 warp and 16 filling yarns that produce a sanded or frosted appearance.

Saran—is a manufactured fiber in which the fiber-forming substance is any long-chain synthetic polymer composed of at least 80 percent by weight of vinylidene chloride units.

Sateen—is a strong, lustrous, medium-weight to heavyweight, spun-yarn satin-weave fabric that is either warp-faced or filling-faced. A warp-faced spun-yarn fabric with a satin weave may be called *cotton satin*.

Satin—is a strong, lustrous, medium-weight to heavyweight, filament-yarn satin-weave fabric.

Satin weave—is a weave in which each warp or filling yarn floats across four or more filling or warp yarns with a progression of interlacings by two to the right or to the left.

Scales—are a horny, nonfibrous layer on the exterior of wool fibers.

Schiffli embroidery—is the application of decorative thread on the fabric's surface to achieve a pattern, as in eyelet embroidery.

Schreiner calendering—etches hundreds of fine lines on a fabric's surface to increase cover, as in tricot, or to add a subtle luster, as in sateen.

Scoured wool—is wool that has been cleaned to remove soil, suint, and other impurities.

Scouring—refers to a finishing step in which soil, excess chemicals, or fiber coatings such as natural waxes or oils are removed.

Screen printing—is a process during which application of color to a fabric's surface is controlled by a specially prepared screen so that dye or pigment paste penetrates the screen in selected areas only. It includes rotary and flatbed screen printing.

Scroop—refers to the natural rustle made when two layers of silk fabric are rubbed together.

Scutching—is a process in which bast-fiber plant stems are passed through fluted metal rollers to break up and remove the woody outer layers.

Sea Island cotton—(*See* Pima cotton.)

Seaweed fiber—is a fiber regenerated from seaweed (*Ascophyllum nodosom*).

Seed fiber—refers to fiber removed from a plant's seed pod.

Seersucker—is a lightweight to heavyweight slack-tension-weave fabric made in a variety of interlacing patterns. It always has vertical crinkled or puckered stripes made by two sets of warp yarns: one set at normal weaving tension, the other set at a much looser, slack tension.

Self-twist spinning—is an alternative method of spinning yarn from S- and Z-twist roving that can be used with staple- and filament-fiber strands.

Selvage—is the self-edge of the fabric where filling yarns end or turn to go through another shed.

Serge—is a general term used to refer to wool or wool-like twill-weave fabrics with a flat right-hand wale.

Sericin—is the water-soluble protective gum that surrounds silk when extruded by a caterpillar.

Sericulture—is the production of cultivated silk.

Serviceability—is the measure of a textile product's ability to meet consumers' needs.

Sewing thread—is a yarn specifically designed for stitching together fabrics or other materials.

Shade sorting—describes a manufacturer's grouping of fabrics by color so that all fabrics of one color match.

Shagbark—is usually a gingham with an occasional warp yarn under slack tension. During weaving, the slack-tension yarns create a single loop at intervals, giving the fabric a unique surface appearance.

Shampooing—(*See* Wet cleaning.)

Shantung—is a rough-textured, plain-weave filament-warp-yarn and irregular-spun filling-yarn fabric that is heavier than pongee.

Shape memory fibers—are fibers with the capacity to change shape in a predefined way.

Shape-retention finish—refers to any finish that controls wrinkling or creasing with heat or resin; it includes crease-retention and durable-press finishes.

Sharkskin—is a wool or wool-like left-handed twill made with alternating warp and filling yarns of two different colors and having a smooth, flat appearance. Occasionally a plain-weave or basket-weave fabric is also called *sharkskin*.

Shearing—cuts away protruding fiber or yarn ends to achieve a level pile, surface nap, or sculptured effect.

Shed—is the space that is formed between warp yarns when at least one harness is raised and at least one harness is lowered during weaving.

Shedding—is the step in weaving during which the harnesses are raised or lowered.

Shifting resistance—describes a characteristic of fiberfill, batting, and wadding in which the fibers do not move or shift with use.

Shin-gosen (shin´ go¯sen)—is an ultrafine fiber, often polyester, with modified cross sections and occasional fiber irregularities. It is produced in Japan.

Shrinkage control—refers to finishes that minimize fabric tension during finishing to reduce shrinkage during use by consumers.

Shrinkage resistance—is the ability of a textile to retain its original dimensions during cleaning.

Shuttle—is the part of some looms that is used to carry filling yarns through the shed.

Shuttle embroidery—is a technique that produces an all-over embroidered pattern on a fabric; it is similar to schiffli embroidery but a more advanced process.

Silence cloth—is a white double-faced fabric used under table linens to minimize noise during dining.

Silk—is the fiber produced by several varieties of caterpillars, including *Bombyx mori*, *Antheraea mylitta*, and *Antheraea pernyi*.

Silk-in-the-gum—(*See* Raw silk.)

Silk noils—refer to staple silk from broken filaments and inner portions of cocoons or waste silk from cocoons in which the caterpillars matured into moths.

Simple calendering—is a mechanical finish. The fabric is passed between two rollers or calenders to remove wrinkles; the simplest calendering process often precedes printing.

Simple yarn—is a yarn alike in all its parts.

Simplex machine—is similar to the tricot machine but uses two needle bars and two guide bars to create a simplex knit.

Singeing—burns fiber ends from the fabric to produce a smooth surface.

Single-figured jersey—is a type of jacquard jersey.

Single-filling knit—is the simplest filling knit; it is made using one set of needles.

Single-jersey fabric—(*See* Jersey.)

Single yarn—consists of one strand of fibers held together by some mechanism.

Sisal—is a leaf fiber produced in Africa, Central America, and the West Indies.

Sizing—is a starch, resin, or gelatinous substance added to warp yarns in preparing them for weaving and fabrics to increase body and abrasion resistance. Sizing also refers to the process of adding sizing compounds to yarns before weaving. (*See also* Slashing.)

Skew—describes an off-grain problem. Filling yarns interlace with warp yarns at an angle less than or greater than 90 degrees.

Skye (sky)—is the process of exposing fabric or yarn to air to oxidize the leuco or soluble colorless form of certain dyes to the pigment or nonsoluble colored form.

Slack mercerization—is a treatment of cotton fabric with sodium hydroxide to increase absorbency; it is especially important as a preparation step in dyeing.

Slack-tension weave—is a weave in which two warp beams are used with one beam at regular loom tension and the other beam at a lower tension for weaving seersucker and terrycloth.

Slashing—See Sizing.

Slippage—is a tendency in some woven fabrics of warp yarns to slide or slip over filling yarns or vice versa and leave open areas in the fabric; it most often occurs in fabrics of low density or smooth filament yarns.

Sliver—is a very weak rope of fibers produced in intermediate steps in the production of spun yarns.

Sliver-pile knit—is a filling-knit fabric in which the pile is created by using fibers from a sliver.

Slub effects—refer to true slub yarns and to yarns that incorporate small tufts of fiber to create an appearance similar to a true slub yarn.

Slub yarn—is a single thick-and-thin fancy yarn.

Smart textiles or smart fabrics—sense and react to the environment or stimuli of an electrical, chemical, thermal, mechanical, magnetic, or other nature.

Smooth-filament yarn—is a yarn of filament fibers that have not been crimped or textured.

Soap—is a cleaning compound made from sodium or potassium salts of fatty acids.

Softener—refers to a compound used to remove hardness ions from water (water softener) or to improve the hand of fabric (fabric softener).

Soft goods—are products constructed of textiles and other flexible materials including apparel, interior textiles, and technical textiles.

Soil—describes contaminants on fabric, yarn, or fiber.

Soil-release finish—is a chemical surface coating on fabrics to improve soil removal during cleaning.

Soil-release polymer—is a chemical present in some detergents that bonds with soil and releases the soil in the wash.

Solution dyeing—describes the addition of colored pigments to polymer solutions prior to fiber extrusion; it is also called mass pigmentation.

Solvent—is a liquid that dissolves other materials; it includes water- and dry-cleaning solvents.

Solvent finishing—refers to processes in which the finishing chemical is dissolved in a liquid other than water.

Solvent spinning—is a type of wet spinning. (*See also* Wet spinning.)

Sorting—is the process of grouping textiles of similar characteristics to avoid creating problems in cleaning or to allow similar treatments.

Sorting wool—refers to dividing a fleece into different-quality fibers.

Sourcing—is the business of identifying, locating, and investigating firms to provide raw materials, intermediate components, and services to enable a firm to supply goods to the market.

Spacer fabric—is a three-dimensional technical fabric made by several methods: weaving, knitting, and nonwoven.

Spandex—is a manufactured fiber in which the fiber-forming substance is a long-chain synthetic polymer consisting of at least 85 percent of a segmented polyurethane.

Special-purpose finish—includes all finishes that improve fabric performance or minimize fabric problems.

Specific gravity—is the ratio of the mass of the fiber to an equal volume of water at 4°C.

Spike yarn or Snarl yarn—is a fancy yarn in which the effect ply forms alternating open loops along both sides of the yarn.

Spinneret—is the thimblelike nozzle through which the solution is extruded to form a fiber.

Spinning—refers to the process of producing a yarn from staple fibers; it also refers to the production of a fiber by extruding a solution through tiny holes in a spinneret.

Spinning solution—(*See* Dope.)

Spiral yarn or Corkscrew yarn—is a fancy yarn in which two plies that differ in size, texture, type, or color are twisted together.

Split-fiber method—is an inexpensive method used to produce tape yarns from olefin film.

Split leather—is one of the inner layers of leather removed from a thick hide.

Spring-beard needle—is a type of needle used in knitting fabrics from fine yarns.

Spun-bonded—is a process of producing a fabric directly from fibers by adhering melt-spun fibers together before cooling.

Spun-laced—is a process of producing a fabric directly from fibers by using water to entangle staple fibers and create a pattern in the fabric.

Spunmelt—is a fiberweb process that combines spun-bonded and melt-blown technology to create fiberweb fabrics.

Spun yarn—is a continuous strand of staple fibers held together by some mechanism.

Stabilization—refers to any finish that is designed to minimize shrinkage or growth of fabric during care.

Stainless steel—is a type of metallic fiber.

Stain-release finish—(*See* Soil-release finish.)

Staple fiber—is any natural or manufactured fiber produced in or cut to a short length measured in inches or centimeters.

Starching—is a process of adding a sizing material to a fabric to add weight or body.

Steam drying—describes using steam to refresh fabrics, remove wrinkles, and soften, deodorize, and sanitize fabric.

Steam washing—describes using steam to boost cleaning, improve detergent action, and remove soil.

Steep twill—is a twill with a wale angle of approximately 63 degrees.

Stencil printing—describes a hand process of adding color to a fabric by using a form to control where the color strikes the fabric.

Stiffness—is the resistance to bending or creasing of a fabric.

Stitch or Loop—is the basic unit of construction in a knitted fabric.

Stitch-bonded fabric—is a multiplex fabric in which fine lengthwise yarns in a warp knit are chain-stitched to interlock the fiberweb base structure or inlaid yarns.

Stitched yarns—are narrow ribbon-like fabrics with one or more rows of stitched thread forming the basic structure of the yarn.

Stock dyeing—refers to a fiber-dyeing process in which loose fibers are colored.

Stockinette (stockinet)—is a coarse-yarn, single-filling, heavy-knit jersey fabric.

Storage—refers to conditions when the textile or textile product is not being used, worn, or cleaned.

Strength—is the ability to resist stress and is expressed as tensile strength (pounds per square inch) or as tenacity (grams per denier). Breaking tenacity is the number of grams of force to break a fiber.

Stretching—is the process of pulling a fiber so that the molecular chains rotate and slide until they become oriented and form crystals within the fiber to enhance certain fiber properties.

Stretch yarn—is a yarn with high degrees of potential elastic stretch and yarn curl.

Striations—are the lengthwise lines present on several manufactured fibers, such as rayon.

Structural design—describes fabrics in which the design is an integral part of the fabric and develops as the fabric is made.

Stuffer box—is a method used to add crimp and texture to filament yarns.

S-twist—refers to a direction of yarn twist that conforms to the slope direction of the central portion of the letter *S*.

Subtractive finish—is a finish that removes some portion of the fabric through either a mechanical or a chemical process to enhance the fabric's appearance.

Suede (pronounced swāᵈd)—is a leather that has been brushed or napped to pull fibrils to the surface and create a softer surface and a more matte luster.

Suede cloth—is a plain- or twill-weave or knitted fabric that is napped and sheared on one or both sides to resemble suede leather.

Suiting-weight fabric—is a general term for heavyweight fabrics of any fiber type or fabric construction.

Sulfar—is a manufactured fiber in which the fiber-forming substance is a long-chain synthetic polysulfide in which at least 85 percent of the sulfide linkages are attached directly to two aromatic rings.

Sulfur dyes—are a class of solubility-cycle dyes used primarily with cotton.

Sunlight resistance—(*See* Light resistance.)

Sun protective finish—(*See* Ultraviolet-absorbent finish.)

Supima cotton—(*See* Pima cotton.)

Supported film—is a composite fabric that combines a fiberweb, woven, or knitted fabric with a film for greater durability.

Supported-scrim structure—is a composite fabric consisting of foam bonded to a yarn structure scrim; fibers may be flocked on the surface to simulate a pile or suede fabric.

Surah (soorʹ-aheᶜ)—(*See* Foulard.)

Surface coating—is a finish, usually metallic or plastic in nature, applied to the face of the fabric; it also refers to a polyamide solution applied to wool fabrics to minimize felting shrinkage.

Surface design—is another term for an aesthetic finish applied to the surface of the textile.

Surfactants—are sulfonate organic compounds used in detergents to assist in soil removal.

Sustainability—describes practices and policies that reduce environmental pollution, do not exploit people or natural resources in meeting the lifestyle needs of the present, and do not compromise the future.

Swivel-dot fabric—is an extra-yarn weave made with a tiny shuttle that wraps extra yarns around some selected warp yarns to create a spot in the fabric.

Synthetic fibers—are produced from synthetic polymers made from basic raw materials.

Synthetic leather—refers to a variety of fabrications or finishes that produce a surface that resembles leather in appearance or texture; some may be brushed to resemble suede.

Taffeta (tafʹ-et-uh)—is a general term that refers to any plain-weave filament-yarn fabric with a fine, smooth, crisp hand. Unbalanced taffeta has a fine rib made by heavier filling yarns and more warp yarns. Faille taffeta has a crosswise rib made by using many more warp yarns than filling yarns. Moiré taffetas have an embossed watermark design. Balanced taffetas have warp and filling yarns of the same size.

Take-up—is the step in weaving when the woven fabric is wound on the cloth beam and warp yarn is let off the warp beam so that more fabric can be woven.

Tanning—is a finishing step in the production of leather to prevent rotting of the hide or skin.

Tapa cloth—refers to a hand-produced fiberweb fabric made from the inner bark of selected trees.

Tapestry (tapʹ-ehs-tree)—is a firm, heavy, stiff jacquard-weave fabric made with several warp- and filling-yarn sets. Tapestry is also used for fabric made by hand in which the filling yarns are discontinuous. In these tapestries, the filling yarn is used only in the areas where that color is desired.

Tape yarn—is an inexpensive yarn produced from extruded polymer film by extrusion or the split-fiber method.

Technical back—refers to the inner side or underside of the fabric as it is made.

Technical face—refers to the outer or upper side of the fabric as it is made.

Technical textiles—include a broad range of materials that are widely used in special applications of a technical nature and that are generally not considered apparel or furnishings.

Temporary finish—describes a finish that is removed during the first care cycle or that has a very short life span.

Tenacity—describes the strength of a fiber; it is usually referred to as breaking tenacity, which describes the force at which the fiber ruptures or breaks.

Tender goods—describe very weak fabrics that have been exposed to some environmental factor or incorrect processing. (*See also* Tendering.)

Tendering—describes the weakening of fibers due to exposure to degradants or a deleterious interaction between fiber and dye or finish.

Tension mercerization—is the treating of cotton yarn, thread, or fabric with sodium hydroxide while under tension.

Tentering—is a finishing step in which the fabric is stretched out to full width and is often combined with other finishing steps like heat-setting. If poorly done, it contributes to bow and skew.

Terrycloth (terry)—is a slack-tension, warp-yarn pile fabric with loops on one or both sides of the fabric. It may have a jacquard pattern and be made with plied yarns for durability. There are also weft- or filling-knit terrycloths.

Tex system—is a direct yarn-numbering system. The yarn size is the weight in grams of 1000 meters of yarn.

Textile—is a general term used to refer to any flexible material that is composed of thin films of polymers or of fibers, yarns, or fabrics or anything made from films, fibers, yarns, or fabrics.

Textile complex—is the global mix of related industries that provide soft goods for the world's population.

Textile Fiber Products Identification Act—regulates use of fiber names in labeling textile products to protect consumers from unscrupulous trade practices.

Texture—describes the nature of a fabric's surface as perceived by sight or touch.

Textured-bulk-filament yarn—is a uniformly bulky filament yarn in which the bulk is added by crimping or texturizing the filament fibers.

Textured yarn—is another term for a textured-bulk-filament yarn; a yarn with notably greater apparent volume than a similar conventional yarn.

Texturing—refers to the process of adding bulk to yarns or modifying fabric surfaces.

Thermal finish—(See Phase-change finish.)

Thermoplastic—describes a fiber's sensitivity to heat; fibers that melt or glaze at relatively low temperature.

Thermosol process—is a method of dyeing synthetic fibers with disperse dyes by padding and by applying dry heat to set the dye.

Thick-and-thin fibers—vary in diameter throughout their length so that in some areas they are thinner and in other areas they are thicker.

Throwing—refers to the process of twisting silk filaments into a yarn or to the process of twisting and texturing synthetic-fiber-filament yarns.

Ticking—is a general term used for fabrics of any weave used for mattress covers, slipcovers, and upholstery. It may also be used in apparel.

Tie-dye—is a resist-dyeing process. Portions of the fabric or yarn are tied to prevent dye absorption in those areas.

Tigaring (tigering)—is a surface napping of knit fabrics to produce a suedelike texture; it also refers to the removal of loose fiber from a pile or napped fabric.

Tissue gingham—is a lightweight, yarn-dyed plain-weave fabric.

Top—is a precursor of a worsted yarn.

Top grain—refers to the outermost layer of leather and includes the grain features of the hide or skin. It is the highest quality of leather removed from a thick hide.

Topical finish—(See Additive finish.)

Torchon (tor´-shohn) lace—is a rugged bobbin lace with very simple patterns.

Torts—include behaviors that interfere with personal rights, such as substandard professional performance or deliberate wrongful acts.

Tow—refers to short flax fibers or to a large assembly of filament fibers to facilitate handling and processing during the production of manufactured staple fibers.

Tow-to-top system—refers to a process of converting filament fibers to staple fibers by cutting or break stretching.

Tow-to-yarn system—refers to a process of converting filament fibers to staple fibers by break

stretching, drawing the fibers, adding twist, and winding the yarn on a bobbin.

Trademark—is a word, symbol, device, or combination used to designate the product of a particular company.

Trade name—is a term used to identify a company's products.

Transition cotton—refers to cotton produced on land where organic farming is practiced but where the three-year minimum for certified organic cotton has not been met.

Translucence—is the ability of a textile to allow light to pass through it.

Triacetate—is a manufactured fiber in which the fiber-forming substance is cellulose acetate in which not less than 92 percent of the hydroxyl groups are acetylated.

Triaxial—refers to a fabric made with three sets of yarns interlaced at 60-degree angles to each other.

Tricot—is a warp-knit fabric made with filament yarns with one or more bars. Tricot has fine, vertical wales on the technical face and horizontal ribs on the technical back.

Tricot machine—is a warp-knitting machine used to produce tricot warp knits.

Trilobal shape—refers to a three-sided fiber cross-sectional shape that is designed to imitate silk.

True crepe—is a fabric made with at least one set of crepe-twist yarns.

True tapestry—is a patterned, unbalanced plain-weave fabric with a discontinuous filling.

Tubular finishing—(See Rope finishing.)

Tuck stitch—is a type of knit stitch in which the previous stitch is not cleared from the needle. It creates a pucker in the fabric and is used in creating patterns.

Tuft density—describes the number of yarn tufts per inch.

Tufting—is a method of producing an imitation-pile surface by stitching yarns to the surface of an existing fabric; it is used to produce carpeting and upholstery.

Tulle (pronounced tool)—is a mesh tricot fabric used as a support fabric or as an overlay in apparel.

Turns per inch (tpi)—is a measure of yarn twist.

Turns per meter (tpm)—is a measure of yarn twist.

Tussah silk—is a type of wild silk.

Tweed—is a general term for wool or wool-like fabrics made of flock or flake novelty yarns in plain, twill, or twill-variation weaves.

Twill flannel—is one of several wool or wool-like fabrics made in a twill weave.

Twill weave—is a weave in which each warp or filling yarn floats across two or more filling or warp yarns with a progression of interlacings by one to the right or to the left, forming a distinct wale.

Twist—is the spiral arrangement of fibers around the yarn axis.

Twistless spinning—is a method of producing staple fiber yarn that eliminates twist and uses starch or sizing to lock fibers in place.

Twist-on-twist—refers to using the same direction of twist in plying two yarns into one yarn as in the production of each individual ply.

Twist setting—is a yarn-finishing process used to help make permanent the very high twist in crepe yarns.

Ultrafine denier—refers to a fiber of less than 0.3 denier per filament.

Ultrasonic cleaning—is a cleaning technique for furnishings that uses high-frequency sound waves to clean the textile.

Ultraviolet-absorbent finish—is a finish that absorbs ultraviolet energy and protects the wearer. It includes optical brighteners, many dyes, and other chemicals.

Ultraviolet protection factor (UPF)—is a measure of the ability of a textile to block damaging ultraviolet radiation.

Unbalanced plain weave—is a plain weave in which the ratio of warp yarns to filling yarns is significantly greater than 1:1; common types are 2:1, 3:1, and 1:2.

Union dyeing—is dyeing a fabric made of two or more fibers to one solid color.

Upholstered Furniture Action Council—is an industry group that issues voluntary standards for upholstered furniture.

Vacuuming—is a cleaning technique for furnishings in which particulate soil is removed from the textile by suction.

Valenciennes (val-en-sehnz´)—is a bobbin lace with a diamond-shaped mesh.

van der Waals forces—are weak attractive forces between adjacent molecules that increase in strength as the molecules move closer together.

Vapor phase—is a type of durable-press finish in which the finishing chemical is applied to the product in vapor form in a closed chamber and cured in the chamber.

Vat dyes—are a class of solubility-cycle dyes used primarily with cotton and some polyester.

V-bed machine—is a type of knitting machine used to produce double-knits.

Velour—is a general term used to describe some woven- or knit-pile fabrics with dense, long, or deep pile.

Velvet—is a warp-pile fabric most often made as a double cloth with five sets of yarns. One pair of ground warp and filling creates one side of the fabric and a second pair of ground warp and filling creates the other side. A fifth set of yarns (pile warp) interlaces between the two sets of ground fabrics. The woven fabric is separated into two complete fabrics when the pile warp is cut. Velvet is usually a filament-yarn fabric.

Velveteen—is a filling-pile fabric with a plain- or twill-ground weave made with long floats that are cut in the finishing process to form a short pile. Velveteen is usually a spun-yarn fabric.

Venetian (veh-ne¯´-shuhn) point lace—is a needlepoint lace with an irregular mesh.

Vicuña—is the fiber produced by the South American vicuña.

Vinal—is a manufactured fiber in which the fiber-forming substance is any long-chain synthetic polymer composed of at least 50 percent by weight of vinyl alcohol units and in which the total of the vinyl alcohol units and any one or more of the various acetal units is at least 85 percent by weight of the fiber.

Vinyon—is a manufactured fiber in which the fiber-forming substance is any long-chain synthetic polymer composed of at least 85 percent by weight of vinyl chloride units.

Virgin wool—is wool that has never been processed into a fabric before.

Viscose rayon—is the most common type of rayon.

Viyella (vî-el´-uh)—is a medium-weight twill-weave fabric made of an intimate blend of 55 percent wool and 45 percent cotton.

Voile (pronounced voyl)—is a sheer, lightweight, low-count, plain-weave spun-yarn fabric in which the yarns have a high, hard (voile) twist to give the fabric a crisp hand. It has a lower count than lawn.

Voile twist—(See Hard twist.)

Vortex spinning—produces a yarn with an outer layer of fibers wrapped around a center of parallel fibers.

Wadding—is a loose assemblage of waste fibers used in textile products as lining and support layers.

Waffle cloth—is a dobby-weave fabric in which the interlacing pattern creates a three-dimensional honeycomb.

Wale—refers to the diagonal line developed by the interlacing pattern of twills or the column of stitches made by one needle in a knit fabric.

Warp—is the group of yarns threaded through the loom in a woven fabric, parallel to the selvage.

Warp beam—is a metal or wood cylinder on which the warp yarns are wound and is a critical part of the loom.

Warp-faced twill—is a type of twill weave in which the majority of the technical face of the fabric is formed by warp yarns.

Warping the loom or Dressing the loom—describes the process of inserting warp yarns through heddles and dents in the appropriate order to create the fabric desired.

Warp-insertion warp knit—is a warp knit in which a yarn was laid in the lengthwise direction as the fabric was being knit.

Warp knitting—is a process in which yarn sets are interlooped in essentially a lengthwise direction to form a fabric.

Warp-pile fabric—is a fabric with pile created by extra warp yarns.

Warp printing—is a process of printing a pattern on warp yarns before weaving.

Warp sateen—is a spun-yarn satin-weave fabric in which warp yarns form the technical face of the fabric.

Warranty—is an implied or written indication that the product is suitable for the purpose for which it was marketed.

Washdown—describes color loss that occurs over time as a fabric is laundered or cleaned.

Wash-off—refers to rinsing soil, excess chemicals, contaminants, or unused dye off the fabric; it is usually done with water.

Wastewater treatment—describes the procedures necessary to return water to a potable and usable condition.

Water—is a common solvent used in fiber processing, finishing, dyeing, and cleaning textiles.

Water-absorbent finish—is a chemical added to a fabric that will increase its ability to absorb moisture.

Water-bath finishing—refers to processes in which the chemical is dissolved in water.

Water-jet loom—is a type of loom in which the filling yarn is inserted in the shed with a stream or jet of water.

Waterproof fabric—refers to a coated or composite fabric that water will not penetrate regardless of the amount of time it is in contact with the fabric or the force with which it hits the fabric.

Water-repellent finish—minimizes the wettability of a fabric; it may result in stain resistance as well.

Water softeners—are compounds used to sequester minerals present in hard water.

Weaver's cloth—is a general term for balanced, plain-weave cotton suitings.

Weaving—is the process of producing a fabric by interlacing two or more yarns at right angles.

Weft insertion—is a single-filling-knit jersey in which a second yarn is laid in a course or knit into the fabric to add stability and that may be napped to create a fuzzy surface on the technical back of the fabric.

Weft-insertion filling knit—(*See* Weft insertion.)

Weft-insertion warp knit—is a warp knit in which a yarn was laid in the crosswise direction as the fabric was being knit.

Weighted silk—designates a silk fabric to which a metallic salt was added (at an amount specified by federal law) to improve hand, dye affinity, or drape.

Weighting—is the treatment of silk with metallic salts to increase the fabric's weight, hand, and dye affinity; it may result in accelerated degradation of the silk.

Wet-adhesive method—uses a chemical adhesive to make laminates.

Wet cleaning—is a cleaning technique for furnishings in which a water-based detergent is worked into the textile and the soiled solution is removed by vacuuming.

Wet-laid fiberweb—is a layer of fibers made from a slurry of fiber and water.

Wet-process finishes—are those applied in liquid form.

Wet spinning—is a fiber-forming process in which the polymer is dissolved in a solvent and the solution is extruded into a chemical bath.

Whitener—(*See* Fluorescent whitening agent.)

Wicking—is the ability of a fiber to transfer moisture along its surface.

Wild silk—refers to naturally grown staple silk that is more irregular in texture and color compared to cultivated silk.

Wilton rugs—are figured pile rugs made on a jacquard loom.

Winch dyeing—is a process for dyeing a loose rope of fabric without tension.

Winding—is the process of transferring yarn from one package to another.

Wool—refers to fiber from various animals including sheep, Angora and cashmere goats, camel, alpaca, and llama.

Woolen yarn—Is a slightly irregular bulky wool or wool-like yarn that has not been combed.

Wool Products Labeling Act—is the federal law that protects the textile industry and consumers from the undisclosed presence of fibers other than wool and that informs consumers of the source of the wool fiber.

Worsted yarn—is a smooth, straight, and uniform wool or wool-like yarn that has been processed to remove short fibers and make the remaining fibers more parallel.

Woven-pile fabrics—are three-dimensional structures made by weaving an extra set of warp or filling yarns into the ground yarns to make loops or cut ends on the surface.

WPL number—refers to the manufacturer's identification number assigned to the firm, as allowed for in the Wool Products Labeling Act.

Wrap-spun yarn—is a yarn with a core of staple fibers wrapped with filament fibers.

Wrinkle resistance—is the ability of a fiber to recover from deformations such as bending, twisting, or compressing.

Wrinkle-resistant finish—keeps wrinkling to a minimum.

Yak—is the fiber produced by the Tibetan ox.

Yarn—is an assemblage of fibers twisted or laid together so as to form a continuous strand that can be made into a textile fabric.

Yarn dyeing—is a process of adding color, usually a dye, to yarns.

Yarn number—describes the size of a yarn.

Z-twist—refers to a direction of yarn twist that conforms to the direction of the slope of the central portion of the letter *Z*.

index